America

SECOND EDITION

America

Volume 2: since 1865

A History of the United States

Norman K. Risjord

University of Wisconsin

Prentice Hall, Englewood Cliffs, New Jersey 07632

Library of Congress Cataloging-in-Publication Data

Risjord, Norman K.
 America, a history of the United States.

 Includes bibliographies and index.
 Contents: v. 1. To 1877 — v. 2. Since 1865
 1. United States—History.   I. Title.
E178.1.R59 1988   973   87–25745
ISBN 0–13–025156–9 (v. 1)
ISBN 0–13–025198–4 (v. 2)

Editorial/production supervision: Marjorie Shustak
Cover and interior design: Lee Cohen
Manufacturing buyer: Ed O'Dougherty
Photo research: Lorinda Morris-Nantz/Kay Dellosa
Cover art: John Ross Key, "Administration,
Mining, and Electrical Buildings from Wooded
Island, World's Columbian Exposition," Chicago
Historical Society

For Bill Kestle, in memoriam—
he brought teachers and books together

America: A History of the United States,
Volume 2: since 1865, Norman K. Risjord

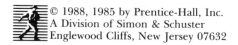

© 1988, 1985 by Prentice-Hall, Inc.
A Division of Simon & Schuster
Englewood Cliffs, New Jersey 07632

Printed in the United States of America

10 9 8 7 6 5 4 3 2 1

ISBN   0-13-025198-4   01

Prentice-Hall International (UK) Limited, *London*
Prentice-Hall of Australia Pty. Limited, *Sydney*
Prentice-Hall Canada Inc., *Toronto*
Prentice-Hall Hispanoamericana, S.A., *Mexico*
Prentice-Hall of India Private Limited, *New Delhi*
Prentice-Hall of Japan, Inc., *Tokyo*
Simon & Schuster Asia Pte. Ltd., *Singapore*
Editora Prentice-Hall do Brasil, Ltda., *Rio de Janeiro*

CONTENTS

1

BITTER REUNION: 1865–1877

2

TYCOONS, SPOILSMEN, AND MUGWUMPS

3

INDUSTRIAL PROGRESS AND INTELLECTUAL POVERTY

4

THE VANISHING FRONTIER

5

THE PEOPLE'S PROTEST: 1892–1900

6

THE NEW AMERICAN EMPIRE: 1865–1903

7

THE PROGRESSIVE IMPULSE: 1900–1910

8

WOODROW WILSON'S PROGRESSIVISM: 1910–1920

9

PROGRESSIVES AND THE WORLD: 1900–1920

10

BATHTUB GIN AND BALLYHOO: 1919–1929

11

HARD TIMES: 1929–1939

12

THE CHALLENGE OF WORLD POWER: 1919–1945   **280**

13

THE COLD WAR YEARS: 1945–1957   **308**

14

AFFLUENCE AND ANXIETY: 1941–1960   **342**

15

THE TURBULENT SIXTIES   **373**

CLIO'S FOCUS

PREFACE

A single-authored textbook spanning the whole of American history is an awesome undertaking. Some might even think it presumptuous. My justification—excuse, if you will—is twenty-five years of teaching the American Survey course. One develops, over that span of time, a sense of organization and a facility for explanation. These qualities were tested before a wider audience through broadcasts on the Wisconsin Educational Radio Network in 1965–1966, 1972–1973, 1982–1983, and 1987–1988. I have also benefited enormously from association with many graduate teaching assistants. Vigilant and sometimes critical, they have induced me to keep abreast of current scholarship. For these reasons it proved easier to cover the ground from Columbus to Reagan than I had anticipated.

This is a traditional piece of history, in the sense that it is chronologically organized and focuses to a large extent on public affairs. This, to be sure, reflects the emphasis and approach of my own teaching. But it will also be of value to the more experimental teacher. With a textbook that supplies the nuts and bolts of history, the teacher can afford to spend class time on areas of special interest or questions of historical interpretation. I feel, moreover, that the main purpose of the introductory survey of American history is to provide students with a rudimentary factual base, while entertaining them enough to encourage further study. It is my hope that this book accomplishes that dual purpose.

In this second edition the text has been expanded by about 10 percent. Most of the added material is in the field of social history. This is in part a response to readers who felt more attention ought to be given to this area of history, but it also reflects the thrust of recent scholarship. Some of the most exciting new discoveries have been in the field of women's studies and the family. These, as well as other important contributions of the past five years, I have tried to incorporate in this edition.

An author incurs many obligations in writing a book, and space permits the acknowledgment of only a few. My wife Connie played the role of historical novice, demanding clarification and explanation of many things that historians tend to take for granted. I am also deeply indebted to the unsung heroes of the profession, those who review and critique manuscripts. Their exacting standards, tempered by fairness and empathy, are a credit to the profession. They are, for this edition, John Snetsinger, California Polytech University; J. Carroll Moody, Northern Illinois University; Thomas E. Siefert, Indiana State University; James E. Sargent, Virginia Western Community College; Louis W. Potts, University of Missouri; Bruce J. Dierenfield, Canisius College; and Peter Wallenstein, Virginia Polytechnic Institute & State University.

My editors at Prentice Hall, especially Steve Dalphin and Marjorie Borden Shustak, did a splendid job of guiding the work through the various stages of production. My contact with Prentice Hall was made through Bill Kestle, Prentice Hall sales representative for Wisconsin and a friend of twenty years. Bill died while the first edition was in production. To his memory it is respectfully dedicated.

Norman K. Risjord

1

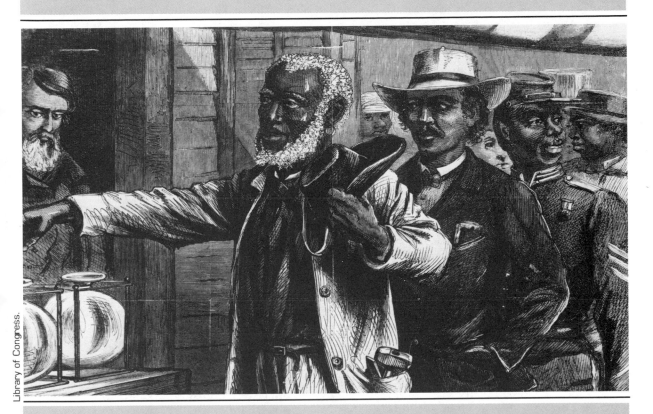

BITTER REUNION:
1865–1877

Charles A. Beard, the most influential historian of the twentieth century, once described the Civil War as "the second American Revolution." The war, in Beard's view, ushered in the triumph of industrial capitalism. It shifted the focus of the economy from farm to factory, the focus of politics from state to national government. The Civil War, in short, created modern America.

Such a broad interpretation leaves many gaps, but it remains a useful framework for exploring the meaning of the Civil War and its aftermath, Reconstruction. The Civil War, for a start, did not bring about industrial growth. In fact, the effort diverted to military service probably slowed economic development. The growth rate of the economy—one measure of industrialization—began to accelerate as early as 1840. The rate of growth in commodity production was about 60 percent in the 1850s, and that rate was reached again in the 1870s. But in the 1860s, increase in manufacturing output was only 23 percent. The North experienced an economic boom during the war, but it was due in part to government deficit spending and in part to inflation. The textile mills of New England were idle much of the time for lack of cotton fiber; it was high prices that maintained high profits. The railroads prospered. They had been built for future demand; not until the Civil War did they use their full carrying capacity.

The war, on the other hand, did bring some important changes. Contrary to what Beard supposed, the war probably changed agriculture more than industry. Before, southerners had always boasted that "Cotton is king!" The war demonstrated that the true king was in fact wheat. Britain found it could do nicely without American cotton because of alternative sources in India and Egypt, but it could not do without American foodstuffs. Despite losing sons and hired hands to the army, the northern farmer was able to feed the city population, the army, and part of Europe as well. He did it by mechanization. The technology for agricultural revolution was available before the war—the steel plow with interchangeable parts, for instance, and the mechanical grain harvester. High food prices and a labor shortage encouraged farmers to buy them. Between 1861 and 1865, the number of machines on northern farms tripled.

War-related industries also grew rapidly. Stimulated by the demand for uniforms, clothing and shoe manufacturers purchased sewing machines. The new devices quickened the shift in both industries from small shops to large-scale factories. The canning industry came of age during the war, largely through military contracts. Borden's condensed milk and Van Camp's pork and beans became standard features of army field rations, and the new tastes acquired by soldiers permanently altered the diets of thousands of families after the war.

⊔ The Political Revolution

Beard's phrase "second American Revolution" refers more to political than economic change. Before the war, government policy catered to rural interests and to the South. Ever since the Polk administration, the federal government had adhered to hard money and a low tariff. In 1857 Congress reduced further the already low rates prevailing since the Walker Tariff of 1846, putting the nation virtually on free trade. Congress left internal improvement projects to the states, though it did provide

---

(*Chapter opening photo*) "The First Vote," pencil sketch for *Harper's Weekly* magazine.

a federal land grant to the Illinois Central Railroad (via the state of Illinois) in 1850. A Homestead Act, designed to benefit the working classes by offering them free farms in the West, fell victim to Buchanan's veto. *States' rights* and *laissez faire* had been watchwords since the time of Jackson. Except for antislavery, southern planters had had no reason to complain. Secession, on the other hand, allowed the North to pass the economic legislation it had long desired. The result was the enactment of something very like the American System of Henry Clay, tailored to meet the needs of a new generation.

ECONOMIC LEGISLATION

The tariff was the first item on the Republican agenda. In February 1861, while the Confederacy was taking form in Montgomery, Alabama, Congress approved a bill introduced by Justin S. Morrill of Vermont that raised tariff rates to the 1846 level. After the war began, military expenses brought further increases, and by the end of the war the average level of rates was 47 percent, more than double the average of 1857. The wall of tariff protection was of particular benefit to the iron and steel industry, which previously had not been able to compete with British products. For the better part of the next century, the United States remained a high-tariff nation.

Internal improvements meant, by 1860, federal support for a Pacific railroad. Republicans committed themselves to the project in the presidential election that year, and secession left them free to choose the central route. In 1862 Congress chartered two corporations, the Union Pacific Railroad, with authority to build westward from Omaha, and the Central Pacific, authorized to lay track eastward from California until the two lines met somewhere in the Great Basin. By the terms of the charters, the government underwrote railroad construction militarily and financially. It guaranteed the right of way, extinguished the Indian land titles, and ordered the army to protect construction workers from Indians. In addition, for each mile of track laid the railroads were to receive a grant of 6,400 acres of public land. This amounted to a swath of alternate sections extending 20 miles on each side of the track (40 miles in the mountains) from the Missouri River to the Pacific. Also, millions of dollars in government bonds were made available to railroad promoters in need of ready cash.

Government generosity, ultimately extended to four transcontinental railroads before subsidies were stopped in 1873, seemed justified at the time. The railroads plunged through terrain inhabited only by Indians and buffalo. It would be some time before the railroads developed enough traffic to make a profit, but in the meantime they served a national need by uniting East and West. As it turned out, the railroads made a good profit from the beginning by selling their land and mineral assets. Government ownership and operation of railroads—a modern alternative—was beyond the realm of nineteenth-century thinking.

Banking and currency also commanded Republican attention in 1862. Since 1846, the government had accepted only gold and silver in receipt of taxes or the sale of public lands, and this hard currency was stored in various subtreasuries. Besides being cumbersome, the system meant that badly needed investment capital was squirreled away in public vaults. Private financial transactions were performed with notes issued by state-chartered banks. Those issued by the larger banks achieved wide circulation, but most were unreliable or circulated only in their own localities. Watching over this unwieldy system was the ghost of Andrew Jackson, who had destroyed the central bank thirty years before.

The U.S. Treasury financed the war in the time-honored way—by issuing paper money. Its notes were called "greenbacks" because of their distinctive color, and they depreciated, as paper money had in every earlier war. The Treasury also issued long-term bonds, but the war proved so fantastically expensive that by 1862 the resources of the financial community were dry. In December of that year, Treasury Secretary Salmon P. Chase outlined a plan for solving in one stroke both the currency question and the banking problem, while at the same time creating a new market for federal bonds. The plan blended private interest with national need in a way that Alexander Hamilton would almost surely have approved. Chase's proposals formed the basis of the National Banking Act passed in February 1863 and amended substantially a year later. By these acts Congress created a system of national banks with federal charters and under the general supervision of the Treasury. Each bank that joined the system was required to purchase at least $30,000 in government bonds, which were then deposited in the U.S. Treasury. These deposited bonds were the security for notes issued by the national banks, and those notes provided the nation with a stable, uniform currency.

The system started slowly, due largely to the huge amount of capital needed to form a national bank, but in 1865, when Congress levied a 10 percent tax on state bank notes, most of the state-chartered banks joined the new program. The national bank system, which remained the nation's primary banking system until the Federal Reserve Act of 1913, was decentralized and privately controlled, thus avoiding the accusations of monopoly and irresponsible power that had destroyed the Bank of the United States. Yet it provided a reasonably stable financial system and a uniform national currency.

Banks, tariff, and Pacific railroad were all designed to appeal primarily to the interests of businessmen and manufacturers. The Republican party, however, did not forget its promises to farmers and workingmen, whose demands since Jackson's time, had focused on cheap land. Even labor unions and workingmen's parties felt their members would have increased bargaining power in the East if workers possessed the alternative of cheap farms in the West. The idea proved to be false, since the average urban laborer was ill-equipped for farming, but it was a politically powerful myth.

The Homestead Act, passed in May 1862, granted 160 acres of public land to any adult male or head of family on the sole condition that he or she live on it for five years. By the end of the war, 1.5 million acres were occupied under the act, and the postwar decades witnessed a rush of homesteaders into the West. There were flaws in the law, to be sure. Many homesteaders failed in trying to farm the arid plains, and the chief beneficiaries often appeared to be lumber and mining companies who used various loopholes to help themselves to huge tracts of land. But the act did answer a long-felt popular demand.

Of even greater long-term social benefit was the Morrill Land Grant Act of 1862, which offered public lands to the states for the support of higher education. Representative Justin Morrill of Vermont had conducted a long crusade in Congress for the bill, but the measure was delayed by the opposition of southerners who feared federal influence in education. The act passed in 1862 was based on population: The states were offered 30,000 acres of public lands for each senator and representative. The eastern states should have benefited as much as the West. In practice, however, the main effect of the law was to stimulate state interest in higher education. This was most pronounced in the West, where public universities financed by land grants were promoted as state enterprises.

Confined at first to "loyal" states, the act was extended to the South after the war. The result was a major stride for higher education, and a sprinkling of land grant colleges that specialized in practical agricultural and industrial arts.

THE FREE LABOR IDEOLOGY

The Homestead Act and the Morrill Land-Grant Act are important clues to Republican thinking. Beginning with Lincoln's "house divided" appeal to northern factory workers, the Republicans claimed to speak for all Americans regardless of social or economic standing. If some of their programs spoke directly to the interests of industrial tycoons and railroad promoters, the Republicans justified them on the grounds that everyone benefited from modern factories and transportation facilities. Free farms and educational opportunity had been the twin goals of the labor movement from its inception, and Republicans responded as soon as they were in power. When labor revised its goals and began aiming for an eight-hour day, most Republicans accepted that idea too. They passed a law establishing an eight-hour day for federal government employees in 1868. Gradually, however, businessmen gained the upper hand in party councils. The contract labor law of 1864, for instance, was passed at the insistence of factory owners who wanted a steady supply of cheap foreign labor. The labor movement's complaint that immigrants undermined domestic wage levels was met by the creation of an Immigration Bureau to encourage still more immigrants.

Actions such as this suggested that the ideology of free labor, on which Republicans had grounded their opposition to slavery and on which they had appealed to businessmen and working people alike, had its limitations. Free labor meant just that. Individuals were expected to rely on their own resources, not on government programs. Freedom meant the elimination of some evils, such as slavery or liquor, not the imposition of some well-intended public policy. In time this view of the role of government in society forced the Republicans to abandon two of their earliest constituencies—factory workers and freed blacks. By the end of the war, workers were beginning to discover that in the competitive jungle of free enterprise, they lacked the strength to bargain effectively with the corporate giants the war and Republican policy had helped to create. It was not long before the newly freed blacks in the South, bereft of government aid and at the mercy of their former masters, made a similar discovery.

⊔ Lincoln, Johnson, and the Radicals

Throughout the war the Republican party was divided over the question of postwar reconstruction. Reconstruction involved two things: the return of the South to the Union with representation in Congress, and the restoration of civil governments in southern states that were occupied by federal armies. Both involved another, even more sensitive, issue—securing civil, and perhaps political, rights for the freed blacks.

The Republican party had never been united in its attitude toward slavery and secession. Abolitionists were not happy with the party's selection of Lincoln, and their suspicions were confirmed by his procrastination on the question of emancipation. As the war progressed, these radical Republicans grew in numbers and volubility, though they never formed a majority. Led by Benjamin F. Wade of Ohio, Charles Sumner of Massachusetts, and Thaddeus Stevens of Pennsylvania, the radicals drafted the wartime confiscation acts and hoped to restructure southern society when the conflict ended. Accepting secession as a fact, they argued that the southern states were "conquered provinces" at the mercy of Congress. Before letting the South return to the Union, the radicals planned to purge it of slavery, secure civil rights for former slaves, and destroy the planter elite that had caused all the trouble.

Moderate Republicans, by contrast, adhered to law and tradition. They worried that some of the wartime measures, such as the confiscation acts, might be unconstitutional. In company with Democrats (who occupied about a third of the seats in Congress), moderates were more aware than radicals of states rights and the interests of loyal whites in the border slave states. Less vindictive than radicals in their attitudes toward the South, moderates were also less confident of the intellectual potential of the freed slaves and less concerned for ensuring their civil liberties. In this the moderates reflected the racial bias that continued to prevail in the North.

LINCOLN AND RECONSTRUCTION

Lincoln, distinctly a moderate when he took office, grew more radical as the war went on. By 1864 he was prepared to throw the weight of his presidential authority behind a constitutional amendment (the thirteenth) freeing the slaves. And by early 1865, he was even suggesting privately that free black men who could read and write be given the right to vote. The president's reconstruction program, however, was more lenient than that of the radicals because it was influenced by military considerations. By being generous rather than vindictive, Lincoln hoped to attract southerners to his cause and further weaken the Confederacy. In contrast to the radicals, who viewed reconstruction as a matter for legislation, Lincoln felt that restoration of

the South could be accomplished by executive orders under the president's war powers. Utilizing loyal minorities that existed in every southern state, Lincoln hoped to create provisional civil governments in the South in the wake of the advancing Union army.

Virginia presented Lincoln with the first opportunity to implement this policy. The mountain counties of western Virginia, populated by small farmers who owned few slaves, had voted against secession. In August 1861, delegates from counties along the Ohio River met at Wheeling to form a legislature of their own and elected Francis H. Pierpont governor. Western delegates subsequently drew up a state constitution, and in 1863 Congress admitted West Virginia to the Union after adding to it the counties around strategic Harpers Ferry. In the meantime, Pierpont transferred his administration to Alexandria, and Lincoln named him provisional governor of Virginia. By the end of 1863, Lincoln had appointed provisional governors to rule the parts of Tennessee, Louisiana, and Texas that were in Union hands.

In an amnesty proclamation, December 8, 1863, Lincoln outlined his program for the reconstruction of the South. He offered to pardon any southerner (except Confederate government officials and high-ranking army officers) willing to take an oath of loyalty to the Constitution. Once the southerner promised loyalty to the Union, he would be granted full citizenship and restoration of his property. When, in any southern state, the nucleus of citizens willing to take the loyalty oath numbered 10 percent of the votes cast in the election of 1860, that state could elect a government. Once the new civil regime abolished slavery, Lincoln promised to recognize it as the legitimate authority in the state.

It was hardly a revolutionary program. The electorate would be that of 1860, which meant a probable restoration of the prewar regimes on the promise only of future loyalty. Freed slaves would have no civil or political rights except those the southern governments might be willing to confer. Arkansas and Louisiana, both in Union hands, promptly accepted Lincoln's terms, formed loyal regimes satisfactory to the president, and elected representatives to Congress. Congress refused to seat them. The radicals had other plans for the South, and Lincoln's failure to consult Congress pushed some moderates to their side.

The radical response to Lincoln's plan was the Wade-Davis bill of July 1864. It proposed to place the southern states under military rule, with northern generals serving as governors. The governor was to enroll all white males, and when a majority of these in any state submitted to a loyalty oath, that state could draw up a constitution and form a civil government. In order to participate in the constitutional convention, either as voter or officeholder, a citizen had to take another "ironclad" oath. The person had to swear by this oath that he had never voluntarily supported the Confederacy or borne arms against the United States. The only persons who could take such an oath were northern "carpetbaggers,"* who had drifted south on the heels of the Union army, and southern unionists, or "scalawags." Some of the southerners were planters and businessmen, but most were poor whites and mountaineers who had nothing in common with the planter-gentry that had engineered secession. By requiring a majority of all white males to take the oath, the Wade-Davis bill ensured a prolonged period of military

rule. By disenfranchising former Confederates, it sought to remake the South into a land of small farmers, black and white.

Lincoln gave the Wade-Davis Bill a pocket veto,** which enabled him to pursue his own program while avoiding a confrontation with Congress. Though it never went into effect, the Wade-Davis bill was a blueprint for the congressional version of reconstruction that was enacted in 1867. In the meantime, Lincoln went ahead with his own version of reconstruction. By the time of his death in April 1865, Virginia, Arkansas, Tennessee, and Louisiana had working governments under it.

Despite occasional disagreements with the radicals, who even toyed with the idea of replacing him with another candidate in the election of 1864, Lincoln moved steadily toward their position in the last months of the war. When Congress took up a constitutional amendment to free the slaves in January 1865, Lincoln used his patronage powers to secure passage. The president's support was vital, for the Thirteenth Amendment squeaked through the House of Representatives by a mere three votes. (This was evidence of the North's continuing racial bias, despite four years of a war in which one of the aims had become the freeing of slaves.) But that was his last great achievement. On Good Friday, April 14, 1865, the president attended a play at Ford's Theater in Washington. John Wilkes Booth, a southern sympathizer, climbed the stairway to the president's box, where the door was unaccountably left unguarded, and shot the president from behind at close range. The nation lost more than a wartime leader; it lost a voice that spoke for compassion and understanding.

It is tempting to speculate what might have happened had Lincoln lived out his term. His reconstruction program would almost certainly have been altered by Congress. Few northerners could see much point in restoring the prewar southern re-

---

* Southerners regarded these northern transients as fortunehunters and scornfully claimed they could put everything they owned into a cheap cloth handbag.

** An act of Congress requires a president's signature in order to become law. If, toward the end of a congressional session, a president delays signing a bill—figuratively stuffing it in his pocket and forgetting it—the measure dies when Congress adjourns.

Library of Congress.

Lincoln's funeral procession down Pennsylvania Avenue.

gimes, and there was a conviction that the South ought to be punished for its rebellion. Even so, it is unlikely, had Lincoln survived, that relations between executive and Congress would have broken down so completely as they did under Johnson, to the point where Johnson became the only president in our history to suffer impeachment. Lincoln resisted the radicals without resorting to name calling, and he kept open his lines of communication. Radical congressmen who detested his policies enjoyed his private company. Lincoln's drift toward abolition during the war, moreover, showed that he was flexible. After the Thirteenth Amendment was passed, it is quite likely that Lincoln would have cooperated with further efforts to confer civil rights

on freed blacks. And cooperation between president and Congress might have resulted in a more successful plan of reconstruction than the one eventually enacted.

JOHNSON
AND THE RADICALS

Johnson differed from Lincoln in politics and personality. Hailing from the Tennessee hill country, where farms were small and slaves were few, Johnson's political ideology was a states rights agrarianism derived from Jefferson and Jackson. A foe of the southern gentry, Johnson sympathized with the radical view that the South ought to be remade into a land of small farmers. But his attachment to limited government prevented him from using presidential powers to enforce such a social revolution. The new president was also stubborn, thin-skinned under criticism, and spiteful in political combat. In public appearances he often adopted the rough speech and crude manners of a frontier stump speaker, evoking mockery and anger rather than sympathetic attention.

Johnson's antipathy toward southern planters encouraged the radicals to think that he might be one of their own. When Senator Benjamin F. Wade, one of the authors of the Wade-Davis bill, suggested to the president in April 1865 the execution of a dozen leading southerners as an example, Johnson raised no objection. He only wondered how, out of several million "traitors," ten or twelve might be selected. The reconstruction plan he announced in May, however, dismayed the radicals. Congress had adjourned and would not reconvene until December 1865. By refusing to summon Congress into special session and proceeding on his own, Johnson indicated that

Andrew Johnson.

Library of Congress.

he considered reconstruction a presidential function, as Lincoln had. Radicals were unhappy also because Johnson's amnesty proclamation was similar to Lincoln's. He retained Lincoln's 10 percent plan, except that he proposed to exempt from amnesty, in addition to political and military leaders, persons whose property exceeded $20,000 in value. This provision would have excluded the planter elite from participating in the restored governments, but Johnson nullified it by granting individual pardons to all who applied.

Johnson detested the planter gentry, but once those grandees had been humbled by military defeat and came to him, caps in hand, for pardons, he felt justice had been done. He also had the southern, poor white's disdain for blacks. He was willing that they be free, but he saw no need for further government efforts in their behalf. Thus, his program for reconstruction, while it recognized the end of slavery, seemed in other respects to turn the clock back to 1860.

Johnson recognized the governments Lincoln had established in Virginia, Tennessee, Arkansas, and Louisiana, and in the course of the summer and fall of 1865 he extended recognition to civil governments in the remaining southern states. By the time Congress assembled in December, the South was "restored," a term Johnson preferred to "reconstructed." The new civil governments embarrassed the president in two ways, however—by enacting black codes regulating the former slaves and by electing to office many of the same men who had governed the Confederacy.

Some sort of legislation was necessary, for the South was in ruins. In addition to Sherman's march through Georgia from Atlanta to the sea, northern armies had cut swaths of destruction through Alabama, Mississippi, and Louisiana. Cities were desolate piles of rubble. In many places, schools and churches had ceased to function. Many white families thought

The Louisiana Black Code

There was wide concern among southern legislators in 1865 that blacks might not be willing to work once they were no longer under the discipline of the lash. Thus the black codes all contained laws regulating labor contracts and prohibiting vagrancy. The following excerpts from Louisiana's Act to Provide for and Regulate Labor Contracts suggest why northerners considered the black codes slavery by another name.

Sec. 1. Be it enacted by the Senate and House of Representatives of the State of Louisiana in general assembly convened, that all persons employed as laborers in agricultural pursuits shall be required, during the first ten days of the month of January of each year, to make contracts for labor for the then ensuing year. . . .

Sec. 2. Every laborer shall have full and perfect liberty to choose his employer, but, when once chosen, he shall not be allowed to leave his place of employment until the fulfillment of his contract. . . .

Sec. 8. Be it further enacted etc. that in case of sickness of the laborer, wages for the time lost shall be deducted, and where the sickness is feigned for purposes of idleness, and also on refusing to work according to contract, double the amount of wages shall be deducted for the time lost. . . .

Sec. 9. Be it further enacted, etc. that, when in health, the laborer shall work ten hours during the day in summer, and nine hours during the day in winter, unless otherwise stipulated in the labor contract. . . .

Sec. 10. Be it further enacted, etc. that for gross misconduct on the part of the laborer, such as insubordination, habitual laziness, frequent acts of violation of his contract, or the laws of the State, he may be dismissed by his employer. . . .

Acts of the General Assembly Regulating Labor, 1865

only of survival. Blacks viewed their sudden change in status from slavery to freedom with a mixture of exhilaration and uncertainty. The first instinct of many of them was simply to move about, to visit distant relatives and friends, to breathe the air of freedom. "They are just a swarm of bees," one observer noted, "all buzzing about and not knowing where to settle." To whites who had lived for generations in dread of slave rebellion, this mass of vagrants was a threat to public order.

The laws concerning freed slaves, known as black codes, did spell out their legal rights. The laws legitimized marriages, gave blacks access to courts, and allowed them to possess property. But, reflecting the fears of whites, the laws also contained vagrancy clauses by which unemployed blacks could be placed under the control of white employers. Some states enacted curfews or required blacks to have passes in order to leave their places of employment. Other laws imposed fines on blacks for trespassing, preaching without a license, possessing firearms, or using alcoholic beverages. Even in the laws that conferred rights, there was racial discrimination. Blacks could marry, but only a member of their own race; they could testify in court, but only if one party to the suit was black. Taken as a whole, the black codes made of the freed slaves second-class citizens.

Such regulations ran counter to the free labor ideology of the Republicans. The freed slaves were tied to their plantations by the authority of the state, given only the freedom to work as a landless peasantry under labor terms set by their former owners. By denying any pretense of equality, the black codes also challenged the Republicans' sense of loyalty. Black people had died in the Union cause; the Union was obliged to protect them from their former masters. "Loyal negroes must not be put down, while disloyal white men are put up," was one moderate Republican's view of it.

The election of former Confederate leaders further weakened the president's position. Some who were elected did not qualify even under Johnson's lenient requirements. Among those elected to Congress was Alexander H. Stephens, vice president of the Confederacy. Such conduct by voters was perhaps to be expected. A proud people convinced of the righteousness of their cause, southerners naturally tried to minimize the effects of the war and preserve as much of their culture as possible. What southerners did not realize was that by rejecting the role of the vanquished, they invited further punishment. By refusing even the pretense of contrition, the South deprived the North of its victory. If nothing was to be changed, the bloodshed was meaningless. That realization gave the radicals in Congress the upper hand.

⊔ The Critical Year: 1866

The extent to which the president and his southern clients had alienated northern opinion was evident when Congress convened in December 1865. Moderate Republicans agreed with radicals that Congress ought to have a hand in reconstruction and that something had to be done to protect the blacks. Congress re-

fused to seat the senators and representatives elected by the Lincoln-Johnson governments and appointed instead a Joint Committee on Reconstruction to investigate conditions in the South. The chairman of the committee, Senator William P. Fessenden of Maine, was a moderate, but Thaddeus Stevens, the radical from Gettysburg, Pennsylvania, who headed the House delegation on the committee, had a powerful voice.

While the joint committee interviewed generals and journalists, former Confederates and freed blacks, building up a file of southern intransigence, the Senate Judiciary Committee drafted the first fragments of reconstruction legislation—a Freedmen's Bureau bill and a civil rights bill. The guiding hand behind these measures was Senator Lyman Trumbull of Illinois, a moderate who, in the previous year, had introduced and floor-managed the Thirteenth Amendment. Distressed by reports of racial oppression in the South, Trumbull decided that Congress had the power to preserve the freedom the amendment promised.

FREEDMEN'S BUREAU AND CIVIL RIGHTS ACTS

The Freedmen's Bureau had been added to the War Department in March 1865 to feed and care for the thousands of refugees drifting into Union army camps. Trumbull's bill, introduced in January 1866, enlarged the bureau's authority, making it the guardian of the rights of the freedmen. The bill also authorized the president to rent 40-acre tracts of unoccupied public land to freed slaves, with the right of future purchase. A companion measure, the civil rights bill, made free blacks citizens of the United States and promised them the "full and equal benefit of all laws and proceedings for the security of persons and property as is enjoyed by white citizens." In the

Senate debate, Trumbull explained that the purpose of this measure was to negate the southern black codes.

Although both measures passed Congress by substantial margins, Johnson vetoed them. He considered both to be special interest legislation, benefiting blacks at the expense of everyone else, and beyond the power of Congress. Literally and even historically, Johnson was right, but politically his veto was disastrous. It meant that he was prepared to leave blacks at the mercy of their former masters. He even rejected Secretary of State Seward's advice that he at least appear less rigid. A furious Congress overrode the veto of the Civil Rights Act (the first time ever for a major piece of legislation) and proceeded to draft an amendment designed to enshrine civil rights in the Constitution. The task fell to the Joint Committee on Reconstruction, which by March of 1866 had completed its investigation of conditions in the South. Drafting an amendment was not easy, for the language had to be broad enough to serve as a platform for congressional reconstruction, yet moderate enough to secure ratification. The committee skirted the issue of black suffrage, for instance, because the North was not yet ready for so bold a stroke. Even so, the Fourteenth Amendment dramatically altered the constitutional history of the United States.

Thaddeus Stevens introduced the committee's handiwork and explained its rationale. The amendment began by defining citizenship in such a way as to make blacks citizens of the nation and of the states in which they resided. It then prohibited the states from abridging the privileges and immunities of citizens, from depriving any person of life, liberty, or property without "due process of law," or denying to any person "the equal protection of the laws." These limitations, explained Stevens, were designed to cure a deficiency in the federal Constitution, which had limited (through the Bill of Rights) only the actions of Con-

gress and not those of the states. The amendment, said Stevens, would allow "Congress to correct the unjust legislation of the States, so far that the law which operates upon one man shall operate equally upon all."

The amendment also encouraged southern states to give blacks the vote by threatening to reduce their representation in Congress if they failed to do so. Stevens considered this the most important feature of the amendment, though he recognized that much more was needed to ensure true independence for the former slave. "Forty acres of land and a hut," he declared, "would be more valuable to him than the immediate right to vote. Unless we give him this we shall receive the censure of mankind and the curse of Heaven."

The most politically important section of the amendment, from the standpoint of the Republicans, was the third. It addressed age-old northern fears of southern political power dating back to the three-fifths compromise in the Constitution which had given southerners a disproportionate vote in Congress and the electoral college. This section barred from political office any southerner who had violated his oath to uphold the Constitution by aiding the rebellion. In effect, it disqualified the old ruling class of the South.

The Amendment passed Congress by partisan votes, with Republicans in favor and Democrats against. The amendment was not a victory for Republican radicals. It was, rather, a distillation of the minimum terms which Republicans, momentarily reunited by Johnson's intransigence, demanded of the South. It did not require black suffrage, disenfranchise former Confederates, or break up the plantations. It demanded only that blacks be given equal rights as citizens and that the South be governed by men loyal to the Union. It was a potential bridge between North and South, between victor and vanquished, that the President might have utilized. Had he done so, the story of reconstruction might have been very different.

JOHNSON'S RESPONSE

Although the Fourteenth Amendment answered some of the constitutional misgivings expressed by the president in his veto of the civil rights bill, Johnson nevertheless objected to it, principally because of the disabilities placed on former Confederates. He thus severed himself completely from the Republicans and placed his political future in the hands of those who were constitutionally deprived of the vote. Taking the cue, the Johnson regimes in the South refused to ratify the amendment—except for Tennessee, which Congress rewarded by seating its representatives.

In August, Johnson's supporters organized a National Union convention in Philadelphia in hopes of launching a new political party. Off-year congressional elections that autumn seemed to present an opportunity for a referendum on Reconstruction policy. The third party movement fizzled, and in desperation the president decided to enter the campaign personally. On August 28 he embarked on a "Swing around the Circle," traveling by railroad and steamboat west to Chicago and returning by way of St. Louis, Indianapolis, and Pittsburgh. Never before had an incumbent president embarked on a partisan tour, and the novelty of the occasion dramatized the president's eccentricity. Losing all sense of proportion, he harangued his audiences, engaged in verbal duels with hecklers, and denounced his radical opponents as "a subsidized gang of hirelings and traducers." Toward the end of the journey, city and state officials openly avoided the president's appearances. He returned to Washington more isolated than ever.

In the fall elections, the voters pronounced judgment: The Republicans carried every northern state. Democrats retained a majority of the congressional delegations only of Delaware, Maryland, and Kentucky. Equally important, the distinction between radical and moderate largely vanished. The Republican party was reunited; it would reconstruct the South in its own way, with or without presidential support.

The lame duck Congress also read the election returns, and that winter it prepared for the new order that would begin on March 4, 1867. First, it moved to take control of its own sessions. To prevent the nine-month gap that had allowed the president a free hand over reconstruction in 1865, Congress passed an act decreeing that the new Congress would begin its session on Inauguration Day, March 4, instead of waiting until the following December. It then moved to restrict the president's power and authority. A Tenure of Office Act (March 2, 1867) prohibited the president from dismissing members of his own cabinet without the consent of the Senate. That same day, by an amendment to an army appropriation act, Congress prescribed that all military orders issued by the president had to be funneled through the Office of General of the Army (Ulysses S. Grant), whose headquarters were to be in Washington, D.C., and who could not be removed or reassigned without the consent of the Senate.

The radicals thus ensured themselves some control over the army, a significant move when one recalls that their blueprint for reconstruction involved a period of military rule. Doubts concerning that intent were instantly resolved when, that same day, March 2, 1867, the outgoing Congress enacted the first of four reconstruction acts. Congress now had control over reconstruction. The president vetoed each of these bills and then watched as Congress overrode his vetoes. The president had become irrelevant; within a year, Congress would seek to remove him altogether.

⊔Congress on the March

The four reconstruction acts Congress passed involved two main principles. Ignoring the existing governments created by presidential order, the acts divided the Confederate states (except for Tennessee) into five military districts, each governed by an army general. Second, the acts outlined the procedure for the restoration of civil government and readmission to the Union (which meant, in effect, having representatives seated in Congress). The district commanders were to enroll all voters, including blacks (but excluding former Confederates who were barred by the Fourteenth Amendment); and they were to hold elections for delegates to state constitutional conventions. The new state constitutions had to include a provision for black suffrage. When a civil government was established, the first legislature elected under it was to ratify the Fourteenth Amendment. When all these conditions were met, the state would be entitled to representation in Congress.

In 1868, six states had complied with these requirements and were readmitted. All had Republican governments, and their readmission was hastened by the Republican desire to have them participate in the presidential election that year. Readmission of the remaining four—Virginia, Georgia, Mississippi, and Texas—was delayed by white efforts to evade the congressional requirements. While whites procrastinated, Congress in 1869 approved the Fifteenth Amendment, which prohibited any state from denying the vote "on account of race, color, or previous condi-

Reconstruction of the South, 1865–1877.

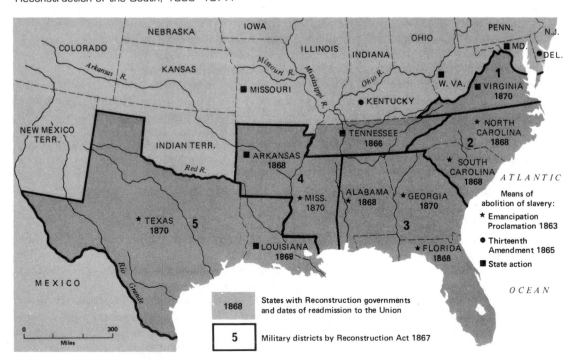

Library of Congress.

A mixed jury of blacks and whites, 1867.

tion of servitude." These four states were required to ratify the Fifteenth Amendment as well, a process completed by 1870.

RADICAL RULE
IN THE SOUTH

Thus began a period of Black Reconstruction—military-radical Republican rule—that lasted in some states for ten years, in others less than two. Though seemingly harsh, the radical program was not as severe as it might have been. No civil war in history has ever ended with so few reprisals. There was only one postwar execution—Henry Wirz, Swiss-born commander of the infamous Andersonville prisoner camp, was hanged for "war crimes."* Con-

---

* More than 12,000 Union prisoners of war died at Andersonville in the last year of the war, out of a total of 30,218 who died in all Confederate prison camps. Less well known is the fact that 25,976 "Rebels" died in Union POW camps.

federate president Jefferson Davis was imprisoned for only two years, and Robert E. Lee was allowed to retreat into the unsung captivity of a college presidency.

The military rule was both brief and light-handed. The federal occupying force numbered only 20,000 men, spread over ten states. The army rarely intervened in civilian affairs; indeed, it cooperated with the Lincoln-Johnson governments until Congress declared them no longer viable. In fact, it can be argued that the army did not exert itself enough. In the summer of 1866 it allowed hideous race riots in Memphis and New Orleans to go on for days. Later, when whites formed vigilante clubs to intimidate blacks, the army stood by helplessly until the president ordered it to act. From the standpoint of the blacks, the tragedy of Reconstruction was that Congress and the army did not go far enough.

Whether Congress had the constitutional authority to impose military rule on the South is, of course, another question. The war had been fought to prevent the

South from leaving the Union—if they were sovereign states and members of the Union, what right did Congress have to evict their governors and install army generals? Cowed by the radicals, the Supreme Court never directly confronted the issue. In 1866 the Court declared in *Ex Parte Milligan* that military courts could not try civilians in areas where the civil courts were open and operating. The case originated in the war, but it seemed to threaten the system of military government the radicals had in mind for the South. Congress promptly retaliated by reducing the number of justices on the Supreme Court and limiting the Court's jurisdiction. Some radicals proposed abolishing the Supreme Court altogether. The Court got the message. In 1867, when two southern states, Georgia and Mississippi, challenged the constitutionality of Reconstruction by asking the court to issue injunctions preventing the president and his secretary of war from enforcing the acts, the Court refused to hear the cases.

JOHNSON'S IMPEACHMENT

The president showed no such discretion. Challenged by the radicals, he planted his feet and fought back. In the summer of 1867, he curtailed the powers of the army commanders in the South and replaced those who were sympathetic to the radical program. In August 1867, he dismissed Secretary of War Edwin M. Stanton. Stanton had worked closely with the radicals in Congress, and as head of the War Department he was the central figure in military reconstruction. Johnson's dismissal did not actually violate the Tenure of Office Act, since Stanton was a Lincoln appointee, but it was certainly a challenge

Johnson's impeachment trial in the Senate.

New York Public Library Picture Collection.

CLIO'S FOCUS: The Captain of the Planter

Captain F. J. Nickols of the *Onward*, the inside ship of the Union fleet blockading Charleston, South Carolina, stared disbelievingly at the vessel steaming out of the heavily fortified port. The craft was flying the stars and bars of the Confederacy as well as the Palmetto flag of South Carolina. As it steered boldly toward the blockading squadron, the name *Planter* could be discerned on its bow. Just as Captain Nickols ordered his gunners at ready, the Confederate vessel raised yet another emblem—a white bedsheet signaling surrender. The *Planter* drew alongside and sixteen ragged fugitives (eight men, five women, and three children) climbed aboard the Union warship.

In charge of the party was Robert Smalls, a slave who had been trained as a river pilot. When the Confederate government chartered the cotton steamer *Planter* to use as a dispatch boat, Smalls, a slave hired by the vessel's owner, went with the ship. He had spent the early months of the war piloting the *Planter* on various missions through the web of waterways between Charleston and Port Royal. He knew by heart the location of the Confederate batteries and the signals used in passing. When the Union Navy seized Port Royal Sound in November 1861, he began to think of escape. From Beaufort, his birthplace, Smalls's mother wrote that the Federals, though they called the Port Royal blacks "contrabands," treated them well and allowed them to work their fields as free people.

The opportunity to escape came on May 13, 1862, when the white officers of the *Planter* went into town, leaving the crew of eight blacks on board. The previous day the *Planter* had taken on two hundred pounds of ammunition and four cannons, a cargo Smalls judged might be of considerable value to the soldiers in blue. Following a prearranged plan, the crew put the vessel under steam, picked up their families at the city's North Atlantic wharf, and sailed into the harbor. With Smalls dressed in the captain's uniform and giving all the proper signals, the *Planter* cleared the Confederate batteries at Forts Sumter and Moultrie and joined the Union squadron. Captain Nickols passed his happy fugitives on to the flag officer at Port Royal, and by nightfall Smalls had delivered his cargo of munitions to the Union depot at Hilton Head.

The abduction of the *Planter* caused a sensation in the North. The Lincoln administration's emphasis on preserving the Union had pushed slavery into the background. Smalls's exploit was evidence that the slaves, at least, understood what the war was about. The antislavery press pounced on the incident with glee. Smalls was the war's first black hero, his deed a clear demonstration that southern blacks had the skill and enterprise to survive in freedom. The abduction had material as well as symbolic value. Loss of the *Planter* deprived the Confederacy of a badly needed supply ship. General Lee himself took note of the loss and issued orders to prevent a recurrence of the "misfortune."

Smalls, commissioned as a second lieutenant, United States Colored Troops, spent the remainder of the war piloting the *Planter* and other Union vessels through the shallow sea island waters. After the war, he and other black veterans formed a cooperative that pooled the meager assets of Port Royal freedmen to purchase a coastal steamer. In command of this vessel, Smalls developed a lucrative trade, profits from which he invested in real estate. By 1868 he was one of the wealthiest men in Beaufort, landlord to much of the town and proud possessor of a stable of racehorses and an elegant carriage.

The regulations adopted by the postwar regime set up under President Johnson and its candid admission that it meant to keep South Carolina a white man's country taught Smalls how fragile a blessing freedom was. In March 1867, while Congress wrote a new reconstruction program, Smalls organized a Beaufort Republican Club, the first in South Carolina. The club, consisting of thirty-eight blacks and three whites, issued a call for a convention to organize a state Republican party. Smalls served as a delegate to that convention and to the convention summoned the following year to draft a state constitution. Smalls's most important contribution to the Reconstruction constitution was a provision for state-supported public education. The article he drafted prohibited racial segregation in the schools and made attendance compulsory for children between the ages of seven and fourteen. On paper at least, South Carolina had the most progressive educational system in the South.

Smalls was a hero to sea island residents not only because of his war record, which he never tired of recounting, but also because he symbolized self-made success. His loyal and predominantly black constituency sent him successively to the assembly (1868–1870), to the state senate (1870–1874), and finally to Congress (1874–1886). Yet he emerged from this lengthy service with little to show. He campaigned for land grants to freedmen, state-support for black business cooperatives, and state and federal protection of civil rights. But neither the white radicals who governed South Carolina in the 1870s nor Republicans in Congress were prepared for such reforms. He managed to hold his seat in Congress after white Democrats won control of the state in 1877, but even there he was an anomaly. In a scandalously fraudulent election in which black votes were thrown out by the boxful, the Democrats finally unseated him in 1886.

Robert Smalls lived until 1915, loyal to the end to the party of Abraham Lincoln, a party that long before had cynically called itself "lily white." It is sad that his party and his country could do no more for such a competent, farsighted leader.

---

to the radicals. The Senate, however, was not then in session, so Johnson had time to maneuver. In a rare display of political cunning, he persuaded General Grant to accept the post.

When Congress returned in December, the Senate refused to approve Stanton's removal. Grant promptly resigned. Johnson angrily denounced Grant for this "treachery," thereby driving the bewildered general into the arms of the radicals. Johnson then selected General Lorenzo Thomas, a braggart with a fondness for the bottle. A rare comedy ensued. Stanton, encouraged by the radicals, barricaded himself in the War Department, refusing to allow Thomas entry. When Thomas, at a Washington social function, announced his intent to take the building by force, Stanton had him arrested. In the midst of this, the House of Representatives voted that the president "be impeached of high crimes and misdemeanors in office." The House subsequently adopted eleven articles of impeachment, the first nine of which related in one way or another to the attempted removal of Stanton. The tenth

article, though it did not allege a crime, was actually the heart of the Radicals' case. It accused the president of attempting, through "intemperate, inflammatory, and scandalous harangues" to bring into "disgrace, ridicule, hatred, contempt, and reproach the Congress of the United States." The eleventh article repeated the charges of the previous ten.

The trial opened in the Senate on March 5, 1868, with Chief Justice Salmon P. Chase presiding. The argument developed by the impeachment managers appointed by the House was that the president was guilty of high crimes and misdemeanors within the meaning of the Constitution. Alternatively, if he could not be convicted of a

Election of 1868.

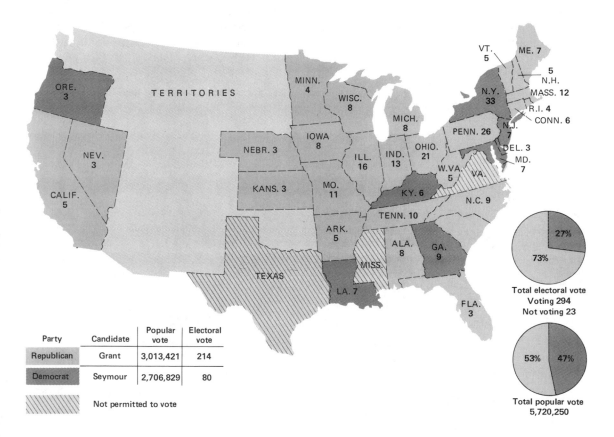

Party	Candidate	Popular vote	Electoral vote
Republican	Grant	3,013,421	214
Democrat	Seymour	2,706,829	80

Not permitted to vote

Total electoral vote
Voting 294
Not voting 23

Total popular vote
5,720,250

crime through judicial procedure, the Senate needed only to decide whether Johnson was "fit to retain the Office of President." The latter argument worried some senators, for it implied that impeachment was a political weapon which might be used against any president who faced a hostile majority in Congress. Republican moderates also worried about the presidential succession. Benjamin F. Wade, president pro tem of the Senate, was next in line if Johnson were removed, and the crusty Ohioan was the most radical of radicals.

On May 16, the Senate voted on the eleventh article, which was the broadest in scope. The vote was 35 in favor of conviction and 19 against—1 vote short of the two-thirds majority required to find the president guilty. The division held firm on two other articles, and the Senate adjourned without bothering with the remainder. The minority that had saved the president consisted of twelve Democrats and seven Republicans. Criticism of the Republican dissenters was harsh but short-lived, as public opinion swung around rather quickly to their point of view.

While the Senate pondered the fate of one president, a Republican convention met in Chicago to nominate another; for 1868 was an election year. The Republican choice was Ulysses S. Grant, a hero in the North and, since midwinter, the darling of the radicals. The general, devoid of political experience, was not eager for the office. Nor was he sure he wanted a Republican nomination, having been a prewar Democrat. He accepted, however, and in the election he swamped the hapless Democratic candidate Horatio Seymour, governor of New York, by an electoral vote of 214 to 80.

Six southern states were readmitted in the summer of 1868, and throughout much of the South the radical program was in place. The new president's task was simply to make it work. That proved a formidable one because the Republican regimes in the South began to crumble almost as soon as they were installed. Radicalism was

"Reconstruction or 'A White Man's Government.'" A Currier & Ives cartoon which depicts a drowning southerner rejecting the helping hand of a freed man, while President Grant advises him to accept the help.

New York Public Library, Aston, Lenox, and Tilden Foundation.

on the wane by 1869, both in Congress and in the reconstructed South.

⊔ Gray Reconstruction

Slavery had locked the black and white races in a love-hate relationship of mutual dependence. Emancipation changed the form of that relationship, but not its substance. Whites, in possession of most of the land and investment capital, were dependent on blacks for labor, and labor was all blacks had to offer. Master became employer; former slave became wage earner or tenant farmer. Freedom, however, did give blacks some mobility and hence some leverage. At the end of the war there was an enormous amount of movement. Even after the wanderlust subsided, black workers did not hesitate to desert an employer if they felt themselves mistreated. For several years after the war, the end of every growing season meant a general rearrangement of population. Some blacks moved into the cities, and others joined the white exodus to the West. But the vast majority stayed in neighborhoods with which they were familiar. Within a couple of years the movement declined and employment relationships became firm. A traveler in South Carolina in 1870 noticed that there was "little or no disparagement of the negro as a labourer among respectable countrymen, who need his services and employ him. On the contrary, there is much appreciation of his good qualities, and much greater satisfaction with what he has done, and may yet be trained to do, as a free labourer, than one might be prepared to find."

THE SHARECROPPER SYSTEM

Although blacks remained in a position of economic dependence after the war, the relationship was more complex than that of employer and employee. Few planters had the ready cash to pay wages, and few blacks were willing to become wage slaves. They hungered for land, even if they could not own it. Sharecropping met the needs of planters and freed blacks. Plantations were divided into rental plots, and the rent was a share of the tenant's crop. That share varied from half to three quarters, depending on the amount of tools and livestock the owner supplied in addition to the land. The system offered a small amount of independence for the tenant, but it also bound him in perpetual poverty. Only by rare good fortune and extraordinary effort could the sharecropper ever save enough money to purchase land of his own.

And ill fortune dogged the southern economy for a decade and more after the war. Cotton was the South's principal market crop, and cotton was no longer king. Cotton had become important in the world economy because textile technology led the Western World's industrial revolution. After 1860 other industries, notably steel and railroads, paced American and European economic growth. Textile manufacture, and cotton consumption, continued at the same level as before. But the South was no longer the key to the world economy. And the South's role in world trade would have been smaller even if there had been no Civil War; the war simply speeded the decline. Small white farmers thus became locked in the same circle of poverty in which the freed blacks found themselves. By 1880, one third of all white farmers in the cotton states were tenants or sharecroppers.

The one thing the Civil War did not change was the concentration of land ownership in the hands of a relatively small number of white planters. The central failure of reconstruction is that the federal government failed to provide land for the freed blacks, a redistribution that would almost surely have benefited poor white farmers as well. Redistribution of wealth was not, to be sure, within the realm of mid–nineteenth-century American thought, but a certain amount might have been accomplished by indirect means. During the war, Congress had already ordered the confiscation of slaves belonging to Confederates. The confiscation of plantations was but a small extension, one in fact advocated by Thaddeus Stevens and other radical Republicans.

In January 1865, General William Tecumseh Sherman, after a conference in Savannah with Secretary of War Stanton, issued Special Field Order Number 15. This military directive set aside for settlement by freed blacks the islands and seacoast from Charleston south to the St. Johns River of Florida and for a distance of 30 miles inland. Each black head of family was to be allowed to have up to 40 acres of land, though ultimate title was left unclear. Sherman and Stanton may have hoped that the lands would be given to the freed blacks, but more likely they expected Congress to set up a program for selling the preempted lands to blacks at low prices. But President Johnson, when the fighting ended, allowed the former white owners to repossess their lands, and a potential model for reconstruction was lost. Congress, even after the radicals won control, made no effort to provide cheap lands for the freed blacks other than those available in the western plains under the Homestead Act.

The failure to provide land for any substantial number of blacks was part of a larger flaw in congressional Reconstruction—that, while it was labeled radical, it was in fact so conservative that it failed to

Black members of Congress, 1869–1873. At left is Senator Hiram R. Revels of Mississippi. The others are members of the House of Representatives, three from South Carolina, and one each from Georgia, Florida, and Alabama.

New York Public Library Picture Collection.

alter the pattern of human relationships in the South. Black suffrage was undeniably a bold step, but otherwise congressional Republicans stood bound in the straitjacket of tradition. They accepted without question the Jeffersonian concept of states' rights (rejecting only its extreme form, secession), reverence for private property, and individualism. The Fourteenth Amendment offered paper guarantees for the rights of the freed blacks, but its enforcement depended on the realities of political power within the southern states. The Reconstruction Acts, far from bringing about any changes in the South, simply shifted the scene of battle from Congress to the states. Black voters and their allies there were left with the burden of determining the ultimate results of the Civil War.

FREED BLACKS
AND THE BALLOT

Blacks understood the challenge before them, and they made as much use as their numbers permitted of the opportunities presented by the Reconstruction Acts. In South Carolina, the first statewide meeting of the predominantly black Republican party adopted a platform calling for free public education, "the division of unoccupied lands among the poorer classes," reorganization of the state's judicial system, and public support for "the poor and destitute." When elections were held in November 1867 for delegates to a constitutional convention, 85 percent of the eligible blacks turned out to vote, and they selected quality leadership. Of the seventy-four blacks elected to the convention, only about half were former slaves. Fourteen were northerners who went to South Carolina after the war in search of political and economic opportunity, and several of these were well educated. Robert Brown Elliott, who would later become a member of Con-

gress, was a graduate of Eton and the Massachusetts School of Law. Among the former slaves chosen to the convention, the majority were ministers or tradesmen, such as the steamboat pilot Robert Smalls, another future congressman.

When the South Carolina constitution was submitted to a popular referendum in the spring of 1868, turnout among eligible blacks was again about 85 percent, whereas less than 60 percent of the registered white voters bothered to participate. Similar enthusiasm enabled blacks to win a majority in the legislature in the elections of 1870 and 1872. In the other southern states, however, the freed blacks, no matter how well motivated, did not have the numerical strength to dominate either the constitutional conventions or the Reconstruction governments. They were dependent on their white allies—northern carpetbaggers and southern scalawags. White Republicans drafted the Reconstruction constitutions and monopolized the top executive and judicial offices in the new governments. The results were as varied as the political mixture—a record of social progress marred by violence, venality, and betrayal.

The state constitutions required by the Reconstruction Acts brought some needed reforms. In addition to extending the suffrage through the addition of black and poor white voters to the poll lists, they reapportioned the legislatures to reflect population changes. Several states, where local officials had been appointed by the governor, made county offices elective. Some expanded the legal rights of women and liberalized penal codes. All provided for a uniform system of free public schools, though only South Carolina and Louisiana prohibited racially segregated school systems. In short, the Reconstruction constitutions brought to the South some of the social and political reforms that had engaged the North in the prewar decades. Next to the constitutional amendments that conferred civil and political rights on freed blacks, they were the main achievement of Reconstruction.

REDEMPTION OF THE SOUTH

The period of radical Republican rule endured in the memories of southern whites for a century afterward. The radical governments were denounced as unconstitutional, fraudulently elected, and hopelessly corrupt. Much of this poor historical image was the work of the white conservatives (Redeemers, they called themselves) who succeeded the radicals. Racially biased and appealing to an all-white constituency, the Redeemers had no difficulty convincing their listeners (and posterity) that radical Reconstruction was a dark day for the South. They drew pictures of governors and legislators making private fortunes through graft and fraud. Corruption was certainly present, but it was no more prevalent than in the North—or in the federal government under Grant.

The debts of the southern states did increase dramatically during the Reconstruction years, but graft was not entirely the cause. The South needed business investment to rebuild, and some states were too generous in their encouragement of business. Alabama purchased the bonds of the Alabama and Chattanooga Railroad in order to encourage construction, and when the railroad defaulted on its debt, the state lost millions. The fiasco was biracial and bipartisan, as both Republicans and Democrats cooperated in the scheme.

The financial problems faced by all southern governments, regardless of who controlled them, were staggering. The total wealth of the South, independent of the loss of slave property, declined by some 40 percent between 1860 and 1870. Emancipation eliminated the major source of state revenue—the tax on slaves—which

had provided the prewar states with nearly half their income. Emancipation also increased tremendously the social services required of the state governments. In South Carolina, for example, a total of 20,000 children, all white, were enrolled in public schools in 1860. The state's reconstruction constitution expanded the state's commitment to public education, and by 1870 there were 120,000 children (50,000 whites and 70,000 blacks) in the public educational system. The resulting taxes, five to ten times the prewar rates, added to the fury of southern whites, who equated taxes with tyranny in the revolutionary tradition.

A depression, beginning with the panic of 1873, was a further cause of debt. In the hard times that ensued, people were unable to pay taxes, and state after state went into debt. Yet in Mississippi, where radical Republicans did not win control until 1874, it was the radicals who introduced the reforms designed to reduce government expenditures. In South Carolina, Republicans exposed and cleaned out their own corruption long before the state was "redeemed" by white Democrats. And in Virginia, where charges of corruption flew as wildly as anywhere, the state not only incurred no Reconstruction debt, but even managed to pay off part of its prewar indebtedness.

The Reconstruction experience varied with each state, and so did the manner and timing of "redemption" by white conservative Democrats. Virginia never did experience Republican rule. In 1868 Virginia Democrats and former Whigs formed the Conservative party, which quickly gained a majority in the legislature and controlled the convention that drafted the Reconstruction constitution. The key to the Conservative success was electoral strength in the predominantly white mountain counties. In North Carolina and Tennessee, the small farmers of the Appalachian highlands generally voted Republican. Some states had a valid two-party system during the Reconstruction years. In Alabama the Democrats won in 1870, yielded to the Republicans in 1872, and returned in 1874. In North Carolina, where blacks numbered only a third of the population, the Republicans held the executive branch of government and the Democrats the legislature from 1870 to 1876. In Florida, on the other hand, Republicans kept themselves in power until 1877 by catering to white interests. Segregation prevailed, no effort was made to secure black civil rights, and only one black, a congressman, was elected to high office throughout the era of Florida's "reconstruction."

Because Reconstruction depended principally on black votes, it was doomed to fail. Freed blacks, even with white allies, were a minority everywhere in the South. After Congress passed an Amnesty Act in 1871, which removed virtually all the political disabilities imposed on former Confederates, "redemption" to white conservative rule was only a matter of time. White violence only hastened the process. Night-riding vigilantes adorned with mystical titles such as Ku Klux Klan or Knights of the White Camellia began intimidating black voters as soon as Reconstruction governments were established. The night riders were most active in those states with a large black voting population, and the violence was directed at the most politically active blacks and their closest white allies. Four predominantly black and solidly Republican counties in Alabama were the scene of almost nightly mayhem in 1869 and 1870. In 1870 all four voted Democratic and gave the Democrats the election.

Not all the violence was secret or organized. The worst riots occurred in South Carolina in 1870–1871, when the state's radical governor organized and armed a black militia. Whites, still shuddering at the memory of John Brown and Harpers Ferry, raided black homes in search of weapons, plundering and beating their occupants. The governor ultimately had to

New York Public Library Picture Collection.
Hooded members of the Ku Klux Klan.

summon help from President Grant and the U.S. Army to restore order, though by the time the army arrived, the weapons had vanished and the rioting had subsided.

Except in Arkansas, where the Republican governor effectively suppressed terrorism with arrests and executions, the Ku Klux Klan was a potent agent of the Redeemers. Alabama, Texas, and Mississippi returned to white conservative rule in 1874–1875 after an extensive campaign of intimidation that frightened blacks away from the polls. It was clear by then that only strong action by the federal government could preserve the social and political gains made by the freed blacks. In 1875 Congress passed a civil rights act guaranteeing blacks equal access to schools and other public facilities and banning their exclusion from jury duty. But enforcement of such guarantees would have taken an army of federal marshals, and the Grant administration was not prepared to take on such a burden.

THE END OF RECONSTRUCTION

The fact is that northern idealism had largely evaporated. The failure to give land to blacks showed that there were limits to northern idealism; the abolition of the Freedmen's Bureau in 1869 signaled its decline. The North never wanted to impose a social and economic revolution on the South, and it soon lost whatever will it had to impose a political revolution. The Republican alliance with the "lower orders," in factory or farm, North and South, had been founded on the free labor gospel—a Christian promise of future reward through hard work and self-discipline in a free environment. In the new age that dawned with the Civil War, the self-help gospel served best those who already had status and wealth, for it justified their success. By the early 1870s, the northern middle class had come to fear the immigrant factory worker and the black field hand as part of the faceless mob of poor who threatened law, order, and property rights. The Republicans, ever the party of the northern middle class, whatever their ges-

tures to factory and field hands, shifted with the groundswell of opinion. The party of political reform under Lincoln was transformed into the party of corporate capitalism under Grant. In the process it abandoned both southern blacks and northern factory workers.

In the South, the Redeemers, with their talk of a New South remade in the urban, industrialized image of the North, appealed to Republican leaders. Republicans of the 1870s felt far more comfortable in the company of wealthy businessmen than in the company of black tenant farmers. And the blacks lost out, because "redemption" brought racial segregation, the denial of civil rights, and the gradual loss of political privileges. Florida in 1885 adopted a new state constitution that specifically disenfranchised blacks, and by 1900 blacks were excluded from the polls everywhere in the South, regardless of the Fifteenth Amendment.

By 1876, when the radical governor of Mississippi fled the state rather than face impeachment by a hostile Democratic legislature, only three southern states remained under Republican rule. The "redemption" of those three—South Carolina, Louisiana, and Florida—by the infamous Compromise of 1877 is part of another story. The Reconstruction era by then had passed.

SUMMARY

Southern secession gave congressional Republicans an opportunity to pass legislation the North had long desired, proposals for economic development once embodied in Henry Clay's American System. The passage of this legislation symbolized the shift in the economy from farm to factory, and it shifted the focus of politics from state to national government. The principal

items on the Republican agenda were a protective tariff to foster manufactures, federal aid for the construction of the transcontinental railroad, a national bank system with power to issue money, and a Homestead Act that offered free land to the nation's toilers, both urban and rural. The burst of legislative activity also set the political agenda for the future. Tariffs, banks, and railroads were the central issues of American politics for the remainder of the century.

Although its commitment to economic growth eventually allied the Republican party with big business, its constituency in the 1860s was composed of the northern middle class and the working people. And Republicans remained concerned, at least through the 1860s, about the fate of blacks in the South. Through the early years of the war, radical Republicans pressured Lincoln to move faster toward emancipation. After the Emancipation Proclamation they quarreled with the president over reconstruction—what to do about the South after the war. Lincoln's approach, set forth in his Amnesty Proclamation of December 1863, was to allow southerners to hold elections for civil governments as soon as 10 percent of the voters in any state were willing to take a loyalty oath. The radical plan, embodied in the Wade-Davis Bill of July 1864, was to impose military rule on the postwar South, disenfranchise the planter-gentry that had caused all the trouble, and build new governments based on middle- and lower-class whites.

After Lincoln's death, Johnson adopted his Reconstruction policy with only minor changes and proceeded to establish civil governments in the South in the course of 1865. The new governments embarrassed the president in two ways, however: They contained a number of ex-Confederate officeholders, and they enacted black codes for the regulation of the former slaves. To many in the North, it seemed as if the war had accomplished very little. Johnson nevertheless adhered to his policy, and the effect was to throw Republican radicals and moderates together. In the spring of 1866, Congress struck at the black codes with a Civil Rights Act, and it reinforced that with the Fourteenth Amendment, which prohibited a state from denying to

its citizens the equal protection of the laws. Johnson's refusal to accept these moderate and obviously needed laws alienated the public, and the radicals won a majority of Congress in the off-year 1866 election.

In the course of 1867, the Congress passed, over Johnson's vetoes, four Reconstruction Acts. These imposed military rule on the South, forced the South to draft new state constitutions that gave blacks the vote, and required the southern states to ratify the fourteenth, and ultimately the fifteenth, amendments as a condition of reentry to the Union. Johnson's obstruction of the reconstruction acts, notably by removing from office his secretary of war, Edwin Stanton, led to his impeachment, though he was not convicted. Shortly after this, in 1868, six states complied with the reconstruction acts (Tennessee having been admitted earlier), and the remaining four were admitted in 1870.

Although it seemed harsh to southern whites, radical Reconstruction benefited blacks but little. They needed more than legal rights; they needed land if they were to have a chance at social and legal equality. But a breakup of the great plantations was beyond the realm of Republican liberalism. Republicans, like most pre–Civil War reformers, felt that freedom meant the elimination of some evil, such as liquor or slavery, not the imposition of some well-intentioned government program. As a result, having freed the slaves and guaranteed their legal rights, the Republicans were inclined to let them fend for themselves. Since blacks were a minority in every southern state, that meant they had to rely on white allies for political survival. After Congress in 1871 restored the vote to whites who had served the Confederacy, blacks were doomed. The radical regimes collapsed one by one, despite sporadic efforts by the Grant administration to shore them up. The last of them were "redeemed" to white conservative Democratic rule in 1877. The white "redeemers" whittled away at black rights, imposed segregation in public facilities, and eventually found ways of depriving blacks of the vote. Civil rights for blacks would have to await the second reconstruction a century later.

READING SUGGESTIONS

Kenneth Stampp's *The Era of Reconstruction, 1865–1877* (1965) is the best introduction to the field. The different approaches to Reconstruction by Lincoln and the radicals during the war are examined by Herman Belz, *Reconstructing the Union: Theory and Policy during the Civil War* (1969); and Hans Trefousse gives a sympathetic portrait of the radicals in *The Radical Republicans: Lincoln's Vanguard for Racial Justice* (1969). Leonard P. Curry's *Blueprint for Modern America* (1968) describes the sweeping legislative program of the Republicans that transformed the nation's political economy.

Dan T. Carter, *When the War Was Over* (1985), examines conditions in the South at the end of the war and the efforts of the Lincoln-Johnson governments. Eric L. McKitrick's *Andrew Johnson and Reconstruction* (1960) is a critical portrait of Lincoln's successor. LaWanda Cox and John H. Cox also examine Johnson's "critical year" in *Politics, Principle, and Prejudice, 1865–1866* (1963). The radical constitutional amendments are the subject of J. B. James, *The Framing of the Fourteenth Amendment* (1956), and William Gillette, *The Right to Vote: Politics and the Passage of the Fifteenth Amendment* (1965). Gillette presents the interesting thesis that the Fifteenth Amendment was passed for the benefit of northern rather than southern blacks.

Michael Les Benedict's *A Compromise of Principle: Congressional Republicans and Reconstruction, 1863–1869* (1974) is a detailed study of the evolution of Radical Reconstruction. Interesting aspects of the story are explored in Robert C. Morris's *Reading, 'Ritin, and Reconstruction: The Education of Freedmen in the South, 1861–1870* (1982) and in Claude F. Oubre's *Forty Acres and a Mule: The Freedmen's Bureau and Black Land Ownership* (1978).

The experience of the southern states under Reconstruction has been drastically revised in the past twenty years. The best survey of the new scholarship is an anthology edited by Otto Olsen, *The Reconstruction and Redemption of the South* (1979), which contains a chapter on each of six states. A particularly good case study, and one that stresses black initiative, is Joel Williamson, *After Slavery: The Negro in South Carolina during Reconstruction, 1861–1877* (1965). Robert Cruden's *The Negro in Reconstruction* (1969) describes black efforts to exercise power throughout the South. The best and most recent study of the black experience in Reconstruction is Leon Litwack's Pulitzer Prize–winning study, *Been in the Storm So Long* (1979). Mark W. Summers, *Railroads, Reconstruction, and the Gospel of Prosperity* (1984), describes railroad politics in the era and the efforts of northern Republicans to spread their version of progress.

Frederic Lewis.

TYCOONS, SPOILSMEN, AND MUGWUMPS

T hose were boisterous years. The post–Civil War decade was noisy, uncouth, bombastic, and exhilarating. Times were good; the economy bounded ahead, surviving a moment of financial panic in 1873. Everything was in motion. Farmers swept onto the Great Plains, while the army drove Indians onto reservations. Steamships jammed with immigrants poured into New York harbor, churning past Bedloe's Island, where the Statue of Liberty would be unveiled in 1886, to unload their human cargoes at the government's processing depot in Castle Garden. East and West, every index of activity surged upward, whether it was the number of steel ingots produced, bushels of wheat grown, churches erected, or outhouses torn down. The rocking chair became a standard feature of American living rooms in those years, so people could move even while sitting still.

The men and women who caught public attention reflected the vitality of the age, its unique blend of audacity, ambition, cynicism, and vulgarity. There was Cornelius Vanderbilt, a hulking old man garbed winter and summer in fur coat and "plug hat," still remembered as a Staten Island ferry boy who had made his riches by manipulating steamship companies and railroads, answering critics with a brazen: "What do I care about the law? Hain't I got the power?" There was Vanderbilt's arch enemy—pious, ascetic, black-garbed Daniel Drew, silk hat pushed to the back of his head, cigar in mouth, blowing a clearing through the haze of tobacco smoke so he could see and read for himself the latest ticker quotations on the Chicago and Northwestern Railroad. There were California's "Big Four"—Collis Huntington, Mark Hopkins, Leland Stanford, and Charles Crocker—two of them hardware peddlers and two dry-goods merchants, planning the construction of the Central Pacific Railroad, longer than any line yet known and crossing some of the most rugged terrain on the continent. There were the telegraph keys on May 10, 1869, clicking "One, two, three—done!" in unison across the nation as the golden spike was driven into a crosstie at Promontory Point, Utah, uniting the Central with Union Pacific in an iron bridge that spanned the continent from sea to sea.

There was also the revivalist Dwight L. Moody, who had come to the pulpit a semiliterate shoe salesman, barely able to pronounce the words in his King James Bible, bellowing to the throng that every ounce of his 280-pound frame "belonged to God." There was liberated Victoria Woodhull, stock market profiteer and confidante of Vanderbilt, in jail for having published in her *Weekly* the story that Henry Ward Beecher, most venerated clergyman of the day, had seduced one of his parishioners. There was the rambunctious Captain Carver, long black hair flying in the wind as he raced to win a bet that he could kill more buffalo in less time than any other man, leaving a trail of rotting carcasses that stretched to the far horizon. And there was Ulysses S. Grant, whose career had been spotted with failure and whiskey until he was picked by Lincoln to command the Army of the Potomac, riding through Central Park in the sky-blue carriage of "Jubilee Jim" Fisk, exhaling billows of fine Havana smoke and enjoying all the perquisites of being president of the United States.

⊔ High Jinks in High Finance

Rapid economic growth, new corporate structures that pyramided capital, and a loose-fisted, amiable government pre-

---

(*Chapter opening photo*) Cartoon of Commodore Vanderbilt. This appeared in the New York *Daily Graphic* a few days after Vanderbilt replied to public complaints about his railroad service with his famous, "The public be damned."

sented fabulous opportunities for fortune hunters. The prince of these was Cornelius Vanderbilt, who began building a steam-driven empire in the 1820s. By 1840 he was worth a million dollars, and his fleet of steamships was extensive enough to earn him the nickname "Commodore." By the 1850s he was manipulating governments like puppets in pursuit of a scheme to build a steamship canal across Central America. And his ruthlessness had become a source of public fascination and dread. When his associates took advantage of his absence on a European tour to seize one of his properties, he wrote:

> Gentlemen:
>   You have undertaken to cheat me. I will not sue you, for law takes too long. I will ruin you.
>
> Sincerely yours,
> Cornelius Vanderbilt

And he did.

THE RAILROAD WARS: VANDERBILT

During the Civil War, Vanderbilt sold or leased his steamships to the government and shifted his attention to railroads. The nation's railroad network, in fact, cried for attention. It hardly deserved the name "network"; it was, rather, a collection of local lines running from the hinterland to the nearest city. Tracks varied in width, so wheels had to be changed when traffic passed from one line to another. A journey from New York to Chicago, a route that would one day become a main line, required a dozen or more transfers. Consolidation required capital, imagination, and iron will; Vanderbilt had all three.

In 1862 Vanderbilt purchased control of the New York & Harlem Railroad, which ran from 42d Street in Manhattan to Brewster, New York, paying $9 a share. To give

himself access to downtown New York, he obtained from the city council a streetcar franchise and connected it to his railroad. This plum raised the value of Harlem Railroad stock to $90 a share. At that point the state legislature, whose collective conscience was as leathery as Vanderbilt's, intervened. The legislature insisted that it had the exclusive right to grant streetcar franchises, and its members secretly sold Harlem stock short in anticipation that the price would fall when Vanderbilt's franchise was annulled.* Sensing a plot, Vanderbilt ordered his agents to buy up every scrap of Harlem stock that was for sale, thus cornering the market. Vanderbilt's corner drove the price to new heights, and when the legislators delivered on their short contracts, they had to pay $179 a share! He had "busted the whole legislature," Vanderbilt later boasted, "and scores of the Honorable members had to go home from Albany without paying their board bills."

By the end of the war, Vanderbilt's consolidated railroads stretched along the Hudson River as far as Albany. He set his sights next on the New York Central Railroad, which ran from Albany to Buffalo on Lake Erie. When the owners resisted his overtures, he severed the connection between his own lines and the Central at the Albany Bridge, forcing New York–bound passengers to walk across the bridge. When critics protested this inconvenience, Vanderbilt replied impatiently:

---

*Bulls and Bears. *Bulls* are people who expect the price of a share of stock (or a commodity) to rise in the future, so they buy now ("buy long") in expectation of making a profit from the future price rise. *Bears* expect the price of a stock (or a commodity) to fall, so they sell now. If a Bear is "short" of stocks to sell, he might enter into a contract to deliver stocks at some point in the future at a stated price ("selling short"). If the Bear is right and the price falls, he buys at the lower price, delivers at the contractual price, and collects his profit. In this case, the legislators used political means to ensure that the price of Vanderbilt's stock fell.

The Bettmann Archive.

The New York stock exchange in its early days.

"Can't I do what I want with my own?" The owners of the New York Central capitulated, Vanderbilt bought control of the line, and the famous "water-level route" (following the Hudson River and the Erie Canal) from New York to the Great Lakes was born. In 1869 the legislature issued a charter that consolidated Vanderbilt's holdings into the New York Central System.

Long before that, however, Vanderbilt had started a new war. The New York Central would be of immensely greater value if it had a monopoly of the overland traffic between the seaboard and the Great Lakes, and from the beginning Vanderbilt had competition. The Erie Railroad, begun in the 1830s, wound for 500 miles across southern New York, connecting the seaport with Lake Erie. In 1857 the Erie fell into the hands of Daniel Drew, the "Great Bear" of Wall Street who had perfected speculation into an art. Drew was not in

the least interested in the Erie as a public utility; he was interested only in manipulating its stock. His practice was to sell the railroad short and then contrive an incident or start a rumor that drove the price of its stock down, whereupon he would deliver on his short contracts at a handsome profit. It was said on Wall Street: "Daniel says 'up'—Erie goes up. Daniel says 'down'—Erie goes down. Daniel says 'wiggle-waggle'—it goes both ways!" An intensely religious man, he would settle with his conscience after fleecing a friend by endowing a church. When his bets went sour, he would lock himself in his house, draw the blinds, and drink whiskey for days on end.

THE ERIE RING

In 1866 Vanderbilt began buying Erie stock, but Drew countered this move by simply printing more. He avoided suspicion by marketing his watery issues[*] through obscure brokerage firms, such as that operated by young Jim Fisk. In 1867 Drew acquired another youthful ally, thirty-one-year-old Jay Gould, who had assembled a small fortune as a stockbroker, and Erie stock mysteriously multiplied. The practice of the Erie Ring, as newspapers dubbed the trio of Drew, Gould, and Fisk, was to buy control of a small and tottering railroad in the name of the Erie and then issue stock on the strength of this new "asset."

Suspecting what was afoot, Vanderbilt persuaded a New York City judge to issue an injunction prohibiting the Erie directors from issuing more stock. Gould got a counterinjunction from another judge, cranked up his printing press, and dumped another 100,000 shares on the market. "Erie went down like a dead heifer," chortled Uncle Dan'l Drew, who as usual had sold short, and there was a near riot in the Stock Exchange. Above the tumult, wrote an observer, "sounded the mad roars of Commodore Vanderbilt." His judge ordered the arrest of the Erie Ring for contempt of court.

Still a step ahead of the Commodore and his deputies, the Erie trio packed up the railroad's books, stuffed $6 million—the profits from the sale of their printing-press stock—into a valise, and fled across the Hudson River to Jersey City. There they took over Taylor's Hotel, renaming it Fort Taylor, and settled in for a siege. Jersey City authorities obligingly provided them with a detail of police guards, and Jim Fisk hired some waterfront loafers for additional protection. Three small cannons were mounted on the riverfront near the hotel, and four lifeboats, each holding twelve armed men, served as a shore patrol. Fisk, wearing naval uniform, assumed command of the Erie navy. To newspaper reporters who crowded into Jersey City, Fisk explained: "Commodore Vanderbilt owns New York. He owns the Stock Exchange. He owns New York's streets and railroads. We are ambitious young men. We saw there was no chance for us to expand in your city, so we came over here to Jersey to grow up with the country." The public loved it.

Inside Fort Taylor, Jay Gould took charge. First, he tried to persuade the New Jersey legislature to make the Erie a New Jersey corporation. Failing that, he packed a big valise with half a million dollars and slipped off to Albany. His object was to persuade the New York legislature to allow the Erie to issue more stock. Vanderbilt sent a counter lobby, and the prices demanded by New York legislators reached unprecedented heights. Gould coupled his handouts with shrewd public relations that portrayed Vanderbilt as a monopolist standing in the way of free competition. Gould got his bill, and Vanderbilt capitulated. Confessing that the Erie war had taught him "it never pays to kick a skunk," he sent a message to Jersey City: "Drew, I'm sick of the whole damned business. Come and see me." A compromise was worked out in which Vanderbilt was reimbursed in part for the $4.5 million he had expended on worthless Erie stock, and the Erie Ring retained control of the railroad.

The aftermath was less comic. In a sudden power grab, Gould and Fisk ousted Drew from the Erie board of directors. Gould had himself elected president of the company; Fisk became vice president and comptroller. With money taken from the Erie treasury, Fisk bought an opera house to serve as the railroad's offices and charged the railroad rent of $75,000 a month. The Erie directors eventually tired of these antics and ousted Gould in 1872. Fisk by then was dead, assassinated on the steps of the Grand Central Hotel by a man

---

[*] Normally, the value of the outstanding shares of a company's stock equals the value of a company's physical assets. Stock issued in excess of the company's value is known as *watered stock*. Pouring profits back into a company to increase its net worth is known as *squeezing the water out* of its stock.

CLIO'S FOCUS: Lydia Pinkham, Queen of the Patent Medicines

Americans have always had a touching faith in nostrums and home remedies. Rural isolation may have been the reason: Most people did not have access to doctors, and had to devise their own cures for ailments. The more successful (or perhaps simply more tasty) of these crept naturally into the marketplace. They were called patent medicines, though the term is misleading. Healers did not dare patent their medicines, because the U.S. Patent Office required a list of ingredients. Since most were a mixture of common herbs, syrup, and alcohol, they could be easily imitated, patent or not. What the owners patented instead were their trademarks, which gave their preparation identity and credibility. An authoritative label was enough for millions who purchased Dr. Williams' Pink Pills for Pale People.

Women, hammered at from infancy with the notion that they were the "weaker sex," were especially good customers. The person who worked this market most successfully was a New England housewife, Lydia E. Pinkham. Her Vegetable Com-

Advertisement for Lydia Pinkham's Vegetable Compound. Sales of her patent medicine made Lydia Pinkham one of the wealthiest tycoons of the age. Chemical analysis indicated that the only active element in the compound was the 13½ percent ethyl alcohol.

New York Public Library Picture Collection.

pound was touted as a cure for every ailment that might afflict female reproductive parts. "Only a woman," declared Mrs. Pinkham, "can understand a woman's ills." The slogan appealed to the feminine mystique.

Lydia Pinkham made the Vegetable Compound on her kitchen stove, and for some years simply gave it away to friends and neighbors. But when her husband went broke in the panic of 1873, she turned professional. The compound, billed as the Greatest Remedy in the World, appeared on the market in 1875. A year later she obtained a patent on the label. The label, a stroke of advertising genius, featured Lydia herself, smiling benignly, dressed in prim black silk trimmed with white lace. The virtue and integrity conveyed by her portrait easily disarmed any critics who might be offended by the words immediately below the picture, which said "Contains 13½ percent alcohol," a notice required by the government. Government officials later discovered that the alcohol was the only operative ingredient; the rest was extract of bark and root.

But the Vegetable Compound was a hit, and Lydia Pinkham exploited her success with shrewd marketing techniques and promotional schemes. By the time she died near the turn of the century, she was one of the country's business leaders.

he had beaten in both love and war.[*] Drew was ruined by the panic of 1873, and when he died the most valuable item in his estate was $130 worth of Bibles and hymnbooks. Jay Gould went on to build a corporate empire that included the Union Pacific Railroad, the Missouri Pacific, the Texas and Pacific, the Wabash, and the Western Union Telegraph Company.

The Erie war was the most spectacular of the speculative high jinks of the Gilded Age, but it was not the only one. Schemers routinely raided corporate treasuries, peddled worthless stock, slipped kickbacks and rebates to favored customers, and bribed politicians. The American marketplace had become a lawless jungle, and before long the competitors themselves realized they

needed some rules and a referee. Government could provide both, but not for some time to come. At the moment—that is to say, in the 1870s—the federal government seemed unable to regulate itself.

⊔ Age of the Spoilsmen

"Party leaders," said Senator William L. Marcy, explaining Jacksonian politics in the 1830s, "claim as a matter of right the advantages of success. They see nothing wrong with the rule that to the victor belong the spoils of the enemy." The Jacksonians had introduced the "spoils system" in the name of democracy. They felt that periodic rotation of officeholders ensured conscientious, honest government because administrators would not have time to become lazy, indifferent, or corrupt. The result, by 1870, was the opposite of what the Jacksonians intended. After the question of Reconstruction was resolved, no issue

---

[*] One comic's eulogy on Fisk: "Last in war, first in peace, and deep in the pockets of his countrymen." Fisk's assassin, Ned Stokes, spent four years in New York's Sing Sing penitentiary, where he was treated as an honored guest.

of substance divided the two major parties. Republicans and Democrats vied for power principally in order to reward their followers. Issues such as tax policy, money and banking, railroad regulation, or labor strife were rarely discussed. At election time, the Republicans contented themselves with rhetorical reminders that southerners and Democrats had once been traitors to the Union, a tactic known as "waving the bloody shirt."

The Democrats could count on the "solid South," once the Radicals were ousted, and they were strong in northern cities and among immigrants. Republicans found most of their support among established nationalities, among Yankees—whether in New England or transplanted—and in the farms and villages of the West. Most voters sided with one party or the other out of parental example and habit. Yet voter interest in politics was extraordinarily high. People thronged to campaign rallies and turned up at the polls in droves. That their choice, quite often, was between tweedledum and tweedledee did not seem to matter. They enjoyed the spectacle, the game, with all its pomp and glitter.

THE RULE OF THE BOSSES

The system made for corruption, but in a curious way, the result was not entirely grievous. The machinery of Congress was so creaky and outdated that the oil of corruption was almost the only thing that made it work. The committee structure dated back to the 1790s. In the House of Representatives, the Speaker controlled all

Popular voting patterns, 1876–1892.

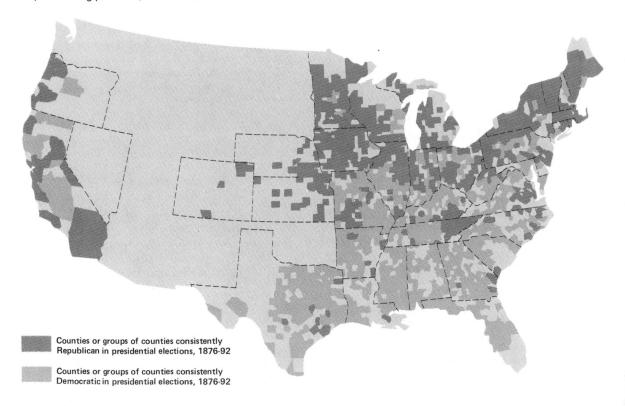

Counties or groups of counties consistently Republican in presidential elections, 1876-92

Counties or groups of counties consistently Democratic in presidential elections, 1876-92

committee appointments and thus held the entire assemblage in an iron grip. Party loyalty and friendship were the keys to a successful political career. Hobbled by favoritism, the congressional committees struggled with an ever-mounting burden of legislation, as the nation's social and economic problems became ever more complex. The first Civil War Congress (1861–1863), busier by far than any prewar Congress, handled 613 pieces of legislation. By the 1880s Congress waded through more 11,000 bills every two years. Needless to say, only the pet projects of committee chairmen stood a chance of passage.

By the mid-nineteenth century, the Senate had become the most important branch of the government, overshadowing even the president. Andrew Johnson's disastrous tenure weakened the presidency, and his successors in the White House, with the possible exceptions of Grant and Grover Cleveland, were a dreary collection of nonentities. Not until Theodore Roosevelt splashed onto the political scene in 1901 would the presidency be revitalized. The Senate, meantime, fell heir to the public veneration accorded its giants of the past—Webster, Clay, Calhoun, and Douglas. That it scarcely deserved it mattered not.

The Senate was the stronghold of the Spoilsmen. Under the arrangement that had seemed reasonable in the 1780s but was merely quaint by the 1870s, senators were chosen by state legislatures. These, in turn, were usually controlled by party machines. So the party head, or "boss" (to use the colloquialism borrowed from the colonial Dutch), had his cronies install him in the Senate. There, through the system known as senatorial courtesy, he was in a position to reward followers with the spoils of office, since the president, in naming customs collectors, postmasters, and judges, almost invariably deferred to the wishes of a state's senators.

In New York, Senator Roscoe Conkling headed a finely tuned Republican machine that rested on a rich bed of patronage, the New York City Customs House. Tall, handsome, and flamboyant, given to wearing white flannel trousers and bright waistcoats, Conkling headed a faction of the Republican party known as the Stalwarts. United by nothing but a fear of change, the Stalwarts directed their best efforts at keeping Grant in the White House forever simply because the aging general himself revered the status quo. The *New York Times* was more discerning than it realized when it gushed that Conkling was "a typical American statesman—a man by whose career and character the future will judge of the political standards of the present."

In Pennsylvania, Republican Senator Simon Cameron held sway, working with Thomas Scott, manager of the Pennsylvania Railroad. Legend had it that the legislature waited upon adjournment until Mr. Scott passed the word that he had "no further business" for it. The political giants of the Middle West were Zachariah Chandler of Michigan and Oliver P. Morton of Indiana. Chandler, a bluff and hearty man, fond of whiskey and poker, was one of the founders of the Republican party. Sent to the Senate in 1857, he resided there, except for one short interval, until his death in 1879. Morton attended the birth of the Republican party in his state, served as governor during the Civil War, moved on to the Senate afterward, and stayed there, a fast and confidential friend of the general in the White House, until his death in 1877. Morton's Republican organization was of particular importance nationally because Indiana was one of the few "swing" states, a political no-man's land where Republicans and Democrats commanded nearly equal support. Morton's organization was the beneficiary of a good share of the governmental thievery of the age simply because a few dollars judiciously distributed in the Indiana backwoods could turn the state's electoral vote and thereby a close national election.

James G. Blaine.

New York Public Library Picture Collection.

Aside from the popular Grant, the nation's favorite politician was James G. Blaine, the "white-plumed knight" from Maine. Blaine entered Congress a Republican during the Civil War, served in the House until 1876, and then moved to the Senate. In nearly twenty years of legislative service, he left no imprint on history, not a single piece of constructive legislation, hardly even a constructive suggestion. His followers, dubbed "Halfbreeds," differed from Conkling's Stalwarts only in that they were less given to apoplexy when civil service reform was mentioned. Yet suave manners, florid oratory, and magnetic personality made Blaine a folk hero, or as close to one as a cynical politician could come. He was nominated for president only once, in 1884, when he suffered the humiliation of losing to Grover Cleveland, the first Democrat elected after the war. But in every other election between 1876 and his death in 1893 he was a formidable possibility, and his role as kingmaker was attested

by his tenure as secretary of state in the 1880s under Presidents Garfield and Harrison.

"When I want a thing," Blaine once remarked to his wife, "I want it dreadfully." Gilded Age politics took its tone from the barons of industry and the speculators of Wall Street who accumulated great wealth and lived in lavish style. The Spoilsmen, on the whole, were not rich men, and they often regarded money as an avenue to power rather than luxury. But their greed was just as intense as that of a Gould or a Vanderbilt, and their wheeling and dealing just as imaginatively flamboyant.

⊔ The Scandals of the Grant Era

Ulysses S. Grant was a genuinely honest man, one of the few in politics in his day. But he was a shy person who required the company of the jaunty freebooters who gathered around him. Raised in poverty, he had longed all his life for the status markers of the rich—thoroughbred horses, fine cigars, and aged whiskey. When such gifts were showered upon him in profusion, he failed to understand that they inevitably bore a price. Naiveté is a dangerous quality in an American president, and Grant was a social innocent. In the summer of 1869, while Fisk and Gould were engaged in a wild and ultimately highly profitable scheme to corner the nation's gold supply, Grant went riding with "Jubilee Jim" in Central Park, conveying the impression that he knew all about the operation.

Fraud and misappropriation of funds were by no means new to the United States government; some of the wrongdoing that was ultimately uncovered in the 1870s dated back to Lincoln's time. But under Grant, the thieves expanded their operations and concocted dazzling new schemes, encouraged by the president's innocence and protected from exposure by the president's own private secretary, Colonel Orville Babcock, a man of wooden conscience and unbridled appetite.

Grant ambled through his first term without serious trouble, at least none that involved the executive branch. For several years the president's chief problem seemed to be subduing the Ku Klux Klan and propping up the unpopular Republican regimes in the reconstructed South. Then, beginning in 1873, scandal after scandal burst around him, rattling him out of his complacency. The cleanup gave birth to a small but important movement for reform. A more perceptive president might have joined the reform crusade, and in so doing

would have given it added respectability. But Grant could not bring himself to desert the providers of good cigars and smooth whiskey.

THE TWEED RING

The first scandal to explode involved local rather than federal corruption. In the fall of 1871, New York City "boss" William Marcy Tweed, together with a number of city officials, was indicted for bilking the city treasury of millions of dollars. The arrests climaxed a two-year vendetta against Tweed by *Harper's Weekly* and its brilliant young cartoonist, Thomas Nast. (Nast invented the donkey symbol for the Demo-

"Can the Law Reach Him—the Dwarf and the Giant Thief." This is a Tom Nast cartoon on "Boss" Tweed.

New York Public Library Picture Collection.

cratic party in 1870 and followed it with an elephant for Republicans in 1874.) The Tweed Ring had engaged in some massive public works. They built a brick wall around Central Park to protect the forest from traffic and provide work for contractors. A city hall estimated at $250,000 ultimately cost $8 million. Tweed and his friends probably received some kickbacks, but so did many contractors.

The root of the problem was that New York City was fast becoming a modern metropolis. It had an urgent need for professional police and fire services (it had a volunteer fire department until 1865), as well as for parks and mass transportation. These needs surpassed its budget, so the city's debt tripled between 1860 and 1870. Tweed, though one of several officials in charge of city finances, was a tempting mark because he was so easy to caricature. He was a huge man, midway between portly and obese, given to lavish entertaining. Stamped by Nast's cartoons as a serio-comic villain, Tweed was a natural target for an ambitious New York Democrat named Samuel J. Tilden, who gathered the evidence that led to the indictments. Although Tweed was convicted only of failing to keep proper accounts, he was sentenced to jail. Freed after a brief term, he was later rearrested. He then escaped, was apprehended after being recognized through a Nast cartoon, and died in prison in 1878. Tilden, on the strength of his "cleanup," went on to become head of the Democratic party and its nominee for president in 1876.

THE CRÉDIT MOBILIER

The public outcry over Boss Tweed was just subsiding in the fall of 1872 when newspaper reporters uncovered a scandalous link between Congress and the newly completed Union Pacific Railroad. The railroad, it developed, had been con-

structed by a separate corporation, the Crédit Mobilier, and the relationship between the two companies was wholly fraudulent. Owned by some of the same men who controlled the Union Pacific, the Crédit Mobilier had grossly overcharged the railroad for construction costs, thereby diverting to the pockets of the railroad's promoters some $23 million in funds that had originally been given to the Union Pacific by the government. A number of prominent congressmen, newspapers discovered, had been given Crédit Mobilier stock in return for a promise not to investigate the company. Congress reacted with appropriate indignation and launched an investigation. The House of Representatives censured one of its members, Oakes Ames, the go-between who had distributed the stock, and then closed ranks, smothering further disclosures.

A presidential election that autumn (1872) presented an early and, as it turned out, premature opportunity for those who wanted to clean up the government. When the Republicans renominated Grant, a reform element, calling themselves Liberal Republicans, bolted the party and held a convention of their own. The Liberal Republicans had a number of able leaders, among them Senator Carl Schurz of Missouri, who for years had been crusading for a federal merit system in place of the spoils system. The Liberals instead chose as their nominee Horace Greeley, publisher of the New York *Tribune*. In 30 years as head of the *Tribune*, Greeley had flirted with every fad that had come along, from vegetarianism to socialism. During the war he had oscillated between wild bellicosity and anguished pacifism. The Democrats, still stigmatized as rebels and traitors, added to Greeley's troubles by endorsing him as their candidate. Grant's henchmen had a field day. In the election Grant, still a hero to most northerners, polled 56 percent of the popular vote, the best showing any candidate had made in a contested election up to that time. Greeley, so badly abused that he confessed "I hardly knew whether I was running for the Presidency or the Penitentiary," died a few weeks after the election.

THE WHISKEY RING

The reform movement failed to get off the ground in 1872 largely because the Grant administration to that point had not been involved in any major scandals. During Grant's second term, however, outrage after outrage burst into public view. The Postal Department was caught taking kickbacks from mail contractors; fraud was uncovered in the Treasury, the War Department, and the Bureau of Indian Affairs. The most spectacular theft of all was that of the Whiskey Ring. Dating back to the war, distillers and Treasury officials had conspired to defraud the government of taxes on distilled liquor. The ring, which

was centered in St. Louis, had come under the investigative eye of the St. Louis *Democrat* in 1869 when Grant appointed General John A. McDonald, an army crony, as supervisor of Internal Revenue for the St. Louis district. McDonald bought off the *Democrat* by taking its publisher into the conspiracy, and expanded ring operations to include distillers throughout the Middle West. To prevent any prying from Washington, McDonald slipped $30,000 in cash to the president's private secretary, Colonel Babcock. Over the next five years the ring deprived the Treasury of some $2 to $4 million. The surplus, after distillers and government officials had taken their allotments, went into the coffers of the Republican party to further Grant's reelection.

In 1874, after scandals of another sort forced the resignation of the secretary of the treasury, Grant named Benjamin H. Bristow to the post. Bristow had little liking for Grant and political ambitions of his own. Alerted to the existence of the ring

Joseph Keppler's cartoon "The Bosses of the Senate."

Library of Congress.

by the St. Louis *Globe*, he began an investigation that resulted in thirty-two raids and the arrest of 238 government officials and distillers. It was the biggest case of governmental wrongdoing in the nation's history.

⊔ Sputtering Reform: Hayes, Conkling, Arthur

The exposure of the Whiskey Ring wrecked any chances Grant might have had for a third term, although he himself seemed willing enough to remain in office. The Republican convention in 1876 was evenly divided between Roscoe Conkling's

Stalwarts, who backed Grant, and the Half-breeds, led by James G. Blaine. With neither side able to prevail, they ultimately compromised on the respectable although not widely known governor of Ohio, Rutherford B. Hayes. The Democrats turned to Samuel J. Tilden, who had earned a reputation as a reformer as well as the governorship of New York as a result of his victory over Tweed. The Democrats had gained steadily in strength since 1872, capitalizing on public disillusion with Grant and the "redemption" of the South by white conservatives. Only three southern states, South Carolina, Louisiana, and Florida, were still under radical Republican rule by 1876. The election was one of the closest ever. After several days of ballot

Election of 1876.

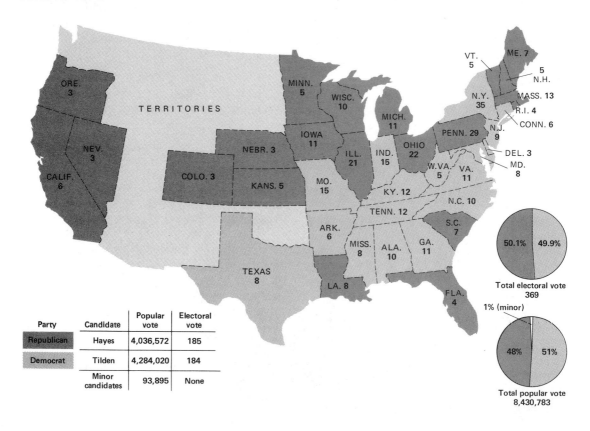

Party	Candidate	Popular vote	Electoral vote
Republican	Hayes	4,036,572	185
Democrat	Tilden	4,284,020	184
	Minor candidates	93,895	None

50.1%   49.9%

Total electoral vote 369

1% (minor)

48%   51%

Total popular vote 8,430,783

counting, during which each side claimed victory, it appeared that Tilden had 184 uncontested electoral votes and Hayes had 165. The number necessary for victory was 185, and 20 were in dispute. One of these was the vote of an Oregon elector; the remainder belonged to the three southern states still under Republican rule.

THE COMPROMISE OF 1877

The reins of Republican power had frayed to the thread of a single electoral vote, but they were not yet broken. Zachariah Chandler, chair of the Republican National Committee, sent telegrams alerting Republican officials in the three southern states to the importance of their count. President Grant ordered the military forces occupying those states to protect the Republican canvassing boards. All three states accordingly returned Republican majorities. While Democrats shouted foul play, Congress created an electoral commission to examine the returns. Republicans had a one-vote majority on the commission, and by a party line vote the commission awarded all 20 votes to Hayes, making him the winner, 185 to 184. By then southerners were again threatening secession, and some Democrats in the North were threatening to delay Hayes's inauguration. Republicans realized that some concessions were in order. The result was a backstairs bargain in Congress on the eve of the inauguration.

The Democrats, for their part of the deal, agreed to let Hayes move peacefully into the White House. In return, Hayes agreed to name a southerner to his cabinet and gave secret assurances that he would withdraw the federal troops propping up the Republican regimes in South Carolina, Florida, and Louisiana. Southerners, in addition, won promises of congressional support for railroad projects in their area. Congress had ended the lavish grants for transcontinental railroads, but an occasional plum was not beyond its means. The bargain offered something for everyone but the freed blacks. Republicans retained the presidency; white southerners completed the "Redemption." By 1876, neither was much concerned about the fate of southern blacks. They were left to the mercies of the southern white majority. And southern states were already devising ways to evade the Fifteenth Amendment and deprive blacks of the vote. The compromise thus represented the Republican party's final desertion of the principles on which it had been founded two decades before.

For the nation as a whole, however, the compromise brought to a close a period in which brute force in politics had too often overcome the usual give and take. It was the last of the great sectional compromises of the century. A solid Democratic South became an accepted fact of American elections. And with open sectional controversy over at last, politicians could return to the most urgent of needs—clean government.

THE LIBERAL REFORMERS AND HAYES

Out of the Liberal Republican revolt of 1872 had grown, by the mid-1870s, a reform movement that sliced through both political parties. The movement was limited in its objectives; it wanted to repair the political system rather than replace it. Liberal reform was middle class in origin, intellectual in character, and thin in ranks. Journalists, such as Edwin L. Godkin of *The Nation* and Whitelaw Reid of the New York *Tribune*, helped to publicize it, and their support lent it substance.

What the reformers wanted was an end to special privilege, whether in government patronage or in subsidies to business. They wanted a freer, more open, more honest, and more competitive political and economic system. Governmental corruption, ran the diagnosis of the liberal reformers, was the product of the spoils system. The remedy was a professional civil service with appointment and promotion based on merit. As economic liberals, they favored freer trade through a reduction in tariffs. In 1876, with the exception of Roscoe Conkling and his Stalwarts, both parties gave lip service to the need for reform.

Rutherford B. Hayes had been a compromise candidate among Republicans, and his administration reflected his divided loyalties. He did bring the reform leader Carl Schurz into his cabinet as secretary of the interior, and he allowed Schurz to place his department on a merit system. On the other hand, he looked away while Treasury Secretary John Sherman, in charge of the government's largest bureau, distributed patronage for his own benefit. Hayes issued an executive order forbidding federal employees from participating in politics and then allowed a Republican committee to send letters to officeholders asking for "voluntary contributions" to the party. Cynics claimed that the biggest cleanup was undertaken by the president's wife, "Lemonade Lucy," who swept the bourbon bottles out of the White House.

With more pluck than anyone expected, Hayes did challenge the powerful Conkling machine in New York. Conkling's power rested on the New York Customs House, where clerks and collectors routinely made small fortunes through bribery and graft. By the rule of senatorial courtesy, presidents felt obliged to clear all appointments at the customs house with Roscoe Conkling, and control of this rich lode of patronage enabled Conkling to control Republican party machinery throughout the state. To challenge Conkling required courage, but Hayes doubtless found in it personal as well as political satisfaction. Without consulting Senator Conkling, he dismissed two of his underlings, collector

Chester A. Arthur and naval officer Alonzo B. Cornell. The president then named Theodore Roosevelt, Sr., who had earned a modest reputation as a reformer, to head the customs house. But the Senate, bowing to Conkling's wishes, refused to confirm the appointment. After the Senate adjourned, Hayes appointed other officers to manage the customs house, thereby claiming a technical victory. The Stalwarts retaliated by electing Alonzo Cornell governor of New York in 1879. Reformers applauded the president's efforts, but everyone else in the Republican party sighed with relief when Hayes announced he would not seek renomination.

GARFIELD, THEN ARTHUR

Roscoe Conkling, made more obstinate than ever by the assault on his bailiwick, went to the Republican convention in 1880 determined to restore Grant and favoritism to the presidency. Blaine's Halfbreeds, together with reformers who called themselves Independent Republicans, had strength enough to block Conkling but not enough to nominate a candidate of their own. The convention eventually turned to James A. Garfield of Ohio, a former general who was too bland to be controversial. Garfield defeated the Democratic candidate in another close contest, which demonstrated anew the balance between the parties in the years after Reconstruction ended. The balance, in turn, helps to explain the political sterility of the age.

After Garfield's term (filled out after his death by his vice president), the presidency bounced from one party to the other every four years for the rest of the century. And between 1876, when Hayes was elected, and 1896, when McKinley was elected, no president enjoyed a friendly party majority in both houses of Congress throughout his term. Balance and sterility fed on each other. Voters refused to give politicians a mandate; politicians, for fear of making enemies, failed to ask for one.

Garfield showed his colors soon after the election when he named James G. Blaine secretary of state and filled his cabinet with Halfbreeds. Independents were dismayed, and Conkling was furious. As if to twist the knife a little further, Garfield nominated a new set of officials to the New York Customs House without consulting Conkling. When the Senate, deferring to a new president, confirmed the appointments, Conkling lost his head and resigned his seat. He intended to embarrass the president and prove the strength of his organization by securing midterm reelection, but he miscalculated badly. A combination of Halfbreeds and Independents in the New York legislature defeated him, and that ended the career of the prince of spoilsmen.

While this drama played itself out in New York, another and more serious tragedy was enacted in Washington. On June 2, 1881, Charles Guiteau, a man with a history of mental troubles, shot and mortally wounded President Garfield. Letters found in the assassin's possession indicated that he was a Stalwart and unhappy with the president's appointments policy. That revelation instantly revived the reform movement. If disappointed officeseekers were going to go around shooting the president, many agreed, it was time to do away with the spoils system. The new president, Chester Arthur, a former ally of Roscoe Conkling, was hardly one to lead such reform, so the Independents turned to Congress.

CIVIL SERVICE REFORM

In the Senate, George Pendleton, Democrat from Ohio, had become the most articulate spokesman for civil service reform.

While he labored to put together a coalition of Democrats and Independent Republicans, the voters took a hand. Turning against the Republicans, in part because of their factional fighting, the voters in 1882 returned a two-to-one Democratic majority in the House of Representatives, a landslide that forecast a Democratic presidential victory in 1884. The Republicans retained a slim edge in the Senate, but the party was both chastened and fearful that it might lose control, after twenty lush years, of the fountain of patronage. Even Stalwarts could see the advantage in a civil service measure that guaranteed tenure to those already in office. The lame duck session that convened shortly after the election approved the Pendleton Civil Service Act by decisive majorities, and in January 1883, President Arthur, having declared independence from his former Stalwart chieftain, signed it into law.

The Pendleton Act established a merit system for appointment and promotion based on competitive examinations. Officeholders already in service had to take the examinations before they could win promotion. The recommendations of congressmen were to receive no consideration in the appointment process, and soliciting political funds from federal officeholders was prohibited. Once "classified" under this system, officeholders could not be dismissed for political reasons. To enforce these regulations, the act authorized the president to appoint a three-person Civil Service Commission.

The act covered only those offices and bureaus containing more than fifty employees, and since most government agencies were smaller than this, the new rules applied to only about 15 percent of federal officeholders. Most of the covered offices were in the vice-ridden Treasury and Postal Departments, however. Coverage was extended in succeeding years, as outgoing presidents sought to provide tenure

Civil Service Reform: The View from Tammany Hall

George Washington Plunkitt, a ward boss in New York City's Tammany Hall political machine, had a refreshing candor, a quality rare in politicians. Seated on his "throne"—a shoeshine stand—he would engage passersby in "plain talks on very practical politics." It was he, for instance, who drew a distinction between "honest graft" and "dishonest graft," honest graft being inside knowledge that enabled one to buy up a piece of property that a government or a public utility was going to need. Here is his appraisal of civil service reform:

> This civil service law is the biggest fraud of the age. It is the curse of the nation. There can't be no real patriotism while it lasts. How are you goin' to interest our young men in their country if you have no offices to give them when they work for their party? Just look at things in this city today. There are ten thousand good offices, but we can't get at more than a few hundred of them. How are we goin' to provide for the thousands of men who worked for the Tammany ticket? It can't be done. These men were full of patriotism a short time ago. They expected to be servin' their city, but when we tell them that we can't place them, do you think their patriotism is going to last? Not much. They say: "What's the use of workin' for your country anyhow? There's nothin' in the game." And what can they do? I don't know, but I'll tell you what I do know. I know more than one young man in past years who worked for the ticket and was just overflowin' with patriotism, but when he was knocked out by the civil service humbug he got to hate his country and became an Anarchist. . . . Isn't it enough to make a man sour on his country when he wants to serve it and won't be allowed unless he answers a lot of fool questions about the number of cubic inches of water in the Atlantic and the quality of sand in the Sahara desert?

Source: William L. Riordon, *Plunkitt of Tammany Hall* (New York: E. P. Dutton, 1948), pp. 15–16.

for their own appointees. Party rotation—the presidency changed hands every four years for the rest of the century—also helped. By 1900 about half of all federal employees were under the civil service system.

Congress in 1883 also grappled with the other target of the liberal reformers—tariff reduction. The outcome was less fruitful. One house approved a rate reduction, but the other restored most of the cuts. The resulting compromise, disparagingly called the Mongrel Tariff, altered the rates but little.

These limited achievements nevertheless heartened the liberal reformers. Independent Republicans, having brought about the political death of their bitter foe,

Roscoe Conkling, were determined to nominate a candidate of their own in 1884. Chester Arthur had made a more impressive president than anyone had expected. He was a tall, handsome man with generous sidewhiskers, always meticulously dressed, a connoisseur of French cooking, and reputed to be one of the best fly-fishermen in the country. He superintended an executive branch relatively free from scandal, and though he proposed little in the way of national need,* he blocked nothing

---

* As we will see in the next two chapters, there was in the 1880s a rising chorus of demand for more currency in circulation, for railroad regulation, and for antitrust laws. Society was also troubled by labor strife and urban violence.

in the way of liberal reform. Independents nevertheless could not forget his unsavory background. Limited in their vision, however, like many reformers, the Independents failed to see that in blocking Arthur they were opening the way for a spoilsman of another sort—James G. Blaine. After resigning from the cabinet in 1881 shortly after Arthur's accession, Blaine resumed his lifelong pursuit of the presidency. And with careful organization and planning, he won the Republican nomination in 1884.

⨆ Cleveland and the Mugwumps, 1884–1888

By 1884, the Democrats, having twice lost the presidency by a whisker, were fully recovered from their Civil War troubles. Less divided than Republicans, they were better prepared to swim with the running tide of liberal reform. Samuel J. Tilden, at 70, was no longer a viable candidate, but the Democrats had a strong and, at 47, relatively young prospect in Grover Cleveland,

also a New Yorker. As mayor of Buffalo, Cleveland had purged that city of well-entrenched rascals. He went on to be governor, and as state executive enhanced his reputation as a reformer. He broke with the bosses of Tammany Hall and administered a successful state civil service program which a youthful Republican Independent, Theodore Roosevelt, guided through the legislature. Cleveland's nomination marked the triumph of liberal reform. His four years as president accomplished its demise.

THE MUGWUMP REVOLT

After the Republicans nominated James G. Blaine, the Independents, heirs to the middle-class idealism of Abraham Lincoln and Horace Greeley, felt they had no choice but to leave a party that had so clearly abandoned the ideals on which it had been founded. Leading the exodus were the reform journals, *Harper's Weekly*, E. L. Godkin's *Nation*, and the *New York Times*. The rebels continued to call themselves Independent Republicans, but a popular nick-

Chester A. Arthur. A food fancier, Arthur was the first president to secure a French chef for the White House.

The Bettmann Archive.

name for them was "Mugwump," derived from an Indian word meaning young warrior. Party wits also claimed it meant an indecisive bird that sat on a fence with its "mug" on one side and its "wump" on the other. For a brief period the description fit the rebels, for they wavered indecisively until the Democratic convention met. Then they threw their support to Cleveland. It was a leap in the dark, because the Democratic platform made no promises about issues. Its assortment of vague generalities was almost identical to that of the Republicans.

In American politics, it was the custom that presidential candidates remain aloof and silent during an election campaign so they did not appear to "hunker" after office too much. Only two nominees had ever toured the country in their own behalf—Stephen A. Douglas in 1860 and Horace Greeley in 1872—and both had suffered humiliating defeat. Cleveland followed tradition by remaining at his desk in the governor's office in Albany. Blaine, however, elected to travel, whistlestopping through New York, Pennsylvania, and the Middle West. Since he had no issues to discuss, his speeches simply embroidered the "bloody shirt."

The campaign soon degenerated into a mudbath in which even the fastidious Mugwumps participated. Mugwump newspapers dredged up an old allegation that Blaine had illegally accepted railroad stocks as a bribe. The allegation could not be proved since Blaine had destroyed the records, but Democrats seized upon it. "Blaine! Blaine! James G. Blaine! Continental liar from the state of Maine!" they chanted. Republicans retaliated by spreading the news that Cleveland, a bachelor, had fathered an illegitimate child twelve years before. The resulting warcry was: "Ma, Ma, Where's my Pa? Gone to the White House, ha, ha, ha!"

After touring the Middle West, Blaine broke his trip home with a stop in New York City. The state's electoral votes were crucial, and the Mugwump defection had hurt. Shortly after Blaine arrived, a delegation of Protestant clergymen came to his hotel to greet him. The cleric assigned to address the candidate droned out a series of platitudes, culminating in a denunciation of the Democrats as the party of "rum, Romanism, and rebellion." Blaine, listening politely but doubtless inattentively, failed to repudiate this slur on immigrants generally, and Irish Catholics in particular, and the Democratic press picked it up. New York went Democrat in the election, and its 36 electoral votes were the margin of Cleveland's victory. The cleric's alliterative bigotry became fixed in American political legend.

THE END
OF LIBERAL REFORM

As colorless in the White House as he had been in the governor's mansion, Cleveland did little to excite or to depress the reformers. He filled his cabinet with loyal Democrats, ignoring the Mugwumps, most of whom drifted back into the Republican fold. Although the Pendleton Act gave the president authority to extend the civil service system, Cleveland refused to do so until near the end of his term, when he had loaded the government with Democrats. His extension of civil service was simply a matter of giving tenure to his own appointees. Two important pieces of legislation won approval during Cleveland's presidency: The Dawes Severalty Act ended the reservation system and offered homestead grants to Indians, and the Interstate Commerce Act instituted the first federal regulation of business enterprise. Neither law originated with the president; the best that might be said was that he did not veto them.

Worried about Treasury surpluses (the national debt, incurred in the Civil War,

THE OPENING OF THE CONGRESSIONAL SESSION.

"The Opening of the Congressional Session." The huge monster "Surplus" with its tail "Tariff Question" crowds the legislative chamber as Congress begins its 1887 session. By the mid-1880s the nation had virtually paid off its Civil War debt, and Congress faced an annual surplus. The surplus was nearly as big a problem as the giant deficits of today. The government could use the money for public buildings, deepening harbors, and the like, but beyond a certain amount such expenditures were sheer waste. Nor could it reduce taxes. The principal federal tax was the tariff, and a reduction in tariff rates caused an outcry from manufacturers and workingmen, who thought they needed protection from foreign competition.

was nearly paid off), Cleveland did urge Congress to cut the tariff rates, and in so doing flashed his credentials as a liberal reformer. When advisers warned that a stand on this issue might weaken his chances for reelection, the president's reply was in the liberal spirit: "What is the use of being elected or reelected, unless you stand for something?" The Republican-dominated Senate blocked revision, but Cleveland's stance ensured that the tariff would be the central issue in the election of 1888.

Cleveland easily won the Democratic nomination in 1888. The Republicans turned to Benjamin Harrison of Indiana, whose chief recommendation was that he came from a "swing" state. In contrast to

the pyrotechnics of 1884, the campaign of 1888 was tepid to the point of dull. Harrison, nicknamed "the human iceberg," matched Cleveland's stolid demeanor. The only novel feature of the election was the participation of businessmen. They had previously remained aloof from party politics but had apparently become alarmed by Cleveland's position on the tariff. Philadelphia dry-goods tycoon John Wanamaker mobilized the business community and raised an unprecedented amount of money for the Republican party. As a result, the volume of campaign literature far exceeded that of any earlier election. How much this affected the outcome is uncertain: Cleveland actually received more popular votes than Harrison, but the Republicans carried New York and Indiana,[*] and hence the electoral college.

What little there was left of the reform impulse faded with Cleveland's defeat. Over the next two years, triumphant Republicans would raise the tariff rates even more and give away the Treasury surpluses in pensions to the Grand Army of the Re-

public. Yet there was brewing all the while a new political revolt in the heat and dust of the rural West and South. This would present a new and far more radical challenge to the political system, and it would end the political sterility that had characterized the Gilded Age.

SUMMARY

Mark Twain labeled the 1870s the Gilded Age, implying that beneath the surface glitter there was a seamy side. Postwar decades are commonly times of pleasure seeking and moral lapse, but the 1870s were even seamier than most. Rapid economic growth, new corporate structures, and lightweight government presented fabulous opportunities for unscrupulous fortune hunters. The huge sums Congress handed out to subsidize the construction of the western railroads were a national scandal, while in the East stock market manipulators looted corporations of their assets.

In national politics the spoils system, originally introduced by the Jacksonians, came to maturity. The Spoilsmen, most of them in the United States Senate, headed state machines that maintained them in office. They used their power to reward their followers with lucrative appointments. The quest for spoils brought the level of political morality to a new low. While Ulysses S. Grant lightly held the reins of government, one scandal after another came to the surface, though not all of them were of Grant's doing. The climax was the exposure in 1875, of the Whiskey Ring, a nationwide conspiracy to defraud the government of taxes that involved hundreds of distillers and revenue agents.

As early as 1872, a group of Republicans who favored reform bolted and formed a third party, called the Liberal Republicans. They stood for tariff reduction and an end to the spoils system through the introduction of a civil service system. Their candidate, Horace Greeley, was easily defeated by Grant; thereafter the Democrats took up the cause of liberal reform. During Grant's second term, Samuel J. Tilden revitalized the Democratic party, which earned him the Democratic nomination in 1876. The contest between Tilden and Republican Rutherford B. Hayes was so close it had to be decided by the House of Representatives. There a sectional bargain was struck by which Hayes gained the White House and in return ended Reconstruction by removing the last federal troops from the South.

A struggle between two Republican factions, the Halfbreeds, led by James G. Blaine, and the Stalwarts, led by Roscoe

---

[*] In both states, voters were famous for selling their votes. When Harrison told Republican national chairman Matt Quay that "Providence has given us the victory," Quay joked to a friend: "Think of the man. He ought to know that Providence hadn't a damned thing to do with it. [Harrison] would never learn how close a number of men were compelled to approach the gates of the penitentiary to make him president."

Conkling, dominated the politics of the Hayes administration. Hayes got into an inconclusive fight with Conkling in an effort to clean out the New York Customs House, the source of Conkling's spoils, but he failed to win support from Congress or the country. James Garfield, elected in 1880, was ostensibly neutral in the Blaine-Conkling war, but he threw his support to Blaine by naming him secretary of state. After Garfield was assassinated in 1881, Blaine was left in control of the party and was its logical nominee in 1884.

Garfield's assassination by a disappointed office seeker helped the liberal demand for civil service reform. The Pendleton Civil Service Act of 1883 established a merit system for appointment and promotion of federal officials based on competitive examinations. The act was limited in effect, but succeeding presidents extended it to the whole federal government by 1900. Republican liberals—called Mugwumps in the 1880s—gained strength from the passage of the act, but they were unable to prevent Blaine's nomination in 1884. The Democrats did nominate a liberal, however: He was Grover Cleveland, governor of New York, who had broken with the bosses of Tammany Hall and administered a state civil service system. Cleveland defeated Blaine in one of the most vicious elections in American history.

Cleveland's administration revealed both the strengths and the weaknesses of the reform movement. He ran an honest and efficient administration, but he had no particular solution for the country's social ills, labor strife and farm depression. He did give approval to two important pieces of legislation—the Dawes Severalty Act, which ended the Indian reservation system, and the Interstate Commerce Act, which began railroad regulation—but neither act originated with the president. In 1888, he embraced tariff reduction. But when he lost the election to Benjamin Harrison, the liberal reform movement was dead.

READING SUGGESTIONS

The traditional view of the Gilded Age as a time of unprincipled politicians and scheming businessmen was best set forth in the works of Matthew Josephson: *The Robber Barons* (1934), and *The Politicos* (1938). Though dated in view, they still make entertaining reading. John A. Garraty's *The New Commonwealth, 1877–1890* (1968) is a more recent view of the period, and it avoids stereotypes. Altina Waller, in *Reverend Beecher and Mrs. Tilton: Sex and Class in Victorian America* (1982), uses one of the most famous scandals of the age as a base for exploring social attitudes of the time. A recent account of party politics in the period is H. Wayne Morgan's *From Hayes to McKinley* (1969). A recent quantitative study is Paul Kleppner, *The Third Electoral System,* *1853–1892: Parties, Voters, and Political Cultures* (1979). Another quantitative study that substantially modifies the traditional image of the Spoilsmen is David J. Rothman's *Politics and Power: The United States Senate, 1869–1901* (1966).

Eric F. Goldman's, *Rendezvous with Destiny* (1952) places the liberal reformers in the broad spectrum of American reform. John G. Sproat's *The Best Men: Liberal Reformers in the Gilded Age* (1968) focuses on the movement itself. Gerald W. McFarland, *Mugwumps, Morals and Politics, 1884–1920* (1975), links the liberal reformers with the Progressives. Good biographies include Allan Nevins, *Grover Cleveland* (1932), and Claude Fuess, *Carl Schurz* (1932).

3

INDUSTRIAL PROGRESS AND INTELLECTUAL POVERTY

Mr. Watson, come here. I want you." The request was commonplace enough. It was the way it was conveyed that was extraordinary: Never before had the human voice been transmitted by wire. The date was March 10, 1876; the site, 5 Exeter Place, Boston. Alexander Graham Bell, aged 29, had obtained a patent on his telephone the week before; now he tested the new device by summoning his 22-year-old assistant, Thomas Watson.

In search of financial backing, Bell took his invention to the exposition celebrating the nation's 100th birthday, which President Grant opened at Fairmount Park in Philadelphia on May 10. The Centennial Exposition was a celebration of the nation's scientific and technical achievements, and Bell's telephone was one of the most popular exhibits. "I hear, I hear!" exclaimed Brazilian emperor Dom Pedro II, leaping from his seat when the talking wire whispered in his ear. Western Union president William Orton, whose telegraph lines could easily accommodate the new communications device, dismissed the telephone as a "scientific curiosity," a mere toy. But he was sufficiently intrigued to hire Thomas A. Edison to see what improvements could be made on it.

Edison, also age 29, had just opened a research laboratory at Menlo Park, New Jersey, with profits earned from a stock-market ticker he had invented. Edison's idea was to bring together teams of scientists and tinkerers and coordinate their efforts to turn out inventions on an assembly-line basis. He would produce "a minor invention every ten days," he boasted, "and a big thing every six months or so." The telephone was his laboratory's first success. Edison discovered that carbon black made a near-perfect transmitter, and his carbon transmitter made Bell's telephone commercially feasible. By then, Orton had already turned down Bell's offer to sell his patent for $100,000, and Bell had found other financial backing. In 1877 he organized the Bell Telephone Association and sold his first bank of telephones to a Boston entrepreneur who set up a switchboard in his office, using the telephones as a communications service by day and burglar alarm at night.

Edison by then was working with a device that recorded sounds on grooved metal cylinders wrapped in tin foil. On November 29, 1877, he shouted the verses to "Mary Had a Little Lamb" into his machine, and when the thing played his voice back, he promptly applied for a patent on the first "phonograph or speaking machine."

Technological advance, of course, was neither new nor exclusively American. Great Britain first experienced self-sustaining economic growth, fed by technology, in the late eighteenth century. By the mid-nineteenth century this "industrial revolution" was altering the pace and direction of life throughout Western Europe and North America. Some of the innovations had profound implications—two such were the telephone and the gasoline engine, also developed in 1876 by a German engineer, Niklaus Otto. A myriad of other improvements were changing patterns of human living, and the Centennial Exposition publicized the most current. Among its exhibits were:

The first commercially produced typewriter, introduced by the F. Remington & Sons Fire Arms Company, and priced at $125.

An envelope-making machine.

Compressed yeast for home baking, introduced by Cincinnati's Gaff, Fleischmann and Company.

A ready-to-apply paint, composed of pigments suspended in linseed oil, prepared by

---

(*Chapter opening photo*) Brazilian emperor Dom Pedro II listening to Bell's telephone at the Philadelphia exposition, 1876.

Edison demonstrating his tin foil phonograph, 1878.

Con Edison.

a machine invented by H. A. Sherwin of Cleveland's Sherwin-Williams Company.

A new beer called Budweiser, which won top honors in the expo competition for its brewer, Adophus Busch of E. Anheuser Company, which had earlier pioneered the refrigerated railcar for the transport of beers.

A new soft drink blended from 16 different wild roots and berries, the concoction of Philadelphia pharmacist Charles E. Hires, who agreed to call it "root beer" in the hope of getting Pennsylvania's hard-drinking coal miners to try it.

⊔ The Rush to Maturity

By any standard, the industrial growth of the United States between 1870 and 1900 was prodigious. The output of manufactured goods increased fourfold in that thirty-year period, and the value of manufactured products doubled. So furious was the pace of growth that the American economy overtook and then outdistanced the economies of western Europe. On the eve of the Civil War, the United States was fourth in the world in the volume and value of manufactured goods. By 1894, it was in first place. By 1900 the United States produced more than the second and third powers, Britain and Germany, combined.

More remarkable still, this growth occurred in a period when the Western world was suffering a prolonged depression. For a quarter of a century, between 1873 and 1897, world markets were glutted with unsold products. Prices fell almost continuously, and there were periodic· bursts of financial panic, business failure, and unemployment. The depression did not slow American growth, but it did make it erratic. Following the panic of 1873, industrial growth slowed, and for several years the annual output of goods held steady. From 1878 to 1883 the economy boomed. This was followed by another interval of stability, and then another forward surge until the crash of 1893 ushered in the worst depression of the century. Then, in 1897, the business cycle turned upward again, bringing a prolonged period of prosperity that lasted until the panic of 1929.

STEEL, OIL, ELECTRICITY: NEW INDUSTRIES

Iron, textiles, flour milling, and lumber, industries that had been the backbone of the economy since colonial times, led the way. But of more interest were new industries, the products of new technologies—steel, oil, and electricity. Steel, formed by adding a small amount of carbon to iron, together with traces of manganese and silicon, was known to the ancients, lost, and then rediscovered in the eighteenth century. It could be made only on a small scale, however, and was used principally for weapons until in the 1850s an Englishman, Henry Bessemer, devised a method for

John D. Rockefeller's first oil refinery in Cleveland, about 1869.

mass production. Bessemer forced a blast of hot air through molten pig iron. The air oxidized ("burned") the carbon present in the iron, thus generating additional heat, and when trace elements were added, steel was the result. The Bessemer process was soon superseded by the open hearth method (also English in origin), which fired a hot gas through molten ore. This was faster, cheaper, and produced a steel free of nitrogen bubbles, which had flawed Bessemer steel. Americans quickly adopted the new techniques. Steel production, a minuscule 70,000 tons in 1870, leaped to more than 4 million tons in 1890.

Petroleum and its associate, natural gas, had likewise been known to the ancients, but no one thought of digging for them until the nineteenth century. Russian engineers dug the world's first oil well at the Caspian seaport of Baku in 1823. The first American well was drilled at Titusville, Pennsylvania, in 1859. The following year, John D. Rockefeller, aged 20, went into the oil business, and by the end of the Civil War his Cleveland refinery was turning out 500 barrels a day. By the end of the 1860s, Rockefeller and other refiners were turning out more than 3 million barrels a year, most of it used for lighting and lubrication.

Thomas A. Edison produced the first practical incandescent lamp in 1879 when he discovered that a carbon filament (of cotton thread) yielded more light with less power than metal filaments. Not content with that, he developed a wiring system of extremely thin copper so that entire cities would be wired at manageable cost. By the end of the year, he had his home village of Menlo Park, New Jersey, strung with wires, and with showman's instinct he lit the entire town by throwing a single switch on New Year's Eve. Edison opened the first central power station in New York three years later, and by 1890 his Illuminating Company was manufacturing a million lightbulbs a year. The new technology threatened to render petroleum obsolete, but the development of the gasoline engine offered new uses and new growth avenues for that industry.

BANKS AND TRUSTS: BIG BUSINESS

New technologies and rapid growth were two elements of America's industrial revolution. The third element was change in the structure of business. Prewar corporations were relatively small, closely held business units. They expanded operations by plowing profits back into the enterprise. Railroads, enormously costly to build, forced the system to become more public. The early railroads were built with a good deal of governmental assistance in the form of tax breaks, loans, and land grants, as well as subsidies from communities that wanted their services. But federal grants ceased in 1871, and state aid dried up after the panic of 1873. As a result, the great era of railroad construction, 1879–1890, was financed principally by private capital. This was pooled by the sale of stocks and bonds to numerous investors on the open market. Railroads were thus the nation's first "big business."

Railroad finance, in turn, stimulated the growth of banking houses, such as J. P. Morgan and Company of New York. The bankers at first served as agents of the railroads, amassing capital and offering construction loans. Later, when the railroads overextended themselves and suffered financial difficulties, the bankers moved in as saviors—at a price. When the panic of 1893 put the Northern Pacific into receivership, Morgan put the line back into business, in exchange for a seat on the board of directors. A decade later Morgan engineered the merger of the Northern Pacific, the Great Northern, and the Burlington railway companies into one corporation that monopolized the railroad traffic of a quarter of the continent.

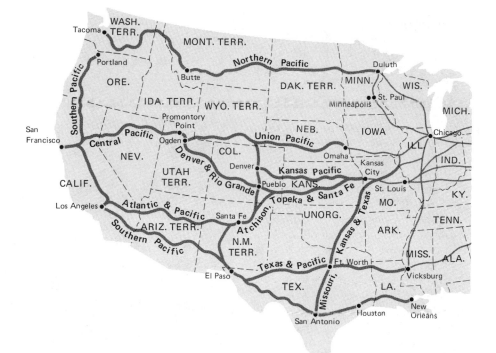

The land-grant railroads, 1863–1900.

Morgan early spotted the potential in the new technologies. He financed the formation of the Edison Illuminating Company, helped it merge with various competitors, and in 1892 engineered the formation of the General Electric Company. Morgan also created the nation's first billion-dollar company in 1901 when he formed the United States Steel Corporation. Significantly, the first president of the corporation, Judge Elbert Gary, was not a steelmaker at all, but a banker.

The bankers failed to make any inroads into oil refining, however, in large measure because John D. Rockefeller straddled the industry like a colossus. Rockefeller did so because he pioneered the most imaginative corporate device of the age, the trust. Rockefeller had been expanding, merging, and buying out competitors since the end of the war, and in 1879 he consolidated his holdings into the Standard Oil Company. The trust, brainchild of Rockefeller's lawyer, Samuel C. T. Dodd, was a legal device that enabled him to control a large number of oil companies without purchasing them. When the trust was formed in 1882, the stockholders of 40 corporations assigned their stock to nine trustees, headed by Rockefeller. The trustees had the power to elect officers of the constituent companies, create new companies, and set management policy. In return for their stock, the holders received trust certificates on which dividends were paid. The improved competitive position of the trust made its certificates more valuable to holders than their stock had been.

Standard Oil expanded with little plan except to eliminate all competition, and the near-monopoly it eventually achieved was what made it famous and created enemies.

But monopoly proved to be not the only, nor even the most important, function of a trust. The Standard's trustees pioneered new forms of management. In their New York headquarters they created eleven departments, each specializing in an aspect of the business—auditing, legal affairs, sales. A comprehensive reporting system kept them abreast of new technologies, and centralized management enabled them to adapt to changing conditions. In the '80s, Standard Oil built a network of pipelines to bring crude oil to its refineries, and in the '90s it began transporting its products by railroad car, rather than in barrels.

Because of these achievements, the Standard Oil Company became a model for centralization in other industries. Before the '80s were over, trusts were formed in sugar, whiskey, meatpacking, matches, and many other industries. In most cases the aim was not the takeover of competition—horizontal combination—but the streamlining of business—vertical combination. Vertical combination involved controlling all stages of production—extraction, refining, and marketing, in the case of oil, for example. The advantages were reliable supplies and sales outlets, reduced transportation costs, and systematic management. "Big business" originated in a desire for efficiency, not for price control.

⊔ An Ideology for Entrepreneurs

The intellectual climate of the Gilded Age accommodated the new industrialists. Postwar eras in our recent past have commonly been periods of conservative temperament, accompanied by a sort of moral lassitude. In the 1920s and 1950s such public moods were apparently a reaction to prewar tensions stemming from strong ideological controversies. In the Civil War era the postwar conservatism was, ironically, an extension—some might say a perversion—of the

New York Public Library.

"The Modern Prometheus." In this 1882 cartoon, free enterprise is depicted as Prometheus, the hero of Greek mythology who stole fire from the gods and gave it to mankind. As his punishment Zeus had him chained to Mount Caucasus where an eagle preyed on his liver all day (the liver being renewed each night). Here the rock is labeled "monopoly" and the iron band that holds Prometheus down bears the label "defective laws." This was one of the first alarms over the growth of big business. The word "trust" had obviously not yet become part of the public vocabulary, or the cartoonist doubtless would have used it.

prewar reform impulse. Prewar reformers had used the rhetoric of Jeffersonian liberalism; words like "progress," "self-reliance," and "equality" came naturally to their lips. They perceived reform to be a matter of eliminating some evil—drink, war, slavery—that fettered free people.

Thus Abraham Lincoln and the Republicans opposed slavery not simply or even chiefly because it was a moral wrong, but because it violated the American promise of opportunity, potentially for whites as well as blacks. But once the evil was eliminated, the individual was expected to fend for himself. The party of Lincoln believed in self-made men, not government-made men.

"Self-reliance" on the lips of an Emerson was an invitation to challenge old ways and invent new; on the lips of a J. P. Morgan, it was a slogan of the rich. And therein lay the changed times. The rhetoric of Jeffersonian liberalism, developed for a thinly populated, highly mobile nation of farmers and shopkeepers, took on new meaning in a complex industrial society. To factory operatives and tenant farmers who needed to band together to protect themselves, the gospel of self-help had little meaning. It served only those who, through luck or cunning, had risen to the top. When Abraham Lincoln told the slaves they would be free, it was a liberal reform. When Andrew Carnegie told his steelworkers they were free to get ahead in the world, it meant nothing because the postwar industrial worker was a machine tender with narrow skills. An ideology that had been developed by liberal reformers before the Civil War served only the needs of wealthy conservatives in the industrial age that followed it. Liberalism had been stolen by conservatives. Historian Clinton Rossiter has called it "the great train robbery of American intellectual history."

THE SLAUGHTERHOUSE CASES

An index of the change was the Supreme Court's gutting of the Fourteenth Amendment. The amendment was the sum of Republican idealism. It and its fellows, the Thirteenth, which had freed the slaves, and the Fifteenth, which had given freed black men the vote, almost alone gave meaning to the Civil War. A series of lawsuits, collectively known as the Slaughterhouse Cases, came before the Supreme Court in 1873. They originated in a Louisiana statute that limited livestock slaughtering in New Orleans to one corporation's premises, which other butchers could use by paying prescribed fees. The purpose was to enable the state to supervise the industry. The butchers, however, brought suit, claiming that the monopoly impaired their right to earn a living and that this right was among the privileges and immunities protected by the Fourteenth Amendment. The court rejected this argument, holding that the Fourteenth Amendment protected only those rights that stemmed from national citizenship. Such rights, it declared, are relatively few. They included, for instance, the right to interstate travel, the right to petition Congress, or the right to ask for federal help when traveling abroad. But most civil rights, including such fundamental liberties as the right to earn a living or to own property, flowed from state citizenship and thus lay beyond the Fourteenth Amendment protection.

The decision thus effectively excluded the federal government from the field of civil rights, a bar reinforced a decade later when the court declared the Civil Rights Act of 1875 to be unconstitutional. When, nearly a century later, Congress sought to reenter the field, it had to do so by way of its power over interstate commerce.* The Slaughterhouse decision did, by implication, leave broad authority to the states to regulate businesses, such as slaughterhouses, in which the public had an interest. But this was not to be. In dissenting from

---

* The civil rights legislation of the 1960s, which prohibited racial segregation in hotels and restaurants and discriminatory hiring practices in businesses, rested on Congress's constitutional power to regulate the flow of persons and goods in interstate commerce.

the majority in the Slaughterhouse Cases, Justice Stephen Field argued that the Louisiana monopoly was a violation of the Fourteenth Amendment because it deprived certain persons of their property without due process of law. Every individual had a natural right, declared Justice Field, to "pursue his own calling," and this right to earn wealth cannot be abridged by a state. Though a minority opinion in 1873, Field's doctrine gradually gained acceptance by the Court. Under it, state laws regulating hours and conditions of labor were systematically thrown out by the Court on the theory that they violated a worker's freedom in choosing job opportunities. It was the conceptual wedding of the Constitution and laissez faire.

SOCIAL DARWINISM

At the same time, Social Darwinism wedded laissez faire to the laws of science. Charles Darwin's *Origin of Species*, which offered the first firm evidence that the world's plants and animals had evolved through natural selection, was published in the United States in 1860. Outside of academic circles, Americans took little interest in it. But they did become intensely excited about a corollary to the evolutionary theorem, that human civilization too progressed from simple to complex, from lower orders to higher, by a competitive process in which only the fittest survived. This notion had been put forth a decade earlier in 1850 by an Englishman, Herbert Spencer. Americans pounced upon Spencer's book, *Social Statics*, because it encouraged middle-class Americans to continue as they were; it was a rationale for their mobile, competitive, lawless society. Some 300,000 copies were sold in the United States between 1860 and 1900.

Spencer postulated that civilization is the product of a gradual yet inevitable evolution. The natural competition among people produced winners and losers, and

the winners were those with more intelligence, industry, or ingenuity. By virtue of this "survival of the fittest," civilization advances. The fittest assume the lead and pull the entire society to a higher order of knowledge, technology, and culture. The theory was deterministic because it assumed that this advance was inevitable. And, with respect to political action, it was conservative (an ironic reversal of the historical determinism set forth by Karl Marx 2 years earlier, in 1848). Because evolution is inevitable, any attempt to manipulate society (by feeding the unemployed, for instance) would retard human progress because it would help the "unfit" to survive. It was a persuasive argument, for it equated laissez faire with civilization; classical economics was underpinned by biology. It elevated self-help to a philosophy.

William Graham Sumner, an Episcopal minister who had become a professor of political and social science at Yale, expounded on Spencer's work in such colorfully titled books as *The Absurd Effort to Make the World Over*. Sumner added a religious touch to Spencer's blend of biology and economics. Sumner argued that the fit were the virtuous, that they survived by their hard work, frugality, temperance, and piety. Survival, in fact, meant success, and success was the reward of virtue. As an ethical system, a guide for human behavior, it was a powerful one indeed, for the promised reward for being good was not in the hereafter, as in most religions, but in the here and now. This compound of biology, classical economics, and ethics constituted an American refinement of Social Darwinism, which received its most eloquent expression in Andrew Carnegie's essay, "The Gospel of Wealth."

THE GOSPEL OF WEALTH

Andrew Carnegie embodied what the gospel promised. A penniless immigrant from Scotland, he rose to be the multimillionaire

Cartoon series ridiculing Darwin's theory of evolution. The first shows the descent of man from pig to bull to man. The second shows Darwin training an ape to jump through a hoop. In the third, the new entrant to society is announced by a shocked butler: "Mr. G-g-g-o-o-orilla."

head of one of the nation's largest steel companies. "The Gospel of Wealth," published in the *North American Review* in 1889, began with a restatement of Jeffersonian liberalism. The sole function of government, Carnegie declared, was to maintain order so as to protect property. If the rich benefited from this, so be it. They had earned the benefits. The losers—the unsuccessful, the poor—likewise deserved their fate, for their condition was clearly the result of some defect in character, a

shortage of wits, or some hidden vice. Poverty, in the mind of Andrew Carnegie, was a badge of lost virtue.

Realizing that such a flinty attitude was certain to antagonize the poor and create unrest, a situation that would endanger the position of the rich, Carnegie searched for ways to temper the system. The wealthy, he decided, were under an obligation, a sort of *noblesse oblige*—an obligation of the privileged—to spend their money wisely, to devote it to the public good. Philanthropy was Carnegie's special contribution to the Spencerian logic. The financing of public works, colleges, and libraries not only provided job opportunities for the poor, but offered them cultural and moral uplift. It also blended with the idea of Christian charity. John D. Rockefeller, a fixture in the Baptist church all his life, summed it up thus: "The good Lord gave me the money, and how could I withhold it from the University of Chicago?"

Whether the poor would be content with whatever blessings might trickle down to them from the endowments of the rich was another question: One cynic described the system as an attempt to feed the sparrows in the barnyard by giving hay to the horse.

SOME NOISELESS DISSENTERS

The broad American middle class accepted the gospel of self-help because its essentials were already deeply engrained in the American culture. In the Gospel of Wealth were echoes of the Puritan ethic, the anti-government whiggery of the Founding Fathers, and the liberal-democratic rhetoric of Jefferson, Jackson, and Lincoln. Most Americans accepted it as a self-evident truth, and they chorused it endlessly in schoolbooks, Fourth of July addresses, and newspaper editorials. Those who dissented made less imprint on their own time than on the next generation.

Lester Frank Ward, sometimes credited with founding the science of sociology, struck at the Social Darwinists' basic premise—that there was some analogy between natural and social evolution. The two, said Ward, are entirely different. Evolution in nature by the process of natural selection is random and wasteful, and since qualities that aid in survival (color, odor, diet, speed) are given preference, natural evolution is inevitable. The evolution of human civilization, on the other hand, is neither ran-

dom, purposeless, nor inevitable. Society, he argued in *Dynamic Sociology* (1884), can be molded by human action. Sociology, in fact, is the science of society, the means for studying and improving the human environment. Where the Social Darwinist would dismiss criminals as losers in the competition for survival, the sociologists would argue that there might be fewer criminals if society cleaned up its slums.

Government, Ward suggested, is not necessarily the enemy of the people. Properly used, it can be a servant. Indeed, it might even be indispensable in preserving the competitive system on which progress rests. Competition, Ward pointed out, destroys itself. Those who succeed gain a dominant position, as Rockefeller did in the oil refining industry. And they naturally extend themselves by ruining or absorbing their competitors. The end product of competition is monopoly, unless the government intervenes with some rules and regulations.

As a social critic, Lester Ward was a conservative. He was concerned with making the free enterprise system work better and more humanely; he had no thought of replacing it with another. The same can be said of the Californian Henry George, whose analysis of the American economy began with the classic trilogy—land, labor, capital. The rich provided capital for production of goods, and the poor contributed labor. The landowner offered no effort; he simply provided space. And therein, George decided, was the root of social inequity. The wealthy, George wrote in *Progress and Poverty* (1879), were not necessarily the most intelligent or most diligent; often they were simply the people who occupied a region first and appropriated the best lands. As more people moved into the area, taking up lower quality lands, the holdings of the original landowner increased in value, whether he made improvements or not. This increase in rent (which is the financial return on land) due to population pressure George called an "unearned increment."

As the title of his book suggests, George was concerned about the persistence of poverty amid plenty. He attributed the disparity in part to the "unearned" rent collected by landowners, and he suggested that the government confiscate this unearned increment through taxes. Since it was unearned, the landowner would not be hurt; he would still receive a fair rent for land and its improvements. The proceeds from such a tax, George estimated, would be enough to finance government; no others would be needed. A "single tax" would siphon excess wealth and relieve the poor of taxes; it was a painless way to make America a more equal and humane society.

George's work became one of the best-selling nonfiction works of its day, and that in itself was a measure of those who found the Gospel of Wealth defective. And it was a measure of their understanding when they seized upon the most superficial of George's ideas, the single tax. A distinction between earned and unearned rent would have been virtually impossible for a government to make, and the expense of collecting would have exceeded the revenue. Even had it worked, the people most affected by it, outside of urban land developers, would have been farmers. Nevertheless, the single tax became a rallying cry for reformers in the 1880s, and Single Tax Clubs sprang up all over the nation.

The importance of Lester Ward, Henry George, and other social critics of the 1880s—Edward Bellamy (who projected a classless society in his utopian novel, *Looking Backward*), Oliver Wendell Holmes, and even future president Woodrow Wilson—lay not in their impact on their own time. It lay in the foundation they built for the future. They started an intellectual revolution that would, within two decades, shatter the easy tenets of Social Darwinism and call into question the simplistic "laws" of classical economics.

That intellectual revolution rested, in turn, on social discontent. The discontent began to rumble in the 1870s, and it rose gradually in volume until it shook the middle-class complacency of those who held to the Gospel of Wealth. The discontent centered among factory operatives and farmers, those who saw no inspiration in the self-made myth. The Gospel of Wealth, after all, was obsolete before it was framed. It postulated a society of artisans and shopkeepers, in which the worker was able to move up the economic ladder as his skills improved. The concept had always been more ideal than real, and with the advent of large-scale factory production, even the ideal vanished.

The vast majority of workers were tied for life to their machines. No more than one in a hundred could expect to win promotion to a managerial post; no more than one in a million could aspire to factory ownership. A steelworker who shoveled coal in one of Carnegie's mills for $2 a day, 66 hours a week, did not have to read Henry George to find out that he was being exploited. Nor did it take much reflection to reach the conclusion that his best chance for survival lay in union with other workers. Farmers, toiling in wheat fields to produce a crop the world had no room for, were not long in reaching the same conclusion. The notion that the poor were in reality victims of exploitation and privilege was heresy in the heyday of Social Darwinism. But from such heresy came the intellectual contours of modern America.

⊔Immigrants, Machines, and Labor

Where did the people come from who tended the machines in the new factories? From the farm, and from abroad. The movement from farm to city had been going on for decades, though as late as 1870 farmers were still a majority of the nation's work force. By 1880 they were a minority, and their ratio continued to decline thereafter. By 1980 farmers constituted only about 4 percent of employed workers. Demographers estimate that in the 1870s and 1880s, the number of residential changes per decade equaled the entire population of the country. Much of it was movement from country to town.

IMMIGRATION AND A LABOR SURPLUS

People who moved across the Atlantic were another source of labor supply. Immigration rose steadily after 1830, and in the period from 1870 to 1900 almost 12 million immigrants made their way to American shores. Immigrants were a particularly valuable resource because four-fifths of them were of working age. European economies had borne the expense of nurturing and educating them; America reaped the reward. In 1890, for instance, immigrants constituted 14.5 percent of the population, but made up 26 percent of the working force. Many moved onto the last frontier, the Great Plains, but as the public lands disappeared, newer arrivals took factory jobs in the East, as the Irish had a generation earlier. Immigrants from Eastern Europe—Poland, Bohemia, Serbia, and Russia—furnished much of the brawn in the nation's textile factories, coal mines, steel mills, and meatpacking plants.

People came in search of opportunity, trying to better their lot in life. Factory wages were dreadfully low by modern stan-

European immigration patterns, 1910.

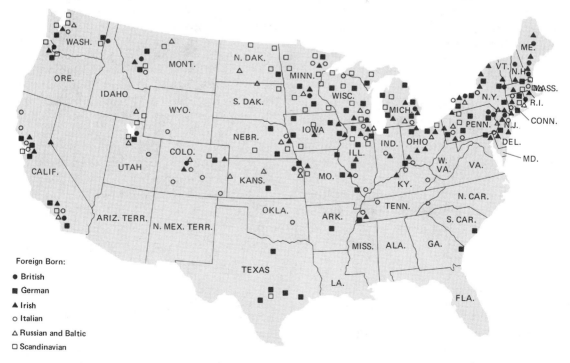

Foreign Born:

- ● British
- ■ German
- ▲ Irish
- ○ Italian
- △ Russian and Baltic
- □ Scandinavian

CLIO'S FOCUS: Chinese Immigration: An Oriental Mythology

Only now, a little more than a century since Congress passed the Chinese Exclusion Act, are scholars beginning to penetrate the crust of mythology that obscures the subject of Chinese immigration. Who were the Chinese who came to America in the nineteenth century? Were they rich or poor, city people or farmers? How did they get to America? What plans and dreams did they have? The answers to these questions were first framed by Anglo-Americans who wanted to keep the Chinese out of the United States. They were thus a collection of self-justifying fictions.

The fictions were essentially three. One is that the Chinese were brought to America by the railroads, beginning with the Central Pacific of California, which needed cheap labor. The railroads, so the story goes, financed the transportation of Chinese immigrants through a credit-ticket system and then deducted the cost from their wages. Second, it was thought that most Chinese immigrants were coolies—illiterate peasants who were accustomed to bondage and willing to work for very low wages. They therefore competed unfairly with Americans of European stock. The third myth is that the Chinese did not plan to stay permanently in America. As a result, they resisted assimilation, clung to their language and their national form of dress, and formed communities of their own, called Chinatowns.

Hugo D. Goldsmith.

Although much work remains to be done, recent scholarship has sketched the outline of a much different picture. First, the notion that the railroad companies scoured China for cheap labor is far too simple an explanation for Chinese immigration. In fact, most Chinese came to America on their own initiative. Conditions in China were probably more important factors in persuading them to leave than the prospect of work in America. The vast majority of Chinese immigrants came from the southern Chinese province of Kwangtung, a province that suffered from extreme social and economic problems. Its population growth was explosive. The number of people in Kwangtung doubled in the course of the nineteenth century, and this growth produced intense competition for land. The losers often became outlaws. The Opium Wars between Great Britain and China (1839–1842) had resulted in the opening of China to international trade and foreign influence. Macao, Canton, and Hong Kong blossomed into great seaports serving many nations. Factories sprang up, and peasants in the hinterland, long dependent for their livelihood on handicraft production, found themselves unable to compete.

These sources of social dislocation were remarkably similar to the changes taking place in Europe in the mid-nineteenth century, changes that impelled Irish, Germans, and Scandinavians to move to the United States. Kwangtung suffered one additional problem. The movement of people into the province from northern China caused a civil war that lasted from 1853 to 1867 and cost perhaps a half million lives. The war gave rise to the coolie trade. Military captives were enslaved and sent as field hands to the plantations of Southeast Asia, South America, and the West Indies. But few were sent to the United States. Most Chinese who came to America paid their own way or, through the credit-ticket system, borrowed the passage money from the railroads. The civil war in China, in fact, may have given the well-to-do as much reason to emigrate as it gave the poor.

There were "pull" as well as "push" factors. The Chinese appear to have had a more favorable view of Western society than has hitherto been supposed. Chinese merchants were well acquainted with Western ways. Merchants, in fact, were among the first to emigrate, and their reports home doubtless encouraged others to make the ocean crossing. American missionaries also helped to portray America as a land of plenty. There is little direct evidence as to what the Chinese expected of themselves in America. But since the forces that impelled them to move were quite similar to the forces at work among European immigrants, it is reasonable to suppose that they shared the same dream—freedom and opportunity. Those who contemplated only a short stay were probably a tiny minority.

The cycles of Chinese immigration offer some clue to their motives. The first Chinese went to California in the 1840s, prior to the Gold Rush. These were mostly merchants and shopkeepers, with a sprinkling of skilled artisans, and they appear to have intermingled with the Mexican and American populations. Migration increased dramatically after the discovery of gold in California in 1848, as Chinese joined the stream of goldseekers flowing into San Francisco. More than 20,000 crossed the Pacific in

1852 alone. Nearly all must have financed their own passage, since railroad construction did not begin for another decade. Chinese traveled to America at the rate of about 4,000 a year for the rest of the 1850s, and most settled in California.

During the early 1860s there was a slowdown in the rate of Chinese immigration, perhaps because of the American Civil War. A third surge of immigration began in the mid-1860s. Most of these people went into railroad construction, but whether they were enticed by this prospect is unclear. The railroad companies did not actively recruit in China. The Central Pacific hired most of its workers from among Chinese already in California. Later, other companies dipped into the labor pool idled by the completion of the Central Pacific. The end of the civil war in Kwangtung was probably at least as important as the railroads for Chinese immigration. Thousands of young men released from military service were looking for new worlds and adventure. About the same time, the introduction of steam navigation in the Pacific made the voyage cheaper and easier. Despite increasing hostility from Anglo-Americans, the Chinese landed on the American Pacific coast in large numbers throughout the 1870s. To stem this human tide, Anglo-Americans created first a mythology and then a law. In 1882 the Chinese became the only people in the world excluded from the United States by an act of Congress.

dards, but to many they seemed a bonanza. A young Polish immigrant who had found work in one of New York's infamous clothing sweatshops told an investigating committee that she earned $4.50 a week. She and her roommate each spent $2 a week on living expenses. "Of course," she added, "we could have lived cheaper, but we are both fond of good things and felt we could afford them." Most East European immigrants came from agricultural backgrounds and had never set foot in a factory. Some failed to overcome the shock and returned home. But the great majority adjusted, aided by habits of hard work and thrift they brought from their homelands and driven by a fear of failure.

The immigrant's lack of labor skills may in fact have eased his adjustment, because the new factories put a premium on discipline rather than skill. Machines encouraged the subdivision of labor, and employers found that simple tasks, endlessly repeated, increased production per man

hour. Shoemaking, once the skilled trade of a village cobbler, became subdivided into twenty or thirty different occupations—beaters, binders, bottomers, burnishers, crimpers, cutters, dressers, edge-setters, and so on—each dependent on a specialized machine. In the Chicago meat-packing plants, as many as 150 men, each with a microcosmic responsibility, handled each carcass between pen and cooling room.

Increasingly, in the later decades of the nineteenth century, employers calculated labor in terms of time rather than skill. The steam whistle summoned the machine tenders to the factory; a locked gate kept them there. Rigid work rules, often enforced by heavy fines, chained them to their tasks. To such conditions the young immigrant, dazed by culture shock and determined to succeed, adjusted as readily—perhaps more readily—as the native-born worker.

Although the increase in labor productivity ought to have resulted in better

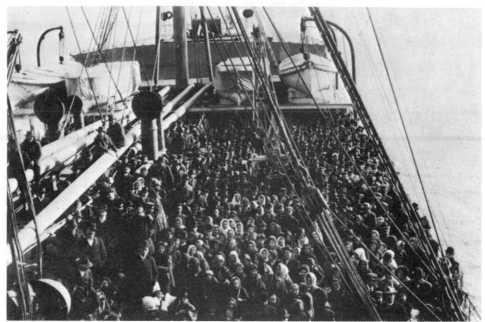

Library of Congress.
A shipload of immigrants.

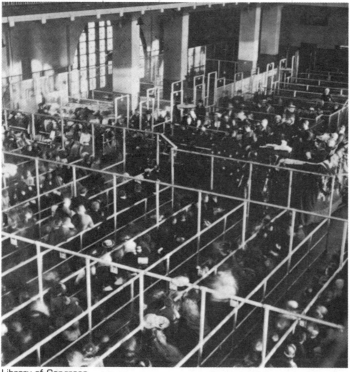

Immigrants being processed at Ellis Island, New York.

Library of Congress.

pay, a labor surplus actually enabled employers to cut wages, and the simplification of tasks provided them with an excuse. Workers had no recourse when wages fell because they were so easily replaced. In Boston, where the introduction of the sewing machine coincided with the arrival of the Irish in the 1840s and made the city the ready-made clothing capital of the nation by the time of the Civil War, a single worker produced about $1,100 in goods a year and earned about $250. In New York, where there were more skilled tailors and fewer machines, a garment maker produced an average of $788 in goods in 1860 and earned $450.

Such managerial greed also brought women and children into the factories in increasing numbers simply because they, like immigrants, were willing to work for low wages. Although the majority of women employed outside the home were domestic servants, as in the past, women by 1870 also made up 10 percent of the industrial work force. In the textile and wearing apparel industries, they constituted almost half. The low wages paid to women were justified on the ground that they had only themselves to support, whereas most men were supporting a family. In the textile industry, however, wages for both sexes were so low that few families could survive unless every member worked. Mill owners understood this and capitalized on it, as the following want ad, taken from a Philadelphia newspaper, indicates:

> SPINNERS, WITH FAMILIES—WANTED—One or two good Jack Spinners, with large families, suitable for work on worsted spinning frames, cards, spooling, or twisting machines, to work in a woolen mill in the country, seven miles from the city. Spinners without such families need not apply.

By the end of the century, children made up 13 percent of the labor force in Massachusetts mills and almost 22 percent in Pennsylvania's.

RISE OF A LABOR CONSCIOUSNESS

Despite these changes in the composition of the nation's work force, more than half of America's industrial workers in 1870 were native-born males. And these too, along with immigrants, women, and children, experienced the dehumanizing effect of machine tending. Labor reformers never tired of pointing out the paradox between the national veneration of free labor and self-help and the reality of industrial "wage slavery." The faith in free labor rested on the assumption that all had an equal opportunity to move up in the world. What happens to that faith, they asked, when the opportunity was no longer there? How, indeed, could work be a virtue when it was no longer "free"? As one labor leader put it: "Are Abraham Lincoln, Andrew Johnson, and N. P. Banks honored because they once toiled with their hands, or because they were fortunate enough to lift themselves into a position where it was no longer necessary?"

There is ample evidence that most of America's wage earners never absorbed the free labor gospel, which received so much lip service from employers and politicians. They resisted factory discipline by failing to report for work, by moving restlessly from job to job, and by engaging in slowdowns and strikes. Absenteeism was rampant. Even the highly disciplined textile mills of New England sometimes ground to a halt on warm summer days for lack of operatives. Payroll records indicate that a quarter of all factory employees stayed home from work at least one day a week. Although the standard work week was six days, it was clear that those who wanted more leisure time took it.

Quitting was another form of rebellion. Government surveys taken at the turn of the century (the first systematic studies made) revealed an astonishing turnover as workers bounced from job to job. The average turnover in most industries was 100

UPI/Bettmann.

Women and children cutting string beans in a cannery.

percent, which meant that a factory owner with a work force of 1,000 had to hire 1,000 new employees every year. When asked why they had quit, only about a third of the workers cited better job opportunities. Most simply said they were "dissatisfied" and in need of a change.

Tending machines was not only dull; it was dangerous. Injuries were common, but rarely was there any way of being compensated for them. Collecting from another penniless worker who may have been at fault was virtually impossible. Collection from an employer required proof that the employer had been negligent. If the injured employee herself or himself had been in any way at fault, the injured person could not sue anyone else, regardless of how negligent another person might have been.

In the preindustrial era, a skilled artisan in a small shop had considerable bargaining leverage. He could take his grievances and pay demands directly to the owner-employer, and his threat to quit caused genuine concern. The machine operator in a corporate-owned factory had no such power. He rarely, if ever, saw the top managers. His complaints were funneled through a shop foreman, who was himself a spoke in the organizational wheel. And if the employee complained too much he was dismissed, for almost anyone could be trained to take his place. In the face of such vast and impersonal power, the workers' only strength was in collective action.

"Big labor," as the union movement eventually came to be called, was a countervailing response to "big business."

BEGINNINGS OF A
NATIONAL MOVEMENT

Organization was slow, in part because self-help and individualism permeated the culture, and the cult of success elevated wealth above industry. Labor leaders countered this by glorifying the dignity of labor and by seeking to instill pride and morale in their followers. Is God "less because His mechanical hand formed the mountains?" roared one union leader in rhetorical query. "No," came the answer. "He is not less because He worked; neither are you."

Rivalries between natives and foreign-born workers, or among immigrant nationalities, also hampered the development of the sense of identification a labor union requires. As a result, labor unions were small and weak, easily crushed when hard times increased job competition. Those who became committed to the union ideal early were soon frustrated, and frustration often led to violence. The violence, in turn, alarmed middle-class Americans who knew nothing of conditions in factories and coal mines and slaughterhouses. With public support, government sometimes intervened to break up strikes, and union leaders found themselves back where they started. The progress of labor organization was more often circular than upward.

Two traditions of labor organization existed in America. One, commonly called "bread and butter unionism," held that unions existed solely for the benefit of their members and that the object of organization was to win tangible benefits, such as higher wages and shorter hours. Trade unions, which were organizations of skilled workers plying a craft, adhered to this view. Unions of craftsmen in the building trades had existed since revolutionary times; by the 1820s, they had citywide organizations in New York and Philadelphia. The other philosophy sought to embrace all types of workers, skilled and unskilled, in a single organization devoted not only to the welfare of workers, but to improving society as a whole. The Workingman's party of the Jacksonian era was actually a blend of the two. It was composed of skilled artisans and simple shopkeepers, but its intellectual interests were broad. Its journalistic voice, *The Workingman's Advocate*, crusaded for cheap land, free education, and hard money. The din drowned out any discussion of wages and hours.

The first nationwide labor organization, the National Labor Union, was likewise a blend of philosophies. Founded in 1866 by William Sylvis of the Iron Moulders Union, the NLU was a loose association of trade unions. Its central concern was legislation limiting the working day to eight hours, and it met with some success. Six states passed laws limiting working hours, and the federal government imposed an eight-hour day on its workshops, ship-yards, and arsenals. But the NLU also sought to reshape and humanize the capitalist system. Among its aims was the creation of producer cooperatives where workers would have a voice in management. This, in turn, drew the NLU into politics. It endorsed the idea of government-issued paper money, for instance, because it thought cheap money would make it easier to finance its cooperatives. Its chief political success was in persuading Congress to repeal the Contract Labor Law of 1864. The NLU believed—correctly, no doubt—that the importation of cheap immigrant labor created competition for jobs and lowered the status of all working people. The union's excursions into politics, however, caused internal dissension, and its refusal to sanction strikes made the discontent worse. The organization was faltering when the panic of 1873 struck, and it collapsed in the depression that followed.

Frederic Lewis.

The burning of the Union Depot and Hotel in Pittsburgh during the great railroad strike of 1877.

All labor organizations suffered in the depression of the mid-1870s, as employers discharged workers, slashed wages, and extended hours. Worker desperation caused the greatest labor confrontation of the century, the railroad strike of 1877. The strike began when the principal railroads connecting Chicago with the East Coast called off a long-standing rate war and announced a 10 percent reduction in wages. When the Baltimore and Ohio Railroad announced an additional 10 percent cut, its workers began a strike at Martinsburg, West Virginia. The strike spread like a grassfire, shutting down the Pennsylvania, New York Central, and Erie railroads. Traffic across the northern portion of the country ground to a halt. When the governor of Pennsylvania sent in state militia to clear the tracks of strikers, the troops

marched into a mob of Pittsburgh strikers with guns blazing. The strikers counterattacked, drove the soldiers into the Pennsylvania railroad's roundhouse, and set it afire. The mob then went berserk, destroying railroad property worth some $5 million.

President Hayes sent in regular army troops, who restored order, and the strike collapsed. Both sides claimed victory, but both may have been losers. Labor emerged with a new sense of solidarity, and it had learned the advantages of striking against an entire industry, rather than individual companies. In the succeeding decade, railroads would remain one of its principal targets. But it lost whatever public sympathy it had had. State legislatures passed conspiracy laws directed at labor unions, and as a way of breaking strikes and boycotts, courts revived the old common law sanctions on conspiracies.

THE KNIGHTS OF LABOR

The return of good times and full employment in the late 1870s revived the labor movement. Standing to benefit was one of the few organizations that had survived the depression, the Knights of Labor. The Knights, founded in 1869 by Uriah Stephens, reflected the utopian labor tradition. Their objective was a universal brotherhood of labor, embracing unskilled as well as trained, immigrants as well as native-born, blacks as well as whites. Because its members were vulnerable, membership rolls were at first kept secret. Making a virtue of necessity, the Knights developed elaborate, mystical rituals. The union struggled on, attracting little attention, until the great strike of 1877, when working people suddenly found the idea of a brotherhood of labor appealing. By 1879 it had over 9,000 members, and by 1882 more than 42,000.

In 1879 the Knights of Labor gained a new president, Terence V. Powderly, the first of America's great labor leaders. Powderly stamped his personality and philosophy on the Knights—as well as some of his flaws. Powderly was an orator, capable of arousing passions with radical rhetoric, but he had little talent for organization. In theory, the Knights were highly centralized, governed by a general assembly with broad powers. In practice, each local managed its own affairs. Some locals were composed of both skilled and unskilled workers, and others were simply trade unions. Some members, in fact, carried trade union cards along with membership in the Knights. Powderly was also an instinctive reformer who toyed with every quick solution that came along, from cheap money to socialism. He had little interest in collective bargaining and hated strikes. Yet his

dynamism carried the Knights for several years, and a booming economy no doubt helped. Militant working people achieved the first big victories for organized labor. This string of victories in the mid-1880s was so remarkable that some have termed it "the great upheaval."

The Knights were of little help in the "upheaval," but they reaped the benefits. It began in the spring of 1884 when unorganized shopmen struck the Union Pacific. The railroad surrendered and recognized the union, whereupon the union joined the Knights of Labor. A miners' strike in Ohio later that year failed, though the miners managed to put together a strike fund that enabled them to hold out for six months. Then, in March 1885, workers of the Missouri Pacific Railroad struck against a pay cut. The strike soon spread to the Wabash Railroad, and traffic in the southern plains came to a standstill. Both railroads were owned by the mighty Jay Gould. When the governors of Missouri and Kansas sided with the strikers, Gould surrendered and annulled the pay cut. A few months later, workers struck again, and this time Gould agreed to recognize the union. Forcing the stock market profiteer to the bargaining table caused a national sensation, for Gould was widely regarded as a villain. The Knights played only a minor role, but they were the most visible institution around. Working people flocked to join, and membership soared to more than 700,000.

THE HAYMARKET RIOT

The triumph was short-lived. Leaders of the Knights of Labor lacked the skill to mobilize such an army, and the public, once the thrill of beating Jay Gould passed, reverted to its normal fear of union violence. In 1886 trade union leaders called for a general strike in support of the eight-hour day. Powderly was against it, arguing that the time was not ripe, but many of

The Voices of Labor

Toiling millions now are waking—
See them marching on;
All the tyrants now are shaking,
Ere their power's gone.

Chorus:
Storm the fort, ye Knights of Labor,
Battle for your cause;
Equal rights for every neighbor—
Down with Tyrant laws!

Anthem of the Knights of Labor.

Tell the world that the men of the Gould Southwest system are on strike! We strike for justice to ourselves and our fellow countrymen everywhere. Fourteen thousand men are out. . . . Bring in all your grievances in one bundle at once, and come out to a man, and stay out until they are all settled to your entire satisfaction. Let us demand our rights and compel the exploiters to accede to our demands. . . .

Knights of Labor appeal, 1886.

QUESTION: You are seeking to improve home matters first?

ANSWER: Yes, Sir, I look first to the trade I represent . . . the interest of the men who employ me to represent their interests.

CHAIRMAN: I was only asking you in regard to your ultimate ends.

WITNESS: We have no ultimate ends. We are going on from day to day. We fight only for immediate objects—objects that can be realized in a few years.

Testimony of Adolph Strasser, president of the International Cigar Makers' Union and one of the founders of the A F of L, before the Senate Committee on Education and Labor, 1885.

the Knights' locals ignored him. The public was frightened by the specter of a nationwide shutdown. And, as it turned out, fear ruled the day.

The strike began on May 1, and it was a fiasco from the start. About 190,000 men laid down their tools, but the walkout was anything but nationwide. Nearly all the strikers were in New York, Cincinnati, or Chicago. In Chicago the situation was complicated by a separate strike against the McCormick Harvester Company that had been going on since February. On May 3 strikers clashed with police, and one man was killed. A protest meeting was called in the city's Haymarket Square. The crowd was disappointingly small and got smaller when rain began to fall. The meeting was about to break up when a formation of police appeared. Someone, evidently an anarchist, threw a bomb, killing one policeman and injuring others. In a fury, the police charged into the crowd with guns blazing. In the aftermath everyone, including Powderly, denounced the bomb throwing. No one thought to criticize the police. Eight anarchists were subsequently convicted, and four were hanged. The only genuine evidence against them was that they were foreign-born.

All labor suffered in the backlash. "We arbitrated with employers as to a scale of wages and hours of labor last May," a Chicago bakers' union reported in late 1886, "but after the general trouble, existing at that time, the employers broke the contract. Some of our men now work 16 hours as a day's labor." The Knights were already on the decline. That spring they had struck against Jay Gould again, and this time they lost. Membership dwindled to 100,000 by 1890. The organization was moribund by the time Powderly retired in 1892.

THE AMERICAN FEDERATION OF LABOR

The Knights were further distracted in their latter years by internal bickering between Powderly and trade union leaders. The trade unions accused Powderly of weakening the movement by catering to the unskilled and ignoring bread-and-butter issues. Long-simmering trade union opposition had culminated in December 1886, when a small group of unionists met in Columbus, Ohio, to organize the American Federation of Labor. Samuel Gompers, a leader of the cigarmakers union and one of Powderly's chief critics within the Knights, was chosen president. The significance of the new organization was not immediately apparent; indeed, it wasted its resources in its early years battling the Knights, rather than employers. But the birth of the A F of L was of far-reaching importance.

It meant, essentially, the triumph of bread-and-butter unionism. The American Federation of Labor was, as its name implied, a decentralized federation of trade unions, in which member unions managed their own affairs. And its aims were limited. It would focus on skilled workers, those with bargaining power, and concentrate on the essentials, wages and hours. Gompers was no reformer, and under his guidance the A F of L was determinedly nonpolitical. It did not even endorse a presidential candidate until 1924, the year Gompers died.

The federation grew slowly, in part because of the hard times of the 1890s. By 1900 it counted perhaps a half million members. It was hardly "big labor"—that concept had to await the 1930s—but it was a start. Most important, it shaped the contours of the American labor movement. Samuel Gompers, like the social critics of his day, Lester Ward and Henry George, was essentially a conservative. He had no quarrel with the free enterprise system; he wanted only labor's fair share. Capital, land, and labor, the trilogy of classical economics, each yielded its return—interest, rent, and wages. Samuel Gompers was satisfied with his third.

Others were not. A genuinely radical movement was brewing by the time the A F of L was founded. This one would call into question the very premises on which American society was founded, and it would provide some imaginative, and sometimes discomforting, answers. Its roots, however, were not in the factory proletariat, as Karl Marx had predicted, but on the farm.

SUMMARY

Self-sustained economic growth began in the United States in the 1840s. After a brief suspension during the Civil War, it took wing again in the 1870s. So furious was the pace of American growth that the economy overtook and then outdistanced the economies of Western Europe. On the eve of the Civil War, the United States was fourth in the world in the volume and value of manufactured goods. By 1900 it was not only first; it produced more goods than the second and third powers, Britain and Germany, combined. Among the new technologies that helped revolutionize the American economy in the late nineteenth century were the Bessemer and open hearth methods of steel manufacture, oil refining, and electric power.

Accompanying the economic growth was a trend toward business consolidation—the formation of large corporations competing in a national market. The pioneer in this was John D. Rockefeller, whose Standard Oil trust dominated the oil refining business. His company became a model for centralization in other industries, such as sugar refining, meatpacking, and distilling. The object in most cases was not to eliminate competition, but to reduce costs and improve efficiency by vertical consolidation—the control of all stages of production, from extraction to marketing.

When trusts were outlawed in 1890 by the Sherman Antitrust Act, business developed a similar device, the holding company. Holding companies held controlling interests in the stock of operating companies, thereby bringing them under centralized management. The purchase of controlling interests required enormous amounts of capital, often furnished by investment bankers. Preeminent among these was J. P. Morgan, who helped organize the General Electric Company in 1892 and the United States Steel Corporation in 1901.

The intellectual climate of the Gilded Age was a friendly environment for the rise of big business. In what one historian has called "the great train robbery of American intellectual history," the rhetoric of Jeffersonian-Jacksonian liberalism, with its emphasis on self-reliance and equality, was adopted by wealthy conservatives to suit their own needs. "Self-reliance" was both intellectual stimulus and moral justification for the person at the top of the economic pyramid; to factory workers or tenant farmers struggling to form unions and cooperative associations, it meant little.

Social Darwinism wedded individualism and laissez faire to the laws of science. Social Darwinism was the thesis of an Englishman, Herbert Spencer, who argued that civilization itself was the product of gradual yet inevitable evolution. The steady improvement resulted from the natural competition among people and the "survival of the fittest." Because the competition was both natural and inevitable, any governmental interference (by feeding the unemployed, for instance) would retard human progress because it would help the "unfit" to survive.

American writers like William Graham Sumner and the industrialist Andrew Carnegie added a religious touch to Spencer's blend of biology and economics. They argued that the virtuous—the industrious, frugal, temperate people—were the most likely to survive in the struggle. And by surviving, they were rewarded with success. This ethical system, in which earthly success was the reward of virtue, Andrew Carnegie called the "gospel of wealth." Social Darwinism had its critics, notably Lester Ward and Henry George, but they had little impact on their own time.

There were enough rags-to-riches success stories in nineteenth-century America (among them Andrew Carnegie's) to lend some credence to the gospel of wealth. But it offered no hope to the millions of poorly paid factory workers, many of them immigrants, who had little prospect of getting ahead, no matter how industrious, frugal, and temperate they were. America's workers in fact resisted the gospel by failing to report for work, by moving restlessly from job to job, and by engaging in slowdowns and strikes.

Working people were becoming conscious of their group identity in the Gilded Age. Paralleling the nationalization of business were efforts to form national labor organizations. The first of these, the National Labor Union, formed in 1866, was a loose affiliation of trade unions that failed after a few years. The Knights of Labor lasted somewhat longer. The Knights preached

the universal brotherhood of labor, but in practice they were an organization of the unskilled because the trade unions ignored them. The Knights experienced some success in organizing railroad workers in the 1880s but declined thereafter. In 1886 Samuel Gompers organized the American Federation of Labor, an association of trade unions that concentrated on "bread and butter" issues—wages and hours. "Big business" thus begot "big labor," though it would be many years before the A F of L rated that label.

READING SUGGESTIONS

The best introductions to industry, labor, and public policy in the second half of the nineteenth century are E. C. Kirkland, *Industry Comes of Age* (1961), and R. Higgs, *The Transformation of the American Economy* (1971). Recent studies of technological change and its social impact are David A. Hounshell's *From the American System to Mass Production, 1800–1932* (1984) and David F. Noble's *Forces of Production: A Social History of Industrial Automation* (1984).

Henry Steele Commager, *The American Mind* (1948), has a good, brief analysis of Social Darwinism and its critics. Irvin G. Wyllie, *The Self-Made Man in America: The Myth of Rags to Riches* (1954), explores the gospel of success. Robert G. McClosky's *American Conservatism in the Age of Enterprise* (1951) is especially good on the conservatism of the courts.

The works of John Higham are the classics in the field of immigration and nativism: *Strangers in the Land* (1955) and *Send These to Me: Jews and Other Immigrants in Urban America* (1970). Stephan Thernstrom, *Poverty and Progress: Social Mobility in a Nineteenth Century City* (1964), studies the comparative progress made by immigrants and native-born Americans.

There is a great deal of fine new scholarship in the field of labor history. Herbert Gutman's

Work, Culture, and Society in Industrializing America (1976) is a pioneering study in the adaptation of workers to industrialism. Also useful are David Montgomery, *Workers' Control in America: Studies in the History of Work, Technology, and Labor Struggles* (1979), and J. R. Green, *The World of the Worker* (1980). In *The Work Ethic in Industrial America, 1850–1920* (1978), Daniel T. Rodgers explores the tension between the ideal of work and the reality. Two recent books examine parts of the work force previously slighted: William H. Harris, *The Harder We Run: Black Workers since the Civil War* (1982), and Alice Kessler-Harris, *Out to Work: A History of Wage-Earning Women in the United States* (1982). Rudy Ray Seward, *The American Family: A Demographic History* (1978), reaches the surprising conclusion that the family remained quite stable in the period 1850 to 1880 and was relatively unaffected by industrialization and urbanization.

On the A F of L, see Philip Taft's *The A. F. of L. in the Time of Gompers* (1970). Harold C. Livesay's biography, *Samuel Gompers and Organized Labor in America* (1978), is also excellent. William M. Dick's *Labor and Socialism in America: The Gompers Era* (1972) looks at some of the alternatives.

4

THE VANISHING
FRONTIER

ever have more noble words been uttered by a more noble being. "I am tired of fighting," he was saying. "Our chiefs are killed. Looking Glass is dead. Toohoolhoolzote is dead. The old men are all dead. . . . It is cold and we have no blankets. The little children are freezing to death . . . I want to have time to look for my children and see how many of them I can find. Maybe I shall find them among the dead. Hear me, my chiefs! I am tired; my heart is sick and sad. From where the sun now stands I will fight no more forever."

The speaker was Joseph, chief of the Nez Percé, the tribe that had welcomed Lewis and Clark and helped the explorers pursue their journey to the Pacific. The tribe boasted that no Nez Percé had ever killed a white man—that is, until the summer of 1877 when the government decided to take away their ancestral lands in the northern Rockies. Even then, the 37-year-old Joseph had counseled peace and prepared his people for removal to a reservation in a tiny corner of present-day Idaho. But when young warriors attacked and killed some whites who had stolen their horses and the army sought to punish them, Joseph sided with his angry people. There followed a tactical retreat unmatched in the annals of warfare. Seven hundred and fifty Indians, half of them women and children, led the U.S. army on a running fight through the treacherous Bitteroot Mountains, across recently erected Yellowstone National Park, and northward across Montana toward the Canadian border.

For almost four months the Indians outwitted and outfought the army, in a total of nineteen engagements scattered over 1,300 miles of Rocky Mountain wilderness. They were trapped at last on October 5, 1877, by fresh troops commanded by Colonel Nelson Miles, and Joseph surrendered.

He was only 40 miles from the Canadian border and the sanctuary established there by the Sioux a decade before.

⊔ The Last of the Indian Wars: Ending a Century of Dishonor

The Nez Percé episode was the last of the Indian "wars"—not the end of bloodshed, but the end of organized Indian resistance. For a decade and a half before 1877, the Indians had fought white encroachment on the last segment of the continent that was still pristine and primitive—the Great Plains and the Rocky Mountains. In 1866 the Sioux fought the Union army, lost, and fled to Canada. In 1876, Sioux warriors, led by Sitting Bull and Crazy Horse, annihilated a detachment of the Seventh Cavalry commanded by General George Armstrong Custer, but the victory won no respite. Cavalry reinforcements stormed across the high plains, killing every Indian they could find. Within a year, Sitting Bull was forced into signing a treaty that surrendered the Black Hills and the game-rich Powder River Valley, and the broken Sioux trudged off to a bleak reservation in the Dakota "badlands." Some of the Sioux warriors enlisted as scouts to help the army catch the fugitive Nez Percé. Crazy Horse, whose tactical genius had become a legend on the Plains, told them not to fight against their own kind. Soldiers clapped him in irons, and when he resisted they stabbed him to death with bayonets.

Such fighting as there was after the Nez Percé war of 1877 resulted when Indians escaped from reservations. The most famous and surely the most persistent of these freedom seekers was Geronimo, an Apache who simply could not tolerate the chronic hunger and stifling confinement

(*Chapter opening photo*) "The Evening Pipe," oil painting by Charles M. Russell, 1891.

Chief Joseph of the Nez Percés.

The Bettmann Archive.

of the barren San Carlos reservation on the headwaters of the Gila River (in eastern Arizona). Between 1881 and 1886 he fled five times from the reservation. Three times he returned voluntarily to support his hungry family; once he was captured by army treachery. He surrendered at last to the persistent Colonel Nelson Miles, who lured him with promises of land and horses. With no intention of keeping its promises, the army shipped him to Florida and then to Fort Sill, Oklahoma. Geronimo spent his last years as an exhibit in Wild West shows.

WOUNDED KNEE

The final event in the string of western racial tragedies occurred in 1890, the year, ironically, in which the U.S. Census Bureau declared the frontier no longer existed. For some years previously reservation Indians had been practicing the ghost dance, a messianistic religion that promised the resurrection of their ancestors, elimination of the white man, and the restoration of their ancient hunting lands. Whites, especially the military authorities in charge of the reservations, regarded the sect as a source of trouble. In December 1890, Nelson Miles, now a general in command of western operations with headquarters in Chicago, ordered the arrest of one of the creed's supposed leaders, Sitting Bull. At Fort Yates in South Dakota Indian police went to Sitting Bull's cabin to arrest him, ghost dancers gathered to resist, and in the scuffle the police shot Sitting Bull through the head. In the tense days that followed, a band of ghost dancers that had left a Dakota reservation was intercepted by the army. The troops, members of the Seventh Cavalry, still haunted by the memory of Custer, forced the group of 120 men and 230 women and children to a cavalry tent camp on Wounded Knee Creek. When the soldiers tried to disarm the Indians, one warrior, who was evidently deaf, appeared to resist. The soldiers opened up with automatic Gatling guns. When the madness ended, 153 Indians lay dead; dozens of others crawled away wounded to die in the bush. The clash between the red and white races, which had begun at Hispaniola in 1492, ended at Wounded Knee in 1890.

THE DAWES ACT

Some called her an "Indian Harriet Beecher Stowe." The compliment was merited but not wholly accurate. Helen Hunt Jackson's book, *A Century of Dishonor* (1881), simply did not have the impact of *Uncle Tom's Cabin*. She had to publish it at her own expense, and even though she mailed a copy to every member of Congress, it is unlikely that many read it. Nor was it widely read by the public. Americans were too wrapped in the myth of the Wild West portrayed by dime novels to trouble themselves with the "Indian problem." Jackson's book was important nonetheless, for it chronicled the dismal history of white–Indian relations—the unnecessary wars, the broken treaties, the officially sanctioned bribery, the stark betrayal. Among those few interested in the "Indian problem" it brought to a head rising dissatisfaction with the reservation system.

The flight of the Nez Percé dramatized the Indians' hatred for the reservations. Most of the reservations were barren land, with little game and few resources. As a result the Indians were totally dependent, reduced to government handouts of food and clothing. Federal agents who governed the reservations were often incompetent, sometimes corrupt. Few had any respect for Indian culture, and they regarded Indian dances and rituals as subversive.

Reformers, for the most part, had no higher regard for Indian traditions. Their solution was to explore the idea, first suggested by Thomas Jefferson, of giving the Indians parcels of land to farm and absorbing them into white society like immigrants. The scheme served the interests of cattlemen and miners who wanted to exploit the Indian lands and break up the reservations. They eagerly joined forces with the reformers. President Grover Cleveland interested himself in the problem, and this tripartite alliance secured passage of the Dawes Allotment Act in 1887. The act provided that the reservation lands, then held collectively by the tribes, could be broken up and distributed in 160-acre parcels to Indian heads of families.

The Dawes Act was in keeping with the individualistic philosophy of the day, but its authors sadly misconceived what the Indians wanted or needed. The Indians were not prepared for assimilation. Most of the western tribes had no knowledge of farming, and the government made no effort to train them. Few could speak English; fewer still understood such elementary features of American culture as the work ethic. The concept behind the Dawes Act was useful enough; it was simply applied to the wrong people at the wrong time. A similar offer to freed blacks at the end of the Civil War would have changed the course of southern history. Blacks would have benefited because they knew how to farm and had absorbed what they wanted of European-American culture. Blacks wanted desperately to participate in American society on an equal basis; the Indians wanted simply to be left alone.

Even so, many Indians might have succeeded if the lands they were given had been fertile. But by the time the Dawes Act was passed, the Indians had been pushed onto some of the most barren, arid terrain on the continent. As a result, they

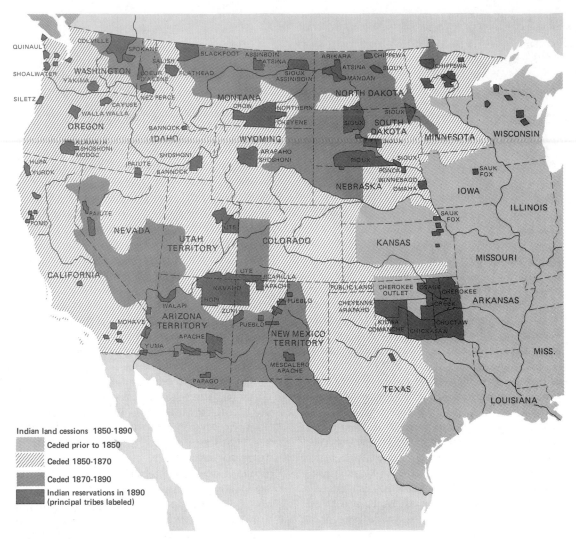

Indian land cessions, 1850–1890.

failed and had to sell out. By 1900 Indian holdings in the West were half what they had been in 1887, and the Indian population was declining to the point where some tribes feared extinction.

"HARRISON'S HOSS RACE"

The federal government, incredibly, led the way in this dispossession. In President Cleveland's last year in office, the govern-

ment purchased from Creeks and Seminoles the middle section of Oklahoma, which had been their preserve since the time of Andrew Jackson. Congress passed a law opening that portion of Oklahoma to homesteaders, and Cleveland's successor, Benjamin Harrison, proclaimed that landseekers could enter the newly purchased lands to stake their claims at noon on April 22, 1889. He sent the army to patrol the border, lest anyone enter sooner to stake out a claim.

Oklahoma Historical Society.
The Oklahoma land rush, 1889.

Oklahoma, by 1889, was the last sizable parcel in the West where a poor settler could still hope to get a free farm. As the appointed day drew near, thousands gathered at the border to participate in "Harrison's hoss race." The noon signal brought a furious rush. Carriages and wagons flew across the prairie, bursting axles on prairie dog villages, toppling over in gravelly streambeds. Trains loaded with the land hungry chugged across the windswept landscape. Many found only disappointment. "Sooners" had entered the territory illegally and hidden on choice parcels until the official entry time. Some were busy plowing their fields when the claim seekers arrived. Those who profited most were the dealers in town lots in communities such as Oklahoma City and Guthrie. Oklahoma City, nothing but a coal-and-water stop for the Santa Fe Railroad on the morning of April 22, was a tent metropolis of 10,000 by nightfall.

In succeeding years the government negotiated further Indian cessions, and in 1904 the entire territory was thrown open to white settlement. That ended any opportunity for the Indians. Many of the plains Indians had been resettled in Oklahoma along with the "civilized tribes" who had been removed there from the South in the 1830s. The discovery of oil in Oklahoma in the 1920s would have provided at least a poetic end to the story, but it was not to be. Whites were the chief beneficiaries of that too. In 1924 Congress granted full citizenship and voting rights to all American Indians, partly as a reward for those who had served in the armed forces during World War I. It proved of little value. Though the Indian population was no longer declining, most Indians continued to live in dire poverty.

In 1934 Congress belatedly recognized the failure of the Dawes Act. It reversed government policy, halted the further breakup of the reservations, and authorized tribal government for those groups that still clung together. The welcome effect was to preserve what remained of Indian language and culture. Problems, of course, remained—poverty, poor education, and the inability of many white Americans to accommodate themselves to a social group that rejected assimilation. But after more than three centuries of dishonor, the government at last gave the Indians a choice in their own destiny.

⊔ Cowboy and Longhorn

By the time Chief Joseph surrendered in 1877, the last frontier was already experiencing dramatic change. The buffalo, which once roamed the grassland in herds that stretched from horizon to horizon, were nearly extinct. The slaughter had begun with the construction of the transcontinental railroad. The railroad hired professional marksmen, such as William F. Cody (Buffalo Bill), to keep their workers supplied with fresh meat. Then came the skin-hunters, who killed and stripped the animals for their hides, leaving the carcasses to the coyotes and vultures. Sportsmen, who measured their pleasure by the numbers of animals killed in a day, finished the job.

The cowboy too was a vanishing species by 1877. The cowboy and the long-horned steer evolved together in the triangle of southern-Texas, formed by the Gulf coastline and the Rio Grande. The triangle is a barren landscape of brown grass and mesquite, searing hot in summer, chill in winter, and dry the year around. The very harshness of the environment shaped the evolution of one of the continent's truly distinctive animals, the Texas longhorn. The creature's ancestors were cattle brought to the New World by the Spanish. Some of these escaped into the wild, multiplied on the Texas grasslands, and later interbred with other varieties brought into the Rio Grande Valley by Mexican ranchers. The result was an animal that was bony, long-legged, and tough, with horns that continued to grow throughout its life. It could withstand the fierce summer heat, endure for long periods without water, and digest practically anything that grew. Commercially, however, it had a serious flaw—it was virtually inedible.

THE CATTLE DRIVE

Spanish breeders (*rancheros*) had been raising cattle in the Rio Grande Valley since the 1600's, and after Texas became independent Americans went into the business.

A western train threading its way through a herd of buffalo.

Smithsonian Institution.

One of the first of these was Richard King, a sea captain from New York who purchased a huge tract of land south of Corpus Christi in 1853. Markets were too distant and transportation too primitive to sell beef, so King and other ranchers exported hides and tallow, which New England artisans made into shoes and candles.

The Civil War brought the western cattle ranch into the national economy and the cowboy into national mythology. Wartime devastation and military consumption depleted the cattle herds of the East, creating new demand for beef. The war also inspired railroad construction onto the western plains, at last giving the ranchers an avenue to market. The man who first spotted opportunity in all this was a cattle dealer from Springfield, Illinois, named Joseph B. McCoy. He wanted Texas ranchers to drive their cattle north across the vast Indian reservation known as Oklahoma to the western terminus of the Kansas Pacific railroad. In 1867 the railroad extended as far as Abilene, a hamlet of a dozen ramshackle log huts, so sleepy that a prairie dog community thrived in the middle of its main street. Bubbling with booster

The cattle and mining frontiers.

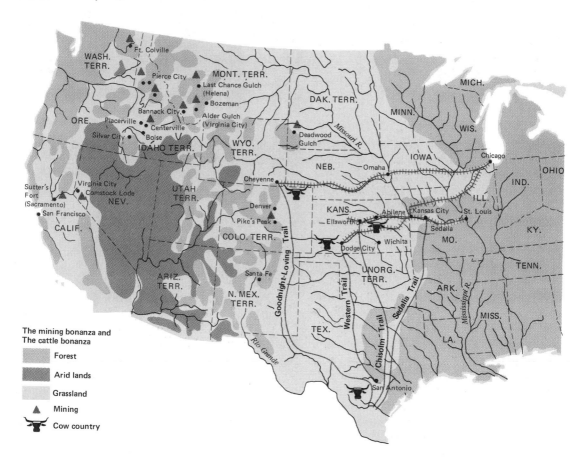

The mining bonanza and
The cattle bonanza

Forest

Arid lands

Grassland

▲ Mining

🐂 Cow country

Photographic Archives, Western History Collections, University of Oklahoma.

Judge Roy Bean described himself as the "Law West of the Pecos." His court house, which doubled as a saloon, was named "The Jersey Lilly." It, as well as his town of Langtry, Texas, was named in honor of a famous singer of the day, Lily Langtry, whom Bean greatly admired but never met.

spirit, McCoy poured his funds into the community, erecting stock pens, loading facilities, and even a hotel, which he named the Drover's Cottage. Then he invited Texas ranchers to embark on the seemingly impossible venture of driving their herds four or five hundred miles across an arid grassland, populated by coyotes, rattlesnakes, and Comanches.

The response was slow not because Texans thought the task difficult, but because earlier attempts to drive cattle in Missouri had been turned back by angry farmers. Nonetheless, by 1868 McCoy's stockpens were filled to capacity, the Kansas Pacific had devised a cattle car for shipment of live animals, and Abilene was booming. In 1871 a half million longhorns moved through Abilene to eastern stockyards. The town declined thereafter as the railroad pushed south and west, making the cattle drives shorter, and creating boomtowns successively out of Newton, Witchita, Fort Hays, and Dodge City.

THE COWBOY MYTH

In remarkably short time, the cattle town and the cowboy became American institutions. The cowboy, like the longhorn, had Spanish-Mexican ancestors. His equipment, from his chaps to his lariat, was Mexican in origin, and his language was studded with Spanish idioms. Only about 12 percent of the 35,000 men who participated in the great cattle drives were Mexican by ancestry; about 25 percent were black. The remainder were uncouth, ill-educated transients of the sort that had populated every earlier frontier. They carried guns but rarely used them, except on rattlesnakes and coyotes. The legendary violence of the cattle towns was largely that—

legend, born of the purple prose of the dime novels that made them famous.

Dodge City had its "boot hill" where victims of "lead poisoning" were buried with their boots on, and it gave the world the first red light district. But gang warfare of the sort portrayed in twentieth-century films was rare. Newton's General Massacre, the greatest carnage on the cattle frontier, involved nine casualties. The famous shootout at the OK Corral in Tombstone resulted in the death of three men. Much of the violence, in fact, occurred not in the cattle towns, where cowboys were routinely disarmed on entry, but in the mining towns of the Far West, Tombstone in southern Arizona, or Deadwood on the edge of the Black Hills. "Wild Bill" Hickok survived stints as marshal of Fort Riley, Hays City, and Abilene, Kansas, only to be shot from behind while sitting at a poker table in Deadwood's Saloon Number Ten. (He was holding two pairs, aces and eights, known ever after as the "dead man's hand.")

By the end of the 1870s, the cowboy and the longhorn were both endangered species, victims of technology. Railroads pushed into the heart of Texas, making the long drives unnecessary. Barbed wire and the steel plow broke up the plains and blocked the old cattle trails. Fencing also permitted selective breeding and thus improvements in the quality of livestock. Ranchers began to import shorthorn Hereford cattle from England, which though less picturesque than the longhorns, brought better prices at the slaughterhouse. And as the cattle drives and the longhorns disappeared, so did the cowboy. The cattleman was, except for his horsemanship, little different from any other farmer.

⊔ The Sodbusters: Farming the Plains

Barbed wire, which first became commercially available in the 1870s, was the enemy of the cowboy, but it was the dirt farmer's lifeline. It enabled him to protect his crops and keep track of his animals. In the East farmers fenced their lands with rock walls, split rails, or thornbushes. None of these materials was available on the Plains. Along with fencing, the dirt farmer needed peace and tranquillity. Civil war in the East and Indian warfare on the Plains slowed the westward drift of population in the 1860s. Peace, postwar prosperity, and barbed wire brought a new spurt in the 1870s. In the thirty years after 1870 more acres were brought under cultivation than had been put to the plow in the preceding two and a half centuries.

Joining the flow of whites from East to West were newly mobile freed blacks from the South. In 1879 some 30,000 blacks followed a former Louisiana slave named Henry Adams to Kansas; some went by steamboat, some went overland along the cattle trails. Native white Kansans, whose prewar free-soil politics had been antiblack as much as antislavery, drove many away, but some managed to hang on. And their example eventually attracted more.

The last frontier also attracted more European immigrants than any earlier westward movement. People from Germany, Scandinavia, and Russia, lured in part by railroad brochures and leaflets, poured into Kansas, Nebraska, and the Dakotas. As late as 1910 more than a quarter of the population of North Dakota was foreign-born, and their children made up another 43 percent.

Regarded for years as a "desert" unfit for white habitation, the Great Plains* did

---

* The Great Plains has three characteristics that distinguish it from other regions of the United States: It is level, treeless, and too dry for most crops, such as corn and cotton. The region begins at about the middle of the Dakotas, Nebraska, and Kansas and stretches west to the foothills of the Rockies. To the east of this—a region sometimes called the "prairie plains" (northern Missouri, Iowa, Illinois, and the southern parts of Wisconsin and Minnesota)—the land is relatively flat and treeless, but it receives enough rainfall for normal agriculture.

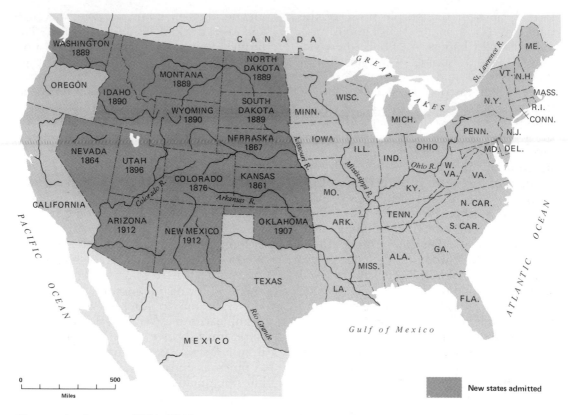

Western development, 1861–1912.

present more problems for the pioneer than any earlier frontier. It was a land of unending grass and few rivers, torrid in summer, frozen over in winter. Trees, which supplied building materials, fuel, and fencing on earlier frontiers, existed only along the widely scattered streambeds. Houses had to be constructed of prairie sod, cut from the earth in bricklike chunks and piled to form walls. The sod house seems a dismal abode to the modern mind, but it had functional utility. It was cool in summer and well insulated in winter. Some were made more attractive on the inside with plasterboard and wallpaper. Oil stoves provided heat, except in remote locations, where buffalo chips had to suffice.

Water was the biggest problem. Geologi-

cally, the Great Plains were formed by erosion from the Rocky Mountains. The soil is therefore loose, and rainfall seeps quickly to the bedrock hundreds of feet below. Rivers were too shallow to be used for transport, so farmers were dependent on the railroads. These problems were not immediately recognized, however, because by chance the movement onto the Great Plains in the 1870s and early 1880s coincided with a period of unusual rainfall. The rains ended in 1886, and then came years of drought, followed by dust storms and a grasshopper plague. Between 1886 and 1890 nearly half the population of Kansas returned to the East. The hardships of the sod house frontier shaped the character of the farm protest. The isolation and lone-

CLIO'S FOCUS: Life on the Sodhouse Frontier

It is hard today to imagine what life was like on the prairie frontier of Kansas, Nebraska, and the Dakotas.

History is the record of the uncommon; it recites the doings of the great and powerful, the thinkers, the shakers, and the leaders. Rarely does it tell about the lives of ordinary people, in part because so few of them left any record of their existence. Their hopes and fears, the dangers they faced, the joys they shared were real enough; they have simply been forgotten. Only a rare memo, preserved by love and luck, affords us a glimpse of "the short and simple annals of the poor."

A recent compilation of diaries and reminiscences written by pioneer women affords a unique insight into life on the Kansas frontier. The endless sea of grass, the violent winters and torrid summers, the monotonous diet of corn, wheat, and potatoes, punctuated with buffalo and beef, the grinding labor of simple survival—all are more poignantly portrayed than in any historian's account. The following excerpts are only a sample of the women's experiences.

A farm family and their sod house, Dakota Territory, 1885.

Nebraska State Historical Society.

In 1879, Emma Smith and her husband E. T. Smith moved west and staked a claim along the South Sappa Creek in Kansas. They set up a campsite and unloaded the cooking gear from the wagon. Emma described the first problem encountered by a Kansas pioneer:

> E. T. and his father set the cook stove on the ground near the creek, but what could we burn for fuel? There was not a tree nor even a bush in sight to furnish us with fuel. But "Grandpa" was elected to supply our needs, so taking a basket and pitchfork he started out and soon returned with a well-filled receptacle of what they called "Chips." Well, I thought I could do almost anything other people could do, so I put on my mittens, and attempted to make a fire. Then I knew why grandfather needed a pitchfork—his fuel was too wet to burn. But I soon learned by experience how and what to gather to make a fire. "Chips" were plentiful, as the plains had for years been an open range, first for buffalo then for cattle in great herds which roamed at will over the prairies. The sod house and cow chips were two great factors in making possible the settlement of this country at so early a date.[*]

Corn was usually the first crop planted and the staple of the first year's diet. Wheat came later, after the tough prairie sod had been twice plowed and harrowed. Chicken reached the table on holidays; dairy products were a luxury that sometimes passed for currency. Bessie Wilson, whose parents homesteaded in McPherson County, Kansas, recalled one festive occasion:

> When it was known that Mr. J. B. Jackson was to be married at Ellsworth on September 6, 1875, some of the neighbors planned a surprise for him and his bride on their return. Mother was asked to bake a cake for the affair. In consequence, we ate our bread without butter for several days in order that father might have enough to take to the store and exchange for the amount of sugar necessary to make a cake. This he did, covering the sixteen miles horseback. Mother's was the only cake at this important gathering, and despite the fact that she had no recipe to go by, and that she used sour milk and soda in the making, it was pronounced by those who partook as being all a bride's cake should be.

The sodhouse and the dugout—a shelter carved out of the side of a hill—usually had a dirt floor, so housecleaning was principally a matter of keeping things swept and tidy. Soap was still an essential for personal needs, washing cooking utensils, and laundry. And making it was a major project. Emeline Crumb followed an old New England recipe. It began with a construction of a hopper of clapboards, lined with straw. Into this went the daily ashes from fireplace and cookstove.

> When the hopper was full, a depression was made in the middle, and clear water poured in each day, until at last the lye began to drip from the groove in the platform. A wooden bucket or stone jar was set under to catch the drippings. When the family did not possess these convenient articles, father went to the woods, cut a proper log, and hewed out a trough, which answered the purpose, just as it did to also water stock, or rock the baby for a cradle.

---

[*] All excerpts from *Pioneer Women: Voices from the Kansas Frontier*. Copyright © 1981 by Joanna L. Stratton. Reprinted by permission of Simon & Schuster, Inc.

If the ashes were leached slowly enough, the lye would be very strong. To be perfect, it should bear up an egg. A fresh egg—not an addled one, which will float anywhere.

When a bright day came—in the right time of the moon—father set the big soap kettle in the back yard, and brought plenty of dry wood near. All the grease and scraps of fat trimmings that had been collected during the year were brought to the place. In the case of grease which had been dried out, such as that from the entrails of hogs, or saved from the cooking, it could be made up at once. There were likely to be some pounds of meaty scraps and rinds, and these were first cooked in a weak lye, by the most particular housewives. When thoroughly cooked, water was put in a wooden tub and the mess turned in and set aside to cool. The debris settled in the bottom, and a mushy grease on top was partly made soap, later to be used as was the more pure grease. When the grease was thus all prepared, the real presiding genius was called to put the finishing touch.
A noted painter was once asked, by a fellow artist, what he mixed his paints with to produce such wonderful results. The reply was "BRAINS." And this was one ingredient of pioneer soap making.
The grease being in an indefinite state, it was a matter of experienced judgment how much to put into the kettle of boiling lye. Not infrequently some eastern dame was invited to superintend the process, who invariably brought her knitting along, and sat in the hickory bottomed rocker, out in the sunshine near the soap kettle, telling of bygone days when men hunted bears and women fought Indians in their absence. When the soap was declared done by the best authority present, it was carefully ladled into a wooden tub containing a few quarts of water, covered and left to cool. If a little salt or rozin had been added it would be hard and could be cut into bars for drying as hard as soap. Turned into a firkin or barrel, and in which it remained until used, it was the popular soft soap. The kind housewives used to scrub their tables and floor. Not the sort used later by politicians.

Fire, the vital center of any prairie home, was also a deadly enemy, more dangerous by far than Indians and wolves. J. C. Ruppenthal, whose parents established a homestead near Wilson, Kansas, in 1877, recalled the curious mixture of thrill and terror inspired by prairie fire:

In the days of endless sweep of prairie, of grass without limit for many, many miles, the ripening of the grass in early fall or its premature drying from drought was signal for renewal of nightly vigilance in watching the horizon all around. Every light against the sky told of a prairie fire in that direction. The direction of the wind, either from or opposite the direction of such fire, or sidewise, the unsteadiness of wind with possibility of veering so as to bring fire toward the home—all these were noted. The last act at night, after seeing that the children were all asleep, and all quiet among the livestock in sheds, pens and corrals, was to sweep the entire horizon for signs of flame.
Many times, on awakening in the dead of night, the room was light with reflection from the sky, shining thru uncurtained windows from some fire ten or twenty or fifty miles away. Often in the small hours mother watched from window to window to see if the light died away, indicating that the fire had gone out, or had grown brighter threatening a wider scope of blackened prairie behind it.
At times the flames themselves were visible at night up to twenty or twenty-five miles away, as they crept up hills in the buffalo grass, or flared longer in redtop bunch grass, and when the fire rolled down into a hollow in big blue stem grass, though the flames might not be seen, the general red glare in the sky told somewhat of the heat and light from the tall grass below. Despite the fear inspired by a prairie fire, there was a fascination to watch a fire by night, advancing, brightening, showing masses of solid flame or myriads

of tiny jets that flickered and went out, to flash again farther along. At times the silhouettes of men fighting could be seen against the background of distant flames.

About half of all the pioneers who braved the Kansas frontier gave up and returned to the East. The final heartbreak for many was grasshoppers. Mary Lyon, who settled in Kansas in 1872, described with wry humor the day the insect plague descended:

August 1, 1874, is a day that will always be remembered by the then inhabitants of Kansas. . . . For several days there had been quite a few hoppers around, but this day there was a haze in the air and the sun was veiled almost like Indian summer. They began, toward night, dropping to earth, and it seemed as if we were in a big snowstorm where the air was filled with enormous-size flakes.

They devoured every green thing but the prairie grass. They ate the leaves and young twigs off our young fruit trees, and seemed to relish the green peaches on the trees, but left the pit hanging. They went from the corn fields as though they were in a great hurry, and there was nothing left but the toughest parts of the bare stalks. Our potatoes had to be dug and marketed to save them.

I thought to save some of my garden by covering it with gunny sacks, but the hoppers regarded that as a huge joke, and enjoyed the awning thus provided, or if they could not get under, they ate their way through. The cabbage and lettuce disappeared the first afternoon; by the next day they had eaten the onions. They had a neat way of eating onions. They devoured the tops, and then ate all of the onion from the inside, leaving the outer shell.

The garden was soon devoured, and when all of these delicacies were gone, they ate the leaves from the fruit trees. They invaded our homes, and if our baking was not well guarded by being enclosed in wood or metal, we would find ourselves minus the substantial part of our meals; and on retiring to bed, we had to shake them out of the bedding, and were fortunate if we did not have to make a second raid before morning.

Lillie Marcks, 12 years old when the grasshoppers scoured the prairie, described a scene that would have driven almost anyone "back home":

Riding his pony like the wind, father came home telling us more tales of destruction left in the path of the pests. They hit the house, the trees and picket fence. Father said, "Go get your shawls, heavy dresses and quilts. We will cover the cabbage and celery beds. Perhaps we can save that much." Celery was almost an unseen vegetable in that time and place—they wished to save it. They soon were busy spreading garments and coverings of all sorts over the vegetables.

The hired man began to have ideas. Everyone was excited trying to stop the devastation. Bonfires began to burn thru the garden. "Now I'll get some of them," Jake said. Picking up a shovel, he ran thru the gate. Along the fence they were piled a foot deep or more, a moving struggling mass. Jake began to dig a trench outside the fence about two feet deep and the width of the shovel. Father gathered sticks and dead leaves. In a few minutes, the ditches were filled with grasshoppers, but they soon saw the fire covered and smothered by grasshoppers. Think of it, grasshoppers putting out a fire.

Ella, my five-year-old sister, was shooing and beating them off the covered garden by means of a long branch someone had given her. I was ill and so excited over all of the battle and could only be up a few seconds at a time. Then all at once, Ella's voice rang out in fear. "I'm on fire!" Forgotten was my fever. I ran to the door and saw a flame going up the back of her dress. In less time that I can tell this, I ran to her and tore off her dress from the shoulders down. Then I turned and looked at the writhing mass of grasshoppers on the garments covering the vegetables and called, "Ma! Ma! Come here! They are eating up your clothes!"

liness of this unique frontier help explain the melodramatic fervor in which the protest was voiced.

RURAL DISCONTENT: MONEY AND CREDIT

New technology compensated in part for the harsh environment, but machines also brought problems of their own. As world agriculture became mechanized, Canada, Russia, Australia, and Argentina became major food exporters along with the United States. The result was a food glut in the Western world that drove down farm prices beginning in the 1870s. Lower farm prices reduced European land values and encouraged European farmers to migrate to the cities and to the United States. The profits from food exports, which gave the United States a favorable balance of trade in all but two years between 1873 and 1900, provided surplus capital for investment in industry. As a result, factories and cities blossomed on both sides of the Atlantic.

Everyone seemed to benefit except the farmers themselves. Tillers of the soil soon found themselves trapped on an economic treadmill. The more successful they were in increasing production, the greater the food glut and the lower farm prices fell. Farmers were forced to seek new ways of increasing production in order to stay even. For a quarter of a century, from 1873 until 1898—a period sometimes called the

Agricultural regions of the United States.

Forest, Hay and Pasture

Forest and Hay

Wheat

Spring Wheat

Hard Winter Wheat

Corn and Winter Wheat

Corn

Cotton Belt

Subtropical Crops

Hay and Dairying

Middle Atlantic Truck Farming

Grazing and Irrigated Crops

Great Depression—farm prices remained low. Wheat that sold for a dollar a bushel in the 1870s often went for less than fifty cents in the 1890s. Corn likewise fell by half, and cotton went from fifteen cents a pound in the 1870s to five cents in the 1890s. At such prices, as farmers grimly observed, it was cheaper to burn their crops for fuel than to buy coal.

A symptom of the hard times was the rise in farm tenancy. Tenant farming had never been part of the American way of life. Americans had always aspired to own their own farms, and low prices for public land had generally made it possible. After the Civil War, however, few freed slaves had the capital to purchase land. Most had to rent parcels of plantations they had previously worked as slaves. Elsewhere, farmers went into debt to buy land and machinery, and when low prices drove them into bankruptcy they lost both. In 1880 a quarter of all farmers did not own the land on which they labored; by 1900 the figure had risen to a third.

Americans have never been given to suffering in silence. Before long, the Great Plains and the South were echoing with farm protest. The price depression hurt farmers precisely because they had become capitalists. The frontier farmer of Jefferson's day for the most part functioned outside the market economy. He and his family produced on the farm nearly all the food and clothing they needed to subsist; a small "cash crop" such as flour or whiskey brought the cash needed for tools and gunpowder. Depression touched them scarcely at all. Post–Civil War farmers, on the other hand, were businessmen. In order to buy machinery that enabled them to increase production, they had borrowed. When the price of their products declined, they found it increasingly difficult to pay their debts. A debt of $1,000 incurred for a harvester could be paid off with a thousand bushels of wheat when wheat was $1 a bushel. But when wheat fell to 50 cents, the farmer had to raise twice as much wheat to pay the same debt. That is what did not seem fair.

From the beginning, the farm protest focused on money and credit. The nation's credit system was, in fact, stacked against the farmer. The stringent requirements set up by Congress for national banks meant that the system was centered in the North and East. Few businessmen outside the urban North had the capital to establish a bank. National banks, moreover, were responsible for most of the nation's paper money. As a result, the rural South and

Show Me!

Western pioneers invented the tall story (1845) and sometimes engaged in tall talk (1850s), but being a practical people living in a harsh environment, they also wanted the lowdown (1880s). Missourians were notorious for their insistence on hard evidence:

> I come from a state that raises corn and cotton and cockleburs and Democrats, and frothy eloquence neither convinces nor satisfies me. I am from Missouri. You have got to show me.

Missouri Congressman Willard Vandiver speaking at a naval banquet, 1899.

West were chronically shy of money and credit. That, in turn, meant that farmers paid higher interest rates.

The farmer-businessman, ironically, was the victim of his own self-reliant competitiveness. Each was an independent producer raising crops for a free market. Because the market was competitively free, prices hovered near the cost of production, the breakeven point between survival and insolvency. Manufacturers evaded the "iron laws" of economics by forming pools, cartels, and trusts, and they persuaded Congress to impose tariffs that would keep out foreign competition. Unorganized farmers bought tools and machines in a protected market, often from firms large enough to impose a set price, and they sold in an open market where the price of their crops was determined by world demand, as set in London or Amsterdam. Organization was clearly needed. Industry and labor, with their trusts and unions, afforded a ready example.

SPECIAL GRIEVANCES

Farmers also had some special grievances, prime among them the railroads. The railroads were natural monopolies. Each line controlled all the traffic in its vicinity. Only when the lines converged, as they did at major urban centers, was there competition. As a result, shipping costs did not necessarily depend on distance. A farmer shipping his wheat a short distance to a milling center might pay more per ton/mile than someone who had a choice of lines in shipping goods from one city to another. As small shippers, moreover, individual farmers had no bargaining leverage. John D. Rockefeller extracted rebates from the railroads on his shipping costs because he

The Union Pacific was so poorly constructed because of the race to secure government financing that much of the line had to be rebuilt.

U.S. Geological Survey, Department of Interior.

could guarantee them a steady supply of large quantities of oil. Farmers had to pay whatever rates the railroads demanded, and the guideline on that was simply what the traffic would bear. Freight rates in the West and South, as a result, were two or three times higher than in the North and East. The problem was particularly oppressive on the Great Plains, where the rivers were too shallow for steamboats and distances too great for wagons. There the farmers were utterly dependent on the railroads—facilities, ironically, that had been built largely with public funds.

The railroads' grain elevator monopoly was another source of contention, especially in the Middle West. Railroads often operated storage elevators as part of their transport operations. Usually the railroads purchased grain from farmers at the elevator, shipped it, and resold it to the millers. As a result, farmers had to accept the railroad's price for their grain, or take it home and eat it.

While grain growers of the prairies fumed at railroads, southern cotton growers had a special grievance of their own—the crop lien system. This vicious practice stemmed from the shortage of credit, especially among tenant farmers, who had few tangible assets to put up as security for loans. Such people went to village shopkeepers at the beginning of each planting season and borrowed the seeds, tools, and materials they needed. As security they put up the one asset they had: their prospective crops. The merchant, in effect, held a lien on the crop for the amount of the loan, and the size of the loan depended in part on the prices the merchant decided to charge for the goods he sold on credit. The merchant also dictated the choice of crop, and he usually insisted upon cotton since that was the easiest for him to market. Thus the southern farmer was tied even tighter to a one-crop system, and that in turn added to the world glut and further depressed prices. When the cotton was har-

vested, it was turned over to the storekeepers for sale. So long as they recovered their investments, they had little regard for price. In fact, a low return meant that the farmer would be back, cap in hand, the following spring. Poor whites as well as black sharecroppers found themselves trapped in this peculiar form of bondage.

The solution to all these problems was organization. By uniting, farmers could gain some leverage against the railroads. By forming cooperatives, they might escape the tyranny of village merchants. By acting in concert, they might even bring some pressure to bear on government, which despite its adherence to laissez faire, always seemed ready to serve the interests of promoters and businessmen.

⊔ The Farmers Organize

The earliest of the farm organizations was the Patrons of Husbandry, founded by officials of the U.S. Department of Agriculture in 1867. The original purpose of the Grange,* as it was commonly known, was to educate farmers in new methods of cultivation, but as the problems farmers faced became clearer, it turned to other activities. It sponsored a number of cooperatives in the Middle West, where farmers could buy implements and seed at low prices. None of them worked very well, but the efforts provoked discussion and heightened the farmers' awareness of their plight.

THE GRANGER LAWS

The Grange was scrupulously nonpartisan, but it could not avoid politics altogether. Many of the farmers' problems—railroad

---

* *Grange*, derived from granary, or barn, referred to the lodges of the organization and ultimately became the common name for the organization itself.

regulation, taxes, credit, and money—required political solutions, and Grangers used their association to pressure legislators. In state capitals the Grangers allied themselves with small businessmen, small-scale shippers who were also victims of railroad discrimination. Under these twin pressures, legislatures in several states—Illinois, Iowa, Wisconsin—passed laws prohibiting rate discrimination and rebates, and they set up commissions to enforce the regulations. In the pre–Civil War era, state regulation of canals and turnpikes was common, but in the postwar atmosphere of Spencerian laissez faire, the "Granger laws," as such regulations were called, were a novelty. They were also a foretaste of the coming century.

In the South the principal farm organizations were the Southern Alliance and its black counterpart, the National Colored Farmers' Alliance. Each claimed a million members by the end of the 1880s. Farmers in the plains states organized themselves into the Northwestern Alliance, born in Chicago in 1880. The alliances were avowedly political, advocating government regulation of railroads, easier credit, and cheap money that would raise farm prices. The Southern Alliance, strongest of the farm organizations, devised an ingenious alternative to the crop lien dilemma. It proposed government loans to farmers at 1 percent interest, with the farmers' crops put up as collateral. A farmer could store his crop in a government warehouse until he found a favorable price, and in the meantime he could borrow up to 80 percent of the crop's value. The idea, a bit ahead of its time, failed to win the interest of Congress, but it was far from impractical. The Commodity Credit Corporation, created in 1933, functioned on much the same concept, with commendable results.

Such ideas, however, failed to win an audience. Congress and the president seemed deaf to the rising protest. Neither of the national parties showed much interest in new ideas or imaginative alternatives. Republicans were wedded to the self-help gospel, which made the only function of government maintaining law and order. Democrats, whose intellectual legacy of states rights and limited government dated back to Andrew Jackson, were even more committed to laissez faire. William Graham Sumner, philosopher of laissez faire, was a Democrat, not a Republican. In 1887 Democratic President Grover Cleveland vetoed a small congressional appropriation to help drought-stricken Texas farmers on the ground that "though the people support the Government, the Government should not support the people." The louder the demand for change, the more the political system seemed to stiffen against it.

The Granger laws, themselves the first tangible result of the farm protest, were among the earliest victims. The railroads battled the regulations from the political stump to the state courts, and when the laws passed anyway, the railroads did what they could to make them unpopular. In Wisconsin the railroads reduced train service until the legislature repealed the law. Elsewhere the railroads fought the regulations in court. The Grange scored one early court victory and then succumbed to judicial conservatism. *Munn* v. *Illinois* (1877) involved an Illinois statute that regulated the rates grain elevators could charge for storage. Munn, an elevator operator, went to court complaining that the law, by regulating his income, deprived him of his property without due process of law in violation of the Fourteenth Amendment. The court rejected his contention, holding that the grain elevator business (and, by implication, the railroads), though privately owned and managed for private profit, was a business "affected with a public interest," and was therefore subject to public supervision.

The concept was bold, providing the basis for the regulation of business enter-

Library of Congress.

A railroad smoking and library car about 1900. The train was a "palace on wheels" for the wealthy.

prise. It was too bold, in fact, for the men who formulated it. Within a few years the court ruled that freight rates prescribed by states must be reasonable, and reasonableness could only be determined by the courts. This ruling, in effect, enabled the railroads to take the state commissions to court every time they tried to set a rate. Then in 1886, in the case of the *Wabash, St. Louis, & Pacific Railway* v. *Illinois*, the court held that the states could not fix rates on shipments that passed beyond their borders; only Congress could regulate inter-

state commerce. Since 75 percent of the nation's rail traffic crossed state lines, this decision virtually excluded the states from the field of regulation. With it, the Granger Laws were dead.

THE INTERSTATE COMMERCE ACT

The *Wabash* decision did increase the pressure on Congress to impose some federal regulations on railroads. If Congress alone had authority in the field of interstate commerce, some felt, perhaps it was time that it exercised its power. Businessmen who used the railroads joined in the cry, and the result was the Interstate Commerce Act (1887), passed with support from both political parties. The act prohibited rebates and pooling agreements and made it unlawful to charge more for a short haul than for a longer one. The act stated that rates must be "reasonable and just," and it compelled railroads to publish their rate schedules. To enforce the regulations, the act created a five-man Interstate Commerce Commission, with authority to prosecute violators in court.

The Interstate Commerce Act was of enormous long-range significance, for it was the first breach in laissez faire. The ICC was the first federal regulatory agency, the forerunner of the alphabet bureaucracy. But the act was of little short-run help to farmers and other small businessmen who used the railroads. The long-haul, short-haul abuse proved impossible to eliminate without bankrupting small lines, and the ICC soon authorized railroads to ignore this provision. Rate setting also proved difficult, because the Supreme Court had already ruled that the reasonableness of rates was a matter for judicial determination. Thus railroads invariably took the ICC to court, and the courts more often than not sided with the railroads. In the mid-1890s the Supreme Court deprived the ICC of rate-setting authority altogether, and after that the commission was nothing more than an information-gathering agency.

Enough of this failure was evident by 1890 that the rising coalition of reformers—farmers, small businessmen, Knights of Labor, and a sprinkling of journalists—began to discuss new and more radical methods of political action. Every branch of government seemed closed to them. So sealed was the political system, so resistant to change, that it seemed to be ruled by conspiracy, by a secret coalition, perhaps led by Wall Street bankers who bought and sold politicians and judges like shares of stock. To break this conspiracy, the people needed a party of their own, an institution that would represent their interests against the bankers and the giant trusts. From this notion emerged the Populist revolt, a political protest movement that shook the complacency of the Gilded Age and infused a new dynamism into American politics.

SUMMARY

In the years prior to the Civil War, the frontier had leaped across the plains and mountains from the Missouri River to California. Afterward, settlement closed in from east and west on the last frontier. Gold and silver miners occupied the mountains; cattle ranchers moved onto the plains. The Indians resisted encroachment on their lands, as they had east of the Mississippi. But because the western Indians were skilled horsemen, the last frontier witnessed some of the fiercest of all the Indian wars. The Sioux fought the Army intermittently through the 1860s and 1870s, surrendering at last in 1877. That same year the Army ended the Nez Percé War by capturing Chief Joseph after a 1,300-mile chase. The final event in the string of western racial tragedies was the massacre of Sioux at Wounded Knee, South Dakota, in 1890. That was also the year in which the U.S. Census Bureau declared that the frontier was over.

The Indian and the buffalo were replaced on the western plains by the cowboy and the longhorn, both the products of Spanish ancestry and the south Texas environment. When the railroads pushed onto the plains after the Civil War, enterprising cattlemen drove their longhorns from Texas across the Indian territory (Oklahoma) to railheads in Kansas. The advance of the railroad created boomtowns successively out of Newton, Wichita, Fort Hays, and Dodge City. And each became a source of western legend. Barbed wire ended the day of the cowboy. It blocked the cattle trails and permitted the selective breeding of shorthorn cattle from England, which fetched better prices than the tough and lean longhorn. Fencing also allowed farmers to move onto the plains, and the cattle frontier yielded to the sodhouse frontier.

The last quarter of the nineteenth century was a difficult time for farmers in both the West and South. The reason was low farm prices, especially for the staple exports, wheat and cotton. A chronic shortage of credit and unfair practices by the railroads added to their problems. For a time, the farmers tried organization. It gave them leverage against banks and railroads, and it enabled them to put pressure on government.

The Grange, formed in 1867, was the first of the farm organizations, and in the 1870s it persuaded several states to pass laws—called Granger laws—regulating the railroads. Another farm organization, the Northwest Alliance, was popular in the Plains states, and the Southern Alliance appealed to both black and white farmers in the South. In 1887 Congress, responding to the demands of small businessmen as well as farmers, passed the Interstate Commerce Act, which set up the Interstate Commerce Commission to regulate the railroads. Despite these limited victories, many farmers by 1890 were disillusioned with the political system and looking for ways to form a political party of their own.

READING SUGGESTIONS

Robert M. Utley's *The Indian Frontier of the American West, 1846–1890* (1984) is the best introduction to that subject. The Indian wars in the West are chronicled in S. L. Marshall, *Crimsoned Prairie: The War between the United States and the Plains Indians* (1972). The mining frontier is covered by Rodman W. Paul, *Mining Frontiers of the Far West, 1848–1880* (1963), and W. S. Greever, *The Bonanza West: The Story of the Western Mining Rushes, 1848–1900* (1963). On the cattle kingdom, see Robert R. Dykstra, *The Cattle Towns* (1970), and Joe B. Frantz and J. E. Choate, *The American Cowboy: The Myth and the Reality* (1955).

Fred A. Shannon, *The Farmer's Last Frontier:*

Agriculture 1860–1897 (1945) is sound economic history, but heavy reading. A bit easier is Gilbert C. Fite's *The Farmer's Frontier, 1865–1900* (1966). The Middle West has been cultivated by Allan G. Bogue in *From Prairie to Cornbelt* (1963), and the Great Plains have been worked by Everett Dick, *The Sod-House Frontier, 1854–1890* (1937). C. Vann Woodward's classic *The Origins of the New South* (1951) has excellent chapters on southern agriculture and the crop lien system. Lee Benson, *Merchants—Farmers—and Railroads* (1955), suggests that urban businessmen were more important than farmers in the drive for government regulation of railroads.

5

THE PEOPLE'S PROTEST: 1892–1900

The saloons of Omaha had laid in an extra supply of liquor. After all, it was the Fourth of July, and a political convention was in town, the city's first. But neither the festival nor the whiskey could distract the delegates from their holy mission. The nation's malcontents—the Alliancemen, Grangers, Knights, suffragettes, single-taxers, and socialists—had been meeting annually since 1889. At Topeka, Kansas, in 1890 they had adopted the name People's party. Now, in 1892, they were gathered in Omaha to select a candidate for president.

⊔ 1892: The People's Party

The major parties seemed to have deserted the people. Republican Benjamin Harrison was no different from his opponent, Grover Cleveland; both, in the Populist view, were the servants of Wall Street financiers. "We meet in the midst of a nation brought to the verge of moral, political, and material ruin," thundered Minnesota's Ignatius Donnelly from the rostrum of the Omaha Coliseum:

> Corruption dominates the ballot-box, the Legislatures, the Congress, and touches even the ermine of the bench. . . . Our homes [are] covered with mortgages . . . the land [is] concentrating in the hands of the capitalists. The urban workmen are denied the right of organization for self-protection. . . . A vast conspiracy against mankind has been organized. . . . If not met and overthrown at once it forebodes terrible convulsions.

The delegates responded with the fervor of a camp meeting warring on the Devil. To the tune of "Save a Poor Sinner, Like Me" they sang that "the railroads and old party bosses together did sweetly agree" to deceive and exploit "a hayseed like me."

It was a revolt of the poor; the Populist message was one of class appeal. Their platform proclaimed "the union of the labor forces of the United States. . . . The interests of rural and civic labor are the same; their enemies are identical." And prime among those enemies were banks and railroads. The Omaha platform demanded government ownership and operation of the railroads and reclamation of all railroad lands that were not in actual use. To break the power of banks, the Populist platform demanded that the government issue the nation's currency, including silver coin, and that it ensure a money supply amounting to at least $50 per person. The platform proposed a graduated income tax to spread the wealth, and postal savings banks to provide ready depositories for the poor. Then came a battery of pro-labor recommendations: restricted immigration, shorter work hours, and laws against the use of Pinkerton-type labor spies.* Finally it offered some suggestions for political reform: popular participation in the legislative process through the initiative and referendum, limiting the president to a single term, and popular election of United States senators.

The Populists proudly admitted to being "hayseeds," but it would be a mistake to dismiss them as rural fanatics. Their platform was in fact a concerted, well-conceived response to the social problems that

---

* The Pinkerton National Detective Agency, founded in 1850 by Alan Pinkerton, the Chicago police department's first detective, became nationally famous in 1861 by uncovering a plot to assassinate Abraham Lincoln on the eve of his inauguration. After the war the agency was commonly employed by employers to spy on their workers. One Pinkerton agent managed to infiltrate the infamous Molly Maguires, an Irish terrorist organization in the Pennsylvania coalfields. Nineteen members of the society were hanged as a result of his testimony.

Magazine artist's conception of the mob attacking the Chicago railroad yards during the Pullman strike.

accompanied the industrial and agricultural revolutions. With the exception of women's suffrage (which, ironically, had been endorsed at some earlier Populist meetings), the Omaha platform set the dimensions of reform for the next quarter century. The only important feature of the platform that did not ultimately become law was government ownership of the railroads and communications utilities. And during World War I, the government even flirted with that.

The Populists nominated James B. Weaver for president, an unfortunate choice because he was aged and a veteran of lost causes. Weaver polled more than 1 million votes in the election, about 9 percent of the total, and he picked up twenty-two electoral votes. The number of Populists in the Senate increased to five in the election of 1892; the number of congressmen to ten. And Populists elected governors in Kansas, Colorado, and North Dakota. Illinois elected a Democrat as governor, John Peter Altgeld, who agreed with every principle in the Omaha platform. The Populists were thus the first third party to carry a state in a presidential election since the Republicans made their debut in 1856.

The electoral map, however, revealed some serious weaknesses. Populists got almost no support in the East, despite their appeal to labor. Gompers and the A F of L ignored them, and the Knights were dying. Nor did they fare well in the prosperous farm states of the Middle West, whose corn, hog, and dairy complexes were little affected by the world farm price depression. In the South they elected a few congressmen and state legislators by allying with Republicans, and that was a dangerous alliance. Most southern Republicans were black, and the association of blacks and poor whites was an explosive mixture.

Most of the popular votes and all the electoral votes won by Populists came from the western plains and the mountain states, where they allied with Democrats. Unlike the connection with blacks, the alliance with western Democrats was one of convenience rather than ideology. The mountain states—Colorado, Idaho, Nevada—were silver producers, and their product had fared as badly in the depression as cotton or wheat. The Populist demand for silver coinage attracted voters there and formed the basis for the political alliance. "Free silver"—that is, the coinage of silver without charge by the government—was only one idea among many in the Populist platform of 1892, but it commanded votes and attention. It would ultimately dominate the movement. The source of its strength requires separate explanation.

⊔ Greenbacks and Free Silver

The search for "cheap money" originated with the depression and the slump in farm prices. A plow that cost $150 could be obtained by growing a thousand pounds of cotton when cotton was 15 cents a pound. When the price fell to 5 cents, the farmer had to grow three times as much in order to buy the same implement. He was working harder and receiving less; it was as simple as that. The fall in farm prices revalued the dollar upward; it had more purchasing power. During the 1870s and 1880s, farmers and their allies searched for various forms of "cheap money" in the hope of deflating the dollar. When the dollar was worth less, cotton and wheat would cost more. "Cheap money" was currency with the face value of a dollar, but not its intrinsic value—silver or paper dollars that had less value in people's minds than a gold dollar. Being of less value, these dollars would bring less when exchanged for a commodity such as wheat, and that raised the price of wheat. Whether this theory would have worked in practice we shall never know, because it was never given a fair trial. What we do know today is that the infusion of substantial amounts of currency into the economy—whether silver, paper, or government-engraved oak leaves—would almost certainly have caused inflation. And that is precisely what the farmers wanted.

CHEAP MONEY
AND THE CRIME OF '73

The principal form of paper currency was notes issued by the national banks. By law, the national banks had to hold in their vaults certain amounts of gold and government bonds as "backing." The holder of national bank notes could take them to a bank and exchange them at any time for gold—or for a government bond that was redeemable in gold. Being "good as gold," the national bank notes were not cheap money. Nor did they solve the nation's monetary needs. Because they were tied to the gold supply, they could not be issued in sufficient volume to meet the needs of an expanding economy.

Notes issued by state-chartered banks were common before the Civil War, but Congress levied a tax on these in 1865 that drove them out of existence. The only other form of paper currency was greenbacks, government notes that had been issued to finance the war. The government

American money from wampum to paper. (1) Wampum was strings of beads made from shells. It was used by eastern Indians for decoration and ceremonial gift exchange. (2) A United States silver dollar of a design used through much of the nineteenth century. (3) A national bank note issued in 1902. Observe that the note is the obligation of a particular bank, the German National Bank of Pittsburgh, and not of the system. (4) This beautiful Indian-head $10 gold piece, or "eagle," was sculpted by Augustus Saint-Gaudens and put in circulation in 1907.

(1) (2) (3) (4)

New York Public Library Picture Collection.

promised that it would ultimately redeem these in gold, but it did not say when. Throughout the war and for some years after, the Treasury did not have enough gold on hand to make the offer. Bankers would exchange gold for greenbacks, but never dollar for dollar. So the value of greenbacks fluctuated throughout the war, and by 1865 a greenback dollar was worth about 67 cents—that is, 1,000 greenback dollars would purchase 670 gold dollars. In that sense, the greenback was "cheap money."

When the depression struck in 1873 and farm prices began to fall, greenbacks took on political importance. In 1874 the Greenback, or National Independent, party was formed at Indianapolis. It opposed the redemption of greenbacks, which Congress was contemplating, and advocated further issues of paper money. The Greenbackers got a mere 80,000 votes in the presidential election of 1876, though four years later, with James B. Weaver (later the Populist candidate), they did somewhat better.

Congress in 1875 passed a law providing for the redemption of the greenbacks, and though the act was subsequently repealed, President Hayes's secretary of the treasury, John Sherman, systematically collected gold with a view to redemption. At last the offer was made: Beginning January 1, 1879, the Treasury would exchange gold for greenbacks, dollar for dollar. The offer alone restored public faith in greenbacks, and they continued in circulation. But they were no longer "cheap money."

By then inflationists' attention had already turned to silver. Since Alexander Hamilton's day, the United States had been on a bimetallic standard. Banks backed their paper money with either silver or gold. The system worked because the ratio of value between the two remained relatively stable. An ounce of gold was worth sixteen times as much as an ounce of silver. In foreign trade, however, gold was the standard by which accounts were kept and debts were paid. Nations deeply involved in foreign trade, such as Great Britain, found bimetallic calculations cumbersome, and in the course of the century the Western world moved toward a single gold standard. Following this trend, Congress in 1873 demonetized silver and placed the United States on the gold standard.

By chance this action coincided with major silver discoveries in the West. The growth in supply and the lessened demand, since the government was no longer using silver for coins, caused the price to fall. Silver miners, suspecting a Wall Street conspiracy of "gold bugs," began denouncing the Crime of '73 that had ended silver coinage. Simultaneously, rural inflationists thought they saw in silver a new form of cheap money. If silver were coined at the old ratio of 16 to 1, they reasoned, it would be overvalued because the market price for silver was actually about 20 to 1. Thus a silver dollar would be worth only four-fifths of a gold dollar, or 80 cents—cheap money.

THE FREE SILVER CRUSADE

As the price of greenbacks rose to a par with gold in the late 1870s, farmers forged an alliance with western silver interests. The mountain region was still in the territorial stage in the 1870s, but it found a powerful spokesman in Richard (Silver Dick) Bland of Missouri. In 1878 Congress yielded to the rising demand for Free silver (the coinage of silver without charge) and passed the Bland-Allison Act. This measure authorized the secretary of the Treasury to buy limited amounts of silver for coinage, and it made the silver dollar legal tender. Treasury Secretary Sherman promptly announced that the silver dollars could be redeemed in gold, just like the greenbacks. Whatever the intrinsic value of the silver dollars, they were thereafter "good as gold." It was also evident, however, that if silver coinage were unlimited—that is, if the government had to coin all the silver brought to it—the Treasury could not long maintain its offer to exchange silver for gold. So the rallying cry of the Populist platform of 1892 was: "The free and *unlimited* coinage of silver at the ratio of sixteen to one!"

Comparative prosperity in the early 1880s silenced the inflationists for a time, but renewed depression and rising farm protest in the late 1880s revived the movement. Congress responded to all the pressures by approving a gigantic "package deal" in 1890. The Sherman Antitrust Act, a sop to small businesses that felt threatened by the gigantic trusts, declared "every contract, combination in the form of trust or otherwise, or conspiracy in restraint of trade or commerce among the several States . . . illegal." Those injured by such conspiracies could collect triple damages in suits at law. To mollify "big business," Congress approved the McKinley tariff, which pushed the rates to new heights. Indeed, the McKinley tariff was designed not simply to harass foreign competition, but to eliminate it.

Finally, Congress in 1890 yielded to the silver interests by passing the Sherman Silver Purchase Act, which required the treasury to purchase the estimated annual output of the nation's silver mines and pay for it with greenbacks. The Treasury did not have to coin the silver, but it still faced some hard decisions. As the number of greenbacks in circulation increased and bars of silver piled up in its vaults, it would eventually have to make a choice. There was simply not enough gold available to back both silver and greenbacks. The Treasury would have to set the greenbacks afloat, or redeem them with silver. That is precisely what the inflationists wanted.

The problem came finally to Grover Cleveland, victor in the presidential election of 1892. His response alienated Populists as well as Silver Democrats, and that set the stage for the political "revolution" of 1896.

⊔ Grover Cleveland: Labor Violence

No president is popular in hard times, and Grover Cleveland took office for the second time just weeks before a Wall Street panic—the panic of 1893—ushered in the worst depression of the century. By early 1894, 600 banks had closed their doors, 74 railroads were in receivership, more than 15,000 businesses had failed, and the unemployed numbered 2.5 million (20 percent of the labor force).

Cleveland's initial response to the panic was to summon Congress into special session in the summer of 1893 to repeal the Sherman Silver Purchase Act, which he thought was the principal cause of the nation's troubles. He secured the repeal, but it cost him the support of his party's silver wing. And it failed to stop the flow of gold from the Treasury. As Treasury receipts fell and the government plunged into the red, people lost faith in government paper and began presenting it for redemption. By 1894 the Treasury's gold reserves were so low that it faced the choice of suspending its offer to redeem dollars in gold or paying its debts in silver. Unable to accept either alternative, Cleveland went to Wall Street for a loan. A consortium of bankers, headed by J. P. Morgan, supplied the gold in exchange for government bonds. It was only a temporary expedient, and within a year Cleveland was back at the bankers' door, cap in hand, asking for more.

LABOR: COXEY'S ARMY AND THE PULLMAN STRIKE

The cozy relationship between the president and the titans of finance contrasted sharply with the near-panic with which he

New York Public Library Picture Collection.

Coxey's army marches on Washington.

handled labor strife. Corporations responded to the depression by cutting their work forces and slashing wages. That sent men into the streets in protest; in 1894 alone there were more than 1,300 strikes, many of them violent. Cleveland let state authorities handle the problem until an army of unemployed descended on Washington. Their leader was "General" Jacob Coxey, an Ohio businessman, who conceived the idea—forty years ahead of its time—of putting the unemployed to work on public projects and financing the endeavor with paper money. In support of his "good roads bill," he organized a march on Washington from his home in Massillon, Ohio. The idea caught on, and from all corners of the nation groups of men walked, drove, or hitched rides on freight

trains, while rumors of impending revolution swept the nation's capital. When it reached the Capitol grounds, Coxey's army, 400 strong, was met by a battalion of police. Coxey was arrested for walking on the grass, and his followers were dispersed with horses and nightsticks.

The uproar over Coxey's army was just subsiding when, in May 1894, workers struck the Pullman Palace Car Company in Pullman, Illinois. George Pullman, inventor of the railroad sleeping car, considered the company-owned town that surrounded his factory to be a model community. But the atmosphere was more like a prison. The company owned all the land, controlled the bank and utilities, set rents in the company-owned houses, and hired spies to report on malcontents. Said one resident: "We are born in a Pullman house, fed from the Pullman shop, taught in the Pullman school, catechized in the Pullman church, and when we die we shall be buried in the Pullman cemetery and go to the Pullman hell."

When the company slashed wages without reducing rents or other prices in the company town, the workers struck. In June 1894, the American Railway Union, formed in the previous year by Populist Eugene V. Debs, joined the strike. The ARU organized a boycott of Pullman cars among the western railroads, and by the end of June it effectively brought to a halt all traffic between Chicago and the Pacific Coast. To that point the strike was peaceful, and the Illinois governor, John P. Altgeld, who sympathized with the strikers, declined to interfere.

Cleveland's attorney general, Richard Olney, found the situation intolerable. He persuaded the president that the federal government ought to act, on the theory that the strikers were interfering with the mails and the flow of interstate commerce. Olney secured an injunction from a federal court ordering the strikers back to work. When U.S. marshals read the court order in the Chicago railyards, the strikers simply jeered. In early July, Olney sent in federal troops to enforce the court order, and suddenly everything changed. The strikers went on a rampage, overturning trains and setting the yards afire. Governor Altgeld ultimately had to send in state troops to restore order. In the meantime, the governor dispatched two blistering telegrams to President Cleveland protesting federal interference in a local affair. The confrontation made Altgeld an instant hero among reformers and Silverites. Had he been native-born (he had emigrated from Germany), he would have had an excellent chance for the Democratic nomination for president in 1896.

In the aftermath, Debs was arrested for disobeying the federal court order. He car-ried his case all the way to the United States Supreme Court, contending that the injunction—a device by which courts can prohibit an activity that will cause foreseeable injury or property damage—had never been applied to a labor strike. The Supreme Court, in the memorable decision of *In Re Debs* (1895), not only upheld the use of injunctions against labor, but accepted Olney's argument that implicit in the power to regulate interstate commerce is the power to eliminate obstructions, such as a union boycott. Until its use was restricted by Congress in 1932, the injunction was a major weapon used by courts and corporations against organized labor.

ALLIANCE WITH BUSINESS

While willing to prosecute labor organizations, Cleveland and his attorney general declined to enforce such rudimentary business regulations as the Interstate Commerce Act or the Sherman Antitrust Act. They watched as the Supreme Court stripped the ICC of one power after another until the commission became, in the words of one dissenting justice, "a useless body . . . shorn, by judicial interpretation, of authority to do anything of an effective character." Under pressure from small producers, the government did proceed against the sugar trust, the E. C. Knight Company, which controlled 98 percent of the nation's sugar refining. Olney, who believed the Sherman Antitrust Act to be "no good," refused to enter the case, and the Supreme Court floundered its way to the curious conclusion that manufacturing (because it takes place within a single state) is not interstate commerce and therefore beyond the power of federal regulation. That decision, coming in the same year as the Debs case, 1895, completed the alliance between government and business.

By that date, too, western Democrats, feeling betrayed by their president, were laying plans to seize control of their party. Populists watched this developing rebellion within the Democratic party with interest.

⊔ A Rising Social Conscience

In 1890, Jacob Riis, a Danish immigrant turned journalist, published a photographic essay entitled *How the Other Half Lives*. Riis was among the first to explore, study, and describe life in the American slum, the degraded byproduct of urbanization. In grim detail and impassioned prose, Riis portrayed the crowding, the filth, and the decadence of New York tenements. Riis, who had come to America in 1870 and wandered for years in near poverty before landing a job with the New York *Evening Sun*, had no patience with the Social Darwinist notion that poverty resulted from laziness and ignorance. It was the other way around, Riis suspected: Environment shaped character. To improve morals, instill dignity, and inspire hard work, society had to clean up its slums. This was the germ of an idea that, embellished by others, would come to be called Reform Darwinism. The theory rested on the notion that individuals interact with their environment, adapting to changed

Life in the "Gay Nineties": The beach at Coney Island, New York, 1896.

The Bettmann Archive.

Culver Pictures, Inc.
Life in the "Gay Nineties": The cakewalk was the first of the African-influenced rhythms that led to ragtime and jazz.

conditions. The corollary was that an improvement in the environment—more space to breathe, fewer taverns and bawdyhouses—would evoke improvements in human behavior.

Jacob Riis never developed a systematic social theory, and he shared many of the racial and ethnic prejudices of his time. But the popularity of his works and the inspiration they offered to others suggest that by the 1890s people were turning away from Social Darwinism and beginning to listen again to those who spoke of human suffering and social justice.

SETTLEMENT HOUSES

Even before Riis burst into print, settlement houses were attempting to improve the quality of life in the nation's over-crowded cities. The settlement house idea originated in England in the 1870s, where social workers decided that blighted urban areas needed community centers that would serve as meeting places, playgrounds, and medical dispensaries. English settlement houses eventually set up language programs for immigrants, arts and crafts facilities, and adult education centers.

A settlement house was established in New York City in 1886, and over the next three decades some 300 centers dotted the urban landscape. The most famous by far was Hull House, founded in Chicago by Jane Addams in 1890. Jane Addams was heir to the humanitarian impulses of the preceding generation. Her father, a long-time Illinois legislator, was an abolitionist and a Republican. Also a believer in educating females, he sent her to Rockford

National Archives.
Jane Addams at her desk in Hull House, Chicago.

Seminary after she finished grammar school. There she received some training in the Greek and Roman classics, along with a heavy dose of evangelical religion. The latter served principally to hone her speaking skills. Selected to represent the school in a statewide oratorical contest, she placed fifth, which was not a bad showing considering that another entrant, William Jennings Bryan, had to settle for second. Her father also financed a tour of Europe as part of her education, a privilege reserved almost exclusively to young men. She visited the usual galleries and monuments, but her most indelible memories stemmed from walks through the slums of London, Paris, and Naples. On a second visit, in company with a Rockford classmate, Ellen Gates Starr, she visited an English settlement house, where a colony of

young men became a part of the community of the poor and organized clubs, lectures, and concerts. It was a practical, well-defined, immensely rewarding way to relieve human misery, more effective in its limited way than evangelical preaching.

Back in the United States, Addams and Starr began looking for a suitable building for a settlement house of their own. They found one in the former country home of Charles J. Hull, which had since become surrounded by tenements and factories, the area populated by Russian and Polish Jews, Italians, Germans, Irish, and Bohemians. Human needs were so great that there was no discussion of where to begin. Children playing in the streets suggested the need for a kindergarten and social activities. Starr organized a reading circle for young women. A superb organizer and shrewd politician, Addams eventually expanded her operation to include a dozen buildings covering half a city block. It boasted a well, a playground, and a summer camp in the country. Hull House had an adult-education program that ranged from college-level literature to cooking and home management. It sponsored concerts and lectures, and it provided both recreation and day care centers for children. The staff of Hull House, mostly women, used the facilities as a laboratory for social research. Hull House alumnae became leaders in the post-1900 Progressive movement.

THE SOCIAL GOSPEL

The churches also showed a new concern for the urban poor. In the 1880s, Washington Gladden, minister of the First Congregational Church in Columbus, Ohio, began preaching a gospel that differed sharply from the ethics of Social Darwinism. Unbridled competition, said Gladden, merely rewards the unscrupulous; the behavior it encourages contradicts Christian love and charity. Gladden argued that the churches ought to side with the poor and the working people, and help them to form unions and other self-help organizations. Gladden's movement, known as the Social Gospel, swept through the Protestant churches in the 1890s.

Among those affected was Walter Rauschenbusch, pastor of a Baptist Church in New York's infamous Hell's Kitchen. "One could hear human virtue cracking and crushing all around," he wrote of the slum, and the experience sent him to reading Edward Bellamy, Henry George, and other dissident writers of the Gilded Age. By the time he left his pastorate in 1897 for a professorship at Rochester Seminary, Rauschenbusch had achieved a blend of the Social Gospel and Reform Darwinism. The churches, he argued, should assume a lead-

ership role in evolution and work for the improvement of the social environment. "Translate the evolutionary themes into religious faith," he declared, "and you have the doctrine of the Kingdom of God." A Populist of the cloth, Rauschenbusch advocated farm and labor cooperatives, the single tax, and trade unions.

Roman Catholics and Jews, their numbers increasing annually with the tide of immigration, had their own versions of the Social Gospel. Both religious organizations catered to the needs of impoverished immigrants in the tenement districts of New York, Chicago, Cincinnati, and St. Louis. They operated orphan asylums and manual labor schools, and played a critical role in the assimilation of eastern and southern European immigrants. During the 1890s, committees of Reform Judaism, operating under various titles, undertook to bring the Jewish faith into accord with the discoveries of modern science and the needs of an urban society.

POPULIST IDEOLOGY

This intellectual ferment was the climate within which the Populist movement grew in the 1890s. The Populists, to be sure, were a rural interest group with specific goals for the solution of farm problems, but they shared with urban reformers a concern for social inequality and injustice. And they formulated out of this a coherent ideology, one that challenged for the first time in an important way the American success myth, the gospel of self-help, and laissez faire. Kansas Governor Lorenzo Lewelling stated the challenge baldly before a Kansas City audience: "It is the duty of government to protect the weak, because the strong are able to protect themselves."

At the core of Populist ideology was the concept of "alienated man." The preindustrial worker, Populists hypothesized, had dignity and importance, an identity with

---

CLIO'S FOCUS: God's Country: Preserve It or Conserve It?

Americans in the nineteenth century never doubted that theirs was "God's country." Nor did many doubt that God had endowed the continent with rich resources for their benefit. This view was shared by the first federal agency created to assess the nation's resources, the United States Geological Survey office, established in 1878. The first director of the USGS was Clarence King, a Yale geologist who had organized the massive 40th parallel survey a decade earlier.

King's survey was a turning point in American exploration and exploitation. Prior to the Civil War, the exploration and mapping of the West had been done chiefly by the Army, whose efforts had culminated with the California and Mexican boundary surveys of the 1850s. The Army's chief interest, however, was in topographical maps for military purposes. King's project had been to conduct a scientific survey of a little-known portion of the West—the Great Basin from the Sierra Nevadas to the Continental Divide. Following the 40th parallel, he had examined a swath of country 100 miles wide and 800 miles long. King had obtained Army approval and congressional financing, but he had taken with him only civilian scientists, most of them from Yale. The project took two years, 1867–1869, and the books that resulted from it—on mining, geology, bird life, botany, and paleontology—constituted the most thorough and professional examination of the western environment ever done.

King himself made some original contributions, notably by advancing the theory, now widely accepted, that the Great Basin originally contained two gigantic lakes (of which the Great Salt Lake is a remnant) formed by melting glaciers. But he never forgot the economic implications of his survey. In the midst of the project he published a report on the potential of Nevada's silver mines as a demonstration of the practical value of his work. Among the economic consequences of his survey was the discovery of the enormous coal formations in Wyoming and Colorado, which remain a source of profit and controversy today.

The establishment of the United States Geological Survey office was the product of an alliance between university scientists and the Smithsonian Institution in Washington. Its goal was the scientific management of resources to ensure maximum utilization. When King resigned in 1880 to go into the mining business for himself, John Wesley Powell became director of the USGS. Powell had been the first man to raft the Colorado River and make a scientific study of the Grand Canyon. Powell altered the focus of the USGS, for he was more interested in such things as water conservation and more willing to battle lumber and grazing interests. Nevertheless, the agency remained committed to the utilization of the wilderness.

About that time, however, the wilderness itself got a champion in John Muir. Scottish-born and Wisconsin-bred, Muir loved wild country and wild creatures. He saw value in preserving wilderness for its own sake. At the University of Wisconsin in the

1860s Muir became acquainted with the writings of Emerson and Thoreau. Their transcendentalism offered him a way of interpreting the value of the wilderness, for the philosophy presupposed the essential unity of God, nature, and the human spirit. Landscape itself, Muir decided, had a "spiritual power." By turning to the wilderness, an individual could purge the "sediments of society" and become a "new creature."

After two and a half years in Madison, he exchanged the "Wisconsin University for the University of the Wilderness." He warmed up with a thousand-mile hike to the Gulf of Mexico and then headed for California. In San Francisco he asked for directions to "any place that is wild" and was sent across the bay to Oakland. He soon ended up in the Sierras. Enamored of the Yosemite Valley, he camped there for a year, his one companion a volume of Emerson's essays. Muir settled in California in the 1870s and soon found his life work—the education of Americans on the need to preserve the wilderness. He early noticed the destruction done by grazing in the Yosemite Valley. "As sheep advance," he wrote in his journal, "flowers, vegetation, grass, soil, plenty, and poetry vanish."

Muir's articles brought him to the attention of Robert Underwood Johnson, an associate editor of *Century*, one of the nation's leading magazines. Johnson journeyed to San Francisco, contacted Muir, and the two went camping in Yosemite. There, over a campfire, they agreed that Yosemite ought to be made into a national park, as Yellowstone had been in 1870. Muir wrote two articles advancing the idea, which *Century* published in 1890. Johnson lobbied in Congress, and a bill creating the park passed in September of that year. In 1892, Muir helped to form the Sierra Club "to enlist the support of the people and the government in preserving the forests and other features of the Sierra Nevada mountains." Wilderness preservation now had both a propagandist and an organization. Both soon collided with the resource managers.

In 1891, Congress passed the Forest Reserve Act, which authorized the president to create forest reserves (later called National Forests) by withdrawing from the market portions of the public domain. President Benjamin Harrison quickly established fifteen reserves covering more than 13 million acres. Muir hoped the government would preserve the forests in their pristine state, but Gifford Pinchot, who had joined the Bureau of Forestry in 1890, had other ideas. A graduate of Yale, Pinchot had been schooled by several of the scientists who had worked with King on the 40th parallel survey. He had also done graduate work in Europe, where timberland was carefully managed for maximum sustained yield. Pinchot's object was scientific forestry, the management of forests to ensure the nation a steady supply of lumber. When compared to the wasteful practices of the lumber companies, then slashing their way across Michigan and Wisconsin, it was a step in the direction of conservation, a term Pinchot appropriated for himself.

Muir at first agreed with Pinchot, for on the surface his methods appeared to be a way for the nation to have its forests and use them too. But he soon came to see that even selective cutting altered the forest ecology by disrupting the living arrangements of both plants and animals. A cutover forest, no matter how well managed, was no longer wilderness. The break, which was to leave the American conservation movement permanently divided, came in 1896. In the meantime, in 1894, Muir lost a potential ally when timber and mining interests allied with resource managers to force the resignation of John Wesley Powell as director of the United States Geological Survey.

In 1896, the Interior Department began developing a policy for the management of the forest reserves. To make a study of the western woodlands, it appointed an advisory commission consisting of scientists from Harvard and Yale, a representative from the USGS, and Gifford Pinchot. Muir agreed to assist the commission's survey in an ex-officio capacity. The differences between Muir and Pinchot surfaced when the commission started to draw up its report. Muir claimed that the purpose of the survey was to determine which parts of the West needed protection and to induce the government to expand the reserves. Pinchot, supported by the delegate from the USGS, contended that the commission's function was to prepare the way for opening the reserves to managed development.

The break became complete in 1897, when Pinchot pronounced himself in favor of allowing sheep grazing in the National Forests. The transcendentalist and the forester went their separate ways, and each could point to successes. In 1901, President Theodore Roosevelt named Pinchot chief forester and custodian of the reserves. Muir also befriended Roosevelt, went camping with him in Yosemite, and in 1908 persuaded him to preserve the Grand Canyon as a national park. The ideological conflict between Muir and Pinchot outlived them both and is very much alive today.

his work. He often labored side by side with his employer, took pride in the skill with which he fashioned his cabinet, carriage, or cutlery, and often participated in its sale. The factory worker, by contrast, was wedded to his machine, his every movement dictated by the mechanical repetition of the machine, his employer a distant and alien force. Industrial capitalism, in short, destroyed the individual, suppressed his human faculties, and left him isolated in a clanking world of nonstop machinery.

The goal of Populist thinkers was to restore richness and vitality to the lives of common people. This could not be done, they felt, under the existing form of social organization because industrial capitalism was not responsive to human needs. They did not, however, envision the violent overthrow of the existing order; the Populists were not revolutionaries. What they proposed instead was more concern for human rights by those in power and the formation of cooperative production and marketing associations. They hoped to replace the jungle of competition with the Eden of cooperation.

The solution was vague, even utopian, and its workability a matter of conjecture. But Governor Lewelling's policies afford us a clue as to how the Populists might have functioned had they won national power. In December 1893, he directed an

Separate But Equal?

In 1896, in the case of *Plessy* v. *Ferguson*, the Supreme Court wrote the "separate but equal" doctrine into American constitutional law. It remained the law of the land until 1954, when the Court overturned it in the Brown school desegregation case. The Plessy decision involved the constitutionality of an 1890 Louisiana statute that required separate railway carriages for whites and blacks. The question was whether the act violated the Fourteenth Amendment, which prohibited the states from denying their citizens the equal protection of the laws. We provide excerpts from both the majority opinion and the dissent of Justice John Marshall Harlan.

> The object of the amendment was undoubtedly to enforce the absolute equality of the two races before the law, but in the nature of things it could not have been intended to abolish distinctions based upon color, or to enforce social, as distinguished from political, equality, or a commingling of the two races upon terms unsatisfactory to either. Laws permitting, and even requiring their separation in places where they are liable to be brought into contact do not necessarily imply the inferiority of either race to the other. . . .
>
> Justice Harlan, dissenting. . . . The destinies of the two races in this country are indissolubly linked together, and the interests of both require that the common government of all shall not permit the seeds of race hate to be planted under the sanction of law. What can more certainly arouse race hate, what more certainly create and perpetuate a feeling of distrust between these races, than state enactments which in fact proceed on the ground that colored citizens are so inferior and degraded that they cannot be allowed to sit in public coaches occupied by white citizens? That, as all will admit, is the real meaning of such legislation as was enacted in Louisiana. . . .
>
> I am of the opinion that the statute of Louisiana is inconsistent with the personal liberty of citizens, white and black, in that state, and hostile to both the spirit and letter of the Constitution of the United States. . . .
>
> *Source*: *Plessy* v. *Ferguson*, 1896

executive proclamation at municipal authorities throughout Kansas. The governor's subject was unemployment; contemporaries labeled his proclamation the Tramp Circular. Unemployment was not only the chief symptom of the depression; it was the chief symbol of the Populist critique. Industrial capitalism had created not only "alienated man," but "superfluous man."

Lewelling traced the history of unemployment back to the Elizabethan Poor Law. For 300 years, he explained, people wandering in search of work had been treated with suspicion and hostility, told to "move on," or jailed without cause. Poverty and unemployment, declared Lewelling, were not the fault of the individual; they were the product of the social and economic system. In America, "the monopoly of labor-saving machinery, and its devotion to selfish instead of social use, have rendered more and more human beings superfluous, until we have a standing army of the unemployed numbering in the most prosperous times not less than one million able-bodied men." Attacking the Kansas statute that punished persons "without visible means of support," Lewelling directed municipal authorities to act with compassion, concluding: "Let simple poverty cease to be a crime."

Placed alongside such heady notions, President Cleveland's little homilies on self-help and obedience to law seem pale indeed.

⊔1896: The Revolution That Wasn't

American voters have never had difficulty finding scapegoats in hard times, and more often than not their wrath falls on the president and his party. Grover Cleveland, it must be said, had done nothing to turn aside that wrath; indeed, his chill indifference seemed to encourage it. Even Cleveland, though, must have been unprepared for the strength of the blow. The occasion was the off-year congressional elections of 1894. For the previous two years, the Democrats had controlled both houses. They were turned out en masse. It was the greatest transfer of congressional seats from one party to another in history. Republicans emerged in the House of Representatives with a solid majority of 132. Democrat Champ Clark of Missouri, noting wryly that the voters were mainly angry at the president, called it "the greatest slaughter of innocents since Herod."

The election also ended the party balance that had characterized the politics of the Gilded Age, and it ushered in a period of Republican dominance. For the next sixteen years both Congress and the presidency (after 1896) were to be in Republican hands. The election also showed that, despite the hard times, voters were not yet willing to embrace the Populist alternative. The Great Plains, hotbed of Populist agitation, returned forty-four Republicans and only two Populists to Congress. The debacle left both Democrats and Populists ready to cement an alliance. The glue was silver.

WILLIAM JENNINGS BRYAN

The catalyst was a 36-year-old Silver Democrat from Nebraska, William Jennings Bryan. After serving two terms in Congress in the early 1890s, Bryan made a try for the Senate in 1894 and suffered defeat. For the next two years he edited the Omaha *World Herald* and toured the country, charming audiences with his golden voice and silver philosophy. In an editorial of November 1894, Bryan laid the foundation for the fusion of the Democratic and Populist parties by endorsing nearly every feature of the Populist platform. He dwelt most on free silver, since that was the issue that evoked widest agreement between Democrats and Populists, but he did not avoid the more radical Populist proposals, such as government ownership of corporations. Democrats preferred "regulation and control" to socialism, he admitted, but they "will prefer the government ownership of railroads to the railroad ownership of government if they have to choose between the two." His conclusion showed how far western Democrats had moved from the Jacksonian liberalism of President Cleveland: "It will be easy, therefore, to agree upon the strict regulation and control of the railroads and other corporations by both federal and state governments."

The coup by which Silverites captured the Democratic party was carefully planned. Bryan spread his name and his program, appealing to a broad assortment of people. "Free silver," he told urban audiences, was merely the first step in a general "restoration of just conditions in this country." He even offered a hand to labor by announcing that he intended to make Samuel Gompers a member of his cabinet. When the Democrats gathered in Chicago for their convention in 1896, the rebels found themselves with a solid majority of delegates. Challenging the president, they inserted a free silver plank into the platform and then organized a floor debate on the question. Bryan, speaking last, delivered an oration that won him instant immortality.

On behalf of the common people, so long ignored by politicians, Bryan declared war against vested interests everywhere: "We have petitioned, and our petitions have been scorned; we have entreated, and our entreaties have been disregarded; we have begged and they have mocked when our calamity came. We beg no longer; we entreat no more; we petition no more. *We defy them!*" His was the language of class appeal, a rallying cry of producers against the money changers, expressed in the self-justifying imagery of an evangelist. It rose at last to the climactic challenge:

> Having behind us the producing masses of this nation and the world, supported by the commercial interests, the laboring interests, and the toilers everywhere, we will answer their demand for a gold standard by saying to them: "You shall not press down upon the brow of labor this crown of thorns; you shall not crucify mankind upon a cross of gold!"

The Democrats nominated Bryan on the fourth ballot. To appease their eastern wing they chose as vice-presidential candidate a New England banker, Arthur Sewell. Free silver was the only part of the Populist program the Democrats specifically adopted, and many Populists had deep misgivings about the alliance. When the People's party met at St. Louis later that summer, however, the fusionists had their way. The party endorsed Bryan while reaffirming the Omaha platform. But it rejected the Democrats' nominee for vice president and chose instead Tom Watson of Georgia, an idealist who had stayed home to avoid the taint of compromise. Watson relented, however, and campaigned for Bryan in the weeks that followed.

MARK HANNA AND THE REPUBLICANS

Republicans underwent some changes of their own in the crucial election year. The architect was Ohio industrialist Marcus Alonzo Hanna, a new kind of political boss. He lacked the flamboyance of the Spoilsmen, and he carefully avoided corruption. His forte was organization, his model the business corporation. He aimed to make the Republican party as efficient and effective as Standard Oil. And by cultivating delegates well in advance of the party convention, he secured the nomination of his candidate on the first ballot. That candidate was William McKinley, congressman from Ohio, as colorless and given to truisms as Grover Cleveland, but sturdy and reassuring as a Greek-columned bank.

While Bryan stormed the country by rail, delivering 570 speeches to some 5 million people, Hanna quietly organized a fundraising committee to "fry the fat" out of American business.* Alarmed by western radicalism, businessmen had been drifting into the Republican party for some years. Mark Hanna cemented the alliance between Republicans and business and turned fundraising into an art. He collected a campaign chest of $3.5 million. Standard Oil alone gave $250,000, a sum equal to the Democrats' entire budget.

Hanna spent his money principally on "education" leaflets that claimed to unravel the mysteries of the money question. His campaign literature was effective because there was a good deal of hard-money sentiment among eastern shopkeepers and factory workers. Neither wanted to be paid

---

* "Fat frying" originated in the election of 1888, when Philadelphia dry goods merchant John Wanamaker organized Republican committees to solicit funds from businessmen. One of his agents explained the method: "I would put the manufacturers of Pennsylvania under the fire and fry all the fat out of them."

William Jennings Bryan
campaigning in 1896.

The Bettmann Archives.

in "cheap" dollars. Republican economists claimed that a silver dollar coined at the ratio of 16 to 1 would have an intrinsic value of only 53 cents. Republican campaign workers passed out buttons that looked like silver dollars, emblazoned with the eagle emblem and the motto: "In God We Trust—for the other 47 cents."

Cultivating an image of cautious solidity, McKinley waged his campaign from the front porch of his home in Canton, Ohio. The party brought the voters to him—some three-quarters of a million of them carried into Canton on nine thousand railroad cars. In bunches they stood behind a white picket fence and listened to McKinley talk vaguely of hard work and the honest dollar.

THE ELECTION

Bryan avoided the Populists in the campaign and ignored their platform, except for free silver. He was being neither hypocritical nor unreasonable: He could already count on the South and most of the West; what he needed for victory was support in the urban East and in the small towns of the Middle West. And there populism—with its image of hayseed radicalism—was the kiss of death. The election results proved it.

McKinley won by 600,000 votes, the largest margin any candidate had obtained since 1872. He carried every northern state from Maine to the Dakotas, plus California and Oregon. Significantly, McKinley car-

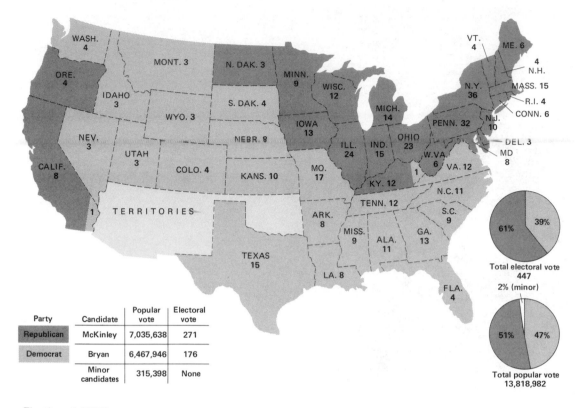

Party	Candidate	Popular vote	Electoral vote
Republican	McKinley	7,035,638	271
Democrat	Bryan	6,467,946	176
	Minor candidates	315,398	None

Total electoral vote
447
2% (minor)

Total popular vote
13,818,982

Election of 1896.

ried states with heavy immigrant populations—such as North Dakota, Minnesota, Wisconsin, and Iowa—because immigrants blamed Democrats for the depression and responded to the Republican promise of a "full dinner pail." Also moving into the Republican camp were the boom cities of the West—Chicago, St. Paul, Omaha, and Kansas City.

The popular image of the two parties that was formed in 1896 lingered for many years. The Bryan-led Democrats clothed themselves in the rhetoric of the down-and-out, but they did it with the style and language of the camp meeting. Such rhetoric, with its overtones of prohibition and nativism, appealed to the rural South and West, but meant little to the ethnic groups

of the Middle West and Northeast. Not until Woodrow Wilson replaced Bryan as leader of the party in 1912 and reformers such as Al Smith of New York undertook to improve working conditions in the sweatshops did the Democrats win much support among urban people and immigrants.

Republicans, traditionally the party of small-town natives and transplanted Yankees, broadened their appeal in 1896. The "full dinner pail," the promise of reward for those who adhered to the traditional virtues of hard work and frugality, identified them with the American heritage itself. That is, so long as the dinner pail remained full. By a stroke of fortune, the business cycle turned upward in 1897, inaugurating three decades of general prosperity. Blessed by good times, the McKinley formula of patriotism, individualism, and sturdy reliability was powerful medicine, as appealing to the Germans of Cincinnati and the Poles of Chicago as it was to the Daughters of the American Revolution. The result was three decades of Republican ascendancy, broken only briefly by a Democratic revival in 1910–1920, until a new depression created new doubts about the old virtues.

COLLAPSE OF THE POPULIST REVOLT

The aftermath of 1896 can be quickly told. The People's party held annual conventions for the next few years, but its influence was gone. Fusion with the Democrats, as the purists had predicted, siphoned much of its vitality. Many who cooperated with the Democrats stayed with the Democrats. But the movement was also a victim of its own contradictions.

For one thing, its perception of class unity was flawed. The interests of rural and urban labor are not necessarily the same. In the 1890s the chief aim of farmers was higher farm prices. For eastern workers, this would have meant higher food prices. Conversely, stronger labor unions and higher factory wages might have meant higher prices for farm machinery. Even within the farm protest movement, interests were not always identical. Efforts to unite the Farmer's Alliances, for instance, stumbled on the pebble of butter substitutes. Midwestern dairy farmers were campaigning for laws forbidding the use of margarine (invented by French chemists in 1869), while southern farmers favored its use because it was less expensive than butter and provided a market for their corn oil.

Race was another source of disunity. Early efforts by southern Populists to bring black farmers into the party gave southern Democrats an opportunity to resurrect the race issue. Confronted with the threat of black equality, southern poor whites forgot their economic troubles and voted Democrat. Burned by this experience, Populist leaders avoided black voters thereafter. In later years, after their party had vanished, former Populists became some of the most impassioned southern demagogues.

Populism, in short, was rooted in depression, and it could not survive in an atmosphere of prosperity. Populist thinkers penetrated to the heart of the problems created by modernization, and they formulated some imaginative solutions. But their support rested on the unemployed and the debt-ridden, and these elements quieted in the sunnier times, though they did not disappear altogether. The Populists also erred in allowing the money question to dominate the debate. That issue evaporated when major gold discoveries in Alaska, Australia, and South Africa increased the world's money supply and incidentally stimulated economic recovery. The silver issue distracted attention from other features of the Omaha platform—paper money, railroads, and regulation of big business. These remained matters of public concern and would be picked up by other reformers.

Populism, after all, was only the vanguard of a large and growing concern for social change in the 1890s. The demise of the People's party was only the end of an organization. The reform impulse remained alive, and with softened rhetoric it was broadening the base of its support. The new movement, which by 1900 had adopted the name Progressive, commanded support among Republicans as well as Democrats, urban shopkeepers and small-town professional men. It eventually enacted the Populist program, and more.

SUMMARY

The formation of the People's party and its entry into the presidential contest of 1892 was the culmination of farm protest that had been brewing for two decades. Although the Knights of Labor and various reform groups sent delegates to the Populist convention at Omaha in 1892, the party was governed by the farmers' organizations, notably the Southern Alliance. Its platform, however, extended beyond farm grievances. It was a reasoned response to the social problems accompanying the industrial and agricultural revolutions. The Populists demanded government control of money, government ownership of the railroads, and a graduated income tax. They also asked for immigration restrictions and shorter working hours. Their platform outlined the dimensions of political reform for the next quarter of a century.

In the election, the Populists polled more than 1 million popular votes and 22 electoral votes, and they elected governors in three states. Their best showing, however, was in the mountain states of the West, where they had cooperated with Silver Democrats. After 1892, free silver came to dominate the movement. The free silver crusade had originated in an effort to reduce the intrinsic value of the dollar. Because of the fall in farm prices, due to the depression, farmers found they had to grow more in order to pay their debts. By devaluing the dollar, they hoped to raise prices and make it easier to pay debts. Silver coinage, which had been stopped by the government in 1873, seemed one way to cheapen the dollar. Western silver miners, looking for an additional market for their silver, naturally agreed. In 1890 Congress yielded to these pressures and passed the Sherman Silver Purchase Act, which required the Treasury to purchase silver with paper money. By increasing the amount of paper in circulation, Populists and Silver Democrats hoped to force the government to back its paper with silver as well as gold, thus returning to a bimetallic standard.

Grover Cleveland, the winner in 1892, inherited this problem along with a depression resulting from the panic of 1893. Cleveland persuaded Congress to repeal the Sherman Silver Purchase Act, but he still had to borrow gold from the New York banks in order to keep the nation on the gold standard. That alienated the Silver Democrats and divided his party. Unemployment and labor strife added to his troubles. In 1894 General Jacob Coxey led an "army" of unemployed in a march on Washington, only to be met by police violence. That same year, a strike against the Pullman Palace Car Company in Chicago turned violent when the federal government interfered with troops, and the governor of Illinois strongly protested the federal interference in his state.

Amid these social and political tensions, the conservatism of the Gilded Age yielded to a reawakened spirit of reform. A Social Gospel movement stirred the nation's churches. Settlement houses for the benefit of the poor appeared in several cities. These signs of reawakened social conscience in the cities paralleled the Populist movement in the South and West.

In 1896, the Silver Democrats seized control of the party and nominated William Jennings Bryan for president. Although the only Populist principle Bryan endorsed was free silver, the Populists also made him their candidate. The voters, however, turned to the Republican candidate, William McKinley. The Populists' radical image and wild rhetoric had frightened the middle classes in the East and Midwest.

The Populist party disappeared soon thereafter, a victim of both its own internal tensions and the return of prosperity.

READING SUGGESTIONS

A good brief overview of this period is to be found in Samuel P. Hays's *Response to Industrialism* (1957). Two histories of reform also provide a broad perspective, though from different points of view: Eric F. Goldman, *Rendezvous with Destiny* (1952), and Richard Hofstadter, *The Age of Reform: From Bryan to FDR* (1955). On the Populists, John D. Hicks, *The Populist Revolt* (1931), is still useful, but the best discussions of the Populist ideology and impact are Norman Pollack, *The Populist Response to Industrial America* (1963), and Lawrence Goodwyn, *The Populist Moment* (1978). For progress in the cities in this period, see John C. Teaford's *The Unheralded Triumph: City Government in America, 1870–1900* (1984).

The political battles of the 1890s can also be approached through biography. The best of these include Allan Nevins, *Grover Cleveland* (1932); H. Wayne Morgan, *William McKinley and His America* (1963); Paul Glad, *The Trumpet Soundeth: William Jennings Bryan and His Democracy* (1960); and C. Vann Woodward, *Tom Watson, Agrarian Rebel* (1938).

For reform currents paralleling the Populist movement, see Henry S. Commager, *The American Mind* (1950); Jane Addams's autobiography, *Forty Years at Hull House* (1935); and C. H. Hopkins, *The Rise of the Social Gospel in American Protestantism, 1865–1915* (1940).

6

THE NEW AMERICAN EMPIRE:
1865–1903

M ay 1, 1898, 5:40 A.M., Manila Bay, the Philippines. Commodore George Dewey peered across the short expanse of water and trained his glass on the ten Spanish warships lying at anchor against the backdrop of the slumbering city. Dewey turned to the captain of his flagship: "You may fire when you are ready, Gridley." The great guns of the U.S. Asiatic Squadron opened fire, and seven hours later, when a ceasefire was ordered, the Spanish fleet was a sinking clump of gnarled steel. Eight of Dewey's sailors had suffered minor injuries; none was killed. Spanish power in the Philippines, a colony Spain had claimed since the time of Magellan, was destroyed. The United States had thrust itself suddenly and forcefully into the Far East. "The guns of Dewey at Manila have changed the destiny of the United States," exclaimed the Washington *Post*. "We are face to face with a strange destiny and must accept its responsibilities. An imperial policy!" Strange names and haunting memories would be part of that destiny—Pearl Harbor, Korea, Taiwan, and Vietnam. How did it happen?

⊔ The Birth of an Imperial Policy

PACIFIC EXPANSION

The notion of a "China market," a land of teeming millions whose rulers lived in golden splendor, is as old as Marco Polo. American merchants, ever alert to trading outlets, dispatched a vessel to China shortly after the American Revolution ended, an economic declaration of independence. A flourishing trade in sea otter pelts ensued. A by-product of that trade was the American discovery of the Hawaiian Islands (English ship captains had been the first Euro-

peans to visit the islands). Yankee skippers found Hawaii a convenient steppingstone across the Pacific. Yankee missionaries followed, and the Americanization of the islands was begun.

China's emperors were wary of foreign trade and foreign influence, but Great Britain, through war in the early 1840s,* forced them to open their doors to the merchants of the world. In 1844, the United States and China signed a treaty placing their mutual exchange on a "most favored nation" basis. This meant that no other nation could be "more favored"; that is, concessions granted to a third party (Britain or Germany, for example) by either of the two original signatories (China or the United States) were automatically extended to the other. The object was free commercial competition, and it became the foundation of American Far Eastern policy.

A decade later Commodore Matthew Perry, negotiating with poised cannon, forced the Japanese to open their mercantile door. Sent by President Millard Filmore, Perry sailed into a Japanese port in November 1853 and demanded a commercial treaty "as a right, and not . . . as a favor." He left word that he would return in the spring for a favorable reply. Perry's demand precipitated a civil war in Japan, but he got his treaty. It allowed American entry into two Japanese ports and provided for the return of shipwrecked American seamen.

The initial American penetration of the Pacific was motivated by desire for trade. After the Civil War, the State and Navy departments interested themselves in terri-

---

* It was called the Opium War (1839–1842) because it began when Chinese officials destroyed opium British merchants had brought illegally into the country from India. The treaty that ended it gave foreigners special privileges in China and set the stage for the Western exploitation of China.

(*Chapter opening photo*) A newspaper artist's rendition of the explosion of the battleship *Maine* in Havana harbor.

tory. The American empire had always expanded westward toward the Pacific; a leap over a few miles of water seemed a natural continuance. In 1867, Secretary of State William H. Seward purchased Alaska from Russia at a price of $7.2 million, and later that year a naval warship, the U.S.S. *Lackawanna*, took possession of Midway Island in the central Pacific. Inhabited only by birds and seals, Midway was another steppingstone to the Far East.

Secretary Seward was also interested in the annexation of Hawaii, but stung perhaps by the newspapers' ridicule of his Alaska acquisition as "Seward's icebox," he settled instead for a treaty of commercial reciprocity. The Senate rejected that, but in 1875 another reciprocity treaty was signed and approved. By the agreement, each country admitted the products of the other duty-free. The effect was to give Hawaiian sugar a preference in the American sugar market. American businessmen moved into Hawaii, established large-scale sugar plantations, hired Japanese immigrants to work them, and multiplied Hawaiian sugar exports tenfold in the next twenty years. In 1887, as a price for renewing the agreement, the United States demanded and received a lease on Pearl Harbor as a naval base. By then the Hawaiian economy was utterly dependent on the American market, and formal annexation was only a matter of time.

A similar process was at work in Samoa, another native-ruled archipelago in the South Pacific. President Grant, ever susceptible to promoters with grand ideas and large-scale maps, fell under the spell of the head of a company that ran steamships between San Francisco and Australia. This gentleman alerted the president to the excellent potential of the harbor at Pago Pago on Samoa. Grant dispatched a series of naval officers who ingratiated themselves with the islanders and returned with various treaties, none of which could pass muster in the Senate. In 1878, the Senate finally accepted a minimum obligation: The United States would give Samoa diplomatic support whenever it became embroiled with another government, in return for the right to establish a naval coaling station at Pago Pago. At that point the United States had no financial interest in the islands. Their economy was, in fact, dominated by a German mercantile firm. After Germany's chancellor, Bismarck, became converted to colonialism in 1884, the Germans extended their influence in the islands. Americans responded with awakened interest at first, and then with rising alarm. A "Samoan crisis" was averted by an agreement by which the United States, Britain, and Germany established a tripartite protectorate over Samoa, while guaranteeing its "independence." The treaty also guaranteed American rights in Pago Pago. As it turned out, Americans were there to stay.

CARIBBEAN OUTREACH

American interest in the West Indies and Central America was also an outgrowth of continental expansionism. Beginning with the "All Mexico" movement of 1848, American slavery expansionists had viewed the Caribbean Basin as a likely target. Private armies of filibusters paraded into the Antilles and Central America throughout the 1850s. And in 1854, emissaries of the State Department, meeting at Ostend, Belgium, even issued a semi-official demand for Spain's surrender of Cuba.

Secretary Seward picked up the theme after the Civil War. He negotiated the purchase of the Virgin Islands from Denmark and a lease on a naval base in Santo Domingo. Both agreements were rejected by the Senate, already grumbling about the money wasted on Seward's icebox. (The United States ultimately did purchase the Virgin Islands in 1917.)

President Grant shared Seward's interest, if not his finesse. In 1869, Grant dispatched his acquisitive secretary, Orville Babcock, to investigate possibilities in Santo Domingo. After a false start or two, Babcock returned with a treaty of annexation and a plan for ultimate statehood for the island. The cost to the United States was a gold payment on the Dominican debt. Babcock also carried an alternative agreement that simply gave the United States a fifty-year lease on a naval base on the island. The Senate rejected both. Babcock's arrangements had an unsavory odor, and the addition of an all-black territory presented some delicate racial problems. Carl Schurz, speaking against the treaties, reflected the biases even of a liberal reformer. To govern tropical islands as "satrapies" (Oriental dictatorships), he declared, would corrupt the American republic. To admit them as states meant receiving people who "have neither language, nor traditions, nor habits, nor political institutions, nor morals in common with us." Such thinly disguised racial bias would be heard again in the great imperial debate of 1899–1900.

In the 1880s, Secretary of State James G. Blaine tried to revive American interest in the world south of the border, focusing principally on the idea of pan-American union. Nothing came of it, in part because Americans were preoccupied with internal problems—trusts, railroads, free silver, and labor strife. Genuine interest in the world abroad, with its attendant expansionism, awaited the decade of the 1890s.

ROOTS OF EXPANSIONISM

There were several reasons for the outburst of American war fever in the 1890s. The passage of time was one of them. A generation had passed since the Civil War ended. The hell of war (the phrase was General William Tecumseh Sherman's) was largely forgotten. Time, too, had

healed the sectional wounds and drawn the nation together; unity in patriotic purpose was once more possible. And time had seen the ending of the frontier, the completion of the energy-consuming conquest of the continent that had absorbed European-Americans from the moment they arrived on North American shores. The momentum of conquest could be deflected in new directions, and the advance agents of empire, in the Caribbean and the Pacific, had already shown the way.

Latent racial bias, reinforced by Social Darwinism and the works of historians who glorified the Anglo-Saxons, was also a factor. By the 1890s the theory of Social Darwinism was being adapted to the international arena. Nations, like individuals, so the argument ran, are also engaged in a struggle for survival: They must grow in influence or they will wither and die. Theodore Roosevelt, soon to become McKinley's assistant secretary of the Navy, thought that nations needed a good scrap once in a while just to stay in shape; otherwise they risked degenerating into an assortment of "self-centered weaklings and spineless moneygrubbers."

Historians and political theorists provided the Social Darwinists with additional ammunition by elaborating a theory of Anglo-Saxon supremacy. Democracy, so the argument ran, was born in the forests of northwestern Europe, carried to England by the Anglo-Saxons, and migrated from there to America. The theory presupposed that those peoples had a unique gift for stable, democratic government, and the corollary was that those same peoples had an obligation to teach the rest of the world. An exquisite digest of this thesis was Rudyard Kipling's poem, "The White Man's Burden." Its title revealed both its assumptions and its biases. Written in 1899, Kipling's poem was an argument for American annexation of the Philippines.

Less elevated, but more candid, was the economic argument for expansionism.

Trade had always been a factor in American diplomacy; in the 1890s it became a central concern. The United States became the leading industrial power in the world in the course of the decade, and by 1900 it poured out more manufactured goods than the second and third powers—Britain and Germany—combined. It also experienced the woes of industrialization: unemployment and market surpluses. And with the unemployment came labor strife. "I am not a pessimist," wrote President Cleveland's secretary of state, "but I think I see danger in existing conditions in this country. What is transpiring in Pennsylvania, Ohio, Indiana, Illinois, and regions west of there, may fairly be viewed as symptoms of revolution." The fundamental problem, as the secretary saw it, was that "our mills and factories can supply the demand by running seven or eight months out of twelve." To keep the mills running for twelve months a year and the work force employed, the government had to "enable our people to compete in foreign markets with Great Britain." This did not necessar-

ily mean establishing colonies. In fact, most Americans wanted to decolonize the world, to eliminate some of the imperial trade barriers in order to enhance American opportunities.

Either way—whether it established an empire of its own or smashed the empires of others—the United States had to play a larger role in world affairs. No one repeated this theme more insistently than Captain Alfred Thayer Mahan. An instructor at the U.S. Naval Academy, Mahan published a book in 1890 entitled *The Influence of Sea Power Upon History, 1660–1783*, in which he traced the rise of the Dutch and British empires, stressing the role of naval power in achieving national greatness. Mahan accepted the thesis that a healthy economy required foreign markets; he argued that these could be held in the face of fierce international competition only by maintaining a strong navy. Command of the seas, in turn, required foreign bases and island coaling stations. "No nation," wrote Mahan, "certainly no great nation, should henceforth maintain

The White Man's Burden

In 1899, the English poet Rudyard Kipling wrote a poem to help persuade the United States to annex the Philippines. Its stanzas reflected the sense of Anglo-Saxon superiority that permeated both British and American imperialism.

Take up the White Man's burden—
　Send forth the best ye breed—
Go bind your sons to exile
　To serve your captive's need;
To wait in heavy harness
　On fluttered folk and wild—
Your new-caught sullen peoples,
　Half devil and half child.

Take up the White Man's burden—
　Ye dare not stoop to less—
Nor call too loud on Freedom
　to cloak your weariness;
By all ye cry or whisper,
　By all ye leave or do,
The silent, sullen peoples
　Shall weigh your Gods and you.

Rudyard Kipling, "The White Man's Burden," 1899. Reproduced by permission of The National Trust for Places of Historic Interest or Natural Beauty and Macmillan London, Ltd.

the policy of isolation. . . . Whether they will or no, Americans must now begin to look outward."

FROM LARGE POLICY TO JINGOISM

At the time Mahan was writing, the American Navy was inconsequential. Among the naval powers of the world, the United States ranked below Chile. Americans had long been hostile to the notion of sea power; Congress and the public, in fact, viewed the Navy as a form of coastal defense. In 1890, when a Naval Policy Board was formed to study naval requirements, the board's cautious recommendation was for the construction of a few "sea-going coastline battleships."

Mahan made some influential converts, however. Among them were Massachusetts Senator Henry Cabot Lodge and Lodge's young friend and disciple, Theodore Roosevelt. In addition to sea power, Lodge advocated building a canal across Central America, the purchase of the Danish West Indies, and firmer control over Hawaii and Samoa. Roosevelt was even more enthusiastic. If he could have his way, he blurted to Mahan, he would "hoist our flag over the island [Hawaii] leaving all details for after action." Years later, in retirement after his presidency, Roosevelt would employ similar language to explain how he acquired the Panama Canal. Its advocates named it the "large policy," and Congress responded with increased naval appropriations in the 1890s. By the end of the decade, the nation boasted a formidable armada of seventeen battleships, six armored cruisers, and a host of support vessels. It was a force equal to Germany's and second only to the Royal Navy of Britain. Roosevelt, appointed assistant secretary of the Navy by McKinley, knew what to do with it. "Peace," he told the Naval War College

in 1897, "is a goddess only when she comes girt with sword on thigh."

The new mood was soon evident in the conduct of American foreign policy. "We planted a Gibraltar in the heart of the Pacific," trumpeted one senator when the United States acquired the rights to Pearl Harbor. Generously endowed by nature and strategically situated, Hawaii was a tempting target for a number of imperial powers. The United States simply moved in first. In 1887 American landowners in the islands, with the support of the State Department, forced the king to agree to a constitution that limited his powers and made his ministers responsible to a senate controlled by American landowners. When the Hawaiian king died in 1891, his sister, Queen Liliuokalani, a nationalist, succeeded to the throne. When the queen attempted to recover some of the royal powers, the American planters, with the connivance of the American minister to Hawaii, plotted a revolution. The uprising broke out in early 1893, and with the help of 150 marines from an American cruiser that happened to be lying in the harbor, the planters overthrew Liliuokalani. The new government quickly drew up a treaty of annexation, which President Harrison submitted to the Senate in February. It seemed likely to pass until incoming President Grover Cleveland withdrew it after learning that the vast majority of Hawaiians remained loyal to the queen.

That move, however, was Cleveland's only bit of foreign philanthropy. Once settled in the White House, he proved as bellicose as any of his predecessors. A boundary dispute between two Latin American countries, Venezuela and British Guiana, presented him with an opportunity. The undefined boundary between the two had become a matter of concern when gold was discovered in the region, and each side had inflated its claims. Venezuela, being the weaker, had offered to submit the controversy to arbitration; Britain had refused. In 1895, a cleverly drafted pamphlet by a paid agent of the Venezuelan government brought the issue to American attention. Twisting the British lion's tail* was always popular with the American electorate, and in early 1895 Congress passed unanimously a joint resolution urging the president to press for arbitration. Cleveland turned the subject over to Secretary of State Richard Olney, the Boston lawyer who had concocted the legal basis for smashing the Pullman strike the year before.

In preparing his case against the British, Olney used the Monroe Doctrine.** The principle of nonintervention set forth in the doctrine, said Olney, meant that Britain could not forcibly deprive Venezuela of territory. Britain was therefore obliged to submit the question of ownership to a third party. And Olney made it clear who he thought ought to be the arbitrator. The United States, said he, "is practically sovereign on this continent [South America], and its fiat is law." Olney sent this memorandum to London on July 20, 1895, and requested a reply before the opening of Congress in December. The tone of the note made it a virtual ultimatum.

British Foreign Secretary Lord Salisbury waited until November before drafting a reply. He informed the United States that Britain was not bound by the Monroe Doctrine and that a boundary dispute was none of the United States's business. Salisbury was right on both counts, but President Cleveland was not the man to yield on that score. He made public the exchange of correspondence and asked Congress for authority to set up a commission to determine the boundary and enforce it. The issue had become, he said, a matter of "national self-respect and honor." Cleveland's message received enthusiastic public support, and Congress promptly gave him the authority he requested. Faced with more serious problems in Ireland and South Africa, the British backed away from a confrontation in South America and agreed to arbitration. Cleveland and Olney had risked a war and won. "Jingoism," some would call it, borrowing—with unconscious irony—the term from a British verse written during a Russian crisis a few years before:

> We don't want to fight, but by Jingo if we do,
> We've got the ships, we've got the men, and got the money too.

Jingoist diplomacy, the casual resort to threat and intimidation, was a risky game. The next confrontation, in fact, led to war.

⊔ Cuba and the War with Spain

A revolution in Cuba sparked the combustion. Cuba was still a Spanish colony, a remnant of the once-glorious Spanish Main. Commercially, however, it was dependent on the United States, and millions of dollars in American capital were invested in its sugar and tobacco plantations. It was a restive colony, with periodic uprisings that invariably won sympathy in the United States. Revolution broke out anew in February 1895, and shortly thereafter a Cuban

---

* The lion was a symbol of the British crown. To twist its tail was to annoy it. This was a favorite tactic of American politicians in the nineteenth century, especially those with Irish voters in their constituencies.

** The Monroe Doctrine was largely forgotten after Monroe announced it in 1823. It had been invoked by the American government only twice—by President Polk when he ordered the British out of Oregon in 1845, and by Secretary of State Seward when he asked the French to withdraw from Mexico at the end of the Civil War. After Olney's resurrection of the doctrine in 1895, however, it became a centerpiece of American foreign policy.

junta set itself up in New York to dispense propaganda and solicit money.

The Spanish commander in Cuba, General Valeriano Weyler, facing a hostile civilian population that was helping the guerrillas, set out to depopulate the countryside and force people into the cities. This removal left thousands homeless and hungry, and the American press described the suffering in lurid detail. The "yellow press," big-city tabloids with sensational headlines, exploited the Cuban story to the utmost. William Randolph Hearst's New York *Journal* and Joseph Pulitzer's New York *World*, already engaged in a circulation war that caused occasional street fights among newsboys, vied with one another for the number of artists[*] and reporters retained on Cuban assignment. One *Journal* reporter made screaming headlines when he spirited Evangelina Cisneros, a Cuban gentlewoman being held by the Spanish, out of the Havana jail and into the paper's offices in New York.

The battle over silver in 1896 momentarily drowned the clamor over Cuba, but the outcry resumed after Bryan's defeat. By 1897 intervention in Cuba, which inevitably risked war with Spain, was being openly discussed. The appeal was both humanitarian and patriotic. Intervention would help a neighbor in trouble while simultaneously ejecting one more decadent European monarchy from the New World. Newspapers affiliated with Protestant churches and the tabloids led the cry; business and trade journals were more cautious. The economy turned upward in early 1897, and most businessmen feared that war might interrupt the cycle.

---

[*] Hearst even employed Frederic Remington, famed for his dramatic paintings of cowboys and Indians. When Remington cabled Hearst from Cuba that everything there was quiet and no one anticipated war, Hearst wired back: "You furnish the pictures and I'll furnish the war."

REMEMBER THE *MAINE*

President McKinley, as his "front porch" campaign attests, was not a man to court trouble. Nor, on the other hand, was he a man to resist pressure. Publicly he ignored a congressional resolution that he recognize the rebel government; privately he pressured Spain for concessions. Spain did make several gestures. It recalled the general, whom the press had dubbed "Butcher" Weyler, and it promised a certain amount of home rule for Cuba, though not outright independence. Most important, so far as McKinley was concerned, Spain refused to give Cubans the right to negotiate trade agreements. The State Department was still digesting the meaning of these concessions when, in January 1898, McKinley decided to send the battleship *Maine* on a "courtesy call" to Havana. The reason was that rioting had occurred in Havana earlier that month, but McKinley's true motive was apparently to keep control of the situation. Apparently he felt he had to do something to keep Congress from doing something worse. In any case, it was a risky step. In an area engulfed in revolution, an incident of some sort was inevitable, and using such incidents as an excuse for extravagant demands was common to the diplomacy of the day. Only three months earlier, Germany had demanded and received a 99-year lease on the Chinese port of Kiaochow as compensation for the murder of two missionaries.

On February 15 it happened: The *Maine* exploded and sank to the bottom of Havana harbor, taking with it some 260 American seamen. How it happened remains a mystery. A Navy Board investigated and reported on March 28 that a submarine mine had exploded outside the ship and set off the ship's magazines. The Spanish government denied responsibility and cooperated in the investigation. That the Spanish were responsible is highly unlikely, since an incident of that sort was almost certain to trigger intervention. In all probability it was an accident.

American jingoes preferred to blame Spain. Senator Lodge called it a "gigantic murder, the last spasm of a corrupt and dying society." "Remember the Maine!" trumpeted the yellow press. Hearst's *Journal* claimed that its own investigation of the disaster revealed it was caused by a Spanish mine. In late February, Assistant Secretary of the Navy Theodore Roosevelt, anticipating war, cabled Commodore Dewey in Hong Kong instructing him to begin offensive operations in the Spanish Philippines when the conflict began. The order was apparently given on Roosevelt's initiative, but the president did not countermand it. McKinley took no steps of his own toward war, however, which led Roosevelt to fume privately that McKinley had the backbone of a chocolate eclair.*

The president dragged his feet with good reason. He was aware of the instructions given to Commodore Dewey, and aware also that great power rivalries in China had made the Far East a powderkeg. (The Germans had their eyes on Spain's Far Eastern colonies, and a German squadron actually followed Dewey from Hong Kong to Manila Bay.) Fearful that the dispute over Cuba might blow up into global conflict, McKinley warned jingoes in Congress to move cautiously. But the war fever seemed to have a momentum of its own. In mid-March, a senator who had made an unofficial visit to Cuba reported that of the 400,000 persons who had been driven into concentration camps, "one half have died and one-quarter of the living are so diseased that they cannot be saved." Outside the camps, he told the Senate, all was desolation.

The *Wall Street Journal* reported that the speech had "converted a great many people in Wall Street." On March 25, a trusted friend in New York sent McKinley a telegram that read: "Big corporations here now believe we will have war. Believe all would welcome it as a relief to suspense." The changed attitude in Wall Street left the president virtually alone in his resistance to war. In the end he yielded to the combined pressure of press, public, business interests, and Congress. Not that he opted for war; he simply gave up efforts to avoid it.

On March 27, McKinley cabled a virtual ultimatum to Madrid. Spain must abandon the resettlement policy, grant an armistice, and enter into peace negotiations, the outcome of which must be Cuban independence. Spain replied on March 31 with an announcement that resettlement was being abandoned and an armistice would be granted if the rebels asked for one. It shied from independence, however, saying only that the Cuban parliament, established as a result of Spain's prior concessions, would pacify the country. On April 9, Spain unilaterally declared an armistice. Two days later, McKinley sent Congress a message saying that negotiations with Spain were unsatisfactory and asking for authority to intervene in Cuba. For a week Congress debated exactly what this meant, and finally on April 19 passed resolutions stating that Cuba ought to be independent, that Spain must withdraw, and that the president had the power to enforce this demand. On April 24, Spain declared war. The next day Congress did the same, making it retroactive to April 21, the date the president signed the Cuban resolutions.

Appended to the resolutions was an amendment drafted by Senator Henry M. Teller of Colorado stating that the United States had no intention of governing or controlling Cuba. The Teller Amendment reflected the blend of idealism and patriotism with which Americans entered the war. The United States had no important

---

* Roosevelt later took it back. But he also is alleged to have said, "McKinley keeps his ear so close to the ground that it's always full of grasshoppers," and there is no record that he ever took that back.

interests at stake; even investments in Cuba were probably as secure under Spanish rule as under independence. New interests and worldwide responsibilities would result from the war, but these were largely unforeseen at the beginning. It was simply a war against a doddering and decadent European empire, waged in the spirit of republican idealism and blessed by the humanitarian gesture of helping a small neighbor win its independence. It was an unnecessary war, an avoidable war, but it was not simply Mr. McKinley's war. This one belonged to the American people. With the exception of World War II, it was the most popular war they have ever fought.

THE "SPLENDID LITTLE WAR"

Commodore Dewey's victory at Manila Bay, the opening engagement of the war, was not the fluke it seemed. The Navy had provided Dewey with some of its newest ships in anticipation of offensive operations against the Philippines, and the army sent an occupation force from San Francisco even before it learned of Dewey's victory. On its way across the Pacific, the squadron dispatched a cruiser to the Spanish Marianas to seize Guam. Unaware that war had been declared, the Spanish garrison on Guam took the opening American salvo for a salute. When they discovered their error, they surrendered. On August 13, the occupation army of 11,000 men entered Manila against only token Spanish resistance.

Meanwhile, a naval blockade had been set up around Cuba, and an invasion army was assembled at Tampa Bay, Florida. A brief invasion scare swept the east coast when the Navy reported that it was unsure of the whereabouts of the main Spanish fleet, which had last been seen heading west from the Azores. Newspapers evoked

The Spanish American War in the Caribbean.

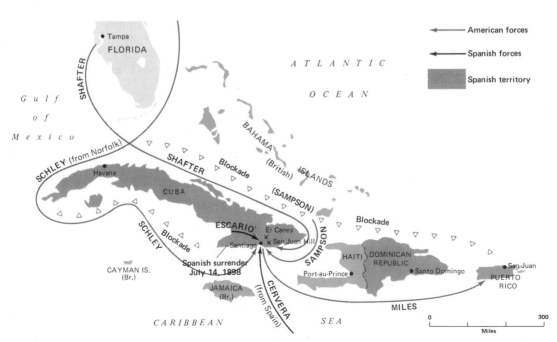

Library of Congress.

The charge up San Juan Hill, as seen by artist Frederick Remington, who had been sent to Cuba by newspaper publisher William Randolph Hearst.

memories of the Armada, and seaboard cities mounted watches. Amidst the hubbub Senator Henry Cabot Lodge remained calm. With a New England Brahmin's disdain for foreigners, Lodge declared that if the Spanish landed in the middle of New York City, they would be absorbed into the local population and be engaged in selling oranges by the time they reached 14th Street. Fortunately, the Spanish fleet turned up in Cuban waters and slipped through the blockade into Santiago harbor.

On June 15, an army of half-trained volunteers landed on the coast of Cuba a few miles east of Santiago, accompanied by a contingent of newsmen, foreign dignitaries, politicians, and well-wishers. The commanding general, 300-pound William R. Shafter, was soon prostrated by the Cuban heat. Day-to-day supervision rested with "Fighting Joe" Wheeler, a relic of the Con-

federacy. The most colorful of the army units was the First Volunteer Cavalry Regiment—the Rough Riders—commanded by Colonel Leonard Wood and new volunteer Lieutenant Colonel Theodore Roosevelt.[*] The unit quickly lost its cavalry status when its horses were drowned in the landing, but Roosevelt, who wrote an account of its adventures (*Rough Riders*, published in 1899) ensured its enduring fame—and his own. On July 1 and 2, the army smashed its way to the top of San Juan and Kettle hills, which surrounded Santiago.

With American guns trained on them from the hilltops, the Spanish ships fled

---

[*] Tradition, firmly attested by Texans, has it that Roosevelt recruited the regiment in the saloon of the Menger Hotel, across the street from the Alamo in San Antonio. In addition to cowboys and some Indians, the regiment included some Ivy League college boys.

the harbor. The Battle of Santiago (July 3, 1898), a running sea fight along the Cuban coast, resulted in the destruction of the entire Spanish fleet. One American sailor was killed by a stray shell fragment. On July 16, the Spanish army, now without naval support, surrendered, and two days later Spain sued for peace. Before the American momentum could be halted, an expeditionary force siezed Puerto Rico. So light was the Spanish resistance that humorist Finley Peter Dunne's saloonkeeper-philosopher Mr. Dooley characterized it as a "moonlight excursion." An armistice was signed on August 12, 112 days after war was declared. American losses in battle were 345 men killed, although yellow fever, which ravaged the army after the fighting ended, pushed the final toll to nearly 6,000.

The speedy American victory was due principally to the ineptitude of the Spanish and their antiquated military hardware. The American Army had shown itself to be utterly disorganized and lacking in leadership. After the charge up San Juan Hill, it was so low on supplies and morale it could hardly move. It was saved only by the panicky flight of the Spanish fleet. The Navy, though better equipped than the Army, had flaws of its own. In the Battle of Santiago, only 3 percent of American shells scored hits. All this escaped the public, however. To Americans, the war was an exhilarating summer escapade, accompanied by the stirring strains of John Phillip Sousa's new march, "The Stars and Stripes Forever." The national emblem had been planted around the world. Secretary of State John Hay summed it up best. It was, said Hay, "a splendid little war."

⊔ An American Empire

The Spanish-American War was part of a worldwide drift toward imperialism in the 1890s. It paralleled the partition of Africa by Europeans and the threatened partition of China. Americans, with the exception of such "large policy" exponents as Mahan and Roosevelt, never fully subscribed to the European style of empire building. Nor, on the other hand, were they immune to European imperialist attitudes. Tarzan, the fictional creation of the English novelist Edgar Rice Burroughs, and arch symbol of the "white man's burden" in the "dark" regions of the world, was as popular in America as he was in England.

ANNEXATION OF HAWAII AND SAMOA

The first result of the drift toward imperialism was the annexation of Hawaii. The status of the islands had been in doubt ever since President Cleveland withdrew the annexation treaty from the Senate in 1893. Dewey's victory at Manila Bay and the prospect of annexation of the Philippines enhanced the importance of Hawaii. "We need Hawaii just as much and a good deal more than we did California," McKinley confided to his secretary; "It is manifest destiny."

While the nation celebrated Dewey's victory, proponents of annexation by resolution—first employed with Texas in 1845—had several advantages. It avoided further negotiations with Hawaii, where Yankee sugar planters maintained tenuous control, and it required only a majority of both houses for passage. Approved by Congress and the president in July 1898, Hawaiian annexation broke the pattern of America's anticolonial past and set a precedent for further overseas acquisitions. In the peace settlement that ended the Spanish-American War, signed at Paris in December 1898, the United States demanded and received the cession of Puerto Rico, Guam, and the Philippines, the latter technically "sold" to the United States for $20 million. Shortly

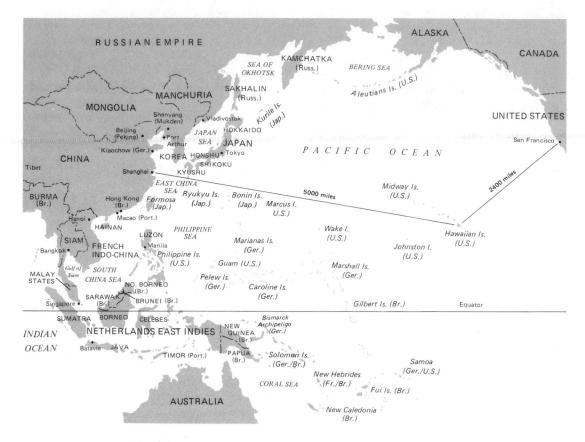

The United States in the Pacific, ca. 1900.

thereafter, the U.S. Navy took possession of uninhabited Wake Island as a further steppingstone across the Pacific, and Congress approved the annexation of American Samoa. The American empire was in place.

THE PLATT AMENDMENT: CUBA

By the treaty of Paris, Spain conceded the independence of Cuba, and the United States lived up to its pledge to let the island go. It did so, however, only reluctantly. The U.S. Army remained in Cuba until 1902. It did worthwhile service. It helped the Cubans set up agencies for effective government, it furthered public education, and it undertook an islandwide sanitation campaign to reduce the ravages of mosquito-borne plagues such as malaria and yellow fever. Nevertheless, for all their good deeds, the longer Americans stayed, the more reluctant they were to let go.

In 1901, Secretary of State Hay formulated a plan for linking the United States and Cuba that eventually became known as the Platt Amendment. Attached by Congress to an army appropriation bill, the plan was later incorporated, at the insistence of the United States, into the Cuban constitution of 1902. For good measure, the Platt Amendment was also incorporated in a Cuban-American treaty of 1903. The amendment restricted Cuba's right to enter into treaties with countries other than the United States, gave the United States power to intervene to maintain law and order, and presented to the U.S. Navy various coaling stations, notably the station at Guantanamo Bay.

The Cubans were not at all happy with the Platt Amendment and accepted it only when Secretary of State Elihu Root promised that the right of intervention was "not synonymous with intermeddling." But it was, as it turned out. When the Cubans signed a treaty extending to the British some of the trading privileges enjoyed by the United States, the American minister in Havana strongly objected. And when a new revolution broke out in 1906, the United States did not hesitate to send troops to restore order. The Platt Amendment remained in effect until 1934. Among its legacies is the radical, Yankee-baiting Cuba of today.

THE PHILIPPINES

The real test of American imperialist mettle was the Philippines. Missionary zeal and manifest destiny had brought the islands into the American orbit, or so the president declared. McKinley explained to a group of visiting clergymen how he reached his decision to retain the Philippines. The United States, he said, could not return them to Spain, for that would be "cowardly." It could not turn them over to another imperial power, for that would be "bad business." And it could not leave them to themselves, because "they were unfit for self-government." After praying to "Almighty God for light and guidance," it came to him "that there was nothing left for us to do but to take them all, and to

---

Mr. Dooley on Imperialism

Mr. Dooley, the fictitious Irish tavernkeeper created by humorist Peter Finley Dunne, had some choice comments on American expansionism.

> Hands across the sea and into someone's pockets.
> There's one consolation—if the American people can govern themselves, they can govern anything that walks.
> To the Filipinos:
> We can't give you any votes because we haven't more than enough to go around now, but we'll treat you the way a father should treat his children if we have to break every bone in your bodies. So come to our arms.

Peter Finley Dunne, *Mr. Dooley in Peace and War* (1899).

CLIO'S FOCUS: Emilio Aguinaldo and the Philippine Revolution

The United States annexed the Philippines in 1898 because neither President McKinley nor Congress thought the Filipino people were prepared for self-government. Both were shocked when the Filipinos rejected the American move and rose up in rebellion. The mistake originated in American racial biases. It was not the first or the last such error.

The Filipino struggle for self-government, in fact, had begun in 1896, two years before Commodore Dewey's victory at Manila Bay. The Filipinos had organized a secret political society, and when the Spanish tried to suppress it, fighting broke out. The poorly armed Filipinos lost the opening skirmishes on the outskirts of Manila, but they managed to defeat a Spanish army when it ventured into the interior of Luzon. The hero of that affair, 25-year-old Emilio Aguinaldo, was made generalissimo

Culver Pictures, Inc.

Emilio Aguinaldo.

and president of the revolutionary government. A moderate and a realist, Aguinaldo saw that his forces lacked the strength to push the Spanish out of the Philippines, so in 1897 he agreed to a truce. In return for a Spanish promise to introduce liberal reforms, including freedom of speech and press, the Filipinos laid down their arms. Aguinaldo went into exile.

Aguinaldo chose Hong Kong for his residence, and there in the spring of 1898 he came into contact with officers of Dewey's squadron. A series of meetings ensued, both in Hong Kong and Singapore, in which American diplomats served as intermediaries between Dewey and Aguinaldo. Dewey informed Aguinaldo that, in the event of war with Spain, then becoming daily more likely, he was under orders to attack the Spanish fleet in the Philippines. But he assured Aguinaldo—so the Filipino leader later claimed—that the United States had no colonial designs on the Philippines. Dewey later denied that any such assurances were given, but it is difficult to believe Aguinaldo would have cooperated with Americans as he did without some expectation that the overthrow of Spanish rule would lead to self-government.

After Dewey's victory at Manila Bay on May 1, the commodore sent an American warship to pick up Aguinaldo and bring him home. On May 19, 1898, Aguinaldo and Dewey met for the first time, and Dewey asked the generalissimo to lead a Filipino uprising against the Spanish, who were still, despite the loss of their fleet, in control of the islands. Aguinaldo agreed, Dewey furnished him with arms, and in the space of a month the Filipinos were in control of everything but the city of Manila. On June 30, an American army of occupation arrived from San Francisco. The American commander shunted Aguinaldo aside and occupied Manila. The Spanish surrendered on August 13. The surrender terms specifically excluded the Filipinos; the Spanish army gave the islands to the American army.

Aguinaldo set up a government for the Republic of the Philippines in a town some twenty-five miles north of Manila. The treatment accorded him in the capture of Manila was the first hint of American betrayal. By October the evidence multiplied, as Dewey and other officials began echoing the administration view that annexation was a necessity. Aguinaldo was thus prepared for the December peace agreement, which formally ceded the islands to the United States. Still, he did nothing. His government controlled the countryside outside Manila, and even the Americans conceded that it commanded the loyalty of most of the Philippine people. Aware of his moral strength and military weakness, Aguinaldo played for time.

The Americans started the fighting. It began on the night of February 4, 1899, when a Filipino approached a picket-guard of a Nebraska regiment. The private who fired the first shot described how it started:

> I yelled "halt!" . . . The man moved. I challenged him with another "halt." Then he immediately shouted "halto" to me. Well, I thought the best thing to do was to shoot him. He dropped. Then two Filipinos sprang out of the gateway about fifteen feet from us. I called "halt" and Miller fired and dropped one. I saw that another was left. Well, I think I got

> my second Filipino that time. We retreated to where our six other fellows were and I said, "Line up, fellows, the niggers are in here all through these yards."
>
> The Filipinos fired back, and the shooting went on through the night. When Aguinaldo offered a truce the next morning, the American commander refused. Instead that morning the American army launched a three-pronged attack on Aguinaldo's headquarters north of Manila. Though badly outnumbered, the Filipino force fought in the open and suffered heavy casualties in a series of battles. Pushed steadily back, Aguinaldo in November 1899 abandoned formal warfare and moved his headquarters into the mountains of northern Luzon. His army dissolved into guerrilla bands, which Aguinaldo directed through a system of codes and couriers. The guerrilla war continued for another year and a half.
>
> The war, begun in treachery, ended in trickery. A U.S. Army officer infiltrated Aguinaldo's camp in company with a band of Filipino mercenaries who pretended to be guerrillas. They seized Aguinaldo and carried him off to an army prison. That ended the fighting. The insurrection cost the U.S. Army some 10,000 casualties, and it cost American taxpayers $600 million.
>
> There is, nonetheless, a happy ending to the sorry tale. In early 1900, while the fighting raged, McKinley sent a commission headed by William Howard Taft to establish a civil government. Taft pacified the islands, instituted a bill of rights that guaranteed basic freedoms, and installed a system of free public education. In 1907 Congress authorized a Philippine assembly, and in the islands' first national election the party advocating cooperation with the United States defeated the party advocating independence. In 1934 Congress passed an act giving the Philippines commonwealth status for ten years, after which they were to have full independence. World War II and the Japanese occupation delayed independence until 1946. And Aguinaldo lived to see it. His memoirs, published in 1957, are a candid yet friendly appraisal of the Philippine-American connection. The reluctant revolutionary who shocked the American people in 1899 became an ally in the end.

educate the Filipinos, and uplift and civilize and Christianize them, and by God's grace to do the best we could by them as our fellow men for whom Christ also died." What the Roman Catholic pope, whose priests had ministered to the souls of Filipinos for nearly 400 years, thought of McKinley's missionary zeal has mercifully gone unrecorded.

In fact, the motives for acquiring the Philippines were strategic and commercial, as the president was well aware. During the depression of the 1890s, American businessmen, prodded by the vision of a "great China market," had taken a lively interest in the Far East. And with the interest went deepening concern that China was falling into the hands of their competitors. Russia had won important trade concessions in Manchuria and had influence with its rulers. Germany had received territorial and commercial concessions in China and made no secret of its ambitions in the Philippines. Britain maintained an official posture of commercial equality in the Far East, a policy the British called "the open door," while silently extending its influence into southern China. Japan menaced Korea, while France moved into Indochina (Vietnam).

In March 1898, President McKinley received a proposal from Britain that the United States and Britain make a joint protest against foreign intrusions into China. McKinley at that point was too busy with Spain and Cuba to reply, but the proposal gave him an opportunity to make Britain's "open door" policy his own. Giving instructions to his peace commissioners on September 16, he told them to demand the Philippines because the islands offered America an opportunity to uphold the principle of commercial equality throughout the Orient. "Asking only the open door for ourselves," he told his envoys, "we are ready to accord the open door to others."

Americans accepted annexation on the assumption they were doing the Filipinos a favor. They were accordingly astonished to find that the Filipinos did not see it that way. Filipinos saw no benefit in exchanging one form of imperial domination for another. The United States established its control of the island only after a savage guerrilla war that lasted for three years.

The Philippine revolution was a shock to Americans. Revolutions that achieved independence from foreign control and annexation to the United States—in West Florida, Texas, Oregon, and California—were part of the national success story. A people that rejected the blessings of American liberty was something new. The peace settlement had sparked a congressional debate on the wisdom of empire; the Philippine insurrection made the controversy more poignant. The imperialists, led by Henry Cabot Lodge, argued in favor of empire on the British model, contending that the United States was obliged, as one of the world's great powers, to shoulder responsibilities. The anti-imperialists, most

prominent of whom was Lodge's Republican colleague from Massachusetts, George F. Hoar, contended that the governing of subject peoples was contrary to American tradition, and that the experience would ultimately undermine our republican institutions. Both sides, ironically, agreed that the Filipinos were an inferior people incapable of self-government. Because of this, declared the anti-imperialists, they could never become citizens; they would be colonists forever dependent on the United States. Precisely because they could not govern themselves, retorted the imperialists, it was our responsibility to care for them.

Although Republicans controlled the Senate, Democratic votes were necessary to secure the two-thirds majority needed for ratification of the peace treaty. William Jennings Bryan, making a special trip to Washington for the purpose, tipped the balance. Though strongly anti-imperialist, Bryan suggested that the Senate approve the treaty and let the voters decide on Philippine annexation. On February 6, 1899, the Senate approved the treaty by the margin of a single vote. And subsequently the American people did speak on the issue, though not with the sentiment Bryan had hoped. In the presidential election of 1900, the issue was starkly presented. The Republican platform favored annexation and suppression of the Filipino rebellion. The Democratic platform advocated Philippine independence. The candidates were the same—Bryan and McKinley—as in 1896, and McKinley won a resounding victory.

By then a national consensus was beginning to form. The debate over empire had, in fact, been a three-way affair. Outside of Congress, various businessmen with interests in the Far East proposed an alternative. The Philippines would have to be retained because to set them free would humiliate the president. But there was no need to acquire other colonies or build an empire on the British model. Colonies were expensive and troublesome. And, if the chief object in having colonies was trade, they were unnecessary. Given fair opportunity and an open door, American merchants and American capital could achieve effective control without the bother of governance. Cuba was a ready example. This solution proved acceptable to the anti-imperialists, and the great debate quickly subsided.

THE OPEN DOOR POLICY

The contours of commercial imperialism had already taken shape by 1900. The target was the vast China market. Worried about the growth of foreign influence in China, Secretary of State John Hay on September 6, 1899, sent a note to each of the powers that claimed a sphere of influence in China—Great Britain, France, Germany, Russia, and Japan—calling on them to allow the United States and one another equal trading rights. As Hay anticipated, he received only grudging replies. Each would agree to commercial equality provided everyone else did. That suited Hay well enough. He had alerted the world that the United States had an interest in China. And he rested on firm ground. Free trade was the oldest, most venerable principle of American foreign policy. The British had already given it a name—the Open Door.

Chinese resistance to foreign intrusion gave Hay an opportunity to reinforce the Open Door policy. The Boxers were a se-

The Boxer Rebellion. American troops are marching past a Chinese temple in Peking.

Culver Pictures, Inc.

cret Chinese society dedicated to eliminating foreign influence, and they had the clandestine support of the empress. In June 1900, the empress dowager ordered all foreigners killed, and the Boxers went on a rampage. Europeans gathered in the legation quarter of the imperial city of Peking, and an international army was formed to rescue them. American troops were sent from the Philippines to participate. In Washington, Secretary Hay worried that the intervention might afford an excuse to carve up China among the colonial powers. Similar expeditions had contributed to the partition of Africa.

In July 1900, Hay sent the second of his Open Door notes. This one went well beyond the plea for equal rights: It was American policy, Hay declared, to preserve the "territorial and administrative" integrity of China and to safeguard "the principle of equal and impartial trade with all parts of the Chinese empire." Thus stated, the Open Door remained the cornerstone of American Far Eastern policy until bombed into oblivion at Pearl Harbor in 1941.

How well it protected China is another question. As with his first note, Hay received only evasive replies. None of the major powers would admit having territorial designs on China. The Russians ignored Hay and tightened their stranglehold on Manchuria. Worried about Russian advances, Japan inquired whether the United States was willing to enforce the Open Door by military means. Washington gave a firm "no," whereupon Japan signed a military alliance with Great Britain, and in 1904 precipitated the Russo-Japanese War. President Theodore Roosevelt mediated an end to the conflict, aided by the mutual exhaustion of the two adversaries, and a peace agreement was signed at Portsmouth, New Hampshire. But Roosevelt's role as mediator did not enhance America's diplomatic leverage in the Far East. Indeed, he tacitly abandoned the

Open Door by recognizing Russia's domination of Manchuria and Japan's occupation of Korea.

The Open Door, then, was less a policy than a statement of principle. It encouraged traders and investors to move into the Far East, but left them to fend for themselves once there. Yankee traders were satisfied with the arrangement. Given equal opportunity, they had long been convinced they could compete with anyone. "The open door," declared the president of the National Association of Manufacturers, an organization created to resist the spread of labor unions, "is the open shop for the world."

⌐Postscript to Global Power: The Panama Canal

America's embrace of commercial imperialism—soon to be labeled "dollar diplomacy"—did not mean that it rejected the concept of territorial dominion. The acquisition of the Panama Canal Zone represented a subtle blend of the two.

The far-flung commitments that resulted from the Spanish-American War revived interest in a canal across the isthmus of Central America, interest that dated back to the gold rush of 1849. In fact, the first need was to eliminate an obstacle that had been erected in the Gold Rush days—the Clayton-Bulwer Treaty of 1850. By that agreement, the United States and Great Britain each pledged not to undertake a canal without the permission of the other. When approached on this subject, the British proved surprisingly tractable. Their war with the South African Boers, coinciding with the Spanish-American War, had evoked much criticism in Europe, especially among Dutch and Germans, and the British were in need of friends. In America, the folklore of the revolution had mellowed, and the Irish vote was sufficiently diluted by other immigrant nationalities so that politicians no longer found it useful to "twist the lion's tail." The Hay-Pauncefote Treaty (1901), by which the United States secured a free hand in the construction and defense of an isthmian canal, marked the beginning of an Anglo-American understanding—a friendship Winston Churchill would call the most important factor in the history of the twentieth century.

The route through Nicaragua pioneered by Commodore Vanderbilt in Gold Rush days had long been the favored site for a canal, but Congress, after considerable debate, settled instead on a Panama route. Aside from offering a shorter distance, coast to coast, Panama had the advantage of possessing an existing ditch, nearly half completed. This was the work of a French company called the New Panama Canal Company. The French company had secured from Colombia, the nation that controlled the isthmus, a concession to build a canal. The concession, originally limited to 1894, had been extended to 1904, but long before that the New Panama Canal Company ran out of funds. It was eager to sell its concession to the United States, and it had two champions in Washington. One was William Nelson Cromwell, partner in the New York law firm of Sullivan and Cromwell and a masterful wirepuller, who served as the company's legal adviser. The other was Philippe Bunau-Varilla, the former chief

Constructing locks on the Panama Canal.

UPI/Bettmann.

engineer of the canal project and a stockholder in the New Panama Canal Company.

Nature also lent a hand in the selection of the Panama route. In 1902, while the Senate was discussing a canal route, Mt. Pelee on the Caribbean island of Martinique erupted, destroying the town of St. Pierre and throwing up enough lava, so it was claimed, to fill up a Central American canal. Champions of the Panama route promptly pointed out that in Nicaragua there were more volcanic eruptions and earthquakes than in Panama. Bunau-Varilla placed on the desk of each senator a Nicaraguan postage stamp featuring a smoking volcano in the middle of Lake Nicaragua. When the real volcano obligingly erupted, accompanied by an earthquake, the Senate voted for Panama. The French canal company, meantime, had agreed to sell its assets for $40 million.

After all this it would seem that Colombia's permission was the least of the problems. That, however, was not the case. The Colombian president agreed to a treaty— the Hay-Herran Treaty—granting the United States the right for a hundred years to a zone of territory across the isthmus of Panama, for which the United States was to pay $10 million down and $250,000 annually. The Colombian senate, mixing fear of Yankee influence with hope for better financial terms, rejected the treaty.

Theodore Roosevelt, who had assumed the presidency when McKinley was assassinated in September 1901, was furious. The United States was being "held up," he declared, by a "Bogota lot of jack rabbits," and one of "the future highways of civilization" was at stake. Newspapers pointed out the obvious solution: the secession of Panama from Colombia and a new treaty with an independent Panamanian government. A number of Panamanians reached the same conclusion; they thought the proposed canal could be a rich asset. In the summer of 1903 Dr. Manuel Amador,

leader of this group, journeyed to the United States to secure help. Bunau-Varilla arranged visits with both President Roosevelt and Secretary Hay. No formal assurances were given, but Amador returned to Panama under the impression that if Panamanians fomented a revolution, the United States would protect them. He also returned with a model Panamanian flag, thoughtfully sewn together by Mrs. Bunau-Varilla from cloth purchased at nearby Macy's.

The administration came away with the impression that a revolution was likely in early November. An American naval squadron, with orders to assure unimpaired transit across the isthmus by preventing armed forces from landing within fifty miles of Panama City, arrived on November 2. Revolution broke out the next day. On November 6 the United States recognized the independent republic of Panama. And on November 18 Bunau-Varilla signed a treaty with Hay granting the United States a perpetual lease on a canal zone ten miles wide in return for $10 million at once and $250,000 annually after nine years. By the agreement the United States also guaranteed the independence of Panama, in effect making the country an American "protectorate." The treaty was signed in haste—Bunau-Varilla, after all, was not a Panamanian and had no authority to negotiate a treaty—for the simple reason that a Panamanian delegation was on the way. Giving the Panamanians a say in their canal seemed to both the Frenchman and the American secretary an unnecessary risk.

Construction of the Panama Canal, a heroic story in its own right, was completed in August 1914. Roosevelt claimed the credit: "I took the Canal Zone and let Congress debate," he boasted in 1911; "and while the debate goes on the Canal does also." An exaggeration perhaps, but also a confession that manifest destiny had degenerated into rank imperialism.

SUMMARY

American interest in the Far East dated from shortly after the revolution. In 1784, a group of New York merchants sent a trading vessel to China. A lively trade in ginseng, furs, lumber, tea, and silver resulted. In 1844, the United States and China signed a treaty placing their mutual exchange on a "most favored nation" basis. The object was free commercial competition, and it became the foundation of American Far Eastern policy. A decade later, Commodore Matthew Perry forced the Japanese to sign a treaty allowing American entry into two ports of their previously closed empire.

After the Civil War, American diplomatic activity in the Pacific increased. In 1867, Secretary of State William H. Seward purchased Alaska from Russia, and the American navy took possession of Midway Island in the central Pacific. In the course of the 1870s, the United States negotiated "most favored nation" trade agreements with the island kingdoms of Hawaii and Samoa, thereby tying both of them economically to the United States. When Hawaiian rulers resisted American influence, an American-sponsored revolution broke out in 1893. Annexation was averted only by a change in American presidential administrations.

Latin America also periodically caught American attention after the Civil War, as it had before. In the 1870s, President Grant tried unsuccessfully to annex the island of Santo Domingo, and in the 1880s Secretary of State James G. Blaine pushed a plan for pan-American union. Despite such moves, foreign affairs in the 1870s and 1880s remained of secondary interest to the American public. Its attention centered instead on internal problems—depression, trusts, railroads, and labor strife. Genuine interest in the world abroad, with its attendant expansionism, awaited the decade of the 1890s.

Several factors account for the burst of American expansionism in the 1890s. Time had healed the wounds left by the Civil War and drawn the nation together. The ending of the frontier released new energies that could be deflected in new directions. In a sense, the leap across the Pacific was an extension of the leap across the continent. Latent racial bias, reinforced by social scientists' theories of Anglo-Saxon supremacy, induced Americans to believe it was their mission to extend their governmental principles to other peoples. And, perhaps most important, there was the need to trade, a realization brought home by the depression of the mid-1890s. Naval historian Alfred Thayer Mahan demonstrated the link between trade, a strong navy, and foreign bases.

A revolution that broke out in Cuba in 1895 was the catalyst for the chemistry of expansionism. The "yellow press" published sensational accounts of atrocities committed by Spanish forces in trying to suppress the revolution. When the battleship *Maine* exploded and sank in Havana harbor in February 1898, American jingoes laid the blame on Spain. Yielding to public pressure, President McKinley asked Congress for a declaration of war in April 1898.

The Spanish-American War was over in four months, though it was another four months before a peace treaty was signed. By that agreement Spain granted Cuba its independence and ceded to the United States Puerto Rico, the Philippines, and Guam. In the course of the war, the United

States annexed Hawaii and the American-protected part of Samoa.

America emerged from the Spanish-American War a world power with global responsibilities. One result was the announcement in 1899–1900 of the Open Door policy, by which the United States sought to preserve free access to the China market. The other result was the construction of the Panama Canal, made possible by an American-sponsored revolution in 1903, by which Panama gained its independence from Colombia and granted the United States a long-term lease on a canal zone.

READING SUGGESTIONS

The best surveys of the rise of American imperialism are Charles S. Campbell, *The Transformation of American Diplomacy, 1865–1890* (1976), and David Healy, *U.S. Expansionism* (1970). Walter LaFeber's *The New Empire: An Interpretation of American Expansion, 1860–1898* (1963), in the tradition of the "Wisconsin school," stresses the economic influences on foreign policy. Ernest R. May's *Imperial Democracy: The Emergence of America as a Great Power* (1961), places America's emergence in the context of international imperialism. Robert L. Beisner, *Twelve Against Empire: The Anti-Imperialists, 1898–1900* (1968), explores the attitudes and the limitations of those who opposed imperialism.

For the Spanish-American War, Frank Freidel's *The Splendid Little War* (1958) is a good, brief introduction. Allan R. Millett and Peter Maslowski, *For the Common Defense: A Military History of the United States of America* (1984), place the war in the context of the nation's military development. Leon Wolff, *Little Brown Brother* (1961), covers the tragic story of the Filipino insurrection. The pacification of the Philippines is the subject of P. W. Stanley, *A Nation in the Making: The Philippines and the United States, 1899–1921* (1975), and the Cuban experience is treated by David Healy, *The United States in Cuba, 1898–1902* (1963).

On the Open Door policy, see Kenton J. Clymer, *John Hay: The Gentleman as Diplomat* (1975), and for the Panama affair, look at Howard K. Beale, *Theodore Roosevelt and the Rise of America to World Power* (1956).

7

THE PROGRESSIVE IMPULSE: 1900–1910

It was not easy being a Republican in Kansas in 1896. Populist oratory seared the prairie, and William Jennings Bryan was the hero of the day. But William Allen White, 28-year-old editor of the *Emporia Gazette*, felt equal to the challenge. He wrote ringing editorials denouncing Populism and worked hard to earn money to buy an elegant house for his young wife. Nonetheless, White lost his temper when he was cornered on the streets of Emporia by a group of fifteen or twenty Populists, who jeered and jostled him until his white linen summer suit was a mess. Aflame with rage, he stalked into his newspaper office, dipped his pen in acid, and dashed off an editorial. "What's the matter with Kansas?" he sputtered.

We all know; yet here we are at it again. We have an old moss-back Jacksonian who snorts and howls because there is a bathtub in the State House; we are running that old jay for governor. . . . We have raked the old ash heap of failure in the state and found an old human hoop skirt who has failed as a businessman, who has failed as an editor, who has failed as a preacher, and we are going to run him for Congressman-at-Large. . . . We have discovered a kid without a law practice and have decided to run him for Attorney General. Then, for fear some hint that the state had become respectable might percolate through the civilized portions of the nation, we have decided to send three or four harpies out lecturing, telling the people that Kansas is raising hell and letting the corn go to weeds. . . .

Oh, this is a state to be proud of! We are a people who can hold up our heads! We don't need population, we don't need wealth, we don't need well-dressed men on the streets, we don't need cities in the fertile prairies; you bet we don't! . . . Whoop it up for the ragged trousers; put the lazy, greasy fizzle who can't pay his debts on the altar, and bow down and worship him. . . . What we need is not the respect of our fellowmen, but the chance to get something for nothing.

White slammed the editorial onto a spike, strode down to the railroad station, and caught a train for Colorado and a brief vacation. He returned a week later to find himself a national celebrity. "What's the Matter With Kansas?" was being reprinted by newspapers across the country; housewives, bankers, even the Speaker of the House of Representatives wrote him letters of congratulation. White had voiced the middle-class values of hard work, thrift, and self-help. America had always been a middle-class society, a nation of enterprisers and entrepreneurs. Industrialization and the growing complexity of the economy broadened the middle class by creating a host of new specialists—engineers, technicians, salesmen, accountants, civil service functionaries.

For such people, the Populist class appeal had no meaning, and Populist mistrust of business enterprise was unsettling. They were not averse to change: The reshaping of America was a middle-class tradition, as homespun as an Andrew Jackson or an Abraham Lincoln. But they insisted that change be made within the framework of middle-class values and without violating the spirit of free enterprise. That is why William Allen White became an instant celebrity in 1896. He spoke for the urban middle class, and these were the people who would have to support the cause of reform in urban, industrial America.

⊔A Reform Mentality

There was much to trouble the American middle class in 1900. Prosperity had returned, but memories of the depression lingered. Those with occupations created by advancing technology were not wholly secure. Labor strife, farmer radicalism, urban corruption, and unprecedented immigration added to the unease. To the new middle class, nearly all of them white, Prot-

---

(*Chapter opening photo*) Theodore Roosevelt, who regarded the presidency as "a bully pulpit."

estant, and Yankee—or at least second-generation North European—immigration seemed a particular threat. By 1900 immigrants were streaming into the country at the rate of a million a year, and native-born Americans viewed the newcomers as very different from themselves. Since colonial times, immigrants to America had come mainly from the British Isles, Germany, and Scandinavia. The new immigrants of 1900 came mostly from Eastern Europe, Greece, and Italy. The "old" had been mainly Protestant and farm-minded; the "new" were Roman Catholic or Jewish and congregated in cities.

In the past, immigrants had been, for the most part, people of low income. They had always congregated in groups determined by nationality and language, and they had always earned lower wages. But this same pattern, when followed by the new immigrants, was perceived as clannish and alien. The native Protestant middle class blamed immigrants for living in filthy, crime-infested ghettoes and condemned them for following machine politicians. The *Passing of the Great Race*, a 1916 book which attempted to demonstrate that North European peoples were superior to others, was a digest of these apprehensions. In response to what was perceived as a threat, the "native" middle class formed organizations such as the Daughters of the American Revolution, insisted that the public schools inculcate American values, enlarged urban police forces, and advanced Prohibition to encourage sobriety among the newcomers. In short, much of what passed for Progressive reform was a response to misplaced fears.

THE PROGRESSIVE IDEOLOGY

The label "Progressive" was coming into use by 1900. It set middle-class reformers apart from Populists and from Mugwump

liberals. The Progressives had much in common with the Mugwumps of the 1880s. They were middle-class, predominantly urban, often well-educated, and committed to free enterprise capitalism. But Progressives were more receptive than liberals of the Gilded Age to the use of government to attain social ends. Liberals, going back to Jefferson and Tom Paine, had always feared government power. The Jacksonian slogan, "The world is governed too much," was a distillation of liberal thought. The Progressives also opposed power, but the power they feared was the tyranny of utilities, railroads, banks, and trusts. Against such enemies they saw government as a potential ally. They proposed to use government to regulate, humanize, or tear apart these new tyrants, and in so doing they gave a new definition to the term "liberal."

The Populists had sought to unite producers and failed. The Progressives found unity in being consumers, and succeeded. Merchants, farmers, professionals, and factory hands had conflicting interests as producers; as consumers of water, electricity, rail services, and manufactured goods, they had much in common. Much of the governmental activity promoted by Progressives was aimed at consumers—pure food and drug laws, lower tariffs, antitrust legislation, railroad rate regulation, honest government, and lower taxes.

These programs in fact reflected less an ideology than an attitude. The Progressives were activists, out to change the world. They rejected the abstract, formal logic of laissez faire and its scientific concomitant, Social Darwinism. They preferred instead the truth that comes from experience and common sense. They believed not in natural laws that explained all behavior, but in changing processes that had to be constantly reinterpreted. "The life of the law," declared the great jurist Oliver Wendell Holmes, "has not been logic; it has been experience." Holmes viewed the United

States Constitution as a living being, an organism capable of adapting to the needs of modern times. "The case before us," he once observed, "must be considered in the light of our whole experience and not merely in that of what was said a hundred years ago."

Through the use of history and experience, Progressives thought they could understand the social processes and manage them for human benefit. Thus poverty was not a function of character, as Andrew Carnegie believed, but a product of environment, lack of education, and the economic system. Through "creative intelligence," said educator John Dewey, human beings could improve their surroundings and enhance their lives.

THE NEW ECONOMICS

Classical economics, the bedrock of Victorian conservatism, was another target of reformers. Economists John R. Commons and Richard T. Ely at the University of Wisconsin rejected the classic supposition that economics contained eternal truths, such as the "law of supply and demand." They considered economics a pragmatic, inductive science, susceptible to experiment. And instead of accepting the exis-

---

"The Fourteenth Amendment Does Not Enact Mr. Herbert Spencer's Social Statics"

Justice Oliver Wendell Holmes, a fixture on the Supreme Court for thirty years, was known in his day as the "great dissenter." In one of his most famous dissents, *Lochner* v. *New York* (1905), he objected to the tendency of judges to interpret the Constitution as embodying free enterprise. The Lochner case involved a New York statute that limited the hours of bakery employees to ten a day or sixty a week. The court majority held that the New York law violated the due process clause of the Fourteenth Amendment because it deprived bakery employers and employees of their freedom of contract.

This case is decided upon an economic theory which a large part of the country does not entertain. If it were a question whether I agreed with that theory, I should desire to study it further and long before making up my mind. But I do not conceive that to be my duty, because I strongly believe that my agreement or disagreement has nothing to do with the right of a majority to embody their opinions in law. It is settled by various decisions of this court that state constitutions and state laws may regulate life in many ways which we as legislators might think as injudicious or if you like as tyrannical as this, and which equally with this interfere with the liberty to contract. Sunday laws and usury laws are ancient examples. A more modern one is the prohibition of lotteries. The liberty of the citizen to do as he likes so long as he does not interfere with the liberty of others to do the same, which has been a shibboleth for some well-known writers, is interfered with by school laws, by the Post Office, by every state or municipal institution which takes his money for purposes thought desirable, whether he likes it or not. The Fourteenth Amendment does not enact Mr. Herbert Spencer's Social Statics.

Justice Oliver Wendell Holmes, Dissenting, in *Lochner* v. *New York*, 1905

tence of poverty and explaining it with such dismal "truths" as the iron law of wages,[*] they sought to enter ethical and humanitarian factors into their equations.

At the University of Chicago, economist Thorstein Veblen took aim at Adam Smith's "invisible hand." This was the metaphor Smith had used to demonstrate that private selfishness (the profit motive) in a freely competitive situation brings public good (maximum production). Not always, or even often, said Veblen. To make a maximum profit, Veblen pointed out, business requires stable prices. And to maintain those prices, businesses adjust production to perceived demand. That results in something less than maximum production or maximum social benefit. The same is true, Veblen noticed, with regard to investment. The very wealthy do not invest any income in excess of need, as classicists had theorized; instead, they indulge in "conspicuous consumption," and spend their wealth on palaces and yachts. One solution, Veblen suggested in *The Theory of the Leisure Class* (1899), would be a graduated income tax so that the government might make productive use of that excess wealth for the benefit of all.

Veblen and other pioneers of the new economics found flaws in the theory of laissez faire, but they had no intention of discarding it. The Progressives were nothing if not capitalists. Their object was to repair the free enterprise system, to make it work more smoothly, more humanely, more effi-

ciently. Businessmen in fact participated in the movement and benefited from it. Many recognized that the competitive game needed a referee, and they welcomed government regulation. Some regulations amounted to publicly financed quality-control mechanisms. The federal Meat Inspection Act of 1906, one of the biggest victories of the consumer movement, blessed an industry with government inspection and approval of its product. What businessman could object to that?

Progressives certainly thought of themselves as reformers, but to label them conservatives is not amiss. By changing the American political and social system, they helped to preserve it. Theirs was a response to the challenges of industrialism, another step in modernization. Their legacy is the world we live in today, a world of bureaucrats and technicians, giant corporations and limited provisions for social welfare. One historian has labeled this blend "corporate liberalism," and it would seem to be as good a description as any.

⊔ New Aims and New Elements: Women and Blacks

Progressives resembled the Mugwumps in many ways and borrowed liberally from the Populists, but their movement differed from the earlier ones in two important respects. Where popular support for the earlier movements was limited, progressivism had broad mass appeal. Second, as part of the mass appeal, progressivism attracted elements of society that had never before had much impact on the course of events—women, blacks, and industrial workers.

The mass appeal was due in part to the work of journalists writing in mass circulation magazines such as *McClure's, Collier's, Cosmopolitan,* and *Everybody's.* Lincoln Steffens, editor of *McClure's,* in 1902 began a

---

[*] In his *Essay on the Principles of Population* (1799), English clergyman Thomas R. Malthus, using the population increase of the American colonies as a basis, argued that population increases exponentially (1, 2, 4, 8, 16, 32), whereas food production increases only arithmetically (1, 2, 3, 4, 5, 6), and predicted an inevitable world food crisis. A few years later, economist David Ricardo posed an "iron law of wages," which declared that wages had to hover at the subsistence level because of overpopulation and competition for jobs.

series on urban corruption, which he later published as a book titled *The Shame of the Cities.* In that same year, Ida Tarbell began in *McClure's* her devastating "History of the Standard Oil Company," which exposed the ruthless methods by which John D. Rockefeller had built his business empire. The reading public gobbled *McClure's,* and other magazines followed its lead. *Everybody's* looked into stock market practices, *Collier's* published a piece on patent medicine frauds, and *Cosmopolitan* commissioned David Graham Phillips's article "Treason of the Senate," which brought to light the cozy ties between Congress and big business.

The writing was often sensationalized, the facts sometimes blurred. Theodore Roosevelt dismissed the journalists as "muckrakers," referring to a character in John Bunyan's *Pilgrim's Progress* who turned down a celestial crown and kept his muckrake so he could devote his life to stirring up dirt. But the journalists were the literary voices of progressivism. By exposing the flaws in American society, they prompted demands for reform.

WOMEN AS PROGRESSIVES

Women were among the most devoted disciples of the muckrakers, for it was they who subscribed to the mass-circulation magazines. Much of what the muckrakers exposed, moreover, seemed to be within the female province. There were still strong taboos against the appearance of women in the public arena, whether on the stage or in the lecture hall. But by 1900 women had found a way to circumvent the restrictions. Woman was the heart of the family, they pointed out, and no one disagreed; woman was responsible for family unity and family integrity. It followed that any threat to the family was also within her sphere, even if it meant that she had to emerge from the home to confront it.

Among the more obvious threats were liquor, impure food and drugs, child labor, and vice. Women might also be expected to interest themselves in schools, libraries, utility rates, and streetcar facilities. These subjects comprised almost the entire agenda of Progressive reform at the municipal level.

The temperance movement, female-dominated since its inception in the 1830s, gave many women their first experience in the public arena. The Women's Christian Temperance Union (WCTU), organized in 1874, became under the leadership of Frances Willard (1839–1898) a vehicle for broad-scale social change. The WCTU was involved in women's suffrage, dress reform, populism, and labor agitation. Although the WCTU won few victories until after 1900, when concern for drinking excess became mingled with middle-class alarm over immigration and urban vice, it was a foundation stone for Progressive reform.

Women's clubs were another bridge from domestic to public life. The club movement began about 1890 and flourished throughout the Progressive era. The club movement was part of the search for order so characteristic of the age. While men formed professional organizations such as the American Medical Association, women organized the General Federation of Women's Clubs and the National Consumers League. The clubs also served psychological needs, for they provided an outlet for the energies of middle-class women. Such women often felt caught in what Jane Addams called "the snare of preparation." They were intelligent and educated, yet barred from occupations that carried responsibility and authority.

The clubs at first focused on intellectual and spiritual uplift, but before long they became interested in community problems. They often started with charity work, moved to the investigation of wrongs, and ended by promoting corrective legislation.

International Museum of Photography at George Eastman House.

Children tending machines in a textile mill.

The General Federation of Women's Clubs campaigned for pure food and drug laws, conservation of natural resources, higher age of consent laws, and abolition of child labor.

The most effective of the women-dominated instruments of change was the National Consumers League, an organization that was essentially the lengthened shadow of one person, Florence Kelley. Educated at Cornell and a graduate of Northwestern University Law School, Kelley had her social conscience pricked by a stay in Europe (during which she was briefly married to a Marxist) and a sojourn at Hull House. While studying law, she led a crusade that resulted in the passage of an Illinois law limiting women to an eight-hour day in factory work. The act also created the state position of factory inspector, to which Governor Altgeld appointed her in 1894, the year of the Pullman strike. She moved to New York in 1899 to head the National Consumers League and began a nationwide campaign for food and drug regulation and laws regulating the working conditions of women and children.

The work of a University of Wisconsin sociologist, Edward A. Ross, provided a strong theoretical underpinning for Kelley's consumer crusade. In *Sin and Society* (1907), Ross pointed out that morals had not kept up with technology and the growing complexity of business organization. As a result, wrongs that went unrecognized were being committed every day—stock watering, price discrimination, kickbacks, adulteration of food, failure to install safety devices. Company managers, small cogs in a giant wheel, did not feel responsible for such wrongs, and the true owners, the stockholders, were remote and often unaware. "There is nothing like distance to disinfect dividends," said Ross. To correct this, the public had to realize that "sin evolves along with society. . . . Our social organization has developed to a stage where the old righteousness is not enough. We need an annual supplement to the [Ten Commandments]."

The Pure Food and Drug Act and the Federal Meat Inspection Act, both passed in 1906, were the outstanding successes of the consumer movement, Kelley's lobbying efforts, and the journalism of a muckraker, Upton Sinclair. In 1906, Sinclair published *The Jungle*, a novel set in the Chicago meat-packing plants. It described the piles of meat stored in great rooms aswarm with rats, and the inattention of workers when the meat, rats, and rat poison all went into the sausage hopper together. The irrepressible Mr. Dooley offered his version of what happened when President Roosevelt read the book: "Tiddy was toying with a light breakfast an' idly turnin' over the pages of the new book . . . Suddenly he rose from th' table, and cryin': 'I'm pizened,' began throwin' sausages out iv the window . . . since then the President, like the rest iv us, has become a viggytarian." With Roosevelt's hearty backing, Congress passed both pieces of consumer legislation later that year.

Women played a major role in the Progressive movement, but they were also targets of Progressives' concern. Since the Civil War, women had been moving into the industrial work force, and by 1900 they were taking over clerical and secretarial jobs as well. By that date, 21 percent of all American women (28 percent in the cities) worked outside the home. Coupled with this was a growing independence in living arrangements. One third of the unmarried female workers lived apart from their parents by 1900. There was thus a widening gap between the behavior of women and the traditional belief that their place was in the home. When journalists, charity workers, and reformers discovered the working girl in the 1890s, they were shocked; they instantly regarded her as a problem. They labeled women who worked and lived away from home as "homeless women" or "women adrift." The double meaning of such terms reveals the assumption that women living outside the family were on the edge of disrepute, that they were a potential source of urban disorder. Most writers on the subject also agreed that acquired characteristics—such as poor health from overwork—could be transmitted through heredity to children. The work life of young women thus endangered their future lives as mothers.

There was less agreement on what to do about it. Conservatives argued that women should be returned to their proper sphere, the home, while feminists applauded the new independence and demanded that all occupations be opened to women. Progressives generally took a middle view; they accepted the fact of the working woman, but they wanted to protect her living environment and improve her working conditions through state regulation. Typical of such legislation was an Oregon statute that limited women's work to ten hours a day. This statute led to a crucial test for all such social legislation before the Supreme Court in the case of *Muller* v. *Oregon* (1908).

The National Consumers League, chief sponsor of the law, obtained the services of Louis Brandeis to present its case. A brilliant attorney worth nearly a million dollars by the time he was forty, Brandeis had been inspired by the labor strife of the 1890s to seek means of making the law serve factory workers as well as it served their employers. The brief he presented to the Supreme Court in *Muller* v. *Oregon* was a landmark in American jurisprudence. Only 2 of its 104 pages dealt with legal logic and precedent; for Brandeis's argument, there was no precedent. Instead, he disgorged upon the startled justices a huge array of social statistics, gathered by factory inspectors and investigative committees both in Europe and the United States. The data demonstrated that laws limiting working hours were within the state's "police powers." They protected the health, safety, morals, and welfare of the people.

The legal fraternity branded Brandeis a dangerous anarchist, but the Supreme Court voted unanimously that the ten-hour law was constitutional. By singling out women for special treatment, both the act and the Brandeis brief revealed a chivalry that many women today would find unacceptable. The importance of the contest is that for the first time, the Supreme Court accepted the principle that the law might evolve in accordance with new social needs. Its acknowledgment of statistical evidence, moreover, formed an important precedent for the Court's reliance on similar data in ordering the desegregation of schools a half-century later.

BLACK PROGRESSIVES: THE NAACP

In 1908, the year of the Brandeis brief, muckraker Ray Stannard Baker did a series on black living conditions published under the title *Following the Color Line*. Baker ended with the conventional praise for Booker T. Washington and his program for elevating blacks in American society. To Baker's amazement, his series was vigorously criticized by blacks themselves. Baker soon discovered there was a fundamental shift under way in the thinking of the black community. Booker T. Washington was not the god he had once been thought to be.

Born in slavery, Booker T. Washington rose to fame through his own abilities and white benevolence. He had been educated by kindly whites, and the school he ran, Tuskegee Institute, subsisted on white charity. The private benevolence of whites, however, was accompanied—and perhaps made possible by—a rigid system of public segregation that made blacks second-class citizens. Realizing that racial bias permeated American society, Washington decided that the best hope was to work within the system, rather than against it. Invited to address the white-organized Atlanta Cotton Exposition in 1895, Washington took the opportunity to set forth his philosophy. Blacks ought to accept social segregation and political disenfranchisement, Washington argued, because there was little they could do about it anyway. They should concentrate instead on economic advancement, on obtaining the skills to get ahead in the world. Once they had im-

New York Public Library Picture Collection.

Booker T. Washington.

proved their position and won respect, social and political equality would come naturally. Washington's remarks appealed to his all-white audience; it was precisely what southerners especially wanted to hear. A black population with manual skills and a proper deference was the southern ideal. The "Atlanta compromise" was applauded everywhere: Booker T. Washington became the spokesman for America's black community.

Washington's policy had some success. In the decade after 1900, the illiteracy rate among blacks fell from 44 to 30 percent, while the number of southern farms under black ownership increased four times as fast as the growth of the black population. But these small advances were more than matched by heavier social and political repression. Southern political oratory became more outrageously racist than ever before. Former Populists, such as Tom Watson of Georgia, became professional race-baiters, touring the lecture circuit to harangue audiences with their outrageous views. Deepening racism can be seen in the increase in lynchings. Mob executions averaged 187 a year during the 1890s. The rate fell after 1900, but only because fewer whites were murdered. Some lynchings were announced in advance, and people came by train to witness the spectacle. Such was the mood that when Theodore Roosevelt invited Booker T. Washington to dinner at the White House in 1901, the southern press went wild. "Entertaining that nigger," roared South Carolina Senator (Pitchfork Ben) Tillman, would "necessitate our killing a thousand niggers in the South before they will learn their place again." By 1910, lynch mobs had filled about half of Tillman's quota.

The government's policy not only condoned segregation; it encouraged it. In 1896, the U.S. Supreme Court in *Plessy* v. *Ferguson* upheld a Louisiana Jim Crow law with the doctrine that "separate but equal"

facilities on railroads were constitutional. In succeeding years, southern legislatures provided for racial segregation in every conceivable public facility, from schools to toilets and drinking fountains. They also sought to dismantle the Fifteenth Amendment, which had given blacks the right to vote. The device was the grandfather clause, pioneered by Louisiana in 1898. This was a proviso in the state's election law that confined voting rights to persons whose grandfathers could vote prior to the Reconstruction Acts. Since only whites could meet that qualification, blacks were automatically disenfranchised. Every southern state but Tennessee followed suit.

After 1900, blacks became increasingly disenchanted with Tuskegeeism, as Ray Baker discovered. The most articulate of these was W. E. B. DuBois, Massachusetts-born and a Harvard Ph.D., who taught at Atlanta's black university. DuBois considered Booker T. Washington's program only another form of slavery, a mechanism by which southern industrialists obtained a cheap, submissive labor force. Tuskegeeism, said DuBois, provided "a voteless herd to run the machines and wash the dishes for the new aristocracy. Negroes would be educated enough to be useful but not enough, or not in the right way, to be able to assert self-respect." In *The Souls of Black Folk* (1903), Dubois blasted industrial education and suggested instead that a black elite, "the talented tenth," be cultivated to instill self-confidence and tear down the barriers that held blacks in submission.

In 1909, Washington's critics formed the National Association for the Advancement of Colored People (NAACP), and DuBois became its director of research and publications. DuBois and his white allies focused on the grandfather clauses, and in 1915 they succeeded in having the Supreme Court declare them unconstitutional. Left untouched by this decision, however, were

New York Public Library Picture Collection.

George Washington Carver. As director of agricultural research at Tuskegee Institute, Alabama, Carver developed hundreds of products that could be made out of southern crops, notably peanuts, sweet potatoes, and soybeans. His discoveries increased the market value of those crops and encouraged a more diversified crop-system.

the parallel "understanding" clauses by which black voters, as a condition of registration, could be called upon to explain features of the state or federal constitutions to the satisfaction of white registrars. Nor was the NAACP able to prevent lynchings or see that the guilty were prosecuted afterward. When blacks moved north to escape repression, they met other forms of racism in housing and job discrimination. The mass movement of blacks northward in search of jobs during World War I triggered terrible race riots in St. Louis and Chicago. Blacks made little progress in the Progressive era, but among themselves they did experience an awakening. And they found new, more militant leadership in DuBois. That at least was something on which to build.

CURING THE ILLS OF DEMOCRACY: THE CITIES AND THE STATES

The attempt to reform city government preceded the Progressive movement by some years. For a century and more, Americans had complained about their cities. Not only were they full of sin and corruption, but they were also full of anonymous, unneighborly people, many of them newcomers to the American experience, who tolerated boss rule. The "cleanup" of a city was considered such a major achievement that it frequently launched a reformer's political career. Grover Cleveland and Theodore Roosevelt each came to national attention as a result of their efforts at municipal reform, Cleveland in Buffalo in the 1880s,

Roosevelt as New York City's police commissioner in the 1890s.

In 1888, the British observer James Bryce decided that "there is no denying that the government of cities is the one conspicuous failure of the United States." Middle-class reformers, who tended to blame urban problems on corrupt politicians who catered to the poor, promptly took up the cry. In 1890, Andrew D. White, president of Cornell University, wrote that "without the slightest exaggeration . . . the city governments of the United States are the worst in Christendom—the most expensive, the most inefficient, and the most corrupt." Four years later, the old liberal reformer, E. L. Godkin, claimed that the condition of the cities was "bringing democratic institutions into contempt the world over, and imperiling some of the best things in our civilization."

A closer examination suggests that the cities were getting a bad rap. The 1870s and 1880s, after all, saw the erection of New York's Central Park, the Brooklyn Bridge, and the Boston Public Library,

each a brilliant synthesis of art and engineering, and each a product of municipal enterprise. The cities, of course, had their problems. In the last quarter of the nineteenth century, they grew at an explosive rate, averaging in some cases a 50 percent increase every ten years. The advent of the streetcar allowed people to move into suburbs, thereby creating new demands on municipal facilities. It was in this period that the major cities installed water mains and sewage lines on a scale that dwarfed the famed aqueducts of Rome. One modern scholar states flatly that at the turn of the century "in America's cities, the supply of water was the most abundant, the street lights were the most brilliant, the parks the grandest, the libraries the largest, and the public transportation the fastest of any place in the world." Most important, they accomplished all this while remaining solvent and financially sound. In 1900, municipal bonds were safer investments than bonds issued by railroads or many other giants of the business world.

Why, then, the bad image? It was, in

A horse-drawn streetcar of the 1890s. The beginnings of public transportation allowed people to move to the outer edge of cities and to form the first suburbs.

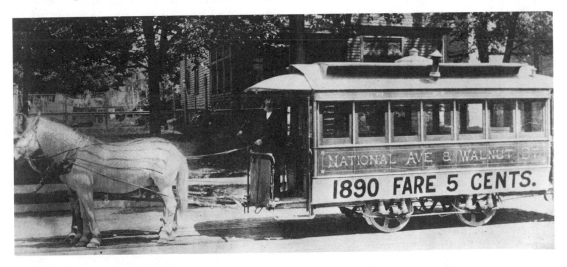

NATIONAL AVE & WALNUT ST.

1890 FARE 5 CENTS.

State Historical Society of Wisconsin.

CLIO'S FOCUS: Daniel Burnham and the City Beautiful

Make no little plans. They have no magic to stir men's blood and probably themselves will not be realized. Make big plans; aim high in hope and work, remembering that a noble, logical diagram once recorded will never die, but long after we are gone will be a living thing, asserting itself with evergrowing insistency. Remember that our sons and grandsons are going to do things that would stagger us. Let your watchword be order and your beacon beauty.

This advice, given by Daniel Hudson Burnham (1846–1912) in the course of an otherwise long-forgotten speech, was a measure of the man. He was physically large, he was among the giants of American architecture, and his plans for America's cities were nothing if not big.

The idea of city planning itself was new. Like Topsy in *Uncle Tom's Cabin*, cities in the nineteenth century were not conceived; they "jes' growed." And the pattern of development was governed not by logic, but by the speculative opportunities of building contractors and streetcar companies. Such chaotic land usage offended the Progressives' sense of order. The filth and lawlessness made Progressives uneasy. And the consequent emergence of boss-led machines inspired them to reform. Reform Darwinism suggested the means—a clean, pleasant, orderly environment was a prerequisite to the restoration of moral order. The City Beautiful was a natural concomitant to progressivism. Daniel Burnham was its architect.

Burnham's opportunity to plan big came in 1893 when he was chosen chief architect for Chicago's Columbian Exposition, a world's fair commemorating the four hundredth anniversary of Columbus's discovery of America. Burnham's concept was to make the fair everything the city was not. In the midst of Chicago's smoke, soot, and grime, Burnham built a White City—monumental edifices in the classic style, plastered with stucco and painted a gleaming white. Where Chicago was cramped, monotonous, and ugly, Burnham's vistas were big, broad, and beautiful. And, to the astonishment of all, he completed it in a few short months.

The fair was a huge success; "city planning" became the order of the day. Every urban center aspired to become the City Beautiful. In 1901, Burnham was placed on a commission to redesign the center of Washington, D.C., between the capitol and the Potomac. The result was the construction of the grand mall that forms an axis between the capitol and the Washington Monument. Burnham was next commissioned to prepare a plan for San Francisco after the city was destroyed by earthquake and fire in 1906. In 1909, Chicago engaged him to form a master plan for that city. And before his death in 1912, he reshaped Manila and Baguio in the Philippines.

Following Burnham's advice, the architects of the City Beautiful laid plans of monumental proportions. They razed tenements and built great plazas and broad avenues punctuated with monuments. Nearly every city developed a civic center plan—public buildings spaced around a broad plaza containing fountains and gardens. The movement, to be sure, had its disadvantages and its critics. There was an air of detachment in the planning, an isolation from the daily needs of the people. The grandiose buildings of the civic center held the spellbound citizen at arm's length. Monuments sometimes clogged important traffic arteries.

In the years after Burnham's death, the City Beautiful yielded to the City Efficient, as planners concentrated on such mundane things as traffic flow, industrial zones, and planned neighborhoods. The City Efficient was another expression of urban progressivism, and although its adherents scoffed at many of the projects of the City Beautiful, they shared some of the same goals. City planners in a later age, in fact, would strive for both beauty and efficiency. For each rested on Daniel Burnham's masterful insight that the physical arrangement of a city vitally affects the welfare and happiness of the people who live in it.

large measure, precisely that—a matter of image. Cities had always had a bad reputation among rural-minded Americans. But their problems seemed worse at the turn of the century because they were exaggerated by certain elements vying for control. Most cities at the turn of the century were a triangle of tension among three groups: the professional civil servants, such as policemen, firemen, water and sewage engineers; middle-class businessmen, who normally dominated the executive branch, as well as the independent park, library, and debt-retirement commissions; and neighborhood retailers, often of immigrant background, who controlled the legislative branch, the board of aldermen, or city council. The urban legislature was the chief forum for the working-class ward politicians, and it was it and they who were the chief targets of the city's critics.

THE "NEW" IMMIGRANTS

European immigrants, streaming through New York's Ellis Island port of entry in record numbers, heightened the concern of middle-class reformers for law, order,

and the future of the cities. Immigration had been rising almost steadily through the nineteenth century, and it peaked in the first decade of the twentieth, with people arriving at the rate of about 1 million a year. It was not just the numbers but also the character of the new arrivals that worried Progressives. Progressives themselves drew a distinction between "old immigrants" and "new." "Old immigrants," who had arrived in the country before 1890, were mostly from northern and western Europe. They were farmers or tradesmen and mostly Protestant (except for the Irish); they were therefore easily assimilated into American society. (Progressives conveniently overlooked the anti-immigrant movements of the pre–Civil War years.) By contrast, the "new immigrants," coming to the United States after 1890, were from southern and eastern Europe for the most part, and they were predominantly Catholic, Jewish, or Eastern Orthodox in religious faith. Few had any skills; laborer, farmhand, and servant were the most frequently cited occupations. Unskilled factory jobs drew them to the cities of the Northeast and Midwest, where they congregated in ethnic ghettoes and (so it seemed to middle-class reformers) resisted assimilation.

The portrait of the "new immigrants," like the Progressives' perception of the city, was overdrawn and given to lurid stereotypes. It is true that the regional and religious character of American immigration did change about the turn of the century, but the impact on American society was not as great as middle-class reformers had feared. To begin with, the country itself was larger than ever before. The 8.2 million immigrants who arrived between 1900 and 1909 constituted only 10 percent of the population, whereas the 2.8 million Irish and Germans who arrived in the 1850s amounted to 12.1 percent of the overall population.

Another factor of note is that the "new immigrants" were mostly males. Only the Jews migrated as families. Most of the others—Italians, Slavs, Greeks, and Rus-

sians—were young men, lured to the United States by economic opportunity, driven from Europe by the threat of coerced military service. Many of these had no intention of staying. They hoped only to earn enough money to buy a farm in the old country, finance a sister's dowry, or secure education for their children. More than 30 percent of the people who arrived in the United States after 1900 returned to their European homelands.

Nevertheless, the nation's foreign-born, driven by poverty into the poorer sections of the nation's cities (just as the Irish had been a generation earlier), contributed to the rising alarm over urban corruption. Cleaning up the cities became a major aim of Progressives. Their concern climaxed with the publication in 1904 of Lincoln Steffens's tale of boss rule, *The Shame of the Cities*. The reform of the cities centered on efforts to bypass the elected officials,

Urban congestion in New York City—Mulberry St. ca. 1900.

Library of Congress.

whose roots were in the ethnic ghettoes and who governed by selling favors. One Progressive answer was the city manager, a professional administrator indirectly responsible to elected officials but independent enough to govern without bribery or favoritism. A number of cities experimented with such devices, but with limited success. Municipal reform was generally sporadic and short-lived. When reformers tired of the game, the bosses crept back. Indeed, many of the urban political machines described by Lincoln Steffens actually provided useful social services. They found people jobs, lent a sympathetic ear to the needs of the poor, and conveyed a sense of belonging. Not until the federal government entered the field of social welfare, beginning in the 1930s, did a cleanup of the cities, of the sort demanded by Progressives, become possible.

Part of the problem was that cities were puppets of the states. The states prescribed the forms of urban government and hence limited the amount of change that could be introduced. And all too often the trail of graft and corruption led from municipal courthouse to state capitol. States, like cities, were often controlled by a political machine, such as that led by Tom Platt in New York or Boies Penrose in Pennsylvania. The bosses of 1900 were less flamboyant than the spoilsmen of the Gilded Age, and they thrived on franchises and tax favors rather than the "spoils" of patronage. But that, in a sense, made them the more insidious, because they were seldom seen or heard. "Invisible government," Progressives called it. They aimed to restore state government to the people.

Wisconsin led the way. Robert M. LaFollette, a self-made lawyer, spent an undistinguished ten years in Congress before deciding to run for governor in 1898. Wisconsin, which had coasted for years under the mellow governance of old-guard Republicans and conservative Democrats, was never the same again. Pungent, sarcastic, piercing, his fists banging home his points, Fighting Bob could play an audience like a violinist at a concert. Some called him a Populist, but LaFollette never put class against class or catered to farmers. He spoke to the middle class, and he knew its enemies—railroads, lumber barons, and stand-pat politicians. His 1898 fight was the opening shot of the Progressive movement. He lost that battle, but he came back in 1900 and won.

As governor, LaFollette pushed through an indifferent legislature a host of novelties:

An industrial commission, the first of its kind, to supervise the safety and well-being of factory workers.

Workers' compensation, an insurance system for compensating workers for job-related injuries without regard to fault.

A state railroad commission that slashed rates and forbade rebates.

A direct primary for the popular selection of party nominees.

A conservation program that vastly enlarged the state forests.

Tripled appropriations for the state university.

By 1906, when LaFollette moved from the governorship to the United States Senate, his name was magic. He had built a machine that dominated the state as effectively as Tammany ever controlled New York, but without the graft. "If I owned Pennsylvania as Bob LaFollette owns Wisconsin," growled Boies Penrose, "my life would be a perpetual holiday. All that he has to do before election is to telephone home and send his latest photograph." Much of LaFollette's strength was due to the fact that business benefited from his program nearly as much as consumers. Railroads learned that lower rates generated more shipping business, and they saved money because they no longer had to give kickbacks to customers and free tickets to politicians. Utilities favored state regulation because it was more uniform and less drastic than municipal codes. And by stressing efficiency and using experts in government, LaFollette created a political climate that attracted new business. So successful was his program that it was widely imitated in other states as the "Wisconsin idea." Oklahoma, when it entered the union in 1907, incorporated the entire program into its state constitution, adding for good measure statewide prohibition of liquor. This reform, however progressive, had not occurred to anyone in Wisconsin.

⊔ Theodore Roosevelt: Patrician Progressive

The beginnings of progressivism in the cities and states are hard to pinpoint, for municipal reform in the 1890s often seemed only an echo of the Populist uproar. Progressivism in the federal government can be dated more precisely: It began with the accession of Theodore Roosevelt to the presidency. After a maverick career in the state assembly and the New York police department, Roosevelt had capitalized on his war reputation to win the New York governorship in 1899 (taking a page from George Washington's biography, he had worn his military uniform to the Republican nominating convention). Never a man to take orders, Roosevelt as governor soon ran afoul of party boss Tom Platt. In 1900, the Platt machine saw an opportunity to rid itself of Roosevelt by sending him to Washington, and a combination of friends and enemies landed him the vice-presidential slot on McKinley's reelection ticket. McKinley's campaign manager, Mark Hanna, whose political philosophy was capsulized in the admonition "Stand pat," foresaw trouble. "Don't any of you realize," he asked associates after the nominating convention, "that there's only one life between that madman and the Presidency?"

In September 1901, that life was taken by an anarchist's bullet, and "that madman" became president.

ROOSEVELT AS PRESIDENT

Actually, Roosevelt and Hanna developed a quite cordial relationship. At the end of Roosevelt's presidency, a friend could recall only one occasion when the two argued. The subject was the Grangers, the agrarian reformers of the seventies. Hanna thought they were useful citizens; Roosevelt claimed they were maniacs. Roosevelt also got on well with the Republican conservatives in Congress, such as Senator Nelson Aldrich, who represented Rhode Island technically and Wall Street in reality. Such relationships were not a pose, for Roosevelt was a man of deeply conservative instincts. In the 1890s he had denounced populism as "semi-socialistic" and Bryan's speeches as "criminal." He respected labor's right to strike, but he thought mobs of workingmen ought to be handled by "regulars, or by good State Guards, not over-scrupulous about bloodshed." He thought political radicalism could best be handled by "taking ten or a dozen of their leaders out, standing . . . them against a wall, and shooting them dead."

But Roosevelt also had the patrician's disdain for greedy merchants, as well as the patrician's attitude of responsibility toward the downtrodden. He abhorred disorder, but he was shrewd enough to see that reform was society's safety valve. He also learned, early in his career, when he was soundly defeated by Henry George in the New York mayoralty election of 1886, that reform had vote-getting appeal. As a member of the New York assembly, he befriended Jacob Riis and toured the city's sweatshops, where entire families worked from dawn to dusk in tenements, sewing clothing or rolling cigars for distant bosses. As governor, he consulted with the leaders of organized labor and signed into law a bill establishing an eight-hour day for workers on government contracts.

Roosevelt's contribution to progressivism was not so much in deed as in style. The White House, long a dull and stodgy mansion visited mostly by politicians and millionaires, hummed with activity. Roosevelt's children romped through its hallways. Artists, writers, muckrakers, and professors crowded the social calendar. Social critic Edward A. Ross paid a visit, and Roosevelt agreed to write a preface for his book, *Sin and Society*. The nation's foremost black, Booker T. Washington, came to dinner, and for the first time a Jew, Oscar Strauss, was named to the cabinet. By hobnobbing with reformers and talking the language of progressivism, Roosevelt made the movement respectable. And that was no mean accomplishment. Populism had failed in part because it never achieved respectability; it never overcame the hayseed image. With Roosevelt, reform was the fashion.

By his sheer vitality, Roosevelt reinvigorated the presidency. Since Andrew Johnson's time, the presidency had been a low-key office, inhabited for the most part by dull mediocrities. Roosevelt regarded the office as a "bully pulpit," and he used its power to the utmost. In 1902, when the mineowners' unwillingness to compromise had produced a coal strike in the anthracite fields of Pennsylvania, Roosevelt drove the owners to the bargaining table by threatening a federal takeover of the mines and hailed the resulting settlement as a "square deal" for all. Never before had a president intervened in a labor dispute on the side of the workers. Yet he did so without alienating businessmen. In 1904, even though Democrats nominated a gilt-edged conservative, Judge Alton Parker, to contest Roosevelt's reelection, corporate funds poured into Roosevelt's campaign coffer. Among his contributors were such giants as Rockefeller, Morgan, Gould, and Harriman. A

masterful politician, Roosevelt had the knack of running with the hare while hunting with the hounds, of masking a deep-seated conservatism in the rhetoric of reform. Nowhere was this more evident than in his policy toward the trusts.

THE TRUST ISSUE

A new wave of business consolidation had swept the country in the late 1890s, aided by the genial unconcern of the McKinley administration and the emasculation of the Sherman Act by the Supreme Court. Trusts were no longer in use; the new device was the holding company. Delaware and New Jersey statutes that allowed one corporation to own stock in another made it possible. James "Buck" Duke's American Tobacco Company (1890) had shown the way. To control a subsidiary, a holding company did not need to own all its common stock. The most that was needed was 51 percent, and often less would do. Even so, the formation of a conglomerate required immense amounts of capital. As a result, investment bankers became an important ingredient in the 1890s consolidation movement.

J. P. Morgan pioneered the technique when he organized the General Electric Company in 1892 and rescued the Northern Pacific Railroad from insolvency the following year. Morgan's standard price for such financial services was a seat or two on the board of directors of the new corporation. The result was a chain of interlocking directorships among industrial corporations, railroads, and banks. Rockefeller owned, besides Standard Oil (reorganized as a holding company), iron mines in Minnesota and banks in Wall Street. When Morgan organized the United States Steel Company in 1901—the nation's first billion-dollar corporation—he installed a banker, Judge Elbert Gary, as president. Indeed, it was said of Gary, an archconser-

New York Public Library Picture Collection.

J. P. Morgan in 1904.

vative union buster, that he "never saw a blast furnace till he died."

The trend toward monopoly worried Progressives. Smaller businessmen felt they were being squeezed out. Consumers blamed rising prices on the lack of competition. Reformers fretted that business was getting too big for public control. The amount of capital involved in the formation of U.S. Steel, after all, was enough to run the federal government for two years. Roosevelt was sensitive to these concerns. He had entered office without any clearly defined ideas on the question of big business, except that he did not want to see the country dominated by a "vulgar tyranny of mere wealth." At the same time,

he recognized that bigness was not only inevitable but had certain advantages—professional management, mass production, standardization, and research investment. So he compromised. "We draw the line against misconduct, not against wealth," he told Congress in his annual message of December 1902. In short, there were "good" trusts and "bad" ones.

In practice, this meant undertaking a few highly publicized prosecutions against railroad, oil, and meatpacking trusts that had unduly exploited the public. His first and most spectacular effort was the prosecution of the Northern Securities Company, a holding company organized by J. P. Morgan and railroad baron James

J. Hill. It had controlling interest in the Northern Pacific, the Great Northern, and the Burlington railroads—in short, a near monopoly of the railroad traffic between the Mississippi and the Pacific Northwest. Nor could anyone deny that the monopoly involved interstate commerce and was therefore subject to the Sherman Antitrust Act. The Supreme Court agreed, and in 1904 it ordered the Northern Securities Company dissolved. The decision was the first effective enforcement of the Sherman Act.

The popularity of this approach was demonstrated in the election of 1904. Roosevelt, who campaigned on the promise of a Square Deal for everyone, won by the largest popular majority given a presidential candidate up to that time. Winning the presidency in his own right strengthened and emboldened him. When Congress assembled in December 1905, he demanded railroad regulation, a pure food and drug act, and conservation legislation. He got all three. The Hepburn Act (1906) expanded the powers of the Interstate Commerce Commission, specifically by giving it authority to fix railroad rates. The decisions of the ICC were still subject to judicial review, a concession Roosevelt had made to secure the support of conservatives such as Senator Aldrich. But it proved of little significance because the courts after 1906 generally accepted the factual findings of the ICC and forced the railroads to prove that their rate schedules were reasonable. In essence, the Hepburn Act became the foundation of twentieth-century railroad regulation.

THE CONSERVATION MOVEMENT

Conservation of natural resources, the remaining item on Roosevelt's agenda, was a relatively new concern among Americans. Land, water, minerals, and timber had always seemed limitless on this abundant continent; exploitation, not preservation, was the American creed. That myth collapsed in 1890, when the Census Bureau announced that there was no longer any significant portion of the United States which contained fewer than two persons per square mile. In that same year Congress, responding to the pleas of John Muir and other conservationists, created Yosemite and Sequoia national parks, and the following year it authorized the president to set aside forest preserves. President Harrison initiated the National Forest system by enclosing 13 million acres of wilderness, but little else was done until Roosevelt.

Conservation was an issue tailored to the Roosevelt style. It was popular among urban Progressives because it suited their recreational needs without cramping their business interests, and it could be instituted by executive order. Resurrecting the musty Forest Reserves Act of 1891, Roosevelt added millions of acres to the National Forest system, withdrew from private development thousands of water power sites, and then asked Congress for authority to do more. Congress in 1906 approved legislation authorizing the creation of Mesa Verde National Park in southern Colorado, with its priceless pre-Columbian Indian ruins, the Grand Canyon National Monument, and a dozen other natural marvels. When, in 1907, a coalition of western politicians serving lumber and mining interests forced the repeal of the 1891 Forest Reserves Act, Roosevelt issued a "midnight proclamation" before the repeal went into effect setting aside 23 new reserves and dared Congress to dismantle them.

In 1905, Roosevelt placed the Bureau of Forestry, headed by Gifford Pinchot, in the Agriculture Department to enhance its status. Pinchot, who coined the term "conservation" as applied to natural resources, was the quintessential Progressive. He set up bureaus and commissions, staffed them with geologists, hydrologists, foresters, and engineers, and made conservation a profession. Pinchot's object was not simply to preserve resources, but to manage their use. Conservation, in short, meant fighting forest fires, instructing lumbermen on tree selection, and damming rivers for hydroelectric power and flood control. This suited the president, and after they were educated to the long-range potential of such a program, it suited lumbermen, ranchers, and irrigation farmers as well. Sensing rising public interest, Roosevelt in 1908 called a National Conservation Congress. It was attended by 44 governors and resulted in the establishment of conservation commissions in nearly every state. Roosevelt's program had its faults, but he did more than any other single figure in the nation's history to awaken Americans to their natural heritage.

⊔ Taft

Roosevelt declined another term in 1908 and went off to Africa to hunt big game. To "carry on the work substantially as I have carried it on," he handpicked the Republican nominee that year, William Howard Taft. Carrying on was a tall order. Roosevelt had moved leftward on the political spectrum in the last years of his presidency. He had begun denouncing businessmen as "plutocrats" and "malefactors of great wealth," and he talked of the need to subject wealth to social control. At his urging, the Justice Department tackled the two biggest and most feared of the trusts—the Standard Oil Company and the American Tobacco Company. Businessmen were outraged, as were Republican conservatives. "We bought the son of a bitch," complained steel magnate Henry Clay Frick, who had contributed liberally to Roosevelt's 1904 campaign, "and then he did not stay bought." So deep and bitter was the division within the Republican party by 1908 that Roosevelt himself would have

had difficulty holding it together. Taft, a ponderous man in both mind and body,[*] never had a chance.

Taft, who had served successfully as governor of the Philippines and secretary of war, was identified with Roosevelt policies, and he talked the language of progressivism. When William Jennings Bryan, the Democratic nominee for the third and last time, hammered at trusts and tariffs, Taft matched him promise for promise. Taft won easily, though Bryan improved substantially on the Democratic showing of 1904. More significant was the accompanying congressional election, in which Progressive Republicans made important gains in the Middle West. Until then, only a minority clustering around Wisconsin's Senator LaFollette, Republican insurgents were becoming a force to be reckoned in the new Congress. The success of Taft's administration depended in large measure on his ability to hold his own party together.

From the insurgents' point of view, Taft started off well enough. He proposed a federal incorporation law and a federal commission to oversee business practices. When these proposals died in Congress, Taft moved vigorously against business combination. In his four years in office he instituted forty-six antitrust lawsuits, more than Roosevelt had initiated in eight years.

THE PAYNE-ALDRICH TARIFF

To redeem his campaign promises on the tariff, Taft summoned a special session of Congress in the spring of 1909 to secure a revision of the rates. The tariff had be-

---

[*] Taft's weight was Washington legend. As governor of the Philippines, Taft once cabled the State Department: "Took long horseback ride today; feeling fine." Secretary of State Elihu Root cabled back: "How is the horse?"

THE PROGRESSIVE IMPULSE / 169

come a major concern among Progressives, who claimed that the wall of high duties protected domestic monopolies from foreign competition and raised prices of consumer goods. One suggestion, circulated as the "Iowa idea," was to eliminate duties on goods produced by trusts. In the House of Representatives the administration's tariff bill, sponsored by Ways and Means Chairman Sereno Payne of New York, put a number of products on the duty-free list and substantially reduced protection for the trust-dominated industries, steel, farm implements, sugar, and lumber. The Payne bill slipped through the House, but a Senate committee, headed by Nelson Aldrich, restored the high rates. The Senate approved the mongrel bill over the angry bellows of Progressives.

Incredibly, the House conferees accepted the Senate version with only minor changes, and Taft signed it into law. Taft's view was that because the act expanded the free list, it was better than nothing. Republican Progressives blamed him for not using White House influence and the threat of a veto to secure a better bill. Besides widening the rift in the Republican party, the Payne-Aldrich debacle handed the Democrats a golden issue. Making the tariff their own, they campaigned in the off-year elections of 1910 in the name of the hard-pressed consumer, and swept into control of both houses of Congress. That election ended sixteen years of Republican rule and left Taft in political isolation.

THE BALLINGER-PINCHOT AFFAIR

A tempest over conservation widened the breach between Taft and Republican Progressives. Gifford Pinchot, head of the Forestry Service since 1900 and a wealthy friend of Roosevelt's, believed that the nation's forests ought to be scientifically managed to afford maximum benefit in timber

production and use of water resources. During his tenure, the Forestry Service worked closely with lumber companies and irrigation interests. These groups, in turn, used their political influence in behalf of the Forestry Service, making Pinchot one of the most powerful figures in the capital. The Roosevelt-Pinchot approach to resource management, because it seemed to make conservation a science and a business, was popular among Progressives.

President Taft, however, took a narrower view of the role of the president than Roosevelt did, and he had little interest in Roosevelt's forest and water programs. Taft's Secretary of the Interior, Richard A. Ballinger, moreover, was a conservationist of another stripe. He was a preservationist, a "nature lover," as Pinchot scornfully called him, who thought that unique and beautiful wilderness areas ought to be withdrawn completely from commercial use. What was not withdrawn, he thought, ought to be developed by private interests at their own expense, rather than "managed" by a government bureau. Even during Roosevelt's presidency, Ballinger and other preservationists clashed with Pinchot when they tried unsuccessfully to prevent a valley in Yosemite National Park from being dammed and flooded as a water reservoir for the city of San Francisco.

When Ballinger opened to private development land and reservoir sites previously set aside by Roosevelt, Pinchot went to Taft to protest. Finding the president unresponsive, he organized a conservation association to whip up public feeling. When Pinchot publicly accused Ballinger of conniving with the Morgan-Guggenheim syndicate in handing out Alaskan coal-mining rights, Taft was forced at last to choose between the two. He dismissed the chief forester, who promptly dashed off to Africa to complain to Roosevelt. Congress investigated and cleared Ballinger of wrongdoing, but pointed questions by Louis Brandeis, who represented Ballinger's accusers, left the impression that the secretary was selling out Roosevelt's whole forest program to private interests. Once again, Taft, who wanted nothing so much as to be free of the entire mess, was tarnished in the eyes of Progressives.

REPUBLICAN RIFT

An uprising among Progressive Republicans in Congress in the spring of 1910 completed the rift in the party and forced Taft at last to choose sides. The issue involved the powers of the Speaker of the House; since Jefferson's time, the Speaker had had the power to appoint the members of all standing house committees. In addition, as chairman of the rules committee, the Speaker had control over all legislative traffic. As a result, the House was controlled by a small oligarchy beholden to the Speaker. In the 1890s, Speaker Thomas Reed had ruled the House so imperiously that he was nicknamed Czar Reed. After their electoral gains of 1908, Republican insurgents were increasingly restless under the hand of Speaker Joseph Cannon of Illinois, who professed to be deeply puzzled by "all this babble for reform."

In March 1910, George W. Norris of Nebraska led a coalition of Republican insurgents and Democrats that removed the Speaker from the rules committee and stripped him of the power to appoint members of the standing committees. Taft held aloof from the dispute, doubtless thinking it was not his place to intervene, but insurgents interpreted his silence as support for the Speaker. Their anger flashed to the surface, and they began publicly accusing the president of selling out to business interests. That drove Taft into the arms of Aldrich and Cannon. At that juncture, Roosevelt returned from abroad with a boat full of trophies that included nine lions, five elephants, thirteen rhinoceroses, and seven hippopotamuses. Seldom have the resources of a continent been so effectively utilized. Roosevelt himself was too nearsighted to be capable of such efficient marksmanship; it developed that every time the former president leveled his rifle, three other rifles leveled at the same instant. "Mr. Roosevelt," explained the safari leader, "had a fairly good idea of the general direction" from which the animal was bearing down upon him, "but we couldn't take chances with the life of a former president." Surveying the American scene, Roosevelt pronounced himself distressed with Taft and accused the president of having "completely twisted around the policies I advocated and acted upon." Insurgency at last had a leader, one with broader public appeal than LaFollette or Norris. The stage was set for the dramatic three-way confrontation of 1912.

SUMMARY

The Progressives were middle-class reformers, predominantly urban, often well-educated, and committed to free-enterprise capitalism. They intended no radical changes in the political and social system; they simply wanted to make it work more effectively, more honestly, and more humanely. But they were more receptive than liberals of the nineteenth century to the use of government to obtain social ends. Liberals of the age of Jefferson and Jackson had feared power wielded by government. The Progressives also opposed power, but the power they feared was not political authority, but the daily tyranny exercised by utilities, railroads, banks, and trusts. Against such enemies they saw government as a potential ally. This change in attitude marked the difference between nineteenth century and twentieth-century liberalism.

The concerns of the Progressives were those of middle-class consumers. They wanted pure food and drug laws; lowered tariffs; antitrust laws; railroad regulation; prohibition of child labor; and honest, responsive government. Their reforms improved the political and social system, and in doing so helped to preserve it. The Progressive legacy is the world we live in today, a world of bureaucrats and technicians, giant corporations, and limited provisions for social welfare.

Women played an important role in the Progressive movement, and this too helped distinguish it from earlier liberal reform movements. Influenced by the muckrakers, the popular journalists who exposed the flaws in American society, women formed clubs and leagues for social betterment. Their organizations at first focused on social evils that most affected the home and family—liquor, impure food and drugs, and child labor. Success in these realms soon led to demands for political rights of their own, notably the right to vote and hold public office.

Reform of municipal and state governments was one of the central concerns of the Progressives. Both cities and states, they discovered, were controlled by boss-led machines, which ruled by favoritism and ballot-rigging. Efforts to clean up the cities met with only spotty success. The political machines provided some vital services to immigrants and the poor, notably in helping them adjust to urban life and finding them jobs. Not until the state and federal governments undertook such ser-

vices, beginning in the 1930s, was it possible to rid the cities of bosses. At the state level the Progressives did institute some lasting changes, most of which were embodied in the widely imitated Wisconsin idea—regulation of railroads and utilities, workers compensation for injuries on the job, the direct primary, and forest conservation.

President Theodore Roosevelt embodied progressivism at the national level until his retirement in 1909. Though a conservative by instinct, Roosevelt also had the patrician's disdain for greedy businessmen as well as the patrician's attitude of *noblesse oblige* toward the downtrodden. Though his accomplishments as president were modest, he spoke the language of progressivism and hobnobbed with reformers. And that in itself helped make reform fashionable. Among Roosevelt's accomplishments were the settlement of a coal strike in 1902 with a "square deal" for workers; enforcement of the Sherman Act against some highly visible railroad, oil, tobacco, and meatpacking trusts; the Hepburn Act (1906), which expanded the powers of the Interstate Commerce Commission; the Pure Food and Drug and Federal Meat Inspection acts (1906); and a government commitment to conservation.

Roosevelt's successor, William Howard Taft, had Progressive credentials, but he lacked Roosevelt's political skill and personal charisma. Though committed to tariff reduction, one of the Progressives' principal concerns, he accepted the Payne-Aldrich Tariff (1909), which altered the rates scarcely at all. That action alienated Progressive Republicans and allowed the Democrats to make an issue of tariff reform in the election of 1910. Taft further alienated Republican Progressives by ignoring their efforts to reform Congress and by mishandling the Ballinger-Pinchot affair, a dispute over conservation policy. When

Roosevelt returned from an African hunting trip in 1910, he threw his support to the Republican insurgents, declaring that Taft had "completely twisted" the policies Roosevelt had begun. That set the stage for the formation of a new third party, the Progressive party.

READING SUGGESTIONS

Interpretive introductions to progressivism, which put the movement in the perspective of twentieth-century reform, are Eric Goldman, *Rendezvous with Destiny* (1952), and Richard Hofstadter, *The Age of Reform* (1955). The best work on Progressive thought is David W. Noble, *The Progressive Mind, 1890–1917* (1970). The Progressive concern for order and efficiency is explored by Samuel P. Hayes, *Response to Industrialism* (1957), and Robert Wiebe, *The Search for Order* (1967). John D. Buenker, *Urban Liberalism and Progressive Reform* (1973), emphasizes the importance of urban, ethnic voters in the movement, while Paul Boyer, *Urban Masses and the Moral Order* (1978), relates municipal reform to the middle-class Progressive concern about the behavior of the immigrant poor. I am particularly indebted to Professor Boyer for pointing out the connection between progressivism and the City Beautiful movement. Donald J. Mrozek provides a different slant on progressivism in his *Sport and American Mentality, 1880–1910* (1983), which relates the rise of organized sports in this period to progressive rationalism and the drive for efficiency.

The role of women in progressivism can be traced in William L. O'Neill, *Everyone Was Brave: The Rise and Fall of Feminism in America* (1969), and in Sheila M. Rothman, *Woman's Proper Place: A History of Changing Ideals and Practices, 1870 to the Present* (1978). Another facet of the story of women is told by Ruth Rosen in *The Lost Sisterhood: Prostitution in America, 1900–1918* (1982). On blacks in the Progressive era, see August Meier, *Negro Thought in America, 1880–1915* (1963). The two principal black leaders of the time are the subject of Louis R. Harlan, *Booker T. Washington: The Making of a Black Leader, 1856–1901* (1972), and Elliot M. Rudwick, *W. E. B. DuBois: A Study in Minority Group Leadership* (1960).

The classic study of progressivism in the national government is George Mowry's *The Era of Theodore Roosevelt* (1958). It should be supplemented by John M. Cooper's imaginative synthesis, *The Warrior and the Priest: Theodore Roosevelt and Woodrow Wilson* (1983).

WOODROW WILSON'S PROGRESSIVISM: 1910–1920

Woodrow Wilson was born of Scots Presbyterian stock in the Shenandoah Valley of Virginia, the first southern-born president since Andrew Johnson. The physical environment of Virginia and the social environment of a clergyman's household were weighty influences on him: Wilson was a curious blend of Jeffersonian liberal and Presbyterian moralist. He had from early life an image of himself as a great statesman ministering to the needs of the world. After finishing college he went to law school, because the law was the traditional entry to a political career. After only a year of practice he returned to school, selecting this time Johns Hopkins University, where emphasis on research had attracted some of the most dynamic social scientists in the country. Wilson received a Ph.D. in 1886, taught at several colleges, and published half a dozen books. In 1902 he was made president of Princeton University.

Wilson brought to Princeton the academic professionalism (specialization of fields and emphasis on research) that had been pioneered by Johns Hopkins, Harvard, Michigan, and Wisconsin. He revised the curriculum and established departments for each academic discipline. He tried to change the social and physical setting by abolishing the elitist eating clubs and housing students in quadrangles, each with its living quarters, classrooms, and faculty, on the model of England's Oxford. Opposed by furious alumni, Wilson backed down. He emerged from the fracas with the reputation of a reformer, however, for the public interpreted his assault on the eating clubs as an attempt to democratize the university. In 1910 he got into an ill-conceived fight over the location of the graduate school, and facing defeat, resigned. His Princeton record was a preview of his public life. He began with drive and vision, and tempered it with a willingness to compromise when necessary. Then he stiffened up, made every issue a moral one, and preferred to risk defeat rather than compromise.

In 1910 New Jersey Democrats, in need of a spotless "front man" to cover their own seamy record and supposing that a college professor would be easy to manage, asked Wilson to run for governor. He agreed, and in the course of the campaign he blossomed into a Progressive. He attacked the trusts, demanded state authority over utility rates, favored direct election of senators, and called for a workers' compensation act. Upon winning the election, he repudiated the conservative party bosses and pushed through the legislature nearly all the measures he had promised. All this was accomplished within one year. Then, with an eye on the White House, he set out on a national speaking tour to make himself better known to party leaders and to the people.

⊔ The Climactic Election of 1912

Theodore Roosevelt also began to work his way toward the White House in 1910. Somewhere on his busy African venture he had found time to read a book by Progressive journalist Herbert Croly entitled *The Promise of American Life* (1909). The work was a critique of progressivism, or at least a critique of the way Progressives handled bosses and trusts. Curing the ills of democracy with more democracy, Croly argued, was merely a romantic effort to turn back the clock. The nation was too large, its economy too complex for effective popular participation. The bosses inevitably would return to power. What was needed instead was a professional governing elite trained to cope with the complexities of modern society, as well as a strong national leader to oversee the public inter-

---

(*Chapter opening photo*) President Woodrow Wilson delivering his inaugural address.

est. Breaking up the large corporations was likewise a losing proposition in Croly's view, for the efficient, the imaginative, or the ruthless would inevitably resurface. Far better to regulate the great corporations to ensure that they did not take advantage of their size to abuse competitors and the public. With a conscious reference to Alexander Hamilton's elitist, probusiness philosophy, Croly suggested that his program be called the "new nationalism."

ROOSEVELT AND THE NEW NATIONALISM

Roosevelt already held most of these ideas. *The Promise of American Life*, as one historian has remarked, did not change his thinking so much as clarify it. In August 1910, at Osawatomie, Kansas, Roosevelt outlined his program. He called it the New Nationalism. The president, he said, must be the steward of the public welfare, above parties and special interests, and all citizens must put national need above personal or sectional advantage. Private property, he went on, is "subject to the general right of the community to regulate its use to whatever degree the public welfare may require." Finally, the New Nationalism recognized that "combinations in industry are the result of an imperative economic law"; hence the solution is not to prevent them, but to control them in the interest of the public welfare. Lest anyone think he had abandoned progressivism, Roosevelt also endorsed the litany of reforms embodied in the Wisconsin idea.

There remained, however, crucial differences between Roosevelt and Republican insurgents such as LaFollette. New Nationalists wanted a bureaucratic state; insurgents remained suspicious of big government and favored instruments of direct democracy (initiative, referendum, and recall) so the people could control the bureaucrats. New Nationalists recognized that business, labor, and agriculture were competing interests and sought to harmonize them through a strong, disinterested executive. Insurgents favored a mass politics in which citizens, rather than competing among one another, were united by their roles as taxpayers and consumers. Thus Roosevelt's performance at Osawatomie did not instantly galvanize Progressives, even of the Republican variety. When insurgents formed the National Progressive Republican League in January 1911, it was with the idea of winning the Republican nomination for Senator LaFollette.

THE BULL MOOSE PARTY

When LaFollette became ill on a speaking tour in the spring of 1912, Roosevelt made his move. He entered several state primaries and won enough delegates to make a decent showing at the Republican convention. But he could not defeat Taft without LaFollette's support, and LaFollette refused to release his delegates. Taft was nominated on the first ballot, and the Progressives bolted the party. Roosevelt and his followers convened in Chicago in August 1912 and formed the Progressive party. Feeling strong as a bull moose, so he said, Roosevelt appeared in person to accept the new party's nomination. The platform adopted by the Bull Moose party was the most advanced set of principles since the Populist platform of 1892. A merger of LaFollette insurgency and the New Nationalism, the platform advocated the various instruments of direct democracy listed in the Wisconsin idea plus a new one—women's suffrage. It also included a shopping list of welfare measures—workers' compensation, prohibition of child labor, regulation of the working conditions of women. Although the Progressives recommended government regulation of business to solve the trust problem, Roosevelt obscured the issue by suggesting in his acceptance speech that the Sherman Act be retained and occasionally applied.

On the Democratic side, Wilson won the nomination he so eagerly sought, but only after forty-six tedious ballots. William Jennings Bryan, who recognized the hopelessness of his own cause and threw his support to Wilson early in the convention, was eventually rewarded with the post of secretary of state. Wilson called his program the New Freedom, but it differed from Roosevelt's principally on the trust issue. Wilson and his chief campaign adviser Louis Brandeis thought that business was already too big to be regulated, that business would control the regulatory commissions. They wanted to strengthen the antitrust laws and restore open competition. The Democratic platform also stressed the need for banking reform and a reduction in the tariff.

The election was a triumph for progressivism rather than for Wilson. Taft, the only conservative candidate in the field, ran a poor third behind Wilson and Roosevelt and uncomfortably close to the Socialist candidate Eugene Debs. (Although the combined vote for Roosevelt and Taft exceeded Wilson's, Wilson won because of the split in Republican ranks.) The Democrats retained control of both Houses of Congress, so the way was clear for the New Freedom.

⎵ The Wilson Synthesis

Theodore Roosevelt, it has often been observed, shaped the modern presidency by using its powers and its prestige. He rose above social and sectional interests and spoke for a popular majority. But Roosevelt was never able to master the entrenched conservatives in Congress. By popular appeals he was able to force Congress to act, but he rarely worked with it and never led it. Roosevelt's triumph was essentially personal, and the office lost its vigor when he retired.

The modern presidency owes as much to Wilson as to Roosevelt. Wilson too spoke for a national constituency—not because people loved him as they did the warm and expansive Roosevelt, but because they admired him. Wilson had an extraordinary gift for articulating reform ideals and a reputation for translating promises into programs. He also had the advantage of a friendly majority in Congress. Making full use of it, Wilson worked closely with Democratic leaders. He outlined the program, helped them draft bills, and used his presidential influence to secure passage. Wilson thus broke down the wall between executive and legislature that had weakened the government throughout the nineteenth century. The result was a flood of legislation that marked the climax of the Progressive movement.

THE UNDERWOOD TARIFF

Congressional Democrats had been working on both tariff and banking reform for more than a year. Tariff reduction bills had passed Congress in 1911 and 1912, only to be vetoed by Taft because they were not "scientific," though what he meant by that was not exactly clear. In February 1913, on the eve of Wilson's inauguration, the Sixteenth Amendment became part of the federal Constitution. The amendment authorized Congress to impose a federal income tax. By ensuring the government a revenue, it eliminated one of the objections to tariff reduction. In April, after close consultation with Wilson, House Ways and Means chairman Oscar Underwood presented a bill that reduced the rates to an average of 25 percent and placed steel and farm machinery on the free list. The Underwood bill breezed through the House, but it ran into a swarm

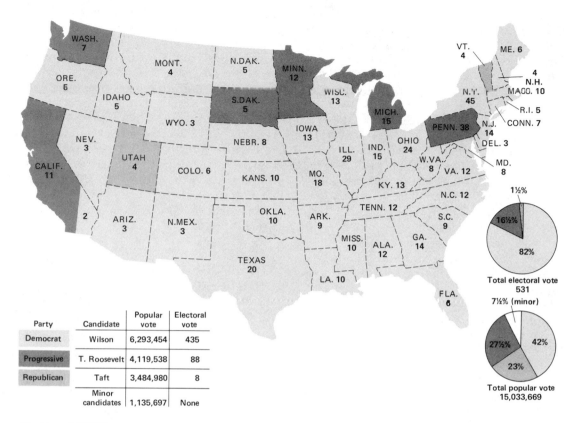

Party	Candidate	Popular vote	Electoral vote
Democrat	Wilson	6,293,454	435
Progressive	T. Roosevelt	4,119,538	88
Republican	Taft	3,484,980	8
	Minor candidates	1,135,697	None

Total electoral vote
531
7½% (minor)

Total popular vote
15,033,669

Election of 1912.

of lobbyists in the Senate. The president then intervened, publicly expressing sorrow that the people had no lobby in Congress. LaFollette and other Progressives launched an investigation of the property holdings of senators that might be affected by tariff rates. The opposition melted, and the Underwood bill became law.

The Underwood Tariff was the first significant reduction in the rates since the Civil War. It also contained the first federal income tax, a graduated levy ranging from 1 to 6 percent. Such a tax had been specifically authorized by the Sixteenth Amendment to the Constitution, approved by Congress in 1909. Unfortunately, the new

tariff never had a chance to prove itself. The war in Europe that broke out the following year disrupted trade, and the Republicans, who came to power after the war, restored the old rates. All the same, it demonstrated that Wilson had a grasp of his office and meant to redeem his campaign promises.

THE FEDERAL RESERVE SYSTEM

Banking reform had been in the works for some years. The financial panic of 1907 had convinced even conservatives that the banking system needed to be strengthened. Senator Aldrich's solution was to create a huge central bank, something like the Bank of England, that could serve as a banker's bank, a reservoir of funds when the system was in need. That solution was unacceptable to Democrats, who saw it as a means of further concentrating power in Wall Street. Democrats were also concerned about monetary reform, though by 1912 they had given up the idea of free silver. The trouble with the national bank notes was that the quantity in circulation was inelastic. The Civil War legislation that had set up the national bank system had provided that the notes were to be backed by gold and government bonds. Thus the number that could be printed depended on the amount of gold and bonds held by the national banks. As a result, the money supply was too limited for the needs of an expanding economy. Wilson mediated among these competing interests and worked out a compromise. The Federal Reserve Act (1913) was thus another victory for the president.

The act established a system of twelve reserve banks, privately owned but supervised by a presidentially appointed Federal Reserve Board. The banks were not to carry on normal banking activities; rather they were (and still are) banker's banks, reserves for members of the system. In time of fiscal crisis, weak banks, instead of closing their doors and setting off a panic, would be able to borrow funds from the Federal Reserve. The system was authorized to issue Federal Reserve notes, intended to serve as the nation's basic circulating medium. Forty percent of each Federal Reserve note represented gold in the vaults of the system. The remainder was backed by commercial paper (checks, IOUs). The number of notes that could be issued depended on the amount of commercial paper in existence at any given time, and that in turn reflected the amount of business transacted. The result was elastic currency that expanded or contracted with the needs of the economy. To enable the Federal Reserve Board to have some control over this expansion and contraction, the law gave it authority to set the rediscount rate—that is, the interest rate that Federal Reserve banks charged member banks for loans. The rediscount rate—essentially the price of money—in turn affected the rates banks charged their customers. The power over interest rates did not give the Federal Reserve Board complete control of the business cycle. But it was an experimental start, a foundation on which to build.

THE FEDERAL TRADE COMMISSION

With the banking problem resolved, Wilson turned to the trusts. Here again, flexibility was the key. The approach to the problem that he had advocated in the election campaign was embodied in the Clayton bill, introduced in 1914. The bill identified and prohibited a whole range of "unfair" business practices. If a corporation committed such a practice, favoring one customer over others with lower prices, for instance, it presumably would be subject to criminal prosecution by the Department of Justice. The bill satisfied no one. Businessmen objected to the bill's many "don'ts" without a government agency to tell them what was legal and what was not. Bryan Democrats objected that the bill did not actually break up any trusts. Roosevelt Progressives wanted a regulatory commission.

Wilson seemed confused by these contradictory signals from within the ranks of Progressives, until Louis Brandeis pointed to a solution. A bill such as Clayton's, which listed a series of prohibitions without clear means of enforcement, would not work. What was needed was a federal trade commission with broad authority to investigate

Library of Congress.
Louis Brandeis.

and suppress restraints of trade. A bill creating such a commission had already been introduced in Congress. Although it reflected the thinking of the New Nationalists, Brandeis persuaded Wilson to lend it his support.

After endorsing the commission concept, Wilson cut the Clayton bill adrift, and the Senate tore out several of its stronger provisions. Nevertheless, the two acts, passed in September and October 1914, represented a bold synthesis of the New Freedom and New Nationalism. The Federal Trade Commission Act created the FTC as a watchdog agency with power to investigate unfair business practices and to issue "cease and desist" orders. The FTC act did not define what was meant by unfair practices; the Clayton Act did that. The Clayton Act made illegal such practices as price discrimination, interlocking directorates in competing corporations, and the purchase of stock by one corporation in another when the result would be reduced competition. The Clayton Act also con-

tained some labor provisions, the result of a decade-long campaign by the A F of L. It exempted labor unions from the antitrust laws (the Supreme Court in 1908 had found an interstate boycott organized by the A F of L to be in violation of the Sherman Antitrust Act), and it restricted the use of injunctions to prevent strikes.

Samuel Gompers, president of the A F of L, called the Clayton Act "labor's Magna Carta," though in fact the courts in succeeding years issued injunctions as freely as ever. Rural Progressives were disappointed that the act did not result in the immediate dismantling of the giant holding companies, but Wilson had never committed himself to that approach. He was willing to tolerate big business as long as he could also control it. The success of his compromise depended on how the FTC was administered and by whom. That it eventually fell into the hands of the very interests it was supposed to watch over was not entirely Wilson's fault.

WILSON AND SOCIAL JUSTICE

Wilson's willingness to accept ideas that he had denounced less than two years before showed he was willing to learn and change as situations changed. His learning experience was evident in other ways. Wilson had taken office with an ill-defined but certainly very limited program in mind. It centered on the liberal notion of restoring free competition and somehow controlling the "money trust." For the social justice proposals the Progressive party advocated, Wilson had no special interest. He had refused to support women's suffrage or restrictions on child labor because he thought these were state, rather than federal, problems. He openly favored racial segregation and worried about the constitutionality of federal labor legislation. After he secured tariff and banking reform and a Federal

Trade Commission, he thought his job was done.

Major Republican victories in state elections that autumn set him rethinking. There was political appeal in social justice, and Roosevelt, who had already abandoned the Bull Moose insurgents, was a likely candidate for the Republican nomination in 1916. In 1915 Wilson signaled a change when he signed into law, although reluctantly, the LaFollette Seamen's Act, which provided special safety and compensation standards for that dangerous occupation. In January 1916, Wilson named Louis Brandeis to the Supreme Court, a move that delighted Progressives in both parties. Later that spring he reversed himself on the question of farm credits, a measure he had previously vetoed, and the result was passage of the Federal Farm Loan Act. Most important, Wilson threw his support behind a workers' compensation law for federal employees and a bill prohibiting the products of child labor from passing into interstate commerce.

The child labor law was especially significant, for never before had Congress exercised the commerce power in this way. The Supreme Court had consistently held that factories, and hence presumably the working conditions within them, are not interstate commerce because a factory does not move. Products do move, often across state lines, and if Congress could prohibit the sale of certain products because they were made under substandard factory conditions (such as with child labor), there was no limit to what it could do in the field of labor legislation. Such free-ranging power was too novel for a Supreme Court on which Oliver Wendell Holmes and Louis Brandeis were the only Progressives, and in 1918 the Court declared the child labor act unconstitutional (*Hammer* v. *Dagenhart*). Not until 1939 did the court reverse itself and concede the Progressive view that the commerce power could be used to achieve social aims.

It must be said that Wilson's role in this spurt of social legislation was secondary. He initiated none of it, and though his support was sometimes crucial, it usually came at the last minute. The legislation reflected the momentum of the Progressive movement, not presidential leadership. Wilson's role in the foundation of domestic policy declined after 1914 largely because he became preoccupied with foreign affairs. Progressivism was losing momentum by 1917, and America's entry into World War I finished it.

⊔ Prohibition and Women's Suffrage

Two aspects of the reform movement did benefit by American entry into World War I: the temperance movement and the feminist movement. The two had long been associated. Women had been the dominant force in the temperance crusade from the beginning. Temperance, however, hampered the suffrage movement because liquor interests, fearing that women might vote dry, used their influence and money to block suffrage laws.

THE PROHIBITION MOVEMENT

Temperance movements had come and gone through the nineteenth century, but the reform failed to attract public interest until the 1890s, when medical science interested itself in the physical effects of drinking. Researchers discovered that alcohol was a depressant, rather than a stimulant as previously supposed, and it had a harmful effect on the brain, heart, liver, and other organs. Life insurance companies, their discipline improved by the development of actuarial tables, discovered that over 7 percent of adult deaths were attributable to liquor. Social statistics of this sort were great for Progressive reformers, who were already aware that liquor contributed to crime, poverty, and political corruption. Others worried about the avalanche of immigrants after 1900 and concluded that without liquor the immigrant masses would be less susceptible to crime and boss rule, more easily assimilated into American life. Scientific premises, concerns about morality, and middle-class anxiety combined to make temperance a likely Progressive cause.

In 1895, the Anti-Saloon League was formed to coordinate the activities of the many local temperance societies formed by the WCTU and other organizations led by women. The league catered to the middle class by focusing on the production and distribution of liquor rather than its consumption. The saloon was a fat target because it catered to the immigrant poor, bred gambling and prostitution, and in the cities served as a political clubhouse for machine politicians. The Anti-Saloon League grew explosively. Within a decade it had an organization in nearly every state, and it boasted a publishing house of its own that generated 400 tons of literature a month. By 1915, it had a paid staff of 1,500 and blanketed the nation with perhaps 50,000 volunteer speakers.

Until 1913, the league concentrated on local governments, trying to secure state prohibition laws, or at least local option laws that would permit counties to vote themselves dry. In that year, with half the counties in the nation dry, the ASL began a push for a constitutional amendment that would permit a federal ban. War in 1917 gave the movement added impetus. The ASL demanded prohibition as a war measure in order to conserve grain. And it began attacking the personal consumption of liquor, as well as its manufacture and sale. In 1918, Congress yielded to the twin pressures of patriotism and well-financed lobbying and approved the Eighteenth

Amendment. By then, twenty-seven states were dry, so the ASL had to secure the approval of only nine more to win ratification. That was accomplished within a year. In 1919 Congress approved the Volstead Act, which prohibited the manufacture or sale of beverages containing more than .5 percent alcohol. That level meant that even beer and wine were illegal, which was probably a mistake because it made the law more difficult to enforce. But, as with so many Progressive regulations, enforcement problems were simply not foreseen.

LIBERATING WOMEN

The entry of women into the public sphere through temperance societies, club activities, and consumer associations helped raise women's consciousness of themselves and their place in society. Feminism, broad in appeal and rich in social implications, was evident long before it surfaced in the suffrage movement.

An early sign was the elimination of the clothing that had bound women and endangered their health for centuries. Layers of petticoats, girdles, high necklines, and long hemlines gave way to simpler, shorter, lightweight garments. Some worried that bare arms and legs would arouse the lust of men, and that the new freedom of women would afford opportunities for all sorts of lascivious activity. Women's dresses, the *New York Times* pontificated in 1914, had approached "the danger line of indecency about as closely as they could." Both sexes adjusted easily to the new styles, in part perhaps because change was the order of the day. New marvels—the automobile, motion pictures, airplanes, subways, rayon, and radioactivity—pounded the senses and stirred the mind. In such a world, a change in clothing styles providing more ample room for movement seemed only natural. Men's clothing, for that matter, underwent similar change, as

Culver Pictures, Inc.

Helen Keller, deaf and blind since infancy, with her "teacher" Anne Sullivan and movie actor Charles Chaplin on a visit to Hollywood in 1918. Helen Keller was one of the most admired women of the age.

spats, high starched collars, and stiff coats yielded to lighter, less formal styles.

Less restrictive clothing in turn allowed more physical activities. In sports women had been confined to croquet, slow-motion lawn tennis, field hockey, bicycling, and sidesaddle horseback riding. Now, football, which came into its own in the Progressive years, was almost the only athletic endeavor that remained closed, as women took up golf, swimming, baseball, and even mountain climbing. Skimpier clothing, which allowed women to climb into vehicles without ladies' maids to help manage their skirts, enabled them to drive automo-

biles. Driving, in turn, opened new horizons and new avenues of self-expression.

Other signs of growing feminine independence were the rising divorce rate and the declining birth rate. Divorce was extremely difficult to obtain in the nineteenth century because of church opposition and widespread belief in the sanctity of the family. Even in the Progressive years, there was concern for the future of the family. But the divorce rate increased anyway. Liberals rationalized that divorce was good for the family as an institution because it allowed bad marriages to be terminated and replaced by good ones. Since there seemed to be no way to prevent divorce, that view eventually came to prevail.

The decline in the birth rate was not due to feminism, but free women found additional reasons for wanting fewer children. The birth rate had begun to decline as early as 1800 and was further depressed by industrialization and urbanization. When women went to work in factories, as they began to do in the mid-nineteenth century, they married later in life and had fewer children. Women who moved to the city felt less need for large families. Children were an economic asset on the farm, where output bore a nearly one-to-one relationship to the number of people available to do the work, but in the city, children could be an economic burden unless they were put to work in the sweatshops. These influences continued, and even accelerated, in the Progressive years.

The more sophisticated economy was also producing more job opportunities for women, such as secretarial work, clerking, and nursing. While these positions were menial compared to the opportunities available to men, they lured women out of the home and discouraged pregnancies. For both homemakers and officeworkers, new knowledge of contraceptives helped to liberate women. Contraceptive devices existed in the Victorian age, but since they were illegal and religious leaders forbade their use, even physicians knew little of how they worked. In 1912 Margaret Sanger embarked on a one-woman crusade to raise that veil of ignorance. A nurse in New York City, she saw women die after trying to abort pregnancies. She found that the immigrant poor knew nothing of venereal disease or personal hygiene. To correct this, she wrote a series of articles for the Socialist newspaper *Call*, but the series had to be canceled when the Post Office threatened to deny *Call* the use of the mails.

Undaunted, Sanger went to Europe to study contraceptive techniques. On her return she began publishing a magazine called the *Woman Rebel*. Although she did not give explicit directions for contraception, she was indicted under the Comstock Act, which called for a jail term for anyone using the mails to discuss sex practices. She fled to Europe again and returned more radical than ever. In 1916 she was sent to jail for operating an illegal birth control clinic. By then her crusade was attracting attention, and she received financial support from middle-class women who wanted to limit their own families as well as control the growth of the immigrant masses. In 1921 Sanger formed the American Birth Control League, which enlisted physicians and social workers in a public discussion of the necessity for and means of contraception. Her movement then obtained respectability, and the repeal of state laws barring the sale of contraceptives was only a matter of time.

THE SUFFRAGE MOVEMENT

Movements such as Margaret Sanger's were too radical to attract the support of the majority of women. Many women, for instance, worried that the use of contraceptives threatened their status as wives and mothers. Others, deeply imbued with the cult of womanhood, feared that if they were put on an equal footing with men they would lose the special virtues of the female personality—charity, tenderness, and piety. There was, however, one reform that did have potential mass appeal—the right to vote. Suffrage did not threaten traditional values; indeed, it was demanded as a matter of justice, an extension of democracy. It was sought also as a means of defending the home, not threatening it. Even without the vote, women in the Progressive years had become active in politics by pushing for changes that affected the family and its surroundings. The vote, it

Abolishing the Home

Charlotte Perkins Gilman was not content with winning legal and political rights for women. She felt that women could never be truly free and independent so long as home and motherhood were objects of reverence. Her arguments anticipated the radical feminism of a half-century later.

Our eyes grow moist with emotion as we speak of our mothers—our own mothers— and what they have done for us. Our voices thrill and tremble with pathos and veneration as we speak of "the mothers of great men"—mother of Abraham Lincoln! mother of George Washington! and so on. Had Wilkes Booth no mother? Was Benedict Arnold an orphan?

. . .

Our physical environment we share with all animals. Our social environment is what modifies heredity and develops human character. The kind of country we live in, the system of government, of religion, of education, of business, of ordinary social customs and convention, this is what develops mankind, this is given by our fathers.

What does maternal instinct contribute to this sum of influences? Has maternal instinct even evolved any method of feeding, dressing, teaching, disciplining, educating children which commands attention, not to say respect? It has not.

. . .

We have made great progress in the sense of justice and fair play; yet we are still greatly lacking in it. What is the contribution of domestic ethics to this mighty virtue? In the home is neither freedom nor equality. There is ownership throughout; the dominant father, the more or less subservient mother, the utterly dependent child; and sometimes that still lower grade—the servant. Love is possible, love deep and reciprocal; loyalty is possible; gratitude is possible; kindness to ruinous favoritism is possible; unkindness, hate, and rebellion is possible; justice is not possible.

Justice was born outside the home and a long way from it; and it has never been adopted there.

. . .

The home, in its arbitrary position of arrested development, does not properly fulfill its own essential functions—much less promote the social ones. Among the splendid activities of our age it lingers on, inert and blind, like a clam in a horse-race.

It hinders, by keeping woman a social idiot, by keeping the modern child under the tutelage of the primeval mother, by keeping the social conscience of the man crippled and stultified in the clinging grip of the domestic conscience of the woman. It hinders by its enormous expense, making the physical details of daily life a heavy burden to mankind.

. . .

Change this order. Set the woman on her own feet, as a free, intelligent, able human being, quite capable of putting into the world more than she takes out, of being a producer as well as a consumer. Put these poor, antiquated "domestic industries" into the archives of past history; and let efficient, modern industries take their place, doing far more work, far better work, far cheaper work in their stead.

Charlotte Perkins Gilman, *The Home* (1903)

was argued, would make them more effective reformers. Whether true or not, a large number of women came to believe it.

The suffrage question was late in coming, in part because women had other causes in the early years of the Progressive movement and in part because the Woman Suffrage Association was all but dead. Susan Anthony, last of the nineteenth-century sufragettes, had retired in 1900, and no one of comparable energy had taken her place. What success the organization had was at the state level. By 1912, nine states—all of them in the West, where there were few women—allowed women to vote.

The revival of the suffrage movement began in that year—1912—with the return home of Alice Paul, a young Quaker who had gone to England for advanced study in the field of social work. Swept into the English suffrage movement, she was converted to militancy by Emmeline Pankhurst, who advocated direct action. Pankhurst's followers took to arson and sabotage to make their point. They set fire to the house of a cabinet member and fired rifles at railroad trains. When arrested, they went on hunger strikes. Alice Paul returned to the United States impressed with the idea of direct action and convinced that a constitutional amendment, rather than state action, was the better course. In March 1913, she organized a march in Washington to coincide with Woodrow Wilson's inauguration. The demonstrators were attacked and beaten by gangs of men. Police and even soldiers had to intervene to stop the riots, and the sympathies of

Woman suffrage before the Nineteenth Amendment.

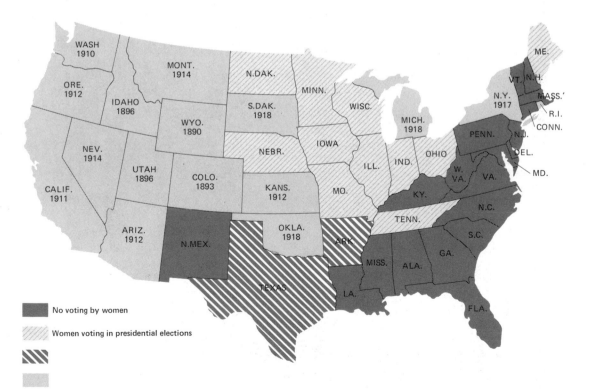

women everywhere were aroused. When Alice Paul organized the National Women's party, contributions came in from tens of thousands of women, reflecting the stifled desires of homemakers who were too shy to march the streets with placards.

The older Women's Suffrage Association continued its efforts at state legislation, but when it lost a crucial battle in New York in 1915 (due largely to massive opposition from liquor interests), it too became converted to the idea of a federal amendment. That same year the Suffrage Association chose as its president Carrie Chapman Catt, a dynamic leader with a talent for organization. She rekindled enthusiasm in the association's locals, built up a treasury of millions, and announced a timetable for congressional passage of the amendment and state ratification. When New York re-

versed itself and gave women the vote in 1917, victory seemed near. No one could any longer deny that women wanted the vote.

The war destroyed the last remaining male argument—that women lacked the education and experience to shoulder public responsibilities. The wartime labor shortage opened new job opportunities for women, who moved into factories, entered municipal work, sold war bonds, and became medical volunteers. Even President Wilson agreed that they had earned the right to equal citizenship.

At that point, Alice Paul's Women's party became a liability. Refusing to abandon their militant tactics, women picketed the White House and condemned "Kaiser Wilson" for trying to make the world safe for democracy while ignoring it at home.

Suffragettes on their way to Wilson's inauguration, 1913.

UPI/Bettmann.

Sophia Smith Collection.
Leaders of the suffrage movement: Jeanette Rankin and Carrie Chapman Catt.

The president could not change his position without appearing to surrender to
pressure. Carrie Catt rescued him by denouncing the tactics of the Women's party,
which enabled Wilson and members of
Congress to dismiss the WP as a handful
of cranks that did not represent the mass
of patriotic, responsible women. Wilson
publicly announced his support of the suffrage amendment, basing it on the need
for national unity in the war emergency.
Congress in 1918 approved the Nineteenth
Amendment, and hard lobbying by the
Suffrage Association secured its ratification
in time for women to vote in the presidential election of 1920.

A majority of women who voted cast
their ballots for Republican Warren G.
Harding, and that in itself was a sign that
the women's vote would make little difference in American politics. Neither the

hopes of the suffragists nor the fears of
their opponents bore fruit. Feminists
themselves were the most distressed by
this. Some years later, pacifist Jane Addams
sorrowfully observed that congresswomen
were distinguished only by their common
enthusiasm for military appropriations.
(This was not wholly true, although Addams did not live long enough to find out.
The only member of Congress who voted
against American entry into both World
War I and World War II was Jeanette Rankin of Montana.)

The greater pity is that the feminist
movement itself died away after 1920. Alice Paul began a movement for an equal
rights amendment and Carrie Catt started
the League of Women Voters, but it was
many years before either organization
achieved any importance. Social feminism,
which had done so much in the field of

labor legislation and consumer protection, faded away. The women's clubs turned to local interests; the Consumers League declined. The suffrage movement had absorbed feminists' energies, and when it reached its goal the energy and the unity were gone.

Women achieved much in the Progressive years, more than at any other time in the past. Much more remained to be done in terms of social equality and economic opportunity. Those goals, however, would have to await another time, for the great generation of reformers—Jane Addams, Florence Kelley, Charlotte Perkins Gilman, Carrie Chapman Catt, Alice Paul—left no heirs.

⊔ Progressivism: An Appraisal

Progressivism was a middle-class movement, preoccupied with the things that affected the middle class—big business, corruption, rising prices, product safety, and railroad regulation. If Progressives did anything for working people, immigrants, and the poor, it was on the order of afterthought. Women and blacks benefited from the atmosphere of reform, but their achievements were largely of their own doing. As historian William L. O'Neill has observed: "Middle-class people were quick to judge the poor, and sometimes even the rich. They seldom looked as closely at themselves."

As has already been noted, progressivism was less a reform than a modernization movement, a response to the complex needs of an industrialized, urban society. If the response was at times flawed, the flaws became evident only with experience. To meet the needs of modern society, Progressives—even skeptical ones like Herbert Croly—relied on scientific data and professional management. Expertise and efficiency were their watchwords. There

were two flaws in this approach. One was the assumption that social problems could be scientifically managed, or—put another way—that scientific management was something more than a balance of competing interests. Conservation, for example, was (and is) a matter of competing interests—exploitive (lumber, mining), developmental (hydroelectric power, irrigation), utilitarian preservation (hiking, canoeing), and preservation for its own sake (preserving the world's gene pool, thermal balance, oxygen supply). As practiced in the Progressive era, conservation meant the "scientific" use of resources for the maximum benefit of competing interests such as lumbering, ranching, farming. Not only were "nature lovers" omitted, but so were small entrepreneurs, who could not get the government's attention.

The other flaw was that the workability of such regulation depended on the disinterestedness of the regulator. The expert, the bureaucrat, must have nothing but the public good at heart. The Progressives had evidence that this was wishful thinking. The first federal regulatory agency, the Interstate Commerce Commission, soon settled into a cozy alliance with the railroads. Wilson's Federal Trade Commission followed the same path. Instead of policing business practices—assuming that is what Wilson and Brandeis expected it to do—it launched friendly investigations to determine whether proposed mergers and combinations were allowable. The FTC also encouraged the establishment of trade associations that tried to set prices within each industry and limit competition. Small businessmen as well as large benefited from the statistics and other information gathered by the FTC.

The same thing happened with other Progressive agencies. A Tariff Commission (1916) was intended to remove trade policy from the political arena, where it was subject to special interest lobbying. The law authorized the president, with the advice of experts on the commission, to raise or

CLIO'S FOCUS: The Radical Left: Threat That Never Was

One of the curiosities of the Progressive era is that, with all the ferment of reform, radical ideas—Marxism, socialism—never won much appeal. A Socialist party was formed in 1901, and for a time it seemed to prosper. Within a decade it boasted 40,000 members and published 100 newspapers. The city of Milwaukee in 1910 elected a Socialist mayor and sent a Socialist, Victor Berger, to Congress. In 1912 the Socialist presidential candidate, Eugene Debs, had financing enough to charter a train, the Red Special, to tour the country. But the Socialists never developed much electoral strength. At their peak they attracted only 6 percent of the popular vote.

They failed because they were unable to recruit working people, as the European Socialist parties did. American trade unions were content to work within the capitalist system, concentrating on "bread and butter" issues. Immigration shattered nascent feelings of working-class unity. Native-born workers resented the competition of lower-paid immigrants, and the immigrants themselves resisted the concept of a proletariat. Having come to America to better themselves, they were determined to do so. Only when they discovered how difficult that was did the foreign-born flirt with socialism, and by then the radical movement was dead.

Socialism in America failed also because radicals warred among themselves over doctrine and tactics. The central dispute concerned the likelihood and desirability of violent revolution (in Europe, a similar dispute had separated evolutionary Socialists from revolutionary Communists). The dispute seems to be endemic to any radical movement—Samuel Adams grappled with it in the days of the Boston Tea Party and so did the Students for a Democratic Society (SDS) in the 1960s. The dilemma is this: In a society where poverty and human misery, while present, are not pervasive (unlike France of 1789 or Russia of 1917), radicals are forced to adopt militant language and take forceful action in order to call attention to the wrongs they perceive. The militancy in turn alienates moderates, the very people whose support is needed to effect change. Those in the radical ranks who counsel prudence are scorned by the militants for compromising principle. Militants, moreover, even if they never win control of the radical movement (revolutionaries were expelled from the Socialist party in 1913), invite repression from outside, from people who take the radical rhetoric at its face value and never understand how truly weak the militants are. Nothing illustrates this so well as the story of one native-born radical movement, the Industrial Workers of the World.

The IWW was formed in Chicago in 1905 by an odd, and ultimately incompatible, assortment of labor leaders and political radicals. Rejecting the trade unions as conservative and divisive, the IWW spoke for the proletarian masses, in the model of the 1880s Knights of Labor. Some of the delegates to the IWW convention, such as Marxist law professor Daniel DeLeon, represented nothing but themselves. The largest organization represented was the 27,000 member Western Federation of Miners, but the miners withdrew from the IWW when they lost a fight to control the union's presidency. In 1908, the "worker" element tossed out DeLeon and his fellow Socialists for advocating political action. The "overalls brigade"—mostly loggers and miners from the Pacific Northwest—preferred "direct action," such as strikes and industrial sabotage. They were given to militant rhetoric and radical slogans, but they had only the haziest notion of what they would substitute for the status quo.

The Wobblies—as they were popularly called—were strongest in the Pacific Northwest because, despite the region's recent frontier experience, that was the part of the country where the gap between "haves" and "have nots" was most vivid. Every American frontier has had its speculator-developers who manipulated government in order to secure an advantage over their less imaginative or less scrupulous fellows. But by the time the Pacific coast was settled, manipulation had become a fine art. Congress cooperated by giving huge land grants to railroads and by extending the homestead principle to big business with the Timber and Stone Act of 1878. As a result, by 1900 the biggest landowner in Montana was Anaconda Mining, the largest in Washington was the Northern Pacific Railroad, with Weyerhauser Lumber second, and the largest landowner in California was the Southern Pacific Railroad. Young men who drifted west in search of opportunity found instead only menial work in companies managed by distant power structures. The IWW's activism gave those people an outlet for their frustration.

Possessed of little popular support and only the most rudimentary organization, the Wobblies voiced their protest on street corners and in market squares. Ignoring them might have silenced them, but city governments were not up to such a sophisticated counterrevolutionary technique. So they enacted ordinances prohibiting sidewalk speeches, and that presented the Wobblies with a more compelling grievance—free speech. The first big confrontation occurred in Spokane, Washington, in 1908–1909. It began with a protest by migrant workers against employment agencies that charged "a dollar for a job" and split the fees with employers, who fired workers as fast as they hired them. When the city council passed an ordinance prohibiting street meetings and then exempted the Salvation Army, the IWW brought people out of the forests and wheat fields to "Fill the Jails of Spokane."

Among those arrested was Elizabeth Gurley Flynn, age seventeen, who had come west from New York to lend her oratorical skills to the cause. In jail that winter she wrote a newspaper article exposing the fact that police had turned the women's section into a brothel. When the mayor countered with some derisive remarks, she sued him for defamation. In March 1910, Spokane surrendered. The council announced that street speaking would be allowed, and jailed Wobblies were released. Over the next few years, the Wobblies carried their free speech movement across the Northwest, but with only minimal results, such as the state of Washington agreeing to regulate employment agencies, and Spokane cleaning up its jail. The Wobblies lacked the organizational ability (or desire) and the staying power to effect deep or lasting reform. And their rhetoric invited repression.

In 1917 the Idaho legislature passed a "criminal-syndicalist" act. The act defined criminal syndicalism as "the doctrine which advocates crime, sabotage, violence, or

Brown Brothers.

Elizabeth Gurley Flynn
addressing strikers, 1913.

unlawful methods of terrorism as a means of accomplishing industrial or political reforms." Although the IWW rarely used such methods, its members frequently advocated them—so the law in effect made it a crime to belong to the IWW. Washington and Oregon enacted similar laws, and juries began sending Wobblies to jail.

The Wobblies, who had occasionally come under gunfire from ill-trained and panicky deputies, grew increasingly desperate under the official repression. World War I, and the patriotism it fostered, made their opponents ever bolder. The all but inevitable confrontation took place at Centralia, Washington, on Armistice Day, 1919. The IWW union hall had already been attacked several times by townspeople. When the American Legion organized a parade route that took the marchers past the union hall twice, the Wobblies decided another raid was coming. They laid plans of their own. Their expectations turned out to be correct.

During a pause in the parade, Legionnaires broke ranks and smashed their way into the IWW union hall. They were met with a hail of gunfire that killed three Legionnaires and left several others wounded. Eleven Wobblie leaders were convicted and sent to jail. The movement had never posed a threat to existing government and was by 1919 on the decline. Federal and state authorities hunted Wobblie leaders for several years thereafter until they became too scarce to find and the public lost interest. Radicalism, for the moment, was dead.

lower tariff rates within certain limits. Wilson's successors in the 1920s stocked the commission with protectionists, and the only advice they got was to keep the rates high. Some critics of progressivism have suggested that the regulatory agencies were intended all along to be servants of big business, that progressivism was in fact a "triumph of conservatism." Some businessmen, it must be said, did anticipate such a result, but most were no more foresighted than the reformers they fought. The Progressives genuinely believed they were ending privilege and forcing business to serve the public interest. Their mistake was in believing that the government would always be in the hands of Progressives: In the 1920s, it was to be in the hands of businessmen.

Even so, the Progressives were godfathers to the twentieth century. They revitalized the presidency and created the notion that government could be a profession. The bureaus they set up, even if they did not function exactly as they intended, became models for later reformers who hoped to cure social ills through government management. And their humanitarian legislation, protecting consumers and the rights of working people, broke new ground. On that too, later reformers would build.

SUMMARY

The presidential election of 1912 was the climax of the Progressive movement. The Democrats nominated Woodrow Wilson, former historian, college president, and Progressive governor of New Jersey. When the Republicans nominated Taft for a second term, insurgents bolted and formed the Progressive party. The new party nominated Roosevelt for president and adopted a platform that reflected his New Nationalism. Distinguishing between "good" and "bad" trusts, Roosevelt was opposed to breaking up big business simply because it was big. He wanted instead to regulate business to ensure that it did not abuse its size and power. Wilson's platform differed little from Roosevelt's except on the trust issue. Wilson contended that business had already grown too big to control; it ought to be broken up so that it would be obliged to control itself through competition. Wilson won the election, carrying with him into office a Democratic congress. The way was clear for Wilson's program, which he called the New Freedom.

Tariff reduction was the first item on the Democrats' agenda, and they accompanied it with the imposition of an income tax, authorized by the newly ratified Sixteenth Amendment. They then tackled banking and monetary reform, coupling the two in the Federal Reserve Act (1913). The act established twelve reserve banks that were to serve as bankers' banks, reserves that would help stabilize the nation's banking system. The act authorized the Federal Reserve Banks to print notes, backed by commercial paper as well as gold, to be an elastic currency to replace the old national bank notes.

On the trust question, Wilson combined the New Freedom approach with that of the New Nationalism. The Federal Trade Commission Act (1914) set up the FTC as a regulatory agency to monitor "unfair" business practices. The Clayton Antitrust Act (1914) defined what those "unfair" practices were. It prohibited such devices as interlocking corporate directorships, price discrimination, and the purchase of stock in a company in order to gain competitive favors.

After the outbreak of war in Europe in 1914, Wilson became preoccupied with foreign affairs and lost interest in further reform. As a result, the final achievements of his presidency—the prohibition and women's suffrage amendments—came about largely because they had built up a momentum of their own. The two were also politically intertwined. Women had long been at the core of the temperance movement, in large part because the abuse of alcohol was one of the most obvious threats to home and family. Fearing the votes of women, the liquor industry threw its resources into the fight against women's suffrage. Middle-class Progressives, worried about urban poverty and disorder, joined women in the temperance crusade. By the time war broke out, more than half the counties and municipalities in the

country were dry. The need to conserve grain during the war gave the movement added impetus, and in 1918 Congress approved the Eighteenth Amendment authorizing prohibition.

The women's suffrage movement, dormant since the Civil War, was revitalized in 1912. It gained new leadership and new militancy. It also gained broad financing from women around the country whose interest in politics had been stimulated by the reform impulse. The war opened new economic opportunities for women, which helped to undermine the argument that they were incapable of sound political judgment. The war also gave Wilson an excuse to reverse himself and endorse women's suffrage as a means of restoring unity and tranquillity. Congress approved the Nineteenth Amendment in 1918, and hard lobbying by the Suffrage Association secured its ratification in time for women to vote in the presidential election of 1920.

READING SUGGESTIONS

The history of Woodrow Wilson's presidency is well told by Arthur S. Link, *Woodrow Wilson and the Progressive Era, 1910–1917* (1954). Two more recent interpretations of the period are Otis L. Graham, Jr., *The Great Campaigns: Reform and War in America, 1900–1928* (1971), and John M. Cooper, *The Warrior and the Priest: Theodore Roosevelt and Woodrow Wilson* (1983). George Mowry, *Theodore Roosevelt and the Progressive Movement* (1947), examines the Bull Moose party. David P. Thelen, *Robert LaFollette and the Insurgent Spirit* (1976), views the Progressive party from another angle. Melvin I. Urofsky's *Louis D. Brandeis and the Progressive Tradition* (1981) is the most recent study of the architect of the New Freedom.

William L. O'Neill, *Divorce in the Progressive Era* (1967), and David M. Kennedy, *Birth Control in America: The Career of Margaret Sanger* (1970), chronicle those two aspects of the women's movement. The women's suffrage movement is chronicled by William L. O'Neill, *Everyone was Brave* (1969), and by Aileen Kraditor, *The Ideas of the Woman Suffrage Movement, 1890–1920* (1965). J. H. Timberlake, *Prohibition and the Progressive Movement, 1900–1920* (1963), and J. R. Gusfeld, *Symbolic Crusade: Status Politics and the American Temperance Movement* (1963), tell the story of the temperance movement.

9

Brown Brothers.

PROGRESSIVES AND THE WORLD: 1900–1920

The United States burst upon the world stage in the 1890s with a suddenness that seemed to startle even Americans themselves. Once the thrill of conquest passed, they surveyed their new empire with something akin to embarrassment. Maintaining colonies and dependencies was contrary to republican ideals of freedom and self-determination. The imperialist impulse vanished almost as quickly as it had risen: No territory was ever claimed and no colonies were acquired after 1900. (The Virgin Islands were purchased from Denmark in 1917, but they were quickly formed into a federal territory.) The armed forces were returned to peacetime levels. No colonial office was set up to administer the empire. The Pacific Islands—Guam, Midway, Wake, and Samoa—were governed by naval officers responsible to the Navy Department. In 1902, Congress passed an Organic Act for the Philippines that set up an island legislature, and in 1916 Congress gave the Filipinos virtual self-government, although the United States reserved ultimate sovereignty over the islands.

⊔Dollar Diplomacy

World problems intruded nonetheless, and Americans discovered that responsibilities, once shouldered, could not easily be discarded. They discovered also that the habit of intervention was not easily broken. The Far East demonstrated both. The Open Door failed to deter the Russian economic and military advance into Manchuria and Korea. Worried about Russian aggression, Japan in 1902 signed an alliance with Great Britain by which the British recognized Japan's interests in Korea. Each also agreed to go to the defense of the other if either became involved in a conflict with more than one other country. With its back door secured, Japan pounced on the Russian fleet at Port Arthur in southern Manchuria and drove the Russians out of Korea in 1904. To prevent the Japanese from achieving total domination in the Far East, President Roosevelt became involved and brought the parties to a peace conference at Portsmouth, New Hampshire, in 1905. The price of Japanese restraint was high. The Russians ceded to Japan the southern half of Sakhalin Island and agreed to evacuate Manchuria. The United States, by separate understanding (the Taft-Katsura Agreement in 1905), recognized Japan's control of Korea in return for a Japanese pledge not to meddle in the Philippines. Roosevelt preserved the balance of power in the Far East, but without enhancing American influence. Indeed, Roosevelt himself was soon to conclude that the United States foothold in the Far East, the Philippines, was becoming a liability.

THE ROOSEVELT COROLLARY

The Caribbean Basin likewise commanded American attention, even after the army evacuated Cuba in 1902. The Spanish-American War made it, in effect, an American lake, and construction of the Panama Canal increased security concerns. After establishing a protectorate over Panama, Roosevelt had no further territorial ambitions in the area. But he could not tolerate European intervention. That was a distinct possibility because of the instability, corruption, and indebtedness of the governments of the West Indies and Central America. Several of them owed sizable amounts of money to British and German investors. In 1902 British and German warships blockaded Venezuela in an effort to

---

(*Chapter opening photo*) The "great white fleet" sent by President Roosevelt on a 'round-the-world goodwill mission in 1907.

force that country to pay up, and Roosevelt had to threaten force to bring the two European powers to the arbitration table. Britain, whose own rivalry with Germany was forcing it to establish closer relations with the United States, suggested that it would gladly support the Monroe Doctrine if the United States would see to it that occasions for intervention did not arise.

A crisis in the island republic of Santo Domingo two years later gave Roosevelt an opportunity to implement this suggestion. After a prolonged civil war Santo Domingo defaulted on its foreign debt, most of which was owed to European bankers. To forestall intervention, Roosevelt sent Admiral Dewey to the island to work out an agreement. The protocol placed the republic in a form of receivership, comparable to an insolvent corporation. Its debt was scaled down by half; the United States

took over its customs collections and allocated half of the proceeds to the Santo Domingo government and half to its creditors. In his December 1904, message to Congress, Roosevelt justified the takeover on the argument that if the United States was going to enforce the Monroe Doctrine and prohibit European intervention in the western hemisphere, it was obliged to use its "international police power" to ensure that no causes for intervention arose. The policy was soon known as the Roosevelt Corollary to the Monroe Doctrine.

The corollary had no historical foundation, for no American government had ever claimed that the Monroe Doctrine forbade temporary European intervention for the purpose of collecting debts. In fact, European gunboats had periodically made menacing gestures without serious objection from the United States. The Roosevelt

The United States in the Caribbean, 1898–1941.

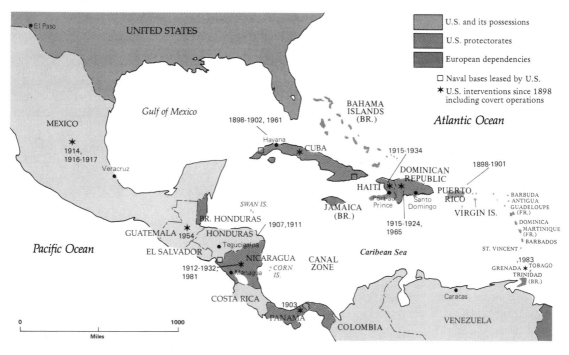

Corollary was not a distillation of long-developing American policy; it was—like the Monroe Doctrine itself—a statement of aspirations. It was also a warning to European governments that the United States was prepared to fill the banking requirements of this hemisphere. The consensus that emerged from the great imperial debate of 1900 pointed in the same direction. American businessmen happily took the cue: Between 1900 and 1917, American trade with Latin America tripled. By 1910, Americans controlled 43 percent of all the property in Mexico and perhaps as much as half of the net worth of Cuba.

In the Taft administration (1909–1913), the marriage between commercial interests and power politics was consummated. Taft's secretary of state, corporation lawyer Philander C. Knox, openly encouraged businessmen to invest in Latin America and in China in order to aid development and encourage pro-American sentiment. Critics called it "dollar diplomacy." The policy ended in further intervention to protect American investments. Nicaragua was a classic case. In 1909, that Central American republic found itself unable to pay its debts, so the State Department arranged to have the Nicaraguan debt refinanced by American banks. The United States then took over customs collection to ensure that the banks were repaid. When a revolution in 1912 threatened the regime, Taft sent in 2,000 marines to restore order. The marines remained until 1933; the customs receivership lasted until 1941.

WILSON'S INTERVENTIONS

In the election campaign of 1912, Woodrow Wilson denounced dollar diplomacy, but his objection was to its commercialism. Wilson saw nothing wrong with intervention. Indeed, he felt the United States had a "peculiar duty" to educate the Latin Americans in self-discipline. The former

schoolmaster told the British ambassador: "I am going to teach the South American republics to elect good men." Wilson's methods, however, differed little from those of Taft. Turmoil in Haiti and its neighbor the Dominican Republic convinced Wilson that intervention was the only way to prevent anarchy and starvation. He sent the marines into Haiti in 1915 and into the Dominican Republic the following year. In Haiti, a U.S.-supervised election resulted in the election of a pro-American president, who promptly placed the republic in a customs receivership. In the Dominican Republic, Americans continued to manage the customs, as they had since Roosevelt's day. Troops remained in the Dominican Republic until 1924 and in Haiti until 1934. In both republics the financial supervision lasted until 1941. Such paternalism left a smoldering resentment, a harvest of bitterness the United States still reaps.

THE MEXICAN FIASCO

The disastrous consequences of Wilson's well-intentioned meddling were not immediately evident, except in Mexico. There it produced a fiasco of the first order. A revolution in Mexico in 1911 brought to the presidency a reformer, Francisco Madero, who set out to destroy the special privileges of the upper classes. In February 1913, the conservative head of the army, General Victoriano Huerta, with the support of American business interests, overthrew Madero and then had him murdered after promising him safe conduct out of the country. Wilson, who became president a month later, disapproved of both Huerta's conservatism and his means of gaining power. Refusing Huerta diplomatic recognition, Wilson settled on a policy of "watchful waiting" in the hope that a more democratic regime would come to power.

While Wilson waited, reform elements

in Mexico settled on Venustiano Carranza as their leader. Carranza, in turn, recruited the services of Francisco Villa, a bandit revered by the peasants of northern Mexico, who referred to him affectionately as Pancho. Villa, at the head of a peasant army that could live on sagebrush and cactus, made himself master of northern Mexico. Another peasant leader, Emilio Zapata, took possession of the southern half.

With the Huerta regime crumbling, Wilson ended his watchful vigil. The occasion was an incident in Tampico in April 1914. American sailors on a supply mission were arrested. They were soon released and Huerta offered an apology, but Wilson chose to turn the incident into a crisis. On the theory that the United States had been insulted, he demanded a 21-gun salute. When that was refused, Wilson sent a naval squadron into Mexican waters. Then, learning that a German vessel carrying arms was heading for Vera Cruz, Wilson ordered his squadron to seize the port. Marines occupied Vera Cruz after a short but sharp fight that cost a hundred lives. Under this fresh humiliation, the Huerta re-

gime disintegrated, and in August 1914 Carranza became president. Wilson promptly extended diplomatic recognition, only to receive the frosty reply that Carranza wanted no American help in governing his country.

Within a few weeks, Carranza and Villa had a falling out, and the civil war began anew. This time the sides were evenly matched, however, and for more than a year the two armies jockeyed and skirmished through the hills of northern Mexico. Then Villa, as cynical as he was desperate, decided to involve the United States in the hope that intervention would topple Carranza. In January 1916, Villa's men stopped a train in Chihuahua, pulled sixteen Americans from it, and shot them. When no outcry resulted, Villa descended on the border town of Columbus, New Mexico, cut up the surprised cavalry garrison, and burned the place to the ground.

While the American public screeched for revenge and Congress discussed war, Wilson ordered his border commander, General John J. (Black Jack) Pershing, to lead an expedition into Mexico to capture

Reaping the Wind of Dollar Diplomacy

Now and then an isolated protest against dollar diplomacy could be heard. The following one, the more remarkable because it was raised in a time not otherwise known for foresight, has a strangely modern ring to it.

In these smaller countries of the South, controlled by our soldiers, our bankers, and our oil kings, we are developing our Irelands, our Egypts, and our Indias. So far they are weak and we have been able to hide them from others. But at the rate the world is moving they can hardly be expected to remain always powerless and isolated. Our North American Christian civilization will find its final test in the way we treat our next-door neighbors. We are piling up hatreds, suspicions, records for exploitation and destruction of sovereignty in Latin America, such as never failed in all history to react in war, suffering, and defeat of high moral and spiritual ideals. How can the United States expect to be the one exception to the rule?

Samuel Guy Inman, in The Atlantic Monthly, *July 1924.*

Brown Brothers.

Pancho Villa.

Villa. It was to be done, said the secretary of war, "with scrupulous regard to the sovereignty of Mexico." Unfortunately, Wilson's scruples did not extend to the point of asking the president of Mexico for permission to intrude into his country. The Mexican commander of the border garrison at Palomas, in fact, prepared to resist until Pershing bought him off by hiring him as a guide.

The military column that crossed the Rio Grande in March 1916 was a motley mixture of technology. The troops rode on horseback; supplies were carried by truck; and the commander rode by car (his driver and aide was Lieutenant George S. Patton, only a few years out of West Point). Pershing's legal authority was the principle, recognized in international law, of "hot pursuit," but the trail had turned cold by the time his men tramped through the ashes of Columbus. Villa's army, too small to do battle, stood by sullen and hostile. During the summer, the "punitive expedition" managed to kill several of Villa's gen-

erals in running fights, but the guerrilla leader himself eluded capture. Lieutenant Patton, exhibiting the flamboyance that would make him a national hero in World War II, defeated one guerrilla detachment after riding into battle in an automobile.

In November, Villa seized Chihuahua City, pillaged it for a week, and then disappeared again into the mountains. The feat demonstrated that Pershing's expedition had accomplished nothing, except perhaps to make Villa a popular hero. In January 1917, President Wilson, increasingly concerned about the war in Europe, ordered Pershing home. A month later, the British turned over to Wilson an intercepted German dispatch offering Mexico a military alliance should the United States enter the European war. The Zimmermann note outraged Americans. Had they reflected further, they might have realized that their own government had helped create the problem.

⊔ The Road to World War

Wilson's slide into the European war followed a similar pattern. Lofty ideals and an urge to refashion the world led to intervention, and the intervention produced only disillusion.

NEUTRALITY

When war broke out in August 1914 between the two great European alliance systems, the Allies (Great Britain, France, Russia, and eventually Italy and Japan) and the Central Powers (Germany, Austria, and eventually Turkey), President Wilson issued a proclamation of neutrality. Neither Wilson nor any other responsible American wanted to enter the war (except Theodore Roosevelt, who was eager to fight, but because he admired German efficiency, took a few weeks to decide which side he was on). Most Americans viewed the war as added evidence that European civilization was corrupt, decadent, and imperialistic. Bankers, industrialists, and farmers all prospered as Europe systematically destroyed itself, but they were not sure that American intervention would bring financial benefit to themselves.

Even so, few Americans were truly neutral in spirit. Those of German or Irish background (an Irish revolution against British rule broke out in 1916) generally sympathized with the Central Powers; most others, including the president, sided with the Allies. Most Americans saw Germany as aggressive, militaristic, and autocratic, and German atrocities seemed to confirm this impression. In their drive for Paris at the outset of the war, German armies slashed across Belgium, violating that country's neutrality. When the Belgians resisted, the Germans responded with harsh reprisals against the civilian population. In late August 1914, the Germans destroyed the city of Louvain after civilians ambushed a German convoy. This and other atrocity stories filled American newspapers through the winter of 1914–1915. And British propaganda agencies made the most of it, portraying the Germans as barbarians and themselves as the bulwark of democracy.

President Wilson, an admirer of English institutions, believed from the outset that a German victory would menace world law and order. If Germany won the war, Wilson predicted, "it would change the course of our civilization and make the United States a military nation." "Colonel" Edward M. House (the title was purely complimentary), a Texas cotton planter who had become Wilson's intimate adviser, shared Wilson's suspicion of Germany. The dispatches of ambassador to Britain Walter Hines Page reflected the British view of the war. Wilson was also motivated by a genuine idealism. He ardently believed in a free world, free of trade barriers, free of imperial domination. And he felt it was America's mission to promote a better world guided by the Progressive ideals of democracy and social justice.

Wilson's initial difficulties, however, were with the British. "Ruling the waves and waiving the rules," as they had in Jefferson's day, the British imposed a loose (and therefore illegitimate) blockade of Germany and extended the definition of contraband to include raw materials and foodstuffs (which, in fact, were the only things Germany needed to import). Wilson protested but eventually accepted the British restrictions. As a result, American trade with Germany dwindled, while exports to Britain and France quadrupled. As part of his neutral posture, Wilson prohibited private loans to the belligerents, but he did permit interbank credits. Through such credit lines, the Allies were able to finance the purchase of munitions and other goods. In October 1915, Wall Street bankers asked Wilson for permission to make direct loans to the belligerents, and Wilson consented. By the time America entered the war, bankers, headed by the House of Morgan, had loaned the Allies nearly $4 billion (about $20 million was loaned to Germany). The Morgan loans represented a considerable financial stake in an Allied victory, though there is no evidence that this affected Wilson's decisions. More to the point, the banking credits turned the United States into an arsenal for the Allied war machine, and that in turn forced Germany to attempt to stop the flow of supplies.

In February 1915, Germany announced that it was creating a war zone around the British Isles. Allied vessels in the zone would be sunk; neutrals were warned to stay clear or they might be attacked by mistake. Germany lacked the surface vessels to enforce such a blockade, but it did have submarines. Wilson warned the Germans they would be held accountable for the loss of any American lives and property. He based his stance on a strict interpretation of the law of the sea. International law held that an attacker had to give warning to a passenger or merchant vessel so passengers and crew could disembark into lifeboats. Since the chief advantage of a submarine was that it could make a surprise attack, such a requirement was impractical. Moreover, British merchant vessels were fully armed, so a submarine that surfaced to give warning would be a sitting mark. By holding Germany accountable to international law while allowing Britain to interpret the law to suit itself, Wilson, in effect, chose his side. The Germans had no illusions; from 1915 on they did not regard the United States as neutral.

SINKING OF THE *LUSITANIA*

German submarines sank several British vessels that spring, some with Americans on board. Then, on May 7, 1915, an *unter-seeboot* (U boat) torpedoed the British passenger liner *Lusitania*, which exploded, capsized, and sank, carrying 1,198 people to their deaths, among them 128 Americans. In the hold was a cargo of munitions, including 4.2 million rounds of ammunition. Wilson, under heavy pressure from jingoes, including Theodore Roosevelt, decided to make an issue of it. He sent three notes to the Germans, each more belligerent than the last, culminating in the demand that the Germans cease submarine warfare. Secretary of State Bryan, who had pointed out in cabinet meetings that relying on passengers to cover contraband was like putting women and children in front of an army, resigned in protest. Wilson replaced him with Robert Lansing, a man who favored intervention on the side of the Allies. Lansing's counsel would make it even more difficult for the president to remain neutral.

Anxious to prevent American entry into the war, the German government sent orders to its U boat commanders to cease attacks on passenger liners. Before the message passed through to all, the British passenger liner *Arabic* was sunk on August 19, 1915, with the loss of two American lives. In response to Wilson's protests, the German kaiser made public the order not to sink liners, and the German ambassador to Washington pledged that no more unarmed passenger ships would be sunk. The *Arabic* pledge was a diplomatic victory for President Wilson, but it did not entirely solve the submarine problem.

William Jennings Bryan was not the only one who saw that an obvious solution was to discourage Americans from traveling on vessels belonging to belligerents. In early 1916, Congress took up the Gore-McLemore resolution, which would prohibit Americans from traveling on armed merchant vessels. The president, arguing that the resolution would destroy the "whole fine fabric of international law," insisted that Americans had a right to travel anywhere they wished. He made the resolution a test of party loyalty, and both houses voted it down.

In March 1916, a submarine sank the ferry *Sussex* in the English Channel, mistaking it for a minelayer. Wilson threatened to sever diplomatic relations, and this time Germany responded with the *Sussex* pledge. It promised not to attack merchant vessels without warning. This greatly reduced U boat operations and eased tensions. But it also meant an uninterrupted flow of supplies into the Allied trenches.

ELECTION OF 1916

The *Sussex* pledge allowed the Democrats to close ranks. The party had threatened to break apart earlier that year over the president's preparedness program. Since the outbreak of the European war, there

USA.
1917

FINLAND
Indep. July, 1917

Lake Ladoga

NORWAY

Helsinki

SWEDEN

Oslo

Stockholm

Petrograd

ESTONIA
Indep.
Feb. 1918

NORTH SEA

LATVIA
Indep.
Nov. 1918

Riga

RUSSIA
1914

Edinburgh

Battle of Jutland
May-June, 1916

DENMARK

Riga offensive
Sept, 1917

LITHUANIA
Indep. Feb, 1918

Memel

Smolensk

GREAT
BRITAIN
1914

BALTIC SEA

Copenhagen

Kiel

Masurian Lakes
Sept, 1914

Vilna

Konigsberg

London

Hamburg

Amsterdam

NETH.

Danzig

Minsk

Tannenberg
Aug, 1914

Berlin

Brussels

Cologne

BELG.
1914

GERMANY
1914

Leipzig

POLAND
Indep. Nov. 1918

Pinsk

Warsaw

Brest-Litovsk

Paris

GERMAN INVASION
AUG-SEPT, 1914

Dresden

Lublin

Kiev

Metz

Mainz

Prague

Cracow

Lemberg

Kerensky offensive
July, 1917

LUX.

Strasbourg

GALICIA

Brusilov offensive
June, 1916

FRANCE
1914

Rhine R.

BAVARIA

Munich

Danube R.

Vienna

Galicia offensives
Aug, 1914

UKRAINE

Berne

SWITZ.

Pressburg

Vittorio-Veneto
Oct-Nov, 1918

Graz

Budapest

Odessa

Milan

Piave June, 1918

Venice

Trieste

AUSTRIA-HUNGARY
1914

RUMANIA
1916

Genoa

BLACK
SEA

Invasion of Serbia
1914

Belgrade

Bucharest

Danube R.

Marseilles

BOSNIA

SPAIN

ITALY
1915

Sarajevo

CORSICA

Withdrew from
Triple Alliance 1914

Rome

MONTENEGRO
1915

SERBIA
1914

BULGARIA
1915

Sofia

Constantinople

ALBANIA

OTTOMAN EMPIRE
1914

SARDINIA

MEDITERRANEAN

PORTUGAL
1916

Salonika

Gallipoli

GREECE
1916

Dardanelles campaign
1915-1916

Smyrna

Naples

SICILY

SEA

Athens

CRETE

1916 Date of entry into the war

────── Maximum advance of the Central Powers

── ── ── Maximum Russian advance

••••••••• Line of the Brest-Litovsk Treaty Mar, 1918

────── Armistice lines, eastern front Dec., 1917

0 ──────── 500
Miles

Central Powers   Allied Powers   Neutral Powers

World War I, 1914–1918.

had been those who advocated that America ought to be prepared, even if it did not intervene. Wilson had at first ignored the preparedness campaign, and then backed it. In the summer of 1916, with the president's support, Congress doubled the size of the army and authorized a naval shipbuilding program. Bryan Democrats from the South and West threatened to desert the president. They were placated, however, by the *Sussex* pledge and by a tax measure that inflicted the cost of arming on the rich through a rise in income taxes and a special tax on munitions makers. The Bryan wing was also able to insert a strong peace plank into the Democratic platform that summer and to establish the party slogan for the coming presidential campaign: "He kept us out of war." They then closed ranks in favor of Wilson's reelection.

Republicans were even more bitterly divided. The eastern wing, led by Roosevelt and Lodge, favored huge military appropriations and denounced Wilson for his faint-hearted policies toward both Germany and Mexico. Midwesterners, led by LaFollette and Norris, insisted on peace, even at the price of abandoning American rights on the seas. Roosevelt made a strong bid for the nomination, but the party chose instead moderate Progressive Charles Evans Hughes, an associate justice of the Supreme Court. Roosevelt—his militarism more a liability than an asset—campaigned for Hughes. It was clear that the vast majority of Americans still wanted no part of the war. Trying to hold his party together, Hughes, whom the Democrats named Charles "Evasive" Hughes, had trouble distinguishing himself from Wilson. Even so, there was enough Republican support in the country to make the election close. Hughes carried most of the Northeast. Wilson, who won by the slim margin of twenty-three electoral votes, carried the South and the trans-Mississippi West.

Strengthened by his victory, Wilson redoubled his efforts to mediate the war. In December 1916, he asked both sides to state their war aims, in the hope of finding some common ground. The Germans, who no longer trusted Wilson at all, refused to reply; the British, among other things, demanded that Germany be made to pay the entire cost of the war. The hideous irony is that losses had become so high and human misery so deep that neither side could afford to quit. After the Allies stopped the initial German thrust at the Battle of the Marne in September 1914, the war had settled into trenches along a line that extended from the English Channel to the Swiss border. Modern weapons—exploding artillery shells, poison gas, machine guns—turned it into mass genocide. France alone had lost 1 million men by the end of 1916. All told, the war would cost Europe 9 million human lives. American diplomat and historian George F. Kennan has remarked that such was the rising cost that any of the belligerents would have been better off to surrender in 1916 than to win in 1918. Yet they could not even afford to negotiate. Politicians feared their people had suffered so much that they would not tolerate anything short of victory.

On January 31, 1917, Germany gave its response to Wilson's mediation by ordering the resumption of unrestricted submarine warfare. The German government knew the move would bring American intervention, but they could not hope to win without cutting off Britain's supplies. And they hoped that a major offensive in the summer of 1917 would "bring England to her knees" before the United States could get its troops across the Atlantic. Wilson severed diplomatic relations but declined further action until Germany committed an overt act.

A series of overt acts ensued. In February, several American merchant vessels were sunk. Toward the end of that month, the British intercepted, decoded, and turned over to Wilson a note from German foreign secretary Alfred Zimmermann to the German ambassador in Mexico. The minister was instructed to offer Mexico a military alliance against the United States, with the promise that Germany would help Mexico recover the territory it had lost in 1848. In light of Wilson's Mexican fiasco, the message had to be taken seriously. The cabinet voted unanimously in favor of war. On April 2, the president went before a hushed Congress to ask for a declaration of war.

He reviewed Germany's transgressions: its violations of international law, its slaughter of innocent Americans, its meddling in Mexico. But realizing that these offenses were rather flimsy grounds for all-out war, he also sought to place the American declaration on broad principle. The "Prussian autocracy," Wilson said, was a threat to popular government everywhere: "The world must be made safe for democ-

racy." At root was his conviction that if the world was to be made a better place—democratic, disarmed, and freely exchanging goods—the United States had to enter the war. If it remained a bystander, it could not hope to influence the peace settlement or the postwar world. The war did not yield the results Wilson expected—but then, wars seldom do.

⊔America at War

The nation was not totally unprepared for war, but to government officials struggling to mobilize, it surely seemed that way. The preparedness measures of 1916 had at least begun the expansion of the navy for the monumental task of transporting 2 million men to France. The increases in the army ensured at least a cadre of trained professionals ready to train others. There re-

A trainload of army ammunition trucks heading for the war front.

State Historical Society of Wisconsin.

mained a shortage of officers that forced the army to set up special training camps that turned out "ninety-day wonders." Though far from smooth, the mobilization was remarkably swift. Fifteen months after the United States entered the war, it had 1 million men in the trenches of eastern France. Americans arrived in time to blunt the great German offensive of 1918 and spearhead the Allied counteroffensive that ended the war.

MOBILIZING FOR WAR

To reach such numbers, conscription was necessary, for the army numbered only about 200,000 in April 1917. In May, Congress passed a Selective Service Act requiring the registration of all males between the ages of 20 and 30 (later changed to 18 and 45). The act permitted the president to accept the services of volunteers but did not compel him to do so. The distinction was important, for Theodore Roosevelt, aged 58 and half-blind, had raised a division of his own and was demanding to be sent to France. The last thing Wilson wanted was a politician in the trenches. The first contingent of the American Expeditionary Force, commanded by Black Jack Pershing, arrived in Paris in June.

Training the 4.8 million men ultimately inducted into the armed forces followed Progressive standards of virtue and efficiency. Secretary of War Newton D. Baker, a veteran reformer, applied the techniques of community organization to the military camps. Around each camp was a social settlement with health facilities and recreational opportunities. Each camp was surrounded by a five-mile "sin-free" zone, and the law forbade drinking by soldiers anywhere. Prophylactics were distributed freely to reduce venereal disease, and horrifying movies showing the effects of VD encouraged their use.

As a result of these heroic measures, the American Expeditionary Force was, as someone remarked, "the cleanest army since Cromwell's day." Even so, the number of deaths due to disease (62,000) exceeded the combat fatalities (51,000), as in all earlier wars. Most of the disease-related deaths were from influenza and pneumonia. A particularly virulent flu virus swept the world in 1918, carrying off more than 21 million people (1 percent of the world's population). In the United States, where a half million died in the epidemic, schools were closed, parades were banned, hospitals were jammed, and supplies of coffins were exhausted in Baltimore and Washington.

Mobilization of the economy likewise followed Progressive lines, notably the New Nationalist emphasis on the coordination of business and government. As early as 1916, Congress created the Council of National Defense, composed of six cabinet members with an advisory commission made up of industrial, railroad, and labor leaders. The council took a complete inventory of America's industrial plant so that priorities could be established in the event of war and standardized the manufacture of munitions. In July 1917, the CND gave way to the War Industries Board which, after a halting start, eventually came under the leadership of Wall Street financier Bernard Baruch. One of the twentieth century's outstanding administrators, Baruch gathered around him a hundred business executives and harnessed the nation's industrial machine, forming priorities, setting prices, making purchases for the Allies, and conserving resources.

A Food Administration under the direction of Herbert Hoover, who had earned a reputation for administrative talent as head of the Belgian Relief Commission, did a similar job in mobilizing agriculture. Hoover, despite a small work force, had three objectives: to feed the American populace, to feed its army, and to feed its allies, especially France, which had been devas-

National Archives.

Woman operating a harvester, formerly a man's job.

tated by the war. By setting high farm prices to encourage production and by appealing to the patriotism of American housewives, Hoover accomplished all three. The export of American foodstuffs in 1918 and 1919 was triple the prewar average. The governmental agencies were dismantled after the war, but the experience was long remembered. When the Great Depression struck in the 1930s, there were some who wanted to meet the emergency with similar devices. Some of the early measures of Franklin Roosevelt's New Deal were based on wartime precedents.

Mobilizing American society—that is, uniting it in behalf of the war effort—produced less fortunate results. Because of the prewar neutralism of "hyphenated Ameri-

cans" (a disparaging term that came to be applied not only to people of recent German extraction but to all foreign-born), the Wilson administration decided the public needed some convincing. With characteristic Progressive efficiency, it created a bureau to do the job. A Committee on Public Information was formed with Progressive journalist George Creel at its head. The committee churned out 75 million pieces of literature ranging from advertisements in campus newspapers ("Are you going to let the Prussian Python strike at your Alma Mater as it struck at the University of Louvain?") to scholarly essays blaming Germany for all the world's troubles. Creel also supported a corps of volunteer speakers, called Four-Minute Men, who gave pep talks in churches, schools, and courthouses,

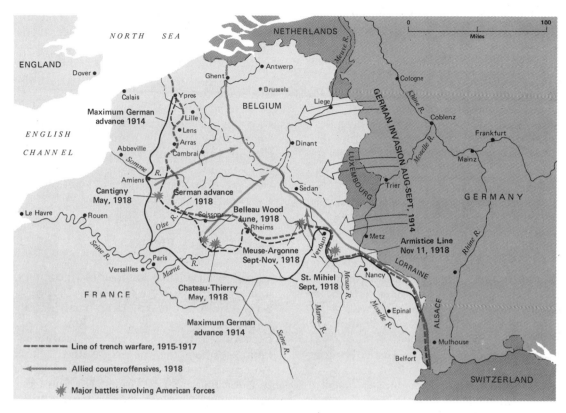

World War I: The American Contribution.

and on street corners. Drawing the movie industry into the war effort, the CPI promoted such films as *The Kaiser*, *Beast of Berlin*, and *Pershing's Crusaders: Our Colored Fighters*. The latter was aimed at black morale, a serious problem because blacks were kept in segregated regiments, usually under white officers, and given only the most menial tasks.

Encouraged by the official hysteria, superpatriots took it upon themselves to purge American society. German books were burned, German china smashed. In Illinois a German "hyphenate" who opposed the war was wrapped in an American flag and lynched. Sauerkraut was renamed "liberty cabbage." People who refused to buy government bonds had their houses

splashed with yellow paint, or were forced to kneel and kiss the flag. Indeed, much of the bigotry characteristic of the 1920s originated in the wartime excesses.

Congress added measures of its own. An Espionage Act (1917) banned treasonous matter from the mails and prohibited "false statements" that impeded the draft or military training. An even more restrictive Sedition Act (1918) made it unlawful to obstruct the sale of war bonds or use "profane" or "abusive" language against the government. The Justice Department, under Attorney General Thomas W. Gregory (who once declared: "Free expression of opinion is dangerous to American institutions"), enthusiastically enforced these loosely worded laws. More than 1,500 people were prosecuted, and the number who were intimidated can only be guessed. Victor Berger, Socialist congressman from Milwaukee, was sentenced to twenty years in prison for violating the Espionage Act, and Eugene Debs was given ten years for an oration in favor of free speech. An elderly South Dakota farmer was given five years for urging a local boy not to enlist. Government agents periodically raided the headquarters of the Socialist Party and IWW.

Never before—not during the Civil War, nor in John Adams's "reign of witches"—had the federal government made such a determined effort to mold the public mind. It was Progressive efficiency run wild. Even the Supreme Court was attuned to the times. In *Schenck* v. *United States* (1919), the Court unanimously upheld the conviction under the Espionage Act of a man who had counseled resistance to the draft. Speaking for the Court, Justice Holmes pointed out that freedom of speech was not absolute, that a person, for instance, does not have a right falsely to shout "Fire!" in a crowded theater. Similarly, said Holmes, Congress has a right to prohibit words that "create a clear and present danger" to national security. Holmes's "clear and present danger" test was in fact intended to limit the occasions when Congress might interfere with free expression, and the following year both he and Brandeis dissented from an opinion upholding the constitutionality of the Sedition Act. Holmes's doctrine nonetheless enabled courts to stifle criticism of the government for many years. Not until the 1950s did the Supreme Court begin to back away from Holmes's test and overturn the convictions of persons accused of seditious utterances.

FIGHTING IN FRANCE

Through all of this, the American military machine sent a torrent of men and supplies across the Atlantic. American participation in the Great War was late and limited, but decisive. American money and munitions had propped up the exhausted Allies; American troops ultimately enabled them to claim victory. In March 1918, the German army, freed of its eastern commitments by the withdrawal of Bolshevik Russia from the war, opened a major offensive. By the end of May it had pushed across the Marne River and seized Chateau Thi-

Lafayette, We Are Here

Just nine days after the first contingent of the American Expeditionary Force landed in France, one of General Pershing's staff officers gave an Independence Day address at the tomb of Lafayette, the French aristocrat who had served so gallantly in the American Revolution. His tribute became one of the most famous remarks of the war.

. . . and here and now in the presence of the illustrious dead we pledge our hearts and our honor in carrying this war to a successful issue. Lafayette, we are here.

Colonel Charles E. Stanton, July 4, 1917.

erry, only fifty miles from Paris. There the American Expeditionary Force, now four divisions strong, fought its first important battle. In June it pushed the Germans back across the Marne and then held Belleau Wood through three weeks of furious German counterattack. By mid-July the German thrust was spent, and in September, with the AEF now numbering more than a million, the Allies began an offensive along the whole front, from the North Sea to Lorraine. In early November, a revolution toppled the German kaiser, who fled to Holland, and an armistice ended the fighting on November 11, 1918. The battle lines at the time ran roughly along the border of Belgium and Luxembourg; Germany itself had not been invaded. The Germans, exhausted but unconquered,

had every reason to suppose that the final peace settlement would be, as Wilson had proclaimed in 1917, a "peace without victory" for either side.

⨆ The Versailles Treaty

In an address to Congress in January 1918, President Wilson presented Fourteen Points which he thought ought to be part of a fair and lasting peace. Included in the first five points were familiar features of American foreign policy—freedom of the seas, free trade, and reduction of armaments. Points 6 to 13 dealt with the map of Europe, the breakup of the Dual Monarchy of Austria-Hungary and of the Ottoman Empire. These imperial agglomera-

Doughboys in the trenches, 1918.

AP/Wide World Photos.

tions were to be replaced by republics representing the cultural and linguistic nationalities of Eastern Europe. The principle of national self-determination, an ingredient in American foreign policy since the beginning of the republic, received new emphasis. The fourteenth point was a proposal for a postwar League of Nations, or, as Wilson phrased it, "a general association of nations affording mutual guarantees of political independence and territorial integrity to great and small states alike."

THE FOURTEEN POINTS AND SECRET TREATIES

The Fourteen Points were what Wilson meant by a "peace without victory," and overnight they made him the moral spokesman for the world. Though phrased as ideals, the Fourteen Points were a realistic expression of American national interests. If approved, they would have opened the world to enterprising Yankee traders. It was worldwide Open Door policy, and precisely for this reason, it caused some misgivings among the Allies. Both Britain and France had extensive empires to manage and defend. Disarmament and free trade challenged the very purpose of empire; national self-determination subverted its very being. Both Britain and France, moreover, were determined to make Germany pay reparations for war expenses and damages. As shrewd and cynical French Premier Georges Clemenceau expressed it: "God gave us the Ten Commandments, and we broke them. Wilson gives us the Fourteen Points. We shall see."

A peace conference to which neither Germany nor Communist Russia was in-

Captain Eddie Rickenbacker, flying ace, 1918.

Library of Congress.

UPI/Bettmann.

The Big Four at Versailles. From left to right they are: Vittorio Orlando (Italy), David Lloyd George (Great Britain), Georges Clemenceau (France), and Woodrow Wilson.

vited opened in the royal palace of Versailles outside Paris in January 1919. Wilson decided to attend, hoping his physical presence would give him greater influence. It probably did, but it also put him in the position of having to bargain for his principles. A bigger mistake was his alienation of Congress. The American delegation, a thousand strong and laced with historians, geographers, and diplomats eager to reorder the world, contained no Republicans of importance and no senators. This oversight—the more astonishing because Republicans had won control of both houses of Congress in the November 1918 election—ensured that whatever settlement Wilson agreed to in Paris would be subject to partisan scrutiny.

In the first of his Fourteen Points, Wilson had called for "Open covenants of peace, openly arrived at." By the time he sailed for France, he was aware that this ideal had been seriously compromised by his allies. Early in the war, the Allies had exchanged secret treaties promising each other territorial gains at the expense of

Germany, Austria, and Turkey. Later Japan was lured into the war with the promise of winning control of German islands in the Pacific, and Italy entered the fight on the assurance of gaining Austrian territory on the Adriatic. The treaties, in addition to being secret diplomacy, revealed that America's allies, far from fighting to save the world for democracy, expected to profit from the war. The treaties were unearthed by Russian revolutionaries after they overthrew the tsar in March 1917 and published with ill-concealed glee. President Wilson was apparently aware of them even before the United States entered the war. Compounding Wilson's difficulties, British and French leaders had made extravagant promises to their people that Germany would be made to pay the cost of the war. Reparations, as such payments were called, were to become the thorniest issue of all.

At the conference, Wilson soon discovered that open diplomacy was fine in theory and utterly impractical. After a series of commissions and councils proved unwieldy, the Big Four—Wilson, Lloyd

CLIO'S FOCUS: Sergeant York

"How many prisoners have you?" asked the astonished American officer as he gazed at the long line of Germans stumbling down the hill. "Honest to God, lieutenant, I don't know," came the answer. And with that candid reply, America had its war hero. Sergeant Alvin C. York caught the fancy of the nation not only for his bravery, but for his refreshing innocence in a world filled with cynical diplomats and inept generals.

A product of the Tennessee mountains, York was a deeply religious man, whose Bible told him that war was wrong. When the Army summoned him in 1917, he retreated into the hills to grapple with his conscience. He knelt and prayed, he later explained, "all the afternoon, through the night, and through part of the next day. And as I prayed there alone a great peace came into my soul and a great calm

Wide World Photos.

Sergeant Alvin York.

came over me and I received my assurance. He heard my prayer and He came to me on the mountainside. . . . I began to understand that no matter what a man is forced to do, so long as he is right in his own soul, he remains a righteous man." Alvin York went to war. He carried his Bible and a conviction that he would not be harmed.

York's division, the 82nd, landed in France in May 1918 and was assigned as backup support for a French army defending the city of Tours. York went on patrol and survived a gas attack. He was promoted to corporal and put in command of an eight-man squad. In September the division was transferred to the Argonne Forest to participate in what was to be the final offensive of the war. It went into action on October 8; its assignment was to capture a railroad, which the Germans used for supplies. The task involved crossing an open valley several hundred yards wide and scaling a ridge of ragged, steep hills. On top of the ridge was a battalion of German machine gunners. As dawn broke, they had an unobstructed view of the valley.

The 82nd moved into the valley and was immediately pinned down by machine-gun fire. York's captain sent a detachment to outflank the Germans. It consisted of York's and two other squads. Sergeant Bernard Early, an Irishman from Connecticut, was in charge. Skirting the valley, the patrol followed an abandoned trench that led them to the rear of the German lines. On the far side of the ridge, they came upon a German major conferring with two other officers. Around them sat some twenty German messengers and stretcher bearers eating breakfast. It was the headquarters of the machine-gun battalion.

The Americans fired and dashed forward with fixed bayonets. Most of the Germans surrendered. Hearing the shooting, the machine gunners on the ridge swiveled and fired into the camp. Sergeant Early fell with six bullets in him; dead too were two other corporals. Only York and seven privates remained.

Caught in the open but saved by his nearness to the German prisoners, York lay in the mud and fired back. His marksmanship, honed in the Tennessee backwoods, was phenomenal. "Every time one of them raised his head," he explained, "I just teched him off." It was like a shooting match back home, "but the targets were bigger. I just couldn't miss." Then, while bullets spattered in the earth around him, he stood up and began firing "offhand," mountain style. "Somehow I knew I wouldn't be killed." When his rifle barrel overheated, he threw the weapon on the ground and pulled out his Colt .45 automatic. A German lieutenant and five of his men rose out of a trench part way up the hill and raced toward him. York brought them down one by one, beginning with the last man, "the way we shoot wild turkeys at home. You see, we don't want the front ones to know we're getting the back ones. I knowed, too, that if the front ones wavered, or if I stopped them, the rear ones would drop down and pump a volley into me." He killed all six.

The fire from the ridge slackened and York turned around, sensing that someone was shooting at him from behind. There stood the German major, empty pistol in hand. He had missed with every shot. The major advanced and asked:

"English?"

"No, not English."

"What?"

"American."

"Good Lord," said the major. "If you don't shoot any more, I'll make them surrender."

York had by then killed twenty-one Germans. The major blew a whistle, and the machine-gun crews came down from the ridge, their hands in the air. York and his half-dozen men searched them, lined them up, and marched them back across the ridge. On the way they came upon other machine-gun nests. York pushed the major out in front of the column and got him to call to the Germans to surrender. All but one did. York shot him. "I hated to do it," he said. "He was probably a brave soldier boy. But I couldn't afford to take any chance, so I had to let him have it."

York's battalion, meantime, had moved across the valley. He met his lieutenant at the edge of the ridge. The lieutenant counted his prisoners as they filed by: There were 132. Word quickly spread that York had "captured the whole damned German army."

The next day, after the railroad was taken, York asked for permission to go back to the hillside. "I had been doing a heap of thinking about the boys we had left behind in the fight. There was just a chance that some of them might be only wounded and still lying out there in pain and need help something terrible." He returned with two stretcher bearers, but found nothing. Medical teams had already cleared out the dead. "All was terribly quiet in the field. Oh, my, it seemed so unbelievable. I would never see them again. I could only pray for their souls. I prayed for the Greeks and Italians and the Poles and the Jews and the others. I prayed for the Germans too. They were all brother men of mine."

The adventure made Sergeant York a national idol overnight, but not simply because of his courage, his religious devotion, or his humanity. York struck a resonant chord in the American psyche. A little more than a century before, Andrew Jackson and his buckskin-clad frontiersmen had withstood the furious onslaught of British regulars at the Battle of New Orleans. Jackson's Tennessee sharpshooters slew some 1,300 redcoats, while losing only 7 of their own. That victory had symbolized the "new man," the American—hardy, bold, and self-reliant, able to overcome singlehandedly the disciplined but unthinking minions of the monarchs of Europe. The symbol, reinforced time and again by the conquest of the West, had begun to fade with the passing of the frontier. Sergeant York gave it fresh life. Here, in a new national emergency, appeared once again a sharpshooting Tennessee "volunteer," outwitting and outfighting an "entire army" of European professionals.

George of Britain, Clemenceau of France, and Orlando of Italy—began meeting secretly to frame an outline. A treaty was presented to representatives of the newly formed German republic in May 1919, and agreed to by the National Assembly at Weimar in June. Agreements with Austria, Hungary, Bulgaria, and Ottoman Turkey followed.

WILSON'S ACHIEVEMENTS

The Versailles Treaty and the territorial agreements that accompanied it appeared to impose heavy penalties on Germany, penalties that seem particularly unjust when it is recalled that Germany had agreed to a ceasefire without ever being invaded. In fact, however, it represented a compromise between the demands of the Allies and the Fourteen Points. Germany lost territory in the east to reborn Poland, and on its western frontier was obliged to return Alsace and Lorraine to France. The portion of Germany that lay west of the Rhine River was made a demilitarized buffer zone between Germany and France. Germany's military forces were so limited as to make future war impossible. Humiliating as it was to the Germans, none of this violated the Fourteen Points in any important way. The land cessions, with the exception of the Danzig corridor which gave Poland access to the sea, were generally in accordance with the Wilsonian principle of ethnic self-determination. Revolutions in the fall of 1918 had overthrown the Hapsburg monarchy and established republican governments in Austria, Czechoslovakia, and Poland. Yugoslavia, an amalgam of Serbs, Croats, and Slovenes, remained a kingdom under the old Serbian royal family. The Versailles Treaty's recognition of these new popularly governed republics was likewise in accord with the Fourteen Points.

Wilson also managed to temper the imperial demands of the Allies. The German colonies in Africa and the Pacific, as well as former Ottoman possessions in the Near East (Syria, Jordan, Palestine) were transferred to the League of Nations. Various Allied governments—Britain, France, Japan—undertook to manage the colonies under League mandate. Thus, the Allies obtained the substance of power while Wilson preserved the principle of anti-imperialism. The mandate system worked well enough to be retained by the United Nations when it was created in 1945.

It was on the issue of reparations that Wilson was not firm enough. He persuaded the Allies to drop their demand that Germany bear the entire cost of the war, but he did agree that Germany should pay for all damages to civilian property in France and Belgium and pensions for all Allied veterans. This alone was an astronomical sum that drained Germany of gold within a few years and caused raging inflation that wrecked the Germany economy. In addition, France was allowed, as compensation for the destruction of its coal mines, to take possession of the rich mines in German's Saar Province for fifteen years. This too added to Germany's postwar economic difficulties.

Wilson felt his greatest achievement at Paris was wringing agreement from reluctant and cynical Europeans for a postwar international organization to preserve the peace. With that accomplished, he felt he could make concessions on other matters. The world organization could smooth the rough edges of the peace settlement. At his insistence the covenant, or constitution, for the League of Nations was embedded in the peace treaty. The League was not given a military force of its own, but it could enforce its will through economic sanctions. In an extremity, it could call on its members to contribute peacekeeping forces. Article X, which Wilson called the "heart of the Covenant," obliged all members "to respect and preserve against exter-

New independent nations   Plebiscite area

Allied occupation zone

Europe after the Versailles Treaty.

nal aggression the territorial integrity and existing political independence of all Members of the League." That provision, in effect, made the League a mutual security alliance. Presumably it was directed at the two powers that were not represented at Versailles and not invited to join the League, Germany and Soviet Russia.

THE LEAGUE OF NATIONS

President Wilson returned from Paris in May 1919 and submitted the treaty to the Senate for approval. The Senate was already aware of the provisions; indeed, a partisan opposition had already begun to form. In March, Senator Henry Cabot Lodge circulated a petition stating that the League did not serve American interests. He obtained the signatures of thirty-nine senators, enough to prevent the necessary two-thirds vote. Lodge, who had earlier favored a postwar world organization, was apparently impelled by a desire to embarrass the Democrats and especially the president, whom he loathed. He had to move cautiously, however, for the League was a popular idea. A majority of newspapers supported it, and a number of state legislatures endorsed it.

The Senate sent the treaty to the Foreign Relations Committee, which Lodge headed, and his strategy soon became evident. For weeks he pondered the document while public interest flagged, and then he held lengthy hearings, in which his committee became a forum for criticism of the treaty. Most of the critics focused on Article X, claiming it deprived Congress of its power to declare war and made the United States the policeman of the world. When the treaty finally emerged from Lodge's committee, it contained fourteen amendments, or reservations. Most were limitations on Article X, and most were mild enough to be acceptable to senators, Democrats as well as Republicans, who had an honest desire to protect American interests. Approval of the treaty therefore depended on the president's willingness to compromise.

Wilson told the Lodge committee he was unwilling to accept alterations because that would require approval of the other signatories. Once the revision process started, there might be no end to it. In September, Wilson set out on a national tour to revive public support for the treaty. He received a warm, even enthusiastic, reception, but he failed to win over any senators. In fact, his insistence that the Senate must accept the treaty as he had written it simply made his opponents more defiant than ever. The president would have served his cause better if he had remained in Washington and searched for a compromise with the "mild reservationists."

Worse still, the tour ended in tragedy. Exhausted by thirty-six formal addresses and numerous whistle-stop appearances, the president collapsed while he was delivering a passionate oration in Pueblo, Colorado. A few days later in Washington he suffered a stroke that left him partially paralyzed for months. Sick and shielded from Congress and the press by his overly solicitous wife, Wilson became more stubborn than ever. When one senator finally penetrated to the sickroom to plead for compromise, Wilson raised himself on his one good arm and growled, "Let Lodge compromise."

The initial test for the treaty came in November 1919. With the Lodge Reservations attached, it failed even to get a majority. All but four Democrats voted against it. A second vote, on a resolution to approve the treaty without amendments, likewise failed to win a majority. There was still room for agreement, however, for more than two-thirds of the Senate had voted in favor of a treaty in some form. Those who did not want a League of Nations with or without amendments were only fourteen in number. Yet through the winter the president stood firm. If the treaty failed, Wilson, his faith in progressivism undimmed, hoped to turn the election of 1920 into a public referendum on the League of Nations. The final vote came on March 19, 1920. With the Lodge reservations—only slightly modified—attached, the Senate voted in favor of the treaty by 49 to 35. It failed for lack of a two-thirds majority. In the minority were 23 Wilsonian Democrats. The president had doomed his own offspring. It was, as one historian has remarked, "the supreme infanticide."

⊔ Wilson's Failure in War and Peace

In retrospect, there appear to be a number of reasons why America's intervention in the Great War proved so disappointing. One was President Wilson's failure to secure Allied agreement on war aims prior to American entry. Britain and France were exhausted at the end of 1916; Wilson had the leverage to dictate a framework for peace as a price for American entry. His "peace without victory" speech of January 1917 showed the direction of his thinking, but it was no binding commitment on the Allies. And the cavalier treatment accorded the Fourteen Points completed American disillusionment. Britain and France were as responsible as anyone for America's postwar retreat into isolationism.

Wilson's political mistakes were also costly. He wounded the pride of the Senate by refusing to take any senators to Paris with him, and his refusal to compromise on amendments to the Versailles Treaty doomed it. Some of the opponents of the League of Nations, such as Robert LaFollette, felt the United States had enough troubles of its own without shouldering the problems of the world, and that, at least, was a position that can be respected. But other Republicans, Lodge among them, were clearly more interested in embarrassing the president than in the nation's interests.

Americans by the autumn of 1919 had simply lost interest in "making the world safe for democracy." For more than two decades they had been summoned to one cause after another; weariness was setting in. The Black Sox scandal—the news that eight Chicago ballplayers had been bribed by gamblers to throw the 1919 World Series—generated more interest in 1920 than Wilson's public referendum on the League. The League of Nations was the last gasp of progressivism. With its defeat, idealism succumbed to apathy.

SUMMARY

The imperialist impulse that had brought on the Spanish-American War vanished almost as quickly as it had risen. After 1900, the United States claimed no more territory and acquired no new colonies. No colonial office was set up to administer the empire. Despite the bold talk of a vast China market, American investments in China were few.

The United States continued to make waves in the Caribbean, however. Presidents Roosevelt and Taft pursued a policy of "dollar diplomacy" in the region. The government encouraged business investment there and protected those investments with force when necessary. When Caribbean republics got into financial difficulties, the United States took control of their customs offices and managed their finances for them. When revolution threatened, the U.S. Marines were sent in to restore order. Cuba, Nicaragua, Haiti, and Santo Domingo were occupied for years, in some cases for decades, by American marines.

Woodrow Wilson denounced dollar diplomacy in the campaign of 1912, but he could not break the habit of intervention. He meddled in Mexican politics until he alienated virtually all parties in Mexico. When one Mexican revolutionary, Pancho Villa, cynically raided an American border town to attract attention, Wilson sent a punitive expedition into Mexico in 1916. The expedition occupied northern Mexico but failed to find Pancho Villa.

After 1914, the central question in American foreign policy was whether to intervene in the war in Europe. The United States declared its neutrality when the war broke out, but it was never neutral in spirit. American sympathies lay with the Allies from the beginning. Americans viewed

Germany as aggressive, militaristic, and autocratic. German atrocities in Belgium, magnified by British propaganda, confirmed this impression. Wilson and his most intimate advisers were also long-time admirers of the British.

Wilson's first step away from neutrality came in the spring of 1915, when he authorized American banks to loan money to the Allies. That enabled Britain and France to purchase large amounts of war materials in the United States, and it forced Germany to try to stop the flow of supplies. In February 1915, Germany announced a war zone around the British Isles, to be enforced by submarines. When a German submarine sank the British passenger liner *Lusitania* in May 1915, sending 128 Americans to their deaths, Wilson sent severe protest notes. After further sinkings and more protests, Germany in March 1916 gave the Sussex Pledge, by which it suspended submarine warfare. The Germans eventually decided they had to resume the use of submarines in order to win the war, however. They began sinking ships again in February 1917. The United States declared war in April.

The American military contribution, though late in arriving, proved decisive.

The American Expeditionary Force, a million strong by the summer of 1918, helped to blunt a German offensive and then spearheaded a counteroffensive that drove the German army back to its frontier by November 1918. An armistice halted the fighting on November 11.

Wilson hoped that his Fourteen Points, announced in January 1918, would serve as the basis for a peace settlement. He desired a generous peace, a "peace without victory" guaranteed by a League of Nations. The Allies had other ideas, and the Versailles Treaty was in reality a compromise between Wilson's idealism and the Allies' desire for retribution. The treaty imposed heavy penalties on Germany that left it economically in ruins.

At Wilson's insistence, the treaty did include provision for a League of Nations. And that, for the United States, proved to be the most controversial part of it. Republicans opposed the League simply because it was Wilson's idea. The public, disillusioned by the outcome of the war, was generally indifferent. Wilson, angered and ill, refused to compromise, and in March 1920 the Senate rejected the treaty. The United States never did join the League of Nations.

READING SUGGESTIONS

A good introduction to the diplomacy of the Progressives is Howard K. Beale, *Theodore Roosevelt and the Rise of America to World Power* (1956). Raymond A. Esthus's *Theodore Roosevelt and the International Rivalries* (1970) offers a more recent look, and his *Theodore Roosevelt and Japan* (1966) is the definitive piece on that topic. Warren I. Cohen, *America's Response to China* (2nd ed., 1980), is a brief but stimulating interpretation. Relations with Latin America are the subject of two books by Dana G. Munro: *Intervention and Dollar Diplomacy in the Caribbean, 1900–1921*

(1964), and *The United States and the Caribbean, 1921–1933* (1975). John M. Blum, *Woodrow Wilson and the Politics of Morality* (1956), contains a good brief description of Wilson's Mexican venture.

Wilson's biographer, Arthur Link, provides the most comprehensive account of the diplomacy leading to World War I. Those who do not want to wade through his multivolume biography might try his shorter study, *Wilson the Diplomatist* (1957). The most recent overview is Robert H. Ferrell's *Woodrow Wilson and World*

War I (1985). Lloyd C. Gardner places Wilson's actions in the context of twentieth-century presidential foreign policy in *A Covenant with Power: America and World Order from Wilson to Reagan* (1984).

David M. Kennedy, *Over Here: The First World War and American Society* (1980), covers the home front in the war, and Edward M. Coffman, *The War to End All Wars* (1968), is the best source for the military operations. For the peace settlement, consult the works of A. J. Mayer, *Political Origins of the New Diplomacy, 1917–1918* (1959), and *Diplomacy of Peacemaking: Containment and Counterrevolution at Versailles, 1918–1919* (1967). Still useful for the fight over the League of Nations is Thomas A. Bailey, *Woodrow Wilson and the Great Betrayal* (1945).

10

BATHTUB GIN
AND BALLYHOO:
1919–1929

In May 1920, only weeks after the U.S. Senate pronounced the death sentence on Wilsonian progressivism by rejecting the Versailles Treaty, the senator from Ohio, Warren G. Harding, was invited to address the Boston Home Market Club. Harding was not associated with the tariff, or any other political principle for that matter. But he was known to be a political ally of Massachusetts' favorite son, Henry Cabot Lodge. And his speaking style was in the ornate tradition of Massachusetts' heroes Daniel Webster and Edward Everett. What the nation required now, he said, is

> not heroism, but healing, not nostrums but normalcy, not revolution but restoration, not agitation but adjustment, not surgery but serenity, not the dramatic but the dispassionate, not experiment but equipoise, not submergence in internationality but sustainment in triumphant nationality.

Such windy alliteration might have passed unnoticed but for one word that captured the mood of a Wilson-weary nation: normalcy. Few realized that normality was the word for which Harding groped, nor would they have cared. Americans in 1920 wanted only to be left alone, free of great crusades and summons to arms, free to pursue the material side of happiness. Instead, the end of the war and demobilization had heightened social tensions. The year in which the Senate struggled over the League of Nations, 1919, was a year of sharp inflation, unemployment, labor strife, and a Red Scare. Normalcy was only a hope; the man who composed the word remained, for the moment, buried in the Senate.

⊔ Search for Normalcy

President Wilson, isolated and ill, distracted by his fight with the Senate over the Versailles Treaty, could not tackle the problems of demobilization. Both Wilson and the Republican majority in Congress expected the country to return to peacetime pursuits without the benefit of government planning. The American Expeditionary Force was brought home and disbanded; soldiers were given $60 and a railroad ticket home. The armada of supply vessels, which the War Shipping Board had purchased or built since 1916, was sold. Railroads were returned to their owners, though with enhanced powers for the ICC. The War Industries Board dismantled its economic empire in a single day.

Near chaos resulted. Four million men and women, discharged from military service, descended on the labor market. Unemployment soared. And because goods were scarce while industry reconverted, so did prices. The cost of living by 1920 was double that of 1913. Even those who were employed felt the pinch; they demanded higher wages, met refusal, and went on strike—four million of them in the course of a year. The public confused the chaos with subversion. Russian Bolsheviks formed the Third Communist International (Commintern) in 1919 to spread Marxist ideology. A Bolshevik takeover in Hungary and uprisings in Germany made it seem as if a worldwide Communist revolution was at hand. Many Americans saw Communists at the root of their own troubles.

THE STRIKES OF 1919

Employers took advantage of the public mood and raised the specter of communism whenever they faced a labor demand. No one was better at that tactic than Judge Elbert H. Gary, chairman of the board of United States Steel and leader of the nation's largest nonunionized industry. When in September 1919, 343,000 workers in the

---

(*Chapter opening photo*) Flappers doing the Charleston.

Chicago-Gary steel district walked off the job seeking recognition of their union, Gary sounded the alarm of Bolshevism, and pointed to the A F of L's chief organizer in the steel mills, William Z. Foster, a former Wobbly. The outcry diverted public attention from the workers' genuine grievances, notably low wages and twelve-hour days. (Foster did become a Communist in 1921 and later became the party's national leader.) In November, the company imported thousands of southern blacks as strikebreakers and got the Indiana state guard to protect their entry into the plant. Striking workers, already torn by ethnic and religious rivalries, rioted. Ultimately federal troops had to be called in to restore order. General Leonard Wood, war hero and Republican presidential contender, declared martial law, and the A F of L surrendered. Unionization of the steel industry was delayed until 1937.

Though less violent, a strike by Boston police in September 1919 had more psychological and political impact. Police unions were not unheard of, but the public was uneasy about them. What happened to the community when its own guardians went on strike? Dissatisfied with their pay and working conditions, the Boston police organized a social club and asked the A F of L for a charter. The police commissioner promptly suspended the club leaders, and the entire force went on strike. After two days of disorder, Massachusetts Governor Calvin Coolidge sent the state guard into Boston. Acknowledging defeat, the police prepared to return to work. But the commissioner refused to reinstate them and began hiring a new force. When Samuel Gompers offered to mediate, he received the following reply from the Yankee governor: "There is no right to strike against the public safety by anybody, anywhere, any time." The statement made Coolidge an instant celebrity; among those sending congratulatory telegrams was President Wilson himself.

The antilabor stance of the Wilson administration in its last years was further illustrated that autumn when the United Mine Workers, under their newly elected president, John L. Lewis, called a strike in the bituminous coal fields. The miners, who had entered into a nonstrike agreement during the war, had not had a pay raise since 1917. Attorney General A. Mitchell Palmer, acting on Wilson's recommendation, secured a court injunction. Lewis called off the strike, saying: "We cannot fight the government."

THE RED SCARE

Attorney General Palmer, with an eye on the Democratic nomination in 1920, was also a central figure in the Red Scare. A law passed in the last month of the war authorized the Labor Department to arrest and deport any aliens who advocated revolution or belonged to a revolutionary organization. The secretary of labor was quietly rounding up aliens when a bomb scare in April 1919 lent urgency to the matter. The black maid of a Georgia senator had her hands blown off when she opened a package mailed to the senator's house. An investigation uncovered 36 bomb packages mailed to members of the cabinet, to justices of the Supreme Court, and to business leaders. Newspaper headlines added to the general fright, and Attorney General Palmer took charge. Working closely with special assistant J. Edgar Hoover, a 24-year-old lawyer who in two years would become the assistant director of the Federal Bureau of Investigation, Palmer began investigating radical organizations. By tapping telephones and prying open letters, Palmer and Hoover obtained evidence to secure secret arrest warrants for some 3,000 aliens. On the night of January 2, 1920, coordinated raids by government agents in 33 cities netted several thousand radicals. In a second series of raids on January 5, FBI agents arrested everyone found in the offices of revolutionary organizations, alien or not. In some cities they even locked up those who came to visit arrested persons.

The Palmer raids resulted in the arrest of more than 5,000 people, about a third of whom were prosecuted by the states. Ultimately, 556 were deported. The IWW, already subject to mob assault in the towns of the Pacific Northwest, as well as harrassment from federal and state authorities, disappeared altogether. The Communist and Socialist parties went underground.

The hysteria died down almost as soon as it had risen, in part because of the official excesses. In the spring of 1920, a committee of distinguished lawyers denounced the Justice Department and accused the attorney general of committing illegal acts. To provide legal services for the victims of government oppression, the American Civil Liberties Union was founded by some distinguished reformers, among them defense attorney Clarence Darrow, muckraker Upton Sinclair, settlement house pioneer Jane Addams, and lecturer Helen Keller, the self-made miracle who had lost her sight and hearing in infancy. That summer the Democratic national convention skipped over Palmer and nominated for president a bland Progressive, James Cox of Ohio. So completely had the public mood changed by the fall of 1920 that the most outrageous piece of anarchism of all caused only a momentary outcry. On September 16, someone detonated a wagonload of explosives in Wall Street in front of the J. P. Morgan Bank, killing 38 people, injuring 200, and causing $2 million in property damage. Newspaper headlines shrieked once more, but the clamor died rather quickly.

The Red Scare itself was a victim of normalcy. Even fear had succumbed to apathy. Warren G. Harding, the Republican candidate in that presidential election year, fitted the national mood perfectly. Harding had told the Ohio Republican committee that

first endorsed him: "I venture to announce now no platform, nor to emphasize any obvious policy. Men in Congress make records which speak for them." Harding's record in Congress revealed nothing but a slavish adherence to the leadership of Henry Cabot Lodge and Boies Penrose. And that, in fact, suited the Senate leaders very well. Harding was, in the phrase of Pennsylvania's Senator Penrose, "a man who will listen." Harding began far back in a strong field that included General Leonard Wood, heir to the Roosevelt following, and Herbert Hoover. Months before the convention, Harding's campaign manager, Harry Daugherty, predicted that the leading candidates would block one another and that, about eleven minutes after two on the last night of the convention, "ten or twenty weary men sitting around a table" would settle on Harding. The prophecy, redrafted by the press to read "fifteen men in a smoke-filled room," proved to be exactly right. Harding won the nomination, listened to the bosses who advised a "front porch" campaign in the McKinley style, and swamped Democrat Cox with 61 percent of the popular vote. It was the most lopsided victory since James Monroe had captured every electoral vote but one exactly a century before.

⊔ The Harding Debacle

Harding was not a man prepared to deal in the abstract or the philosophical; he preferred to deal in people. Even in that realm, his judgment was questionable: He filled the White House with cronies who shared his liking for bourbon and poker.

CRONIES AND CROOKS

A few of his cabinet were able men. Secretary of State Charles Evans Hughes handled the twin diplomatic problems of the day, German reparations and naval arms limitations, very well. Treasury Secretary Andrew W. Mellon, a Pittsburgh banker, managed his department with skill, although most of his budgetary recommendations centered on reducing taxes on the rich. The most energetic member of the cabinet was Commerce Secretary Herbert Hoover, who took an obscure bureau and made it a centerpiece of government. Hoover persuaded industry to standardize so that plumbers could interchange pipe fittings and mechanics could swap carburetors. Recognizing that, with Europe in shambles, America had become the world's banker, farmer, and fabricator, Hoover sent the Commerce Department abroad. In some places his commercial attachés attracted more attention than the State Department's diplomats. Commerce, always a feature of American foreign policy, became in Hoover's hands a diplomatic art.

But that was it. The rest of Harding's cabinet were listless nonentities or profiteering scoundrels. Lesser offices went to friends from Ohio, soon dubbed the Ohio gang, who looked for guidance to Attorney General Harry Daugherty. The Ohio gang dealt in pardons, paroles, protection to bootleggers, and general graft. The head of the Veterans Bureau bilked his agency of $250 million through deals with hospital building contractors, while the war's human debris—300,000 disabled and 70,000 mental patients—waited for medical service. When honest contractors complained, Harding summoned his Veterans Bureau chief, extracted some of the story from him, and allowed him to go abroad to resign in February 1923. When the Senate began an investigation a month later, the bureau's counsel committed suicide. Harding himself was not part of the thievery, but he could not have been totally unaware of it. Later that spring he confessed to journalist William Allen White: "I can take care of my enemies all right. But my friends, my God-damn friends, White, they're the ones that keep me walking the floor nights!"

In June 1923, the president left Washington for a speaking tour of the West and a vacation in Alaska. With him were a trainload of reporters and Secret Service men, his wife, and his physician, a man from Harding's home town of Marion, Ohio. Harding's purpose was to recover some of his popularity and to escape the troubles of Washington. And there certainly were troubles brewing.

One Senate committee was burrowing into the affairs of the Veterans Bureau and another was sniffing around the Interior Department. And then there was Nan Britton, the hometown girl who had been infatuated with Harding since the beginning of his political career. There had been trysts with Nan, mostly in New York hotels, from 1916 until 1922. Their child, a daughter, was born in 1919. Britton, who described the affair in a book, *The President's Daughter* (1927), claimed that Harding never denied paternity or showed any unwillingness to support her. A private investigator, who also burst into print after Harding died, claimed that Mrs. Harding was fully informed of the whole affair. Whether true or not, there were many who noted a tense atmosphere in the White House after 1922. In the summer of 1923, when the president headed for the West Coast, Nan Britton set out for Europe— at the president's expense, or so she alleged.

The speaking tour was not a success; Harding daily became more tense and nervous. Commerce Secretary Hoover, along for the ride apparently, complained of the incessant card playing. He became so sick of bridge that he never played the game again. In Seattle, Harding had difficulty finishing an address and spent a night in pain; his physician diagnosed it as food poisoning. On board ship to San Francisco, he came down with pneumonia. On August 2 he was sitting in a hotel room recovering from that when he suffered a stroke and died. The private investigator who had been shadowing Nan Britton later claimed he had been poisoned by his wife. More likely, he died the natural, if untimely, death of a man who had overlived and underexercised.

TEAPOT DOME

Two months later, Senator Thomas Walsh of Montana, who had been looking into the affairs of Interior Secretary Albert Fall of New Mexico, went public with his findings. One scandal after another rocked the government in the months after Harding's death as the sins of the Ohio gang came to public view. The most spectacular was Walsh's revelation of the Teapot Dome. This scandal involved oil lands located at Teapot Dome, Wyoming, and Elk Hills, California. Presidents Taft and Wilson set these public lands aside to ensure a future oil supply for the navy. In 1922 Interior Secretary Fall leased the lands to oil companies, among them the Mammoth Oil Company,* headed by Harry F. Sinclair.

The Senate learned of the leases and ordered an investigation. Senator Walsh at first suspected nothing more than a dispute among conservationists, much like the Ballinger-Pinchot affair of the Taft years. When he learned the extent of the conspiracy, he began public hearings in October 1923. It developed that Fall had accepted "loans," "little black bags" full of cash, and prize cattle for his New Mexico ranch from the oilmen. The government got the leases invalidated, but it failed to secure a conviction of the oil tycoons. Fall was ultimately convicted and sent to prison for accepting a bribe—the first and, until the Nixon presidency, the only member of a president's cabinet to be so punished.

Attorney General Daugherty, leader of the Ohio gang, fought back by ordering the FBI to investigate senators who were investigating the executive department, but in 1924 he too was forced to resign. Brought to trial for accepting money from a German company whose assets had been seized during the war, Daugherty refused to testify on grounds that he was protecting the confidence of the president. He was acquitted, but others in his circle committed suicide or went to jail.

⊔ The Coolidge Years

"Keeping Cool with Coolidge," one of the hit songs of the 1927 Broadway musical *Good News*, was on the mark: Calvin Coolidge was cool. A flinty-faced Yankee who never uttered three words when two would do,** Coolidge was the very opposite of Harding; an occasional cigar was the extent of his vices. The expression on his face, as William Allen White remarked, was one of "looking down his nose to locate the evil smell which seemed forever to affront him." He replaced Harry Daugherty as attorney general with Harlan Fiske Stone, dean of the Columbia Law School (and later a distinguished member of the Supreme Court), and he engaged in a general governmental housecleaning. Coolidge, who earned a term of his own in 1924 by defeating conservative Democrat John W. Davis, brought the nation five and a half years of impeccable, not to say unobtrusive, governance.

Coolidge's approach to language had its advantages, both for Coolidge and his listeners, because the man went to the presidency with neither policy nor philosophy.

---

* The company was later known as the Sinclair Oil Company, with a dinosaur as its symbol. Both companies are commemorated today in a mammoth statue of a dinosaur perched atop the Black Hills between Sinclair, Wyoming, and Rapid City, South Dakota.

** A pleasant young woman who had the misfortune to be placed next to him at dinner while he was vice president said: "Mr. Coolidge, I've made a rather sizable bet with my friends that I can get you to speak three words this evening." Coolidge replied, "You lose."

His public speeches were an assortment of truisms that could have been garnered from the century-old *McGuffey Eclectic Reader*. One caustic biographer remarked that Coolidge, early in life, "cut the umbilical cord between thought and speech." He had no sympathy for the down and out, and less understanding of how they got there. "When more and more people are out of work, unemployment results," he once declared.

TRIUMPH OF LAISSEZ FAIRE

All this may explain his popularity. His predominantly white, small-town constituency shared the same values: hard work, frugal living, honesty, and piety. And they felt they could do very nicely without government. Coolidge was their man.

Under Coolidge, policy was set by people who did have ideas and plans—that is to say, special interests. Coolidge willingly agreed. After five months in office, he told the country: "The business of America is business," by which he meant that any form of rewarding activity, from farming to teaching, was a form of business. But it was not farmers and schoolteachers he appointed to office; it was businessmen. He loaded the Tariff Commission (a Progressive carryover) with corporate executives, who made their decisions in the light of their own interests. Coolidge, in any case, accepted their recommendations only when they favored higher rates. To the Federal Trade Commission (another Progressive legacy), Coolidge named only safe conservatives, as Harding had before him. William E. Humphrey, appointed to head the FTC in 1925, publicly advocated self-regulation of business, which of course meant nonregulation. He worked closely with Commerce Secretary Herbert Hoover to help businessmen form trade associations that divided up markets and reduced competition. Laissez faire, the ideal of the day, was selectively applied, as it had been so often before.

In such a climate, wealth was the key to power. Other interest groups, such as farmers, had no part in the governmental decision making. And farmers were in acute distress throughout the twenties. Theirs was the blue note in the Jazz Age. The decline in farm prices and income was attributable in part to improvements in agricultural technology. With gasoline tractors, hybrid seeds, and commercial fertilizer, American farmers could produce more food than the world could eat—at least that part of the world which could afford to eat. There was also reduced consumption as prosperous, educated Americans trimmed their diets. Changes in women's clothing styles sharply reduced the demand for cotton. Mechanized farmers survived. Small, inefficient farmers became tenants or headed for the city in search of work. In 1927 and again in 1928, Congress passed bills to have the government buy up farm surpluses for storage or marketing abroad. Each ran into a presidential veto. Coolidge contended that Congress did not have the power to single out a special interest for governmental benefits. That this could be stated with straight face was a true measure of his sense of humor.

SPOTTED PROSPERITY

For the middle and upper classes, on the other hand, the Coolidge years were years of sustained prosperity, for which the president, by not doing anything disruptive, could at least take indirect credit. The booming economy, together with the high rates imposed by the Republican Fordney-McCumber tariff of 1922, provided the government with more tax receipts than Coolidge's frugal budgets required. Treasury Secretary Mellon was able to pay off nearly half the nation's war debt, while persuading Congress to cut corporate and personal income taxes. Not all shared equally in the prosperity—there was chronic technological unemployment, as machines took over more and more jobs—but among the employed, the benefits of prosperity were probably more equitably distributed than ever before. Real per capita income rose from $522 in 1921 to $716 in 1929, which meant that the average American was 40 percent better off at the end of the decade. The prosperity contributed to the euphoria of the Coolidge years, which the middle class of a later time would look back to nostalgically as the "roaring twenties." A brief calendar of events offers a glimpse of those years, in which so much of modern American life took shape.

1923. The black revue *Runnin' Wild* opened at New York's Colonial Theater on October 29, featuring the song "Charleston," which launched a national dance craze. The previous week, *The Ziegfeld Follies*, featuring Fanny Brice and Paul Whiteman and his orchestra, opened at the New Amsterdam Theater. In Philadelphia, Bessie Smith recorded "Down Hearted Blues," a song that would sell 2 million copies and launch the career of the first woman jazz singer. New products introduced that year included the Schick razor, the Maidenform bra, and Sanka coffee. Clarence Birdseye, who had obtained patents on a fast-freezing process, opened a frozen food business that would change American eating habits. Corporations founded that year were Hertz Rent-a-Car, Pan American Airways, Zenith Radio, Pet Milk Company, and the Nielsen rating service for radio broadcasts. Tetraethyl lead was introduced as an additive for gasoline. The federal government introduced a numbering system for U.S. highways. Beer tycoon Jacob Rupert built Yankee Stadium, and the Yankees won their first World series, beating the Giants four games to two. President Coolidge

Culver Pictures, Inc.
Bessie Smith, Queen of the Blues.

ended the year by lighting the first White House Christmas tree.

1924. Grey flannel trousers, known as Oxford bags, were introduced from Britain, and the first Winter Olympics was held in France. In the football game of the decade, Illinois vs. Michigan, Illinois halfback Harold (Red) Grange ran the opening kickoff 95 yards for a touchdown and scored three more times in the next 12 minutes; the final score was Grange 39–Michigan 14. The Galloping Ghost, sportswriter Grantland Rice called him. New products introduced that year included Kleenex and Wheaties; new corporations, IBM and MGM. George Gershwin wrote the score for *Rhapsody in Blue* in three weeks and

AP/Wide World Photos.
"The Galloping Ghost," Red Grange, in action against Michigan, 1924.

performed it, accompanied by Paul Whiteman, at New York's Aeolian Hall. Macy's held the first Thanksgiving Day parade, and the price of a brand new Model T Ford was $290.

1925. On New Year's Day, Knute Rockne's Notre Dame, with its Four Horsemen in the backfield, defeated Stanford in the Rose Bowl. The Yale University Athletic Association took in more than a million dollars in a single ticket season. The U.S. Post Office introduced air mail service, and the *Grand Ol' Opry* went on the air in Nashville. Popular songs included "Yes Sir! That's My Baby" and "Five Foot Two, Eyes of Blue." A. Phillip Randolph organized the Brotherhood of Sleeping Car Porters. The first motel opened in San Luis Obispo, California. The Florida real estate boom crumbled when investors discovered that lots they had purchased were under water. New products included Scotch tape; the newest pastime was contract bridge. Al Capone, after gunning down archrival Dion

O'Bannion in his flower shop, took over as boss of Chicago bootlegging, and Pretty Boy Floyd began a twelve-year career in which he would rob thirty Midwestern banks and kill ten people.

1926. Gertrude Ederle became the first woman to swim the English Channel and beat the world record by nearly two hours. Her feat was a major blow to the "weaker sex" image that had oppressed women for centuries. In New York, silent screen star Rudolph Valentino, whose sideburns and slicked-down hair had set the standard for masculine sex appeal, died at the age of 31. Also dead that year, of blood poisoning, was escape artist Harry Houdini, who had made headlines just weeks before his death by remaining under water in an airtight case for 91 minutes. Broadway musicals included Sigmund Romberg's *Desert Song*, and the first sound movie, *Don Juan*, starring John Barrymore, opened at the Manhattan Opera House. Genes, as instruments of heredity, were proved to exist, and physicist Robert H. Goddard fired the first liquid-fueled rocket. New products on the market were Prestone antifreeze, synthetic rubber, the permanent wave, zippers, and cellophane. A Scottish inventor made the first successful demonstration of television, though it would be two decades before the device was ready for the market.

1927. Charles Lindbergh flew the Atlantic, Babe Ruth hit sixty home runs, and Alvin (Shipwreck) Kelly sat on a flagpole in Baltimore for a record-breaking 23 days, 7 hours. Henry Ford's Model T, the Tin Lizzie, was supplanted by the more powerful, better-geared Model A. Twenty million automobiles were on the highways that year. Duke Ellington began his career at Harlem's Cotton Club, and Grauman's Chinese Theater opened in Hollywood. Other novelties: trans-Atlantic telephone service, the first coast-to-coast radio broadcast (the Rose Bowl game), electric juke boxes, Coney Island's roller coaster, Wonder Bread, Hostess Cupcakes, and Gerber baby food. In Chicago, 145,000 people, the largest stadium crowd ever to witness a sporting event in America, jammed Chicago's Soldier Field to watch a Dempsey-Tunney rematch. Gene Tunney had won the heavyweight boxing title from Jack Dempsey the previous year. In the rematch, the famous "long count" fight, Tunney rose from a knockout blow (after Dempsey, the Manassa Mauler, failed to retreat into a neutral corner, thus delaying the referee's count) and won the fight. At the other end of Chicago, Al Capone recorded an income of $105 million, an all-time record for a private citizen.

1928. Amelia Earhart became the first woman to fly the Atlantic, though she was accompanied by two men who insisted on doing the driving. (She later flew it alone to prove that she could.) Anthropologist Margaret Mead, aged 26, revolutionized her field with her book *Coming of Age in*

Samoa. George Gershwin introduced his *An American in Paris* in New York's Carnegie Hall, and the radio variety comedy *Amos n' Andy* made its debut on Chicago's WMAQ. Walt Disney's *Steamboat Willie* was the first animated cartoon with a sound track. It also provided Americans with a new national idol, Mickey Mouse. At least 1,565 Americans died from bootleg liquor that year, and hundreds more were blinded. Federal agents were making 75,000 arrests a year in attempting to enforce Prohibition.

Accompanying this explosion in new lines of business and new products was a revolution in advertising. Newspaper advertising dated back to the time of Benjamin Franklin, and in the intervening century it had changed but little. In 1900, advertisers used either poster-style displays to obtain single brand-name publicity or they tried "salesmanship in print" with hard-selling copy full of reasons for trying a particular product. By about 1914, a few advertisers were selling the benefit, rather than the product—illumination instead of lighting fixtures, prestige instead of automobiles, sex appeal instead of soap. (Woodbury's pathbreaking slogan "The Skin You Love to Touch" first appeared in 1911). By the 1920s, such methods dominated the industry. The new approach was to appeal to consumer needs and values, rather than product superiority. Advertisements increasingly dwelt on "participatory" anecdotes and illustrations, such as, "Are you sure you know your type?" "Little dry sobs through the bedroom door," and "And he wondered why she said No!" The approach succeeded because it responded to the fear of failing to keep pace. Business was getting bigger, technology more complicated, the family more distended, and religion less comforting. Personalized advertising allowed people to feel they were abreast of the quickened tempo of change. Noting that the "inferiority complex" had become an important target of advertising, a J. Walter Thompson executive in 1930 thought that it was due to "the fact that this standardized age has made people feel inferior."

⊔ Social Tensions of the Twenties

The twenties was a time of boundless energy and inventiveness. But the decade also had its seamy side. Beneath the glitter were the baser elements of nativism, bigotry, and political apathy.

NEW MORES

"Blow some my way," said a woman to a man lighting a cigarette in a Chesterfield ad of 1925. And the fast-growing field of advertising could count another triumph: It had broken a taboo by suggesting that women smoked. Women did, but in the classic mode of the double standard, the subject was never discussed in public. Taboos were falling like dominos in this dawn of modern times. The theories of Sigmund Freud, though not widely read, were widely discussed in drawing rooms and at cocktail parties. Public displays of affection became common, especially in the automobile. Women were bolder, more outspoken. "Of course a flapper* is proud of her nerve," wrote a woman in the *New York Times* under the heading "Flapping Not Repented Of"—"she is not even afraid of calling it by its right name. She is shameless, selfish and honest, but at the same time she considers these three attributes virtues. Why not? She takes a man's point of view as her mother never could, and

when she loses she is not afraid to admit defeat, whether it be a prime lover or $20 at an auction."

The flapper, as activist and as symbol, was a compromise of tensions among women. The women's suffrage amendment had been a feminist victory, but it had not been won for feminist reasons. Feminists—advocates of female equality—had merely succeeded in persuading middle-class women, who had been a potent force for reform in the Progressive era, that the vote would give them a healthier, broader, and more influential domestic life. Insofar as feminists hoped that womanpower could change the world, they were disappointed and frustrated. Evidencing the tension was a split between the major women's organizations. Alice Paul's Congressional Union, which had been the most radical of the suffrage organizations, became the National Woman's Party. Its chief political aim was an amendment to the Constitution guaranteeing equal rights for women. The more conservative women's suffrage association reorganized itself as the League of Women Voters. The League, together with the Federation of Women's Clubs (which themselves began to devote more time to contract bridge than to child labor and pure foods), cast doubt on the desirability of a constitutional amendment, fearing that it would undermine the special treatment with respect to wages and hours that working women had achieved during the Progressive era.

The flapper was, in a sense, a common denominator of the two viewpoints. The flapper was bold, venturesome, and independent. But she also reflected the same disillusionment as males did in the aftermath of the "war to end war." One member of the new womanhood bluntly observed that the previous generation had always put off its own ambitions until some job of reform had been done. "They were all going to return to their personal knitting

---

* The origins of the word *flapper* remain obscure. One authority claims it referred to a young bird learning to fly. Others say it was an early reference to teenagers, referring specifically to the pigtails worn by young girls, which flapped as they walked.

Library of Congress.

Enforcing laws regulating beachwear.

after they had tidied up the world. Well look at the world! See how they tidied it up! Do you wonder that our generation says it will do its personal knitting first?" Thus, even though the vast majority of women in the 1920s adhered to the traditional role of wife-companion, they were able to assert their individuality in new ways. Their grandmothers had violated sensibilities by invading saloons and their mothers had marched for suffrage; the new generation broke tradition in its own way by smoking, dancing, bobbing its hair, and raising its skirts. In 1928, the *Journal of Commerce* estimated that the number of yards of cloth required for a woman's costume was a half to a third of the amount needed before the war. The new freedom of movement was especially evident among the young. Couples thought nothing of hopping into an automobile and driving twenty miles for an evening of dancing in another town. The advent of the closed automobile (10 percent of all cars in 1919,

nearly 90 percent by 1929), moreover, made even privacy mobile and added to the relaxation of Victorian standards. Petting, first brought to public attention by F. Scott Fitzgerald's tale of collegiate life, *This Side of Paradise* (1920), became a symbol of the new freedom.

The automobile did more than affect the birth rate.* It lowered church attendance by providing alternative ways of spending a Sunday, and it rearranged the landscape. In 1916, the federal government began appropriating funds for highway construction, and by the end of the 1920s, nearly one fourth of the road mileage in the country had some type of surfacing. The automobile offered new outlets for American restlessness. "A stream of tourists bowls or bumps along the open trails from Maine to California," wrote a *New York Times* reporter in 1922. "Camp fires and tent villages mark its daily course. It draws Main Street across a continent and changes a sparsely-settled countryside into a vast and populous suburbia." The commuters' suburb, miles from the city center, was another offspring of the automobile. Previously residential urban patterns had been dictated by the streetcar; the automobile enabled the city to sprawl into the countryside, gobbling farmland and converting sleepy villages into busy suburbs.

SCIENCE AND RELIGION

Technology was the great accelerator for social change, and those who prided themselves on being up to date pored eagerly through the latest accounts of scientific progress. In 1921, Albert Einstein, whose

---

* The birth rate in the United States had been declining since the early nineteenth century and continued to do so in the 1920s. But the '20s were the first decade in which the rate of decline was less than in the previous decade. How much the automobile was responsible for this, of course, can only be guessed.

general theory of relativity had been published only six years before, visited the United States. Thousands of New Yorkers turned out to greet his party at the dock. The following year a team of astronomers from California's Lick Observatory tromped into the desert of western Australia in order to verify Einstein's theory by taking pictures of an eclipse of the sun. The displacement of star images due to the sun's gravity was exactly what the Einstein equations predicted, the first sound evidence that he was right. Across the country, Einstein became a familiar name, a synonym for genius, and relativity became standard drawing room fare. " 'Science says,' " grumbled the *Nation* magazine in the middle of the decade, "will generally be found to settle any argument in a social gathering, or sell any article from toothpaste to refrigerators."

While science received the credit for social change, it also received the blame from those who were bewildered by the pace or distressed at the direction. The immorality of youth, complained elderly conservatives, was due to the decline of religion. Religion, in turn, had been undermined by science,

Clarence Darrow at the Scopes Trial, 1925. In cross-examination he took Bryan apart "like a dollar watch."

notably Darwin's theory of evolution. Evolution, said the traditionalists, not only ran counter to the biblical description of Creation, it bestialized humankind by making man the descendant of apes. The most vocal champion of this view was the aging apostle of prairie economics and mountain religion, William Jennings Bryan, who led a single-minded crusade against the teaching of evolution in the public schools. Most of Bryan's support came from rural America, the Midwest and the South, where people clung to traditional ways. In Florida, North Carolina, and Texas, state boards of education forbade the teaching of evolution; in Tennessee, the legislature made it a criminal offense.

Bryan took a personal interest in the Tennessee law. After the lower house of the assembly passed his anti-evolution bill in the spring of 1925, he went to the state to build public pressure. Lecturing a meeting on the subject "Is the Bible True?" Bryan thundered: "It is true! Every word of it. Every comma. Every miracle recorded in the Bible actually happened. The Bible is the word of God, who dictated it verbatim to the Apostles!" Copies of the speech were given out in the Tennessee senate, which passed the bill by a wide margin. The governor thought it absurd but signed the bill on the theory that it would soon be forgotten. After all, legislatures often approved of foolish things. The governor was wrong: An anti-evolution law was too luscious an opportunity for those who could see fame and profit in staging a "battle" between science and religion. It was, as one journalist noted, an "age of ballyhoo."

The American Civil Liberties Union, newly formed and in need of a cause, ran ads in Tennessee newspapers offering to provide a legal defense for any teacher who violated the law. In tiny Dayton, a local booster read the ad and decided the town could use some publicity. He located a young general science teacher, John

Thomas Scopes, who was willing to admit he had discussed evolution in his high school class. The sheriff arrested Scopes, the promoter telephoned the ACLU, and the ACLU hired the famous defense attorney Clarence Darrow. Bryan returned to aid the prosecution. Journalists and movie cameramen crowded into town, and for twelve incredible days in July 1925 the nation witnessed a climactic battle between science and religion. Scopes was convicted—he confessed, after all, to breaking the law—but Bryan, who took the witness stand to testify as an expert on the Bible, was made to look a fool. He died only a few days after the trial ended. Religious fundamentalism, however, remained very much alive.

NATIVISM

Religious primitivism was only one of the shadows in the 1920s' darker side. Intolerance and bigotry, never far from the surface in America, seemed more prevalent than ever before, perhaps because they became fused with nationalism. The war had nourished this unholy union; the Red Scare of 1919 consummated it. States hounded radical organizations throughout the 1920s. The discovery that persons of foreign birth, especially Jews, made up a good portion of the members of the Communist and Socialist parties revived ancient prejudices. The most celebrated case was that of Nicola Sacco and Bartolomeo Vanzetti, two Italian-born radicals, who were accused of participating in a payroll robbery in South Braintree, Massachusetts, in April 1920, in which a bank guard was killed. Recent findings indicate that at least one of the two men, Sacco, may have been guilty, but the court at the time showed little concern for hard evidence. Their trial was a mockery, as the judge allowed the state's attorney to make their political radicalism the cornerstone of his case. Sacco

Library of Congress.

The Ku Klux Klan parading down Pennsylvania Avenue in Washington, D.C., 1925.

and Vanzetti went to the electric chair in 1927.

The most sinister form of 1920s nativism was the Ku Klux Klan. The Klan of Reconstruction days had died in the 1870s. It was revived in 1915 by William J. Simmons, a traveling preacher and insurance salesman, who obtained a charter for his secret organization from the state of Georgia. Simmons described the KKK as a "high class, mystic, social, patriotic benevolent association," dedicated to "white supremacy" and "Americanism." More broadly aimed than the original Klan, Simmons's "invisible empire" directed its attacks against Jews, Roman Catholics, and immigrants, as well as blacks. The second Klan grew slowly until 1920, when Simmons hired a promotional genius named Edward Clarke. Clarke organized a nationwide drive for white males willing to put up $10 for a membership and another $6 for hood and robe. Membership salesmen were given the lofty title of Kleagles, and each was allowed to pocket $4 of the $10 fee. Seldom has the blend of modern advertising and the profit motive had such instant and overwhelming success. Kleagling became one of the growth industries of the decade, and Clarke, who had the white sheet concession, became a millionaire. At its height in 1924, Klan membership reached 4.5 million, and it either controlled or heavily influenced the governments of Texas, Oklahoma, Arkansas, California, Oregon, Indiana, and Ohio.

IMMIGRATION RESTRICTIONS

Another form of nativism, less vicious but even broader in appeal, was the drive for immigration restrictions. Like Prohibition, this was a legacy of the Progressive movement. Urban reformers and labor leaders joined to limit the trans-Atlantic tide of humanity that, to Progressives at least, appeared to be responsible for urban blight, crime, and unemployment. In 1917, Congress passed, over President Wilson's veto, an act imposing a literacy test. This, it was thought, would exclude large numbers of

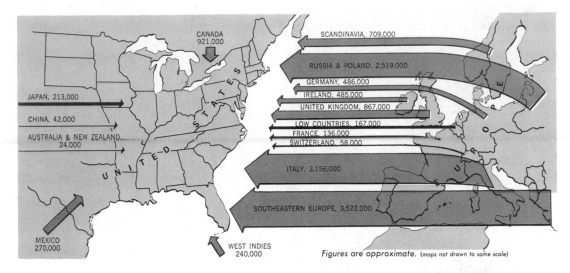

CANADA
921,000

SCANDINAVIA, 709,000

RUSSIA & POLAND, 2,519,000

GERMANY, 486,000

IRELAND, 485,000

JAPAN, 213,000

UNITED KINGDOM, 867,000

CHINA, 42,000

LOW COUNTRIES, 167,000

AUSTRALIA & NEW ZEALAND,
24,000

FRANCE, 136,000

SWITZERLAND, 58,000

ITALY, 3,156,000

SOUTHEASTERN EUROPE, 3,522,000

MEXICO
270,000

WEST INDIES
240,000

Figures are approximate. (maps not drawn to same scale)

Sources of immigrants, 1900–1920.

peasants from Eastern Europe. The act had little effect, for people willing to move several thousand miles were also willing to learn enough English to pass a test. More than 900,000 immigrants arrived in the United States in 1920, and American consuls reported that millions more were preparing to leave their war-ravaged countries. In 1921 Congress passed a Quota Act that limited the number of persons each nation could send to the United States to 3 percent of that nationality present in the United States in 1910.

There is nothing inherently wrong with immigration restrictions; any country has the right to avoid overpopulation. The wrong was in the effort to freeze the ethnic mix. The National Origins Act of 1924 revealed the bias behind it all. That act, which remained in effect until 1950, prohibited Oriental immigration and limited European nationalities to 2 percent of the foreign-born according to the census of 1890. The choice of that year discriminated heavily against the predominantly Roman Catholic, Orthodox Catholic, or Jewish nationalities of southern and eastern Europe,

which did not begin migrating to the United States in significant numbers until after 1890. Because of the difficulty in determining the national origins of the native-born population, the quota system did not go into effect until 1929. The onset of the depression that year further discouraged immigration. In fact many immigrants, unable to find work in America, returned home. For the entire decade of the 1930s, the net immigration was only 68,789.

BLACK AMERICAN NATIONALISM

In the cities of the eastern seaboard in the 1920s, blacks replaced immigrants at the bottom of the social ladder. Black migration to the North had begun in the 1890s, but it increased dramatically during the war and after. The attraction was jobs, an environment in which there were fewer social taboos, and the opportunity to exercise political rights. Conditions in the South also drove people north. The boll weevil decimated southern cotton agriculture and sent farmers into the cities in search of work. Whites took jobs traditionally reserved for blacks, and blacks went to the North.

The war greatly enhanced job opportunities for blacks in the North. The demands of munitions factories on the one hand and the military services on the other, coupled with a virtual halt in immigration, created a severe manpower shortage. Blacks, who had previously been relegated to service occupations even in the North, suddenly found openings in railroad yards, mines, munitions works, and steel mills. Reports and letters sent home about the opportunities awaiting in the North encouraged others to leave, and the momentum of the migration carried into the 1920s. By 1930, about 20 percent of the nation's black population lived outside the South.

Northern whites reacted violently to the black migration. In the summer of 1919, fighting broke out in Chicago when blacks tried to use a Lake Michigan beach. Violence soon erupted in twenty-four other cities. Fifteen whites and twenty-three blacks were killed and hundreds injured by the end of what black publications called the "red summer." What was new about this rioting—besides the fact that it was northern, and most race riots in the past had been in the South—was that the blacks struck back. Previously, race riots had been largely a matter of white assaults on black neighborhoods. In Chicago and elsewhere in 1919, gangs of black youths ranged into white tenement districts, beating, burning, and looting. The violence bespoke a new militancy, born, perhaps, of new-found pride.

The new spirit among Afro-Americans

Jim Crow laws were rigidly enforced in the South.

Library of Congress.

was evident also in the popularity of the first black nationalist movement in the United States. Its leader was Marcus Garvey, a Jamaican immigrant who founded the Universal Negro Improvement Association in 1914. A nationalist who believed that God and Christ were black, Garvey opposed integration as a white scheme to ensure a subservient labor supply. His solution was a return to Africa and the establishment of a black empire. After the bloodshed of 1919, millions of blacks flocked to his standard. To drive the European colonial powers out of Africa, Garvey formed a black army and air force and began buying ships. His dreams crumbled, however, against the rock of world resistance, and the U.S. government took him to court for using the mails for fraud. He spent two years in jail and was then deported to Jamaica. Garvey's movement, short-lived though it was, was particularly significant because it originated in the ghetto. The black press, the churches, and the leaders of rights organizations nearly all opposed him. His movement arose from a broad and growing sense among blacks that racial prejudice permeated not only the South, but all America.

Pride of racial identity was expressed in other, less violent ways. From the black neighborhoods of upper Manhattan Island came an outpouring of artistic and literary work that won the title of the Harlem Re-

"To Make a Poet Black, and Bid Him Sing!"

Countee Cullen (1903–1946), the adopted son of a Harlem minister, was one of the most extravagantly praised of the poets of the Harlem Renaissance. He published his first volume of verse, *Color*, in 1925, the year he was graduated from New York University. The common theme in his poetry is the burden of dark skin color, which conceals the whiteness of the soul within.

> *I doubt not God is good, well-meaning, kind*
> *And did He stoop to quibble could tell why*
> *The little buried mole continues blind,*
> *Why flesh that mirrors Him must some day die,*
> *Make plain the reason tortured Tantalus*
> *Is baited by the fickle fruit, declare*
> *If merely brute caprice dooms Sisyphus*
> *To struggle up a never-ending stair.*
> *Inscrutable his ways are, and immune*
> *To catechism by a mind too strewn*
> *With petty cares to slightly understand*
> *What awful brain compels his awful hand.*
> *Yet do I marvel at this curious thing:*
> *To make a poet black, and bid him sing!*

naissance. The renaissance spoke for the New Negro, who no longer asked for equality (for that implied that whites had power to confer it). Equality existed already; the problem was that whites had yet to recognize that fact. As poet Langston Hughes expressed it: "We younger Negro artists who create now intend to express our individual dark-skinned selves without fear or shame. If white people are pleased we are glad. If they are not, it doesn't matter. We know we are beautiful." Some of the militance showed in their writings. The verses of Claude McKay were a call for a revolution against bigotry. The lyrics of Countee Cullen and the short stories of Claude McKay explored the black condition and its cycle of discrimination, ignorance, and poverty.

The Harlem artists received support and encouragement from white writers, but they were not widely read. The common white perception of Harlem was of an assortment of nightclubs operating in defiance of Prohibition and featuring primitive "earth rhythms" called jazz. Jazz was not an inappropriate symbol of the black renaissance, for its unusual chord progressions were African in heritage as much as American. Yet it was only a facet, one side of the gem; that whites accepted it for the whole said something else about the 1920s.

PROHIBITION

President Herbert Hoover called it a "noble experiment," but Prohibition was that only in principle. In practice, it made law evasion fashionable, financed criminal syndicates, divided Americans into "wets" and "drys," and contributed to political sterility.

The Eighteenth Amendment to the Constitution, approved by Congress in December 1917 and ratified by the requisite number of states within little more than a year, prohibited the manufacture, transport, or sale of intoxicating liquors. The Volstead Act, passed over President Wilson's veto in October 1919 to implement the amendment, defined "intoxicating liquors" as any beverage that contained more than .5 percent alcohol. That was the first mistake, for the act outlawed even beer and wine. The majority of Americans accepted restrictions on distilled liquor; those who wanted to repeal the Eighteenth Amendment—"wringing wets" in the phrase of the day—were few in number. But in that majority were many, especially among the foreign-born, who regarded beer and wine as normal mealtime fare. Because it ran contrary to cultural traditions, Prohibition was impossible to enforce.

The other flaw in the legislation was that it prohibited the manufacture or sale of liquor, but not the consumption. In eco-

How to Make Bathtub Gin

Bathtub gin was usually made in gallon jugs, rather than in bathtubs. Juniper juice, which gives gin its distinctive flavor, was available at most drugstores or supplied as a gift with the alcohol by one's bootlegger. This recipe cost the maker about 2 cents an ounce and was ready to drink upon mixing.

2 parts alcohol (hospital alcohol or grain alcohol)
3 parts water
1 teaspoon juniper juice
1 tablespoon glycerin to smooth it

nomic terms, it curtailed supply but not demand. Seldom has free enterprise responded so swiftly or so effectively to market opportunities. The manufacture and transport of liquor—bootlegging—became big business, and because it was illegal it was dominated by criminals. Gangsters such as Al Capone in Chicago and Dutch Schultz in New York consolidated the liquor trade on the same principles that big business was using to consolidate the automobile, steel, and electric power industries. Prohibition did not create organized crime, but it did make criminals wealthy.

It also added to social tensions. Rural, Protestant America generally favored the law and abided by it. Most of the opposition came from cities and states with sizable foreign-born, Roman Catholic populations. New York, Wisconsin, and Maryland even went so far as to repeal their own state liquor regulations, leaving enforcement of Prohibition entirely to the federal government. Many middle-class people supported Prohibition while patronizing their local speakeasies, on the theory that it kept the factory workers sober and thus docile and industrious. White southerners favored it because it kept liquor out of the hands of blacks. Humorist Will Rogers, noting this, remarked: "Mississippi will vote dry and drink wet as long as it can stagger to the polls."

The Republican party, whose constituency was white, Protestant, and middle class, supported Prohibition, but the issue tore the Democrats apart. Since the 1890s, the Democratic party had been an uneasy coalition of incompatible interest groups. Its traditional southern following was rural, lilywhite, Protestant, and socially conservative. Its northern support, on the other hand, was predominantly urban and contained a hearty number of the foreign-born and Roman Catholics. Prohibition added a wet-dry confrontation to this sectional tension. The strains surfaced in the presidential nominating convention of 1924. Southerners and westerners lined up behind William Gibbs McAdoo; northern Democrats backed New York governor Alfred E. Smith—Irish, Catholic, and "wringing wet." For 95 wearisome ballots, the two sides struggled without result. At that point both Smith and McAdoo withdrew from the contest, and on the 103rd ballot the convention selected a little-known corporation lawyer named John W. Davis. Davis was swamped by Coolidge in the election. Indeed, it mattered little who won, since candidates and platforms were virtually indistinguishable. Four years later, the northern wing got the upper hand and nominated Al Smith, but he lost to Herbert Hoover in an election that pitted urban wets against rural drys. If the politics of the twenties was sterile, it was in part because the political parties themselves fell victim to internal divisions and to the social tensions of the decade.

⊔ A Fragile Prosperity

There were some remarkable similarities between the 1920s and the 1870s. Both were postwar decades in which gaiety and glitter hid a seamy underside, and the majority of Americans seemed interested only in the pursuit of gain. They were alike in another respect: Each was a time of rapid economic growth. The classic industrial revolution of the nineteenth century was built on coal and steam and paced by the construction of the railroads. Economic growth in the 1920s was stimulated by a new form of power, electricity, and new materials, such as aluminum and plastics. It was paced by the spread of automobiles and radios.

Industrial production doubled between 1921 and 1929, and national income rose by half. These profits were not evenly distributed, however. Wages of factory workers went up only 8 percent in the course of the decade. Where did the profits go?

CLIO'S FOCUS: On the Air

In a decade of technological marvels and phenomenal growth, nothing attracted more wonder, or grew more rapidly, than radio. The various components for voice transmission had been developed before the war—the microphone, the transmitter, the vacuum tube, the circuit, and the high-frequency alternator. Radios had become standard equipment on ships early in the century, though their transmissions were usually in Morse code. The Radio Act of 1912 empowered the secretary of commerce to award operators' licenses and assign wavelengths to stations. Naval, amateur, and government transmissions were kept separate.

Until the early 1920s, most radio sets were home-made—a chunk of germanium crystal hooked to a coil of copper wire and batteries, with the whole attached to a piece of board. The headset, priced at $1.98, was the most expensive component. When the whole family wished to listen to the crackles and squeaks coming from faraway places, the headset was placed in a bowl, which converted it into a primitive loudspeaker.

The first station to undertake commercial broadcasting was WWJ Detroit in the summer of 1920. That autumn, the Westinghouse Company started KDKA in Pittsburgh in order to stimulate sales of radio sets. On November 2, both stations carried the Harding-Cox election returns. In 1921 the University of Wisconsin station, WHA, began broadcasting radio concerts, and WJZ Newark carried the World Series. That winter—the winter of 1921–1922—radio swept the country. A San Francisco newspaper breathlessly described the discovery that millions were making: "There is radio music in the air, every night, everywhere. Anybody can hear it at home on a receiving set, which any boy can put up in an hour." In February, President Harding had a radio installed in his White House study.

Transmissions were still crude. Microphones were morning-glory-shaped horns eight feet long and three feet across. "You shouted into the big end," one announcer recalled, and to be sure of being heard "you stuck your head halfway down into it." Phonograph music was transmitted "by putting the morning-glory horn of the phonograph player against the morning-glory horn that was the microphone." But few seemed to care. Five hundred stations were founded in 1922 and 60 million radio sets were sold.

By 1924, there were some 1,400 stations—filling the air, as one critic put it, with "shrieks and groans, cross-talks, muddled and garbled music and announcements" that created "a radio reign of terror." Secretary of Commerce Herbert Hoover declared his license book "filled" and refused to license any new stations. Hoover also opposed advertising, which he thought would be the "quickest way to kill broadcasting." The first commercial had hit the airwaves in 1922—a plug for Long Island real estate aired by a New York station for $100. Advertisers themselves were unsure whether the public would accept their intrusions. The first commercials were simple credits, such as the following: "Tuesday evening means the Ever-Ready Hour, for it is on this day and at this time each week that the National Carbon Company, makers of Ever-Ready flashlight and radio batteries, engages the facilities of these fourteen radio stations to present its artists in original radio creations."

As broadcasters soon discovered, the public had little objection to radio advertising. The founding of the National Broadcasting Company in 1926 consummated the marriage of radio and commerce. Wholly owned by RCA, General Electric, and Westinghouse, NBC's purpose was to stimulate the sale of radio sets. By the summer of 1927, NBC had 40 stations in its network, linked by telephone lines. The pool of listeners attracted sponsors. NBC's very first offering, a 4½-hour variety show on November 15, 1926, was sponsored by Dodge automobiles.

The founding of CBS the following year institutionalized the sponsor system. Unlike NBC, CBS had no radio manufacturers among its stockholders; it depended entirely on advertising revenue. And figures told the story. In the 1927–1928 season, NBC had 39 company-sponsored programs, and CBS had 4. The following season, 65 sponsors bought time on the two networks. The first radio survey, conducted on January 1, 1929, by a Massachusetts Institute of Technology professor, found that one-third of all American homes had radios, and the potential audience numbered 41.4 million people. The quality of programming, to be sure, still left much to be desired. In 1930, one literary critic claimed that most of the programs were intended only to "tickle the tastes of the mentally deficient." But for better or worse, radio had wrought a profound change in American life.

They were retained by corporations for further growth or given out as dividends, which increased 100 percent in ten years. Either way, stockholders benefited, and the result was rising interest in stocks. The "great bull market" became, in turn, the symbol of the prosperity of the 1920s.

That prosperity, however, was fragile. In part because the benefits of rising productivity were not shared in the form of higher wages, America's business community was approaching the time when it could produce more than people could afford to buy. That phenomenon, known as underconsumption, was one of the major factors in the depression that struck in 1929.

Business also became less competitive in the 1920s. The 1870s had witnessed the rise of the trust; in the 1920s the holding company came into its own. In the course of the decade 25 percent of American factories fell under the control of holding companies. The purpose of consolidation was to reduce competition so that each company would have better control of its markets. That enabled it to adjust production to demand or manipulate demand through advertising. Scientific management was the slogan of the day; business had become a profession. And by turning the Commerce Department into a bureau of vital statistics for the business world, Secretary Hoover gave the new profession the government's blessing.

Trade associations were another way of eliminating competition. These were fellowships binding the companies involved

AP/Wide World Photos.

Aimee Semple McPherson (1890–1944), a tall, red-headed dynamo from Canada, who had been converted to Pentecostal Protestantism at the age of 17. In 1917 she moved to the United States with her daughter, her mother (who was also her manager), a leaky tent, and a reputation as a faith healer. After five years of criss-crossing the United States by train with her revival troupe, she opened her famous Angelus Temple in Los Angeles. The temple boasted 5,000 seats, 2 balconies, a sky-blue ceiling, and a dome glistening with crushed seashells. The temple was the center of her "Foursquare Gospel," which by 1926 was the International Church of the Foursquare Gospel with more than 80 branches in the United States and Britain. By the end of the decade she possessed her own radio station to spread the Word. Evangelism became big business in the 1920s.

in an industry; the American Chemical Institute, for instance, is a trade association. Secretary Hoover actively encouraged them because they promoted standardization, eliminated waste, and spread technical information. At the same time, the trade associations cut competition among their members by fixing prices and apportioning markets. This meant that businesses not only failed to share the rewards of productivity with the labor force, they also failed to share them with consumers by lowering prices. The benefits went to stockholders, and the great bull market rolled on until the bubble burst.

THE CRASH

The stock market crash did not cause the Depression. An economic downturn was already under way by the summer of 1929, months before the Wall Street panic. There was a drop in consumer spending, a rise in retail inventories, a decline in factory output—all the classic symptoms of recession. Nor was it surprising. The economy had been booming since 1922; readjustment was overdue. Fluctuations in the business cycle appear to be as inevitable as they are unpredictable. The business cycle, moreover, is an international phenomenon. In the 1930s the Depression affected the entire world, throwing out of work people who had never heard of Wall Street. The stock market crash deepened and prolonged the Depression. The crash was a national trauma, a shattering of the American dream. Its sequel was public caution, even pessimism. Businessmen were hesitant to invest, companies afraid to employ, and consumers slow to buy. The Depression went on for a decade, until it was ended by World War II.

THE GREAT BULL MARKET

The stock market had become part of the culture of the twenties, as characteristic of the decade as talking movies or ballroom dancing. Not everyone "played the market"—even at the height of the mania only about 3 percent of American households owned stock—but nearly everyone followed it. The market was the topic of the day in 1928–1929. The interest in the stock market reflected another trait of the twenties—the conviction that God intended Americans to be rich. The Florida real estate boom was an early example. People bought worthless scrubland not because they expected to live on it, but because they expected the price to rise. And for a time the prices did rise, simply because other believers entered the market. The supply of buyers slowed in the spring of 1926, and a devastating hurricane later that year—which swamped Miami and killed 400 people—ended the bonanza. But it

failed to dim the faith of Americans in get-rich-quick schemes.

The price of securities had begun to rise in 1924. In May of that year the *New York Times* average of the prices of twenty-five industrial stocks was 106; by the end of the year it was 134—that is, an average of $134 per share. By the end of 1925 it stood at 181. There were sound reasons for the increase. Business was brisk, profits good, dividends high. Many companies found that public subscriptions of stock were a useful way of raising capital to expand. American business literally "went public" in the 1920s, and the public responded enthusiastically. Collecting dividends was an effortless way to get rich. As the price of stocks continued to rise, many people began doing what only professional speculators had done before—buying not for the dividends, but in order to resell at a profit. It was an even quicker way to get rich.

By trading on margin, even those with little money to invest could enter the market. Margin enabled people to reap the benefit of a price increase without the expense of having to own the stock itself. Under this system, the speculator had to provide cash for only a fraction of the value of a stock, usually 25 percent. The rest was borrowed from a brokerage house, using the stock as security. When, a few months later, the stock went up in price, the investor could sell it, pay off the brokerage loan, and have doubled the initial cash outlay. Brokers profited because their interests rates ran as high as 12 percent. That level soon attracted the major New York banks, which set up brokerage houses of their own. They borrowed money from the Federal Reserve System at 5 percent and lent it to speculators at 12 percent.

The system also had a built-in panic button. If the price of stock went down rather than up, the margin trader had to sell quickly to pay off his loan. So any deflation of the market was likely to trigger a wave of panicky selling. Stock market panic threatened the nation's banking system. Since the brokerage loans were secured only by stock, the banks, when it was all over, were left with worthless pieces of paper. Bank failures were common in the early years of the Depression.

In 1927 the boom began in earnest. By the end of that year, the *New York Times* industrial stock average stood at 245, a net gain of 69 points for the year. In the spring of 1928 prices moved upward by leaps and bounds, and the volume of daily sales doubled. Broker's loans on margin rose from $3.8 billion at the beginning of the year to $6 billion by the end.

PANIC

There were some who realized the boom could not last forever, but no one knew how to slow it without causing panic. President Coolidge was cheerfully oblivious to such things; Treasury Secretary Mellon was a staunch advocate of inaction. The Federal Reserve Board was too timid to act, and powerless in any case. Its one weapon against speculation was the rediscount rate, the interest it charged member banks for funds. By raising that, the Federal Reserve Board would have forced banks to increase the interest rates they charged their customers and thus discouraged brokers' loans. After much worrying, the board finally increased the rediscount rate in the summer of 1929. But by then the speculation was out of hand.

Herbert Hoover later claimed in his memoirs that he had become concerned about the "tide of speculation" as early as 1925. If so, he kept his views to himself. His election in 1928, in fact, triggered a new wave of buying. The mania reached its height in the summer of 1929, as the market average surged 110 points in just three months, reaching 449 on August 31. Brokers' loans exceeded $7 billion.

The great bull market came to an end in early September. Professionals sensed a crash and began to pull out. Public enthusiasm remained high, however, and the market stayed up through the month. Brokers' loans, in fact, set a new record. The break came on Thursday, October 24, when 12,894,650 shares changed hands amid wild confusion. So frantic was the trading that the ticker fell behind, and lack of information added to the panic. In succeeding days trading remained heavy, but prices held as bankers tried to shore up the market by buying stocks. Then, on October 29, Black Tuesday, panic struck. More than 16 million shares changed hands, and perhaps many more that were not recorded. Even the great corporations suffered. In the course of a week American Telephone and Telegraph went from 304 a share to 72, U.S. Steel fell from 262 to 22, and General Motors went from 73 to 8. In the aftermath of the panic, it seemed to many that American society itself had come unraveled. It was certainly the end of an era.

SUMMARY

The first task the United States faced at the end of the war was demobilization— dismantling the armed forces and returning to a peacetime economy. Reflecting the public's desire for a quick return to "normalcy," the government demobilized quickly and without much planning. The result was economic dislocation, unemployment, and inflation. Adding to the chaos were labor strikes and a Red Scare, the latter touched off by the Bolshevik Revolution in Russia and the founding of the Comintern in 1919. Tired of the tension and even more tired of Wilson, the electorate in 1920 turned to a safely conservative, utterly nonideological Republican, Warren G. Harding.

Harding's presidency was a disaster, though the dimensions of the wrongdoing were not fully known until after his death in 1923. Then investigations revealed corruption and favoritism masterminded by the president's friends from Ohio. Most spectacular of the scandals was the Teapot Dome; in this particular deal, oil company executives had bribed the secretary of the interior to lease them government-owned oil lands. Harding's successor, Calvin Coolidge, cleaned out the "Ohio gang" and administered the country for five years with silent, unobtrusive efficiency. Businessmen dominated the government under Coolidge, as well as the regulatory commissions set up by the Progressives, but the middle class generally benefited from the Coolidge prosperity.

The 1920s were a time of pleasure-seeking, but beneath the surface there lurked some serious social tensions. Among these was a crusade against the teaching of evolution in the schools, backed by traditionalists who feared for the decline of religion. Leading the crusade was William Jennings Bryan, who engaged in a memorable forensic duel with defense attorney Clarence Darrow at the Scopes trial in Dayton, Tennessee, in 1925.

Nativism, nourished by the war and the Red Scare of 1919, was another social tension of the decade. Its most overt form was the Ku Klux Klan, which had been revived in 1915 and flourished through the 1920s. Immigration restrictions were another. The Quota Act of 1921 and the National Origins Act of 1924, in addition to limiting the number of immigrants, discriminated against those from Roman Catholic countries of southern and eastern Europe.

Black migration to the North during and after the war added to racial tensions and brought riots. Black reaction to discrimination and prejudice was evident in the popularity of Marcus Garvey's back-to-Africa movement, which had wide support in the northern ghettoes. A black protest literature developed chiefly as part of the Harlem Renaissance, the flowering of the arts in the cultural center of black America.

Prohibition was another social tension of the decade. The Volstead Act of 1919 was so extreme in its attempt to outlaw all liquor, even beer and wine, that it invited opposition. Flouting the law became fashionable. The manufacture and transport of illegal liquor became big business, and because it was illegal it fell into the hands of gangsters. Prohibition exacerbated the nation's social and regional tensions, as rural South and West tended to be dry and urban North and East tended to be wet. It also divided the Democratic party and rendered it nearly helpless.

Prosperity was the conditioning factor of the 1920s, but it was a fragile one. There were pockets of distress, notably in agriculture and coal mining. Moreover, wages remained low because labor unions were weak, and working people could not afford to buy many of the products of industry. The consequent surpluses, due to underconsumption, helped cause the economic readjustment that turned into a lengthy depression. The readjustment began in the summer of 1929. In October it affected the stock market, which had been advancing rapidly for two years in a speculative mania. The market crash ended the buoyant optimism that helped feed the prosperity; its psychological impact deepened the depression.

READING SUGGESTIONS

The classic picture of the 1920s as a time of both frivolity and disillusion was first drawn by Frederick Lewis Allen in *Only Yesterday: An Informal History of the 1920s* (1931). Although the stereotype has been modified by more recent writing, Allen's brief and breezy account is still fun. Paul A. Carter, *Another Part of the Twenties* (1977), examines some of the social tensions of the decade. William E. Leuchtenberg, *The Perils of Prosperity, 1914–1932* (1958) is probably the best scholarly account of the period.

The Harding and Coolidge presidencies receive sympathetic treatment in the works of Robert K. Murray: *The Harding Era: Warren G. Harding and His Administration* (1969), and *The Politics of Normalcy: Governmental Theory and Practice in the Harding-Coolidge Era* (1973). Murray's *The Red Scare: A Study in National Hysteria, 1919–1920* (1955) describes the postwar repression and the Palmer raids.

The youth cult is the subject of Paula S. Fass, *The Damned and the Beautiful: American Youth in the 1920s* (1977). The status of women in these years is treated by Carl Degler, *At Odds: Women and the Family in America from the Revolution to the Present* (1980), and by William H. Chaffe, *The American Woman, 1920–1970* (1972). Roderick Nash, *The Nervous Generation: American Thought, 1917–1930* (1970), and Nathan Irvin Huggins, *Harlem Renaissance* (1971), cover aspects of the 1920's thought and writing. E. David Cronon, *Black Moses: The Story of Marcus Garvey* (1955), explores the back-to-Africa phenomenon.

For the social tensions of the '20s, consult John Higham, *Strangers in the Land: Patterns of American Nativism, 1860–1925* (1955); Robert A. Divine, *American Immigration Policy, 1924–1952* (1957); David Chalmers, *Hooded Americanism: The History of the KKK* (1965); and N. F. Furniss, *The Fundamentalist Controversy, 1918–1931* (1954). Ray Ginger's *Six Days or Forever?* (1958) is a wonderfully vivid account of the Scopes trial. George M. Marsden puts the trial in perspective in *Fundamentalism and American Culture: The Shaping of Twentieth Century Evangelicalism, 1875–1925* (1980).

George Soule, *Prosperity Decade: From War to Depression, 1917–1929* (1947), is a good introduction to the economy of the 1920s. Alfred D. Chandler, Jr., treats the changes in business organization in *Strategy and Structure: Chapters in the History of American Industrial Enterprise* (1962). The plight of organized labor is the theme of I. Bernstein, *The Lean Years: A History of the American Worker, 1920–1933* (1960). John Kenneth Galbraith, *The Great Crash* (1955), is a good brief introduction to the coming of the Depression.

11

HARD TIMES:
1929–1939

Each year seemed worse than the last. In 1930, national income was $68 billion, down from $81 billion in 1929, and there were 4 million unemployed. In the course of the year, 1,352 banks closed their doors, and for the first time in American history more people moved out of the country than came in. Unemployment reached 8 million in 1931, and 2,294 banks closed. Automobile sales were so bad that in Detroit, two out of three adult men (four out of five among blacks) were unemployed. In 1932, unemployment doubled again, to 16 million. Wall Street's Dow Jones Industrial Average of stock prices fell in mid-year to 41, down from its high of 381 in September 1929. U.S. industrial production was one-third of its 1929 total. Some 1,616 banks failed in 1932; 20,000 businesses declared bankruptcy; and there were 21,000 suicides.

The depth of human misery was beyond measure. The search for work was at first hopeful and vigorous, then grim, and finally desperate. After family savings trickled away, borrowing began—from friends and relatives, from landlord, from corner grocer. When bonds of blood and friendship became frayed, there was the dole. Silent and humiliated, the head of the family joined a line of shame-faced men shuffling slowly forward to receive a loaf of bread or bowl of soup from some hard-pressed charity. Community relief sources were soon exhausted. By 1932, the city of Toledo was able to provide only two cents per meal per person per day. In New York City, entire families received an average of $2.39 a week in relief payments. In most rural areas, there was no relief available at all. "I don't want to steal," a Pennsylvania man wrote his governor, "but I won't let my wife and boy cry for something to eat. . . . How long is this going to keep up? I cannot stand it any longer. . . . O, if God would only open a way." For many, God was the only recourse; human institutions had failed them.

⊔ The Depression: Hoover to Roosevelt

"We in America today are nearer the final triumph over poverty than ever before in the history of any land," Herbert Hoover had declared during the presidential contest of 1928. In the hard times that followed, people remembered those words and mocked him with bitter irony. The shantytowns of migrants who roamed the land in search of work became known as Hoovervilles. Newspapers, which covered sleeping hobos, were called Hoover blankets, and the inside-out pockets of beggars were Hoover flags. No president is popular in a time of depression, but none ever has been so reviled as Hoover. What his critics failed to see was that he was the first president in history to propose federal initiatives to combat a depression.

FEDERAL INITIATIVES

Presidential policy in all previous depressions had been to let the economy work itself out of trouble. Van Buren in the 1830s and Grant in the 1870s had rejected proposals that the government print paper money; Cleveland in the 1890s refused public works projects. Hoover was raised in the same tradition. Life is a race that goes to the swift, he said in the 1928 campaign. Free public education ensures that each gets an equal start; government is simply "the umpire of fairness in the race." His phrase "rugged individualism" became the political watchword of the 1920s. Yet he could bend with the times. When the Depression began, he met with business leaders and won pledges from them to maintain wages. And they did. Though

---

(*Chapter opening photo*) Abandoned farm in the Oklahoma dust bowl.

AP/Wide World Photos.

Hooverville, 1933. The shacks of the unemployed are scattered around this waterfront site in Seattle, Washington. Previously occupied by a shipyard, it had once been one of the busiest industrial sites on the Pacific Coast.

production fell and unemployment rose, wages remained fairly stable until 1932. In 1930 Hoover asked Congress for an appropriation of more than $100 million for public works to relieve unemployment, and he stepped up construction of two massive federal projects in the West, the Boulder and Grand Coulee dams. The scale of his efforts was too small to affect unemployment noticeably, but important precedents had been set.

Hoover also established government agencies to cope with the depression. In 1930 he created the Federal Farm Board to buy up and store farm surpluses. This too was a new departure: Hoover's predecessor had vetoed a similar proposal on the grounds that it was special interest legislation. The Farm Board did not work very well, in part because the stored surpluses themselves had a depressing effect on prices, but it was a foundation for the farm program of Hoover's successor, Franklin Roosevelt.

Reconstruction Finance Corporation. In December 1931, Hoover asked Congress to create a special corporation that could make loans to troubled businesses. This too was a departure. In 1932 Congress chartered the Reconstruction Finance Corporation, endowing it with a half billion dollars and giving it authority to borrow up to $2 billion. The idea was that

The Hobo

If there was a single symbol of the Depression, it was the hobo, the man (or occasionally woman) who left home and sometimes family to roam the country in search of work. He rode in empty railroad cars, slept in city parks, begged food at people's back doors. He was harrassed by railroad police, scorned by town officials, and often found jail the most comfortable spot he had seen in weeks. Louis Banks, raised on a small cotton farm in Arkansas, went to Chicago at the age of fourteen and got a job as a cook on a Lake Michigan steamship. He lost his job in the Depression and took to the road. Here are some of his recollections.

1929 was pretty hard. I hoboed, I bummed, I begged for a nickel to get somethin' to eat. Go get a job, oh, at the foundry there. They didn't hire me because I didn't belong to the right kind of race. 'Nother time I went into Saginaw, it was two white fellas and myself made three. The fella there hired the two men and didn't hire me. I was back out on the streets. That hurt me pretty bad, the race part.

When I was hoboing, I would lay on the side of the tracks and wait until I could see the train comin'. I would always carry a bottle of water in my pocket and a piece of tape or rag to keep it from bustin' and put a piece of bread in my pocket, so I wouldn't starve on the way. I would ride all day and all night long in the hot sun.

I'd ride atop a boxcar and went to Los Angeles, four days and four nights. The Santa Fe, we'd go all the way with Santa Fe. I was goin' over the hump and I was so hungry and weak 'cause I was goin' into the d.t.'s, and I could see snakes draggin' through the smoke. I was sayin', "Lord, help me, Oh Lord, help me," until a white hobo named Callahan, he was a great big guy, looked like Jack Dempsey, and he got a scissors on me, took his legs and wrapped 'em around me. Otherwise, I was about to fall off the Flyer into a cornfield there. I was sick as a dog until I got into Long Beach, California.

Black and white, it didn't make any difference who you were, 'cause everybody was poor. All friendly, sleep in a jungle. We used to take a big pot and cook food, cabbage, meat and beans all together. We all set together, we made a tent. Twenty-five or thirty would be out on the side of the rail, white and colored. They didn't have no mothers or sisters, they didn't have no home, they were dirty, they had overalls on, they didn't have no food, they didn't have anything.

Sometimes we sent one hobo to walk, to see if there were any jobs open. He'd come back and say: Detroit, no jobs. He'd say: they're hirin' in New York City. So we went to New York City. Sometimes ten or fifteen of us would be on the train. And I'd hear one of 'em holler. He'd fall off, he'd get killed. He was tryin' to get off the train, he thought he was gettin' home there.

. . .

I was in chain gangs and been in jail all over the country. I was in a chain gang in Georgia. I had to pick cotton for four months, for just hoboin' on a train. Just for vag. They gave me thirty-five cents and a pair of overalls when I got out. Just took me off the train, the guard. 1930, during the Depression, in the summertime. Yes, sir, thirty-five cents, that's what they gave me.

I knocked on people's doors. They'd say, "What do you want? I'll call the police." And they'd put you in jail for vag. They'd make you milk cows, thirty or ninety days. Up in Wisconsin, they'd do the same thing. Alabama, they'd do the same thing. California, anywhere you'd go. Always in jail, and I never did nothin'.

by shoring up banks, railroads, and industrial enterprises, the RFC would prevent failures and halt the rise of unemployment. Progressive Republican congressman Fiorello LaGuardia of New York City labeled it a "millionaire's dole," but in theory at least the RFC's benefits were to trickle down to people at the bottom. Like Hoover's other efforts it was too little and too late, but this institution too his successor would find useful.

Norris-Laguardia Act. Another sign of Hoover's flexibility was his approval in 1932 of the first major piece of federal labor legislation, an anti-injunction act.[*] The act originated in Congress, where it was sponsored by Representative LaGuardia and Senator George Norris of Nebraska, but Hoover approved it. In doing so he pronounced sentence on "rugged individualism," because the act put the government behind the labor movement. It made "yellow dog" contracts (by which workers agreed not to join a union) unenforceable in federal courts, and it forbade courts from issuing injunctions against legitimate union activities such as strikes and picketing.

Hoover's record in office was meager but not barren: He was parent or godfather to more progressive legislation than Harding and Coolidge combined. Yet the public failed to see this. To Americans, Hoover was a stubborn proponent of the status quo, utterly indifferent to the plight of the poor. This public impression was due in part to Hoover's insistence that the economy was fundamentally sound. At first he attributed the downturn to the speculative

mania that had brought the Wall Street crash, and he expected things to improve after a brief adjustment. When times did not get better, he blamed world conditions. This faulty diagnosis led him to make statements that people neither forgot nor forgave. "The fundamental business of the country, that is, the production and distribution of commodities, is on a sound and prosperous basis," he said shortly after the stock market crash. And in the spring of 1930 he assured the country that the crisis would be over in sixty days. To the public, such announcements—which Hoover himself did not believe—sounded as if the president was either ignorant or indifferent to the real state of affairs.

Hawley-Smoot Tariff. The faulty diagnosis also led to some fatal policy decisions. In 1930, Hoover lent his support to a tariff increase as a way of helping farmers and manufacturers by keeping foreign goods off the market. The Hawley-Smoot Tariff, signed by Hoover over the protests of 1,000 economists, raised the tariff rates by about a third. European nations retaliated by raising their tariffs, American exports dropped, and industrialists were no better off than before. Farmers, who had been coaxed into supporting the measure by duties on agricultural imports (of which there were none), suffered even more.

THE BONUS MARCH

The other source of Hoover's poor public image was his attitude toward relief. Unemployment was the starkest tragedy of the Depression; relief was the biggest human need. Both public and private resources were soon exhausted. During the first years of the depression, the only public relief was provided by cities. They regarded their programs as temporary and deliberately kept funds low for fear that recipients might quit looking for work. They soon

---

[*] Ever since the Pullman strike of the 1890s, businesses had sought to prevent strikes by obtaining court orders enjoining or preventing them. Courts frequently issued such orders on the theory that strikes led to injuries and property damage. The effect was to put the force of the law on the side of management.

found that they could not afford to do otherwise. Tax revenues dwindled because property owners could not collect rents from their unemployed tenants. Cities cut their own employees, stopped buying books for their libraries, and even shot zoo animals in order to stay financially afloat. Cities were forced to ration relief. In 1932, New York City's weekly allowance for a family was $2.39, and only half the families who qualified for an allowance received one. In Detroit, allowances fell to 15¢ per day per person before giving out entirely. President Hoover insisted that no one was starving and cited as proof a decline in the death rate. One angry social worker replied, "Have you ever seen the uncontrolled trembling of parents who have starved themselves for weeks so that their children might not go hungry?" Newspapers reported the story of a rural schoolteacher who told a little girl who looked sick to go home and eat something. "I can't," the youngster said. "It's my sister's turn to eat."

By 1932, states and cities were borrowing from the Reconstruction Finance Corporation to keep themselves afloat. Through all of this President Hoover staunchly insisted that relief was a local problem, to be solved by voluntary agencies and local government. If Washington undertook the burden of curing economic distress, he announced in 1931, it would subject the nation to a huge and remote bureaucracy, and the community would lose control of its own destiny. This may have been the only true prophecy Hoover ever made, but it was small comfort to the hungry.

The Bonus March of 1932 produced a dramatic confrontation between president and people on the issue. The march grew out of a belated recognition by Congress that it had not done enough for the veterans of 1918. In 1925 it offered them insurance certificates worth $1,000, payable in twenty years. In 1932 Democrats, in an effort to align themselves with the American Legion in an election year, introduced a bill in Congress to pay off the policies as a relief "bonus." Unemployed veterans converged on Washington, many of them with their families, to press for the plan.

A tent village with a population of 10,000 appeared on the flats along the Potomac River. By June 1932, thousands of other veterans camped in the city's parks, dumps, and warehouses. The Senate rejected the bonus bill, but it did provide money to send the veterans home. All but about 2,000 left. The president ordered the army to disperse the rest. A force of cavalry and infantry armed with machine guns and bayonets, commanded by Army Chief of Staff Douglas MacArthur, blasted through the marchers' tent camp and burned it to the ground. Newsreel films captured it all, and the public wondered at the president's curious view of governmental authority in hard times. Banks and industries had received tariff subsidies and RFC loans; the unemployed got bayonets and gunfire.

1932: A NEW DEAL

The Republicans renominated Hoover in 1932, but without enthusiasm. The Democrats, sensing a rare opportunity for victory, turned to Franklin Delano Roosevelt, governor of New York. Roosevelt, a distant cousin of the Republican Roosevelt, had paralleled Teddy's career for a time. He had served as assistant secretary of the navy under Wilson and stood as vice president on the Cox ticket in 1920. The parallel ended when he contracted infantile paralysis the following year and was crippled for life. In 1928 his friend Al Smith persuaded him to run for governor of New York to complement Smith's bid for the presidency. Roosevelt won New York, while Smith lost both it and the presidency. Roosevelt was reelected in 1930 by the largest majority ever given a gubernatorial candidate in that state. His state unemployment

Bettmann Archive.
Women celebrating the end of prohibition.

relief program placed him symbolically in opposition to the president. The nominating convention went through its ritualistic battle between wets and drys, ending with a reaffirmation of the 1928 victory for wets, and then nominated Roosevelt on the fourth ballot. Few knew anything of Roosevelt's plans or ideas, but there was a clue to his personality in his acceptance. Breaking all precedent, Roosevelt flew to Chicago to accept the nomination in person. His speech, otherwise unexceptional, ended with a ringing declaration: "I pledge you, I pledge myself, to a new deal for the American people. . . . This is more than a political campaign; it is a call to arms."

The outlines of the New Deal were not immediately evident. Roosevelt brought no ideological blueprint to the campaign; in-

stead, he brought an open mind and a tactical pragmatism. "It is common sense," he told his associates during the campaign, "to take a method and try it. If it fails, admit it frankly and try another. But, above all, try something." Roosevelt seemed to sense that the nation had arrived at a turning point. The old order was dead. A certain amount of experimentation was needed before a new order was established. At an early press conference, he likened himself to a football quarterback. He knew what the next play would be, but beyond that he had no fixed plan because "future plays will depend on how the next one works." The New Deal was not "creeping socialism," as its enemies sometimes called it, nor did it involve a "planned economy," as some of its adherents liked to think. It was rather a collection of improvisations—

UPI/Bettmann.

Enroute to the Inauguration. Roosevelt greets the passing crowd, while Hoover sits solemn and dejected.

some rather hastily conceived, and many that did not work. But it shaped American politics for decades to come.

Roosevelt swamped Hoover in the election, winning 57 percent of the popular vote and carrying the electoral college by 472 to 59. The Democrats had won control of Congress in 1930, and Roosevelt's popularity added to their strength (they would control Congress until 1946). The promise of a New Deal, however, failed to brighten the popular mood. That winter of 1932–1933 was the worst yet. Unemployment reached a new pinnacle, and hunger turned to starvation in some of the eastern cities. Congress rushed through two new

amendments to the Constitution—the Twentieth, which advanced inauguration day to January (beginning in 1937) and did away with the lame duck session of Congress, and the Twenty-First, which repealed Prohibition.

Then, in February 1933, the banking system, tottering since 1929, collapsed. People had lost faith because of bank failures, and began withdrawing their money. More banks closed their doors, and the panic spread. On February 4 Louisiana's governor declared a statewide bank holiday, and state after state followed suit. On the morning of Roosevelt's inauguration, Wall Street itself closed down; by then banks were closed or working on restricted hours in 47 states. The economy seemed to have ground to a halt. People, deeply frightened, looked to Washington for hope.

Roosevelt's inaugural address was aimed at just that. "This great Nation will endure as it has endured," he promised, "will revive and will prosper. So, first of all, let me assert my firm belief that the only thing we have to fear is fear itself." Roosevelt's leadership rested on his extraordinary ability to communicate with people via radio or newsreel. He was able to express grand ideas in simple language and to project his own warmth and confidence. He instituted a series of fireside chats on radio that took him into the living room of every American home. He was able to communicate the

A fireside chat.

National Archives.

feeling that government was interested, was concerned for people's welfare, and was doing something to revive prosperity. And people believed.

⊔ The First New Deal, 1933–1934

Historians have found two not entirely consistent patterns in the Roosevelt program. One was a preoccupation with economic recovery and a willingness to work with business interests to that end. Among Roosevelt's group of advisers—dubbed the Brain Trust by newspapers because several had come from university campuses—were men who advocated state-regulated monopolies like those in Europe. These planned ventures could limit production in order to keep prices up. The approach promised much for bankers and industrialists and their trade associations, but little for labor and nothing for consumers. The other pattern in Roosevelt's program was a concern for social justice, a desire to put people to work on a permanent basis and to eliminate poverty. Roosevelt experimented with both approaches, often simultaneously. Recovery dominated the first New Deal; social justice became uppermost after 1935, shaping quite literally a second New Deal.

RELIEF FOR BANKS, FARMERS, AND THE UNEMPLOYED

The banking crisis was the first concern, and Roosevelt's solution provided a clue, not fully appreciated at the time, as to what the New Deal would be. Radicals such as Louisiana's Senator Huey Long advocated government operation of the banking system. Roosevelt never considered it. Two days after his inauguration, he closed all the banks in the country pending congressional action. He convened Congress in special session on March 9 and presented an emergency banking bill. The bill gave the Treasury power to supervise the re-opening of sound banks and gave the president broad powers over the buying and selling of gold. The bill slipped through Congress in six hours flat; the House vote was unanimous, the Senate vote nearly so. Congress was as frightened as the people. On Sunday evening, March 12, the president went on the radio in the first of his fireside chats to explain that the banking system was fundamentally sound. Sixty million people listened, and they believed. The next morning the banks opened their doors to lines of people waiting to deposit their money. "Capitalism," wrote one of the Brain Trust, "was saved in eight days." That may have been putting it too simply, but the fact remains that Roosevelt started

his presidency in a desire to save, not change. That bankers and business failed to see it that way was always a mystery to him.

To reinforce public confidence in the banking system, Congress created the Federal Deposit Insurance Corporation (FDIC), which insured private bank deposits up to $5,000. Even if a bank failed, its depositors were guaranteed recovery of their funds. There has never been a serious run on American banks since that day, and the very banks that fought Roosevelt then make the FDIC a central feature of their advertising today.

By March 16, the president was beginning to hit his stride. On that day he sent to Congress an agricultural adjustment bill aimed at solving the "farm problem." Since the 1870s, American farmers had produced more food and fiber than the world

Dairy farmers dumping milk in the hope of raising prices.

State Historical Society of Wisconsin.

could consume or afford to buy. Low farm prices and rising tenantry had been a problem even in the prosperous twenties. Roosevelt proposed to reduce farm surpluses and raise prices by offering farmers money payments to limit production. Unfortunately, by the time the Agricultural Adjustment Act cleared the Congress in May 1933, crops were already in the ground, and the first job of the Agricultural Adjustment Administration (AAA) was to persuade farmers to plow them up. The destruction of 10 million acres of cotton in the South and 6 million pigs in the Middle West fixed the image of the AAA in the public mind, but in the long run the AAA must be deemed a qualified success. Farm income rose by about 50 percent in Roosevelt's first term, and indebtedness dropped sharply. The decline in production and consequent increase in prices was due as much to drought as to the government's program, but farmers benefited nonetheless. When the Supreme Court, still loaded with Harding-Coolidge-Hoover appointees, declared the AAA unconstitutional (*United States* v. *Butler*, 1936), farm prices fell and angry farmers burned the Court in effigy.

The unemployed also commanded attention in that frantic spring of 1933. In May, Congress appropriated a half-billion dollars in relief money to be channeled through state and local agencies. To supervise the expenditure, Roosevelt created the Federal Emergency Relief Administration (FERA), and placed at its head Harry Hopkins, who had managed Roosevelt's state relief program in Albany. Hopkins was a curious blend of humanitarian and cynic, a chain-smoking social worker with an eye for women and racehorses. By Roosevelt's second term he would be the most important man in the administration, and during World War II he would serve as Roosevelt's personal emissary to Winston Churchill and Joseph Stalin.

Setting up shop in a hallway of the Re-

construction Finance Corporation amid discarded packing crates, Hopkins spent over $5 million in his first two hours in office. FERA fed the hungry and clothed the naked, but such stopgap measures were not enough. In the fall of 1933, Hopkins went back to the president to explain the need for a federal agency that would take people off the relief rolls and put them to work. The president authorized him to set up the Civil Works Administration, and Congress appropriated more funds. Within a month, Hopkins had put to work as many men as the nation had mobilized in World War I. At its height in January 1934, the CWA employed 4,230,000 persons, building or improving airports, highways, schools, and playgrounds. The projects were short on capital and thin on planning—critics coined the word "boondoggle" to describe them[*]—but they offered millions hope and self-respect in that winter of despair.

The CWA, however, alarmed Roosevelt, whose instincts were essentially conservative. The president shied from the notion that the government owed every man a job (much less every woman) and feared he might be creating a permanent class of government-paid reliefers. In the spring of 1934, the CWA was disbanded, and FERA took up the relief burden once more.

THE NATIONAL INDUSTRIAL RECOVERY ACT

The farm and relief programs were stopgap measures to cope with the immediate emergency. In June 1933, Congress undertook a more comprehensive remedy for the Depression, the National Industrial Recovery Act, the last important legislation of

---

[*] Some insist that "boondoggle" was actually coined by a 15-year-old Eagle Scout in the 1920s to describe Scout handicrafts and was later picked up by enemies of the New Deal.

the "Hundred Days."[*] The act created the National Recovery Administration, whose mission was to form a partnership of government, business, and labor. Working with the trade associations that had been formed in the 1920s, the NRA was to help draft codes of fair competition that would allocate production and end price cutting. Since collusion among competitors was contrary to the antitrust laws, the act promised release from the antitrust laws for businesses that joined the NRA.

The NRA never did work very well, in part because, like the AAA, it was founded on the notion of raising prices by limiting production. Many companies joined simply to evade the antitrust laws, and the larger corporations dominated the trade associations. Labor was clearly a junior partner in the bargain. Section 7(a) of the act guaranteed the right of labor to bargain collectively, but the initiative was left to the unions, which had been greatly weakened by the Depression. Before long businessmen and workers alike were referring to the NRA as the "national run around," and few mourned when the Supreme Court found that the code-making authority was an unconstitutional delegation of Congress's power and laid the NRA to rest (*Schechter* v. *United States*, 1935).

The National Industrial Recovery Act also attempted a more long-term solution to the problem of relief. Title II created the Public Works Administration (PWA) and gave it $3.3 billion for the construction of public buildings, roads, sewer systems, and other public utility projects. The PWA was to hire private contractors to undertake the construction, and through them its expenditures were to trickle down to the unemployed. Thus the PWA represented another partnership between government and business, one devoted more to long-range recovery than to immediate human needs. Administration of the agency further delayed its impact. The PWA was placed under the jurisdiction of Interior Secretary Harold Ickes, a Republican, who scrutinized every blueprint. Though it eventually put 4 million men to work, the PWA had little impact on unemployment until 1935.

Two other agencies created by Congress in this frantic Hundred Days session of Congress (March–June 1933) were an imaginative blend of conservation (in the Progressive tradition) and relief. The first of these was the Civilian Conservation Corps (CCC), which aimed at putting young men from families on relief to work on soil conservation and reforestation projects. They lived in work camps and received room and board plus $30 a month, of which $25 automatically went to their families. By 1940, when the CCC came to an end, more than 2 million young men had served in the program. It had helped relieve one of the deepest tragedies of the Depression— young people who could not afford to go to school and who lacked the skills to get a job. An unanticipated social dividend was that the CCC provided a disciplined cadre of leaders when the armed forces had to be expanded at the outbreak of World War II.

THE TVA

The other conservation-relief agency was the Tennessee Valley Authority (TVA), one of the boldest, most controversial, yet most successful of the New Deal experiments. The TVA originated in Progressive Republican Senator George Norris's decade-long fight for government operation of the Wilson Dam on the Tennessee River at Muscle Shoals, Alabama. The government had begun the dam during World War I with a view to producing electricity

---

[*] A reference to the classic Hundred Days which was the climactic end to the Napoleonic Wars, from Napoleon's escape from the island of Elba on March 1, 1815, to the Battle of Waterloo on June 18.

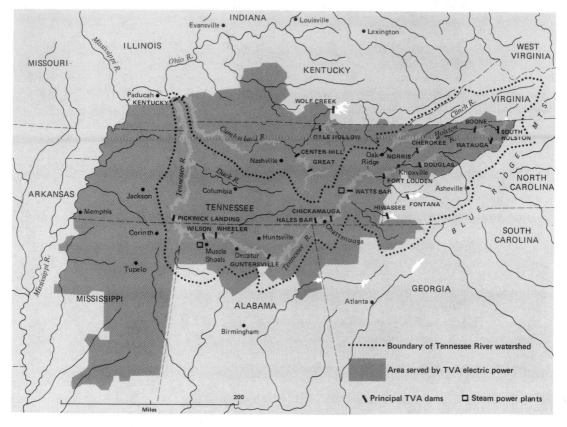

The Tennessee Valley Authority.

for the manufacture of munitions. By the time it was completed, however, it had generated more political controversy than electricity. President Harding, embarrassed at finding this embryo of socialism in his government, tried to sell it to Henry Ford, but Norris persuaded Congress to block the sale. Norris countered with a bill authorizing the government to produce and sell electricity, but it fell victim to the vetoes of Coolidge and Hoover. While Roosevelt was governor of New York, he became interested in public power when he discovered that private utility rates were five or six times higher than they were in neighboring Ontario, Canada, where a publicly owned power system drew electricity from

Niagara Falls. After his election as president, Roosevelt invited Norris to accompany him on a visit to Muscle Shoals, and from that tour emerged the idea of the TVA.

The bill the administration sent to Congress in April 1933 was breathtaking in scope. It proposed nothing less than the rehabilitation of an entire region—the valley of the Tennessee River and its tributaries, which drained all or portions of seven states: Virginia, North Carolina, Georgia, Alabama, Mississippi, Tennessee, and Kentucky. To undertake this task, the act created the Tennessee Valley Authority, a public corporation independent of the government (except that the president would appoint its director), which combined the authority of government and the flexibility of private business. The TVA was given funds to improve five existing dams and build twenty new ones with the dual purpose of producing cheap electricity and conserving soil and water through flood control.

Progressives such as Norris also hoped that the TVA might serve as a yardstick by which to measure private utility rates. The TVA's rates were lower than those of private utilities, but its critics attributed that to the fact that the TVA paid no federal taxes and made only voluntary contributions to local governments. Nevertheless, private utilities were forced to meet the challenge, and the nation's average electric bill dropped 23 percent over the next seven years, where it had dropped only 2 percent in the previous seven. By 1950, the government had invested 1 billion dollars in TVA dams, and by then too it had recovered every penny of the investment through increased tax receipts in an area that had previously been one of the poorest in the nation. The TVA also produced an unanticipated dividend during World War II: Its inexpensive electricity facilitated the development of the atomic bomb at Oak Ridge, Tennessee.

MANIPULATING THE DOLLAR, 1933–1934

Most of the early measures of the New Deal were aimed at raising prices as a way out of the Depression. The most direct way of accomplishing that was by devaluing the dollar in terms of gold, and that was precisely what the agrarian Bryan wing of the Democratic party advocated in 1933. Roosevelt entered office without a commitment on this question (as on most others), but the banking crisis forced him to act. By a series of executive orders and laws in March and April 1933, the president in effect took the United States off the gold standard. Roosevelt prohibited the banks from redeeming currency in gold coin, and prohibited the export of gold. Congress purchased the gold stocks of the Federal Reserve system with government bonds and declared void all private contracts that required payment in gold. These moves dropped the dollar to 85 cents on foreign exchanges, thereby making American goods cheaper for foreign buyers.

In October 1933, after a new drop in prices wiped out the summer's gains, Roosevelt went on the radio to announce his conversion to the idea of a "commodity dollar." The idea, he explained to a baffled public, was to reduce the intrinsic (gold) value of the dollar to bring it in line with the reduced value of commodities. A shirt that cost $1 in 1926, for instance, sold for 50¢ in the Depression; thus the purchasing power of the dollar had doubled. If the gold content of the dollar were cut in half (a theoretical cut because dollars could not be exchanged for gold anyway), a dollar would be equal to one shirt instead of two, and a shirt would once again cost $1—or so the theory went. In January 1934, Congress passed the Gold Reserve Act, giving the president the authority he needed. Roosevelt reduced the gold content of the dollar by about 40 percent, giving the country a "59¢ dollar" and the Republicans a political warcry. The dollar was simultaneously devalued in foreign exchanges, and the the United States began paying a higher price for gold. When Roosevelt entered office, the price of gold was about $20 an ounce. He instructed the RFC (an agency he had inherited from Hoover and used in ways that left the former president aghast) to begin buying the world's gold. The RFC steadily raised the price it was willing to pay and finally pegged gold at $35 an ounce, a price that held until 1971.

How effective Roosevelt's efforts at inflation through devaluation were is hard to say. Prices did rise in 1935–1936, but that may have been due as much to other New Deal efforts. In the end the currency experiment proved only that the "gold bugs" were wrong. It was possible to have a stable and ultimately prosperous economy with a currency backed by nothing but the people's faith. The ghost of William Jennings Bryan could rest at last.

THE FIRST NEW DEAL: AN ASSESSMENT

Some of Roosevelt's early measures were bold and innovative, and he showed a concern for people and their welfare. There were, moreover, echoes of progressivism not only in the field of conservation, but in the regulation of business. The Securities and Exchange Commission (1934), created by Congress as a watchdog for Wall Street, was reminiscent of Woodrow Wilson's Federal Trade Commission. A Reciprocal Trade Agreements Act (1934), which authorized the executive to arrange mutual tariff reductions with other countries, steered the country in the direction of freer trade.

But that was it. Recovery, not reform, was the goal of the First New Deal. The administration was quite willing to work closely with big business, as it did through the NRA. Its agricultural program mostly benefited the commercial farmers; tenants and sharecroppers received little or nothing. Roosevelt's relief program was humanitarian in motive and short range in view. Even his public works projects, except for the short-lived CWA, were to be self-liquidating; that is, they paid for themselves over time. At one point Roosevelt even suggested to Ickes that the PWA ought to buy up banks that had failed and turn them into Post Offices rather than build new ones. In his first year in office he actually reduced the government payroll. The only money put into the mighty NRA was for secretarial wages. The budget was still in

the red, but that was due to light receipts: The deficit for Roosevelt's first half year in office was lower than Hoover's.

Roosevelt's hesitancy was due in part to the fact that, like Hoover, he did not expect the Depression to last long. Temporary measures, he felt, were enough. He was, on the other hand, open to persuasion and willing to experiment, and he had around him men who were already tossing about some novel—some would say radical—ideas. The theory of the great English economist John Maynard Keynes that government in time of depression ought to incur massive deficits through spending programs that would put money in the hands of consumers (called "priming the pump") already had some believers in the Roosevelt circle. If the depression persisted, Roosevelt would be forced to employ larger and more expensive government programs. The depression did persist, and Roosevelt's leftward shift came to be known as the second New Deal.

⊔ The Second New Deal, 1935–1936

Although the first New Deal had neither ideology nor coherence, its farm program and its efforts to relieve unemployment gave hope to millions. Roosevelt's personal magnetism conveyed assurance that the country was in good hands. The voters responded enthusiastically. In the election of 1934, the Democrats' share of the popular vote actually increased, something no majority party had ever achieved in an off-year election. The Democrats swelled their majorities in Congress and held all but seven state governorships.

The election also brought the first serious criticism of the president. The legislation of the Hundred Days, though opposed by most Republicans, had brought little real opposition. People's sense of urgency induced them to accept almost everything Roosevelt had to suggest. But by early 1934, the scope and novelty of the New Deal were beginning to sink in. Roosevelt had involved the government in every aspect of the economy; through the radio, he had injected himself into every American home. Republicans accused him of usurping power and hinted that the United States might be following the totalitarian path of Mussolini's Italy and Hitler's Germany. (The dictatorship accusation was to shadow Roosevelt the rest of his life— which is to say, the remainder of his presidency.) Businessmen accused Roosevelt of being partial to labor and farmers, an accusation that absolutely astonished the president. Conservative Democrats, such as the 1924 candidate John W. Davis, broke publicly with him, as did his one-time friend Al Smith, whose defection left the deepest hurt of all. These groups formed the bipartisan Liberty League in 1934 to support the election of anti–New Deal congressmen.

Rejected by the Right, Roosevelt had little choice but to seek support from the Left. He may also have felt a need to undermine the radical Left, which had gained strength in the hard times. Communist and Socialist parties had reported membership increases. Demagogues of the radio waves, such as the Catholic priest Charles Coughlin, who blamed the Depression on international bankers, got a wide hearing. Most dangerous of all, from Roosevelt's point of view, was Louisiana's Senator Huey Long, the Kingfish, whose slogan was "Every man a king, but no one wears a crown." In 1934 Long formed the Share Our Wealth Society to promote the idea of confiscating all incomes in excess of $1 million and using the money to furnish every family a guaranteed annual wage. Within a year, Long's movement claimed 7 million members, and the Kingfish clearly had his eye on the Democratic nomination in 1936. Such movements were

nurtured in misery. Roosevelt saw the need to instill a spark of hope. That it meant a switch in tactics bothered him not at all; dramatic reversals often caught his fancy.

LONG-TERM RELIEF AND REFORM

Roosevelt sketched the framework of the second New Deal in his annual message to Congress of January 1935. There were three principal features: relief, labor legislation, and social security. Stopgap measures were not enough, Roosevelt declared; there was no end to the Depression in sight. The government had to undertake a massive, semipermanent public works program that would put the unemployed to work by the millions.

The WPA. Roosevelt could not bring himself to accept the deficit spending theories of Lord Keynes,* but he could agree to some temporary deficits in the interest of relieving human misery. Congress responded by appropriating the astounding sum of $5 billion, and Roosevelt created the Works Progress Administration to spend it. He installed as head of the agency Harry Hopkins, whose name had become a household word as a result of his earlier efforts in the field of unemployment relief.

Hopkins was interested in people, not projects. He also worked on the assumption that painters, actors, and historians had to eat even if they could not build airports and dams. The WPA's Federal Theater Project took plays and vaudeville shows to cities and towns across the country. WPA historians collected town and county records and stored them in fireproof institutions for a wealthier genera-

---

* After reading Keynes' *General Theory of Employment, Interest, and Money* (1936), Roosevelt confessed to the startled Englishman that he had not understood a word of it.

tion to peruse. WPA sociologists interviewed aged blacks and recorded their recollections of life in slavery and post–Civil War freedom. The New Deal did more to promote culture than any other administration in the history of the nation. Such projects attracted both attention and ridicule, but in fact about 80 percent of WPA funds went into construction and conservation projects. Some of those were also ridiculed, and WPA workers were accused of loafing on the job. "We Piddle Around" was a national joke. The point, though, is that Harry Hopkins did put people to work, over 8 million of them by 1941, almost one-fifth of the total labor force. In any given month the average number of WPA workers was around 2 million—2 million men and women able to say they worked for their wages, 2 million people given a stake in society, 2 million who might otherwise have listened to the promises of demagogues and revolutionaries.

Relief was no longer considered a dole, a free lunch in a Hooverville soup kitchen. In coming to terms with the Depression, Americans had also found ways of profitably engaging the unemployed. Two satellites of the WPA are illustrative. The Rural Electrification Administration (REA) employed WPA workers to build power lines that would carry electricity to isolated rural areas. The private utilities had been reluctant to carry their services to the countryside because the number of customers on each line was too few to justify the expense. Electric power revolutionized life on the farm. Another offshoot of the WPA was the National Youth Administration (NYA), which offered young people part-time jobs so they could stay in school.

The Wagner Act. The labor provisions of the NRA codes had not been sufficient. Unions were still on their own in dealing with industry, and with so many people out of work, they had little bargaining power. In 1933 and again in 1934, Senator Robert Wagner of New York introduced a bill offering government guarantees of the right to organize and bargain collectively. Roosevelt had refused to endorse the idea, and Wagner's bill failed to pass. In February 1935, Wagner reintroduced his measure, and the president, after some hesitation, gave it his blessing. Business lobbied vigorously against it, but the Senate approved it overwhelmingly and the House passed it without even a roll call.

The Wagner Act, or National Labor Relations Act, aligned the government with organized labor. It declared that working people had a right to form unions, and it prohibited various unfair practices, such as dismissing a worker who joined a union. The act created the National Labor Relations Board and authorized it to supervise elections in plants and factories to determine which unions would represent employees. Once the employees in a plant voted in favor of a union, the employer was obliged to bargain with it in good faith. Assured of government support, labor unions began a drive to organize the mass industries, notably steel and autos. By 1941, the number of organized workers had doubled, and "big labor" had become a factor in American politics and society. In succeeding decades the Wagner Act was modified to ensure employers some bargaining rights, but it remains today the cornerstone of American labor legislation.

Social Security. Old-age insurance was the third element in the second New Deal. This idea too had been discussed for some years within the Roosevelt circle without getting the president's support. It was hardly new. Old-age pensions were a common feature of the European welfare state, and they had been endorsed by the Progressive platform of 1912. Roosevelt agreed to the principle in 1934 and formed a committee to examine the problem. The committee's bill slipped through Congress in the spring of 1935 with only token opposition.

The Social Security Act set up a pension fund from which workers would receive retirement benefits at age sixty-five. The fund was financed by a payroll tax levied on employers and by deductions from workers' wages. In theory, at least, the program was to be self-financing and independent of the public purse. The other arm of the act was a relief program offering monetary compensation to the unemployed for a certain number of days per year. The program was cautious and experimental. Far from a governmental giveaway, social security was envisioned as an insurance system that workers financed out of their own pockets. In the beginning, it was aimed mostly at factory workers. Professional people, farmers, teachers, and the self-employed were not part of the system. Nevertheless, it was a departure from the gospel of self-help. The government was now ensuring, even insisting, that people provide for their future. Roosevelt soon came to recognize its revolutionary implications. To the end of his days he regarded social security as the supreme achievement of the New Deal.

Progressivism. Three other measures rounded out the second Hundred Days of 1935. The Banking Act of 1935 greatly strengthened the powers of the Federal Reserve Board so that, by manipulating the money supply and interest rates, it could influence the business cycle. A revenue act sharply increased taxes on inheritances and high incomes, leading opponents to accuse Roosevelt of trying to "soak the rich." Finally, the Public Utility Holding Company Act ordered the breakup of the public utility holding company empires, thereby recommitting the administration to trust-busting. These acts also afford a clue to the shifting focus of the New Deal. The

Roosevelt administration in 1935 was still concerned with recovery, but it was more inclined toward long-range solutions than temporary ones. It was far more concerned about the poor and far more critical of the wealthy than it had been in 1933. Now it was closer to the Progressive tradition. Banking and antitrust legislation was something any Wilsonian could applaud. The Wagner Act and social security, though far beyond anything Wilson had dreamed, had roots in the Progressive philosophy. The focus of the first New Deal was on recovery, that of the second was on reform.

ELECTION OF 1936

The second New Deal also provided the Democrats with a ready-made platform for the election of 1936. The party was still unified, despite some defections, and Roosevelt was renominated easily. His running mate, who had been with him on the 1932 ticket, was John Nance Garner, a Texan who represented the party's rural-southern wing.

The Republicans had more difficulty, both with platform and ticket. They could not assault the New Deal directly, for it was popular. Instead, they contented themselves with the promise that they could administer government welfare programs more efficiently. For a nominee, they finally settled on Kansas Governor Alfred M. Landon. Landon had managed to keep the Kansas budget balanced in the hard times by heroic economies and thus stood in at least symbolic contrast to Roosevelt the spender. Symbolism, it turned out, was all Landon had to offer. He accused Roosevelt of threatening the free enterprise system, yet he conceded the need for government action. But what sort of action he could not say. Roosevelt swamped him in the election, polling 27.8 million votes to Landon's 16.7 million and carrying every state but two. In the 1920s, when the nation had been Republican and Maine's rock-bound Republican electorate had trooped to the polls early in order to beat the weather, the myth had arisen that "As Maine goes, so goes the nation." In 1936 Roosevelt's campaign manager Jim Farley gave the old slogan a new twist: "As Maine goes, so goes Vermont."

⎵ The Roosevelt Coalition

The victory revealed more than Roosevelt's popularity; it also reflected some long-term demographic shifts in the American electorate. The foreign-born had been attracted to the Democratic party since the turn of the century. By the mid-1930s, their sons and daughters had come of age, and they did what American children have long done: They voted the party of their parents. Both the foreign-born and second-generation Americans were congregated in the cities of the East and Middle West. During the years of Republican ascendancy those cities generally voted Republican. The shift began with World War I, when Al Smith and other urban Democrats made open appeals to the foreign-born. Internal migration reinforced the shift. Southerners, especially from Appalachia, began moving into northern industrial cities during the war, and the migration intensified in the 1920s. Akron, Ohio, center of the nation's tire industry, became known as "the capital of West Virginia." These voters too were Democrats, as their ancestors had been since before the Civil War. The election of 1924 revealed that Republicans were losing their grip on the nation's largest cities. In 1928, the cities were Democratic for the first time, and Roosevelt vastly increased the Democratic margin in 1932 and 1936.

Besides demographic shifts, the election results revealed the success of Roosevelt's class appeal, especially in the second New Deal. The *Literary Digest* made itself the butt of a national joke after the election because, as the result of a "scientific" poll, it had predicted a Landon victory. The magazine, in fact, failed to survive the national laughter. But its mistake was the result of naive polling methods. It had conducted a postcard straw vote from mailing lists drawn from telephone directories and automobile registration records. It was people who owned neither telephones nor automobiles who elected Roosevelt.

Prominent among these were factory workers in general and blacks in particular. Black Americans abandoned the party of Abraham Lincoln for the first time and moved into the Democratic party en masse. For the most part, they have been there ever since. Labor unions too began to shed the veneer of impartiality imposed by Samuel Gompers, especially the new militant organizations in the mass industries (then in the process of forming themselves into the CIO). Mineworkers, steelworkers, and auto workers turned their unions into fundraising machines for the Democratic party.

The by-product of all this lower-class activity was the rather poor showing of the radicals in the election. After eight years of hard times, with no end in sight, a resurgence of utopianism would have been quite understandable. Huey Long was dead, shot by an assassin on the steps of the Louisiana state capitol, but there were others with panaceas by the basketful.* Nevertheless, in 1936 the Communist party candidate, Earl Browder, received only 80,000 votes. Norman Thomas, the Socialist party candidate, who had polled 884,000 votes in 1932, drew a mere 187,000 in 1936. Roosevelt had taken the steam out of the political Left.

---

*Long died in the arms of Gerald L. K. Smith, an anti-Semitic, pro-Nazi radio demagogue.

CLIO'S FOCUS: Kingfish: The Story of Huey Long

Huey Long was a demagogue and a southerner, but he fit no stereotype. He was no race baiter, and he scorned bigots. His racial attitudes were those of a white southerner of his day. He believed blacks to be inferior and accepted segregation. But he also expected blacks to benefit as much from his programs as whites. Blacks, in turn, supported him, and those who were eligible to vote voted for him.

Like every demagogue, Huey Long made many promises, but unlike the others, he fulfilled most of them. Long delivered paved highways, new bridges, free school books, and an eminent state university. His building efforts saddled Louisiana with public debt, but they provided some badly needed public works in addition to some desperately needed jobs.

Huey Long had a thirst for power that would have awed a Caesar. But whether he was dangerous or whether he was a threat to democracy, as his critics charged, we will never know. His life was cut short, like Julius Caesar's, by an assassin in his own capital.

A myth that Huey Long cultivated all his life was that he was born to poverty. It helped him, of course, identify with the dirt farmers who were his constituents. His father, who raised livestock, was actually one of the larger landowners in his parish. With part-time work as a traveling salesman, Long put himself through Tulane Law School. He was admitted to the bar in 1915 and practiced law in Shreveport until he was elected governor. Huey Long loved politics, and from his sales experience he developed a stump oratory that was vernacular, witty, and persuasive. With virtually no political experience, he ran for governor in 1924 and lost. He ran again in 1927 and won.

Long's rhetoric during the campaign frightened the conservative Democratic establishment, but his program was hardly radical. He instituted a badly needed highway building program financed by bonds and a tax on gasoline. He provided free textbooks for elementary and secondary schools, and he imposed regulations on pipeline companies that drastically reduced rates on home fuel. His enemies, among them the Standard Oil Company, made him more popular than ever with his rural constituency. He also used the governor's patronage powers to create a state machine loyal only to him. Once-critical legislators joined him because he was a source of power and profit. There was some corruption, but no more than in any other city or state machine in the country. When Long's enemies initiated an investigation of corruption in the state in 1934, they found practically nothing. Long was devoted to power, but he used that power for what he perceived as the interests of the common people.

When the Depression struck, Long was prepared. He expanded his construction projects, anticipating by some years the New Deal public works projects. Although he never really articulated the goal, Long aimed to make Louisiana as modern as any state in the Union. This goal was implicit in his firm support for Louisiana State University, which became one of the finest universities in the country. To be sure, he also meddled in its affairs. He selected one president and fired two football coaches. He rarely missed a football game, usually gave a rousing speech at half-time, and occasionally led the band. On one occasion when an LSU home opener conflicted with a Barnum and Bailey circus performance, he called circus officials and demanded that they change the date. When they refused, he reminded them of Louisiana's statute requiring that animals brought into the state be dipped in disinfectant to rid them of disease-carrying ticks. Long threatened to have all circus animals dipped at the border. "Have you ever dipped a tiger?" he asked sweetly over the phone, "or an elephant?" The officials changed the date.

In 1930, midway through his term as governor, Long ran for a seat in the U.S. Senate and won. The Senate would give him national exposure; he may already have had his eye on the presidency. He completed his term in order to push through the remainder of his program, and in 1932 he headed for Washington. His reputation preceded him. As soon as he set up headquarters in the Mayflower Hotel, a delegation of reporters came by for an interview. "What should we address you as?" asked one. "Governor? or Senator?" "Down there," said Long, dragging on his cigar, "they call me 'Kingfish.'" Actually he gave himself the nickname, which he took from the Amos and Andy radio show. Because it made ideal copy for the press, the nickname stuck.

Long had no time for the low-profile deferential behavior expected of a freshman senator. Within a few days of taking his seat, he delivered a major address to the Senate that set newspaper editors and politicians clucking for days. Long entitled his speech "The Doom of America's Dream," which he reinforced with an ominous prediction of violent revolution if the needs of the poor and the unemployed were not met. Boldly he prescribed redistributing wealth through taxation.

Long approved of Roosevelt's record as governor of New York and worked hard for the Democratic candidate in the 1932 election. Roosevelt responded by inviting him to the Roosevelt estate at Hyde Park, New York. The two had much in common. Each had the ability to arouse intense devotion or intense hatred. But that interview was their last friendly one. In the spring of 1933, Long fought virtually every administration proposal. He thought the government should have taken over the banks instead of shoring up the system. He objected to the Agricultural Adjustment Act because it would do nothing for small farmers, and he predicted the NRA would benefit no one but big business. Roosevelt, as intolerant of mavericks in Congress as Long was in his own state organization, summoned the senator to the White House in June 1933 and informed him that he was going to deprive him of further federal patronage in Louisiana. Thereafter Roosevelt used his appointment powers to build up an anti-Long faction in the Democratic party of Louisiana.

Ironically, as his grip on Louisiana loosened, Huey Long's national reputation increased. He was a charismatic radio personality, and his drawing power made him a network favorite. On February 23, 1934, Long announced over a national radio hookup the formation of the Share Our Wealth Society to support legislation he had introduced in Congress. Long's measures included a capital levy tax that would confiscate all family fortunes in excess of $5 million, and an income tax that would confiscate income in excess of $1 million a year. From the revenue derived from these taxes, said Long, the government could guarantee every family an income of two or three thousand dollars a year. "Share our wealth, and make every man a king!"

Huey Long already had his eye on the 1936 election. He planned to contest Roosevelt for the Democratic nomination. If that failed, he planned to form a third party. This, he hoped, would take enough votes away from Roosevelt to give the election to the Republicans. After four years of Republican rule, the people would be ready for anything—and he would be ready for them. The scheme was characteristic—a blend of cynicism and idealism underscored by a thirst for power. Whether it would have worked we will never know. And perhaps it is just as well. On September 8, 1935, Huey Long was shot and mortally wounded in a corridor of the Louisiana capitol building in Baton Rouge. The assassin, an idealistic young physician who apparently feared that Huey Long might some day become president, was immediately shot to death by Long's bodyguards.

THE CIO: A NEW MILITANCY IN LABOR

Prior to 1935, Roosevelt had done almost nothing for organized labor. Even the concessions in the NRA codes had not been his idea. His secretary of Labor, Frances Perkins, the first woman to serve in a president's cabinet, had solid credentials as a reformer (including service in Hull House), but she had little influence on administration policies. Yet among labor leaders, as with so many other people, Roosevelt was able to inspire sympathy when he had no policy. John L. Lewis, leader of the United Mine Workers since 1919 and a Republican by voting habit, visited Roosevelt in 1933 to complain that his union had barely enough members to pay the organization's expenses. Roosevelt consoled him, and armed with nothing more than that, Lewis returned to the coalfields. There, glowering from under craggy eye-

brows, he told the diggers: "The president wants you to join a union."

Within a year Lewis was able to stand before the A F of L convention and boast that the UMW was once again a fighting force of 400,000 miners. Not content, he introduced a resolution to establish a Steelworkers Organizing Committee (SWOC) and grant a provisional charter to the United Auto Workers (UAW). William Green, successor to Samuel Gompers, and other A F of L leaders agreed, and then did nothing. The A F of L was dominated, as it had been in the days of Gompers, by trade unions. Its leadership was wary of the mass industries, whose workers were predominantly foreign-born or black and whose jobs required so little skill that they could easily be replaced. Not to be denied, Lewis went to the Atlantic City convention the following year (1935) with eyebrows twitching in anger. They "seduced me with fair words!" he roared, and "having learned that I was seduced, I am enraged and ready to rend my seducers limb from limb."

Three weeks later, on November 10, 1935, Lewis and the leaders of seven other A F of L unions that were organized by industry without regard to job specification met in Atlantic City to form the Committee for Industrial Organization. Its purpose was to encourage the organization of the mass industries: steel, autos, rubber, cement, aluminum. Besides Lewis, the most important leaders on the committee were Sidney Hillman of the Amalgamated Clothing Workers and David Dubinsky of the International Ladies Garment Workers. Green and the A F of L executive board urged the committee to disband, and when they refused, expelled them. In 1937 the CIO unions, now grown to ten, reorganized themselves as the Congress of Industrial Organizations.

Lewis had chosen the proper moment to rebel. Just as his disagreement with the A F of L's leadership reached its climax, Congress passed the Wagner Act. With the federal government behind them, CIO leaders marched boldly into the great industrial plants and sought signatures for petitions to hold union elections. Their tactic was to concentrate on steel, which since the great strike of 1919 had been the most obstinate of open-shop industries. But workers in other industries, emboldened by the government's sympathetic attitude, would not wait.

The CIO was just organizing itself in February 1936 when a group of laid-off workers organized a sitdown strike at the Goodyear rubber plant in Akron, Ohio. The tactic was a variation of what employers had been doing for years. Workers had little bargaining power in mass industries because they were easily replaced; when they went on strike, employers locked the factory and looked for replacements. Instead of walking out, the Goodyear workers took over the plant and set up a picket line outside that turned back workers from succeeding shifts. The picket line eventually stretched for eleven miles around the entire Goodyear complex. Company officials were helpless because if they asked for military help, as they had been quick to do in the past, the resulting violence would destroy the plant. Goodyear surrendered, recognized the union, and agreed to a wages and hours package.

The idea spread quickly. In December 1936, automobile workers at the Fisher body plant in Cleveland sat down at their machines and declared themselves on strike. A month later, workers at the Chevrolet plant in Flint, Michigan, brought their assembly line to a halt. Both strikes came to resemble a siege. In Flint, police formed a barricade around the plant, and strikers' wives carried food through their ranks. When police tried to disrupt the supply line, striking workers drove them off. The fight went down in labor history as the Battle of Bulls Run. Governor Frank Murphy refused to send in state troops (Roosevelt later appointed him to the Supreme Court), and General Motors surrendered. A month later Carnegie-Illinois Steel Company, the largest component in the United States Steel complex, agreed to a contract with SWOC without a strike. Little Steel, the companies that made up the rest of the steel industry, managed to resist unionization until 1941. By the time the United States went to war at the end of that year, the CIO boasted 5 million members. By that date too, the only sizable American company with an open shop was Ford Motors. And in 1942 Henry Ford, patriarch of the assembly line who had managed to instill in his employees a singular blend of rugged individualism and corporate nonidentity, surrendered to a union—in part because the government threatened not to let him make tanks without one.

THE NEW DEAL
AND THE UNDERSIDE

The shift in the black vote in 1936, like that of labor, reflected a common perception that Roosevelt was "their man." And as with labor, Roosevelt's gestures to blacks were largely symbolic. He brought more blacks into government than ever before. Black professionals, lawyers, journalists, and PhDs served in executive positions in the Departments of Interior, Commerce, and Labor. Mary McLeod Bethune, president of Florida's Bethune-Cookman College, was named to head the Division of Negro Affairs of the National Youth Administration, thus becoming the first black in history to head a government agency. But token gestures such as these were as far as the president would go. He never committed himself to the idea of civil rights, and he condoned official discrimination. The Federal Housing Administration, established to stimulate the housing industry by underwriting mortgages, refused to guarantee mortgages on houses purchased by blacks in white neighborhoods. The armed forces were racially segregated throughout World War II, and so were the CCC camps. For fear of alienating southern whites, Roosevelt never endorsed the two pieces of federal legislation blacks so desperately needed—a law making lynching a federal crime and a constitutional amendment abolishing the poll tax. The poll tax, or capitation tax, was the latest device by which southern states deprived blacks of the vote. A poll tax receipt was required for voter registration, and unsophisticated, poorly educated rural blacks simply did not keep such documents.

Blacks themselves forced the most important civil rights gesture Roosevelt made. In 1941, as the nation geared for war, A. Philip Randolph, president of the Brotherhood of Sleeping Car Porters, proposed a march on Washington to demand equal access for blacks to jobs in defense industries. The proposal was a taste of the postwar civil rights movement in that it was black-inspired and black-led and was a direct action movement. Fearing violence, Roosevelt acted to forestall the demonstration. On June 25, 1941, he issued an executive order banning discriminatory hiring in industries that accepted government defense contracts, and he established the Fair Employment Practices Committee (FEPC) to enforce the rules. The FEPC actually had little power, but it was a landmark—the first federal civil rights agency. It raised hopes, and rising expectations was the central dynamic of the postwar civil rights movement.

Indians fared somewhat better in the New Deal. To head the government's Indian Bureau, Roosevelt appointed John Collier, who had led a crusade through the 1920s for Indian land ownership. The Dawes Act of 1887, aimed at making Indians independent landowners, had accomplished precisely the opposite. Poverty-stricken Indians, many of them unfamiliar with farming techniques, had sold the allotments given them under the Dawes Act to white ranchers and farmers. Since 1887, Indian landholdings had dropped from 138 million acres to 48 million, and almost half of that was untillable desert. In 1934 Collier secured passage of an Indian Reorganization Act that reversed the process by restoring lands to tribal ownership. It also encouraged the tribes to establish councils for self-government, and it made available loans for economic development. Collier's bureau established special schools in the Indian lands that emphasized vocational and agricultural training, and he issued special orders that Indian agents were not to interfere with religious practices or social customs. Indians would continue to live in poverty and hunger, but at least their cultural individuality had won respect. And for the first time after centuries

New York Public Library Picture Collection.

Amelia Earhart. The first woman to fly the Atlantic, she was a national hero in the Depression decade. While on a round-the-world flight in 1937, she ran out of gas between islands in the Pacific and was never seen again.

of slaughter and degradation, they had won a voice in their own destiny.

Women made up one-fifth of the labor force at the beginning of the 1930s, but they continued to labor under a number of social taboos. The Depression and male unemployment pushed many of them back into the home. The protective legislation enacted by the Progressives hindered women as much as it helped them. In occupations in which women made up the majority of the workers (in department store employment, for instance) protective legislation improved their working conditions and sometimes their pay. In male-dominated occupations, that same legislation prevented women from competing because the job involved night work (newspaper printing), or demanded stamina (streetcar conducting), or was considered unsafe (metalworking). One result of the Pro-

gressive legislation then, was to encourage, or even compel, women to remain in those occupations (storeclerking, school teaching) that were already filled with women.

Married women who wished to work, or needed to, encountered additional pressures in the 1920s and '30s. Conservatives denounced married women who left the home to work as a threat to the family and a "menace to the race" because they were likely to have fewer children. As a result, public opinion tolerated the employment of only a few groups of married women, notably blacks, immigrants, and women with grown children. The number of working wives therefore remained small. In 1920, only one-tenth of all wives worked; by 1940, the figure had risen to 17 percent, or about a third of the female work force.

The Depression further discouraged female employment. To both government officials and business executives it seemed patently unfair to allow the wife or daughter of an employed man to work while an unemployed man could not feed his family. Federal law required that whenever a reduction in personnel was necessary in any government office, the first to go would be those whose spouses held another government position. Three-fourths of the time the dismissed spouse was the woman. Although the WPA paid women the same rate as men, it gave men the preference for its jobs. The federal government did fund day-care centers for the first time in the 1930s, but the purpose was not to free women to enter the job market; in most cases it was the more limited humitarian objective of providing children of the poor with hot meals.

What gains women made in the New Deal—and they were token at best—were due largely to the president's wife, Eleanor. An ardent advocate of women's rights, Eleanor Roosevelt as early as 1928 had written an essay advocating equal pay for equal work. In 1933 she persuaded her husband to place a woman in his cabinet,

Secretary of Labor Frances Perkins. But beyond that she could not go, and perhaps did not want to. She apparently realized that her husband had enough problems and enough enemies without tackling women's rights. Even so, she made herself a force in the administration, and by playing an active role demonstrated what women could do. In FDR's first year in office she traveled 40,000 miles, lecturing to women's clubs, appearing at college commencements, and unveiling memorials. So peripatetic was she that in 1935 the Washington *Star* headlined on its society page the news: "MRS. ROOSEVELT SPENDS NIGHT AT WHITE HOUSE."

She also managed, in many ways, to bridge the gap between president and people. She obtained interviews with the president for people with a cause. She kept Walter White, head of the NAACP, posted on the president's views and the impact some New Deal programs might have on blacks. When the Daughters of the American Revolution barred black opera singer Marian Anderson from performing in their Constitution Hall, Mrs. Roosevelt resigned her own membership in the DAR and arranged to have Anderson sing at the Lincoln Memorial on Easter Sunday. Her syndicated newspaper column, "My Day," an unpretentious account of her thoughts and activities, conveyed a sense of intimacy between White House and people. Nevertheless, for all of Eleanor Roosevelt's efforts, the status of women in American society improved scarcely at all in the 1930s.

The New Deal's record, with respect to the victims of legal and social discrimination, meager though it seems, must be viewed in the context of the times. The 1930s was not an age of human benevo-

Marian Anderson. The famous contralto was the first black to perform at the White House.

New York Public Library Picture Collection.

lence. In Germany, Adolph Hitler had risen to power on the notion that the Jews had been responsible for Germany's defeat in World War I. In the United States, bigots such as Father Coughlin and Gerald L. K. Smith echoed Hitler's anti-Semitic venom in weekly radio broadcasts. When the city of Los Angeles complained that Mexican nationals were absorbing a disproportionate share of the city's welfare budget, the Southern Pacific Railroad offered to ship them back to Mexico at $14.70 a head. An estimated 200,000 Mexicans were forcibly sent home in 1933 alone. In Scottsboro, Alabama, that same year, nine young black men were tried for rape, even though medical testimony indicated that their accusers had not been molested. Five were ultimately sentenced to life imprisonment. In such a world the American government was a model of tolerance. Those who assail Roosevelt for not doing more have the advantage of twenty-twenty hindsight.

⊔ The Ebb of Reform, 1937–1939

The reform impulse lost momentum in Roosevelt's second term, in part because the president himself lost his political magic. In the spring of 1937, at the crest of his postelection popularity, Roosevelt made the biggest mistake of his career. Angry at the Supreme Court for overturning much of the legislation of the Hundred Days, Roosevelt in February 1937 sent to Congress a Judiciary Reorganization Bill. In it he asked for authority to appoint a replacement for every judge who failed to retire at the age of seventy.

PACKING THE COURT

Roosevelt stressed the need to speed judicial processes by replacing "aged or infirm judges," but Congress and the public saw it for what it was—an attempt to pack the Supreme Court with friendly judges. The uproar was deafening. People reacted as if Roosevelt had threatened to suspend the Constitution itself.

FDR might have fared better had he been candid, for there were deep philosophical issues involved. The justices of the Supreme Court were Harding-Coolidge-Hoover appointees, and a majority took a narrow view of the constitutional powers of Congress. On the thesis that agriculture and manufacturing were not interstate commerce and therefore not susceptible to congressional regulation, the Court had declared unconstitutional the NRA, the AAA, and several other New Deal programs. But the president apparently decided that legalism was not a good basis for a popular appeal and rested his case instead on the question of old age.

While Congress discussed Roosevelt's plan, the Supreme Court rendered it unnecessary. By a 5 to 4 vote, the Court in April 1937 upheld the Wagner Act (*N.L.R.B.* v. *Jones & Laughlin Steel Corp.*) on the reasoning that the commerce power includes the right to protect the flow of commerce "from the paralyzing consequence of industrial war."* In May, by a similar one-vote margin, the Court upheld the constitutionality of the Social Security Act as a legitimate exercise of the commerce power. The credit for this tactical retreat belongs to Chief Justice Charles Evans Hughes. Hughes had come to realize that the Court could not long continue to thwart the will of Congress and the electorate, and he had swung a fellow moderate to his view even before Roosevelt's reorganization plan was made public.

---

* This was, ironically, a simple extension of the reasoning of the Debs decision (1896), in which the Court had upheld the use of a federal injunction to break up a strike on the ground that the government had power to remove obstructions to the free flow of interstate commerce.

Roosevelt pressed forward with his scheme anyway, but in the end the most Congress conceded was an attractive pension plan that would encourage justices to retire. That proved enough. Retirements enabled Roosevelt to name seven new justices in the next four years, giving the Court a liberal complexion that would last until the Nixon era. Roosevelt won the war, but it cost him heavily in popularity. It also cost him control of Congress.

PANIC OF 1937

Roosevelt made another error in judgment that spring. Things had been looking up; 1936 had been a pretty good year. Unemployment had dropped to around 7 million, stocks were up, and people were vacationing in Florida again. The president, who had never abandoned his dream of a balanced budget, ordered a cut in federal spending on the assumption that the Depression was coming to an end. The WPA cut its job rolls in half, and the Federal Reserve Board raised bank reserve requirements to prevent the boom from getting out of hand. These moves sent the economy into a nosedive in the fall of 1937. Unemployment soared back up to 10.5 million, and Wall Street crashed once again.

Sounding very much like Hoover, the embarrassed president claimed that the downturn was only temporary. He called it a "recession." But he also called for new expenditures. Congress restored funds to the WPA, quadrupled farm subsidies, and embarked on a shipbuilding program. The economy began to revive. Nothing the government did, however, made much of a dent in unemployment. In 1939, on the

Okies stalled on the highway in New Mexico, 1937. "Broke, baby sick, and car trouble!"

Library of Congress. Photograph by Dorothy Lange for the Farm Security Administration.

very eve of World War II, there were still 9.5 million unemployed.

In addition to his own political mistakes, Roosevelt was hampered in his second term by the formation in Congress of a conservative coalition of Republicans and southern Democrats. Southern Congressmen, believers in states rights by tradition and conservative by nature, had felt increasingly uncomfortable with the New Deal. Poor whites and blacks benefited from the administration's farm mortgage and housing programs, but those were not the people with power in the South. Commercial farmers and industrialists controlled the southern states, and these people had much in common with Republicans.

The coalition would dominate American politics for two decades after the war. In 1938, however, it was still in the formative stage, and the administration was able to squeeze through Congress two final measures that tidied up its farm and labor programs. A second Agricultural Adjustment Act undertook to limit farm production by setting marketing quotas that enabled farmers to plan their output, and it sought to utilize farm surpluses by distributing them to educational and other institutions. The Fair Labor Standards Act, passed that same year, established a minimum wage and maximum hours for workers involved in interstate commerce, and it also outlawed child labor at last.

In the off-year elections of 1938, Roosevelt tried to break the developing anti–New Deal coalition by opposing selected southern Democrats in the state primaries. It backfired, as the court-packing scheme had, for it only reinforced southern suspicions of federal interference. Roosevelt's targets became martyrs, and every one was reelected. After this, Roosevelt himself seemed to tire of the game. He also became increasingly preoccupied with foreign affairs and the need for the United States to arm, as the situation in both Europe and the Far East deteriorated steadily. In 1938 the president refused to support a federal antilynching law because he needed southern votes on a naval construction program. That was the symbolic end of the New Deal. In his annual message of January 1939, the president made it official. He had, said he, no further reforms to suggest. Instead, the urgent need was preparation for national defense. The progressive impulse, as in 1917, was already on the wane; war erased it altogether.

THE NEW DEAL: AN APPRAISAL

The New Deal failed if it is measured by the goal it had set for itself—recovery from the Depression. The nation in 1939 was rolling at a better pace than in 1933, but it was hardly prospering. There were still nearly 10 million unemployed. World War II, not the New Deal, ended the Depression. It also proved that economist Keynes was right—the wartime deficits primed the economic pump. (The national debt soared from $60 billion in 1940 to $250 billion in 1945.) Whether such massive deficits were politically possible in peacetime is another question. Roosevelt clearly did not think so; he never embraced the Keynesian theory, as the 1937 recession attests. At the same time, even the modest deficits of 1935 and 1936 had produced some recovery, and the deficits to that point had not created any serious political backlash. In summary, if Roosevelt can be faulted in his fiscal politics it is for being too timid, rather than too bold.

But there are other standards by which the New Deal can be measured. Its thrust was essentially humanitarian, and its principal achievement may have been that it offered hope to the hopeless. The lot of industrial workers improved dramatically not only through wages and hours legislation, but most important through government guarantees of the right to bargain collectively. Organized labor, struggling ever since World War I, experienced the most dramatic growth in its history, and the chief beneficiaries were the low-skilled toilers of the assembly-line industries. The lives of farmers too improved dramatically not only through higher incomes (achieved at the cost of stored surpluses), but through such daily amenities as easy credit and electric power.

By enhancing the position of farmers and wage earners in American society, the New Deal reduced the relative importance of business, which had been so dominant in the previous decade. What emerged from the maze of New Deal experiments was a new political economy, a "people's capitalism" that made socialist alternatives largely irrelevant. And though it could not bring the nation out of the Depression completely, it did insert a number of stabilizers into the economy that have helped prevent any major economic downturn ever since. Among these were bank deposit insurance, the minimum wage, farm price supports, unemployment compensation, and old age pensions. Most important of all, these changes demonstrated that there was a middle way between the extremes of fascism and communism. In a world in which totalitarianism had become the order of the day, Franklin Roosevelt's New Deal demonstrated to Europeans as well as Americans that democracy was still a viable way of government.

SUMMARY

The statistics of bank closures, business failures, and soaring unemployment told the story as the nation slid ever deeper into depression from 1929 to 1933. President Hoover, though a firm advocate of free enterprise and "rugged individualism," did make some moves to combat the decline. In 1930 he stepped up construction on two massive dam-building projects in the West, and he created the Federal Farm Board to buy up and store farm surpluses. At Hoover's behest, Congress in 1932 created the Reconstruction Finance Corporation to make loans to troubled businesses.

But these actions proved insufficient. Worse, Hoover did nothing to provide relief for the unemployed, and unemployment was the biggest single calamity of the Depression. The voters' rejection of Hoover in the election of 1932 was due as much as anything to their perception of his hardheartedness toward the unemployed.

Franklin Roosevelt entered office in 1933 without coherent ideology or firm commitment. The early stage of the New Deal was a makeshift assortment of experiments. The first New Deal, the legislation of 1933–1934, was aimed primarily at recovery. To restore the economy, Roosevelt was quite willing to work closely with business, as in the National Recovery Administration (NRA), when he allowed businesses to make cooperative price arrangements and released them from the antitrust laws. The relief programs of the first New Deal were humanitarian in motive and temporary in nature, based on the assumption that the Depression would soon end. The farm program too was a short-term series of devices for curtailing production. The only bows to the Progressive tradition were stock exchange regulation and a Reciprocal Trade Agreements Act aimed at lowering tariffs.

Roosevelt moved politically leftward in the course of 1934. The shift resulted in part from attacks on him by conservatives, and in part from a felt need to undermine the Depression-born popularity of the radical Left. Roosevelt also reached the conclusion that the Depression had become a more or less permanent condition and that stop-gap measures were not enough. The result was a series of proposals in his annual message of 1935, which historians have called the second New Deal. First among these was long-term relief. Congress appropriated $5 billion, and Roosevelt created the Works Progress Administration (WPA) to administer the program. In addition to construction workers, the WPA employed writers, artists, actors, and historians. The Social Security Act, second of these initiatives, contained a provision for direct relief in the form of monetary payments to the unemployed. In addition, the act created a system of old age and survivors' insurance, paid for in part by a payroll tax on employers. The third initiative was labor legislation in the form of the National La-

bor Relations Act, which provided a federal guarantee of the right to organize and bargain collectively. Inspired in part by the government's support, the mass unions in the American Federation of Labor broke away and formed a national organization of their own, the Congress of Industrial Organizations. The CIO then began a vigorous organizing drive in the largest mass industries, steel and autos.

The second New Deal was also more inclined toward Wilsonian progressivism. The Banking Act of 1935 reorganized and strengthened the Federal Reserve system, and in 1938 the administration began a comprehensive antitrust investigation. That same year the Fair Labor Standards Act rounded out the New Deal's labor legislation, and a second Agricultural Adjustment Act established the modern government farm price support system. Throughout 1938 Roosevelt became increasingly concerned about the deteriorating world situation and the need to rearm. In his annual message of January 1939, he called for an end to reform. World War II ended the New Deal.

READING SUGGESTIONS

The most authoritative, judicious, single-volume treatment of the 1930s is William E. Leuchtenburg's *Franklin D. Roosevelt and the New Deal, 1932–1940* (1963). Paul Conkin, *The New Deal* (1967), is a brief, faintly critical analysis. E. E. Robinson, *The Roosevelt Leadership* (1955), is more critical still. Martin L. Fausold's *The Presidency of Herbert Hoover* (1985) is the most recent effort to refurbish Hoover's image. Richard Hofstadter's *The Age of Reform: From Bryan to FDR* (1955) sees little relationship between the New Deal and earlier progressivism; Otis L. Graham, Jr., *Encore for Reform* (1967), sees substantial continuity. W. Elliot Brownlee's, *Dy-*

namics of Ascent: A History of the American Economy (1979) contains a recent appraisal of the New Deal's success in promoting economic recovery.

For the impact of the New Deal on segments of the population, see Susan Ware, *Beyond Suffrage: Women in the New Deal* (1981); Theodore Salutos, *The American Farmer and the New Deal* (1982); Raymond Wolters, *Negroes and the Great Depression: The Problem of Economic Recovery* (1970); Irving Bernstein, *Caring Society: The New Deal, The Worker, and the Great Depression* (1985); and Monroe Lee Billington, *The Political South in the Twentieth Century* (1975). Thomas K.

McGraw, *TVA and the Power Fight, 1933–1939* (1972), traces the early history of that institution.

The impact of the Depression on the lives of the people is vividly portrayed in Studs Terkel's *Hard Times* (1970), a collection of personal interviews. Secondary assessments of the impact of the Depression are C. Bird, *The Invisible Scar* (1966), and E. R. Ellis, *A Nation in Torment* (1970). Daniel T. Carter's prize-winning *Scottsboro: A Tragedy of the American South* (1969) recalls one of the more sordid incidents of the decade. Alan Brinkley, *Voices of Protest: Huey Long, Father Coughlin, and the Great Depression* (1982), discusses the panacea builders. My sketch of Huey Long borrowed heavily from T. Harry Williams's 1969 prize-winning biography.

13

THE COLD WAR YEARS:
1945–1957

"T he United States has not the option as to whether it will or will not play a great part in the world. It *must* play a great part. All that it can decide is whether it will play that part well or badly." The words were Theodore Roosevelt's, and he was referring to America's entry into World War I. Most Americans of 1919 would have agreed with Roosevelt, but few were willing to shoulder the responsibilities the role entailed.

⊔ Isolation

The nation's experience in World War I was a disillusioning one. The behavior of America's allies in the peace settlement resurrected age-old American prejudice. Europe, they decided, was decadent beyond redemption; it ought to be shunned because it could not be saved.

WAR DEBTS

In the years following the Great War, petty disputes over war debts deepened American mistrust. The government lent the Allies millions during the war, and property-conscious Americans naturally expected to be repaid. They were unmoved by the Allies' contention that debt payments ought to be linked to Germany's payment of reparations, and they were stunned when the European press sneeringly referred to Uncle Sam as "Uncle Shylock." Shocked and disillusioned, Americans withdrew into themselves in the 1920s.

The federal government, even under the inept Harding and the lackadaisical Coolidge, was more assertive. It even showed flashes of statesmanship. It never officially conceded the Europeans' point that war debts must be tied to reparations,

but it intervened twice to rescue the broken German economy. Through the Dawes Plan (1924) and the Young Plan (1929), the American government arranged for loans to Germany that enabled it to keep up at least token debt payments, though most of the debts were still outstanding when the next war began in 1939. Under pressure of the Depression, President Hoover in 1931 declared a moratorium on reparations and war debts. The public continued to grumble, echoing Coolidge's terse complaint: "They hired the money, didn't they?" But the government let the issue fade away, recognizing that the demands placed on Germany had already given rise to a political movement, National Socialism, that was a dangerous blend of nationalism and militarism.

DISARMAMENT

Arms limitation was the other thrust of American diplomacy in the 1920s. At the root was self-interest as well as idealism. Japan was making itself into a military power in the Far East. The United States, already maintaining a two-ocean navy, had no desire to engage in a shipbuilding contest with this rival. At the invitation of Secretary of State Charles Evans Hughes, delegates from nine nations with interest in the Far East (except for the Soviet Union), met in Washington, D.C., in the winter of 1921–1922. The chief accomplishment of the conference was a Five Power Naval Treaty by which the United States, Britain, Japan, France, and Italy agreed to a ten-year freeze on the construction of capital ships (large warships) and the scrapping of some existing vessels. The agreement set the maximum capital tonnage of the United States and Great Britain at 500,000 tons, that of Japan at 300,000 tons, and those of France and Italy at a maximum

---

(*Chapter opening photo*) Pearl Harbor, December 7, 1941.

of 175,000 tons each. The first disarmament agreement of modern history,* the Washington Treaty prevented for the moment a naval armaments race. It also froze the balance of power in the Far East.

The other product of the Washington conference was a Nine Power Treaty, by which all the major imperial powers agreed to respect the sovereignty and territorial integrity of China and refrain from seeking special trading privileges. The world committed itself for the first time to the American principle of the Open Door in China. That Japan agreed to this was particularly significant, because ever since the Russo-Japanese War of 1904–1905, the Japanese had been encroaching on the Chinese province of Manchuria. Japan fought on the side of the Allies in World War I, and as a goodwill gesture Wilson's secretary of state, Robert Lansing, signed an agreement recognizing that Japan's nearness to China gave it special interests. By signing the Nine Power Treaty, Japan in effect agreed not to exploit this privilege. China, for the moment, was secure.

But only for the moment. The concessions made by Japanese officials at Washington angered Japanese nationalists. They felt humiliated by the terms of the naval limitation treaty, which guaranteed their inferiority to the United States and Great Britain. Under pressure from such people, the Japanese government scrapped no ships of importance and within a few years began building anew. When their fleet approached the tonnage limitation agreed upon at Washington, the Japanese demanded revision of the treaty. In 1934, they renounced the treaty altogether. The American government, serene and frugal in the 1920s, preoccupied with domestic deficits in the 1930s, did not even build its navy to the authorized treaty strength until 1938, a year before World War II broke out in Europe. The failure of this experiment at arms limitation caused many a recrimination during and after World War II.

Another source of sardonic mirth during and after the war was the Paris Peace Pact of 1928. Invited by France to join in a bilateral renunciation of war, Coolidge's secretary of state, Frank B. Kellogg, instead suggested a general statement outlawing war to be signed by all nations. Although eventually signed by more than sixty governments, the Kellogg-Briand Pact had no mechanism for enforcement. And it proved to be no restraint whatsoever on the military ambitions of Germany, Italy, and Japan in the 1930s.**

ISOLATIONIST DIPLOMACY

Conciliation and disarmament, the twin thrusts of American diplomacy in the 1920s, fit well with the public wish to be isolated from international troubles. Isolationism actually deepened toward the end of the decade as a result of the work of historians. As early as 1920, scholars had begun to question the notion, put forth by Allied war propaganda and given official currency by the Versailles Conference, that Germany had started the war. Revisionist works published in the late 1920s and early 1930s argued that Germany may have been the country least responsible for the war. Russia and Austria, said the revisionists, were most to blame, and Allied propaganda, coupled with American naïveté, brought the United States into the conflict.

Never slow to capitalize on a popular cause, the U.S. Senate in 1934 set up a committee to investigate American entry

---

* Unless one chooses to count the series of nineteenth-century agreements among the United States, Britain, and Canada that first limited and then prohibited warships on the Great Lakes.

** Taking this as a lesson from the past, American negotiators in the numerous arms limitation talks that have taken place since World War II have consistently demanded the right of inspection and other devices for enforcing the agreements.

into World War I. Headed by North Dakota Senator Gerald P. Nye, who combined a midwesterner's isolationism with a progressive's mistrust of businessmen, the committee concluded that a coalition of bankers and munitions makers ("merchants of death," in the committee's ringing phrase) had pushed the United States into war. The committee's research was flimsy and its allegations unsupported, but it did not matter. It fit the public mood. A year later, in 1935, Congress passed the Pittman Resolution, the first brick in wall of neutrality legislation designed to isolate the United States from war. In the event of an outbreak of war somewhere in the world, the resolution prohibited the export of munitions from the United States, made it illegal for American ships to carry arms to a belligerent, and empowered the president to warn Americans not to travel on the vessels of warring nations. Had the resolution been passed twenty years earlier, it might have kept the United States out of World War I.

Given the mood of Congress and the public in the mid-1930s, the Roosevelt administration could not have engaged in energetic diplomacy even if it had wanted to. In fact, it did not; the president was preoccupied with the Depression. During his first year, for example, he refused even to cooperate with Europe's efforts to stabilize currency values. In 1934, however, he shifted slightly under the gentle prodding of Secretary of State Cordell Hull and endorsed a measure to improve the nation's foreign trade. The Trade Agreements Act empowered the president to negotiate agreements that would go into effect without the approval of Congress, and it authorized him to lower American duties by as much as 50 percent in order to obtain concessions from other countries. The State Department swiftly negotiated mutual tariff reductions with seven European and six Latin American nations, and American exports inched upward.

The opened doors were of considerable importance to Latin America, whose economy had been blasted by the Depression and the decline in world trade. To shore up economies south of the border, the administration in 1934 established an export-import bank with a federal endowment. The bank made loans to help stabilize Latin American currencies and exchange rates. In his inaugural address Roosevelt had pledged the United States to the role of being a good neighbor in foreign relations, and the term soon became associated specifically with his Latin American policy. The Good Neighbor Policy meant more than economic cooperation—it meant "hands off" politically. President Hoover had quietly abandoned Teddy Roosevelt's corollary and dollar diplomacy without publicly renouncing the right of intervention to protect American investments. FDR completed the switch.

At a Pan-American conference in Montevideo, Uruguay, in December 1933, Secretary Hull promised that the United States would not again interfere in the internal affairs of Latin American countries. In 1934, Roosevelt terminated the Platt Amendment, which had given the United States the right to intervene in Cuba, and he officially recognized a revolutionary regime in El Salvador. In the mid-1930s, when Mexico appropriated American-owned oil lands, Secretary Hull demanded only that Americans be adequately paid. A satisfactory arrangement was soon worked out. The Good Neighbor Policy, which has since become a fixture of American diplomacy, at least in principle, was one of Roosevelt's more shining successes.

⊔ The Breakdown in World Order, 1935–1939

The Good Neighbor Policy was not an abandonment of isolationism, however. In fact, it was a form of isolationism. It was quite acceptable to the pacifists, who by 1935 were conducting marches to protest the presence of ROTC units on university campuses. They scoffed at Woodrow Wilson's internationalism as an attempt "to make the world safe for the Morgan loans." Such introversion had elements of danger by 1935, however, for the international order was breaking down. Diplomacy was yielding to force of arms.

MILITANT NATIONALISM

The breakdown was traceable to a militant form of nationalism that had risen in Italy and Germany in the 1920s and infected much of Europe in the Depression years. The common word for it was *fascism*, a term coined by Italy's dictator, Benito Mussolini.* It was an ideology of authority, in which government assumed total control of a society and its economy. In Mussolini's Italy, in fact, business interests were directly represented in the government. In Germany, an even more virulent form of fascism appeared with the rise of the National Socialist party. For the Nazis, patriotism was almost a religion, complete with dogma, form, and ritual. Frenzied and fanatical as religious converts are apt to be, the Nazis made race the core of their doctrine. They contended that whites of north European ancestry were superior to all other peoples. Capitalizing on the wave of anti-Semitism that had swept Eastern Europe in the 1920s (oddly enough, it had affected Poland and Russia more than Germany), the Nazis blamed German Jews for German defeat in World War I. They also blamed the Jews for Germany's economic woes of the '30s. Jews fled Germany by the thousands, but few found refuge in the United States, for Congress refused to expand the tiny immigration quotas set up in the 1920s.

---

* *Fasces* were sticks the ancient Roman rulers used to symbolize authority.

Nazi leader Adolph Hitler came to power in Germany in 1933 and soon thereafter began rearming his country, in defiance of the Versailles Treaty. Emboldened by Hitler's stand, Mussolini, seeking to expand the Italian empire, attacked the poverty-stricken African country of Ethiopia. The League of Nations protested, but the most it could bring itself to do was impose a limited trade embargo on Italy. While world attention focused on Ethiopia, Hitler in 1936 sent German troops into the Rhineland, the part of Germany that bordered on France and which the Versailles Treaty had made into a demilitarized buffer zone. In 1936 Hitler and Mussolini formed what Mussolini called a Rome-Berlin axis around which the rest of Europe would revolve. When civil war broke out in Spain that year, the two dictators sent arms to the fascist forces of General Francisco Franco, who eventually prevailed over a democratically elected government.

The situation in the Far East also deteriorated. Japan, without ever subscribing to the Fascist ideology, had also been arming for aggression. In 1931 the Japanese army seized the Chinese province of Manchuria and converted it into a Japanese puppet state called Manchukuo. In response, the American secretary of state, Henry L. Stimson, announced a Non-Recognition Doctrine, by which he upheld the Open Door Policy and refused to recognize as legitimate any partition of China. The doctrine alerted Japan to the fact that America was a potential foe without helping China at all. In succeeding years, Japan withdrew from the League of Nations, renounced the naval limitation treaty, and claimed the right to approve all foreign loans to China. In 1937, Japan attacked China outright, triggering a Sino-Japanese War that eventually became merged into World War II.

What prompted this Japanese outburst? A variety of things. Japan had an explosive birth rate in the 1920s and '30s, and it felt that it needed more room for its people. It also had few natural resources of its own and relied heavily on foreign trade to survive. Neighboring China had both the space and the resources. Japan also coveted the rich supplies of rubber, tin, and oil available in Indochina, Malaya, and the East Indies. These resources had been appropriated by France, Britain, and the Netherlands. Was not Japan as entitled to them as Europe? After all, reasoned the Japanese, the United States presumed to dominate the Western Hemisphere through the Monroe Doctrine. Why could they not have a Greater East Asia Co-Prosperity Sphere of their own?

American leaders were less concerned with the morality of Japan's position than with its threat to their own interests. A vision of a "great China market" had dazzled Americans ever since the 1890s. Although American trade with China was actually less than its trade with Japan, China's future seemed rosier—especially if the country were unified by the emergent nationalist Chiang Kai Shek. Moreover, if Japan succeeded in gaining control of China, Japan would be less dependent on American products. In 1937, Roosevelt's secretary of commerce told the president that if Japan won control of China's cotton crop, the American South would be ruined. Realizing that the country had neither the strength nor the will to halt Japan's aggression in China, Roosevelt contented himself with some trade restrictions. He did not, however, interrupt the sale of oil and steel, the two American products Japan needed most. The trade restrictions nonetheless caught the attention of the Japanese. They came to view the United States as the main barrier to their ambitions in the Far East and that notion led ultimately to Pearl Harbor.

APPEASEMENT: MUNICH

As the world staggered from crisis to crisis in the mid-1930s, it became apparent that the neutrality laws enacted by Congress were too stringent. The mandatory arms embargo, for instance, prevented the administration from providing aid to the Ethiopians or to the democratic forces in Spain. Under administration pressure, Congress enacted a new Neutrality Act in 1937. This retained the embargo on arms, ammunition, and credit, but it gave the president some discretion in determining whether a war existed. It also permitted belligerent powers to purchase nonmilitary goods from the United States, provided they paid cash and transported the goods in their own vessels. When Japan attacked China shortly after the act was passed, Roosevelt utilized his new latitude by refusing to announce officially that war existed in the Far East. That enabled the administration to supply arms and credit to the Chinese. In October 1937, Roosevelt tried to awaken Americans to the growing international danger. In a speech in Chicago, he proposed an international quarantine on aggressor nations. The president obviously hoped that his slogan "Quarantine the aggressors" would catch on as the phrase "Good Neighbor Policy" had. Instead, public reaction ranged from hostile to indifferent. Another Wall Street panic that year and rising unemployment reminded Americans that they had problems enough of their own.

Far from quarantining aggression, the British in the fall of 1937 embarked on a policy of appeasing Germany's grievances in order to establish a new European accord. Hitler, they argued, was only seeking to unravel the Versailles Treaty, which had been unfairly imposed on Germany. Some even saw Hitler as the main barrier to the spread of Soviet communism. Roosevelt supported Britain's efforts to achieve an international understanding. Unfortunately, the goodwill gestures only seemed to whet Hitler's appetite. In the spring of 1938, he announced the "reunion" of Germany and Austria (his Third Reich was supposedly heir to previous German empires that had dominated Central Europe),

Brown Brothers.
Adolph Hitler on the eve of the war.

and he laid claim to a German-speaking portion of Czechoslovakia. Flying to Munich, Germany, in September 1938 for a personal meeting with Hitler, the British and French prime ministers agreed to the dismemberment of Czechoslovakia in return for Hitler's promise to make no further territorial demands.*

British Prime Minister Neville Chamberlain returned to London promising the world "I give you peace in our time." But Roosevelt was under no such illusion. He began a major ship-building program in the fall of 1938, and his fiscal requests for 1939 included almost $2 billion for defense spending. In March 1939, Hitler occupied the rest of Czechoslovakia, and a month later Italy attacked nearby Albania. Abandoning appeasement, the British and

---

* Munich has remained for half a century the classic example of appeasement serving only to whet an aggressor's appetite, and its lesson that aggression must be forcefully resisted has been a theoretical cornerstone of American Cold War policy. But the "lessons" of history are seldom clear. There were those who argued at the time—and others have since—that Hitler's policies would ultimately have brought him into conflict with the Soviet Union, and that the world would have been better off if the Western democracies had simply let the two battle each other to exhaustion. Those who feel that the war against Hitler was justified because of his Jewish policies are morally right and historically hindsighted. Not one of the Allies—the United States included—went to war on behalf of the Jews.

CLIO'S FOCUS: The War of the Worlds

The Czechoslovakian crisis of September 1938 left Americans badly shaken. It had been a media event, and it had much the same impact that the Kennedy assassination would have on a later generation. During the German occupation of Austria that spring, CBS had achieved live hookups with London, Paris, and other European capitals. The correspondents maintained in each city were coordinated by Edward R. Murrow in London. When the crisis broke on September 12 with Hitler's demand for a German-speaking portion of Czechoslovakia, both CBS and NBC were ready with live coverage. For the next eighteen days, until the Munich Pact was signed on September 30, they carried more than 300 shortwave pickups. Every ultimatum, every rumor of war was carried into American living rooms. And when it was over, only 12 percent of Americans thought the Munich agreement was a good one; 76 percent believed that if war broke out in Europe, the United States would join in. Americans were prepared for the unthinkable. What they were not prepared for was a hoax.

It began as a Halloween prank. The prankster was 25-year-old actor-producer, Orson Welles. Welles had a Sunday evening drama hour, which he broadcast from CBS's Studio One. It had no sponsors because its opposite on NBC, the Chase and Sanborn Hour, featuring ventriloquist Edgar Bergen and his wisecracking puppet Charlie McCarthy, was the most popular show of the week. Radio censuses credited the Chase and Sanborn Hour with about 35 percent of the listening audience and Welles's Mercury Theater with 3.6 percent. The last Sunday in October fell on the day before Halloween, and Welles, inspired by the Munich crisis, decided to do H. G. Wells's science fiction thriller, *War of the Worlds*. Unfortunately, the script, produced between Tuesday and Thursday of the previous week, came out flat. Science fiction didn't lend itself to radio; the Martians failed to come across on the air. Then someone suggested making it a simulated news broadcast, with Welles and other actors imitating announcers and government officials. They even found someone with a voice like Roosevelt's. So the script was rewritten in the two remaining days.

To protect himself and alert the audience, Welles opened and closed the broadcast with explanations that it was only a play. What he failed to take into account—because the rating services had never disclosed the fact—is that audiences switched dials during commercials. So only a tiny audience heard the opening disclaimer. Several minutes into the broadcast, a Charlie McCarthy skit ended on the other network, a coffee commercial succeeded it, and millions of NBC's listeners flipped their dials to CBS. What they heard was a CBS news announcer purporting to broadcast from a farm in New Jersey where a spaceship had landed. He was talking to a Princeton professor, played by Welles himself. The professor ventures the opinion that the spaceship is definitely from some other world. While they are talking, a hatch unscrews and snakelike tentacles emerge from the craft, followed by a hideous face. Amidst excited voices in the background, the CBS announcer, sobbing and retching, describes the creature's gleaming eyes and drooling, pulsating lips.

The announcer loses control. A second announcer calmly shifts the program back to New York and plays Debussy. Thereafter the music is periodically interrupted with news bulletins. New Jersey police have advanced on the thing and have been incinerated in a sheet of flame. Then the second announcer, who by this time has lost his professional cool, returns with the announcement that the spaceship was only the lead craft in an invading army from Mars. He goes on to reveal that Martians have annihilated the New Jersey National Guard. Successive bulletins reach him that the president has declared a national emergency, that the army air corps is wiped out. Then an operator breaks in with news that Newark has fallen and advises refugees to use highways 7, 23, and 24.

In the final scene, the last surviving CBS announcer is standing on a New York rooftop, his voice ravaged by gas, describing a cloud of black smoke that is drifting over the city. Panic-stricken people are racing through the streets and dropping like flies. The smoke envelops him, and he too goes off the air. Then comes the voice of an unknown operator somewhere in the country trying to contact New York. Isn't anyone there? And that voice too falls silent.

Then came the half-hour station break, and a CBS announcer told the audience it was listening to Orson Welles and his Mercury Theater. But by then hardly anyone was paying any attention. Thousands of screaming people had taken to the streets; thousands of others jammed telephone switchboards. Governors were trying to tell people that martial law had not been declared. Train and bus terminals in New Jersey and Pennsylvania were filled with wild-eyed people trying to buy tickets to anywhere. A survey by Princeton University subsequently determined that of the more than 6 million people who heard the broadcast, 1.7 million believed it was a genuine newscast, and 1.2 million were sufficiently alarmed to take some action.

Back in Manhattan, New York police closed in on the CBS building. Welles signed off in Studio One by reminding everyone that it was Halloween, opened the door, and was swarmed upon by blue-clad police. Intense questioning ensued, and when the police decided that no law had been broken, they turned Welles and his assistants over to the press. Next morning's headline read:

RADIO WAR TERRORIZES U.S.
PANIC GRIPS NATION
AS RADIO ANNOUNCES
"MARS ATTACKS WORLD"

The story even drove Hitler off the front pages for two whole days, and Welles rocketed to national fame. Invited to a White House function, he was taken aside by the president, who said: "You know, Orson, you and I are the two best actors in America." Not sure whether the president was serious or not, Welles merely bowed.

French signed treaties guaranteeing the independence of Poland, the country next in Hitler's line of march. To the east, Soviet dictator Joseph Stalin concluded that Britain and France were too weak to be of help. He decided to make his own peace with Hitler to buy time for a Soviet arms buildup. A truce with the Soviet Union suited Hitler, because it meant he could impose demands on Poland without fear of Soviet interference. The result was a Nazi-Soviet nonaggression treaty signed in Moscow on August 23, 1939. A week later, September 1, German armies rolled across the Polish frontier, and two days later Britain and France declared war. Europe once again had fallen into the abyss.

THE ROAD TO PEARL HARBOR, 1939–1941

Roosevelt promptly declared American neutrality, and he promised Americans that his administration would do all it could to stay out of the war. The president may have been sincere in his promise, but he was never fully neutral. He had warned both Germany and Italy before the fighting started that the United States would send aid to Britain and France in the event of war. Germany's lightning conquest of Europe forced Roosevelt to step up the aid until all pretense of neutrality vanished. He did not always keep the people informed of his steps toward war, and for that he was severely censured by postwar historians. (Roosevelt's defenders argue that the president was simply able to accept, more rapidly than other Americans, the responsibilities of world power. Even if that is true, his actions laid the foundation for the "imperial presidency" of the postwar era.)

Blitzkrieg. The western front was quiet during the winter of 1939–1940, as German armies completed the conquest of Po-

land. Then, in April 1940, the Germans demonstrated what technology had done for the art of war. Airborne paratroops descended on Denmark and Norway, while mechanized panzer divisions swept across the Netherlands, Belgium, and northern France. The Germans called it *blitzkrieg*, lightning war. France surrendered in June 1940, and Britain stood alone. To soften Britain for invasion, the Germans in September 1940 began round-the-clock bombing of British cities. For six months an airborne battle raged between the German Luftwaffe and the Royal Air Force. When it became apparent that Britain could not be crushed, Hitler sent his armies into eastern Europe to conquer the Balkans (Hungary, Rumania, and Bulgaria had already sided with Germany), and he began preparations for an attack on his ancient foe, Communist Russia.

As Hitler's plans for world conquest slowly unfolded, American isolationism began to evaporate, though as late as the spring of 1941 fewer than 10 percent of Americans thought the United States should enter the war. Support for Britain, even at the risk of entering the war, climbed steadily, however, reaching 60 percent in the opinion polls during the Battle of Britain. Quick to lead whenever he had a following, Roosevelt in September 1940 made a deal with the British in which he gave them fifty American destroyers (vital in keeping open the Atlantic sea lanes) in exchange for 99–year leases on base facilities in the Caribbean and Newfoundland.* During the autumn of 1940, he ordered the American Navy to intercept "aggressor" vessels in the mid-Atlantic,

---

* The American presence during the war on such Spanish-speaking British possessions as Trinidad led to some interesting cultural cross-pollination, symbolized by the wartime song hit "Rum and Coca Cola." The famous Caribbean steel band of today was created when the Trinidadians discovered the musical qualities of an empty American oil drum.

One World

In 1942 Wendell Willkie, who had been Roosevelt's opponent in the election of 1940, embarked on a goodwill trip to the Soviet Union. His object was to reassure Soviet leaders as to America's political unity and productive capacity. From Moscow, Willkie continued on around the world, touching five continents in fifty days. In Beirut he talked to the Free French leader Charles de Gaulle, and he interviewed Chiang Kai Shek in Chungking. He came back to America with a profound insight, a realization that the war had ended the old imperial system, that future peace could be preserved only on the basis of equality among peoples. He voiced this prophetic thought in his account of the trip, a best-selling book entitled *One World*.

> When I say that in order to have peace this world must be free, I am only reporting that a great process has started which no man—certainly not Hitler—can stop. Men and women all over the world are on the march, physically, intellectually, and spiritually. After centuries of ignorant and dull compliance, hundreds of millions of people in eastern Europe and Asia have opened their books. Old fears no longer frighten them. They are no longer willing to be Eastern slaves for Western profits. They are beginning to know that men's welfare throughout the world is interdependent. They are resolved, as we must be, that there is no more place for imperialism within their own society than in the society of nations. The big house on the hill surrounded by mud huts has lost its awesome charm.

Wendell Willkie, *One World* (New York: Pocket Books, 1943).

thereby offering greater protection to British convoys. He kept the order secret, however, which had the twin advantages of avoiding isolationist criticism and allowing the Germans to discover America's territorial limits through hard experience.

Roosevelt had to take public opinion into account because 1940 was an election year, and he was making an unprecedented bid for a third term in office. Aware of the public mood, Roosevelt and the Republican candidate, Wendell Willkie, outdid one another in promising peace and neutrality. During the campaign Roosevelt flatly told a Boston audience: "Your boys are not going to be sent into any foreign wars." Because the candidates were in general agreement, the third term, which violated a tradition dating back to George Washington, was the major issue of the campaign. Roosevelt nonetheless won handily, 449 electoral votes to 82.

Lend Lease. By the end of 1940, Britain was out of funds and it was clear that the "cash and carry" principle of the neutrality laws had to be abandoned. With heavy presidential pressure, Congress in March 1941 passed the Lend Lease Act. This act authorized the president, at his discretion, to lend military hardware to countries in need. Explaining the measure in a fireside chat, Roosevelt said it would make the United States "the great arsenal for democracy." It meant in effect that the United States was underwriting the British war effort. When Germany invaded the Soviet Union in June 1941, Roosevelt extended lend lease to that country as well.

The Atlantic Charter. By midsummer 1941 it was clear that American entry into the war was only a matter of time. Anxious to establish war aims before this happened, Roosevelt sought a meeting with Britain's

AP/Wide World Photos.

Winston Churchill gives his victory salute. Churchill, on his way home from the Atlantic Conference, August 1941, greets a British cruiser off Iceland. Churchill frequently wore a naval uniform.
He first had contact with Roosevelt during World War I when Churchill had been First Lord of
Admiralty and Roosevelt was assistant secretary of the Navy. When they began a confidential
correspondence in the 1930s, Churchill always signed himself "Former Naval Person."

wartime prime minister, Winston Churchill. The two met on an American warship
in Argentia Bay, Newfoundland. The statement of principles they agreed upon,
known as the Atlantic Charter, was a joint
expression of "their hopes for a better future for the world." The principles included these:

That no country would benefit territorially
by the war

That all peoples had a right to choose their
own government (a principle that helped dissolve the British Empire after the war)

Economic collaboration in the postwar world

Freedom of the seas

Like Wilson's Fourteen Points, the Atlantic
Charter became the moral beacon of the
war. The difference was that Roosevelt
committed the Allies to a selfless peace *before* the United States entered the war.

The question nevertheless remains:
How clear and present was the danger?
Did German aggression represent a threat
to American security or American interests? Hitler was never a direct threat to
American security, whatever his dreams
for a new world order. He could not even
cross the English Channel, to say nothing
of the Atlantic. And after Germany attacked the Soviet Union, even Britain was
safe. Had the Soviet Union collapsed and

yielded its rich resources, especially oil, to the Germans, Hitler would have posed a bigger threat. But when the German thrust ground to a halt short of Moscow and Leningrad in the fall of 1941, a Soviet collapse became less likely. Indeed, from that point on, it became increasingly unlikely that Hitler could even win the war.

What then was Roosevelt's concern? A commencement address he gave at the University of Virginia in the spring of 1940 affords a clue. There Roosevelt drew a picture of the United States surrounded by a hostile world, like a prisoner in a cage given morsels of food at the whim of his captors. That Roosevelt's central concern was economic—America's prosperity rather than its security—is evident also from the internal memorandums of the administration. Roosevelt and his cabinet advisers certainly abhorred Hitler's racial theories and his persecution of the Jews (mass executions had not yet begun), but there is no evidence that moral considerations influenced their decisions. They worried less about Jews than about German penetration of the Latin American market.

The Tripartite Pact. On the other hand, concern for a world dominated by Axis aggressors was not entirely unreasonable. In September 1940, Germany, Italy, and Japan signed a formal alliance in which it was agreed that Germany and Italy would lead in the establishment of a new order in Europe and Japan would lead in the establishment of a new order in Greater East Asia. They further agreed to assist one another if one of the three was attacked by a party not yet in the war. Though it did not explicitly say so, the Axis pact was aimed directly at the United States. The Axis hope was that the United States would give way rather than fight both Germany

World War II: Alliances.

Allied nations

Axis nations

Neutral nations

and Japan. It was wrong, for the pact only hardened American attitudes. It was further evidence to Americans that the true aim of the Axis was world domination. And that, Roosevelt felt, would be detrimental to American interests, even if the United States were not attacked.

⊔ Pearl Harbor: America at War

In July 1941, American attention shifted back to the Far East when the Japanese completed conquest of French Indochina, which they had invaded the previous year. The move seemed part of a broad strategy of conquest, a step toward British Malaya and the oil-rich Dutch East Indies. The American response was swift and violent. Roosevelt froze Japanese assets in the United States, closed the Panama Canal to Japanese shipping, and forbade the export to Japan of vital materials, including oil. Faced with the dilemma of retreat or war with the United States, Japan's moderate premier, Prince Konoye, offered a deal in September 1941. Japan would withdraw from Indochina and undertake no further expansion southward if the United States would recognize the status quo in China and drop the trade embargo.

Roosevelt and Hull responded with a ringing defense of the territorial integrity of China and demanded that Japan withdraw from the country altogether. Japan could not possibly agree, for to do so would have meant a return to a Far East dominated by Western imperial powers. Some historians have faulted Roosevelt for being unnecessarily hard, pointing out that he might have struck a deal that left Japan with some enclaves on the coast of China and freed himself to concentrate on the greater menace, Nazi Germany. In Roosevelt's defense, however, it must be remembered that the United States had stood for

the independence and integrity of China for more than forty years. To strike a bargain that partitioned China would have been a dishonorable desertion of a friend. The memory of the British-French surrender at Munich, moreover, was still bright. Roosevelt and Hull could not afford a Far Eastern Munich.

Events thereafter moved swiftly. In October, Prince Konoye resigned, General Tojo became prime minister of Japan, and orders were given for the attack on Pearl Harbor in Hawaii, headquarters of the American Pacific fleet. The attack fleet sailed on November 25. Five days earlier the Japanese ambassador to the United States presented a final offer: a withdrawal from Indochina in return for American recognition of Japan's domination of China. Secretary Hull responded with a reiteration of the Open Door Policy. The blow fell on Sunday, December 7, and when the "day of infamy" was over, eighteen major warships, including three battle wagons, were sunk or seriously damaged, about 180 U.S. aircraft were destroyed, and 2,043 Americans were dead.

The remaining mystery is why Pearl Harbor was caught so utterly unprepared. The mystery is deepened by the fact that the United States had cracked the Japanese government's secret code (Operation MAGIC) and thus had access to Japan's internal messages throughout 1941. As a result, American officials knew that an attack was coming, though they were not sure where it would fall. Some postwar historians accused Roosevelt of deliberately leaving Pearl Harbor undefended in order to invite an attack that would unite the nation. The attack did enrage and unite Americans, spelling Japan's ultimate doom, but there is no evidence that Roosevelt and military officials conspired to invite it. A better thesis is that information pointing to an attack on Pearl Harbor became lost in "intelligence static," the maze of information developed by Operation

MAGIC.* But inexperienced intelligence analysis is only part of the story. Much of the blame must rest on the army and navy commanders at Pearl Harbor. As one of Roosevelt's biographers, Robert E. Sherwood, phrased it, there is in the end no "adequate explanation of why, with war so obviously ready to break out somewhere in the Pacific, our principal Pacific base was in a condition of peacetime Sunday morning somnolence instead of in Condition Red."

MOBILIZING FOR THE FIGHT

The United States was not totally unprepared for war. Thanks to Roosevelt's shipbuilding program, the Navy was nearly equal in strength to that of the Japanese and could replace its losses more easily. It suffered severely at Pearl Harbor, but it lost none of its aircraft carriers, which fortunately were at sea at the time of the attack. And carriers proved to be the critical weapon in the contest for the Pacific. As a result of the Selective Service Act of 1940, the first peacetime draft in the nation's history, the Army was a formidable force of 1,600,000 in December 1941. The Army Air Corps possessed 9,000 planes, though only 1,100 were fit for service.

Even with these advance preparations, victory depended on the mobilization of American industry. The extent to which that was achieved was phenomenal. By the end of the war, the military services had trained and equipped more than 15 million men and women, the Air Force had 72,000 planes in service, and the Navy operated a fleet of more than 4,500 vessels. Thanks to wealth and organizational talent, the American soldier in World War II was the

healthiest, best-paid, best-fed, and best-equipped fighting man in the world. Some of the German equipment was superior to American, but British and American scientists gave the Allies an edge in new technology, including long-range radar, high-altitude bombsights, proximity fuses for artillery and anti-aircraft shells, and the atomic bomb.

Snafus** aplenty accompanied the mobilization. Unable to accept an all-powerful planning agency such as the War Industries Board of World War I, Roosevelt went through a series of ineffectual ad hoc committees between 1939 and 1941. In January 1942 the president created the War Production Board, headed by Donald Nelson, which gradually assumed control of the entire economy. Searching for executive talent to head the war mobilization boards, the government turned to business executives (Nelson, for instance, was executive vice president of Sears, Roebuck). Government salaries were too low to attract such men, so they came "on loan" from their corporations at a dollar a year and continued to receive their corporate salaries. A first-term senator who chaired a Committee investigating the Defense Program objected to the practice. How, asked Senator Harry Truman, can the government ask young men to risk their lives on the battlefield when it cannot ask industrialists to give up their huge salaries in order to serve the public? Truman's query was a lingering echo of New Deal reform. In the war emergency, the administration was more interested in efficiency than social fairness. "Old Dr. New Deal," Roosevelt told a press conference shortly after Pearl Harbor, had been replaced by "Dr. Win-the-War." The new physician attended the birth of the military-industrial complex.

Federal spending between 1941 and 1945 totaled about $320 billion, which was

---

* In 1947 Congress created the Central Intelligence Agency to coordinate the analysis of strategic intelligence to prevent such problems in the future.

** Coined during the war, "snafu" was an acronym that stood for "situation normal all fouled up."

roughly twice the amount the federal government had spent in all the years since it was established in 1789. About 41 percent came from tax receipts; the rest was borrowed. The national debt climbed from $49 billion in 1941 to $259 billion in mid-1945. The deficit spending at least demonstrated that Lord Keynes was right: The massive infusion of money primed the economic pump and restored prosperity.

Despite such spending, the government was able to prevent severe inflation. Inflation was a constant threat because personal income rose steadily and consumer goods were in short supply as manufacturers turned to war production. (Automobile manufacturing, for instance, was suspended altogether.) The government combatted inflation by raising taxes and fixing prices. An Office of Price Administration (OPA) imposed ceiling prices on everything from clothing to food, and it rationed such items as gasoline,* sugar, meat, and shoes. Congress also made collection more efficient by introducing the withholding tax on personal incomes, and it discouraged profiteering by imposing a 90 percent excess profits tax on corporations. As a result of these efforts, the rate of inflation was less than 5 percent yearly throughout the war.

Fearful that wage increases might trigger inflation, the government carefully regulated labor-management relations. The president created the War Labor Board, with representatives from labor, management, and the public, to mediate labor disputes. As it turned out, the WLB's principal job was holding the line on wages. Early in the war, leaders of the A F of L and CIO gave a no-strike pledge. Wildcat

strikes occurred periodically, but the days lost due to work stoppages amounted to less than one-tenth of 1 percent of the total working time—a record that not even British labor equaled. Thus, although personal income did rise dramatically during the war, it was due to full employment and overtime rather than wage increases.

The most dramatic violation of the no-strike pledge came in May 1943 when John L. Lewis called a strike in the coal mines. President Roosevelt seized the mines, but the mineworkers struck again when the WLB refused to grant the wages they demanded. When Roosevelt threatened to ask Congress to draft the miners into the military, they returned to work. But upon the threat of a third strike, the WLB gave them everything they wanted. Lewis's antics cost labor dearly in the long run. Public sympathy, so crucial to the success of the sitdown movement of 1937, cooled noticeably. Congress passed an act authorizing the president to seize any struck war plant, and states passed laws regulating labor practices. It all portended a postwar reaction against organized labor.

THE HINGE OF FATE, 1941–1943

Winston Churchill flew to Washington shortly after the United States declared war, and on New Year's Day, 1942, the United States, Britain, and the Soviet Union entered into a "grand alliance." Roosevelt and Churchill also made public an earlier decision to concentrate first on Germany. They considered Germany the greater menace because it was known to be experimenting with secret weapons, such as rockets and atomic energy. In addition, the Soviet Union, battling German armies only a few miles from Moscow, was in desperate need of help, and Britain afforded a convenient base of operations. Saving the lives of Jews, on the other hand,

---

*Gasoline was plentiful, but it was rationed in order to save tires. When the Japanese conquered the Dutch East Indies in 1942, they cut off a major source of America's rubber. Synthetic rubber, developed with massive government funding, was one of the major new industries born of the war.

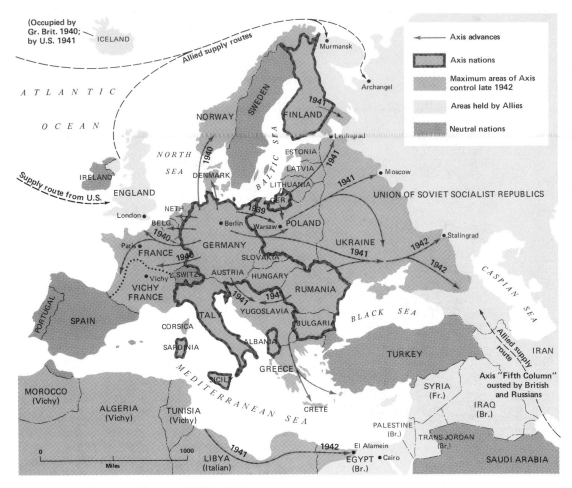

World War II: European Theater, 1939–1942.

was not a high priority with either Roosevelt or Churchill, even though by 1942 Nazi Germany was already placing Jews in concentration camps and beginning the first executions that would lead ultimately to the extermination of more than 6 million Jews and millions of non-Jews.

The situation remained critical through most of 1942. In May, a German army under General Erwin Rommel, which had landed in North Africa the previous year, began a desert offensive that menaced the Suez Canal. During the summer, the Ger-

mans renewed their offensive in Russia, sweeping into the oil-rich Caucasus. In the North Atlantic German submarines, hunting in packs, were sinking three ships a day. Particularly vulnerable was the long sea lane to Russia around the North Cape of Norway. About one-fourth of the vessels that plied the Soviet lifeline were sunk by submarines or by Norwegian-based German bombers.

In the Far East, the situation was equally desperate. Within days after Pearl Harbor, Japanese forces descended on the Philippines, British Malaya, and the Dutch East Indies. In April, the American army defending the Philippines, cornered on the Bataan peninsula, surrendered. Its commander, General Douglas MacArthur, escaped by submarine to Australia. Later that month Japanese forces penetrated Burma and severed the Burma Road, the Ameri-

can supply line to China. Until a new overland route was opened, Americans kept Chiang Kai Shek fighting by flying munitions over "the hump"—the Himalyas, highest mountains in the world.

As the months raced by, however, the Axis thrust slowly lost momentum. In May 1942, an American carrier task force inter-

World War II: Japanese Advances, 1941–1942.

cepted a Japanese squadron in the Coral Sea, just north of Australia, and inflicted heavy losses. The Battle of the Coral Sea was the first in history fought exclusively by carrier-based aircraft, and it set the pattern for the Pacific fighting. In early June, Admiral Chester Nimitz intercepted another Japanese task force heading for Midway Island. In a ferocious air battle, Nimitz sank four Japanese carriers and some lesser ships while losing only one. In August, American Marines landed on Guadalcanal in the Solomon Islands, marking the first American offensive in the Pacific.

During the summer, a British army under General Bernard Montgomery stopped the German advance in North Africa a few miles short of Suez. On October 24, at the Egyptian village of El Alamein, Montgomery began a counteroffensive of his own. On November 8, an American army landed on the western coast of North Africa, hoping to trap Rommel and his German-Italian army in a gigantic vise. That autumn, too, the momentous Battle of Stalingrad opened on the Russian front, and when it ended Germany was weaker by 22 divisions (750,000 men). Slowly, yet inexorably, the hinge of fate (it was Churchill's phrase) had begun to turn.

⊔ Unconditional Surrender, 1943–1945

The decision to land American troops in North Africa represented a compromise of the British and American strategies for winning. Mindful of the deadly trench warfare of World War I, the British were reluctant to make an early cross-Channel thrust. They preferred to work at Hitler's "soft underbelly," the Mediterranean. Though left unsaid, it was also a fact that the Mediterranean was traditionally a British sphere of influence, and Churchill was determined that the British Empire would play a major role in the postwar world. American strategists preferred a direct assault on Germany, but in 1942 they lacked the resources to mount a cross-Channel invasion. They also agreed that some move was necessary to bolster Soviet morale—thus the landing in North Africa.

CASABLANCA

The North African campaign also committed the Allies to a Mediterranean War— that is, the invasion of Sicily and Italy. In Tunis, the American army was a short hop from Sicily, and it seemed more efficient to use it there than to transfer it back to Britain. Roosevelt and Churchill, meeting at Casablanca, Morocco, in January 1943, made the decision to proceed with the invasion of Sicily and Italy and to delay the cross-Channel landing until 1944. Stalin felt betrayed, but by early 1943 there was no longer a danger that the Soviets would collapse. An entire German army had been surrounded, ground to pieces, and forced to surrender at Stalingrad, and the Soviets were preparing a spring offensive.

The other decision made at Casablanca was to demand the unconditional surrender of the Axis. It was an unusual demand, for in the past wars had usually been ended by an armistice and a peace conference. It has been argued that the demand for surrender prolonged the war because it discouraged peace initiatives by German and Japanese moderates. Perhaps it did, but it is difficult to see how the Allies could have settled for anything less than the destruction of the Nazis and all they stood for, no matter how the war was brought to a close. The demand for unconditional surrender reflected the moral quality of the contest.

The invasion of Sicily in July 1943 knocked Italy out of the war. The Italian king, who had never had much stomach for the Rome-Berlin Axis, forced Mussolini

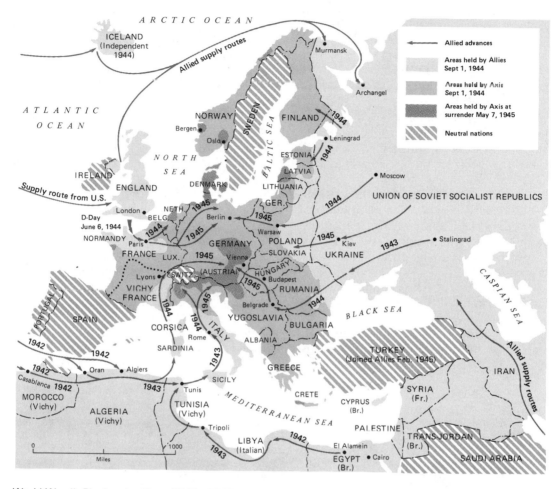

World War II: Closing the Ring, 1942–1945

to resign and agreed to a surrender. The surrender meant little militarily, for German troops seized the country and prepared to defend it. Italy became occupied territory, like the rest of Hitler's Europe. Sicily was taken in three short weeks, due in part to the tactical brilliance of General George Patton, a master of mechanized blitzkrieg.

On September 9, 1943, the American Fifth Army landed at Salerno, Italy, just south of Naples, while the British Eighth Army landed on the toe of the Italian boot.

The Germans dug in, and the mountainous Italian terrain proved ideal for defense. A bloody winter war ensued as the British-American force inched its way toward Rome. In retrospect, it would appear that the main justification for the Italian campaign was to wear down the Germans and make the cross-Channel invasion easier. If so, that objective was accomplished with the capture of Rome on June 4, 1944. The landings in France came two days later. Instead of stopping at Rome, the British-American force continued to push up the Italian peninsula, expending lives for little profit.

VICTORY IN EUROPE

Two years of preparation preceded the cross-Channel invasion of France. While the buildup of men and supplies went on, Allied air forces pounded Germany with round-the-clock air raids. As early as May 1942 they were able to mount the first thousand-plane raid, striking the German rail center of Cologne. The main effect of the raids was to interrupt German transportation and fuel supplies. By 1944, the Luftwaffe was virtually grounded for lack of gasoline.

General Dwight D. Eisenhower, who had masterminded the North African campaign, was in overall command of the invasion. The armada that assaulted the sandy beaches of Normandy, France, on June 6, 1944, was the largest ever assembled—600 warships, 4,000 landing craft, and a prefabricated harbor that handled 326,000 men and 50,000 vehicles within one week. By the end of July, Normandy was secured, and General Patton, commanding the American Third Army, broke through the German lines and sped for Paris. So fast did Patton move that the Germans had no time to organize a defense. A special truck unit had to be formed just to keep Patton supplied with gasoline. Paris fell on August 25, and Patton swept on toward the German border while other British-American armies moved through Belgium and the Netherlands.

In December 1944, Hitler counterattacked, using the last resources he had, including the aged and the young. The Germans penetrated about fifty miles through the forests of eastern Belgium and Luxembourg, surrounding one American division and pushing others back. Newspapers called it the Battle of the Bulge, but by January 1945 the dent in the American

The Holocaust. When the allied armies finally reached central Germany and Poland, they found the victims of the Nazi concentration camps. The slaughter of Jews had gone on to the very end.

AP/Wide World Photos.

lines was repaired and the attack resumed. The Americans crossed the Rhine River on March 7, and by the end of April they were at the Elbe River, only 53 miles from Berlin. By that time the Soviets, who had pushed across eastern Europe in 1944, had Berlin surrounded and were pounding it to rubble with artillery. On April 30 Hitler committed suicide in his bomb-proof bunker, and German troops began laying down their arms. Germany formally surrendered on May 8.

VICTORY IN THE PACIFIC

The Pacific was a different war, requiring different strategies. Even after the Japanese advance was blunted at the Coral Sea and Midway in the spring of 1942, prospects for American victory were uncertain. Japan had had two decades in which to fortify the Marshall, Gilbert, and Caroline islands, which it governed under League of Nations mandate. These archipelagoes in the South Pacific were thousands of miles from the Japanese home land and constituted an outer perimeter of defense. The Marianas, of which Guam was the largest, and the Philippines constituted an inner perimeter. Once that was penetrated there were chains of fortified islands—the Bonins and the Ryukyus—that had to be subdued before American forces could launch an attack on the Japanese homeland. It appeared that the conquest of the Pacific would take time (some estimated ten years) and cost many American lives (some said more than a million).

The Japanese empire was more vulnerable than it looked, however. Not every island in an archipelago had to be captured.

Marines landing on a Pacific island.

U.S. Marine Corp.

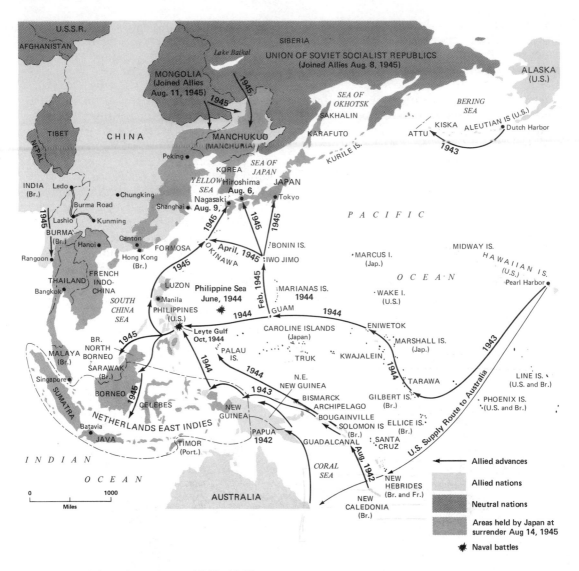

World War II: Assault on Japan, 1942–1945.

Americans found that often one would do. It could be used as a staging base for an assault on the next island group. In bypassing islands, the Americans isolated Japanese troops, neutralizing them as effectively as if they were prisoners of war. At Rabaul on the island of New Britain the Japanese had stationed a force of 100,000 men. The war went right by them, and they never fired a shot. A war some feared might last ten years was finished in three and a half.

Guadalcanal in the Solomon Islands was the first target. The fighting was ferocious because the numbers were about equal and both sides were learning the art of jungle warfare. But it was cleared of enemy by February 1943. Through the rest of that year McArthur and the Army, with help from Australian and New Zealand forces, fought their way up the coast of New Guinea, aiming for a landing in the Philippines, while the Navy and Marines perfected their island hopping, capturing Tarawa in the Gilbert Islands (November 1943), and Kwajalein and Eniwetok in the Marshalls (February 1944).

In June 1944, the Navy moved into the Marianas, Japan's inner perimeter of defense, with a landing on the island of Saipan. Japan committed its main carrier task force to the defense and saw it annihilated in the Battle of the Philippine Sea (June 19). In October, General MacArthur and the Army landed on the Philippine island of Leyte. Japan committed the remainder of its fleet, including battleships, and for three days (October 23–25) the greatest sea fight in history raged in Leyte Gulf. When it ended, Japan's navy was no more.

From airfields in the Marianas American bombers could reach the Japanese homeland. The "softening up" process began in the spring of 1945. The final steppingstone was the island of Okinawa, only a hundred miles from the Japanese coast. The landing on Okinawa, April 1, 1945, brought forth the last of Japan's air force. Suicide pilots, the kamikaze, filled their planes with explosives and tried to crash them into American ships. For ten lurid, terrifying weeks, kamikaze filled the skies over Okinawa: 3,500 suicide pilots purchased with their lives 36 American vessels. But by June 21, Okinawa was secured.

Development of the atomic bomb made

"I Shall Return." Those were General MacArthur's famous words when he left the Philippines in March, 1942. When the American army returned to Leyte in October 1944, MacArthur splashed ashore at the head of his men and announced: "People of the Philippines, I have returned!"

UPI/Bettmann.

Operation Overlord

the invasion of Japan unnecessary. American scientists had been working on an atomic device since 1942, when a group of physicists at the University of Chicago achieved the first self-sustaining nuclear chain reaction. The decision to use the weapon fell on Roosevelt's successor in the White House, Harry S Truman. Roosevelt had made Truman his vice presidential running mate in the election of 1944. The pair defeated the Republican ticket headed by Thomas E. Dewey of New York, but Roosevelt died of a cerebral hemorrhage on April 12, 1945, less than three months into his fourth term.

Truman was attending a conference of Allied leaders at Potsdam, Germany, on July 18, 1945, when the first atomic bomb was tested in the desert near Alamogordo, New Mexico. Truman conveyed the news to Churchill, Clement Atlee (soon to be Churchill's successor), and Stalin. The conference accordingly issued an ultimatum *1947* calling on Japan to surrender or face "the utter devastation of the Japanese homeland."

Japan was already moving in the direction of peace. Tojo fell from power in mid-1944, and in the spring of 1945 the emperor appointed Baron Kontaro Suzuki premier and ordered him to end the war. The Suzuki government was struggling with the Japanese military, which wanted to fight to the end, when it received the Potsdam ultimatum. To gain leverage against his opponents, Suzuki declared that the ultimatum was "unworthy of public notice." Unaware of Japan's internal power struggle, Truman ordered the bomb dropped. On August 6, a bomb flattened 4 square miles of Hiroshima, killing 80,000 Japanese outright and condemning to death another 80,000 with burns and radiation sickness. On August 8, the Soviet Union declared war on Japan and invaded Manchuria. The following day, another atomic bomb leveled the city of Nagasaki. On August 14, after suppressing a cabinet rebellion of militarists who wanted to fight on, the Suzuki government agreed to surrender. On September 2, a great Allied fleet entered Tokyo Bay, and later that day, on the deck of the battleship *Missouri*, the Japanese foreign minister, General MacArthur, and representatives of the Allied governments signed the articles of surrender.

Why the bomb? Some of the physicists who developed the atomic bomb objected to its use. They asked Truman instead to stage a public demonstration of the awesome power of the weapon, so the Japanese at least would know what they faced. Truman never gave the idea serious consideration. "I regarded the bomb as a military weapon," he later explained, "and never had any doubt that it should be used." The president's military advisers estimated that the invasion and conquest of Japan would cost a million American lives; Truman justified use of the bomb on grounds of saving those men. As to the morality of warring on helpless civilians, the conscience of the United States had already been dulled by the massive firebomb raids on Japanese cities. More Japanese civilians, in fact, were killed by firebombs than by atomic bombs. Truman's decision was simply the logical outcome of Allied decisions to win the war as quickly as possible through whatever technology was available. Admiral William D. Leahy, chief of naval operations, thought that "FDR would have used it in a minute to prove that he had not wasted two million dollars."

One intriguing factor remains. Use of the bomb had diplomatic as well as military implications, for with a nuclear monopoly it was at least technically possible for the United States to impose its will on the rest of the world. "God Almighty in His infinite wisdom dropped the atomic bomb in our lap," was the way one senator expressed it. Truman was certainly aware of his power; aides noticed a surge of self-confidence after he received news of the first atomic test while at Potsdam. It is too much to say that he ordered the atomic bomb used on Japan as a demonstration and a warning to the Soviet Union. But he did expect that possession of the bomb would improve his bargaining position in negotiations with the Soviets. That he thought this suggests that even before the hot war against the Axis ended, a cold war of Soviet-American tensions had begun.

SUMMARY

American policy in the 1920s and 1930s has long been described as isolationist, but there was more interaction with foreign countries than is commonly supposed. In the 1920s the United States participated actively in arms limitation negotiations. The Treaty of Washington (1922) limited the number of capital ships maintained by the world's sea powers, and it contained an agreement signed by the major imperial powers to respect the sovereignty and territorial integrity of China. The Kellogg-Briand Pact of 1928 attempted to put an end to war by outlawing it.

None of these arrangements worked very well, and that helped to intensify American isolationism in the 1930s. Japan embarked on a ship-building program and renounced the limitation treaty when it reached its limits. In 1931 Japan violated the territorial integrity of China by occupying Manchuria.

After Hitler came to power in Germany in 1933, the situation in Europe deteriorated as well. Hitler began rearming Germany in defiance of the Versailles Treaty. In 1935, Mussolini, dictator of Italy, attacked Ethiopia, and in 1936, German troops occupied the previously demilitarized Rhineland. In 1936, Germany and Italy formed an alliance Mussolini described as a "Rome-Berlin axis."

Through all of this the United States remained determinedly isolationist, the mood deepened by congressional revelations that bankers and munitions makers had been responsible for American entry into World War I. Between 1935 and 1937, Congress adopted neutrality legislation designed to insulate the United States from foreign war. The law required the president to impose a munitions embargo when war broke out abroad, and belligerents were allowed to purchase nonmilitary goods only on a cash and carry basis.

After Japan attacked China in 1937 and Germany occupied Austria in 1938, President Roosevelt began to try to alert the American public to the impending danger. Roosevelt also embarked on a naval construction program in 1938. After war broke out in Europe in September 1939, Congress began to dismantle the neutrality laws. In September 1940, after German armies had occupied most of the European continent, the United States loaned Britain fifty destroyers to help protect the Atlantic sea lanes, and in March 1941 Congress passed a Lend Lease Act to provide war material to Britain and France. Lend Lease was extended to the Soviet Union after Hitler invaded Russia in June. Discussions with Japan concerning a settlement in the Far East broke down in the fall of 1941 when the United States refused to accept the Japanese occupation of China. Japan's attack on Pearl Harbor, on December 7, 1941, brought the United States into the war.

The United States and Britain agreed that the defeat of Germany would take first priority. The first American assault was made in North Africa in November 1942. After German and Italian armies were cleared from North Africa, American and British armies invaded Sicily and then Italy in July and September 1943.

The Mediterranean campaign delayed the cross-Channel invasion of Europe, to the distress of the Soviet Union, but the landing in France was finally made in June 1944. By that time ·Soviet armies had turned back the German advance and were pushing the Germans into Poland and Rumania. While the British swept through the Netherlands, American armies raced across France, survived a German counterattack (the Battle of the Bulge) in December, and crossed the Rhine in March 1945. Soviet armies reached Berlin in April and pummeled the German capital until Germany surrendered on May 8, 1945.

In the Pacific, the Japanese advance was halted by the naval Battle of Midway in June 1942, and the United States launched its offensive with a landing in the Solomon Islands in August. Thereafter the Army under General Douglas MacArthur worked its way toward Japan by way of New Guinea and the Philippines, while the Navy and Marines island-hopped across the Pacific. The Marines landed in the Marianas, Japan's inner perimeter of defense, in June 1944, and MacArthur landed in the Philippines in October. The Philippine landing brought out the remains of the Japanese Navy, and the United States Navy destroyed it in the Battle of Leyte Gulf.

In the spring of 1945, U.S. Army and Marines penetrated Japan's innermost defenses with landings at Iwo Jima and Okinawa, surviving on the latter a suicide (kamikaze) attack by the remnants of the Japanese Air Force. In July the atomic bomb was successfully tested, and after Japan appeared to ignore a warning to surrender, President Truman ordered a bomb dropped on Hiroshima on August 6. A second bomb leveled Nagasaki on August 9, and Japan agreed to a ceasefire. The formal surrender took place on the battleship *Missouri* in Tokyo Bay on September 2, 1945, six years to the day after World War II had begun.

READING SUGGESTIONS

The best overviews of American diplomacy in the 1920s and 1930s are Jean-Baptiste Duroselle, *From Wilson to Roosevelt* (1963), and Roland N. Stromberg, *Collective Security and American Foreign Policy from the League of Nations to NATO* (1963). Selig Adler, *The Isolationist Impulse* (1957), describes the attitudes of Congress and the public, while the road to war can be traced in Robert H. Ferrell, *American Diplomacy in the Great Depression: Hoover-Stimson Foreign Policy* (1957), and John E. Wiltz, *From Isolation to War, 1931–1941* (1968). Lloyd C. Gardner, *Economic Aspects of New Deal Diplomacy* (1971), presents a revisionist interpretation. Another suggestive, brief, and readable bit of revisionism is Bruce M. Russett, *No Clear and Present Danger: A Skepti-cal View of United States Entry into World War II* (1972).

Wartime mobilization is nicely described by Gerald D. Nash, *The Great Depression and World War II: Organizing America* (1979), and Richard Polenberg, *War and Society: The United States, 1941–1945* (1972), is a good account of the home front. Albert Russell Buchanan, *The United States and World War II* (2 vols, 1964), is an authoritative treatment of the military phases of the war. A well-written account of the naval battles is Samuel E. Morison, *The Two-Ocean War* (1972). Gordon W. Prange, *At Dawn We Slept* (1981), and Cornelius Ryan, *The Longest Day* (1975), are particularly recommended as vivid accounts of the attack on Pearl Harbor and the Normandy D-Day landings. Also recommended is Barbara Tuchman's splendidly written *Stilwell and the American Experience in China* (1970).

The sordid story of the Japanese internment is told by Roger Daniels, *Concentration Camps USA: Japanese Americans and World War II* (1971). The development and use of the atomic bomb is recorded by M. J. Sherwin, *A World Destroyed: The Atomic Bomb and the Grand Alliance* (1975); Gar Alperovitz, *Atomic Diplomacy: Hiroshima and Potsdam* (1965), links Truman's use of the bomb with the onset of the Cold War.

12

THE CHALLENGE OF WORLD POWER: 1919–1945

am biased in favor of God, the Republican Party, and free enterprise," Henry R. Luce once declared. He might have added that he was also for country and Yale, his alma mater. Proprietor of the *Time-Life-Fortune* publishing complex, Luce not only spoke *for* "middle America," he spoke *to* it. On February 17, 1941, Luce published an editorial entitled "The American Century" in *Life* magazine. This was ten months before the Japanese attacked Pearl Harbor, and the majority of Americans were strongly anti-Hitler and eager to aid Britain, but still unwilling to enter the war.

Luce's essay was a call for intervention, but it was more: It was a summons to "a truly *American* internationalism." Luce scorned the "internationalism" of a Napoleon, a Lenin, or a Hitler, who sought to dominate the world by conquest or subversion. America could dominate the twentieth century, he declared, through morality, generosity, and example. It had had a chance to do so in 1919 and denied it; it had another chance in 1941. Already, Luce pointed out, America was the intellectual, scientific, and artistic capital of the world. American jazz, American slang, Hollywood movies, and American patented products were familiar to people "from Zanzibar to Hamburg." "We are already a world power in all the trivial ways," said Luce; it was time to assert our moral leadership.

How? Point one. America must promote freedom of the seas and world trade to encourage the spirit of free enterprise around the world. Point two. America must export its technical and artistic skills, its engineers, doctors, artists, scientists, and educators. Point three. America must undertake "to be the Good Samaritan of the entire world," feeding those whom the "worldwide collapse of civilization" has rendered hungry and destitute. And point four: A "vision of America as a world power includes a passionate devotion to great

American ideals—freedom, equality, self-reliance." The nation must be a "powerhouse of ideals."

The key to Luce's essay is the phrase "American internationalism." At its debut on the world stage, America was not to be one among equals; it was to be in a starring role. A global policy would be pursued on America's terms. Allies would be welcomed when they cooperated, ignored when they did not. This was isolationism in another form—a unilateral policy in a global arena, much like the Monroe Doctrine and the Open Door. It had broad appeal both to the new liberal internationalists born of the war, such as Harry Hopkins, and to conservative, tradition-minded isolationists such as Senator Arthur Vandenberg of Michigan. It was a vehicle draped in red, white, and blue that enabled Americans to undertake world responsibilities when the shooting war against the Axis gave way to the "cold war" of Soviet-American confrontation in 1945–1946.

⊔ The Wartime Conferences

The United States entered World War II with the vision of making it a war to end all wars. This was to be accomplished through global adherence to the Atlantic Charter principles of freedom of the seas and national self-determination and by the formation of an international organization to resolve disputes. Once such an organization was established, Secretary of State Cordell Hull declared with almost mystical optimism, "there will no longer be need for spheres of influence, for alliances, for balance of power, or any other of the special arrangements through which, in the unhappy past, the nations strove to safeguard their security or to promote their interest."

American millennialism quickly ran afoul of Soviet realism. While the world

---

(*Chapter opening photo*) The Korean War: the flow of soldiers and refugees.

was preoccupied with the German attack on Poland in 1939, Stalin had taken advantage of his pact with Hitler to seize territory that had been part of the Russian empire before World War I—eastern Poland; the Baltic states of Latvia, Lithuania, and Estonia; the Rumanian province of Bessarabia; and portions of Finland. When the United States entered the war in 1941, Stalin, with a German army on the outskirts of Moscow, grimly insisted that the Soviet Union would demand the Baltic provinces as well as part of Poland at the end of the war. Stalin's territorial ambitions placed Roosevelt in a dilemma: He had to choose between self-determination for Eastern Europe and cooperation with the Soviet Union. In the end he chose the latter, hoping, with characteristic optimism, that the defeat of Germany would soothe Stalin's fears and end his desire for pro-Soviet buffer states in Eastern Europe.

Roosevelt really had little choice. After the massive Soviet victory at Stalingrad in early 1943, it was evident that Russian armies would roll over Eastern Europe before Britain and the United States could achieve a victory over Germany in the West. By mid-1943, Roosevelt realized he could not keep Stalin from taking what he wanted in Eastern Europe. Roosevelt's mistake, if any, was in failing to communicate this reality to the American people. As a result, it came as a shock to Americans when their war for freedom ended in the slavery of Eastern Europe.

THE TEHERAN CONFERENCE

The three allied leaders—Roosevelt, Churchill, and Stalin—met for the first time at the Iranian capital of Teheran in November 1943. The atmosphere was tense but cordial. Stalin had been bitterly resentful over the failure of Britain and the United States to open a second front in France during 1943, but he was appeased by the explicit promise of a landing in May or June of 1944. Stalin also promised to enter the war against Japan after the European war ended, but he made it clear he expected territorial concessions in return.

Late in the conference Roosevelt invited Stalin to his quarters for a private discussion of the problem of Eastern Europe. Roosevelt told the Soviet leader that, while the United States adhered to the principle of self-determination, it was not prepared to go to war for the preservation of Poland or the Baltic states. He pointed out that there were large numbers of people in the United States of Polish, Latvian, Lithuanian, and Estonian birth and that they had considerable voting strength. For the benefit of American public opinion, said Roosevelt, it was important that some sort of referendum be held in those countries in accordance with the principle of self-determination. Stalin said he understood, and the subject was dropped. How much he understood is open to question. Roosevelt's effort to talk to him as one party boss to another may only have reinforced Stalin's contempt for Americans. On the other hand, as we shall see, he did allow postwar elections in Eastern Europe, and in some countries non-Communist governments were elected in the presence of Soviet armies. He may well have felt that he lived up to his agreements.

At Teheran, Stalin also gave a vague commitment to participate in the United Nations at the end of the war. This the American delegates considered crucial. The conference broke up in an atmosphere of mutual goodwill, but the good feelings did not last. Stalin felt he had vital interests in Eastern Europe, interests that, ironically, were the result of Soviet weakness. For three years the Soviet Union had borne the brunt of the fighting, while Britain and the United States fiddled with what seemed to be peripheral operations in the Mediterranean. And the cost was horrendous. Soviet war deaths, civilian and military, totaled 16 million; 70,000 villages were destroyed; and a quarter of the nation's machinery was wrecked. With some justice, Stalin looked to his enemies in Germany and Eastern Europe for recompense. With less justice, but not without reasons, he was determined to dominate Eastern Europe, by force if necessary, to secure a buffer against future German militarism. The United States might have accepted this had force not been necessary. American leaders recognized the Soviet need for friendly governments on its borders. Americans insisted only that those governments be democratically chosen. And that could not be. History, tradition, culture, economics—all dictated that any freely elected government in Eastern Europe would be anti-Soviet. Therein lay the germ of the Cold War.

THE YALTA CONFERENCE

Poland was the focus of the dispute over Eastern Europe because it was of symbolic as well as strategic importance to both sides. Britain and France had gone to war in 1939 to preserve the independence of Poland. The United States had millions of Polish-American voters. The West generally viewed Poland as a bulwark against Asia. If Poland fell into Soviet hands, there was nothing to prevent the Red Army from sweeping across Europe once the American troops returned home. Stalin viewed Poland just the other way around: It was a bulwark against Germany, which had attacked his country twice within thirty years. By the time the next wartime conference met, at the Crimean resort of Yalta in February 1945, Stalin had set up and given official recognition to a Communist regime at Lublin, Poland.

Despite building suspicions, keeping the alliance together was still the top priority as Roosevelt, Churchill, Stalin, and their aides assembled at Yalta. American military officers wanted the Soviet Union to enter the war against Japan in the hope that this would induce Japan to surrender without an invasion. Saving American lives was a military priority throughout the war, a policy of which Stalin was acutely and angrily aware. Pressed by Roosevelt at Yalta, Stalin agreed to enter the war against Japan three months after Germany surrendered, a time lapse the Russians needed to transfer troops to eastern Siberia.

It was further agreed to divide Germany into four zones of occupation, the fourth being given to the French, who had maintained a shadow government* and a fighting force in Britain under the command of General Charles de Gaulle. Stalin demanded $20 billion in reparations from Germany, but Roosevelt and Churchill, who were anxious to avoid a repetition of the 1920s quarrel over reparations, managed to get that question postponed.

Poland was the thorniest issue at Yalta, but there too Roosevelt came away feeling he had won a minor victory. Stalin demanded much for himself and more on behalf of Poland. He wanted the country moved 100 miles to the west, as far as the Oder and Neisse rivers so the Soviet Union could keep the territory it had seized in eastern Poland. This meant forcing Germany to give Poland Silesia, with its rich coalfields, plus East Prussia and Pomerania as far west as the Baltic port of Stettin. Considering the atrocities the Germans had committed in Poland, the proposal was not entirely unreasonable. Britain and the United States refused to condone the transfer, but there was nothing they could do to prevent it. Roosevelt did manage to extract a promise that free elections would be held in Poland. Since the nature of the Polish government, rather than its bound-

---

* Known as the Free French government, it spoke for the many French people who resisted the German occupation.

U.S. Army Photograph C-543.

The Big Three at Yalta. Roosevelt, obviously in ill health, shows the strains of a war presidency. He died two months later.

aries, was the true issue, he came away from Yalta mildly satisfied.

The satisfaction quickly evaporated in the face of Soviet deception: Stalin broke every promise he made on Poland. He refused to allow non-Communist leaders from Poland's exile government in London to participate. He made no move to hold elections, and he stood by while the Lublin government suppressed freedom of speech and press. Elsewhere in Eastern Europe, his agents began to undermine non-Communist governments that had been elected in Hungary and Czechoslovakia. By the end of the year it was clear he did not intend to allow any but Soviet influence into Eastern Europe. His excuse was that the Western allies had imposed their capitalist system on the countries they had "liberated," such as Italy and Belgium.

In later years the decisions at Yalta would become a major political issue in the United States, as Republicans accused Roosevelt of giveaways that verged on treason: the giveaway of Eastern Europe, the agreement to divide Germany in such a way that Berlin, the capital, lay deep inside the Soviet zone, and the surrender of territory in the Far East as an inducement to the Soviets to enter the war against Japan when the atomic bomb made their assistance unnecessary. Roosevelt's defenders argued that the president was aged and ill, unable physically and mentally to resist Soviet demands. Roosevelt, it is true, was not in top form at Yalta. The war had aged him visibly, and he died of a stroke on April 12, 1945, just two months after the conference ended. That illness weakened his resolution, however, is unlikely.

Yalta is best understood when it is remembered that Roosevelt in fact had little to "give away." Eastern Europe was already in the hands of the Red Army. It was not Roosevelt's to "give away." He could not prevent Communist domination without starting World War III, an alternative that was neither morally defensible nor politically possible. As to the giveaway of Berlin—still today a hot spot in the Cold War—Roosevelt never possessed the power to do that either. At the time of the Yalta Conference American armies had not even crossed the Rhine, the main barrier to the invasion of Germany, while Soviet armies were sweeping across the plains of eastern Germany. Americans crossed the Rhine on March 7, Soviets moved into the suburbs of Berlin on April 21, and the two armies met at the Elbe River, some hundred miles west of Berlin, on April 25. To be sure, General Eisenhower had ordered General George Patton into southern Germany to prevent the Nazis from escaping to the mountain recesses of the Alps, but it is doubtful that Patton would have beaten the Russians to Berlin even if he had been ordered to do so. And, finally, the territorial concessions in the Far East were nothing more than the recovery of islands Japan had taken in 1905. If Soviet entry into the war against Japan was made unnecessary by the atomic bomb, that was not evident—even to American military leaders—until the bomb was successfully tested, five months after Yalta.

In short, Roosevelt, dealing from weakness at Yalta in the areas that most concerned him, extracted from Stalin what assurances he could. If the conference was a failure from the American point of view, it was because Stalin failed to keep his promises. Although Roosevelt came away with his usual sunny optimism, there is good evidence that even he was disillusioned with the Soviet dictator in the weeks before his death. With Roosevelt's death, the problem of Soviet relations settled on the inexperienced shoulders of Harry S Truman. Aware of his shortcomings, Truman put on a bold front. His tough demeanor, in turn, intensified the hostility between East and West.

BIRTH OF THE UNITED NATIONS

One promise Stalin made at Yalta he did keep—that the Soviet Union would participate in a postwar world organization. To Americans at the time, that promise was important. Roosevelt and his advisers were eager to avoid the mistakes of the past, and one of those mistakes they thought was the compartmentalization of the world in the 1930s. Trade barriers and political isolation, they felt, had created a climate of suspicion in which fascism had thrived. Thus a major aim of American diplomacy was a postwar world of open commercial and political intercourse. The first of these goals was accomplished in a conference at Bretton Woods, New Hampshire, which established the International Monetary Fund and the World Bank, each designed to stabilize the world's currencies in relation to the dollar as a step toward freer trade. Secretary of the Treasury Henry Morgenthau persuaded the Soviets to participate in the conference, largely on the promise of obtaining a massive postwar reconstruction loan.

The American government began discussing a postwar world organization just weeks after Pearl Harbor, and by the end of 1942 opinion polls indicated that three-fourths of the country favored it. In April 1945, a conference at San Francisco, attended by delegates from fifty nations, drafted the United Nations charter. The new world body resembled the old League of Nations. It basic form was a general assembly in which each member had one vote, regardless of size or population. The assembly was to be a forum for world opinion. Decision-making authority reposed in the Security Council, made up of five permanent and six rotating (elected) member nations. The permanent members were (and are) the United States, the Soviet Union, Britain, France, and China (Chiang Kai Shek's China was included at Roosevelt's insistence, though no one felt it had the status of a world power).

The Big Five concept reflected both Soviet and American desires. Stalin would not participate in the world organization without preferential treatment. Roosevelt felt that, regardless of American ideals, the Big Five would have to run the world until it recovered from the war. To reinforce the importance of the Big Five, the UN charter prescribed that critical decisions of the Security Council required unanimous consent, which in effect gave each of the members a veto power. This provision was inserted, interestingly, at the insistence of the United States. Still preoccupied with the mistakes of the past, the administration wanted to avoid a battle over the UN in the Senate, such as Wilson had faced over the League of Nations. The veto undermined potential criticism from isolationists by allowing the United States to veto UN measures that threatened its vital interests. That the Soviet Union was the earliest and most persistent user of the veto was an irony that escaped most of Roosevelt's Republican critics.

THE POTSDAM CONFERENCE

While the world organized itself into a loose federation at San Francisco in April 1945, President Truman faced the Soviet

The Big Three at Potsdam. They are Joseph Stalin, President Truman, and British Prime Minister Clement Atlee.

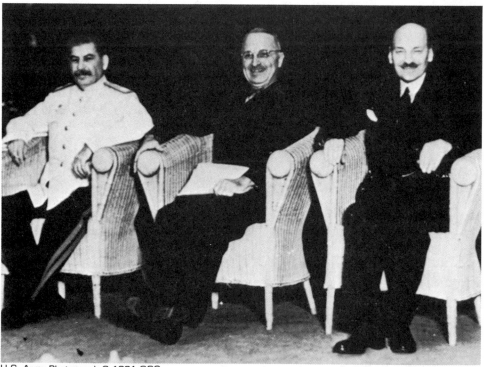

U.S. Army Photograph C-1861-OSC.

problem. Compensating—unconsciously perhaps—for his newness and inexperience, he adopted a tough posture. At his first foreign policy conference with his military advisers on April 23, he declared that agreements with the Soviet Union on Po land had "so far been a one-way street and this could not continue." Later that afternoon he had a meeting with Soviet Foreign Minister Molotov and shouted at the astonished Russian in the language of a Missouri mule skinner. When Molotov complained that he had never been talked to like that in his life, Truman retorted: "Carry out your agreements and you won't get talked to like that." But strong language proved to be Truman's only weapon. In June, the United States bowed to reality and extended diplomatic recognition to the Communist government of Poland.

In an atmosphere of deepening suspicion, the Allied leaders met for the final wartime conference at Potsdam, Germany, in July 1945. The conference confirmed the division of Germany into four zones of occupation—British, French, Soviet, and American[*]—and the division of Berlin into occupation sectors. A compromise on the Soviet demand for reparations allowed Stalin 25 percent of the capital equipment in the western zones and a free hand in his own zone, which he promptly stripped. Stalin also confirmed his pledge to enter the Pacific war by August 8. And that was the extent of agreement at Potsdam. Soviet demands for control of the Turkish straits leading from the Black Sea to the Mediterranean were turned aside, as was a Soviet

---

[*] The British occupied the northwest, including the Ruhr. The French held the Saar Basin in the southwest. The Soviets occupied the eastern portion, and the United States held southern Germany, principally Bavaria. A standing joke of the time was that the British got Germany's industrial heart, the French got the coal mines, the Soviets got some of the finest farmland in Europe, and the United States ended up with some of the prettiest scenery in the world.

demand for a share in the postwar occupation of Japan. Truman, in fact, returned from the conference determined not to participate in any more "joint set-ups" with the Russians because they understood nothing but force. General MacArthur, he decided, would be given complete control of Japan after it surrendered.

⊔ Cold War Begins, 1945–1949

By the end of 1945, it was clear that the Grand Alliance had collapsed. Stalin closed Eastern Europe to Westerners, made menacing gestures toward Turkey, and refused to withdraw Soviet troops from northern Iran until he received oil concessions. In the Far East, Soviet armies, before withdrawing from China, turned over a stockpile of arms to the Chinese Communists, enabling them to reopen their civil war with Chiang Kai Shek.

THE IRON CURTAIN

It was Winston Churchill who issued the formal declaration of hostilities. Invited to speak at Westminster College in Fulton, Missouri, on March 5, 1946, the former prime minister told Americans that "from Stettin on the Baltic to Trieste on the Adriatic, an iron curtain has descended across the Continent" of Europe. To lift that curtain and liberate Eastern Europe, Churchill called for an Anglo-American association, an anti-Communist alliance outside the framework of the United Nations. President Truman, sharing the stage with Churchill and nodding gravely in agreement, added weight to the declaration. Stalin's response was instant and angry. Describing the speech as "a call to war with the Soviet Union," he withdrew from the World Bank and the International Monetary Fund and

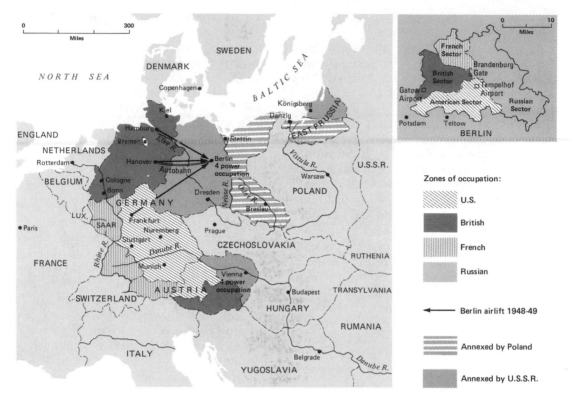

Occupation zones in Germany and Austria, 1945–1954.

announced a five-year plan to make Russia self-sufficient in the event of another war. The term "cold war" was not yet in the American vocabulary (it was coined in 1948), but the war had begun.

The next few months demonstrated that Great Britain was not capable of playing much of a part in the grand association of English-speaking peoples Churchill envisioned. It teetered throughout the year on the edge of bankruptcy, propped up mainly by massive American loans. Britain was particularly embarrassed in the eastern Mediterranean, a sphere of British influence for more than a century. Greece and Turkey relied heavily on British financial aid, and both were in difficulties. The Greek monarchy was battling rebels who received supplies from Communist re-

gimes in Bulgaria and Yugoslavia. Turkey, though tranquil internally, was under heavy Soviet pressure. As early as September 1946 the American government began preparing a program for military aid to Greece. The moment of decision came on February 21, 1947, when the British ambassador informed the State Department that Britain could no longer afford aid to Greece and Turkey.

Truman had few options. In the twelve months following the surrender of Japan, the United States had gone through the most rapid demobilization in the history of the world. It cut its armed forces from 12 million men and women to fewer than 2 million. The Air Force went from over 200 to fewer than 50 combat groups. The government, remembering the chaos of

CLIO'S FOCUS: Vietnam in 1945: The Lost Opportunity

Nothing should have been more evident in 1945 than the fact that the war in the Pacific had doomed the old European empires. The swift collapse of the French in Indochina, the British in Malaya, and the Dutch in the East Indies in the face of the Japanese advance destroyed forever the myth of white supremacy. And the guerrillas who fought the Japanese throughout the war were hardly likely to submit to another form of occupation. The United States, anti-imperial by tradition and the arbiter of the Far East after the defeat of Japan, might well have helped to install independent nationalist governments in Southeast Asia and reaped a rich reward in goodwill. In failing to do so, it missed a rare opportunity. In Indochina the missed opportunity was to have tragic consequences for the United States itself.

The Viet Nam Doc Lap Dong Minh Hoi (Vietnamese Independence League) led the resistance to the Japanese occupation. The Vietminh, as it was popularly called, was formed in 1941 by Ho Chi Minh, who a decade earlier had organized the Vietnamese Communist party. Though led by Communists, the Vietminh purported to be a national front organization embracing patriots of whatever political hue in a common struggle against the French and the Japanese. Chinese Nationalist leader Chiang Kai Shek, after some vacillation, allowed the Vietminh to establish a training base in a province of south China under his control. The American Office of Strategic Services (forerunner of the CIA) supplied the Vietminh with arms. In the winter of 1944–1945 a Vietminh force crossed into Indochina and cleared the Japanese from several of the northern provinces. American OSS agents commanded some of the Vietminh units. Several agents became close friends of Ho Chi Minh's.

The result was an atmosphere of goodwill between the United States and the Vietminh as the war in the Pacific came to an end. Ho Chi Minh was deeply impressed by Washington's setting a date for Philippine independence, and he praised President Roosevelt's anticolonial pronouncements. He doubtless hoped that the United States would help him secure independence from France. Shortly after Japan surrendered, he wrote to an American agent urging him to have the United States take the case of Indochina to the United Nations, whose charter promised independence to all nationalities. "If the United Nations forget their solemn promise & don't grant Indochina full independence, we will keep fighting until we get it." On September 2, 1945, Ho Chi Minh formally proclaimed Vietnam's independence, modeling his declaration on the American Declaration of Independence.

The Potsdam conference of July 1945 had decreed that, following the defeat of Japan, British troops were to occupy the southern half of Vietnam and Chiang Kai Shek's forces would take over the northern half. Their mission was to disarm the Japanese and recover allied prisoners of war. Neither army followed its mandate. The British restored the French to power in Saigon, while the Chinese looted the northern part of the country. Ho Chi Minh remained in power in Hanoi, but his country was so devastated he needed help to survive. During the winter of 1945–

1946 he appealed for help to the American state department and wrote several letters to President Truman. He received no response. The Truman administration was clearly more concerned for the goodwill of France than that of a distant Communist in a far corner of the world.

By early 1946, Vietnam was effectively divided. The Vietminh controlled the northern half, and the French ruled the southern half. On March 6 the two reached an agreement whereby Ho recognized French sovereignty over Vietnam in return for a French promise to withdraw their army over a five-year period. Both sides violated the agreement, and by the end of the year the first Indochina war had begun.

The agreement of March 6 ended Ho Chi Minh's efforts to secure the assistance of the United States, although contacts continued. It is intriguing to speculate on what might have happened if the United States had adhered to its own principle of national self-determination, capitalized on the goodwill in Hanoi, and persuaded the French to reach a settlement looking toward eventual independence. Several Americans familiar with the scene have suggested that Ho Chi Minh would in all probability have become "another Tito," a nationalist first and a Communist second. Although he had lived in both China and the Soviet Union in the 1930s, he had no obligations to either country in 1945. And his admiration for the United States appears genuine. That Ho would have been a long-term friend of the United States appears unlikely, but almost any alternative sequence of events would have been better than the one that fate unveiled over the next thirty years.

the rapid demobilization of 1919, tried to slow the process. But the public insisted on speed; Americans were eager for peace and normality.

THE TRUMAN DOCTRINE AND THE MARSHALL PLAN

On February 27, 1947, Truman consulted with congressional leaders of both parties on the possibility of furnishing financial aid to Greece and Turkey. The key was Michigan Senator Arthur Vandenberg, chairman of the Senate Foreign Relations Committee, a former isolationist who had become converted to the "American century" idea. Vandenberg formed a bipartisan congressional coalition in behalf of the

program, but he wondered whether the voters would accept it. Never before had the American government provided massive economic aid to another nation in time of peace. In a later meeting he warned Truman that to gain support for such a policy, he would have to "scare hell out of the American people."

Truman did precisely that. On March 12, 1947, he stepped before network microphones at the House of Representatives to address a joint session of Congress. He outlined the European situation in stark terms. Communism was spreading its tentacles across the continent. Greece and Turkey, he declared, were in the most immediate danger, and he asked Congress for an appropriation of $400 million to help those nations defend themselves. His reasoning: "I believe that it must be the

The Truman Doctrine

On March 12, 1947, President Truman appeared before Congress to ask that it vote to aid Greece and Turkey. Placing the request in the larger context of the Cold War, he predicted that, if Greece and Turkey should fall, "confusion and disorder might well spread throughout the entire Middle East." This prediction was an early version of what President Eisenhower would call "the domino principle."

> At the present moment in world history nearly every nation must choose between alternative ways of life. The choice is too often not a free one. . . .
>
> I believe that it must be the policy of the United States to support peoples who are resisting attempted subjugation by armed minorities or by outside pressures. . . . I believe that our help should be primarily through economic and financial aid, which is essential to economic stability and orderly political processes.
>
> The world is not static and the status quo is not sacred. But we cannot allow changes in the status quo in violation of the charter of the United Nations by such methods as coercion, or by such subterfuges as political infiltration. In helping free and independent nations to maintain their freedom, the United States will be giving effect to the principles of the charter of the United Nations.
>
> It is necessary only to glance at a map to realize that the survival and integrity of the Greek nation are of grave importance in a much wider situation. If Greece should fall under the control of an armed minority, the effect upon its neighbor, Turkey, would be immediate and serious. Confusion and disorder might well spread throughout the entire Middle East.

Harry S Truman, speech to Congress, March 12, 1947.

policy of the United States to support free peoples who are resisting attempted subjugation by armed minorities or by outside pressures."

That statement, soon labeled the Truman Doctrine, laid the foundation for American Cold War policy. Truman might have confined himself to the immediate needs of Greece and Turkey, but he talked instead in universal terms because he felt the need to awaken and invigorate the American people. His all-encompassing declaration would eventually produce Cold War confrontations in lands most Americans would have had difficulty locating on a map in 1947—Korea, Quemoy, Lebanon, Laos, Santo Domingo, Vietnam, El Salvador. Congress and the public responded to Truman's summons. They did so, how-

ever, not in the name of international charity, but in the hope of spreading "the American way."

Extending the foreign aid program to Western Europe was a logical step, and the need for it was already apparent. Secretary of State George Marshall returned from a tour of Europe in the spring of 1947 quite shaken by the signs of disintegration. Germans were still digging out of the rubble; the British lurched from one fiscal crisis to another. In France and Italy, Communist parties were winning votes. In a Harvard commencement oration in June, Marshall announced his plan, and it was an imaginative one indeed. Stopgap measures were not enough, he declared. American assistance should provide a permanent cure. And he asked the European nations themselves to get together and draw up a relief program. The United States would then undertake to provide the money over a period of years. The idea was breathtakingly bold and refreshingly generous. As described by Marshall, it meant a step toward world order. It would be help to peoples in need, without regard to national borders or ideologies.

The plan placed the Soviets in an awful dilemma. They and their satellites in Eastern Europe desperately needed American money, but to accept it under the sponsorship of the consortium envisioned by Marshall risked having the Western powers gain influence in Eastern Europe. Soviet Foreign Minister Molotov attended the planning conference in Paris where European delegates discussed their needs, and he spent most of his time on the telephone to Stalin. When British and French delegates rejected a Soviet suggestion that each nation establish its own recovery program, the Soviets withdrew from the conference. It was just as well, for it is doubtful that Congress would have approved the Marshall Plan if the Soviet Union had been among the beneficiaries. Republican isolationists, led by Senator Robert Taft of Ohio, were already flinging their spears at the plan, calling it an "international WPA." In order to secure congressional approval of the plan, the administration had to present it as a means of preserving Europe from communism. As Truman himself admitted, the Truman Doctrine and the Marshall Plan were "two halves of the same walnut."

Congress ultimately appropriated $17 billion, to be spread among sixteen Western European nations over a five-year period (1948–1952). The effect was dramatic. Western Europe exhibited a unity not seen since the days of the Roman Empire; it recovered and it prospered. The Marshall Plan was unique in concept, unprecedented in its success. But it would not have been undertaken had there been no perception by Americans of a Communist threat.

CONTAINMENT

By the summer of 1947, American Cold War policy was firmly in place; it needed only a conceptual foundation. George F. Kennan, a State Department expert on the Soviet Union, provided that with an article in *Foreign Affairs* magazine entitled "The Sources of Soviet Conduct." Signing himself Mr. X, a device Soviet leaders used to publish official opinion without committing particular officials, Kennan reviewed the history of Soviet expansionism and warned the American people that they must gird themselves for a "long term, patient, but firm and vigilant containment" of communism. Like Truman, Kennan was not certain Americans were capable of such long-term vigilance, so he presented the choice in the language of a patriot-evangelist. The American response to the Soviet challenge, he said, would test the nation's "over-all worth," and the thoughtful citizen ought to "experience a certain gratitude to a Providence which, by providing the American people with this implacable challenge, had made their entire security as a nation dependent on their pulling themselves together and accepting the responsibilities of moral and political leadership that history plainly intended them to bear."

Kennan's own view of containment was more limited. His principal concern was Germany, which he felt was the key to the control of Europe. But his rhetoric was sweeping, and his imagery spoke to the American conscience: It summoned from memory the Puritans' Wilderness Zion, Tom Paine's Asylum for Mankind, the Jacksonians' Manifest Destiny, and Woodrow Wilson's dream of making the world safe for democracy. The American century had to be moral, reverent, and anti-Communist.

A popular theologian, Reinhold Niebuhr, carried this message to the average American through a series of articles in popular magazines. Niebuhr's reasoning ran thus:

The United States had to reject its "sentimental optimism" of the past, pull its head from the sand, and accept its world responsibilities.

Profiting by the mistakes of the past, notably at Munich, the United States must resist aggressors, rather than appease them.

The Soviet Union is the current aggressor, and it is capable of overt aggression or silent subversion.

THE BERLIN AIRLIFT

Soviet moves in Europe bore out what Americans were hearing from the president and the pulpit. In August 1947, Soviet agents rigged the elections in Hungary to ensure a Communist government. In February 1948, a Soviet mission to Czechoslovakia forced the resignation of a non-Communist premier, and two weeks later Soviet agents assassinated the Czech foreign minister. On June 23, 1948, Soviet authorities in East Germany halted all traffic between Berlin and the Western zones. It was a transparent effort to force the United States, Britain, and France out of Berlin; and by resorting to force, the Russians provoked the first crisis of the Cold War.

Stalin imposed the blockade in retaliation for Western moves to establish an independent West German government. Either the Western nations must abandon their plans or evacuate Berlin, leaving the country's historic capital in the hands of the Communist East Germans. What he accomplished instead by the blockade was

The Berlin Airlift. Awed Berliners stare at an American C-74 Globemaster, which had crossed the Atlantic carrying 20 tons of flour for Berlin.

UPI/Bettmann.

American rearmament and a Western military alliance.

General Lucius Clay, American commander in Germany, wanted to shoot his way into Berlin, but Truman instead decided to make use of the still-open air lanes into the city. By supplying West Berlin from the air, he maintained the Western presence in the city and forced Stalin to make the choice between war and peace. The American and British air forces set up round-the-clock missions, flying cargo from airfields in western Germany into Berlin's Templehof Airport. At its peak, the airlift carried into Berlin 13,000 tons of food, clothing, and fuel a day, and it went on for 324 days. It was a triumph of

American technology and a propaganda blow to the Soviet Union, which seemed to be trying to starve innocent women and children.

The blockade hastened the formation of a Western military alliance. In July 1948, President Truman ordered a fleet of B-29s, the super-bomber capable of carrying atomic bombs, to be stationed in Britain. But he refused to give the Air Force custody of the bombs (which were in the possession of the civilian Atomic Energy Commission) because, as he put it, he did not wish "to have some dashing lieutenant colonel decide when would be the proper time to drop one." That same month the United States, Canada, and the nations of Western

Postwar Alliances in Europe and the Middle East.

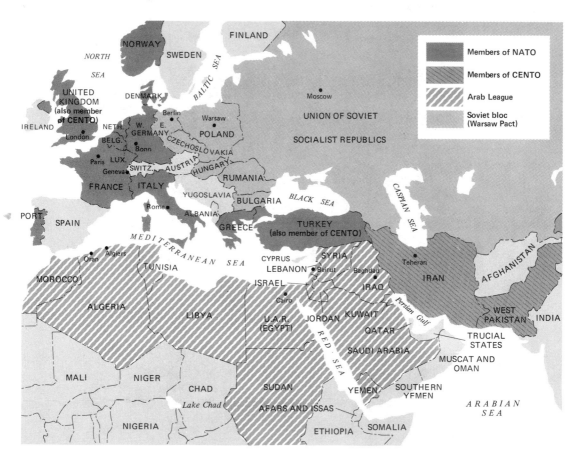

Europe (Britain, France, Italy, The Netherlands, Belgium, Luxembourg, Iceland, Denmark, Norway, and Portugal) began discussing the formation of an Atlantic alliance. A treaty creating the North Atlantic Treaty Organization (NATO) was agreed upon in December and signed in April 1949. A collective security agreement, the treaty declared that an attack on any member of the alliance was an attack on all, and it promised the creation of joint military forces. That summer the Western allies ended their zones of occupation and created the Federal Republic of Germany, with its capital at Bonn. The rearming of West Germany and its admission to NATO were only a matter of time.

In retrospect, both sides bore responsibility for the Cold War. It arose from the interaction of the Soviet Union and the United States, from the thrust and counterthrust of policy decisions. The stakes grew higher with each confrontation, until the two sides stood at the brink of hot war. Fear, rather than ambition, was the dominant factor governing the decisions of each, and that made the rivalry more dangerous because it made reactions more unpredictable. Militant rhetoric added to the tension, as each side overstated its position in order to sway opinion at home and allies abroad. In this Truman had the more difficult job, because his decisions were subject to the approval of American voters. His rhetoric and that of administration officials did more than awaken Americans to their responsibilities; it terrified them. The result was a Red scare that added to international tensions and stifled rational discussion of issues.

⊔ The Red Scare, 1947–1950

Fear of domestic subversion was a natural corollary to the Cold War rationale developed by the advocates of patriot-interna-tionalism. Reinhold Niebuhr had postulated that Soviet moves were prompted by ideology—the Leninist aim of world Communist revolution. It followed that the Soviet threat to world order and hence to American interests was both overt and covert. Internal subversion was as much to be feared as armed aggression, and the Communist coups in Hungary and Czechoslovakia seemed to bear this out.

CHAMBERS AND HISS

The Truman administration reinforced this theory by taking to heart Senator Vandenberg's advice that, in order to secure military and foreign aid appropriations, it had to "scare hell out of the American people." Through the remainder of 1947 and 1948, President Truman ordered a loyalty check of federal officeholders (2,000 resigned rather than submit to investigation, and 212 were dismissed) and sent cabinet members on anti-Communist speaking tours. Attorney General J. Howard McGrath and FBI director J. Edgar Hoover were among the most extreme. "There are today many Communists in America," shrilled McGrath. "They are everywhere— factories, offices, butcher stores, on street corners, in private business. And each carries in himself the death of our society!"

In Congress the House Un-American Activities Committee[*] picked up the scent. Sensing a leftward drift in Hollywood movie plots, the committee summoned actors, writers, and directors for interrogation. Ten who refused to testify were sent to jail for contempt of Congress; three hundred others, whose political opinions were suspect, were blacklisted by Hollywood studio executives. As the committee's

---

[*] The committee was created in 1939 to investigate both Communist and Fascist subversion. When asked on one occasion to define "un-American," committee chairman Martin Dies said it included "anyone who disagrees with the views of this committee."

investigation continued, revelation piled on revelation. In the summer of 1948 Whittaker Chambers, sometime editor of *Time* magazine and a self-confessed former Soviet agent, testified that in the late 1930s he had been given State Department documents by a former department official, Alger Hiss. Hiss, who had resigned in 1947 to become president of a peace foundation, sued Chambers for libel. Chambers thereupon conducted committee members, FBI agents, and assorted newsreel cameramen to his Maryland farm, where he took from a hollowed-out pumpkin microfilm of State Department documents he claimed Hiss had passed to him. Hiss was subsequently tried, convicted of perjury, and sent to prison.

President Truman, failing to see the extent to which he himself had helped to bring on the Red scare, became alarmed at the witchhunt. In the autumn of 1948, he denounced the HUAC investigation as a "red herring" designed to sidetrack his domestic program. That remark only convinced a thoroughly frightened people that

Nixon and the Red Scare. Congressman Richard Nixon and Robert Stripling, chief investigator for the House UnAmerican Activities Committee, look over the microfilm that Whittaker Chambers had hidden in a hollowed-out pumpkin on his Maryland farm.

Truman, like Roosevelt before him, did not fully realize the danger of Communist subversion.

McCARTHY

Public alarm mounted through 1949. The House committee discovered that even the FBI had been penetrated by a Soviet agent. In September of that year, President Truman somberly announced that the Soviet Union had tested an atomic device. American scientists had assured people it would probably take the Soviets ten years to develop an atomic bomb. They did it in four.

Had they stolen that secret too? The answer came in February 1950, when Klaus Fuchs, a British physicist who had worked on the atomic bomb at Los Alamos in 1944–1945, confessed that he had delivered information on the bomb to Soviet agents. Two days after the Fuchs admission hit the headlines, with exquisite timing, Wisconsin Senator Joseph McCarthy told a Republican women's club in Wheeling, West Virginia, that he had a list of 205 Communists in the State Department. The accusation was incredible (McCarthy's list, if one ever existed, may in fact have originated with the administration's own investigation). Nevertheless, it attracted atten-

"Tail-gunner Joe." Joseph McCarthy was a low-level intelligence officer in the South Pacific during the war. Although he had never flown a plane in combat, he persuaded a journalist to take the picture shown above. The photograph, widely printed in Wisconsin newspapers, enabled him to run for a seat in the U.S. Senate in 1946 on the slogan "Congress needs a tail-gunner!" Ironically, the picture shows him in the rear-gun position of a two-man dive bomber, not in the tail-gun position of any kind of plane.

State Historical Society of Wisconsin.

tion among a press and public long since hardened to shocking revelations.

McCarthy made the same accusation the following night in Salt Lake City, only this time the number of Communists was 57. A week later it was 81. But the public was too frightened to disbelieve. Later that spring he testified before a Senate committee headed by the widely respected Millard Tydings of Maryland. Pressed to point out a single Communist in the State Department, McCarthy named Owen Lattimore, Johns Hopkins University professor and expert on the Far East. Tydings investigated and cleared Lattimore after FBI director J. Edgar Hoover affirmed there was no evidence to substantiate McCarthy's charge. McCarthy then went after Tydings. In the fall election of 1950 he helped secure Tydings' defeat by branding the Democrat as a Communist sympathizer. Thereafter no one in Congress and few in the press dared oppose McCarthy.

How great was the Communist danger? Communist espionage was real enough. Major rings were uncovered in Canada and in Britain in the late 1940s, though only isolated agents were found in the United States.[*] Communist subversion, which McCarthy and others confused with espionage, was less real. McCarthy and other Republicans eventually adopted the line that the domestic centralization stemming from the New Deal and the war amounted to "creeping socialism" which, unless halted, would inevitably lead to communism. This was a partisan assault, not a question of national security, but it does afford a clue to McCarthy's motives. Politics was at the core of McCarthy's Red hunt from the beginning. McCarthy had been

elected to the Senate in 1946 after defeating the distinguished Robert M. LaFollette, Jr., in the Republican primary. He had offered the voters nothing except the slogan "Congress needs a tailgunner" (he had actually been an aircraft mechanic in the Pacific during the war). His Senate career had been undistinguished, and when he faced reelection in 1952, he needed an issue. Communism was made to order. He could pose as a patriot while blasting Democrats for being "soft on communism." Their softness, he would soon be saying, was due to their own liberalism, their tolerance of "creeping socialism." That, in turn, would lead to the accusation that the Democrats were guilty of "twenty years of treason."

Even so, the Red scare might have faded as rapidly as the first such scare in 1919 except for new developments in the Cold War. The "fall" of China into Communist hands and the Korean conflict kept alive the Red scare and ushered in the four incredible years of the McCarthy era.

⊔ China and Korea, 1945–1953

The Cold War policy of containment formulated by the Truman administration between 1946 and 1948 was aimed primarily at Europe. The central concern of Truman's secretaries of state, George Marshall and Dean Acheson (who succeeded Marshall in 1949), was that Germany might collapse and create a vacuum for Communists to fill. And, they reasoned, if Germany fell, the rest of Europe would go with it.[**] The first big test of containment, however, came in the Far East.

---

[*] The closest approach to a network was the case of Julius and Ethel Rosenberg, who were convicted of giving atomic secrets to the Soviets on rather dubious evidence. Amid a liberal uproar that still reverberates, the Rosenbergs were sent to the electric chair in 1953, the only persons ever executed for treason in time of peace.

[**] Although President Eisenhower was the first to liken this chain reaction effect to a falling row of dominos (and he was referring to the Far East), members of the Truman administration frequently talked of the spread of communism in similar terms.

THE FALL OF CHINA

When the Japanese troops left China in 1945, the old Chinese rivals, Nationalist Chiang Kai Shek and Communist Mao Tse-tung, resumed their civil war. American military advisers in China predicted that Chiang's corrupt and inefficient government could not win, and American efforts to mediate the conflict failed. Of the military aid the Truman administration provided Chiang Kai Shek, 80 percent was lost, stolen, or fell into the hands of the Communists. By 1949 the Nationalist forces were in full retreat. Mao proclaimed the People's Republic of China in October of that year, and by December Chiang Kai Shek's army was evacuated to the island of Taiwan.

The "fall" of China had a tremendous psychological impact on Americans, greater by far than the "fall" of Poland or Czechoslovakia. Americans had a mystical, romantic view of China, conditioned by missionaries, novelists, and even comic-strips such as "Terry and the Pirates." They had suffered the trauma of Pearl Harbor as a result of their defense of the principle of the Open Door in China. Chiang Kai Shek had so many friends in Congress that newspapers talked of a "China lobby." When Truman cut off aid to the Nationalists on the ground that most of it was ending up in the hands of the Communists, the China lobby roared in anger. Republican Senator Kenneth Wherry, archetype of the patriot-internationalist, insisted that American aid could remake China and render communism irrelevant. "With God's help," he shouted, "we will lift Shanghai up and up, ever up, until it is just like Kansas City!"

The shock of "losing" China contributed to the psychological climate in which McCarthyism flourished. Assuming that someone was to blame, the public listened eagerly as McCarthy pointed to Owen Lattimore and other State Department advis-

ers. McCarthy and other Republicans also accused the Truman administration of having concentrated on Europe while letting Asia go "down the drain." Their policy of "Asia first" had much appeal among former isolationists. Yielding to such pressures, the administration refused to extend diplomatic recognition to Communist China and prevented the Communist regime from replacing the Nationalists in the UN. For more than twenty years the United States maintained the fiction that the Nationalist government on Taiwan was the government of China. This may have been a mistake, because it threw the Chinese Communists into the arms of the Soviets. Stalin had stayed aloof from the Chinese civil war, in part because he mistrusted a Communist movement that he did not control. There were thus deep differences between Chinese and Russians that a more flexible American policy might have exploited. But in February 1950, the two Communist giants signed a Sino-Soviet friendship treaty in Moscow. That brought the Cold War, with its rhythm of thrust and counterthrust, to the Far East.

KOREAN WAR

The first thrust came in Korea, a land divided at the 38th parallel of latitude between a Communist government in the north and a pro-American government in the south. On the morning of June 25, 1950, North Korean armies rolled across the border in an attack on South Korea. Whether or not Stalin ordered the attack remains a mystery. The North Korean government had been created by the Soviets and looked to them for aid, so it is unlikely that they had proceeded altogether on their own. And Stalin had much to gain and little to lose in such a conflict. A quick North Korean victory—which seemed likely since the South Korean regime of President Syngman Rhee was both corrupt and inept—would produce a new, strong, Soviet-oriented Communist state in the Far East. That outcome would frighten Japan, which was discussing a peace treaty with the United States giving American rights to bases on its soil. And it might give China's Mao, already showing independence from Soviet leadership, some cause for concern. Nor had Stalin any reason to fear American intervention. Secretary of State Acheson had publicly stated that the line of containment in the Far East would be drawn at Japan, Okinawa, and the Philippines.

Stalin did not reckon on American public opinion or the pressures put on Truman

by the Red scare. Politically, Truman could not afford to let another country "fall" to the Communists. He and other Democrats had to prove to McCarthy and "Asia first" Republicans that they could stand up to Communists anywhere in the world. Intervention, in turn, provided an excuse for building up American military strength, a policy to which the administration was already committed.

Alerted by American intelligence sources that the North Korean attack was coming, the president was able to respond quickly. Within hours after the attack began, he ordered General MacArthur in Japan to send military aid to the South Koreans, and he ordered the U.S. Navy to protect Taiwan and the Philippines. The State Department had prepared a resolution for submission to the United Nations before the attack began, and on June 25, the very day the North Koreans moved, the UN Security Council approved a resolution branding the North Koreans as aggressors. The resolution was broad enough to provide in advance a UN sanction for anything the United States might decide to do. The Soviet Union did not participate in the discussion of the resolution because it was boycotting the UN for having refused to seat Communist China. (Had its delegate been present he would certainly have vetoed the resolution, thereby depriving the United States of world approval for its intervention in Korea. The Soviet neglect may have been the biggest blunder of the Cold War.)

The following day, Truman ordered American Air Force units stationed in Japan to go to the aid of the South Koreans. The bombing slowed the North Koreans not at all as they pushed the South Koreans down the peninsula. On June 30 Truman ordered American ground units into the fray, stating that it was American policy simply to restore the original border. In making his decision, Truman consulted neither congressional leaders nor NATO

The Korean War.

allies. One of the by-products of the Cold War were the enormous powers assumed by American presidents. Historian Arthur Schlesinger, Jr., later described the phenomenon as the "imperial presidency."

General MacArthur's forces stopped the North Korean advance near the tip of the peninsula and then drove the troops back, turning the retreat into a rout with a dramatic landing at Inchon near the 38th parallel. The American success encouraged Truman to broaden the conflict into a war for liberation and the UN agreed. The administration ordered MacArthur to destroy the North Korean army, and on October 7, American troops crossed the 38th parallel. The Chinese warned that if the American army advanced to the Yalu River, the border between China and Korea, they would enter the war. The warning was ignored. In Korea MacArthur, full of mis-

sionary zeal and given to bombast, announced an intent to unify Korea on American terms. He also hinted of American air raids on Communist "sanctuaries" in China. Within days, the American army encountered the first Chinese soldier. MacArthur talked of having his men "home by Christmas." In late November, the Chinese came in waves, pushing the Americans out of North Korea in two weeks. The battlefront wavered back and forth for the next few months but finally stabilized along a mountain chain that roughly tracked the 38th parallel. There it remained for the next two and a half years.

In Washington, the president and joint chiefs of staff revised their war aims. They would conduct a limited war with the limited objective of reestablishing an independent South Korea. By applying American

Truman and MacArthur meet on Wake Island, October 1950.

UPI/Bettmann.

technology and firepower, they hoped to inflict enough punishment on the Chinese and North Korean armies to bring them to the peace table. MacArthur lacked the temperament for such a war. He demanded total victory, even if it meant blasting China with nuclear weapons. Senator McCarthy and other Republicans in Congress agreed. When MacArthur sided with them publicly, Truman relieved him of command (April 11, 1951). Republicans, the China lobby, and many journalists were outraged. To millions, MacArthur was the greatest living American, and for a time the president felt the blast of the country's anger. Later that summer, however, General Omar Bradley, chairman of the joint chiefs, put the incident in perspective when he told a Senate investigating committee that the war MacArthur wanted "would be the wrong war at the wrong time in the wrong place and against the wrong enemy."

The irony in the savage verbal conflict between Truman and the "Asia first" faction is that it obscured the extent to which the president had met the Communist challenge. With emergency powers granted by Congress and huge defense budgets justified by the war, Truman increased the army by half, doubled the air force, and obtained air bases in Spain, Morocco, Libya, and Saudi Arabia. Extending the Truman Doctrine to the Far East, he provided financial and military aid to the Philippines and to the French in Vietnam, both of whom were fighting Communist insurrections. In Europe, he added Greece and Turkey to NATO and began the rearming of West Germany. At home, the

Truman vs. MacArthur

After being relieved of his command, General Douglas MacArthur returned to the United States. He was still a national hero, and Truman's dismissal of him was widely denounced in Congress and the press. Invited to address a joint session of Congress, MacArthur gave one of the memorable speeches of the age. But after MacArthur's death, Truman had the last word.

In War . . . there can be no substitute for victory. . . . The world has turned over many times since I took the oath on the plain at West Point. . . . But I still remember the refrain of one of the most popular barrack ballads of that day which proclaimed most proundly that

Old soldiers never die, they
just fade away.

And like the old soldier of that ballad, I now close my military career and just fade away— an old soldier who tried to do his duty.

General Douglas MacArthur, address to Congress, April 19, 1951

I fired MacArthur because he wouldn't respect the authority of the President. I didn't fire him because he was a dumb son of a bitch, although he was. . . .

Harry S Truman to newsmen, 1961

government produced the first hydrogen bomb (March 1951), the B-52 jet bomber, and the first guided missiles. The cost was high—a huge and seemingly permanent military establishment and a marriage between government and the corporate giants. Truman's achievements are breathtaking in restrospect, yet his critics contended only that he did not go far enough. Such was the mood of the McCarthy era.

⊔ The Devil and John Foster Dulles

In Paris, General Eisenhower, commander of the combined NATO forces, listened with growing apprehension to the uproar over MacArthur's recall. A moderate by nature, with no formal ties to either political party, Eisenhower scorned the McCarthyites and worried that the "Asia first" Republicans might reduce America's role in Europe. Eastern Republicans urged Ike to return home and enter the presidential contest of 1952. The Republican party had not held the White House for twenty years, and as a war hero Eisenhower was an attractive candidate. In the end Eisenhower decided that both the country and the GOP needed him. He returned and won the party nomination on the first ballot. To placate the party's right wing he chose an ardent Communist hunter, Richard M. Nixon, as his running mate. The Republican platform denounced containment as "negative, futile, and immoral" because it abandoned "countless human beings to a despotism and Godless terrorism." This implied that if Republicans gained power, they would be able to confront the menace and free "enslaved" peoples. The platform appealed to the missionary zeal and moral certitude of Americans. It offered the promise of remaking the world. It was the vision of an American century, and it swept Eisenhower into the White House.

MASSIVE RETALIATION

In his inaugural address, Eisenhower warned Americans: "Forces of good and evil are massed and armed and opposed as rarely before in history. Freedom is pitted against slavery, lightness against dark." It is unlikely that Eisenhower actually perceived the world in such stark terms, but that was the tone of his administration in its early years. The moral posture was principally due to the influence of Eisenhower's secretary of state, John Foster Dulles, whose father (like Woodrow Wilson's) was a Presbyterian minister. A Wall Street lawyer before he entered the diplomatic services, Dulles fought evil with the world as his courtroom, the Soviet Union as the defendant, and Heaven as the judge.

By 1953 the controversy surrounding Truman's handling of the Korean conflict produced a new form of Cold War reasoning. The flaw in the Kennan-Niebuhr concept, it seemed, was that it concentrated too much on Europe. Korea demonstrated that communism could be a threat anywhere in the world. The post-Korea reasoning ran thus:

The line of containment extends around the world. (The Republican promise to abandon containment and roll back communism was only campaign rhetoric.)

Since Communists are governed principally by ideology (rather than, say, national interest or historic attitudes), they are a menace whether Soviet-inspired or not; therefore a Communist movement anywhere in the world has to be countered by American action.

This did not mean, however, that the United States had to police the entire world, because that would be prohibitively expensive (a cardinal tenet among Republicans was that national bankruptcy due to military spending was as great a danger as Communist aggression).

Eisenhower and Dulles had two solutions to this dilemma: (1) They proposed to organize and train local forces so that peoples living along the line of containment could defend themselves. The South Korean army, which American drill instructors had turned into an effective fighting unit, was a model. The local forces could then be gathered into a world alliance system so that the line of containment would be held by mutually pledged allies. (2) The American contribution to this system was to be air power. Atomic weapons were containment's linebackers—a powerful force maintained at an acceptable price. In the words of Eisenhower's Secretary of Defense, Charles E. Wilson, the atom provided "a bigger bang for a buck."

Dulles called the concept of holding the line of containment through air power "massive retaliation." In a speech in January 1954, he explained that America's great strategic reserve enabled the United States "to retaliate instantly and at places of our choosing" whenever the Soviets or one of their satellites became aggressive. The flaw in this policy was that it was not credible. Did anyone *really* believe the United States would flatten the Soviet Union merely because Communists had poked at the line of containment in some remote corner of the world such as Taiwan or Tibet? More to the point, did the United States believe it could bomb Soviet cities without inviting its own destruction? The Soviets had tested a thermonuclear bomb in 1953, and they had the planes to deliver it. As atomic physicist J. Robert Oppenheimer observed, the United States and the Soviet Union were like "two scorpions in a bottle, each capable of killing the other, but only at the risk of its own life."

A series of Far Eastern crises soon exposed the flaws in massive retaliation. In Vietnam (formerly French Indochina), the French had been battling a Communist-led insurrection since 1946. The United States, which had encouraged the French to grant Indochina its independence at the end of World War II, steered clear of the contest until 1950. Then Truman and Acheson discovered that the French were a "free people" battling communism. In 1952, Congress voted a huge aid program for the French. Eisenhower and Dulles continued the aid, even though the State Department informed them that the French were disliked by large elements of the native population.

THE DOMINO PRINCIPLE: VIETNAM

The war went badly for the French, and by the spring of 1954, the Communist rebels, calling themselves the Viet Minh, controlled half the country. In an effort to bring the guerrillas into an open fight, the French put 10,000 of their best troops in an isolated outpost called Dienbienphu. The guerrillas surrounded the garrison and cut off its supplies. The French cry for help presented the Eisenhower administration with its first crucial foreign-policy decision. The president might have let the French simmer in the colonial stew they themselves had created, but he chose instead to regard it as a struggle between communism and freedom. At a press conference on April 7 he explained to the public that all of Southeast Asia was like a row of dominos. If you knocked over the first one, the last one "would go over very quickly." The domino principle remained a centerpiece of American Cold War thinking ever after.

But how to shore up the first domino? One Air Force general thought that a couple of tactical atomic bombs could "clean those Commies out of there," but army strategists thought ground forces would have to be used. Eisenhower was reluctant to intervene without at least British and Australian support. Both turned him down. Congress dug in its heels when it learned that the joint chiefs were divided and allies nonexistent. On May 7, 1954, while the American government floundered, Dienbienphu fell. French colonial rule in Vietnam was doomed.

A conference on Vietnam had opened in Geneva, Switzerland, in April 1954. Joseph McCarthy, as head of a Senate Internal Security Subcommittee, was at the height of his witchhunt that spring. The administration itself had come under attack. It was not politically possible for it to participate in a treaty that yielded territory to Communists. So Eisenhower and Dulles sent only an observer to Geneva and stood by helplessly while the French negotiated a private settlement with the rebel leader Ho Chi Minh. Two agreements, the Geneva Accords and the Geneva Armistice, signed in July 1954, provided for a partition of Vietnam at the 17th parallel of latitude. The French agreed to withdraw south of that line, leaving the Communist Viet Minh in control of the North. The agreements specified that neither South nor North could join a military alliance or allow foreign military bases on its territory. Finally, the agreements provided for elections, supervised by an international commission, to be held within two years to unify the country. The United States did not sign the agreements, but it did promise to abide by them and to support "free elections supervised by the United Nations."

The Vietnam debacle revealed the many deficiencies in massive retaliation. But the main lesson Dulles drew from it was the need for allies to support American intervention. So he set out to find some. The Southeast Asian Treaty Organization (SEATO), formed in September 1954, included Britain, France, Australia, New Zealand, the Philippines, Thailand, and Pakistan. Though modeled on NATO, SEATO was not a military alliance; it was an agreement only to consult with one another in the event a revolutionary movement appeared in the region. It was also essentially a white Western alliance. Only two of the signatories—Thailand and the Philippines—actually resided in Southeast Asia, and the major powers of the region—Indonesia, Burma, and India—refused to have anything to do with it.

BRINKMANSHIP

Massive retaliation received another test in the winter of 1954–1955, when Communist China poked and prodded at the line

The Two Vietnams.

17th parallel—the temporary division between North and South Vietnam established by the Geneva Conference in 1954

Communist countries

Allied with U.S.

Neutral countries

Members of SEATO

Nations having bilateral treaties with the U.S.

Communist bloc

The Alliance System in the Far East.

of containment. The incident involved two tiny islands a few miles from the Chinese mainland, Quemoy and Matsu, which were still garrisoned by Nationalist troops. Outraged by the Nationalist bombing of Chinese ports from American-built planes (a venture inspired by the Republican promise to "roll back communism"), the Chinese began bombarding the islands with artillery. In January 1955, Eisenhower asked Congress for authority to go to the defense of Formosa and "related positions" (meaning Quemoy and Matsu) if they were subjected to armed attack. His reasoning was that Quemoy and Matsu were integral to the defense of Formosa, and if Formosa fell, the entire Far East "would probably come fully under Communist influence." Congress had already bought the domino principle. Declared Wisconsin's Senator Alexander Wiley: "Either we can defend the United States in the Formosa Straits now, or we can defend it later in San Francisco Bay." The resolution, although it gave the president a blank check to commit the country to war whenever he thought it advisable, swept through Congress with only three opposition votes in each house. It was another building block in the imperial presidency.

A major war scare resulted. In March 1955, Dulles declared that the "aggressive fanaticism" of the Chinese was more dangerous than Hitler had been and vowed to stop them with nuclear weapons. Within the administration, officials discussed the possibility of "preventive war"—the destruction of China's military capacity with tactical nuclear bombs. Dulles thought that if civilian casualties were kept to a minimum, "the revulsion might not be long-lived." Eisenhower, however, was not so sure that a nuclear war could be limited, and he vetoed a preventive air strike. The tall talk, however, apparently impressed the Chinese, who gradually ceased their shelling of the islands.

In discussing the crisis with a *Life* magazine reporter, Dulles boasted:

> The ability to get to the verge without getting into the war is the necessary art. If you cannot master it, you inevitably get into war. If you try to run away from it, if you are scared to go to the brink, you are lost. We walked to the brink and we looked it in the face. We took strong action.

"Brinkmanship" apparently succeeded in the Formosa Straits crisis, but it frightened people out of their wits, in America and around the globe. It also chastened Eisenhower, who thereafter rejected all suggestions that there might be a military solution to the Cold War. He also concluded it was time to come to some sort of agreement with the Russians.

Stalin's own paranoia had been largely responsible for beginning the Cold War, and his death in 1953 presented an opportunity for accommodation. Nikita Khrushchev, who became Communist Party chairman after a short power struggle, wanted to ease tensions in order to concentrate on building the Russian economy. He also realized that a face-to-face meeting with the American president would enhance his own prestige. Fearing precisely that, Eisenhower and Dulles stalled, demanding that the Soviets make some advance concession as a gesture of good will. In May 1955, the Soviets obliged by agreeing to a peace treaty with Austria, thereby resolving one of the problems left from World War II. The treaty ended the Soviet-American occupation of Austria and granted the country self-rule, with the proviso that it be militarily neutral. Dulles was still not happy because he feared a summit conference might be misinterpreted by allies abroad and political critics at home. As Ike later recalled, "Well, suddenly the thing was signed [the Austrian treaty] one day and Foster came in and he grinned rather ruefully and he said,

UPI/Bettmann.

The Geneva Summit Conference, 1955. The photo shows President Eisenhower with Soviet Premier Nikolai Bulganin to his right and French Premier Edgar Faure and British Prime Minister Anthony Eden to his left.

'Well, I think we've had it.' " Dulles could see no way to avoid a conference. He warned Ike, though, not to smile while his picture was being taken in company with Russians.

Nothing of substance was accomplished at Geneva in July 1955. The Soviets proposed a unified, neutral Germany. The United States rejected it because West Germany had become the keystone of the NATO alliance. Eisenhower electrified the conference with a proposal for "open skies," so that each side could monitor the military capabilities of the other. Khrushchev denounced it as overt espionage. Tempers remained calm, however, and journalists detected a desire on both sides to lessen tensions. They labeled it the "spirit of Geneva." Whether the "spirit" would affect policy remained to be seen.

THE MIDDLE EAST AND THE EISENHOWER DOCTRINE

The phrase "third world" was coined at a conference of Asian and African delegates at Bandung, Indonesia, in 1955. Most represented people who had recently won their independence from European imperial powers or were in the process of doing so. By describing themselves as a "third world," they declared their independence from both East and West and asserted neutrality in the Cold War. Since most of these nations were undeveloped and desperately poor, Dulles and others in the government and the press worried that they might be susceptible to the virus of communism. Dulles's concern intensified when Chairman Khrushchev paid a highly publicized

Eisenhower on Nuclear War

Richard L. Simon, president of the publishing firm of Simon & Schuster, wrote to President Eisenhower asking him to comment on the recommendation of a newspaper columnist that the government embark on "a crash program for long-range air power and missiles." Here is a portion of Eisenhower's reply:

Dear Dick:

Thank you for your letter, which brings up subjects too vast to be discussed adequately in a letter. Suffice it to say here that I doubt that any columnist—and here I depend upon hearsay because I have no time to read them—is concerning himself with what is the true security problem of the day. That problem is not mere man against man or nation against nation. It is man against war. . . .

When we get to the point, as we one day will, that both sides know that in any outbreak of general hostilities, regardless of the element of surprise, destruction will be both reciprocal and complete, possibly we will have sense enough to meet at the conference table with the understanding that the era of armaments has ended and the human race must conform its actions to this truth or die.

President Eisenhower to Richard L. Simon, April 4, 1956

visit to India. With beaming countenance and jovial manner most unusual for a Russian, Khrushchev, vodka glass in hand, went from one Indian reception to another. Nothing tangible came of the visit, but Americans were put on notice that they faced competition in a new arena. By the mid-1950s, the Cold War had become a contest for the "minds and hearts" of the world's nonwhite millions.

Attention soon focused on the Middle East, where Egypt's president, Gamal Abdul Nasser, proved to be a master at working both sides of the Cold War street. Nasser was becoming a hero in the region by subduing two of Egypt's oldest enemies— the British and the Nile. He expelled the first in 1952, and by 1956 he was planning to dam the second. In need of capital for his Aswan Dam, Nasser applied to the American-controlled World Bank for a loan while preserving his neutrality by purchasing arms from Communist Czechoslovakia. Nasser then formed an anti-Israeli

alliance with Saudi Arabia, Syria, and Yemen, and he refused to repudiate the Czech arms deal. Dulles vetoed the Aswan Dam loan. Nasser retaliated in July 1956 by seizing the Suez Canal from the British and announcing that he would finance the dam from canal revenues.

Dulles, having caused the crisis, now tried to defuse it. He flew to London to try to persuade the British that they would not be hurt by Egyptian management of the canal. But the British had developed a domino theory of their own. They feared that Nasser, if not stopped, would take over all their assets in the Middle East. The French became worried over Nasser's influence among Arabs in Algeria. And the Israelis, already under attack by Nasser-inspired terrorists, saw the Suez takeover as a step toward open war.

The Suez affair lay ticking like a time bomb while world attention turned to Eastern Europe. Anti-Communist riots broke out in Poland in August 1956. The infection spread to Hungary, where the government yielded and promised greater freedom. With the Soviets distracted by the Hungarian revolution and the United States preoccupied with a presidential election, the Israelis struck on October 29. In a matter of hours they destroyed Nasser's army and took most of the Sinai Peninsula. Two days later, on the pretext of saving the canal, British and French troops landed on the Sinai. The quickness with which they arrived, however, blasted their cover story. The whole affair was a British-French-Israeli plot to finish Nasser.

Eisenhower was furious both because of the crudeness of the tactics and because they had plotted behind his back. The Americans and Soviets jointly backed a UN resolution urging a truce and imposing an embargo on Britain and France. Under world pressure, the attackers agreed to a ceasefire and withdrawal from the Sinai. The Soviets, meanwhile, took advantage of the Middle Eastern crisis to crush the revolution in Hungary.

Ironically, the mess Dulles had created in the Middle East rebounded to Ike's political benefit. Americans rallied around the president in time of crisis. In the election that November he defeated the Democratic candidate, Adlai Stevenson, by an even larger margin than he had in 1952. As Stevenson ruefully observed, "Apparently all you have to do to win elections is make fatal mistakes in foreign policy."

The biggest beneficiary of the fiasco was the Soviet Union. Khrushchev had rattled his missiles during the crisis. The Egyptians credited him with forcing the British and French to pull out, and Nasser thereafter looked to the Soviets for support. Nasser emerged with enhanced prestige in the Arab world, and his brand of Arab nationalism gained supporters everywhere. Britain lost what little influence it had left in the region, and the American government felt obliged to move into the vacuum. In January 1957, at the request of the administration, Congress passed a resolution that was soon called the Eisenhower Doctrine. It authorized the president to intervene militarily in the Middle East whenever a legitimate government stated that it was threatened by "international communism" and asked for help. Precisely what "international communism" meant was left to the president to define. No wider authority had ever been given an American president.

The latitude given the president was the more dangerous because Eisenhower never clearly distinguished between "international communism" and simple anti-American or anti-Western attitudes. He had earlier allowed the CIA to topple an anti-American government in Guatemala and an anti-Western regime in Iran. In 1958 he invoked the Eisenhower Doctrine to send marines into Lebanon, where the only threat to the government came from radical Muslims. All this boded ill for the future, but for the moment Cold War tensions eased. Each side had tacitly recognized the other's sphere of interest. The American inability to aid the Hungarians in 1956 ended the rhetoric about freeing "enslaved peoples." The Soviets recognized the West's vital interests in the oil-rich Middle East. They courted Nasser and even sent him some weapons, but they took no overt action when the United States felt its interests truly threatened, as when Eisenhower sent the marines into Lebanon in 1958. The Soviets continued to probe the line of containment, notably in Germany, and Communist uprisings shattered it in Southeast Asia. Tension continued, but by 1957 both sides had signaled an intent to keep the conflict within limits. The first, and most dangerous, phase of the Cold War had ended.

SUMMARY

The United States and the Soviet Union had kept each other at arm's length for many years prior to World War II. Not until 1933 did the United States extend diplomatic recognition to the Communist government in Russia, and relations remained cool thereafter. The formation of the wartime alliance improved things momentarily, but Soviet criticism of British-American military strategy and American suspicion of Soviet intentions in Eastern Europe chilled relations again midway through the war. At the Teheran Conference in 1943, President Roosevelt attempted to extract an oral agreement from Stalin to hold postwar elections in Eastern Europe, but he succeeded only in creating greater misunderstanding. Because of his fear of Germany, Stalin was determined to have pro-Soviet governments in Eastern Europe, and therein lay the germ of the Cold War. The Yalta and Potsdam conferences in 1945 confirmed the division of Europe; by early 1946, the Cold War had begun.

In the course of 1946, the Truman administration developed a set of postulates that guided its Cold War policy. The first of these was that the Munich mistake must not be repeated, that aggression must be resisted, not appeased. The second was the assumption that the Soviet Union desired to control, by seizure or by subversion, portions of Europe and the Middle East. The American response, suggested George F. Kennan, ought to be a long-term policy of containment.

From these premises flowed a series of policy decisions: the Truman Doctrine (1947), by which Congress provided funds to Greece and Turkey to enable them to resist Communist pressure, and the Marshall Plan (1947–1952), a multibillion-dollar aid program for the reconstruction of Western Europe. When Stalin in 1948 blockaded Berlin in an effort to force the American, British, and French armies out of the city, Truman ordered an airlift of supplies. It lasted for 324 days. The Berlin blockade, in turn, stimulated the formation of the North Atlantic Treaty Organization (1949), a mutual security alliance involving Western Europe, Canada, and the United States.

A civil war, meantime, had been raging in China between the Nationalist forces of Chiang Kai Shek and the Communist forces of Mao Tse Tung. In 1949 Chiang Kai Shek retired to Taiwan, leaving the Communists in control of the mainland. In June 1950, Communist North Korea attacked South Korea, and under United Nations auspices, the United States went to the aid of South Korea. The "fall" of China and the Korean War triggered a rethinking of American Cold War strategy. The debate was conducted in the atmosphere of a Red Scare, brought on by the rhetoric of the Truman administration and the accusations of Senator Joseph McCarthy.

The result was a modification of the Truman postulates. Truman's Republican critics accused him of concentrating too much on Europe and allowing communism to advance in Asia. They wanted the containment line extended around the world. To defend such a line with American troops would have been much too expensive, so President Eisenhower, elected in 1952, and Secretary of State John Foster Dulles developed a policy of containing communism through the use of local forces in alliance with the United States, reserving American air power and the threat of "massive retaliation" as the ultimate response to aggression. While this new philosophy was being evolved, Eisenhower in 1953 reached a settlement that ended the Korean War.

Vietnam, where the French had been battling a coalition of Communists and Nationalists for nearly ten years, provided the first test for the Eisenhower-Dulles strategy. In the spring of 1954 a French army became trapped at the remote outpost of Dienbienphu, and the French asked for American help. Eisenhower was unwilling to commit land forces in Asia, and he rejected the idea of air strikes. The French force surrendered, and in a conference at Geneva that summer Vietnam was divided between Communist North and French-controlled South. President Eisenhower thereafter committed himself to giving financial aid to South Vietnam.

The Vietnam debacle cast considerable doubt on the usefulness of massive retaliation as an instrument of policy, but Eisenhower successfully employed it the following year, 1955, by forcing Communist China to cease the shelling of two Nationalist-held islands in the Formosa Straits. Secretary Dulles, meanwhile, extended his alliance system with the formation of the Southeast Asia Treaty Organization (SEATO) in 1954 and the Baghdad Pact (CENTO) of Middle-Eastern countries in 1955. Separate alliances bound the United States to Japan and South Korea.

The war scare over the Formosa Straits, which added "brinksmanship" to the American language, led Eisenhower to the conclusion that it was time to come to some sort of agreement with the Soviet Union. The result was the first Cold War summit conference at Geneva in July 1955. Nothing of substance came from the meeting, but it did serve to lessen tensions. The Cold War had settled into a stalemate in which the United States and the Soviet Union recognized that each had spheres of vital interest. This tacit accommodation became evident in 1956 when the United States settled a Middle East crisis without Soviet interference, and the Soviets crushed a popular movement in Hungary without American intervention. By 1957, relatively tranquil relations between the two superpowers indicated that the first phase of the Cold War had ended.

READING SUGGESTIONS

The best introductions to wartime diplomacy and the origins of the Cold War are Steve Ambrose, *Rise to Globalism: American Foreign Policy, 1938–1980* (rev. ed., 1987), and John L. Gaddis, *The United States and the Origins of the Cold War* (1972). Walter LaFeber, *America, Russia, and the Cold War* (rev. ed., 1976), and Lloyd Gardner, *Architects of Illusion* (1970), are revisionist studies mildly critical of American policymakers. Robert James Maddox, *The New Left and the Origins of the Cold War* (1973), is a critique of the revisionists. John L. Gaddis, *Strategies of Containment: A Critical Appraisal of Postwar American National Security Policy* (1982), is the most recent survey.

For specific features of Truman's response to the Cold War, see R. M. Freeland, *The Truman Doctrine and the Origins of McCarthyism: Foreign Policy, Domestic Politics and Internal Security, 1946–1948* (1972); John Gimbel, *The Origins of the Marshall Plan* (1976); Gregg Herken, *The Winning Weapon: The Atomic Bomb in the Cold War, 1945–1950* (1982); and Timothy P. Ireland, *Creating the Entangling Alliance: The Origins of the North Atlantic Treaty Organization* (1981). For the main features of the Korean war, consult David Rees, *Korea: The Limited War* (1964), and John W. Spanier, *The Truman-MacArthur Controversy and the Korean War* (1959).

Eric Goldman, *The Crucial Decade—and After*: *America, 1945–1960* (1960), is a fast-paced survey of the Truman and Eisenhower presidencies, and it is particularly good on the McCarthy phenomenon. More detailed studies of the rise and fall of Joe McCarthy and the impact of the anti-Communist crusade on civil liberties include: Robert Griffith, *The Politics of Fear* (1970); Athan Theoharis, *Seeds of Repression: Harry S Truman and The Origins of McCarthyism* (1971); and David Caute, *The Great Fear: The Anti-Communist Purge under Truman and Eisenhower* (1978).

14

AFFLUENCE
AND ANXIETY:
1941–1960

Through the early years of World War II, every complaint about a shortage or a shortcoming had been met with the slightly irritated and totally unanswerable query: "Don't ya know there's a war on?" In fact, Americans followed the progress of the war closely through radio broadcasts and newspapers, studying front-page maps where dramatic arrows symbolized advancing armies. Yet Americans also seemed determined to carry on as if there were no war. Irritants, such as labor shortages and rationing, were buried under a host of fads and crazes.

The Jitterbug, successor to the Lindy Hop of the early '30s, was the dance of the day. In the dark year of 1942, Glenn Miller's "Chattanooga Choo-Choo" became the first phonograph record with sales of more than a million. The following year "Pistol Packin' Mama" made hillbilly music (later given the more graceful name country-western) part of the national culture. Although much of the recording industry was idled that year by a musicians' strike, more than a million bootleg recordings of the song were sold before the musicians returned to work.

The musicians' strike helped end the big band era, and the meteoric rise of Frank Sinatra heralded the new era of the solo singer. Overnight Sinatra became a cult hero, with fan clubs numbering in the thousands, made up mostly of teenage girls (bobby-soxers). In the fall of 1943, while the Fifth Army slogged along the muddy roads of Italy, New York City found it necessary to dispatch twenty police cars and 450 policemen to control a crowd of 30,000 bobby-soxers shrieking over Sinatra at Manhattan's Paramount Theater. The following winter tens of thousands of vacationers ignored gasoline rationing and headed for Florida beaches. When gas shortages left them stranded, the railroads diverted trains to Florida to retrieve them. Pearl Harbor united Americans in support of the war; escapism helped them endure its sorrows.

Even so, the fads and fantasies of the war should not obscure the ingenuity and inventiveness with which the civilian sector of the economy continued to make life healthier, easier, and happier for the majority of Americans. Indeed, the amount of nonmilitary scientific and technical progress during the war years is truly astounding. A sample by year:

1943. The "Big Inch" pipeline, connecting Texas oil fields with the eastern seaboard, was completed, as was the War Department's Pentagon, the world's largest office building. Penicillin, discovered by British scientists before the war, was tested in American laboratories for the first time in the treatment of disease, though it would not be available in commercial quantities until 1945. The Pap test for cervical cancer in women, developed by a Greek-American physician, became accepted by American doctors. New products that year included the electric hearing aid, oral contraceptives, and DDT.

1944. A Harvard engineering professor produced the first digital computer, and a Rutgers University chemist discovered streptomycin, first of the mycin "wonder drugs," though like penicillin, it would not be marketed until 1945. Supermarkets introduced prepackaged produce and meats.

1945. A New Orleans physician discovered the parallelism between lung cancer and cigarettes, and television, developed before the war, made its appearance in American homes. New products that year included the ballpoint pen, frozen orange juice, and aerosol insecticides.

Most important of all, nearly all Americans by 1945 were able to participate in the benefits of this scientific and industrial progress. The government's war expenditures had produced an unparalleled prosperity. The nation's gross national product

---

(*Chapter opening photo*) Giants of the Big Band era: Cootie Williams, Harry James, and Benny Goodman.

(the combined output of all goods and services) in 1945 stood at $211 billion, double the 1929 figure, and nearly all the increase had come during the war years. A combination of full employment, progressive taxation, wartime savings, and rationing had ensured that all segments of society shared in the growth. In 1945, the top 8.5 percent of Americans held only 20.9 percent of the nation's personal wealth, down from 32.4 percent in 1929. Glowed one New Deal economist: "The facts show a better break for the common man than liberals in 1938 could have expected for more than a generation." Racial minorities and women were still generally at the bottom of the economic ladder, but they too benefited immensely from the war experience.

⊔ Changing Times: Minorities

American attitudes toward the Japanese had always been colored by racial bias, and Japan's "sneak attack" on Pearl Harbor gave ancient prejudices a new respectability. Newspaper and magazine accounts of the fighting, as well as the Hollywood version of the war, contained numerous references to Japanese racial characteristics— and Americans in taverns and on street corners habitually used racial slurs. It made the war in the Pacific uglier still.

JAPANESE INTERNMENT

After the Japanese attack on Pearl Harbor, hysteria gripped the Pacific Coast. There were rumors of impending invasion; cities were blacked out at night against possible air raids. Fear deepened when journalists reported—falsely, it turned out—that Japanese living in California had conspired in the attack on Pearl Harbor and were planning to subvert the war effort. Japanese

were an inviting target, for they had never been popular among Californians, who looked with suspicion on their frugal living habits and willingness to work for minuscule wages. Under pressure from California, Theodore Roosevelt had negotiated a "gentleman's agreement" with Japan in 1906 that had limited Japanese immigration, and by act of Congress in 1924 Japanese immigrants were not allowed to become American citizens. But by the 1940s, about two-thirds of the Japanese residing on the Pacific Coast were citizens by birth.

In the atmosphere of early 1942, even that right came to have no meaning. The commanding general of the region, John DeWitt, expressed the common feeling: "A Jap's a Jap . . . It makes no difference if he is an American citizen." Responding to such pressures, President Roosevelt in February 1942 issued an executive order instructing the army to intern and relocate all Japanese. By August the army had moved some 110,000 people to camps at Tule Lake, California, and in Oregon. Allowed to take only what they could carry, the Japanese were forced to sell their land and possessions at short notice. The unscrupulous among white Americans were not slow to take advantage.

Though surrounded by barbed wire, the internment camps resembled Indian reservations more than the infamous concentration camps run by the Nazis. Indeed, some were managed by agents of the Indian Bureau. Within the camps there was everything that might be expected—boredom, complaints about the food, strikes, and endless tension as internees debated whether they ought to resist the humiliating treatment or submit to it as a sign of loyalty. The government's policy originated in fear mixed with prejudice, and not in genuine hatred. When the fear subsided, the policy came under attack. In 1943 the army recruited a regiment of Japanese from the camps for fighting in Italy (where they had an outstanding combat

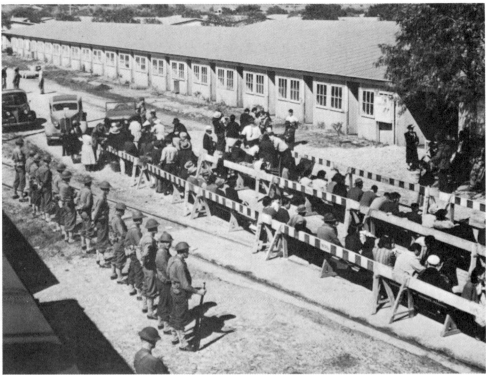

Library of Congress.

Japanese-Americans registering at a detention camp in 1942.

record), and by the end of 1944 the internees were being released. The government closed the camps on January 2, 1945. Although the United States Supreme Court in 1944 upheld the relocation policy on the grounds of military necessity, it stands as a monument to the wartime destruction of civil liberties.

ZOOT SUITS AND PACHUCOS

Mexican-Americans too bore the brunt of wartime tensions and latent prejudice. The war turned California into a boom state. Aircraft and shipbuilding industries sprouted overnight, drawing transients from the farms and villages of the Middle West. The military moved in, absorbing land and port facilities, as the state became a gigantic funnel for troops and supplies moving on to the war in the Pacific. The Mexican community, victim of housing segregation and discrimination in employment, felt the tension without benefiting from the prosperity. Its frustrations were evident in a dramatic rise in juvenile crime as gangs of self-styled toughs, proudly calling themselves *pachucos* (a term that originally meant "marijuana runner"), roamed the sprawling ghetto of East Los Angeles.

To reinforce adolescent group identification, they adopted a distinctive uniform, a lavish costume with exaggerated shoulders and pegged pantlegs known as a zoot suit. The zoot suit spread to urban ghettoes in other parts of the country, but only in

UPI/Bettmann.

The Zoot Suit: Costume of the war years.

BLACKS AND THE BEGINNING OF CIVIL RIGHTS

No other city experienced violence against Mexicans, but there were a number of riots involving black communities. Long the targets of the most vicious forms of American racial prejudice, many blacks viewed the war with detached indifference. One story that circulated widely involved a black sharecropper who, on the day after Pearl Harbor, said to his landlord, "Ah hear dem Japanese gone done dee-clare war on yo' white folks." Blacks who participated in the war effort—and the vast majority certainly did—encountered discrimination in factory employment and in the armed services. The army kept blacks in segregated units under white officers, and the navy assigned them to noncombat duties. The Red Cross routinely segregated its blood plasma into "colored" and "white," a practice galling to blacks who knew that the man who created the Red Cross Blood Bank, Dr. Charles Drew, was a black man.

Blacks who drifted into northern cities seeking work in defense plants created added social tensions. There were racial clashes and beatings in Mobile, Alabama; Springfield, Massachusetts; Beaumont, Texas; and New York City. In most instances blacks were the victims, but in Detroit in June 1943 they fought back. After days of fighting between gangs of white and black youths, blacks responded to a rumor that a black woman and her baby had been killed by a band of whites and swept into downtown Detroit. Whites counterattacked, and the riot spread. Police intervened, using tear gas to break up mobs of whites and guns on blacks. Federal troops finally brought the riot under control. The toll was 35 dead, more than 700 wounded, and 1,300 arrested. These figures would not be matched until the great urban riots of the 1960s.

Despite the home front warfare, World

war-tense Los Angeles did it create panic. Newspapers were filled with crime statistics and portrayed the pachucos as Chicago-style gangsters. The Los Angeles City Council passed an ordinance making it a crime to wear a zoot suit. Sporadic acts of violence climaxed in the first week of July 1943, when a rumor that a gang of pachucos had beaten up a sailor sparked four days of rioting. White servicemen roamed through the Mexican district beating Mexican youths and ripping off their clothing, followed by police who arrested the adolescents for indecency and vagrancy. Politically weak and hence defenseless, the Mexican community was not much better off than the Japanese.

War II was a turning point in the history of American race relations. Nazi racial theories, made hideous by the discovery of the death camps at the war's end, caused Americans to reexamine their own biases. Public anti-Semitism, so common in radio broadcasts of the 1930s, was utterly discredited. In 1942 the great Swedish sociologist Gunnar Myrdal called attention to America's own race problem in *An American Dilemma*, a book for which he won the Nobel Prize. Among Myrdal's more interesting statistics was a poll of black opinion on the war and the discovery that 18 percent sympathized with the Japanese. Southern white businessmen, when asked to choose between racial equality and a German victory, selected the latter by a large margin.

The changing white attitude could be seen first in the military services. Midway through the war the army put a stop to segregation in its PXs, recreational facilities, and troop transports. In the final stages of the campaign against Germany it even experimented with mixed-race platoons, and found the result greatly improved the combat performance of black soldiers. The navy went even further. It not only gave blacks combat assignments (it had consigned them to mess halls at the beginning of the war), it began commissioning black officers.

One by one, the barriers of discrimination crumbled. The Supreme Court declared that blacks had a right to vote in party primaries (the South Carolina Democratic party had sought to make itself a white-only private club), and the American Bar Association opened its ranks to all races. The Daughters of the American Revolution had refused to let Marian Anderson sing in Constitution Hall in 1939 (Eleanor Roosevelt had helped the singer find another location), but she sang there in 1943 to an audience that was one-third black. In 1944, New York's Harlem district

elected to Congress Adam Clayton Powell, a charismatic minister who regarded all of black America as his constituency. By then too, the black press, as well as such militant civil rights organizations as the Congress of Racial Equality (CORE, founded in 1940), were pushing for federal civil rights legislation. Such a law was still thirteen years in the future, a measure of the prejudice that had yet to be overcome.

WOMEN AT WAR

By contrast, no long-range women's movement emerged from the war, even though the war opened many new opportunities for them. Women worked in war plants at every conceivable job. Rosie the Riveter (the title of a 1942 song) became a national symbol—clad in trousers (a costume almost unthinkable before the war), hair enclosed in bandanna, sleeves rolled up for the job ahead. By the end of the war women constituted a third of the industrial work force, and another hundred thousand were in military uniform as WACs (army), or WAVES (navy).* Despite this contribution, male attitudes changed little. One marine officer, when informed that women had been assigned to his post, blurted: "God damn it all. First they send us dogs. Now it's women."

And women made little headway against discrimination during the war. It was government policy that women should be paid the same as men for doing the same work, but the government made no effort to enforce it. Even in federally owned and operated shipyards, the highest pay for women was $6.95 a day; for men, it was $22 a day. And everywhere the chances that a

---

* To the U.S. Marines a marine was a marine, so the corps steadfastly refused to give its female recruits a separate identity, even though civilians suggested such possibilities as mariness, femarine, and marina.

Gordon Parks.

Rosie the Riveter.

Rosie the Riveter: A Diary of a Bomber Plant Worker

There were 16.5 million women in the labor force by 1945, up by more than one-third since 1941. And the war effort enabled them to move into occupations that had been traditionally dominated by males. Women worked on tank assembly lines, fed blast furnaces in steel mills, and welded battleships. "Rosie the Riveter" was one of the legends of the war. One of the "Rosies," Mable Gerken, who was employed in a bomber plant, kept a diary of her experiences. Here are some excerpts.

January 8, 1943

This is the strangest school you can imagine. It is in the center of a huge building about 700 feet long and 300 feet wide. Probably sixty feet high. That's my guess anyhow, right or wrong. A row of bombers being completed take up one half of the building, while small assemblies, blueprint tables, tools and machinery fill the other half.

There are about thirty-eight or forty in the class. New ones coming in each day or so and others leaving to work on production. They are mostly women from twenty to sixty years old, who have no knowledge of mechanics. They tell me the men who apply for work are sent directly to the line. We have two young men teachers, who have worked in the plant for some time. They know their job, but I don't think they consider the fact that we beginners don't know the difference between a rivet gun and a drill. It is very confusing. Also noisy.

January 18, 1943

Well, ten days of school. Filing metal, drilling holes, riveting, bucking, drilling and filing again. This morning at one o'clock, our instructor called eight women aside, including Martha and me.

"You are to go with Mr. George," he said. "You are needed on the line." Did I say once before that I was scared stiff? Well right now I'm petrified. "But," I managed to object, "I don't think I'm good enough to rivet on a bomber."

"You may never see a rivet gun again, I hope," he laughed. He could see I was puzzled so he picked up a rivet gun and showed me how he held it, then handed it to me. "Your hands are too small," he said.

That after ten days! They were not dull days by any means. We had a half hour for lunch and ten minute rest periods. We all sat along the aisle on benches and compared notes and told stories. Some of the women were refined, others not so much so. Some were really tough, and others thought it was smart to act tough. They were housewives, clerks, office girls, waitresses, retired teachers and even a librarian.

They were tall and short, thin and fat. No matter what size, age, color, or background, there is a place for every woman to do her share in winning a war.

January 19, 1943

Well, I had my first big disappointment today. Martha and I were so happy when we went home yesterday. We expected to come back today and finish up where we left off. The line had moved four times since we quit, so our plane was down four positions and looked practically finished. Guess we each expected to build a bomber. We just started over on another plane, and of course, found out that is all we have to look forward to.

The skin [the aluminum exterior of the plane] comes in different sized pieces, each with a number on it. Some are long and narrow, others nearly square. They are put on like shingles on a roof, only they are much larger. The fuselage is built in four sections: the forward section, the center section, the rear half, and the tail section. We are working on the center section. Some sections where the skin laps, the clecos are not strong enough to hold, so we have to put temporary bolts in. Today I pushed the bolts through from the inside and Martha put the nuts on the outside. Tomorrow we will change off.

February 10, 1943

Yesterday afternoon we were on top of the hill near here. We stopped our car and looked in the direction of the plant. There was nothing there except a small town. Houses with trees and shrubs, streets going both ways. You couldn't tell where the mock village stopped and the real one started. It is truly concealed. An enemy aircraft would never suspect that it was built on top of the buildings. The wire covering with imitation grass extends across the street and parking lot. Rumor has it that our plant is one of the hardest to detect from the air.

July 17, 1943

One of the problems, or perhaps I should say one of the adjustments we are going to have to face when this war is over, is the equality of races. Where we have lived, we have had no contact with the colored race, and consequently it shocked me when at rest period today a six foot, husky, black Negro stopped in front of a demure, timid little blond as she was lighting her cigarette. He didn't ask for a light, simply bent over and accepted one as she was lighting her own. As he ambled on down the aisle with two white men, she looked at our astonished faces and explained, "He works in my position."

More and more colored people, both men and women, are coming into the plant. They are working side by side with the whites, and who is to say they are not doing their share in winning the war.

We have a colored team working on the frame section. One is a middle-aged woman, quite dark, with small shoulders and huge hips. She always bends forward as she works, and one can't help thinking of a little boy with a sling shot. The other is rather young and very pretty, with a slender boyish figure. They build their assemblies perfect in thirty-five minutes, which means that every forty minutes we issue them another group. We keep their jobs pulled ahead so they don't have to wait.

One day, the young girl didn't show up. The older woman had to work with a white girl. They were slow getting their assemblies finished, so I kidded the colored woman about it.

"Oh, these slow white trash," she said. "They're just plain lazy." That should hold me for a while.

August 8, 1945

News of Russia declaring war via the grapevine. Then the loud speaker declaring, "President Truman announced 'Russia declares war on Japan.'" Everyone took it calmly. You'd never know from the appearances of the workers that we had been tense over Russia for a long time—that there had been much speculation as to how long it would take to finish us if Russia joined with Germany and Japan.

Public speakers were prophesying, "Watch Russia. As Russia goes, so goes the war." We were watching Russia. But Hitler overstepped when he tangled with Stalin. Russia is on our side for the present. I wonder how long?

August 14, 1945

The war is over. The war is over. The war is over. I jumped out of my "share-the-ride" car today in front of the grocery store. Mrs. Eden shouted at me before my feet hit the ground. "The war is over," she yelled, "The war is over—The war is over."

She grabbed me and we danced around and round singing, "The war is over—The war is over—The war is over." Then I remembered all the rumors of the past. "How do you know?" I demanded.

"President Truman just announced it over the radio; I heard it."

I rushed to the phone and called the plant. I got our department. "The war is over," I shouted. "The war is over." Just like that!

The evening paper says "Two-day holiday for all plant workers."

Mable R. Gerken, *Ladies in Pants: A Home Front Diary* (New York: Exposition Press, 1949), pp. 11, 14–16, 20, 47–48, 94.

woman might be promoted to a better-paying job with added responsibilities were almost nonexistent. One woman put it baldly: "No working woman (in whatever line of work) labors under the delusion that any woman is actually, either socially or economically, equal to men in the U.S. in 1944."

More progress might have been made had there been an active, organized feminist movement at the outset of the war, as there was in World War I. But the cult of domesticity reigned supreme. Indeed, with the social dislocation caused by the war, as people moved to the vicinity of military bases and war plants, the institution of the family, with wife and mother at its core, took on new significance. The public welcomed women in the war plants, but it clearly regarded their work as temporary; it was only "for the duration" of the war. One government publication praised Rosie the Riveter, but described her as a housewife who took a war job only to bring her man home more quickly and make the world a safer place for her children.

In 1943, the federal government appropriated funds to finance day-care centers for the children of working mothers, but it was a stopgap measure in every way. Funds were kept low and administration was ragged. The government openly feared that if the centers became too convenient, they might outlast the emergency and encourage women to stay at work. By 1945, federal day-care centers housed only about 100,000 children, meeting less than 10 percent of the need. When the war ended, the centers were closed. When the state of New York discontinued its day-care program, working mothers picketed the residence of Governor Thomas E. Dewey (Republican nominee for President in 1944 and 1948), who promptly labeled them Communists.

At the end of the war, one-fourth of the women employed in industry either quit or were laid off. The proportion of women in the job market fell from 35 percent to 28.6 percent. Those who did remain in the work force were employed in the clerical, service, and sales positions that had been reserved for them since the turn of the century. For women, as well as for America's racial minorities, the war was an awakening, but little more.

⊔Postwar Stresses

The specter of postwar depression haunted the Roosevelt administration throughout the war. Roosevelt's advisers were well aware that the war alone had ended the 1930s depression, and they had good reason to suppose that, when the war plants were closed and the armies dismantled, there would once again be unbought surpluses, low prices, and unemployment. Some officials recommended a gradual demobilization to ease the strain on the economy, but that proved politically impossible. Soldiers protested, even rioted, at military posts around the world when the army tried to slow discharges, and President Truman himself promised a speedup. By mid-1946, a year after the war had ended, the armed services were reduced from 12.5 to 2 million men and women. To save money, the government canceled $35 million in war contracts after Japan surrendered, and within ten days 2.7 million men and women had been released from war plants.

INFLATION AND LABOR STRIFE

The depression failed to materialize, however, in part because government expenditures, even without war contracts, continued to be high. Congress had also attempted to ease the impact of demobilization through a Servicemen's Readjustment Act (1944), popularly known as the

G.I. Bill of Rights. The act assured veterans the jobs they held prior to the war, and it offered low-interest loans for those starting new businesses. Most important, it offered government scholarships for education. Between 1945 and 1950, over 2 million veterans took advantage of the G.I. Bill to attend college, and millions more returned to high schools and vocational training programs.

These and other government measures prevented any serious unemployment after the war, and pent-up consumer demand prevented any price depression. Indeed, the problem the country faced was not depression, but runaway inflation. Consumers emerged from the war with some $140 billion in savings. Goods remained scarce for some months while industry reconverted, and the combination of big demand and small supply put intense pressure on prices. In the fall of 1945 Congress approved an extension of the Office of Price Administration (OPA), which had controlled prices during the war, but Truman vetoed the measure as inadequate. While the government squabbled, prices soared.

Accompanying the inflation was a wave of strikes in the winter of 1945–1946, as labor sought to hold wartime gains. Organized labor had been bound by the no-strike pledge during the war. Now, with the war ended and consumer goods in short supply, it found itself in a good bargaining position. The walkout began in the oil refineries and spread to automobiles, steel, and the electrical industry. By January 1946, there were 2 million people on strike across the nation. Truman's response was to appoint fact-finding boards, which generally granted the wage increases labor demanded. Just as the crisis eased, John L. Lewis called his United Mineworkers out on strike. Truman seized the coal mines, as Roosevelt had threatened to do in 1943, and negotiated a wage settlement that favored the miners. Six months later, in November 1946, Lewis denounced the settle-ment and threatened another strike. Truman called his aides together and told them: "This time I mean to slap that so-and-so down for good." The government, which was still operating the mines, obtained a court injunction ordering the miners to continue working. When Lewis ignored the order, the court cited him for contempt, fining the union $3,500,000 and Lewis himself $10,000. The encounter marked the end of the cozy relationship between government and labor unions that had developed in the course of the New Deal.

TRIMMING THE NEW DEAL

Labor strife, soaring prices, and international tensions, as the United States and the Soviet Union drifted into the Cold War, presented Republicans with a silver platterful of issues in the fall elections of 1946. They summed them up with the slogan, "Had enough?" And voters, it seemed, had. The Republicans gained control of both houses of Congress for the first time since 1930, and they appeared to be in a good position to recover the White House in 1948.

For the next two years, President and Congress sniped at one another over taxes and expenditures. Republicans lacked the strength to roll back the New Deal, but they did trim at its more ragged edges, eliminating some agencies and consolidating others. The National Security Act (1947) was the most important piece of governmental reorganization, for it framed the military establishment as it exists today:

It joined the War and Navy Departments into a single cabinet-level Department of Defense.

It established the Joint Chiefs of Staff to provide planning and advice for the president.

It created the National Security Council, consisting of the president, the chairman of the joint chiefs, and relevant cabinet officers (depending on the issue at hand) to provide long-range strategic planning and to advise the president in times of diplomatic crisis.

It created the Central Intelligence Agency to coordinate and assess information gathered by various government agencies (a result, in part, of congressional investigation of the intelligence mixup at Pearl Harbor).

Trimming the New Deal's labor legislation was also on the Republican agenda, and the public generally agreed. The strikes of 1946—and especially the antics of John L. Lewis—had convinced many voters that labor unions had become too powerful. The man chiefly responsible for the Taft-Hartley Act was the intellectual and political leader of the Senate, Robert A. Taft of Ohio. The son of a former president, Taft had been brushed aside by Republicans in 1944 in favor of the more attractive Thomas E. Dewey, and he would be again in 1948. But in other years he was Mr. Republican, the embodiment of the party's laissez-faire, small-government ideology.

Formally called the Labor-Management Relations Act (1947), Taft's measure was intended to equalize the advantages labor had secured by the New Deal's Wagner Act. It outlawed certain unfair labor practices, such as the jurisdictional strike (where unions went on strike against one another seeking to win jurisdiction over a factory), and it prohibited labor unions from making political contributions. The Taft-Hartley Act also established a mechanism for settling strikes in key industries. If the president determined that a strike posed a national emergency, he could seek a court injunction postponing it for sixty days, a cooling off period in which the parties could negotiate with government mediation. If there was no settlement within that time, the entire union membership had to vote on the employer's last offer before a strike could be called.

Truman vetoed the Taft-Hartley Act,

calling it a slave labor law, but Congress passed it over his veto. Truman's characterization was too strong, but the broad support for the act in Congress did reflect growing public hostility to labor. In the following years, states, particularly in the South and West, began passing right to work laws that protected the choice of those who did not want to join unions. These laws, in turn, encouraged the drift of manufacturing enterprises into the Sunbelt states, where labor costs were lower and unions weaker. Long-term shifts from smokestack to high-tech industries, from manufacturing to services, also weakened labor unions. Never again would organized labor be as powerful, economically and politically, as it was at the end of World War II.

ELECTION OF 1948: THE FAIR DEAL

Americans were slow to accept Truman, who conveyed neither confidence nor charisma in the early months of his administration. In the face of the Soviet threat in Europe and social tensions at home, Truman seemed to flounder in indecision. "I wonder what Truman would do if he were alive today," was one of many jokes at his expense. When Truman became accustomed to his office, he countered such criticism with bold initiatives in the Cold War—the Truman Doctrine, the Marshall Plan, and the Berlin airlift. Though generally popular in the country, these measures alarmed Democratic liberals, who thought he was too belligerent toward the Soviet Union and too preoccupied with foreign affairs. In mid-1947, former vice president Henry Wallace organized a left-wing movement known as the Progressive Citizens of America. It advocated accommodation with the Soviet Union abroad and renewed reform at home. In December of that year, Wallace announced that he would run for

Truman

Democratic gains from election of 1944

Dewey

Republican gains from election of 1944

Thurmond

Election of 1948.

the presidency on a third party ticket. The breakup of the New Deal coalition seemed to doom any chance Truman had for re-election.

The president, however, managed to hold together the other elements of the New Deal coalition. His veto of the Taft-Hartley Act kept labor in line. In May 1948 he overrode State Department objections and extended diplomatic recognition to the new state of Israel, making the United States the first nation in the world to do so and thereby ensuring himself the Jewish vote in the United States. Truman also courted the black vote by committing himself to civil rights. In early 1948 he recommended that Congress make the wartime Fair Employment Practices Commission permanent, make lynching a federal crime,

protect the right to vote, and prohibit discrimination in interstate transportation facilities. In separate actions he ordered the desegregation of the armed forces, a program that was finally completed in 1952.

The president's civil rights program caused another split in the Democratic party. Southern congressmen were outraged and talked openly of switching their electoral votes to a southerner. Their moment came at the Democratic convention of 1948, when Minnesota delegate Hubert Humphrey led a successful fight to insert a civil rights plank in the platform that committed the Democrats to a program even stronger than Truman's. Several southern delegations walked out and subsequently formed the Dixiecrat party, which backed South Carolina Governor

Strom Thurmond for president. What remained of the Democratic party nominated Truman, but without much spirit. With both Left and Right peeling off, Truman appeared to be helpless.

What happened instead was the greatest upset in American political history. Being an underdog was a role that suited Truman's personality and his style of oratory. He traveled some 32,000 miles by train, delivering an average of ten speeches a day at "whistlestop" towns across the country. The Republican nominee, Dewey, spoke mainly to friendly audiences of Republican fundraisers and committed himself to nothing in the way of principle or policy. Until election eve, pollsters and journalists predicted a Republican victory. Truman won by an electoral vote of 303 to 189, with 39 Deep South electoral votes going to the Dixiecrats. Wallace polled a mere million popular votes (half in New York) and no electoral votes, and that was the secret to the election. The defectors had taken only the extremists, and they allowed Truman to occupy what historian Arthur Schlesinger, Jr., called "the vital center"— a blend of anticommunism abroad and modest reform at home.

Truman's program had been evolving for two years, principally through requests for legislation that the Republican Congress had largely ignored. In his inaugural address he described his program as the Fair Deal, an extension of Roosevelt's New Deal. It did indeed go well beyond the New Deal, for it included civil rights legislation, federal aid to education, and a national health insurance program. All that, however, was too progressive for Congress, where a coalition of Republicans and southern Democrats held sway. Truman wrested a few measures from Congress— a federal housing act, an increase in the minimum wage, and an extension of social security to include the self-employed—but his most innovative proposals were buried in committees. By 1950 the Cold War and the Red scare commanded public attention; the Fair Deal was simply forgotten.

EISENHOWER AND THE FALL OF McCARTHY

"There is only one real issue for the farmer, the laborer, and the businessman," Senator Joseph McCarthy declared during the 1952 election campaign, "—the issue of Communism in government." McCarthy oversimplified as usual. Actually Republicans had identified two other issues that year: Korea and corruption. In Korea, peace negotiations had dragged on for more than a year while the fighting continued. By mid-1952 the principal issue was the return of prisoners of war. Some 60,000 Chinese and North Korean POWs did not want to be repatriated to their Communist homelands, and the United States was reluctant to force them. Many Americans wondered if the whole war was worth the price. At home, Truman's jaunty progressivism had turned into a testy defensiveness, as the administration was bombarded with charges of being soft on communism and careless about corruption. The examples of corruption uncovered by Republicans were petty and isolated—one of the president's aides was found to have accepted a deep freezer from a man who did business with the government—but they lent substance to the Republican charge that the Democrats' long tenure in office had made them careless.

The campaign that year, 1952, was a superficial one. The foreign policy debate triggered by General MacArthur's dismissal and the allegations of Senator McCarthy posed questions requiring critical decisions, but neither of the presidential candidates—Dwight Eisenhower and Adlai Stevenson—was willing to discuss them. Eisenhower confined himself to generalities about restoring morality to government while allowing his running mate, Richard

Nixon, to ride shotgun on the campaign bandwagon. (Nixon's charge that Stevenson "got a PhD from Dean Acheson's College of Cowardly Communist Containment" suggests the level of the debate.) Stevenson, ducking such birdshot, tried to separate himself from Truman and the Fair Deal and succeeded only in confusing everyone. Eisenhower's promise two weeks before the election that he would go to Korea in order to end the war may have clinched his victory, but most Americans in 1952 simply voted for a change.

The immediate victor, however, was Senator Joseph McCarthy, for the election also gave the Republicans a majority in the Senate. With Republicans organizing the upper house, McCarthy became chairman of the Senate Subcommittee on Government Operations, giving him a forum for his witchhunt, a budget, and a government-paid staff. Eisenhower had avoided any criticism of McCarthy during the election campaign, and his silence was taken as approval.

In office, Eisenhower and Dulles set out on a Communist hunt of their own. To deflect criticism of the State Department, Eisenhower named a leading McCarthyite to head the department's personnel program, the chief result of which was to prevent any intelligent discussion within the department of Dulles's policies. Eisenhower also loosened the standards for dismissal of government employees. Where Truman required evidence of disloyalty, Eisenhower authorized dismissal on the grounds that an individual's appointment "may not be clearly consistent with the interests of national security," which was not only vague, but placed the burden of proof of innocence on the employee. Under this guideline, Eisenhower claimed to have removed 2,200 "security risks" in his first year in office. In actuality, nearly all those removed were charged not with disloyalty, but with alcoholism, drug addiction, or sexual perversion. The theory was that such flaws made them "risks" because they were vulnerable to blackmail and other forms of intimidation.

The administration's purge made McCarthy's performance respectable, and the senator made the most of it. In the spring of 1953 he and his subcommittee's legal adviser, Roy Cohn, investigated the Voice of America, a government radio station beamed at Eastern Europe, claiming it was a front for leftists. Shortly thereafter, Cohn and another of McCarthy's aides, G. David Schine, toured United States Information Agency libraries in Europe and found 30,000 "subversive" books. Despite the absurdity of the charges, panicky bureaucrats removed thousands of volumes from library shelves. That June, Eisenhower told a Dartmouth College commencement audience: "Don't join the bookburners!" But when asked to elaborate, he insisted he was not referring to McCarthy.

Within a year, McCarthy, who had neither the ambition to organize a following nor the intellect to lead one, destroyed himself. By early 1954 he was spewing his venom on the administration itself, adding one year to his original accusation of "twenty years of treason" (the Roosevelt-Truman administrations, 1933–1953) and thereby implicating the first year of the Eisenhower administration in the coverup of communism. Many Republicans were horrified. Through it all, Senate minority leader Lyndon Johnson had kept silent. But when McCarthy unearthed a "pinko" dentist at one of the army's training posts and the army countered with the release of documents revealing McCarthy's attempt to obtain special privileges for his former aide Schine (who had been drafted), Lyndon Johnson suggested that the hearings of McCarthy's subcommittee be televised. For thirty-six days, the nation watched as McCarthy bullied witnesses, ignored legal procedures, and interrupted testimony with constant cries of "Mr.

UPI/Bettmann.

Senator McCarthy waves a document as "evidence" that Democratic presidential candidate Adlai Stevenson had a record of associations with subversive groups and endorsed "the suicidal Kremlin-shaped policies of this nation."

Chairman, point of order!" In January 1954, the Gallup poll reported that a record 50 percent of Americans approved of McCarthy; by May, his rating had fallen to 35 percent. That summer a Republican senator introduced a resolution of censure, and after carefully orchestrated proceedings (Johnson let only southern conservatives speak for the Democrats), it won approval. McCarthy lived for another three years, but after December 1954 he was politically dead.

⊔ Affluence and Apathy: The Fifties

The fall of McCarthy signaled a change in the national mood. For a generation, Americans had been summoned by one call after another—the New Deal revolution, hot war, cold war, the Communist purge—

and, consciously or not, they felt the need to relax. By the mid-1950s, they were engaged in a frenzied pursuit of normalcy.

STATION WAGON SUBURBS

One index was the birth rate. The number of children born annually increased steadily from 1940 to 1957, and in that interval the birth rate rose by 50 percent, the biggest increase in births ever recorded anywhere. The phenomenon is even more remarkable because the marriage rate declined over those same years, meaning that people were simply having larger families. Why the urge to have children? Affluence, principally. Throughout the 1950s the average annual rate of unemployment was 4.6 percent, a figure that meant almost full employment. In addition, a shortage of young workers (due to the war and the low birth rate of the 1930s) meant opportunity for rapid advancement, at least for white males. The post–New Deal welfare state, from government-insured bank deposits to home loans, gave people the security that encouraged them to spend beyond their incomes. And easy credit enabled them to do so. Financial well-being encouraged early marriages and large families.

The flight to the suburbs, the most prominent demographic shift of the decade, was both cause and effect of the baby boom. People migrated toward open spaces in part to provide a healthier, more spacious, morally elevated neighborhood in which to bring up children. The accommodating environment, in turn, encouraged them to have more. Social critics denounced the suburbs as sprawling agglomerations of nearly identical dwellings, mass-produced by a developer whose sole aim was profit. The accusation was true enough, but it was also true of the midtown apartments and row houses from which the suburbanites fled. If nothing else, the move to the suburbs stimulated an unprecedented housing boom. By 1960, one-fourth of all the houses in the nation had been built within the previous decade. The construction industry set the pace for the decade's prosperity because it entailed so much spinoff demand—for plumbing fixtures, furniture, appliances, landscaping supplies, and so on.

The flight to the suburbs accentuated the importance of women in the family, but it did not much alter their role in society. The number of women in the work force dropped sharply after the war as returning veterans took their places, but it began to rise again in 1947, and by 1950 it had returned to World War II levels. Women continued to enter the work force during the 1950s, and by 1960, 40 percent of the adult female population was employed outside the home. However, in the 1950s the majority of working women were married (60 percent), whereas before the war the female work force was mostly single. When queried as to their motives, working women in the 1950s emphasized financial necessity. The installment buying, charge accounts, and credit cards of America's new suburban life-style had put new burdens on family finances, and women found that their efforts made a valued contribution to family well-being. Although this trend challenged the traditional view that the woman's proper place was in the home, female employment remained family-oriented. Most women were not after careers, and the jobs available to them did not encourage it. The cult of domesticity, though shaken in the 1950s, continued to reign.

Yet even those women who stayed at home found their situation different. As incomes rose and demand increased, and as credit facilities became more complex, women found themselves becoming real business managers of their households. Women began to make the key decisions on family spending. Advertisers sensed this and increasingly geared their appeals to women. By the end of the decade even the automobile—once as masculine as the chain saw—was being designed to appeal to women. Stuffed with children, dogs, and grocery bags, the station wagon was the ultimate symbol of suburban domesticity.

POPULAR CULTURE

Another outgrowth of mass affluence was mass leisure. The average work week dropped from 44 hours in 1940 to 41 by the mid-1950s. Paid vacations, enjoyed by fewer than half of American workers in 1940, were nearly universal by the 1950s, and in the same interval the average vacation doubled from one week to two. Tourism and entertainment became major industries. By 1950, Americans were spending as much money on entertainment as on rent. And even when a person spent leisure time productively, the effort was eased by power mowers, power cultivators, and power tools.

The motion picture industry at first benefited from the new leisure. Attendance at movies reached a peak in 1948 that has not been equaled since, despite an increase in population. Thereafter the movies yielded to other forms of recreation—camping, for instance, which became a major pastime as tent and back-packing technology improved. Most of all, movies yielded to television. The number of television sets in American homes numbered about 4,000 at the end of the war and 40 million a decade later.

The early 1950s have been called, with some justice, the golden age of television. The tremendous potential in the medium was evident in the superb satire of Sid Caesar and Imogene Coca ("Your Show of Shows"), the quality documentaries of Edward R. Murrow's "See It Now," and the original, live dramas of "Playhouse 90." But variety and originality soon gave way to bland imitations punctuated only by violence ("The Untouchables") and greed ("Queen for a Day"). The Red scare, with its systematic blacklisting, was in part responsible. Countless actors, writers, and directors lost their jobs; imaginative ideas were shunned as potentially controversial.

The very success of TV also contributed to its decline. Instantly accessible to everyone with no more physical or mental effort than the flip of a switch, it had enormous commercial potential. By the mid-1950s, advertisers had gained almost total control of programming. The networks screened program material for appeal in terms of age, sex, income, or sheer volume, and the predicted audience was then sold to a corporate sponsor. The public became the commodity to be bought. The ratings system, which tied the per-second cost of advertising to viewer percentage points, completed the process. Both program and audience became numbers.

In its early days, television was perceived as the most egalitarian of media, the universal communicator that would melt away class and regional differences and restore family intimacy. It did both, but in ways that were unexpected. Television was a force for communicating *to* people, but it tended to eradicate communication *among* people. A family might gather before a television set for an evening, but there was little genuine contact with one another. As the necessity for communication declined, so did communication skills. By the 1960s, educators were blaming television for a long-term drop in the reading and writing abilities of students. Even bodily functions became dependent on the flickering screen. The TV dinner, first introduced in 1954, bent both diet and cooking to media requirements. City water supply officials, puzzled by drops in city water pressure at regular intervals, discovered that the pressure drops coincided with television commercials and the simultaneous flushing of thousands of toilets. Television may have reflected the '50s culture as much as it influenced it, but it also changed America. It oversimplified life and encouraged life to imitate the medium. It homogenized people and impaired communication. Not since the automobile has any mechanical device wrought so much change in human life.

THE YOUTH DECADE

In the affluent suburbs, wealth trickled from parents to children, creating a new market in the American economy. Phonographs, long-playing record albums, penny loafers, and sugar-coated breakfast cereals were part of a multimillion-dollar business. In this decade given to the young, 1955 was a vintage year. Television introduced Captain Kangaroo and the Mickey Mouse Club, and Bill Haley revolutionized American music with "Rock Around the Clock."

UPI/Bettmann.

Elvis Presley. The young Elvis ecstatically slaps his guitar during a television rehearsal. He was preparing for a live appearance on "The Ed Sullivan Show," CBS's popular Sunday evening variety show, October 28, 1956.

Rock and roll was the core of the youth culture precisely because it was avant garde, just as jazz had been in the 1920s. Like jazz, it was derived from black musical forms, from rhythm and blues, and that made it the more fanciful and romantic. Rock and roll was a lighthearted challenge to adults and their suburban world. The advice to "rock around the clock" was also sexually suggestive, a herald of the sex revolution of the 1960s. Elvis Presley, who wriggled to stardom in 1956 with "Love Me Tender" and "Heartbreak Hotel," added his own stock to the growing merger of music and sexual license (and ultimately

to the association of both with the use of narcotics).

Though self-consciously distinctive, the youth culture of the 1950s did not break with dominant values. The rock songs of Elvis Presley and the country-western ballads of Johnny Cash (who also appeared in 1956) depicted poignant moments of life, but rarely touched on social problems or challenged such institutions as marriage, religion, or patriotism. Rock and roll did not even alter traditional dance styles until Chubby Checker invented The Twist in 1959. Nonetheless, rebellion lay just beneath the surface. Once politicized, it became the youth revolution and the counterculture of the explosive 1960s.

THE EISENHOWER CONSENSUS

The 1960s were another decade, however, and for the moment all America seemed wrapped in a cult of conformity. The young, for all their subterranean rebelliousness, were known as the "silent generation." Imitating their parents, most directed their lives toward marriage, a split-level home, a new car, and membership in a country club. It was a decade, as one novelist put it, of happy people with happy problems. Sociologist Daniel Bell, in *The End of Ideology*, celebrated the end of radical leftist ideology. Marxism, Bell explained, was born in nineteenth-century industrial Britain; it was irrelevant to twentieth-century postindustrial America. Instead of failing, as Marx had predicted, capitalism had worked. Class conflict was obsolete and unnecessary. Instead of conflict, said Bell (and many economists and historians agreed with him), there was growing equality and a natural harmony in America—a consensus—as capitalists became professional managers and workers moved into the middle class. Differences of interest and opinion could now be resolved without resort to radical solutions.

The principal threat to this consensus, according to Bell and others, was the deluded adherents of Marxism. To preserve its unique destiny, the United States had to prepare for a lengthy struggle with communism. Thus did the ideology of consensus blend neatly with the Cold War rationale for containment. It fitted what people wanted to believe and found acceptance with little discussion. The silence of the "silent generation" itself made for consensus. By philosophy and temperament, President Eisenhower fitted the national mood perfectly. He was a man without strong political persuasion (Democrats, thinking he might be one of theirs, had sounded him out in 1948 and 1952), or any discernible ideology. Blessed with a fatherly grin and a good deal of sound common sense, Eisenhower somehow conveyed an impression of solidity, integrity, and balance.

And he carefully cultivated the image. Upon his arrival in Washington, he joined the National Presbyterian Church (seven previous presidents had been members), even though he had no earlier church affiliation, and he became a Sunday regular. His inaugural parade contained a last-minute entry called "God's Float." In 1954 he issued an executive order that God be added to the U.S. pledge of allegiance so that it read: "one nation, under God, indivisible. . . ." Ike also instituted the practice of opening cabinet meetings with a prayer, though it was sometimes forgotten in the rush of business. When an aide on one occasion reminded him of the oversight, Ike burst out: "Oh, God dammit, we forgot the silent prayer." If such public relations efforts were occasionally superficial, they were nevertheless successful. Even politicians and journalists who disagreed with some of his policies considered him a sincere, decent human being.

When forced to speak extemporaneously, as in a press conference, Eisenhower was capable of rendering the English language nearly incomprehensible. But few cared in a time that avoided debate and resented ideologues. Ike was also shrewd enough to make use of his well-known problems with the language. When his press secretary James Haggerty asked what he planned to tell journalists about the sticky Formosa Straits issue in the spring of 1954, Eisenhower, who wanted to keep his options open and the Chinese off-balance, replied: "Don't worry, Jim. If that question comes up, I'll just confuse them."

Through his first two years in office, Eisenhower was preoccupied with foreign affairs. In the summer of 1953 he finally obtained an armistice in Korea, an agreement that permitted prisoners of war to choose whether they wished to be repatriated. As a result, 21,809 Chinese and North Korean POWs remained in South Korea, and 359 members of the United Nations force, including 23 Americans, chose to remain on the Communist side. The Cold War was central to both foreign and domestic politics until the end of 1954. Dulles dominated the one, and McCarthy dominated the other.

Eisenhower handled McCarthy with cautious indirection. When advisers urged him to speak out against the Wisconsin senator, the president shied away, saying: "I will not get into the gutter with that guy." After the Senate censured McCarthy, however, Eisenhower took command. In his January 1955 message to Congress, he defined his philosophy of modern Republicanism as "progressive moderation and moderate progressivism." When journalists pressed for a further explanation, Ike said he was a liberal with regard to people's rights and a conservative with regard to their pocketbooks.

It was a formula that did not stand close examination, but it gave Eisenhower what he loved most, flexibility. It gave reign to his own instinctive conservatism without unraveling the New Deal. In his first year in office he had stunned the army by slashing the defense budget in order to cut the government's annual deficit. In succeeding years he used his veto power against federal housing, public works, and antipollution programs. On the other hand, he approved legislation that increased social security benefits, raised the minimum wage, and improved unemployment benefits. Eisenhower also supported the interstate highway program (begun in 1956), the largest and most expensive public works program in history. Eisenhower's pragmatic, nonideological approach to

government allowed the Republican party to digest the New Deal revolution. The McCarthy era hysteria faded; little more was heard of "creeping socialism" or "twenty years of treason." Eisenhower worked closely with the Democratic leaders of Congress, Sam Rayburn in the House and Lyndon Johnson in the Senate, both conservative Texans. Even party politics yielded to the national consensus.

But to maintain it, Americans had to ignore or overlook fundamental social ills, such as poverty and racial and sexual discrimination. Eisenhower was willing to do so. He had no feeling for the poor, nor much sympathy for civil rights. But such problems could not be buried forever. Indeed, the civil rights issue simmered throughout Eisenhower's presidency. It was a herald of the tensions of the 1960s and the end of consensus.

⊔ Civil Rights: Black Initiative

Since the war, blacks had been pushing steadily at the social barriers to equality. They were entering professions, such as law, medicine, and education, that had previously been closed to them. Greater wealth, more education, and improved status, in turn, made the legal barriers to equality even more intolerable. By the mid-1950s, blacks were prepared to take the initiative in the fight against discrimination. (The leadership of older civil rights organizations, such as the NAACP, was predominantly white.)

The legal foundation for official discrimination was a decision of the United States Supreme Court in the case of *Plessy* v. *Ferguson* (1896). The Court had ruled that the various features of the Fourteenth Amendment designed to protect the rights and privileges of American citizens did not prevent state governments from providing separate facilities for blacks and whites, so long as the two facilities were equal. The Plessy case involved a southern Jim Crow law that required separate seating on railroad trains, but the principle of separate but equal had been applied to all public facilities, including schools. By World War II, there was not even a pretense that separate could be equal, since budgets for black schools in the South were uniformly lower than those for white schools.

BROWN ET AL. v. BOARD OF EDUCATION OF TOPEKA ET AL.

In 1950, the Supreme Court chipped away at the separate but equal doctrine by ruling that Texas and Oklahoma could not maintain separate law schools for blacks because the black school did not have comparable faculty or library facilities. In 1954 in *Brown* v. *Board of Education of Topeka*, the Supreme Court struck it down altogether, ruling that segregation was inherently unequal, even where physical facilities were equal. In doing so, the Court accepted sociological and psychological evidence concerning the effect of discrimination on black children.

In a second decision a year later, the Court laid on local school boards the responsibility for drawing up plans for desegregation and required that it be done with "all deliberate speed." It declined, however, to set a deadline, and this gave whites an opportunity to delay. All over the South, white citizen councils and other voluntary associations were formed to resist desegregation. President Eisenhower, unfortunately, encouraged the resistance with a public statement that he would enforce the Court's orders regardless of his own beliefs—which implied that he privately disagreed with the decision. By the time Eisenhower left office six years later, some progress had been made in the upper

South and in such border states as Kansas and Delaware, but not a single school district in the lower South had yielded. One—Prince Edward County, Virginia—had even abolished its public school system altogether rather than permit racial mixing.

NONVIOLENT RESISTANCE

In such an atmosphere it is scarcely surprising that southern blacks took matters into their own hands. The heroine of the moment was Rosa Parks, a black seamstress who, feeling more tired than heroic after a day's work, refused to yield her seat to a white person on a city bus in Montgomery, Alabama. Her refusal violated both city ordinance and southern custom. She was forcibly ejected, but four days later, on December 5, 1955, Montgomery blacks began a boycott of city buses. The chief organizer was Reverend Martin Luther King, Jr., a Baptist minister who had recently arrived in the city to accept his first church. Eleven months later, the United States Supreme Court struck down Jim Crow ordinances such as Montgomery's, and the city capitulated to the boycott. In early 1957, Martin Luther King organized the Southern Christian Leadership Conference to promote desegregation throughout the South by nonviolent means. In succeeding years the black-led SCLC would become a major force in civil rights, and King would win the Nobel Peace Prize for his use of nonviolent pressure to achieve social change.

Although urged by many to lend his personal prestige to the civil rights struggle, President Eisenhower remained firmly uncommitted. The battle against intolerance, he declared, had "to be fought—not in the chambers of any legislature—but in the hearts of men." He did agree, however, that the federal government had some obligation to protect the right to vote. In the South, voting registrars systematically dis-

UPI/Bettmann.

Rosa Parks sits contentedly in the front of a city bus in Montgomery, Alabama, in December 1956, having won her battle.

criminated against blacks. In some counties where blacks were a majority of the population, no more than half a dozen were on the registration lists. In 1957 the administration sent to Congress a voting rights bill that empowered judges to jail anyone who prevented a qualified person from voting. Senate majority leader Lyndon Johnson, working behind the scenes, deleted some key enforcement provisions to prevent a southern filibuster and obtain passage. Weak though it was, the Civil Rights Act of 1957 was the first federal law in the field since Reconstruction.

But schools were still the focus of civil rights in 1957. When a court ordered the schools of Little Rock, Arkansas, opened to blacks in September of that year, Governor Orville Faubus mobilized the National Guard. Armed soldiers prevented black

children from entering the city's Central High School. After some delay, Eisenhower decided he could not overlook this challenge to federal authority. He federalized the National Guard and sent in paratroops to enforce the federal court order. The president's concern was constitutional, rather than humanitarian, but he did help topple another stronghold of prejudice.

Emboldened by these modest gains, southern blacks began a broad-scale assault on the Jim Crow laws that required segregation in all public facilities. In February 1960, four black college students sat down at an all-white lunch counter at Woolworth's in Greensboro, North Carolina. They ordered coffee, were refused service, and stayed in their seats until the lunch counter closed. The point was made. Businesses had to treat all customers equally

CLIO'S FOCUS: The Warren Court

The most liberal element in the American political system in the 1950s, a decade of conservatism, may have been the Supreme Court. Under Chief Justice Earl Warren, named by Eisenhower in 1953, the Court embarked on a period of judicial activism unique in its history. To credit (or blame) Warren for this—or even to label it a Warren Court—is somewhat misleading, for Warren was far from the most liberal member of the Court and followed the majority as often as he led it. The Warren Court was the product of its time.

Its roots lay in the "Roosevelt revolution" of 1937–1941, when deaths and retirements allowed Roosevelt to restructure the Court, replacing the conservative justices who in the previous fifteen years had overturned some 200 state and federal laws because they interfered with free enterprise. Roosevelt's appointees—Felix Frankfurter, William O. Douglas, Hugo Black, and Robert Jackson are the best remembered—combined solid legal credentials with New Deal humanitarianism. They regarded as settled the age-old controversy over the power to regulate interstate commerce. "The commerce power," said Justice Jackson in the decision that upheld the constitutionality of the TVA, "is as broad as the economic needs of the nation." On the other hand, they did worry about the effect of governmental power on the liberties of the citizens. The rise of totalitarianism in Europe sharpened their concern. As Justice Frankfurter expressed it in 1943: "All members of the Court . . . are equally zealous to enforce the constitutional protection of the free play of human spirit."

This concern necessarily entailed judicial activism because the field of civil liberties law rested somewhere between the primitive and the nonexistent in 1940. In that year the Court upheld a state's power to compel schoolchildren to salute the flag against their religious scruples. The right of free speech was still subject to the "clear and present danger" test, which meant that Congress could abridge it whenever it felt the nation in danger from abroad. Black rights were subject to the separate but equal concept, and the field of criminal procedure was governed by the Palko rule, which allowed state and municipal police to deny counsel and extract confessions from suspects by "third degree" interrogations.

At the same time, the public temper of that era made it certain that a judicial excursion into the arena of civil liberties would be controversial. The mood of the forties and early fifties was shaped by hot war, cold war, and McCarthyism. It is difficult enough to elaborate a philosophy of civil rights in tranquil times because the people whose rights need protecting are minorities and misfits. In a society at war, on the brink of war, and rent with suspicion, the defenders of civil liberties themselves come under attack. As a result, it is scarcely surprising that the Court's first steps into the field in the late 1940s were hesitant ones. In the years after the war, the Court declared the white primary unconstitutional (the South Carolina Democratic party had declared itself a private, whites-only club); it held that racially restrictive real estate covenants could not be enforced; and it held that, at the graduate school level, separate educational facilities are inherently unequal.

No one—least of all President Eisenhower—foresaw that Chief Justice Warren would quicken the pace and lead the Court into a bold affirmation of individual rights and freedom. Warren had served three terms as a genial, noncontroversial governor of California before Eisenhower discharged a political debt by appointing him to the Supreme Court. The self-confidence Warren instilled in the Court was evident in his first term, 1954, when the Court handed down its decision in the case of *Brown* v. *Board of Education*, which one scholar has called "one of the most daring assertions of court authority in judicial history." The Chief Justice, speaking for a unanimous Court, held that racially separate school facilities are inherently unequal and thus contrary to the Fourteenth Amendment. Warren's decision further shocked conservatives because it accepted as legal evidence the testimony of sociologists and psychologists concerning the impact of segregation on black children. A year later the Court reinforced the Brown decision by demanding that southerners dismantle their segregated school systems with "all deliberate speed"—in effect, a pace enforced by the courts.

While the nation wrestled with the school problem, the Warren Court moved in other directions. In a series of decisions in 1956 and 1957, it met McCarthyism head on by overthrowing federal convictions of alleged Communists and restricting the powers of legislative investigating committees. In *Yates* v. *United States* (1957), it replaced the "clear and present danger" test for legitimate speech with a rather vague, but in the end workable, distinction between revolutionary speech (permissible) and revolutionary behavior (which might not be). In 1962, the Warren Court sought to protect free expression in another way by prohibiting school officials from composing prayers for classroom use (*Engel* v. *Vitale*), a decision that raised a storm of protest from religious conservatives. In that same term it held that the equal protection clause of the Fourteenth Amendment obliges states to reapportion their legislatures periodically, in line with population shifts, in order to preserve the principle of "one man one vote" (*Baker* v. *Carr*).

While controversy swirled around these rulings, the Court struck off into the thorny field of criminal rights, holding that evidence which had been unconstitutionally obtained—by an illegal seizure, for instance—could not be introduced in court (*Mapp* v. *Ohio*, 1961); that indigent criminals who cannot afford their own lawyers are entitled to have one provided by the state (*Gideon* v. *Wainwright*, 1963); and that a confession extracted from a suspect after lengthy interrogation without the presence of a lawyer cannot be used as evidence (*Escobedo* v. *Illinois*, 1964). In the mid-1960s the Court expanded the freedom of newspapers by narrowing the definition of libel, restricted state birth control laws, and ruled antimiscegenation laws to be unconstitutional. By the time Earl Warren retired as Chief Justice in 1969, the Bill of Rights had a very different meaning from what it had in 1940. His niche in history was not won without personal cost, however. A small but noisy band of conservatives cried for his impeachment throughout the 1960s. Eisenhower himself came to regret his appointment, saying it was "the biggest dam-fool thing I ever did." Posterity may not agree.

or cease business. The movement quickly spread, and by the end of that year some 50,000 people had participated in sit-ins, walk-ins, wade-ins, and swim-ins across the South. There were few tangible results (nationwide chain stores, fearing adverse publicity, opened their facilities), but the black community had taught whites an important lesson. No longer could white southerners argue that the civil rights movement had been drummed up by a few northern black organizations in alliance with white liberals. The sit-ins revealed that the mass of southern blacks deeply resented the social and legal biases that hemmed them in. The question now was whether the black protest would remain nonviolent in the face of rising white violence.

⊔ The Decline and Fall of Practically Everything, 1957–1960

Eisenhower faced Adlai Stevenson again in the presidential election of 1956, and he defeated the Democratic candidate even more soundly than in 1952. Ike's percentage of the popular vote was greater than any earlier president had achieved, with the exception of Roosevelt in 1936 and Harding in 1920. He even broke the century-long Democratic stranglehold on the South, carrying Virginia, Tennessee, Texas, Florida, and Louisiana among the states of the old Confederacy. It was a personal victory—Republicans failed to win control of either house of Congress—and it was his last. From that point on, everything seemed to go wrong.

SPUTNIK

In August 1957, the economy slipped into a recession, the first since the Korean conflict, and the popular mood shifted from one of buoyant optimism to apprehension. In October, the Soviet Union stunned the world by launching an artificial satellite that circled the earth, sending back radio beeps. (They called it *Sputnik*, meaning "little moon.") The feat not only demonstrated the sophistication of Soviet technology, but had enormous military implications. It meant the Soviets had developed rockets capable of powering intercontinental ballistic missiles armed with nuclear weapons. The United States was working on ICBMs of its own, but to that point they were largely untested. Public apprehension turned to agony in December 1957 when a navy missile with a hastily improvised satellite perched on its nose exploded on the launching pad. In January an army missile at last carried a satellite into orbit, but it was the size of a grapefruit and weighed only 18 pounds. By then the Russians had orbited a second Sputnik, weighing 1,160 pounds and carrying a live dog. (The reason Soviet satellites were so colossal, it was later learned, was that the Soviets had not learned how to miniaturize electronic circuitry.)

President Eisenhower handled the crisis badly from the beginning. The American military could have undertaken a crash program that would have beaten the Soviets into space, but the president had not thought it worthwhile. When journalists and politicians began fretting about Soviet rocket advances and the possibility of a "missile gap," Eisenhower denied such a gap was developing. He refused to provide any evidence, however. When the issue refused to go away, the president increased spending on various missile programs and compensated for the increase with cuts in army manpower so the defense budget remained the same. Technology did improve, and by early 1960 the president was able to announce that American ICBMs had landed within 2 miles of their targets after 5,000-mile flights. But the uproar over the "missile gap," which the Democrats had turned into a major political issue, drowned him out.

There were moral as well as military implications in the Soviet Sputnik. Earlier in 1957, Harvard economist John Kenneth Galbraith had published a widely read book, *The Affluent Society*. Galbraith criticized America for lacking moral fiber and a sense of direction. We had become, said he, an affluent nation of pleasure seekers who wasted our affluence. Americans spent more money annually on cosmetics than they did on education, more money on bubble gum than on books. Sputnik, which seemed to reveal Soviet superiority in science and technology, bore him out. Through frugality and hard work, the Russians had surpassed us. The shortage of consumer goods in the Soviet Union, once thought to be evidence of communism's shortcomings, now appeared to be a source of strength. The Soviets were pulling ahead while Americans sank into a flabby affluence. A wave of spectacular scandals, ranging from the exposé of network rigging of television quiz shows to the arrest and conviction of the president of the Teamsters Union, intensified doubt about America's moral fiber.

An intense self-examination ensued. The educational system, which for some years had been criticized for failing to teach Johnny reading and arithmetic, was a special target. The U.S. government itself issued a report on *Education in the U.S.S.R.* that focused on the rigors of Russian education and emphasized the amount of time Russian children spent on sciences, languages, and mathematics. The result was a worthwhile examination of educational curriculums across the country and a new emphasis on math and science. Congress passed the National Defense Education Act (1958), which provided funds for instruction in math, science, and foreign languages, and created a loan fund for college students. It was the first step toward federal aid to education.

President Eisenhower seemed bewildered by the uproar. He had suffered a major heart attack in 1955, and he aged visibly during his second term, spending what seemed to many an inordinate amount of time on the golf course. Sherman Adams, a flinty New Englander who had been Eisenhower's assistant ever since the 1952 campaign, took on so many routine White House duties that he became almost an assistant president. He controlled access to the president and accordingly made enemies both in Congress and among the press (which nicknamed him "the abominable no-man"). Then, in June 1958, a House committee revealed that Adams had accepted gifts—paid hotel bills, an Oriental rug, and a vicuna coat—from a New England businessman and had, in return, interceded with government agencies in the businessman's behalf. Eisenhower at first defended his assistant, but after weeks of newspaper controversy, he finally asked for Adams's resignation. The Adams affair, together with the yearlong recession (in which unemployment reached a postwar high of 7 percent) gave the Democrats a powerful boost in the off-year election of 1958. In a spectacular landslide, they gained 47 seats in the House of Representatives and 13 in the Senate, giving them commanding majorities in both houses that they would retain for a decade.

DIPLOMATIC DISASTERS

John Foster Dulles was stricken by cancer in 1957, and though he remained in office until a month before his death in May 1959, he was not the force he had been during Eisenhower's first term. The president himself took up the reins of diplomacy, but bad luck and poor judgment continued to plague him. In the summer of 1958 he sent Richard Nixon on a goodwill tour of Latin America, but the vice president encountered only hostile crowds shouting anti-American slogans. In 1960, Adlai Stevenson visited Latin America and reported that feelings there were inspired not by communism, as the administration believed, but by the U.S. tendency to support "hated dictators" and exploitive business interests. A revolution in Cuba brought the point closer to home.

On January 1, 1959, Fidel Castro climaxed a long guerrilla campaign with a triumphant entry into Havana, and Cuba's right-wing dictator, Fulgencio Batista, fled into exile. American opinion generally favored Castro as a force of democracy in the hemisphere, and the administration cautiously recognized his government. In May 1959, Cuba enacted agrarian reform laws that confiscated some American properties. Eisenhower promptly cut off aid and demanded compensation. Through the rest of that year, Castro's rhetoric became more anti-American, and in February of 1960 he arranged for the sale of sugar to the Soviet Union in exchange for economic and military assistance. Eisenhower ordered a cut in American sugar purchases from Cuba, which made Castro even more dependent on the Soviet Union, and in January 1961 Eisenhower severed diplomatic relations. At that point it mattered little whether Castro was a Communist: He had become an enemy.

Eisenhower spent his last months in office trying to find a way to ease the tensions of the Cold War; he clearly wanted to retire in the role of the great peacemaker. In 1958 he announced that the United States was ending further nuclear testing, and after conducting a final series of tests, the Soviet Union followed suit. The following year, when Nikita Khrushchev, taking advantage of the supposed Russian superiority in ICBMs, ordered the Western allies to leave Berlin within six months, Eisenhower invited the Soviet leader to visit the United States. After a whirlwind tour of

the country, which included a denunciation of bourgeois morality on a Hollywood movie set, an angry outburst at being barred from visiting Disneyland because his safety could not be guaranteed, and a wide-eyed tour of an Iowa corn farm, he met with Eisenhower at the president's mountain retreat, Camp David. Although no progress was made on the question of Berlin, Khrushchev agreed to withdraw his time limit on Western evacuation of the city, and Eisenhower agreed to a summit conference to try to resolve the Berlin question.

Buoyed by this limited success in dealing with the Russians—reporters found in it a "spirit of Camp David"—Eisenhower embarked on an international goodwill tour. In December 1959, he flew around the world, visiting eleven countries from India to Spain. Although he returned with nothing to show except assurances that the world desired peace, Americans responded enthusiastically to his mission. In January the Gallup poll reported that 71 percent of the people approved of the way he was doing his job, his highest confidence rating in three years.

Then disaster befell him once again. On May 5, 1960, only days before the summit conference was scheduled to begin in Paris, Khrushchev announced that the Soviet Union had shot down a U-2, a high-altitude American spy plane. The administration put out the word that it was a weather plane which had drifted off course, whereupon the Soviets produced the pilot, Francis Gary Powers, who confessed on Soviet television that he was employed by the CIA. Eisenhower then disclaimed knowledge of the spy flights, but backtracked when he realized that this implied subordinates were running the administration. At last he bared his breast, acknowledged that U-2s had been flying over the Soviet Union for some years gathering pictorial intelligence, and defended them as an outgrowth of his 1955 "open skies" proposal. He went on to say that the overflights would continue.

The last statement was the blunder. Khrushchev might have accepted a shrug, a sheepish grin, and a promise not to do it again. But he could not accept a public threat of future overflights—it was an intolerable affront to Russian pride. He went to the Paris conference, harangued the American delegation, and stomped out. The conference broke up in confusion.

Thereafter everything got out of hand. In midsummer the Japanese canceled an Eisenhower goodwill trip to their country on the grounds that they could not guarantee his safety. In June, Khrushchev threatened to sign a separate peace with East Germany, thereby reviving the Berlin crisis because access to Berlin would then be in the hands of the East Germans. In July,

Castro threatened to seize all American-owned property in Cuba in retaliation for U.S. "economic aggression," and Eisenhower countered by cutting sugar imports from Cuba by 95 percent. Khrushchev pledged to defend Cuba with Soviet missiles and claimed that the Monroe Doctrine had died a "natural death." So completely did Khrushchev dominate events that in December *Time* magazine named him "man of the year."

The succession of diplomatic crises served as backdrop for the 1960 presidential election. One of the candidates for the Democratic nomination, Senator John F. Kennedy of Massachusetts, promised to "get the country moving again." The promise had strong appeal. To many Americans, it seemed that the nation had been drifting aimlessly for too long.

SUMMARY

Government spending and full employment during the war combined to pull the United States out of the Depression. The gross national product in 1945 stood at $211 billion, double the 1929 figure, and nearly all the increase had come during the war years. Racial minorities and women were still generally at the bottom of the economic ladder, but they too benefited immensely from the war experience in new employment opportunities. By the end of the war, women made up a third of the domestic labor force. Blacks for the first time began to find their way into white-collar jobs and the professions. Racial bias persisted, however, even while whites were repudiating Nazism. It was most evident in the wartime internment of the Pacific Coast Japanese and in the race riots triggered by the movement of black workers into northern cities.

Demobilization in 1945 brought social stresses, just as it had in 1919. The end of wartime price controls led to inflation, and price increases fostered labor unrest. The wave of strikes helped cause a political backlash, and in 1946 the Republicans captured control of Congress for the first time since 1930. For the next two years Congress pecked away at the New Deal, eliminating some agencies and consolidating others. Among its achievements were the National Security Act (1947), which established the Department of Defense and the CIA, and the Taft-Hartley Act (1947), which limited the power of labor unions and set up machinery for settling strikes in key industries.

Truman's upset victory in 1948 paved the way for the Fair Deal. A continuation of the New Deal, Truman's Fair Deal involved added social security benefits, an expanded federal housing program, and high price supports for farmers. Innovations that would have gone beyond the New Deal, such as national health insurance and federal aid to education, failed to clear Congress. One of Truman's most significant accomplishments was in the field of civil rights, where he ordered the desegregation of the armed forces. More might have been accomplished but for the onset of the Korean war and the rise of McCarthyism, which together ended the Fair Deal.

For a full year after Eisenhower's election in 1952, Senator McCarthy dominated the headlines. Eisenhower seemed determined to give McCarthy enough rope to hang himself, which the senator eventually did by attacking the U.S. Army in the spring of 1954. The televised Army-McCarthy hearings exposed McCarthy for the shallow bully he was and ended his witchhunt.

The end of the Korean war and the fall of McCarthy reduced both international and domestic tensions, and the national mood shifted in the mid-1950s to one of relaxed pleasure-seeking. A baby boom, the flight of white society to the suburbs, and the entry of married women into the labor force were the major social trends of the decade. The advent of television and rhythm-and-blues music (rock and roll) were the most important cultural developments. Eisenhower's personality and leadership style suited the times: He offered

solidity and integrity without any discomfiting ideology. He governed, in part, by avoiding controversial issues, and that left important problems to be resolved by a later decade. An example of this is civil rights, a problem brought to public attention by the Supreme Court's 1954 school desegregation decision (*Brown* v. *Board of Education*). White southerners fought judicial efforts to implement the decision throughout the decade, while Eisenhower remained aloof until his authority itself was challenged by the governor of Arkansas in the Little Rock crisis of 1957.

Eisenhower's reelection victory over Democrat Adlai Stevenson in 1956 was the high point of his presidency. Thereafter his political acumen, as well as his luck, gave out. The Soviet launching of an artificial satellite in September 1957 was a severe blow to America's pride and prestige. A mood of doubt and self-criticism seized Americans, as they questioned their educational system, their consumption habits, even their moral fiber. Then came a string of disasters abroad: Fidel Castro's takeover of Cuba in 1959, the downing of a U-2 spyplane over the Soviet Union in May 1960, and the subsequent failure of the Paris summit conference. The president, who aged visibly in his second term, seemed lethargic and bewildered. By 1960 many Americans were ready to listen to the voice of a young Democratic candidate for president, John F. Kennedy, who promised to "get the country moving again."

READING SUGGESTIONS

A lengthy but entertaining overview of this period is William Manchester, *The Glory and the Dream: A Narrative History of America, 1932–1972* (1974). Briefer, and also entertaining, is Eric F. Goldman, *The Crucial Decade—and After, 1945–1960* (1961). A good introduction to the

Truman presidency can be found in Robert J. Donovan's two popularly written volumes: *Conflict and Crisis: The Presidency, 1945–1948* (1977), and *Tumultuous Years: The Presidency of Harry S Truman, 1949–1953* (1982). Also recommended is *Seeds of Repression, Harry S Truman and the*

Origins of McCarthyism (1971) by Athan Theoharis. The best study of McCarthy is Thomas
C. Reeves, *The Life and Times of Joe McCarthy*
(1982).

The best survey of the social and cultural
changes of the fifties is Douglas T. Miller and
Marion Nowak, *The Fifties: The Way We Really
Were* (1977). Also useful is Paul A. Carter's *Another Part of the Fifties* (1983). The dominant social trend of the decade is explored by Kenneth
T. Jackson in *Crabgrass Frontier: The Suburban-
ization of the United States* (1985). The changing
role of women and the family during and after
the war is chronicled in Sheila M. Rothman,
*Woman's Proper Place: A History of Changing Ideals
and Practices, 1870 to the Present* (1978); Carl
N. Degler, *At Odds* (1980); and William H.
Chafe, *The American Woman: Her Changing Social, Economic, and Political Role, 1920–1970*
(1972). The beginnings of the civil rights movement can be traced in Benjamin Muse, *Ten Years
of Prelude: The Story of Integration since the Supreme Court 1954 Decision* (1964).

The Eisenhower presidency has yet to be
mined very deeply by historians. A judicious
but unimaginative survey is Charles C. Alexander, *Holding the Line: The Eisenhower Era, 1952–
1961* (1975). George B. Nash explores the intellect of the time in *The Conservative Intellectual
Movement in America since 1945* (1976). Paul L.
Murphy, *The Constitution in Crisis Times, 1918–
1969* (1972), puts the Warren Court in historical
perspective. A recent biography of the Chief
Justice is G. Edward White's *Earl Warren: A Public Life* (1982). Richard H. Pells, *The Liberal Mind
in a Conservative Age: American Intellectuals in the
1940s and 1950s* (1985), finds the roots of the
"New Left" in the 1950s.

15

Frederic Lewis.

THE TURBULENT
SIXTIES

He had worn a silk top hat in the slow ride with Eisenhower down Pennsylvania Avenue in the open limousine. But now he stood bareheaded, hair tousled by the wind, an image of youth (he was age 43) and vitality. It was January 20, 1961. President John F. Kennedy was delivering his inaugural address. "Let the word go forth," he declared, "that the torch has been passed to a new generation of Americans—born in this century, tempered by war, disciplined by a hard and bitter peace, proud of our ancient heritage." He had been elected on the promise that he would "get the country moving again," and to that end he demanded national sacrifice. "Ask not what your country can do for you," he advised Americans, "—ask what you can do for your country." As a people, he said, we must be willing to "pay any price" to force the Soviets to retreat in Europe.

His was the summons of the warrior, a call for individual sacrifice to the goal of collective strength. It was a spine-tingling reiteration of the dream of "an American century." And it dealt exclusively with foreign policy and the Cold War. Khrushchev's 1959 declaration, "We will bury you," was still ringing in American ears. The Soviet premier intended the remark as a reaffirmation of the classic Marxist principle that communism would inevitably triumph over capitalism (a forecast reinforced by post–World War II statistics on Soviet economic growth), but most Americans took it as a Cold War challenge. John F. Kennedy's call for heroic sacrifice thus hit a responsive chord.

⊔Kennedy:
The New Frontier

Kennedy's victory over Richard Nixon in 1960 was a close one. Of nearly 69 million ballots, Kennedy won by 118,000, a margin of one-tenth of 1 percent. A switch of only 35,000 votes in Illinois and Texas would have elected Nixon. The election was close largely because no issue of substance separated the candidates in the campaign. In nationally televised debates—the first ever in an American presidential election—the two candidates agreed that economic growth and aid to the poor were desirable and that the nation must reassert itself in the Cold War. Nixon was somewhat more warlike in his determination to defend Chiang Kai Shek's island outposts in the Formosa Strait, while Kennedy emerged more bellicose on the subject of Cuba. Kennedy also criticized Eisenhower's defense budgets and promised to expand the nation's military strength.

CLIMAX OF THE COLD WAR

Beneath the subtle nuances that distinguished Nixon's and Kennedy's positions on foreign policy lay a fierce ideological struggle over national priorities that had been going on for some years. Some military leaders, among them Army General Maxwell Taylor, had been arguing that the Eisenhower-Dulles strategy of massive retaliation was too limiting, that the nation needed to build up its conventional arms to fight "brushfire" wars and counteract guerrilla activity, especially in the Third World. Kennedy, who held the Cold War assumption that communism was a worldwide "monolithic and ruthless conspiracy," endorsed this amendment to the Eisenhower-Dulles strategy. And he did so without abandoning the concept of massive retaliation. Shortly after he entered office, Kennedy learned that the "missile gap"—on which Democrats had made political capital since Sputnik soared into the heavens—never existed. The United States and the Soviet Union had a rough parity in

(*Chapter opening photo*) College students burning draft cards during the Vietnam war.

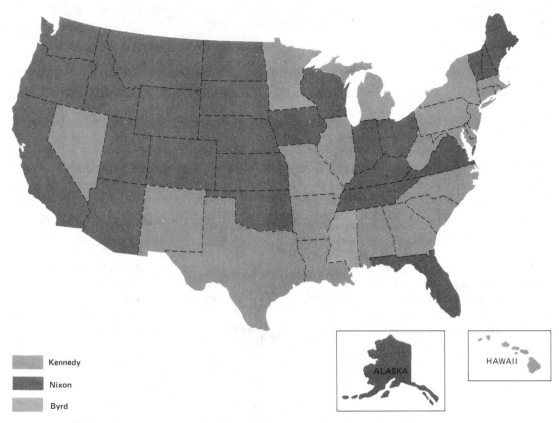

Kennedy

Nixon

Byrd

ALASKA

HAWAII

Election of 1960.

missiles in 1960, and because of Eisenhower's last-minute appropriations, the United States would soon have a clear lead. After silencing Pentagon officials who were prepared to make this news public, Kennedy asked Congress for a special appropriation of $2.4 billion earmarked for missiles. A month later, in May 1961, he requested additional appropriations for conventional weapons. The buildup continued, and by the end of the decade the American military arsenal included 1,000 nuclear-armed intercontinental missiles and 70 nuclear-powered and armed submarines. The nation's explosive power was the equivalent of fifteen tons of TNT for every person in the world. And there was once again rough parity with the Soviet Union, which had responded to the American arms buildup with a buildup of its own.

The Cuban situation presented Kennedy with an early opportunity to recover the initiative in the Cold War. During his last days in office, Eisenhower had severed relations with Cuba and allowed the CIA to plot Castro's overthrow. The intelligence agency, which had scored political coups in Guatemala and Iran earlier in the 1950s, was eager for the job. As a result of interviews with Cuban refugees, the CIA was convinced that Castro was not popular with the Cuban people and that the appearance of an opposition force would occasion a general uprising. It began training Cuban exiles at secret bases in Guatemala. Told of the scheme when he took office, Kennedy gave it his approval.

The result was disaster. On April 17, 1961, the CIA, with monumental ineptitude, landed its Cuban brigade on a beach at the Bay of Pigs, a site so remote from Cuba's major population centers that the landing had no chance of triggering a popular uprising. Its one supply ship was blasted out of the water by Castro's sixplane air force, which the CIA's agents had failed to destroy. Castro himself directed the counterattack that surrounded the beachhead. When Kennedy refused to risk open war by sending in American air support, the mission was doomed. Of 1,500 invaders, only 300 escaped into the hills; the rest were captured and later ransomed to the United States for drugs and medicines.

The failure of the Cuban people to rise up against their government ought to have sparked some discussion within the administration, but it did not. Instead, Kennedy blamed the fiasco in part on American newspapers that had broken the story of the Guatemalan training camps (implying that Castro was dependent for his strategic intelligence on the *New York Times*) and called for greater "self-discipline" among Americans to "match the iron discipline" of the Communists around the world. Ever-pleased with a good try, Americans supported the president's Cuban venture by a margin of two to one.

Despite the bravado, Kennedy was acutely aware that he had failed to get the country "moving." His arms buildup, which was accelerated after the Cuban fiasco, was a long-term project with few visible results. For the moment, its chief dividend was to enable him to negotiate from strength. "We arm to parley," Winston Churchill had phrased it. In his inaugural address Kennedy had declared: "Let us never negotiate out of fear. But let us never fear to negotiate." In this spirit he agreed to meet Nikita Khrushchev in Vienna in June 1961.

The focus of the meeting was the three-power outpost of West Berlin (governed by the United States, Britain, and France) situated in the heart of Communist East Germany. A relic of the wartime conferences that had set up Allied zones of occupation in Germany, West Berlin had become a thriving commercial center with the assistance of massive transfusions of money from West Germany. Although the city had no military significance, it was an embarrassment to the Communists. East Germans by the thousands (a total of 3 million from 1949 to 1961) crossed into West Berlin seeking refuge and better living conditions ("voting with their feet," as American authorities put it). The exodus was not only a standing rebuke to communism, it drained East Germany of its best-educated people. In Eisenhower's last year of office, Khrushchev proposed that the Western powers sign a peace treaty formally ending World War II, recognizing the sovereignty of the two Germanys, and ending the military occupation of Berlin. If the Western allies refused, Khrushchev threatened to sign a separate treaty with East Germany, which presumably would leave that regime in charge of the access routes to West Berlin. The United States, Britain, and France would then have to abandon West Berlin or, by negotiating access to the city, grant recognition, in effect, to the East German government.

Kennedy and Khrushchev got along badly at Vienna. Khrushchev had been issuing inflated claims of Communist superiority for years; Kennedy was determined to yield nothing. On his return, Kennedy made a grim television broadcast in which he declared his willingness to fight if necessary, and asked Congress for additional military appropriations. He mobilized military reserves and ordered an armored unit stationed in West Germany to travel the highway corridor into West Berlin. In August 1961, Soviets and East Germans erected a cement-block wall between East and West Berlin to stem the flow of refugees. Although it was not immediately apparent, that action defused the crisis. During the autumn, Khrushchev silently abandoned his plans for a separate treaty with East Germany. Republicans considered the Berlin Wall a defeat for Kennedy, but it was nothing of the kind. It was, and is, a monument to the inadequacies of communism.

Both sides handled the crisis badly, which added to the public confusion and alarm. Right in the middle, Khrushchev announced that the Soviet Union was ending the three-year moratorium on nuclear testing, and a week later Kennedy declared the United States had "no other choice" but to resume testing itself. He followed that up by recommending the construction of a nationwide system of fallout shelters. A confused public debate ensued as scientists argued over survival statistics[*] and church leaders discussed the morality of shelter owners having to shoot neighbors to prevent overcrowding.

More disturbing, in retrospect, was the Kennedy style of diplomacy the crisis revealed. Instead of approaching the Soviet challenge with multiple options among which force was the last, from the outset Kennedy made it a test of will backed by force, a confrontation in which one side or the other had to back down. This was a very dangerous sort of diplomacy for a nuclear age. Some would say it was not diplomacy at all, but a game of "chicken."[**]

Kennedy's tendency toward diplomacy by confrontation was even more evident in the Cuban missile crisis, a year later.

MISSILE CRISIS AND TEST-BAN TREATY

A missile gap brought on the Cuban affair—not the one so much discussed during the election of 1960, but the reverse, the gap of American superiority over the Soviets. Americans led the Soviet Union in intercontinental missiles at the time of Kennedy's election, and Kennedy's military buildup widened the lead. In addition, the United States, in the wake of Sputnik, had placed intermediate-range missiles in Italy and Turkey. Khrushchev countered with a missile program of his own, and while that was getting started he decided to offset the American advantage by placing some intermediate-range missiles in Cuba. A further advantage, from the Soviet point of view, was that missiles would bolster the Castro regime and deter an American invasion.

During the summer of 1962, the Soviets began constructing launching sites in Cuba. Cuban refugees leaked the first word of these preparations, and photographs taken by U-2 spyplanes confirmed the existence of the bases. Two of Kennedy's options were military invasion, advocated by the military, and a missile swap—Americans removing their obsolete missiles from Turkey in exchange for Soviet withdrawal from Cuba. Kennedy opted for a third strategy that kept open the other two. On October 22, 1962, he went on nationwide television to explain the situation to the American people. Proclaiming his readiness for war if necessary, he demanded an immediate "elimination" of the Soviet bases and proclaimed a naval "quarantine" (in effect, a blockade) to prevent missiles from reaching Cuba. Shortly thereafter the U.S. Navy announced that Soviet vessels,

---

[*] Dr. Willard Libby, holder of a Nobel prize in chemistry, claimed that 90 to 95 percent of Americans could survive an atomic war in modest shelters, such as the one he had built in his backyard. His argument was somewhat weakened, however, when his backyard shelter was destroyed by a brushfire.

[**] "Chicken" was an adolescent automobile game in which two drivers drove head-on until one swerved to avoid a collision.

UPI/Bettmann.
President Kennedy during the Cuban Missile Crisis.

presumed to be carrying missiles, had been spotted in the mid-Atlantic heading toward Cuba. It was the most dangerous moment of the Cold War.

Kennedy acted without consulting with Congress, the Western allies,* or the United Nations. Kennedy, in fact, rebuffed a UN proposal for a moratorium on the blockade to give time for private negotiations. Khrushchev was dumbfounded. He,

---

* In the wake of the crisis, French President Charles de Gaulle withdrew from NATO's unified military command and attempted to build a separate understanding with the Soviet Union. In the early 1980s, French politicians, defending their support for a gas pipeline linking the Soviet Union and Western Europe, cited de Gaulle's tradition of independence from the United States.

after all, had accepted the presence of American missiles on his Turkish border with only modest protest. He denounced Kennedy's blockade-backed ultimatum as "outright banditry," but he could not, would not, risk war. In a conciliatory letter, Khrushchev offered to remove the missiles from Cuba if the United States would end the blockade and agree to respect Cuban independence. The next day, however, he sent a second, stiffer message demanding the removal of American missiles in Turkey in exchange for those in Cuba.

On the suggestion of Attorney General Robert Kennedy, the president's brother, Kennedy responded to the first letter and ignored the second. He agreed to lift the blockade if the Soviets would remove the missiles (in effect, making no concession at all) and made no mention of Turkish bases. The world waited breathlessly, aware that it teetered on the edge of nuclear holocaust. Then the word went out from Moscow, and the Soviet vessels turned around short of the American blockade. "We're eyeball to eyeball," said Secretary of State Dean Rusk, "and I think the other fellow just blinked." After tensions subsided, Kennedy quietly removed the outmoded American missiles in Turkey. Having proved himself the better warrior, Kennedy could afford to be discretely gracious.

The glimpse of holocaust in fact sobered both sides. Within the Soviet Union, Khrushchev was criticized first for initiating the crisis and then for failing to see it through. (The criticism would contribute to his fall from power a year later.) In December 1962, the Soviet leader suggested that the two nations end further nuclear testing. Kennedy was receptive. "One mistake," he had conceded after the Cuban crisis, "can make this whole thing blow up." And on-site inspection, which the Soviets had always resisted as a form of espionage, became irrelevant when American scientists convinced Kennedy that nuclear blasts could be monitored by the same instruments used to detect earthquakes around the world. In June 1963, Kennedy announced the suspension of atmospheric tests as an act of "good faith," and a month later negotiators in Moscow initialed a treaty banning nuclear tests in the atmosphere.

It was a limited step (Kennedy actually increased underground tests to appease conservatives and the military), but an extremely significant one. It was the first formal Soviet-American agreement of the Cold War. It was followed by an agreement to establish a "hot line" telephone between Moscow and Washington to improve communications in time of crisis and lessen the chance of error. Later that year Kennedy announced that the United States would sell surplus wheat to the Soviet Union, a move that not only benefited American farmers, but improved the chances of peace through mutual interdependence. With this series of agreements, the Cold War entered a new phase, described in the language of diplomacy as *détente*.*

SOUTHEAST ASIA

On the other side of the world, Kennedy's policies went through a similar cycle, from confrontation to accommodation. On turning over the reins of power to Kennedy, Eisenhower apologized for the "mess" in Laos, a section of former French Indochina. Though not acknowledged by Eisenhower, neighboring South Vietnam was also a "mess." By 1960, both countries were embroiled in civil war.

The Geneva treaties that had ended the first Vietnam war had called for popular elections within two years to unify North and South Vietnam, after which the French were to evacuate their forces from their one-time colony. Fearing that the Communists might win, the Eisenhower administration encouraged the South Vietnamese premier, Ngo Dinh Diem, to block the elections. When the French withdrew, the United States became the financial and military prop of the South Vietnamese regime. But Diem's government became increasingly unpopular. Diem was American-educated, Roman Catholic, and allied with the country's landlords; he was ruling a people who were mainly Buddhist peasants. By 1958, guerrilla activities against the regime had begun, and in 1960 the National Liberation Front, or Vietcong, an alliance of nationalists and Communists, was formed. Civil war broke out in Laos between the Pathet Lao, an odd assortment of peasants,

---

* A French word, *détente* has no precise English equivalent. It means a relaxation, particularly of strained relations between nations.

schoolteachers, and pro–North Vietnamese Communists, and the Royal Laotian Army, which was largely trained and financed by the American CIA.

Kennedy inherited an Eisenhower plan to intervene in Laos, and for a time he gave it serious consideration. Viewing the conflict in Laos not as a local dispute but as a Cold War confrontation, he warned that "outside" forces were menacing that "independent country." Secretary of Defense Robert McNamara, however, informed him that American conventional forces were not yet strong enough for "brushfire wars." While Kennedy wavered, the Soviets suggested reconvening the Geneva conference. Kennedy agreed, negotiations began, and on July 21, 1962, agreement was reached in Geneva on a neutralized Laos, with a government that included the Royal Army and the Pathet Lao under a neutralist premier. The coalition soon collapsed and fighting resumed, but by then attention had shifted to South Vietnam.

By 1962 the South Vietnamese regime of Ngo Dinh Diem was clearly on the defensive. The Vietcong were in control of large chunks of countryside, and the Vietnamese army units lay huddled in the cities. Whenever the army ventured into the jungle, it was chewed up by guerrillas. President Eisenhower had sent in some American soldiers (disguised as civilians because the 1954 Geneva Accords prohibited foreign military units in Vietnam) to train the South Vietnamese in counterinsurgency. Kennedy increased the number of advisers and eventually sent Special Forces units (Green Berets) to fight the guerrillas on their own terms. By improving the American army's capacity for fighting conventional wars, Kennedy had made intervention not only possible, but tempting.

By mid-1963, however, the president was undergoing a change of heart. He still subscribed to the domino theory, maintaining that American withdrawal "would mean a collapse not only of South Vietnam, but Southeast Asia." But he had also come to view the conflict in political terms. He was urging Diem to undertake political and economic reforms that would improve his popularity among the peasants. In September 1963, Kennedy acknowledged that the United States could not win the war for the Vietnamese. "In the final analysis," he said, "it is their war." That was two months before he died. Whether he would have taken the next step—a negotiated, political solution to the war—can only be guessed.

A BASIC CONSERVATISM

In accepting the Democratic presidential nomination, Kennedy talked of the challenges facing Americans and called for a resurrection of the frontier spirit. The phrase "new frontier" caught on, though as a description of Kennedy's domestic program it was almost meaningless. Even so, that program was both sweeping and imaginative. It built on Truman's Fair Deal, with proposals for federal aid to education and federally subsidized health insurance, and went beyond it. To cure chronic unemployment, Kennedy proposed a manpower training program to help the unemployed develop new skills. He also suggested a Peace Corps, modeled on Roosevelt's Civilian Conservation Corps, to provide teachers and technicians for developing countries in the Third World.

With the exception of the Peace Corps (which Congress saw as a way of battling Third World communism), every one of Kennedy's proposals sank in the mire of congressional conservatism. The Democrats still had majorities in both houses of Congress, but control of that body was in the hands of a coalition of Republicans and southern Democrats. When Kennedy was urged to go over Congress's head and take his program to the people, an aide said:

"The President feels that there is never an appropriate time for opening a cold war with Congress."

While Congress would not appropriate money for domestic programs, it was willing to spend funds for the exploration of outer space. Space not only had a romance of its own, but in the aftermath of Sputnik it was a field of Cold War competition. The administration assumed that the Soviets planned eventually to place a man on the moon, and another technological "first" would have been a shattering blow to American pride—with inevitable voter repercussions. So in the late spring of 1961, with the New Frontier bogged in a congressional quagmire, Kennedy announced a manned space program with the objective of placing an astronaut on the moon by the end of the decade. It was a stunt born of patriotism rather than science, since most scientists agreed that instrumented exploration provided greater rewards for money expended. The public, humiliated by Sputnik and alarmed by talk of a missile gap, accepted the decision enthusiastically. Only former president Eisenhower sounded a sour note. Said he: "Anybody who would spend $40 billion in a race to the moon for national prestige is nuts." Had they been consulted, some of the poor in the nation's dilapidated cities might have agreed.

Beneath the liberal veneer there was a fundamental conservatism to the Kennedy administration. The men closest to the president were essentially technicians, schooled in the art of scientific management and closely tied to the eastern business establishment. Secretary of State Dean Rusk came to his post from the Ford Foundation. Defense Secretary Robert McNamara, an expert in scientific management, had been president of the Ford Motor Company. Treasury Secretary Douglas Dillon was a Wall Street financier who had served in the Eisenhower administration. Prominent liberals in the Democratic party, such as Adlai Stevenson and John Kenneth Galbraith, were buried in diplomatic posts (Stevenson in the UN, Galbraith in India).

Far from a break with the Eisenhower consensus, the Kennedy administration was a continuation of it. Nowhere was this more apparent than in the cozy relationship between government and business. During the Eisenhower years American corporations, working through foreign subsidiaries, had gone far toward "Americanizing" the rest of the planet. By the end of the 1960s, American corporations controlled 80 percent of Europe's computer business, three-fourths of the world's oil, and half of all the modern industry in Great Britain. Foreign aid, which had begun as a device for battling communism in the 1940s, became a source of corporate prosperity in the 1950s and 1960s. A "buy American" clause, added to the foreign aid program in 1968, meant that four-fifths of all overseas assistance came back to the United States through the purchase of American products. Government loans to developing countries through such agencies as the Export-Import Bank and the Agency for International Development (AID) not only opened new markets for American corporations, but made much of the Third World financially dependent on the United States.

Foreign aid, particularly in Latin America, went to the training of military and police units that kept conservative elites in power and preserved a friendly environment for American investments. In this area too, Kennedy's rhetoric soared higher than his record. In his inaugural address he called for "a new alliance for progress" between the United States and Latin America. In what the president described as "a vast cooperative effort," Kennedy envisioned land reform and political democracy in Latin America, aided by American technology and funding. Congress in 1961 appropriated several billion dollars for the program, but its conservative administrators had no intention of stirring up social change in the impoverished region. Instead, they worked through established elites, as in the past, and the alliance soon floundered.

WHITE VS. BLACK

Kennedy's fundamental conservatism was also evident in his attitude toward black civil rights, though on this issue, as in his foreign policy, he grew more flexible, more liberal, as time passed. Although he appointed more blacks to government positions than any previous president, he shared Eisenhower's perception that racial brotherhood could not be forced on the country. He and Attorney General Robert Kennedy aimed only to enforce the voting rights legislation of 1957 and 1960 by filing suits on behalf of aggrieved blacks, in the hope that once blacks got the vote in the South, other segregationist barriers would fall.

Such a policy was too slow and too paternalistic for blacks, who had already won important gains through bus boycotts and sit-ins. In the summer of 1961 the Congress of Racial Equality (CORE) began a series of "freedom rides" through the South to force integration of transportation facilities. Whites responded violently, and the attorney general suggested a "cooling off period." "We had been cooling off for 100 years," protested CORE's James Farmer. "If we got any cooler we'd be in a deep freeze." Working behind the scenes, Robert Kennedy did wheedle a ruling out of the Interstate Commerce Commission that prohibited segregation in interstate travel. But the administration continued to drift from one crisis to another.

Blacks' efforts to help themselves triggered white violence, and white violence ultimately forced the president's hand. In the summer of 1962, federal courts ordered the University of Mississippi to admit James Meredith, a black Air Force veteran. Governor Ross Barnett defied the order and encouraged white vigilantes to attack Meredith and his escort of 400 federal marshals, sent into Mississippi by Robert Kennedy. Meredith was enrolled, but at the price of 2 people dead and 375 injured. In February 1963, President Kennedy at last proposed a new civil rights bill. The heart of it was quicker prosecution of voting rights violations and provision of federal funds for school desegregation. Unmentioned was the broader problem of discrimination in hotels, restaurants, and factories.

To alert the Kennedys and white liberals generally to the shortcomings in their approach, Martin Luther King, Jr., in the spring of 1963 carried his civil rights crusade to Birmingham, Alabama, "the most thoroughly segregated big city" in the nation. Through boycotts, sit-ins, and demonstrations, King hoped to bring about enough "creative tension" to make white businessmen yield. Police authorities responded instead with clubs, fire hoses, and dogs, all well recorded on television. In June, Governor George Wallace of Alabama (the only state in which no black attended any public school with whites) literally stood "in the schoolhouse door" to prevent two black students from entering the University of Alabama. Kennedy had to place the Alabama National Guard under federal orders to protect the students and ensure their enrollment. Later that month Medgar Evers, secretary of the Mississippi NAACP, was assassinated.

Stung into action, Kennedy in June 1963 proposed a new civil rights act prohibiting racial segregation in all accommodations, and in a nationally televised speech he committed himself completely to racial equality in American society. The administration had earlier fretted about a march on Washington announced by Martin Luther King, fearing it might turn into a violent confrontation. After his June address, Kennedy welcomed the march and adroitly turned it into a demonstration of support for his civil rights bill. King cooperated: The throng of 250,000 who gathered in Washington on August 28, 1963, was a model of nonviolence. Standing in front of the Lincoln Memorial, King delivered a peroration worthy of Lincoln, Webster, or Patrick Henry. "I have a dream," he declared:

> I have a dream that one day this nation will rise up and live out the meaning of its creed: We hold these truths to be self-evident, that all men are created equal. I have a dream that . . . the sons of former slaves and the sons of former slaveowners will be able to sit together at the table of brotherhood.

But southern whites remained unmoved and northern whites were too often indifferent. Opinion polls indicated that Kennedy's stand in favor of civil rights had cost him 4.5 million white votes in the South and endangered his political future. "The issue could cost me the election," Kennedy confided to a black leader shortly before his death, "but we're not turning back."

Across the racial barriers, the rights movement had already moved ahead of the president. One bitter black commentator noted that Kennedy had visited Berlin at the height of the Berlin Wall crisis and declared, "Ich bin ein Berliner," but he had failed to visit Montgomery, Alabama, and declare "I am a nigger." While Martin Luther King organized his march on Washington in the summer of 1963, the Student Nonviolent Coordinating Committee (SNCC), a spinoff from King's organization made up mostly of black college students, organized a voter registration drive in Mississippi. White vigilantes killed five of the student leaders, three blacks and two whites. Federal authorities investigated and brought charges and then watched helplessly as southern judges threw their cases out of court for lack of evidence. The summer nightmare had a profound effect

Martin Luther King: "I Have a Dream."

UPI/Bettmann.

on students of both races. Many blacks decided they had to separate themselves from whites of all kinds. Many white students concluded that prejudice and corruption permeated American society, North as well as South. Black power, the New Left, and the counterculture of the mid-1960s were the result.

ASSASSINATION

On November 22, 1963, President John F. Kennedy was shot and killed while riding in a motorcade in downtown Dallas, Texas. A suspected assassin, Lee Harvey Oswald, was arrested, but he in turn was murdered in the Dallas police station by Jack Ruby, a nightclub owner with underworld connections. Ruby was tried and convicted, but the conviction was overturned on appeal. Ruby died before a new trial could be held. The motives of both assassins have never adequately been explained. For Americans who witnessed the president's assassination on television newsreels and the killing of Oswald on live television, it was a traumatic experience unequaled by any other event of the century. The enormity of the crime was only part of it: An image was shattered along with the man.

Kennedy had made an enormous impact on Americans in a thousand days of office. No president since Theodore Roosevelt had conveyed such youthful vitality; none since Lincoln had presented such ready wit. A master of the media, he turned press conferences into happenings as he sparred with reporters and crushed them with facts and figures recited from memory. Even his pastimes, touch football and sailing, were suffused with vigor (which Kennedy pronounced "vigah"). Then, suddenly, it was all gone, and the nation began to come apart.

⊔Johnson: The Great Society

The new president, Lyndon Johnson, was determined not only to hold the country together, but to march boldly into the future. Appearing before Congress just four days after the assassination, Johnson pled for passage of the Kennedy program. A former Senate majority leader whose congressional career went back to the days of Roosevelt, Johnson knew the art of managing Congress. He was also a masterful persuader. Under his insistent prodding, Congress broke the legislative logjam and enacted the New Frontier:

> A tax cut was designed to stimulate the economy and reduce unemployment. It did both. The years 1964 to 1967 were the longest period of sustained prosperity in the post–World War era, and in the same years both inflation and unemployment averaged below 4 percent.
>
> A Civil Rights Act (1964) provided federal aid for the desegregation of schools; it also prohibited discrimination in interstate facilities, such as hotels and restaurants, and in all but the smallest factories.
>
> Medicare (1965) provided hospital care, administered by the social security program, for Americans over age sixty-five.
>
> An Office of Economic Opportunity (OEO) was created to administer a multibillion-dollar program offering loans and grants to communities that had developed plans for improving themselves. The same legislation set up VISTA, a domestic peace corps, and Headstart, a program of preschool training for the children of the poor. Together, these agencies constituted what Johnson called a "war on poverty."

The problem of poverty, brought to the nation's attention by Michael Harrington's book *The Other America* (1962), had engaged Kennedy's attention in the weeks before his death, but the decision that it must be eliminated was Johnson's.

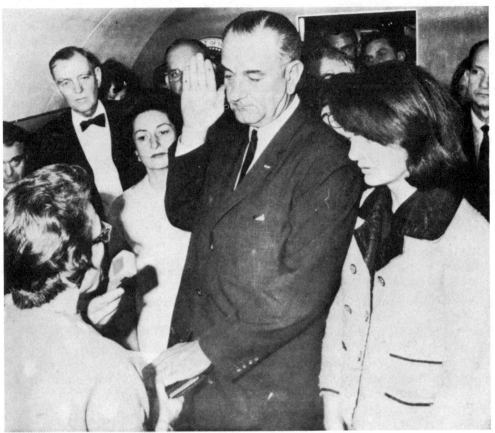

AP/Wide World Photos.

Lyndon Johnson taking the Oath of Office aboard the presidential plane. Kennedy's wife, Jacque-
lyn, stands next to him, as if to endorse the orderly transit of power.

In a commencement address at the University of Michigan in the spring of 1964, President Johnson asked all Americans to join "in the battle to build the Great Society." The label Great Society stuck as a description of Johnson's program. It was a continuation of Kennedy's, updated with recommendations for newly perceived problems, such as poverty, pollution, and urban blight. Though broad in scope, the Great Society was couched in terms of moderate progressivism. By courting conservatives with such money-saving ideas as

turning out the White House lights at night, Johnson politically straddled the middle of the road. He was left with the middle because the Republican party had steered itself to the far right.

In 1964, the Republicans nominated for president Arizona Senator Barry Goldwater, leader of the Republican remnant that had yet to come to terms with the Roosevelt revolution. In the course of the campaign Goldwater advocated selling the TVA, denounced social security, opposed civil rights, proposed giving local military commanders control over nuclear weapons, and advocated the use of nuclear devices to defoliate* the jungles of Vietnam. Instead of countering such nonsense, the Democrats publicized it and let Goldwater destroy himself. Johnson won over 61 percent of the popular vote and carried every state except five in the South and Arizona. The Democrats increased their margins in both houses of Congress and picked up over 500 seats in state legislatures. The Great Society seemed at hand. But it was not to be: Within a year, American society was tearing itself apart.

ANTIWAR PROTEST, 1964—1968: VIETNAM

"Freedom summer," the civil rights leaders called it as they prepared a new voting rights drive in Mississippi in 1964. The eight hundred white students who participated remembered it as the most exhilarating moment of their lives. But the violence and death they encountered were also a shattering experience; Mississippi violated everything they had been taught to believe or value. Their schoolbooks had assured them that in America every person had the right to vote, that in America people lived by the law and criminals were punished. Yet in Mississippi, murderers walked the streets freely and even boasted of their deeds, and those who tried to register to vote were in jail, along with many who tried to help them. They returned disillusioned with a system that could produce great wealth and material comfort, but could not handle injustice.

The colleges of the San Francisco Bay area furnished a goodly share of the stu-

dents who went to Mississippi in the summer of 1964. When the University of California at Berkeley resumed classes in September, a group of students organized a picket line outside the offices of the Oakland *Tribune* to protest the newspaper's racially discriminatory hiring practices. When executives of the paper informed the university that the picketing had been organized on university property, the university banned political recruitment and advocacy on the walkway that was a traditional center of political activism.

That action gave birth to a free speech movement, that through strikes and demonstrations eventually brought the university to a halt. In December, the university faculty yielded to the movement's demands and removed all restrictions on political activity, but by then students were questioning the larger role of the university in modern society. The university, they concluded, was not the island of free inquiry it pretended to be; it was part of "the system," wedded to corporate America by rich contracts for engineering and scientific services.

The student protest movement spread rapidly, and in the spring of 1965 there were demonstrations at a dozen schools across the country. Students protested the universities' parentlike regulations and demanded participation in administration. In March, students by the thousands flocked to Selma, Alabama, to lend support to a voting rights drive organized by Martin Luther King. Even so, in the spring of 1965 the campus revolt was ill-defined and uncoordinated, a product of frustration and disillusionment. Vietnam gave it focus.

Lyndon Johnson accepted without question the Cold War postulates that had been dictating American foreign policy since the Truman years. He considered himself in a global confrontation with international communism in which any breach in the line of containment, whether by aggression or subversion, warranted an American re-

---

*American military advisers constantly complained of the jungle canopy that hid the movements of Vietcong guerrillas from government airplanes and helicopters.

sponse. Defending his Vietnam policy after making the decision to send in American troops, he wrapped together the Munich "lesson" and Eisenhower's domino theory. "We learned from Hitler at Munich," he told a press conference, "that success only feeds the appetite of aggression. The battle would be renewed in one country and then in another country."

The military and ideological potpourri that was Vietnam simmered idly on a back burner during Johnson's first months in office, while the president concentrated on his domestic menu. In August 1964, just as the election campaign was getting under way, Vietnam came forcefully to his attention. On August 2, North Vietnamese torpedo boats allegedly struck at U.S. destroyers patroling in the Gulf of Tonkin. Johnson protested, and when he received reports of another attack two days later, he ordered air raids against torpedo bases and oil storage tanks in North Vietnam. At the same time, Johnson secured approval (by a unanimous vote in the House and an 88 to 2 vote in the Senate) of a Gulf of Tonkin Resolution empowering the president to "take all necessary measures to repel any armed attack against the forces of the United States and to prevent further aggression." The administration relied on this resolution ever after as authority for armed intervention. Johnson's response to the Tonkin Gulf incident was measured and limited, but it did signal the fact that he was prepared to use U.S. armed forces in defense of the South Vietnamese government.

The 1964 election, during which Johnson pledged again and again that he sought "no wider war," delayed further escalation. In January 1965, Johnson's chief foreign policy advisers—McGeorge Bundy, Robert McNamara, and Dean Rusk, all carryovers from the Kennedy administration—informed him that the war in Southeast Asia was going badly and that the president had to choose between "escalation and with-

drawal." The president doubtless felt he had little choice. He had confidence in American military power, and he feared a political backlash if he "lost" Vietnam. Having made his decision, he needed only an excuse. Vietcong guerrillas provided it when on the night of February 7 they sent mortar shells into a compound of American advisers in Pleiku, killing nine and wounding a hundred. Johnson ordered new air strikes against North Vietnam. The theory was that the Vietcong were dependent on the North for supplies, even though American intelligence agents reported that most VC weapons were captured from the inept South Viet army, and that "punishing" the North would induce it to halt supplies.

Intervention had a momentum of its own. In March, the first American combat troops went into South Vietnam to protect the air bases from VC attack. In April, the administration, confessing that the air war had failed to "break the enemy's will," sent in additional troops to set up coastal enclaves. In May the president was distracted by a need to intervene in the Dominican Republic to overthrow an anti-American regime that had seized power there, but by June he was concentrating again on Southeast Asia. That month American forces moved out of their enclaves and undertook the first "search and destroy" mission. In July the Joint Chiefs, which at first had thought 40,000 soldiers ample for the task, projected an American commitment of 193,000 to the war in Vietnam. That figure was reached by the end of the year. And still the war went badly.

Opposition to the war escalated right along with the troop commitments. In March 1965, just days after the first American combat marines splashed ashore, students and faculty at the University of Michigan held a teach-in that explored the origins of American involvement. The teach-in idea spread quickly to other campuses that spring and the following year.

Vietnam War

- ■ Major battles
- △ U.S. bases
- X Areas of guerrilla activity
- ▨ Communist countries
- ▦ Allied with U.S.
- ▤ Neutral countries

The Vietnam War.

By 1967, when the American troop commitment in Vietnam was approaching half a million, the peace movement too had become a small army and extended far beyond the university campuses. In April of that year, 125,000 demonstrators gathered outside the United Nations building in New York, and in October 75,000 blockaded the Pentagon. By then the nation was divided into two hostile camps, and many of those in the undecided middle disapproved of the way the president was handling the war. Johnson's popularity rating in the polls had fallen to 29 percent.

Why did the war become so terribly unpopular so swiftly? Television and news reports for one thing. People were better informed than ever before. With reality staring at them from the television screen, it was hard to romanticize the conflict. World War II had had a storybook quality because the enemy clearly deserved annihilation and the battle moved inexorably toward victory. In Vietnam the enemy was never seen, and the victims on TV news broadcasts were women and children, pathetic and frightened, often suffering from burns received during U.S. napalm raids.

Government falsehoods were another source of public disillusion with the war. Because it was a guerrilla war without defined battle lines, the Army marked its "progress" toward "victory" with "kill statis-

---

Men at War

Lieutenant Philip Caputo, U.S. Marines, was part of the first U.S. combat unit sent into Vietnam on March 8, 1965. *A Rumor of War*, the narrative of his experiences in 1965 and 1966, graphically depicts what that war did to the men who fought it—their loss of confidence, their loss of purpose, their loss of values, and ultimately their loss of humanity.

> . . . A young lieutenant in a motley uniform—Khaki shirt and green utility trousers—walked up to me and introduced himself. From D Company, he was the landing liaison officer. He asked what outfit I was from.

"That's Charley over there." He pointed to where the squad tent was going up, then shook my hand and said, "Welcome to Danang," as if I were a visiting conventioneer. In a column of twos, we trudged past a warehouse and a squadron of parked H-34 helicopters. The pilots stood watching us with an air of veteran insouciance. They were got up in Terry and Pirates costumes: camouflage uniforms, rakish bush hats, low-slung revolvers. I gathered that one of the advantages of being in Vietnam was the freedom more or less to dress as you pleased.

· · ·

Slogging back into the swamp, we saw the enemy dead lying in a neat rank, as if for an inspection. A photographer—I think he was with *Stars and Stripes*—was taking pictures of them from various angles. Amazingly, there were only four of them. *Four*. We had fought for an hour and a half, expended hundreds of rounds of small-arms ammunition, twenty mortar shells, and a full concentration of 155s to kill four men. I remarked on this to someone in company headquarters, who said, "There were a lot of pieces and blood trails around, so we estimate eight VC KIA." When I asked how that figure had been arrived at, the marine replied, "Oh, I guess somebody just counted up the arms and legs and divided by four."

· · ·

There was only a slight chance of being killed in a headquarters unit, but Sullivan probably had not felt any intimations of mortality when he walked down to that river, a string of canteens jangling in his hand. Then the sniper centered the cross-hairs on his telescopic sight, and all that Sullivan had ever been or would ever be, all his thoughts, memories, and dreams were annihilated in an instant.

· · ·

I came to understand why Lemmon and the others had seemed so distant. It had nothing to do with my no longer belonging to the battalion. It was, rather, the detachment of men who find themselves living in the presence of death. They had lost their first man in battle, and, with him, the youthful confidence of their own immortality. Reality had caught up with them, with all of us. As Bradley put it later that evening: "I guess the splendid little war is over."

· · ·

The war started at night. The eight-inch and one-fifty-five millimeter guns commenced their regular shellings, and the VC began their sniping and mortaring. Our patrols slipped down darkened trails to set ambushes or to be ambushed themselves. On the perimeters, sentries listened and looked into a blackness lighted now and then by dull flares. They waited, alternately bored and nervous, for the infiltrators who sometimes probed our lines to lob grenades over the wire or spray a position with carbine fire. They came in twos and threes, and that is how they died and how our own men died—in twos and threes. . . . Men were killed and wounded, and our patrols kept going out to fight in places they had fought the week before and the week before that. The situation remained the same. Only the numbers on the colonel's scoreboard changed.

· · ·

Everything rotted and corroded quickly over there: bodies, boot leather, canvas, metal, morals. Scorched by the sun, wracked by the wind and rain of the monsoon, fighting in alien swamps and jungles, our humanity rubbed off of us as the protective bluing rubbed off the barrels of our rifles. We were fighting in the cruelest kind of conflict, a people's war. . . . Ethics seemed to be a matter of distance and technology. You could never go wrong if you killed people at long range with sophisticated weapons. And then there was that inspiring order issued by General Greene: kill VC. In the patriotic fervor of the Kennedy years, we had asked, "What can we do for our country?" and our country answered, "Kill VC." That was the strategy, the best our best military minds could come up with: organized butchery.

· · ·

Just before the platoon resumed its march, someone found a length of electrical detonating cord lying in the grass near the village. The village would have been as likely an ambush site as any: the VC only had to press the detonator and then blend in with the civilians, if indeed there were any true civilians in the village. Or they could have hidden in one of the tunnels under the houses. All right, I thought, tit for tat. No ceasefire for us, none for you, either. I ordered both rocket launcher teams to fire white-phosphorus shells into the hamlet. They fired four altogether. The shells, flashing orange, burst into pure white clouds, the chunks of flaming phosphorus arcing over the trees. About half the village went up in flames. I could hear people yelling, and I saw several figures running through the white smoke. I did not feel a sense of vengeance, any more than I felt remorse or regret. I did not even feel angry. Listening to the shouts and watching the people running out of their burning homes, I did not feel anything at all.

Philip Caputo, *A Rumor of War* (New York: Holt, Rinehart and Winston, 1977), pp. 52, 126, 162, 192, 229–230, 284–285. Reprinted with permission.

---

tics." The justification for American intervention was that the United States was aiding a free democratic regime that had the support of most of its people, and that the Vietcong were an assortment of malcontents reinforced by infiltration from the North. If the malcontents could be wiped out and the infiltration halted by air raids, the war would end, went the official reasoning. Thus "body counts" told the fortunes of war. When the numbers of VC continued to increase, the Army, still unwilling to admit that the guerrillas might be recruiting among the South Vietnamese

An American infantry adviser alongside South Vietnamese troops, 1964.

The Bettmann Archives, Inc.

peasantry, claimed the increase was due to infiltration from the North. Skeptical journalists began talking of a "credibility gap" between government reports and the reality of the situation.

President Johnson underestimated the economic cost of the war as badly as he miscalculated the political cost. In January 1966, Johnson went before Congress to sketch his domestic program and at the same time ask for supplementary appropriations to finance the war. "I believe," he said, "that we can continue the Great Society while we fight in Vietnam." It had been an article of faith among liberals that the United States could meet its obligations abroad while promoting social welfare at home. As heir to that faith, Johnson had no reason to question it. The nation could afford, as he put it, "both guns and butter."

He was sadly wrong. Congress seized upon the president's optimism and levied no war taxes until 1967. To meet the rising costs of the war, it skimped on domestic programs. The Office of Economic Opportunity, centerpiece of the war on poverty, lost its funds, its impetus, and ultimately its idealists. By the end of Johnson's term, it was just another Washington bureau. The government debt mushroomed, and a cycle of deficits and inflation began that would plague the nation into the 1980s.

FROM CIVIL RIGHTS TO BLACK POWER

Foreign war and domestic violence went hand in hand, though there was not always a causal connection between the two. In August 1965, a subdivision of Los Angeles known as Watts, a black ghetto, exploded into five days of violence. Police and national guardsmen moved in, and when it was over, 34 were dead, 4,000 were under arrest, and much of Watts was in ashes. "We won," a black adolescent told a puzzled Martin Luther King, who was touring

the smoke-blackened streets a few days after it ended. "We won," he explained, "because we made them pay attention to us." A black political leader described it as a "tremendous community tantrum." Blacks, he said, had seen the nation become concerned over discrimination "over there" in Alabama and Mississippi while it ignored what was going on in Watts. Their schools were wretched, their streets filthy, their police force predominantly white and openly bigoted, and neither city nor federal government seemed to care. In the view of black militants, the president talked of urban poverty and sank his money into Southeast Asia.

Like the antiwar movement, the spirit of urban violence spread. The following year, 1966, there were riots in Cleveland, Chicago, and Atlanta. In 1967, 127 cities experienced racial violence, with 77 people killed and more than 4,000 injured. In Detroit, scene of the worst rioting, it took a force of 15,000 federal troops to restore order, the largest force ever assembled to suppress domestic violence in America. The urban rage made the 1960s the most violent decade since the Civil War, but there was a difference from earlier forms of violence. In the past, black had fought against white; in the '60s, blacks fought their environment. Whites, who found themselves in the middle of an uprising, were jostled and cursed and some had their cars tipped over, but few were battered or injured. Nearly all the casualties were black, victims of white police who in some cities fired into the mobs.

The shift in battleground from rural South to urban North made the issues more complex. In the South, the demands of the civil rights movement for open ballots and open schools could be met by changes in the law, and the changes did not immediately threaten the interests of the southern white majority, however reluctant that element might be to concede them. In the North, blacks were demand-

CLIO'S FOCUS: The Movement

Sometimes a story is best told by its participants. The following documents were selected to illustrate the curious mixture of attitudes, emotions, experience, and ideology that made up the antiwar, antiprejudice, anticapital, anti-Establishment protest of the 1960s, which its adherents referred to simply as "the movement."

The Student Nonviolent Coordinating Committee (SNCC), which ultimately became one of the core organizations of the movement, began placidly enough, as indicated by its founding statement of April 1960:

> We affirm the philosophical or religious ideal of nonviolence as the foundation of our purpose, the presupposition of our belief, and the manner of our action.
> Nonviolence, as it grows from the Judeo-Christian tradition, seeks a social order of justice permeated by love. Integration of human endeavor represents the crucial first step towards such a society.
> Through nonviolence, courage displaces fear. Love transcends hate. Acceptance dissipates prejudice; hope ends despair. Faith reconciles doubt. Peace dominates war. Mutual regards cancel enmity. Justice for all overthrows injustice. The redemptive community supersedes immoral social systems.
> By appealing to conscience and standing on the moral nature of human existence, nonviolence nurtures the atmosphere in which reconciliation and justice become actual possibilities. Although each local group in this movement must diligently work out the clear meaning of this statement of purpose, each act or phase of our corporate effort must reflect a genuine spirit of love and good-will.

This idealism collided with reality when northern students went South to participate in SNCC voter-registration drive. The following excerpt was published in a volume entitled *Letters from Mississippi* (1966).

> Gulfport, August 12 [1964]
>
> Dear Mother and Father:
> I have learned more about politics here from running my own precinct meetings than I could have from any Government professor. . . . For the first time in my life, I am seeing what it is like to be poor, oppressed, and hated. And what I see here does not apply only to Gulfport or to Mississippi or even to the South. . . . The people we're killing in Viet Nam are the same people whom we've been killing for years in Mississippi. True, we didn't tie the knot in Mississippi, and we didn't pull the trigger in Viet Nam—that is, we personally— but we've been standing behind the knot-tiers and the trigger-pullers too long.
> This summer is only the briefest beginning of this experience, both for myself and for the Negroes of Mississippi.
>
> Your daughter,
> Ellen

Mario Savio, leader of the Berkeley Free Speech Movement, was one of the first to link racism with the social structure itself. The following excerpt is from an article he published in the December 1964 issue of *Humanity*.

Last summer I went to Mississippi to join the struggle there for civil rights. This fall I am engaged in another phase of that same struggle, this time in Berkeley. The two battlefields may seem quite different to some observers, but this is not the case. The same rights are at stake in both places—the right to participate as citizens in democratic society and the right to due process of law. Further, it is a struggle against the same enemy. In Mississippi an autocratic and powerful minority rules, through organized violence, to suppress the vast, virtually powerless majority. In California, the privileged minority manipulates the university bureaucracy. . . .

Political liberals were among the earliest targets of the New Left because their patchwork programs reinforced the system and often benefited the corporate Establishment. The following selection, which denounces Lyndon Johnson's "Great Society Barbecue," is from an essay by Richard Flacks, a sociology instructor at the University of Chicago. It was published in 1966 under the title *Thoughts of the Young Radicals*.

. . . This is where Mr. Johnson has particularly succeeded and where other Democratic Presidents failed—on the one hand, he has won full-fledged corporation participation in welfare-state policies; on the other hand he has won wholehearted labor, liberal, and ethnic group support for what is, in fact, a center-conservative government. Thus "consensus" is a conveniently bland term which covers a new politics in America—the politics of what might be called "liberal corporatism." . . .

As Oscar Gass has recently suggested, however, this full-scale, if belated and diluted, implementation of the New Deal promise does not necessarily imply that the Great Society will be a place of greater social justice and equality. For the current program is thoroughly circumscribed—it cannot seriously encroach on substantial corporate interests that include the maintenance of less than full employment, a decidedly impoverished public sector, a very strong emphasis on private consumption, and the use of public funds to subsidize private interests. Moreover, a more equitable distribution of wealth is unlikely because the Great Society consensus does not grant legitimate political voice to substantial sectors of the population. . . . The absence of the poor from the Great Society Barbecue keeps the consensus stable—and explains why it neglects egalitarian goals.

By 1966, SNCC saw a connection between American racism and the Vietnam war. The following statement was approved at a January 6, 1966, SNCC conference in Atlanta, just before the organization was taken over by the advocates of Black Power.

We believe the United States government has been deceptive in claims of concern for the freedom of the Vietnamese people, just as the government has been deceptive in claiming concern for the freedom of the colored people in such other countries as the Dominican Republic, the Congo, South Africa, Rhodesia or the United States itself.

We of the Student Nonviolent Coordinating Committee have been involved in the black people's struggle for liberation and self-determination in this country for the past five years. Our work, particularly in the South, taught us that the United States government has never guaranteed the freedom of oppressed citizens, and is not yet truly determined to end the rule of terror and oppression within its own borders. . . .

We recoil with horror at the inconsistency of this supposedly free society where responsibility to freedom is equated with responsibility to lend oneself to military aggression. We take note of the fact that 16 percent of the draftees from this country are Negro, called on to stifle the liberation of Vietnam to preserve a "democracy" which does not exist for them at home. . . .

The following excerpt, taken from a 1967 article by Ronald Aronson and John C. Cowley, is a fair summary of the radical critique of American capitalism.

> The waste economy, in order to expand and perpetuate itself, extends and intensifies exploitation backwards to the worker in the corporation and forwards to the consumer, and in the process it increasingly invades every area and moment of the individual's life—through advertising pressures to buy and consumer credit. . . . More and more, the individual, in obediently supporting his economy, surrenders areas of autonomy. The system's demands on him, the stereotyped and standardized forms of amusement, leisure activity and pleasure, block out any possibility for the development of individual interests, needs, and desires. In short, the economy has had to extend itself deeply into the individual.

What alternative did the New Left envision? That was never very clearly spelled out. Most of the alternative-society proposals that came out of the movement have an ethereal quality to them. Yet they reflect the deep-seated idealism that permeated the movement. The following excerpt, taken from a 1968 essay by two New York graduate students in biology, John and Barbara Ehrenreich, is representative.

> The society we strive for is one in which human goals—individual and social, material and psychological—take priority. Production, education, politics—all must be validated solely by the contribution they make to human welfare, not by whether they yield economic growth, balance the budget, or protect the rights of American investors abroad. In such a society men can become truly human, can exercise all their talents and skills, can relate to other people in a free and open manner. And it is this truly human existence, made possible by directing all our society's resources to human needs that is our ultimate vision and our ultimate goal. The question we must ask then is—what institutions enable us to build such a society? . . .
>
> The prerequisite for a human society is: control of the factories, the banks, the utilities, the networks of transportation and distribution, in the hands of the people. . . . We reject styles of "socialism" in which power is nominally public but decisions are made by a bureaucracy, far removed from the people. Nor would we want popular control to mean that public needs would be ascertained by sociological and psychological studies rather than by direct popular participation in decision-making.

ing equality in jobs and housing as well as more sensitive treatment by officials. Redress of these grievances could come only at a cost to whites—in the real estate industry, for instance, or in the trade unions.

Above all, what blacks desired was to be treated with respect. They did not want to be "given" anything. They felt that job opportunities and a decent living environment were theirs by right, by virtue of being Americans. Black power, though a slogan much misunderstood by whites, meant essentially that. And the first step was to assume leadership of their own rights organizations.

After running into a stone wall of white resistance in Mississippi in the summer of 1964 and in Selma, Alabama, in March of 1965, two militant rights organizations, SNCC and CORE, reexamined their philosophy and tactics. Could the movement remain nonviolent, some asked, or was racism so rooted in American society that only revolution could rip it out? Could blacks continue to work with whites in the movement, or was the white presence simply more liberal paternalism? Both organizations became radicalized. In the spring of 1966 SNCC elected Stokely Carmichael, an avowed revolutionary, chairman of its central committee. White members of the organization, though not expelled, were ordered thereafter to work only in white communities. Some months later CORE formally rejected nonviolence, denounced the Vietnam war, and endorsed the Black Power slogan.

The revolutionaries in the movement were doomed to frustration and failure. Hounded by police on charges of inciting riots, most went to jail or fled into exile abroad. The FBI made special work of the Black Panthers, best known of the extremist organizations, and decimated its leadership in a series of spectacular shootouts. But the movement for black equality achieved more than it knew. If nothing else, it raised the level of white consciousness. Racial slurs, at one time a common feature of the language patterns of middle-class and blue-collar America, became unfashionable. Police forces, whose bigotry had helped to spark urban riots and whose tendency to panic increased the bloodshed, were reformed and retrained. Black mayors were elected in Detroit and Cleveland. As a result of new federal laws and the voter registration drives, the number of black voters in the South tripled between 1964 and 1968. And after a final binge following the death of Martin Luther King in the spring of 1968, the urban rioting ceased. Equality was still a dream, but gigantic strides were taken in the 1960s and the momentum continued into the succeeding decade.

1968: THAT HIDEOUS YEAR

Black novelist James Baldwin once called the 1960s "a slum of a decade." He may have been too harsh, for there were many redeeming qualities about the era, not the least of which was the intellectual ferment stirred by writers such as Baldwin himself. But there was nothing redeeming about 1968. That was, by any measure, a slum of a year. Let us toll the calendar:

January. Violence ruled the land from urban ghetto to university campus. The president was literally a prisoner in the White House. The Secret Service would not let him appear in public because it could not guarantee his safety. On January 5, the United States lost its 10,000th plane over Vietnam. On January 30, date of the Vietnamese New Year holiday of Tet, Vietcong and North Vietnamese forces unleashed simultaneous attacks on 30 South Vietnamese cities, including the capital, Saigon. The timing, scale, and ferocity of the attacks took American commanders completely by surprise. They must have involved weeks of preparations, with masses of guerrillas moving openly through the countryside. Thousands of Vietnamese peasants must have known the attacks were coming; not one informed the government. A VC suicide squad even managed to penetrate the American embassy compound in Saigon, forcing embassy staff members to fight for their lives. A newspaper photographer caught the ambassador himself peering anxiously out of an embassy window, pistol in hand. That picture told a thousand words of failure. American and South Vietnamese troops eventually forced the guerrillas out of the cities, killing many thousands in the process, and General Westmoreland pronounced it a great victory. He also asked the president for another 200,000 men.

March. New Hampshire held the first primary in this presidential election year. Minnesota Democrat Eugene McCarthy, an antiwar candidate, had entered too late to have his name on the ballot, but write-in ballots gave him 42 percent of the Democratic total (versus 49 percent for the president). McCarthy's showing encouraged Robert Kennedy, now a senator from New York, to enter the presidential race as another antiwar candidate.

Racism—which surfaced every time America fought a war in Asia—together with the military's obsession with numbers and "body counts" and the anger and frustration that followed Tet, combined to produce one of the worst atrocities of the war. On March 16, a company of helicopter-borne infantry descended on the Vietnamese village of My Lai, gathered the inhabitants into groups, and "wasted" them with automatic weapons fire. The Army managed to suppress news of the massacre for almost two years, showing that even the Army high command had lost sight of the values it was supposed to be defending.

On March 31, President Johnson bowed out of the presidential contest, stating his hope that he could spend the last months of his political career searching for peace. To encourage the North Vietnamese to negotiate, he ordered a stop to air and naval bombardment north of the 20th parallel. News reporters noted another possible reason for Johnson's withdrawal. Within a few days he would have had to face both Kennedy and McCarthy in the Wisconsin primary, and the university communities in that state had been hotbeds of antiwar feeling. The Johnson campaign committee had sent a man into Madison to arrange appearances for Johnson supporters. But, admitted a committee member, "all we've heard from him since is a few faint beeps, like the last radio signals from the Bay of Pigs."

April. On April 4, Martin Luther King stepped out onto the balcony of his Memphis motel room and was killed by a single rifle shot from an unknown sniper. Fingerprints led the FBI to escaped convict James Earl Ray, who was arrested in Britain, extradited for trial, and sentenced to 99 years in prison. After the assassination, enraged blacks took to the streets in scores of cities, burning and looting. Entire city blocks were flattened in the nation's capital, and it finally took 55,000 federal troops and National Guardsmen to restore order.

June. Senator Robert F. Kennedy, having won Democratic primaries in Indiana and Nebraska, won the crucial California primary on June 4. That night, while he was leaving a hotel victory celebration, Kennedy was assassinated by Sirhan Sirhan, a young Arab who was distressed by Kennedy's position on the Palestinian question.

July. In Rome, Pope Paul issued an encyclical reinforcing the Catholic Church's opposition to artificial means of birth control, apparently in response to a world trend toward legalizing contraceptives and abortions. In California, biologist Paul Erlich published a best-selling book, *The Population Bomb*, warning what was in store for the world if population growth continued unchecked.

August. The Democratic party meeting in Chicago nominated Vice President Hubert H. Humphrey for president, while Chicago police ran amok in the streets clubbing antiwar demonstrators (some of whom had come to break up the convention) and innocent bystanders with uncompromising indifference. In Miami Richard Nixon cashed a decade's worth of political IOUs and won the Republican nomination for president. In Prague, Soviet tanks rumbled into the streets to crush a liberal government that had sought to ease life for the Czech people.

November. The troop commitment in Vietnam reached its peak of 550,000, and the U.S. death toll approached 30,000, putting Vietnam on its way to becoming the third bloodiest war in our history. By an

UPI/Bettmann.

Police grapple with demonstrators outside the Democratic Convention, Chicago, August 28, 1968.

electoral vote of 302 to 191, Richard Nixon was elected president of the United States. It was not a vintage year.

The presidential election did not really turn on the question of war. Both candidates promised to get the country out of it, though neither specified how that might be done. It was clear by the fall of 1968 that a majority of Americans thought the involvement in Indochina had been a mistake. But it was also clear that an even bigger majority rejected the peace movement's demand for unconditional withdrawal, for that would have amounted to an admission that the blood and treasure expended so far had been an utter waste. Thus President Nixon faced a seemingly impossible choice on taking office. The war

could not be "won," nor could it even be long continued. But it dare not be "lost."

On January 25, 1969, a few days after Nixon's inauguration, the National Security Council made a decision to begin withdrawing American troops in advance of negotiations with North Vietnam. The withdrawal would be gradual and described publicly as Vietnamization—that is, allowing the South Vietnamese to fend for themselves, which had been a stated American goal all along. Even so, it would be four more years, four years of on-again–off-again peace talks, four more years of government deception, air raids, and the involvement of Laos and Cambodia, before an agreement was reached and the American commitment ended.

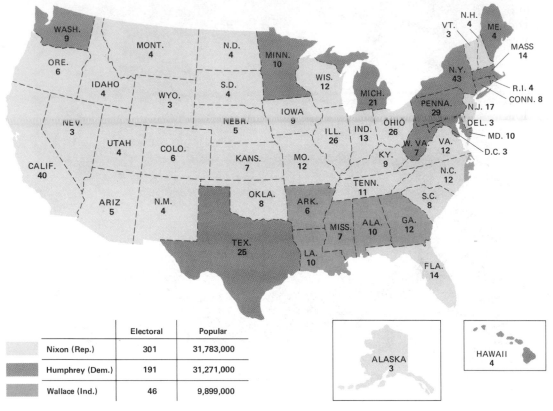

	Electoral	Popular
Nixon (Rep.)	301	31,783,000
Humphrey (Dem.)	191	31,271,000
Wallace (Ind.)	46	9,899,000

Election of 1968.

⊔Rebirth of Reform

The turmoil of the 1960s was accompanied by an intense self-examination. The consensus was gone; change was in the air. Not since the days of the New Deal had there been such intellectual ferment. Yet the upheaval of the sixties differed in important ways from earlier reform movements. In the past, reformers had sought to mobilize distinct economic classes—farmers, workers, small businessmen—with the object of pressuring the government for remedial legislation. In the sixties, social critics rejected government altogether, perceiving the political system to be part of the problem. The main beneficiaries of the reform spirit—blacks, women, Hispanics, Indians—benefited not so much from legislation, as from heightened public awareness of their needs.

THE WOMEN'S MOVEMENT

Since World War II, women had been moving into jobs that had once been closed to them. During the 1950s, the number of women lawyers doubled and the number of engineers tripled, and the trend increased in the 1960s. By the end of the decade, women constituted almost 40 percent of the nation's work force. Despite this progress, they continued to face severe discrimination in the job market. They usually earned less than men doing comparable work, and those with managerial positions rose more slowly than men in corporate hierarchies. The ferment of the sixties, and particularly the civil rights movement, in which many young women participated, helped awaken women to their own plight.

In 1963, Betty Friedan's book *The Feminine Mystique* challenged the century-old cult of domesticity, pointing out the vast discrepancy between the popular image of the happy homemaker, "fluffy and feminine, . . . gaily content in a world of bedroom and kitchen, sex, babies, and home," and the stark reality of most women's lives. Friedan blamed teachers and magazine publishers for brainwashing women into accepting the theorem that shopping, sewing, and sex equaled happiness. Friedan's book brought into the open a growing perception among women that they needed a feminist consciousness that allowed them to examine their condition from a fresh viewpoint. Since 1961, when President Kennedy appointed a special Commission on the Status of Women, federal and state investigators had been compiling a mass of figures demonstrating the economic, social, and legal disabilities that encumbered women. Women's rights leaders had long been aware of the discrimination, but to many women, as well as most men, the statistics were a revelation.

The first fruit of this growing awareness was the addition of a clause prohibiting discrimination on the basis of sex as well as race in the Civil Rights Act of 1964. Actually, the provision had been inserted by opponents of the bill in the hopes of adding to its enemies, but female members of Congress persuaded civil rights–minded liberals to accept it. However, the Equal Employment Opportunity Commission, the federal agency in charge of implementing the act, regarded the sex provision as a "fluke" and chose to ignore it. That

brought women to the realization that they needed a rights organization that could bring pressure on their behalf in the political arena. In 1966, a group of professional women and government workers formed the National Organization for Women (NOW), and they installed Betty Friedan as its first president. NOW focused on state and federal legislation guaranteeing equal rights for women. It also sought to undermine the tradition that a woman had to choose between motherhood and work by urging legislation that would ensure maternity leaves without jeopardy to job security, tax deductions for child care expenses, and publicly financed day-care centers. NOW also supported the right of women to limit the number of children they had through contraceptives and abortion, sparking a controversy that still rages.

By the mid-1960s the women's movement was itself becoming increasingly divided. NOW represented relatively conservative, middle-aged women, many of them in the professions. To many younger women, veterans of the civil rights and anti-war movements, the goals of NOW seemed too limited. True liberation, they felt, required nothing less than the transformation of American society and culture. As a result of their experiences as freedom riders in the South or their attempts to produce tenant rebellions in the urban ghettoes of the North, these younger women had gained a greater understanding of how their own lives were shaped by culture and tradition. Rejecting traditional forms of organization, women's liberation groups developed a network of informal "consciousness-raising" groups. There, in a supportive, noncompetitive setting, women shared information and experiences.

What came out of all this ferment could not simply be called a feminist ideology because major differences remained among feminist groups as to the cause and cure of America's ills. (Socialists had one solution, for instance, and lesbians, quite another.) Nevertheless, there did emerge a feminist critique, a rejection of the notion that childbearing created for women "natural" roles as wives and mothers, a critique of a national value system that associated strength, rationality, and independence with men.

Women's liberationists were also more inclined to take up the confrontational politics that had worked for the civil rights movement. In 1968, they picketed the Miss America contest, protesting the national preoccupation with bust size and congeniality, rather than brain power or strength of character. Activists pushed their way into all-male bars and clubs, contending that such exclusive bastions were themselves a reflection of the "man's world/woman's place" value system. Other feminists began to monitor sex stereotyping in books, while still others lobbied for women's studies programs in high schools and colleges.

Like the black power movement, the feminist revolt inspired some extremist rhetoric, and it created its own backlash among women who found comfort in passive domesticity. But considerable progress was made nonetheless. By the early 1970s, the states were passing equal opportunity laws to end discrimination in employment. The Supreme Court in the early 1970s overturned state laws that limited the use of contraceptives and restricted the right to abortion. Public concern for the rights of women and racial minorities was one of the few impulses of the '60s that survived into the conservative '70s and '80s. It may have been the '60s' finest legacy.

BROWN POWER, RED POWER

The cultural nationalism inherent in black power was contagious. By the end of the 1960s, the nation's Hispanic and American Indian minorities were seeking recognition of their cultural identities. The myth of the great melting pot in which the world's peoples were Americanized in a land of opportunity, they came to feel, cloaked a society that was in truth dominated by a white middle class. Stripped of their language, segregated in urban slums or barren reservations, consigned to menial jobs or government handouts, America's "brown" and "red" races shared the perception that united all the decade's protest movements—that there was a large gap between American ideals and American reality, and that the gap was papered over with hypocrisy.

In 1963, California field workers, led by Cesar Chavez, formed a labor union to seek better pay and working conditions. Unable to strike because they were so easily replaced in their unskilled jobs, the workers organized a nationwide boycott of California grapes and lettuce. The boycott received support from labor leaders and Senator Robert Kennedy, and eventually it worked. In 1966 some of the largest grape growers recognized the union and negotiated labor contracts. By then *La Causa* had become a cultural as well as a labor battle. Following the example of blacks who had succeeded in getting programs in Afro-American Studies started at many universities, Hispanic nationalists (they adopted the name Chicano in 1969) demanded the teaching of Spanish in the schools of the Southwest and Hispanic studies in American universities. Economic progress and cultural pride went hand in hand.

Indians too called attention to their traditions and their past. Best-selling books such as Dee Brown's *Bury My Heart at Wounded Knee* chronicled the centuries of betrayal that had been the story of the American frontier. In the late 1960s, Indians adopted the tactics of demonstration used by the civil rights and antiwar movements. They occupied Alcatraz Island in San Francisco Bay, offering to buy it from the federal government for $24 in beads and cloth (the price the Dutch allegedly paid for Manhattan). Other militants challenged federal control of reservations by seizing the village of Wounded Knee, South Dakota, and still others invaded the offices of the Indian Bureau in Washington.

The result of all this was heightened awareness among the white majority and a new respect for nonwhite, non-European cultures and traditions. In the succeeding decade, pluralism replaced the homogenized melting pot as an American ideal.

THE COUNTERCULTURE

In 1960, University of California sociologist C. Wright Mills published an essay entitled "The New Left" in which he acknowledged that the "old left," which had looked to the Soviet Union for intellectual sustenance, was dead. It had failed to attract any significant support in the American labor movement, and it was deeply embarrassed by the Soviet repression of liberal movements in East Germany and Hungary in the 1950s. The "new left," Mills predicted, would appear on college campuses and draw its strength from middle-class youth. For a time, the civil rights and antiwar movements seemed to bear Mills out. Civil rights marches or service in the Peace Corps were radicalizing experiences for young idealists, who found that injustice and exploitation were the norm, often abetted by the policies of American corporations and the American government. Disillusioned, they returned to the college campuses, shed the sport coats and skirts of middle-class respectability, and adopted a sort of unisex combat gear—blue jeans and army field jackets.

Many rejected the American value system itself and developed an underground counterculture. They scorned the Puritan ethic, with its emphasis on work and thrift and its promise of future reward. The counterculture made a cult of the cool, the passive, self-indulgent being who lived only for the present. Drugs and hard rock music were central to this mystique. Drugs were illegal and hence a challenge, and their use shocked the guardians of middle-class morality—parents, teachers, and police. Rock music, especially the San Francisco style practiced by the group called The Grateful Dead, was the glue of the counterculture, its principal means of communication and interaction. Hard rock was a blend of radical politics, allusions to consciousness-raising drugs, and an excited sense of imminent cultural and political revolution.

Society needs social critics who call attention to its injustices, its flawed assumptions, and its hypocrisies, and much of what the student radicals of the 1960s said was worth listening to. But "the movement," as they came to call it, died of its own excesses. Talking only to each other (the "generation gap" that bound them together also isolated them from the larger society), they convinced themselves that revolution was feasible. They soon discovered that university campuses and rock music hangouts were poor power bases from which to launch one. Frustrated, the more extreme elements engaged in petty acts of grisly violence, such as the Weathermen's[*] Chicago "days of rage" in the fall of 1969 and the bombing of the University of Wisconsin physics building in August 1970. Such tactics split the movement and angered the larger society it was trying to change.

The first sign of conservative backlash came in May 1970 when hard-hat construction workers in New York City attacked a parade of antiwar demonstrators. Fundamentally conservative and avowedly patri-

---

[*] The Weathermen and Weatherwomen were revolutionary sects of the Students for a Democratic Society (SDS), taking their name from a verse by folk rock singer Bob Dylan, "You don't need a weatherman to know which way the wind is blowing."

otic, America's blue-collar workers had no tolerance for the sons and daughters of the rich who posed as revolutionaries. Neither did most other Americans. By the fall of 1970, Nixon's Vice President Spiro Agnew was receiving loud applause when he denounced student demonstrators as "effete snobs" whose "elitist" notions were the product of a national permissiveness. In the election that fall Republicans actually picked up a few seats in Congress, contrary to the tradition that the party in power loses seats in an off-year election.

The demonstrations continued as the Vietnam war dragged on. The demonstrations of the spring of 1970, triggered by the invasion of Cambodia, were in fact the most violent yet. But as Nixon gradually dismantled the draft, the number of demonstrators diminished. And as the '60s gave way to the '70s, the winds of social change were stilled.

SUMMARY

The conduct of the Cold War was the chief issue in the presidential election of 1960, but neither Richard Nixon nor John F. Kennedy was inclined to question the set of assumptions that had governed American decision making since Truman's day. The debate instead centered on Kennedy's accusation that Eisenhower's niggardly military budgets had created a "missile gap" in space weapons and left the ground forces too weak to fight "brushfire wars." Kennedy's promise to "get the country moving again" thus involved both a massive arms buildup and a more forceful diplomacy.

A series of confrontations ensued. First there was the Bay of Pigs disaster in Cuba. Then, in the summer of 1961, came the Berlin crisis, as Kennedy ordered a partial mobilization in response to Khrushchev's threat to give the East Germans control of the access routes to Berlin. A year later, in October 1962, came the Cuban missile crisis, the most dangerous of all Cold War confrontations. Both sides were chastened by the affair, and in 1963 they signed a treaty banning the atmospheric testing of nuclear weapons, the first cold war arms limitation agreement.

While President Kennedy concentrated on foreign affairs, his domestic program sputtered in Congress. Kennedy's New Frontier contained some leftovers from Truman's Fair Deal, such as federal aid to education and health insurance for the aged, as well as some imaginative innovations—a worker retraining program to combat technological unemployment, a Peace Corps to lend American skills to developing countries; and an "alliance for progress" in Latin America. In 1963, responding to the violence caused by the black voting rights drive, Kennedy proposed a civil rights law giving federal protection for the right to vote. Unfortunately, most of these programs failed to get past a conservative coalition of Republicans and southern Democrats in Congress. The shock of Kennedy's death, together with reform in the congressional committee structure, broke the legislative blockade. In the spring of 1964 a Civil Rights Act, Medicare, and a poverty program were all enacted into law. Lyndon Johnson's victory over Barry Goldwater in 1964 confirmed the nation's commitment to what Johnson called the "great society."

And then everything went wrong. The situation in Vietnam, where the American-backed Diem government had been fighting Communist guerrillas since the late fifties, had deteriorated by 1964 to the point where it seemed that only American intervention would prevent a Communist takeover. In August 1964, following an incident in the Tonkin Gulf off the North Vietnamese coast, Johnson had obtained broad authority from Congress to employ American forces. In February 1965 he ordered the bombing of military targets in North Vietnam and then sent in ground forces to protect American airbases. The buildup of American strength continued until by 1968 there were more than half a million troops in Vietnam, and Americans had virtually taken over direction of the war.

Rising protest accompanied the military escalation. The protest stemmed from the government's short-term inability to explain its objectives and long-term inability to achieve results. Adding to the din was urban violence and the revolutionary rhetoric of Black Power advocates.

The social ferment and the heightened public awareness that accompanied it did benefit women and racial minorities. The Civil Rights Act of 1964 opened new avenues of economic opportunity by banning discrimination by race or sex in employment practices. The states followed with equal opportunity laws of their own. Between 1965 and 1974, the United States Supreme Court further liberated women by overturning state laws that limited the use of contraceptives and restricted the right to abortion. Black Power, stripped of its revolutionary rhetoric, was a summons to black pride, a plea for recognition of the unique Afro-American subculture. Other minorities, notably Mexican Americans and Indians, picked up the cry and demanded recognition as well. One of the lasting results of the sixties' ferment was a recognition of the value of cultural pluralism.

By the end of the decade the demonstrations, the riots, and the revolutionary talk were producing a white conservative backlash. Richard Nixon owed his election as president in 1968, in part, to the desire of the "silent majority" of middle-class whites for "law and order." As the '60s gave way to the '70s, the winds of social change were stilled; a mood of conservatism enveloped the country.

READING SUGGESTIONS

The best and most recent survey of the 1960s is Allan J. Matusow's *The Unraveling of America: A History of Liberalism in the 1960s* (1984). Although a comprehensive historical treatment of the Kennedy administration remains to be written, there are good monographs on specific phases of it, among them: Carl M. Brauer, *John F. Kennedy and the Second Reconstruction* (1977), and Herbert Dinnerstein, *The Making of a Missile Crisis* (1976). David Halbersham, *The Best and the Brightest* (1972), is an analytical portrait of the decision makers who embroiled the United States in Vietnam. Arthur M. Schlesinger, Jr., *Robert Kennedy and His Times* (1978), is a splendid biography of one insider by another. The most recent treatment of the Kennedy assassination is Michael L. Kurtz, *Crime of the Century* (1982). Ronnie Dugger, *The Politician: The Life and Times of Lyndon Johnson* (1982), is the best treatment to date of Johnson's senatorial career. Doris Kearns, *Lyndon Johnson and the American Dream* (1976), covers his presidency.

To understand the roots of black protest in the 1960s, the reader might start with *The Autobiography of Malcolm X* (1964). The most recent study of the civil rights movement is Rhoda Lois Blumberg, *Civil Rights: The 1960s Freedom Struggle* (1984); also recommended are Harvard Sitkoff, *The Struggle for Black Equality, 1954–1980*

(1981); Stephen B. Oates, *Let the Trumpet Sound*: *The Life of Martin Luther King, Jr.* (1982), and Mary A. Rothschild, *A Case of Black and White*: *Northern Volunteers and Southern Freedom Summers, 1964–1965* (1982). The rise of ethnic consciousness is traced in Matt S. Meier and Feliciano Rivera, *The Chicanos* (1972), and in Michael Novak, *The Rise of the Unmeltable Ethnics* (1972).

Recent studies of the feminist movement include: Jo Freeman, *The Politics of Women's Liberation* (1975); Sara Evans, *Personal Politics*: *The Roots of Women's Liberation in the Civil Rights Movement and the New Left* (1979); Barbara Deckard, *The Women's Movement* (1979); and Rosalind Rosenberg, *Beyond Separate Spheres*: *Intellectual Roots of Modern Feminism* (1982). Massimo Teo-dori, *The New Left*: *A Documentary History* (1969), is a good anthology of New Left writings. Irwin Unger, *The Movement* (1974), critiques the New Left; Ken Hurwitz's *Marching Nowhere* (1971) critiques the peace movement.

The most recent and objective assessment of the Vietnam war is George C. Herring's *America's Longest War*: *The United States and Vietnam, 1950–1975* (1979). A unique feature of the war is recounted in Kathleen J. Turner's *Lyndon Johnson's Dual War*: *Vietnam and the Press* (1985). Of the many accounts written by participants, the best are Philip Caputo, *A Rumor of War* (1977), written by a Marine lieutenant, and Michael Herr, *Dispatches* (1978), written by a war correspondent.

16

UPI/Bettmann.

WAR AND PEACE:
1970–1980

The constant protest, the outcry from those who had been too long ignored—blacks, Hispanics, women, Indians, gays, and pacifists—nearly drowned out a small voice with a conservative message. It was January 1969, the month of Richard Nixon's inauguration. The voice belonged to Kevin Phillips, a young congressional aide, and he titled his entry *The Emerging Republican Majority*. Despite the author's obscurity and the dull title, the book was important because it both explained and rationalized Nixon's electoral victory.

Two great social movements, said Phillips, were dissolving the Democratic majority that had governed America from the thirties to the sixties. They were also forging a new conservative majority. One was the movement of people away from the traditionally liberal population centers of the Northeast and into the traditionally conservative Sunbelt states of the South and West. The other was the movement into the suburbs of well-paid factory operatives and tradespeople, a generation or two removed from their European origins and concerned principally with the preservation of their newfound status.

Frightened by the uprisings in the ghettoes and the antiwar demonstrations, shocked by stories of drug abuse and sexual license among youth, this was the "silent majority" to whom Nixon had appealed in the election campaign. It responded to Nixon's cry for "law and order" because "law and order" meant putting blacks and youth back in their places. True to Phillips's prediction, this same majority returned Nixon to office in 1972 and installed Ronald Reagan in the White House in 1980 and again in 1984.

The persistence of this national mood reflected something more than a "backlash" against the '60s or even the continued drift of population. At the root of it through the 1970s and '80s was a feeling that government had become the enemy, not the servant of the American people. This was more than a reemergence of old-style individualism; it was a paradox of modern times. By the 1970s, the liberalism born of Progressivism and the New Deal seemed bankrupt. The more government tried to solve the nation's economic and social problems, the more bureaucratic, remote, and inept it seemed. Presidents Nixon, Carter, and Reagan were all elected as outsiders who promised to reconquer the government for the American people. Even as an incumbent President running for reelection, Reagan in 1984 successfully campaigned against the Washington establishment. Mistrust of government and social conservatism were the dominant mood of the time.

⎵Bring Us Together: The Nixon Presidency

During the 1968 election campaign, a little girl's hand-painted plea "Bring Us Together" had given Nixon his theme. He promised to end the strife and heal the nation's wounds. Once in office, however, the promises seemed forgotten. The administration reversed the government's civil rights priorities and cut back Johnson's economic opportunity programs. Wooing southern conservatives who had thrown their support to George Wallace in the election, Nixon named two southerners to vacancies on the Supreme Court, only to have them rejected by the Senate because of their dubious judicial qualifications and segregationist background. The retirement of Earl Warren and other justices, how-

---

(*Chapter opening photo*) President Nixon greeted by Chairman Mao Tse-tung, 1972. The rapprochement between the United States and Communist China may have been the most important event of the 1970s.

ever, gave Nixon five appointments to the Court in his first two years, enabling him to restructure it on more conservative lines. Although Nixon's appointees did not always vote as the president anticipated, the Court under Chief Justice Warren Burger was much different from the liberal, activist "Warren Court."

As the 1970 congressional elections approached, the administration became even more hostile toward its critics. Nixon denounced antiwar demonstrators as a "band of violent thugs," and Vice President Spiro Agnew began a campaign to fix the blame for opposition to the Vietnam war on the television networks. In the meantime, the administration carried on a running battle with Congress. Nixon vetoed hospital construction, urban development, and education bills. When Congress voted funds for Great Society programs, Nixon claimed the right to impound the money to prevent it from being spent.

Nixon's policies revealed the changes that had taken place in American conservatism in the Cold War years. There was the same hostility to social welfare legislation as in the days of Robert Taft and Thomas Dewey, but not the same fear of budget deficits. Where Taft had warned of bankruptcy through military spending, Nixon adopted the Keynesian view that defense expenditures were a way of stimulating the economy. His budget deficit for 1971 was a peacetime record of $23 billion. Nixon also wielded executive power in ways that would have shocked conservatives of the past. In order to curb inflation (then running at about 7 percent), Nixon in 1971 imposed the nation's first peacetime controls on prices, wages, and rents. Faced with a trade deficit that year which made serious inroads on the nation's gold supplies, Nixon severed the connection between the dollar and gold and set the dollar afloat in international markets. The effect was devaluation, the first since Roosevelt's "commodity dollar" of 1934. The "imperial presidency" was in its glory, and scarcely a conservative registered a complaint.

NIXON-KISSINGER FOREIGN POLICY

The war in Vietnam was tearing the nation apart, and only a resolution of that conflict could bring it back together. In sharp contrast to his law and order stance on domestic affairs, Nixon proved surprisingly flexible in foreign policy. In tandem with his National Security Adviser Henry Kissinger, Nixon completed the Cold War shift that had been interrupted by Vietnam—the shift from confrontation to negotiation, from polarity to détente.

There were two lessons to be drawn from the interventionist episodes of the Kennedy-Johnson years. One was the limits of American power. The American military, with all its technology and firepower, could not impose its will on a civilian population without that population's active support. Nor could it shore up a government that lacked the support of its own people. As early as 1967, Nixon had come to the conclusion that the United States was overextended in its global commitments and that "the role of the United States as world policeman is likely to be limited in the future."

Shortly after taking office, he announced plans to Vietnamize the war in Southeast Asia, which meant, in practice, withdrawing American troops. On an Asian tour in August 1969, Nixon explained the rationale for the new policy, a statement the press instantly labeled the Nixon Doctrine. The United States would meet Communist attacks in any area vital to American security, Nixon said, but it could furnish only economic aid and moral support to governments on the edges of Communist territory that were threatened with internal subversion and civil war. "Asian hands must shape the Asian future," he declared. The American troop commitment in Vietnam fell from 475,000 in 1969 to 23,000 by January 1973.

Also drawn from the experience of the 1960s was the realization that Communist regimes were not necessarily identical. They were not bound by a common ideology and were not all committed to the destruction of the United States. One of the central assumptions that had guided American Cold War thinking was wrong. Driving home this lesson was the rift between the Soviet Union and Communist China. Resentful of Soviet domineering and proud of its own revolutionary heritage, China had begun to pursue an independent line in the late 1950s. Conflicting territorial claims and border skirmishes in the sixties deepened the mistrust. By 1970, the two Communist giants were pointing nuclear warheads at each other. The split offered the United States an opportunity for old-fashioned balance of power diplomacy.

Diplomatic "realism" of this sort was Henry Kissinger's strength. A forty-five-year-old Harvard professor who had served as foreign policy adviser to Republican moderate Nelson Rockefeller in 1968, Kissinger was inclined to treat the Soviet Union and China as rival powers with historical interests to protect. He felt it was possible to bargain for limited objectives without fear of a Yalta-style "sellout." Nixon shared Kissinger's view of world affairs. The two had other points in common as well. Both were secretive, suspicious, and power hungry. They disliked bureaucracies, especially the plodding professionals in the State Department. With Kissinger as his National Security adviser, Nixon capped a trend that had been underway since the Truman administration—the restriction of the State Department to administrative functions and the concentration of foreign policy decision making in the White House. With the help of the National Security Council and the Central Intelligence Agency, Nixon and Kissinger felt

they could assess options, make decisions, and undertake covert operations with a speed and secrecy that enabled them to create events, rather than simply react to them. There was flexibility in the arrangement; there was also the opportunity for abuse.

President Nixon's visit to Communist Rumania in August 1969 signaled the new approach. The Soviet repression of freedom in Czechoslovakia the year before had reminded the world once again that communism in eastern Europe was just another form of imperialism. Nixon's visit showed his willingness to exploit nationalist tendencies among Soviet satellites, while negotiating with the Soviet Union itself. Playing the "China card" in the international poker game was simply the next step. An improvement in Sino-American relations would blunt Soviet influence in Asia, would add to the list of Soviet worries, and might even help the United States out of the Vietnam quagmire.

The Chinese themselves made the first overture when in April 1971 they invited and then royally entertained an American table tennis team that had been touring Japan. Weeks later, Kissinger secretly flew to Peking, and in July Nixon announced that he would visit China "to seek the normalization of relations" between the two countries. Nixon's China visit of February 1972, extensively covered by network television, resulted in more fluff than substance. But it did substitute calm discussion for the strident rhetoric of the past. This sudden and complete reversal in policy, unmatched in American diplomatic history, caused scarcely a ripple among the public. Except for remnants of the China lobby, which howled when China was admitted to the United Nations and Taiwan was expelled, Americans seemed to accept the Nixon-Kissinger brand of "realism."

In June 1972, President Nixon followed his China visit with an equally well-publicized visit to the Soviet Union. It was a further signal of his determination to re-place Cold War moralizing with hard-headed diplomacy. The most sensitive topic between Russia and America was the limitation of nuclear weapons. Since the end of World War II, arms limitation talks had been stalemated because the Americans insisted there could be no agreement without on-site inspection of weapons. The Russians saw physical inspection as an excuse for spying. During the 1960s, however, spy satellites had given each side the means to count the missiles of the other without inspection. The Strategic Arms Limitation Talks (SALT) started in 1969 and reached a preliminary agreement in 1971. Nixon signed a formal treaty on his visit to Moscow in 1972. The treaty froze the existing ratio of intercontinental ballistic missiles (ICBMs), but it did nothing to end the arms race. Each side turned to the development of weapons not covered by the limitations—and thus left much for SALT II negotiators later. Nevertheless, SALT I signaled a détente.

The Nixon-Kissinger strategy was less successful in Vietnam, though it did eventually get the United States out of the war. The rapprochement with China was not of any immediate help, in part because North Vietnam was more closely tied to the Soviet Union than to China. Worse still, the North Vietnamese took advantage of the American withdrawal to step up their activities. Nixon tried to counter that by ordering the bombing of the North Vietnamese trails that ran through Laos and Cambodia, a bombing that had to be kept secret because those two countries were technically neutral. When that failed, he ordered on April 30, 1970, a joint American–South Vietnamese invasion of Cambodia. The order precipitated the most violent antiwar demonstrations of all, with eruptions on 448 college campuses. At Kent State University in Ohio, National Guard troops fired into a mob of protesting students and killed four.

Secret negotiations had been underway between the United States and North Vietnam since 1968, but little progress had been made because the North Vietnamese insisted on an unconditional American withdrawal and a Communist voice in the South Vietnamese government. The United States needed some kind of interim settlement, a face-saving device that would permit withdrawal without an admission that the bloodshed—57,000 American lives by 1972—had been in vain.

When the North Vietnamese army mounted an open invasion across the demilitarized zone that separated the two Vietnams in May 1972, Nixon resumed the bombing of the North. The North Vietnamese returned to the bargaining table, and in October 1972, Kissinger announced a preliminary agreement. But South Vietnamese objections sent the negotiators home again. In December Nixon again unleashed his bombers, this time in the indiscriminate bombing of cities and villages. In four years, Nixon dropped 4.6 million tons of explosives on North Vietnam, compared with Lyndon Johnson's 2.8 million tons.

The bombing raids brought the North Vietnamese back to the table, and on January 8, 1973, a peace treaty was signed. Actually, it was little more than an agreement to call it quits; the major political issues were left unresolved. The United States was to withdraw its remaining troops while allowing more than 100,000 North Vietnamese troops to remain stationed in South Vietnam. Kissinger had successfully resisted the formation of a coalition government in Saigon, but he had won South Vietnam no more than a "decent interval" in which to reach a settlement with the Communists on its own.

After the last Americans departed, both sides violated the ceasefire. In the next eighteen months another 50,000 people were killed on both sides. Then, in March 1975, the Communists struck in force. In six weeks, it was all over. The red flag flew in Saigon, which was renamed Ho Chi Minh City. In the midst of the Communist offensive, President Ford asked Congress for $422 million in military aid to the South Vietnamese government. Congress had drawn lessons of its own from the experience. In 1973 it had passed a War Powers Act that required the president, whenever he committed American forces to battle, to secure the consent of Congress within ninety days. And now it refused Ford's request. The "imperial presidency" was also a victim of the war.

Had the blood shed by Americans been in vain? Perhaps not. If the United States had not intervened, South Vietnam would surely have succumbed to the Communists (by ballots or bullets) in the 1950s, and that would have put enormous pressure on Malaya, Indonesia, and the Philippines, all of which were then struggling with Communist guerrillas of their own. American intervention bought time for Southeast Asia, twenty years in which the countries of that region built prosperous economies and stable (except for the Marcos regime in the Philippines) political systems. The domino theory might have been valid when Eisenhower announced it in 1954 (and been even more valid when the State Department first considered the concept in 1950). That there was no domino effect in 1975 after the fall of Saigon may have been one of the unseen and unsung results of American intervention.

Americans themselves took the collapse with surprising calm. Despite the fears of the U.S. government in the 1960s, there was no backlash, no search for scapegoats, as there had been after the fall of China. The speed of the collapse no doubt helped, for it demonstrated what war critics had been saying: The South Vietnamese regime was a hollow shell. If South Vietnam's peasants wanted a Communist government, cynics suggested, perhaps they deserved one.

In summary, Nixon's achievements in the field of foreign policy are impressive indeed. He got the United States out of a war it could not win and dared not lose, and he turned the Cold War onto the path of détente, where, despite an occasional bump and curse, it remains today. Had he retired honorably in the spring of 1973, he might have won history's accolade as one of the greatest of foreign policy presidents. Instead, Watergate earned him history's scorn.

⊔ Watergate and After

The English Liberal Lord Acton had an axiom: "Power corrupts, and absolute power corrupts absolutely." Amid the Cold War tensions of the 1950s and 1960s American presidents had assumed extensive powers, and they had given foreign and domestic intelligence agencies a freedom to operate that presidents in another time would never have permitted. But Lord Acton's dictum came true: Power corrupted the powerbrokers. In the Eisenhower administration the FBI began the surveillance of civil rights organizations, tracking leaders such as Martin Luther King with bugs and wiretaps, looking for misbehavior that might be used against them. FBI Director J. Edgar Hoover kept secret files on the drinking and sex habits of members of Congress, and he remained director long after he reached retirement age in part because no one dared to suggest that he quit. In the same years, the CIA periodically planned the assassination of foreign leaders who were critical of the United States, and the agency played a significant role in the overthrow of democratic but left-leaning governments in Iran (1953), Guatemala (1954), and Chile (1973).

The imperial presidency was all but out of control when Nixon took office, and he was not the man to reign it in. Insecure and hypersensitive to criticism, Nixon gathered around him men who played on his suspicions and anxieties. The two closest to the president, H. R. Haldeman, White House chief of staff, and John Ehrlichman, domestic affairs adviser, had no governmental experience. Haldeman had been in advertising; Ehrlichman was a lawyer. Inexperience, intellectual inbreeding, and unbridled power were a deadly combination.

PLUMBERS AND THE BREAK-IN

Angered by newspaper reports in 1969 of the secret bombing raids on Cambodia and fearful that Johnson holdovers in the government were leaking information to the war protesters, Nixon ordered the FBI to uncover the sources of information leaks. The FBI obligingly tapped the offices and houses of White House and National Security Council staff members, as well as those of four Washington reporters. Simultaneously the CIA began to collect information on thousands of individuals and organizations involved in the antiwar movement. In 1970 a special White House task force, "the plumbers," was set up to locate leaks within the government. When Daniel Ellsberg, a former Pentagon employee who had become disillusioned with the war, gave newspapers classified documents that detailed America's involvement (published as the *Pentagon Papers*), the plumbers were put on Ellsberg's trail. Hoping to uncover derogatory information about Ellsberg, they broke into the office of his psychiatrist, using CIA equipment. The government subsequently prosecuted Ellsberg for releasing classified documents, but it was unable to convict him because the government had procured its evidence illegally.

By 1972, White House staff members had compiled an enemies list composed of prominent persons who had spoken out against the war, and they persuaded the Internal Revenue Service to harrass these people with investigations of their tax records. That spring a special Committee for the Re-Election of the President (CREEP) was formed to collect funds independently of the Republican party to be used exclusively for Nixon's campaign. The head of CREEP was former attorney general John Mitchell, who had directed Nixon's 1968 campaign. Among the staff personnel transferred to the committee from the White House were Gordon Liddy and Howard Hunt, both experienced plumbers. On the night of June 17, 1972, a group of five men—among them James McCord, CREEP security chief—broke into the offices of the Democratic National Headquarters in the Watergate, a complex of offices and apartments overlooking the Potomac River in Washington, D.C. The break-in was clumsy, the men were caught by an alert security guard, and ultimately all seven—including Hunt and Liddy—were indicted.

Although the Washington *Post* established a connection between the Watergate break-in and the Committee for the Re-Election of the President within a few days, both CREEP and the White House denied any involvement. Nixon's press secretary dismissed it as a "third-rate burglary." To conceal a crime is itself a crime. The men surrounding the president nevertheless thought a coverup essential because of the approaching election and because an investigation might reveal some of the administration's other "dirty tricks." To protect the president, Liddy confessed that he had ordered the break-in on his own initiative and that no one in the administration was involved. Since there was no way to get the truth until the burglars were brought to trial, the coverup worked—at least through the election.

South Dakota Senator George McGovern swept the spring primaries and earned the Democratic presidential nomination that year. McGovern was antiwar and favored a worldwide reduction in America's military commitments. His program was hardly radical, but support from antiwar protesters tarred him with the brush of radicalism. *Time* magazine called him "the prairie populist." Nixon swamped him in the election, taking 60.7 percent of the popular vote and capturing every state except Massachusetts. Yet despite the landslide, the Democrats lost only twelve seats in the House, gained two in the Senate, and remained in firm control of Congress. It was not a vote for Nixon, or even for the Republicans; it was a vote against radicalism and turbulence. The "silent majority" had spoken out against the sixties.

THE COVERUP COMES APART

The coverup began to unravel in the early months of 1973. Federal Judge John Sirica, presiding over the burglary trial, clearly disbelieved much of the testimony and threatened to hand down severe sentences. Unwilling to be sacrificed, one of the burglars wrote Sirica, telling the judge that he and other witnesses had committed perjury during the trial under "political pressure." About the same time, White House counsel John Dean, his conscience stricken by the massive illegality that surrounded the president, began talking to Senate committee investigators. In February, the Senate had set up a special committee to investigate the Watergate break-in. It was headed by a venerable constitutionalist, Sam Ervin of North Carolina. In nationally televised sessions the Ervin committee interviewed Dean and other witnesses from May through August 1973. The committee's most sensational discovery was that all White House conversations had been taped by voice-activated recorders.[*] The

tapes, of course, could answer the key question concerning Nixon's role in the coverup: What did the president know, and when did he know it?

Nixon refused to release the tapes, claiming executive privilege, until the Supreme Court ordered him to do so on July 24, 1974. One of the released tapes was the "smoking gun" that connected the president to the coverup: It contained a conversation of June 23, 1972 (six days after the break-in), in which Nixon and Haldeman discussed how to prevent the FBI from investigating the burglary. Informed by Barry Goldwater and other leading Republicans that impeachment was inevitable, Nixon resigned the presidency on August 9, 1974. Among the dozen men eventually convicted and sent to jail for the crime of obstructing justice were Haldeman, Ehrlichman, and Mitchell. It was the worst political scandal in American history.

THE FORD INTERREGNUM

In the middle of the Watergate revelations of the summer of 1973, the attorney general of Maryland revealed that Vice President Spiro Agnew had accepted bribes while serving as governor of Maryland. Faced with a possible prison term, Agnew in October 1973 pleaded "no contest," received a fine and probation, and resigned the vice presidency. Under the twenty-fifth Amendment, which provided for the presidential succession, Nixon nominated Re-

---

[*] The Watergate affair has left two unresolved mysteries. The first is why the break-in occurred. What did the burglars expect to find in a Democratic party headquarters? The other mystery is why Nixon did not destroy the tapes. They were stored in a White House vault and could have been magnetically erased. There is still no satisfactory answer to the first question. As to the tapes, Nixon later explained that to erase them would have been an admission of guilt. Perhaps, but he might also have pled negligence. He had already accepted responsibility for the affair and admitted he had been negligent when he accepted the resignations of Haldeman and Ehrlichman in April 1973.

publican congressional leader Gerald Ford of Michigan as vice president. Ten months later, on Nixon's resignation, Ford became president, the first ever to obtain the office by appointment. Some doubted Ford's intellectual depth and originality, but no one doubted his integrity. In the poisoned atmosphere of Watergate, that in itself was a mark of distinction.

Ford moved quickly to separate himself from Nixon. General Alexander Haig, a former Kissinger deputy who had taken over as Nixon's chief of staff after the resignation of Haldeman and Ehrlichman, was sent to Europe as NATO commander. This freed Ford from Haig while honoring the general, and because the appointment did not require Senate approval, Haig could not be summoned to testify about the last days of Nixon. Ford also offered a conditional amnesty to military deserters and draft dodgers—another break with Nixon, who had campaigned in 1972 against "acid, amnesty, and abortion." But on September 8, 1974, Ford ended his brief honeymoon with press and public when he granted Nixon a full pardon for any crimes he might have committed while in office. To many Americans it was the ultimate coverup, because now Nixon could never be brought to trial or made to testify under oath. It also relieved him from accusations that were potentially more serious than the obstruction of justice—income tax evasion and the diversion of both government and CREEP funds for the renovation of his homes in Florida and California.

Many of Ford's problems, it must be said, were not of his making. He took office at the beginning of a world recession, brought on in part by a fourfold increase in the price of oil imposed by the Arab-led oil cartel, OPEC (the Organization of Petroleum Exporting Countries). The price increase fueled inflation, which reached an annual 14 percent by the end of 1974, while the recession caused unemployment (8.7 percent by the spring of 1975) and slowed economic growth in the decade to almost zero. No president was very successful in finding a solution to the dilemma of stagflation, but Ford never really gave it a try. His answer to inflation was to encourage American consumers to buy less and eat less, a solution that served only to alarm manufacturers and farmers. Though convinced that the nation needed a comprehensive energy plan, he was never able to form one. In the absence of governmental action, market forces took over. Rising prices cut consumption and produced an "oil glut" by the end of the decade. In the meantime, inflation worsened and the economy sputtered.

Although he lacked solutions of his own, Ford was not prepared to accept the ideas of others. The Democrats, smelling victory in the election of 1976, were brimming with proposals, but Ford vetoed almost every one. In his two and a half years in office, Ford vetoed sixty-six different congressional bills, a record for the time involved. Congress, controlled by Democrats, responded by approving only a little over half of Ford's recommendations. Even Nixon had enjoyed a 60 percent success ratio in his last eight months. Ford tried to make a virtue of his relations with Congress, claiming to have arrested inflation by vetoing Democratic spending measures, but the claim only dramatized the two years of national drift.

Ford was somewhat more successful in foreign policy, in part because he followed the directions laid down by Nixon. Kissinger, made secretary of state by Nixon in 1973, was retained and pursued détente with the Soviet Union and China. During a trip to the Soviet Union in November 1974, Ford and Brezhnev pledged to negotiate a new SALT treaty. The two sides quickly agreed on the total number of strategic vehicles each would be allowed, 2,400, but talks stalemated in conflicting United States and Soviet demands concerning the Soviet Backfire bomber and the U.S. Cruise missile. SALT II negotiations were passed on to Ford's successor in the White House, Jimmy Carter.

Détente also allowed Kissinger a new flexibility in the Middle East. Through the 1960s, the United States had perceived the Middle East conflict between Arabs and Israelis in terms of the Cold War, largely because Egypt, Syria, and Iraq accepted Soviet arms and technicians, and all three were forever denouncing the United States. After the 1967 war, however, in which Israel took the Sinai from Egypt, the West Bank from Jordan, and the Golan Heights from Syria, the Arabs became disillusioned with the Soviet Union. In 1972 Anwar el-Sadat, Nasser's successor, expelled the Russians from Egypt and made friendly overtures to the United States. In October 1973, Egypt and Syria pounced on Israel, using the weapon of surprise that had served the Israelis so well in earlier conflicts. Israeli forces fell back but soon recovered the initiative. Within a few weeks, Israeli armies menaced both Damascus and Cairo. Kissinger, playing the role of honest broker, shuttled by air among the three capitals and arranged a truce. A peace settlement eluded him, however, and that problem too was passed on to Ford's successor. Nonetheless, the respect from all parties that Kissinger won and the goodwill toward the United States he created was a solid foundation for subsequent American efforts in the region.

By the end of Ford's term, Kissinger was coming under increasing attack from both Left and Right. Conservative Republicans complained that détente was a one-way street, that the Soviets yielded nothing in Eastern Europe while continuing to cause trouble in the Middle East and Africa. Liberal Democrats accused him of viewing African conflicts, such as the civil war in Angola, through a Cold-War lens. They objected to his cozy relations with military juntas, such as that in Pakistan. Revelation of the CIA involvement in the military coup in Chile in 1973 also damaged the secretary's reputation, for it was evident that both he and Nixon had approved it. Others, such as presidential candidate Jimmy Carter, referred to Kissinger's Lone Ranger style of diplomacy, his tendency to act as his own diplomatic corps, to lurch from one crisis to another, improvising as he went. Whatever the final assessment of the man, it is clear that his singlehanded control of American foreign policy from 1973 to 1977 was an abnormality, made possible only by Nixon's political wounds and Ford's inexperience. It is unlikely that any future secretary of state will have similar freedom of maneuver.

⊔ A Post-Industrial Society

Since the dawn of the Industrial Revolution, the phenomenal pace of Western economic growth had depended on an abundance of cheap energy, supplied by fossil fuels. That era came to an abrupt end in 1973 when OPEC more than quadrupled the price of oil and followed that with further increases in 1975 and 1976. These actions triggered worldwide inflation, threw Third World countries deeply into debt, and slowed economic growth in the industrialized West to a percentage point or two a year.

By 1975, the term *stagflation* had entered the American vocabulary. A clumsy verbal combination of *stagnation* and *inflation*, the term reflected the bewilderment of economists over the performance of the economy in an energy-short world. Slow growth usually brought lower prices, but the 1970s combined the worst of both worlds: slow growth and continued inflation. Adding to the nation's troubles was increased foreign competition, especially from Germany and Japan, whose industries had been entirely rebuilt since World War II, and the growth of multinational corporations seeking cheap labor outside the United States. By the 1970s, much of the footwear purchased by Americans was made in Italy, and much of the clothing was made in South Korea, Taiwan, or Hong Kong.

The industry hardest hit by the new economic order was automobiles. Since the 1920s, the automobile had been part of the "American dream," symbolizing both mobility and status. By 1970 the purchase and maintenance of an automobile absorbed as much as 10 percent of the average family budget; one out of every six American jobs depended on the automobile and related industries. During the 1970s, the dream came apart. The market was already saturated at the beginning of the decade. Every family that could afford a car had one or more. Manufacturers were supplying only replacement vehicles, with some marginal expansion into utility vehicles, such as campers and pickup trucks. Then came the series of energy crises, with skyrocketing prices and waiting lines at service stations. American car-makers, accustomed to building fuel-guzzling, chrome-plated status symbols, were slow to react. Consumers switched to smaller, more fuel-efficient imports. By 1980, of 8 million cars sold, more than 2 million were imported from Europe or Japan. By building smaller, more efficient cars, American manufacturers held their own in the 1980s, but foreign imports still accounted for 25 percent of the market by the end of the decade. Equally portentious, multinational corporations were "farming out" the manufacture of car parts to cheap labor countries, just as the textile industry had done.

The steel industry, centerpiece of America's industrial revolution in the late nineteenth century, suffered an even more severe decline. The allied victory in World War II was due in large measure to the ability of the United States to turn out more steel than Great Britain, Germany, Japan, France, and the Soviet Union combined. In 1950, American steel production amounted to 46 percent of the world's total. By 1980, that figure had shrunk to 17 percent, and by that date nearly 14 percent of American steel was imported. The decline of steel was due in part to the use of lighter materials, such as fiberglass and aluminum in the new fuel-efficient automobiles, but it was also due to the age and inefficiency of American steel plants. Steel executives began closing down their more decrepit plants in the late 1970s, but because of foreign competition they saw no profit in building new ones. In the mid-1980s, despite a generally prosperous economy, unemployment in some steel-making communities of the Northeast hovered near 45 percent.

The troubles of the automobile and steel industries were symptomatic of the broad decline of manufacturing as a segment of the American economy. At the end of World War II, one out of every three American workers was employed in the production of goods. By 1980, fewer than one in four were so employed. Farm employment underwent an even more dramatic decline, although this curve was a continuation of a centuries-long trend. Agriculture employed 17 percent of the workforce in 1940, 6.2 percent in 1960, and 3.5 percent in 1980. Where did the workers go? To the service sector, which by 1980 employed two-thirds of the labor force. Some of the service occupations were ancient and honored, such as law, medicine, and school-teaching. Others were high-tech forms of old occupations. Persons who once might have been maids and gardeners were now staffing fast-food restaurants and laundromats. Still other occupations were new. Computer specialists, whose numbers doubled in the 1970s, were not even listed as an occupation by the Department of Labor in the 1940s. This shift from an economy based on the extraction (farming, fishing, lumbering, and mining) and refinement (steel- and auto-making) of goods to an economy based on human information and services is called *post indus-trial.*

If steelworkers were possibly the biggest losers in this economic transformation, women may have been the biggest gainers. Despite a rather sluggish performance in the 1970s, the American economy managed to create almost 20 million new jobs. And most went to women. In 1960, women held about 35 percent of all available jobs; by 1980, they held about 44 percent, or almost half. To be sure, most of the new jobs were clerical, secretarial, or in retail sales, realms dominated by women since the turn of the century. But as a result of legislation and "consciousness-raising" in the 1960s, women in the 1970s and '80s moved in significant numbers into jobs traditionally reserved for men—bank officers, engineers, real estate sellers, bus drivers, and accountants, to name but a few.

The benefit to women was biracial, another result of the "consciousness-raising" of the 1960s. Black women had always been more inclined than whites to work outside the home, no doubt out of economic necessity. But in the new information society, they were no longer confined to the menial services of maids, laundresses, and sales clerks. Between 1960 and 1976, the proportion of black women who held clerical jobs nearly tripled. By 1980, nearly half of all employed black women were white-collar workers.

The transformation to a post-industrial society also affected the American family, as the female worker changed from "working girl" to "working wife." In 1900, fewer than one in ten married women worked for wages. By 1980, half of all married women worked outside the home, and married women comprised almost two-thirds of the female labor force. During the 1970s, mothers—particularly mothers of young children—were the fastest-growing segment of the workforce. A large proportion of these workers were part-time, and they were simply supplementing fam-ily income. But the figures represented a weakening as well as strengthening of family ties. Nonfamily living arrangements increased rapidly during the 1970s. By the end of the decade, one-fourth of all households were made up of unrelated persons living together. Even the term *family* meant for many Americans a single-parent, single-income household. A quarter of all American children resided with only one parent by 1980, and 70 percent of these households were headed by women, many of whom had never married.

END OF THE '60s OUTLOOK

In earlier decades, adversity had produced anger and cries for government action; in the 1970s, it produced only frustration and resignation, which in fact reinforced the conservatism of those who governed. Nothing so much illustrates this as the change in attitudes among youth. The rebellious young of the '60s were the self-confident prophets of the future, secure enough in their economic status to be able to challenge the ways in which that status had been achieved. It doubted society but never doubted itself. Its mission was to lead the world to a new, if somewhat ill-defined, order. Polls conducted at the end of the 1970s revealed an entirely different mood. A Washington *Post*–ABC News survey found that 70 percent of the respondents felt they were better off than their parents, but only half felt their children would do as well as they. Their children seemed to agree. In a 1981 poll, roughly half of high school seniors queried said that they did not expect to own more in their lifetimes than their parents did. The specter of downward mobility—that each generation might be worse off than the last—was something new to America.

Environmentalists, their popularity itself a legacy of the '60s, added to the national funk of the '70s. Apocalyptic statistics tumbled out of the newspapers. In 1970 it was calculated that combustion was annually sending 140 million tons of grime and hydrocarbons into the atmosphere that would soon create a "greenhouse effect" on the world's climate. DDT was threatening the survival of the nation's symbol, the bald eagle, and some parts of the Ohio River were so full of chemicals that the river was a fire hazard. Urging a cleanup of Lake Erie, scientists claimed that people who fell into the lake would decompose before they could drown. A team of ecologists at the Massachusetts Institute of Technology used computers to determine the ultimate effect of unchecked economic and demographic growth on nonrenewable resources. The predicted results were so catastrophic that the only solution seemed to be "zero growth." Such a solution meant the abandonment of the American dream; it was also particularly depressing to the nation's poor. Zero growth meant persistent unemployment and the pricing of goods, including such necessities as fuel and clothing, beyond their means.

Although its statistics were unnerving and its options unsettling, the ecology movement did achieve some successes. Indeed, the movement was almost the only trace of progressivism in a predominantly conservative decade. In 1969 Congress passed the National Environmental Policy Act, and President Nixon created the Environmental Protection Agency to enforce its provisions. In 1970 environmental groups filed suit under the NEPA to prevent the oil companies from building a pipeline across the Alaskan wilderness. That same year Congress passed a Clean Air Act requiring a 90 percent reduction in auto emission toxicants by 1977, and the Senate rejected President Nixon's proposal that the United States build a supersonic transport plane largely on environmental grounds (excessive noise and pollution of the upper atmosphere). In 1973 Congress passed an Endangered Species Act banning federally financed projects that could destroy or modify the habitats of species "listed" by the Environmental Protection Agency. The act proved to be a powerful legal weapon that has enabled ecological organizations to hold up construction of environmentally disruptive dams and waterways.

Environmentalism was and is a movement predominantly of whites, especially the educated, the liberal, and the affluent. It suited them because it satisfied their social concerns without threatening their living standards or social position. Precisely because it is preservationist, ecology is not a movement that appeals to the unemployed or even to the well-paid blue collar worker who aspires to own a second car or a lake cabin. Nor had it much appeal to racial and ethnic minorities, for it promised neither an increase in per capita wealth nor a redistribution of it.

EQUALITY: HALF-FILLED PROMISES

The civil rights movement reflected the changing priorities of these Americans. In the 1950s and 1960s the movement focused on legal and political rights, especially in the South. In the 1970s it emphasized social and economic equality— employment opportunity, education, and housing—and attention shifted to the North and the West.

The economic advances of minorities in the sixties and seventies can be counted as impressive or depressing depending on one's expectation. There is good evidence that the government's equal opportunity and affirmative action programs were highly effective in promoting the employment of blacks, Hispanics, and women. In the late '60s the U.S. Department of Labor set numerical hiring goals with respect to women and racial minorities and forced them on all companies that did business with the government—some 20,000 to 30,000 in all, including the nation's largest corporations. A 1983 Department of Labor study found that from 1974 to 1980, the employment rate of women and minorities grew much faster among companies covered by affirmative action requirements than among those not covered. The study also discovered that women and minority groups experienced greater upward mobility in cases where the government enforced affirmative action. They began to move from low-skilled service jobs into skilled and managerial positions. It might fairly be concluded that, although the experience of the 1960s had made white males more conscious of the needs of others, governmental prodding was still necessary in the 1980s.

Other statistics revealed similar mixed results. The growth of black-owned businesses and an increase in the number of black executives meant that by the mid-1970s 30 percent of black families had reached the middle income bracket, in comparison with 10 percent in 1964. At the same time, the proportion of white families in that bracket was 56 percent. Nor did increased wealth alter living quality much, since few black families moved out of densely populated urban cores. Those who did usually moved into suburbs already housing blacks, areas being abandoned by whites. There was hope for the future: During the 1970s, blacks made up 9 percent of the college population, not far off the 11 percent of the total population they constituted. And there was discouragement for the present: The income of black families remained about 58 percent of that of white families through the decade. In 1980, 55 percent of all black children were born out of wedlock, and 41 percent of all black households were headed by single females (unmarried, divorced, or deserted). The decline in factory jobs and the premium placed on education in the post-industrial society placed the poor in America at a greater disadvantage than ever. And much of this new burden, together with its destabilizing influences, was born by the black and Hispanic populations.

Politics mirrored society's mixed results. The change was most dramatic in the South. In 1962, before the voting rights drive began, there had not been a single elected black official in the states that had made up the Confederacy. By 1970, there were thirteen black congressmen and 198 state legislators. The number of black officials in northern cities also increased dramatically. By the early 1980s, Detroit, Cleveland, Philadelphia, Atlanta, Los Angeles, and Chicago had all been served, for varying lengths of time, by black mayors. On the other hand, as the civil rights movement pushed into the North, new forms of white backlash appeared. The busing of students to achieve racial balance in schools was an explosive issue throughout the 1970s. Busing disrupted neighborhood and ethnic loyalties, and in the view of suburban whites, subjected children to the malignant environment of the inner city. In 1972, President Nixon, with an eye on a right-wing challenge to his reelection being mounted by segregationist candidate George Wallace, came out against the crosstown busing of students. Federal courts continued to issue busing orders into the early 1980s, but white elected officials have been decidedly unenthusiastic about enforcing them.

Even with voting rights secured, blacks have had difficulty influencing American politics because of low voter turnout. In most elections, only about 40 percent of those eligible have actually participated, as against approximately a 50 percent turnout for whites. Though small, the black vote has been solid. In 1976, blacks gave Jimmy Carter 94 percent of their vote, and in 1980 they were the only ethnic-religious group to adhere to the Democratic cause. Their solidity has earned them new respect, and it has emboldened their leaders.

In 1984, Rev. Jesse Jackson became the first black candidate for the Democratic presidential nomination.

The feminist movement that had begun in the 1960s climaxed in 1972 with the passage by Congress of the Equal Rights Amendment to the Constitution. Thereafter the movement became less strident and better organized, as it lobbied for state ratification of the amendment. The transforming influence of the "liberation" movement was told in the statistics of the 1970s: The annual marriage rate declined by more than 10 percent between 1968 and 1978 as women postponed marriage in favor of careers or cohabited without formal ceremony; and the divorce rate increased by 50 percent as feminine independence placed greater demands on marriage partnerships. It seems likely that the number of abortions also increased, though reliable statistics are lacking. In 1973 the Supreme Court (dominated, ironically, by Nixon appointees) ruled that states could prohibit abortions only in the last three months of pregnancy and that they could regulate abortion for health purposes only in the second three months. During the first three months, a woman and her doctor had the right to decide. The main beneficiaries were the poor and unwed, for whom illegal abortions had been dangerous and expensive.

All these changes gave rise to fears of a "sexual revolution" that would undermine traditional values and threaten the very existence of the nuclear family. By the end of the 1970s, traditionalists had zeroed in on the Equal Rights Amendment as the incarnation of social evil. After passage in 1972, the ERA had quickly received approval in 35 of the 38 states needed to ratify, and then it became mired in the legislatures of the remaining 15. Traditionalists clouded the issue with hysterical predictions that the amendment would eliminate privacy in bathrooms, allow homosexual marriages, put women into combat, and deprive housewives of their husbands' sup-

port. A concerted effort by women's groups persuaded Congress in 1979 to extend the time limit for ratification by three years. State legislatures, confused by the propaganda of conflicting interests, did nothing more, and on June 30, 1982, the amendment died.

Surveying the wreckage, Betty Friedan, whose *Feminine Mystique* (1963) had helped trigger the movement, wondered openly if the leaders of the movement had not fallen for a feminist mystique that created a chasm between feminists and those women who still looked to the home and family for their identity. The latter group included not only full-time housewives and mothers, but the many women who held static, unfulfilling, or part-time jobs. By the extremities of their rhetoric, thought Friedan (herself a target of some of that rhetoric), feminist leaders had made it easy for conservatives "to lump E.R.A. with homosexual rights and abortion into one explosive package of licentious, family-threatening sex." In *The Second Stage* (1981), Friedan declared an end to the "first stage," in which women's aim had been full participation in the professional and political world of males. She proposed a "second stage" in which women would work with men, rather than against them. She described this stage as "a mode that will put a new value on qualities once considered—and denigrated as—special to women, feminine qualities that will be liberated in men as they share experiences like child care." Whether Friedan's prognosis is accurate remains to be seen. What is clear is that one phase of the women's movement ended with the death of ERA. Another is beginning.

⊔ The Carter Presidency

The damage to the Republican party done by Watergate was evident in the midterm election of 1974, when the Democrats increased their margin of control to about three-fifths of the seats in each house of Congress. Democrats seemed certain to capture the presidency in 1976, and as a result there were many contenders. Jimmy Carter, a former governor of Georgia, seized an early lead in the primaries and held on to win the nomination by venting the popular feeling that the political system had gone awry. He criticized the "politicians" in Washington, promised to reorganize the federal bureaucracy, and called for a government "as good as the American people."

Such talk, together with the fact that he had never held federal office, gave him the image of being an outsider untarnished by the corruption in Washington. In fact, Carter was no outsider at all; he had close connections with what its critics call the Eastern Establishment. Since 1973 Carter had been a member of the Trilateral Commission,* an international organization of corporation executives, publishers, and scholars formed by Chase Manhattan chairman David Rockefeller. The connections gave Carter access to potential campaign contributors and media contacts. *Time* magazine, which had impaled McGovern in 1972 on the pitchfork of populism, gave Carter favorable treatment throughout the primary campaign, as did the larger eastern newspapers.

After the election, Carter drew heavily on the Trilateral Commission in constructing his administration. Commission members included Vice President Walter Mondale, National Security Adviser Zbigniew Brzezinski, Secretary of State Cyrus Vance, the secretaries of the treasury and defense, and several lesser officials. Governmental gadfly Ralph Nader described Carter's cabinet as "conservatives, old-line establishment, traditional in-house advocates for

certain interests and completely main line." Carter's victory over Gerald Ford in 1976, in short, represented neither an alteration of the power elite nor a shift in direction for the government.

THE POLITICS OF LOWERED EXPECTATIONS

The Carter presidency is more significant for what it finished than for what it started, in both domestic and foreign policies. As if to pronounce a requiem on the New Deal and the Great Society, Carter called for no new reform initiatives, promised to streamline existing programs to eliminate waste, and called for a balanced budget by 1980. He also began dismantling the maze of bureaucratic regulations in the banking, trucking, and airline industries that stifled competition and increased both costs and prices. Carter's neoliberalism, however, still differed from the conservatism of Nixon and Ford. He abandoned the claim to "inherent" presidential powers with respect to national security and encouraged Congress to correct some of the intelligence agency abuses revealed in the investigations of 1975. The Foreign Intelligence Surveillance Act of 1978 required court approval for any kind of governmental electronic surveillance of American citizens. Carter also appointed to federal office more women, Afro-Americans, and Hispanic-Americans than any previous president.

What legislative proposals Carter did make, Congress buried. Carter's poor relations with Congress were not entirely of his own making. In the wake of Vietnam and Watergate, Congress was resistant to any sort of executive leadership, and unfortunately it lacked firm leadership of its own. But Carter added to his difficulties. He had portrayed himself in the election campaign as an outsider, and many in Congress preferred to treat him as one. His

---

*So named because it draws its members from the advanced capitalist "trilateral" world of North America, Western Europe, and Japan.

White House staff—the "Georgia mafia" of Hamilton Jordan, Jody Powell, and Bert Lance—were genuine outsiders, with no experience, and not especially adept at handling Congress. Bert Lance, an Atlanta banker and Carter's closest friend, proved particularly embarrassing. When Carter named him budget director in 1977, a congressional investigation revealed that Lance had engaged in some highly questionable, though not illegal, banking practices. Carter ultimately asked for Lance's resignation, but his wavering raised some questions as to how good he was at spotting the immorality he kept talking about.

Congress rejected Carter's drafts for labor law reform and for tax reform, and it gutted his energy program. The "energy crisis," provoked by the OPEC price rises in the mid-1970s, was the most compelling issue of his presidency. In 1977 he asked Americans to treat the problem as "the moral equivalent of war." But aside from some appropriations for solar energy research, the most Carter could wheedle from Congress was the repeal of oil and gas regulations that had kept fuel prices low. The increase in fuel prices to the world market level did reduce consumption. Oil companies, however, received a multi-billion-dollar windfall (the differential between the international cartel price and the cost of production). Rising fuel prices also set off a new inflationary trend. By 1980, Carter's economic policies had produced two twentieth-century firsts. The peacetime inflation rate reached 18 percent, and the prime interest rate stood at 20 percent.

Bewildered by the constant friction with Congress and the criticism of the press (those that praised him through the election campaign quickly turned on him), Carter went into seclusion at the presidential retreat of Camp David in the summer of 1979 to ponder his failures. Upon emerging, he summarily dismissed four cabinet secretaries and reassigned several others. The "massacre" raised new questions about his leadership abilities, but relations with Congress did improve. With the help of Democratic liberals, Carter obtained the passage in 1980 of the Alaskan Wilderness Act, the most important piece of legislation of his presidency. The act placed in a wilderness preserve some 100 million acres of forest, and it placed mining, drilling, and lumbering restrictions on many millions more. Presidents have departed office with lesser legacies.

FOREIGN POLICY

In his election campaign Carter indicated that he had absorbed the "lessons" of Vietnam. He accepted the fact that America could not always shape overseas events to its liking, and that it needed to work more closely with its European allies and Japan. In 1977 he declared the Cold War ended and suggested that communism was no longer an international menace. "We are now free," he declared, "of that inordinate fear of communism which once led us to embrace any dictator who joined us in our fear. For too many years we have been willing to adopt the flawed principles and tactics of our adversaries, sometimes abandoning our values for theirs. . . ." Thus, in foreign policy as in domestic, Carter broke with his Democratic predecessors. His neoliberalism was Kissinger's *realpolitik* tempered with concern for human rights. The human rights emphasis was a simple reassertion of American values, which had been cast in doubt by Vietnam and Watergate; except for some verbal jousting with Latin American dictators and the Marcos regime in the Philippines, it never served as a foundation for policy.

Building on the Kissinger initiatives, Carter's new look foreign policy compiled an impressive record of achievement. In September 1977, the president completed negotiations that had begun under President Ford with Panama concerning the future of the canal. Two treaties were signed and approved by the Senate. One provided for the return of the canal to Panama in the year 2000. The other guaranteed the canal's neutrality in peace and war, including, by Senate amendment, the right of the United States to intervene for its defense. Panama protested the reservation but accepted it to avoid a fight. The treaties mended an old wound and improved the image of the United States in Latin America.

Although National Security Adviser Zbigniew Brzezinski was inclined to be tough with the Soviets (in part because of his Polish background, some thought), Secretary of State Cyrus Vance guided foreign policy in Carter's early years, and Vance was a firm advocate of détente. He picked up the SALT II negotiations where Kissinger had left them, and on June 18, 1979, Carter and Breszhnev signed the SALT II treaty at a summit meeting in Vienna. The treaty limited the number of ICBMs in each nation's arsenal and called for a reduction in the number of missiles by 1981. It died in the Senate when the Soviets invaded Afghanistan in 1979, but each side has since adhered to the missile limits it imposed.

While negotiating with the Soviets, Carter kept his "China card" close at hand. In December 1979, he established formal diplomatic relations with the People's Republic of China. Then, he withdrew formal recognition of the Chinese nationalist government on Taiwan (Formosa) and renounced the mutual defense treaty that had originally bound the United States to Chiang Kai Shek. American-Taiwanese relations still remained cordial, in part because Taiwan had become a major source of inexpensive labor for America's multinational corporations.

The signing of a Middle East peace treaty between Egypt and Israel was Carter's most spectacular triumph. Following a dramatic visit to Israel by Egypt's presi-

Jimmy Carter at the highpoint of his presidency, March 26, 1979. Carter joins hands with Egyptian President Anwar Sadat and Israeli Prime Minister Menachem Begin in celebrating the signing of an Egyptian-Israeli peace treaty.

UPI/Bettmann.

dent, Anwar el-Sadat, the two countries had begun negotiations in late 1977. When the process lost momentum in the summer of 1978, Carter invited the two men to Camp David, the presidential retreat in the mountains of Maryland. There, through Carter's good offices, an agreement was reached in September 1978. Israel agreed to withdraw in gradual stages from the Sinai peninsula, which it had held since 1967, and the two countries agreed to establish full diplomatic and trade relations. Egypt recovered its territory and won a needed respite from war, though at the price of alienating its Arab allies. Israel secured its "back door" and neutralized the most powerful of its enemies. The negotiating process halted there, however, and in the wake of the 1982 Israeli invasion of Lebanon, peace in the Middle East remains as elusive as ever.

Less dramatic, but nonetheless important, was Carter's refusal to involve the Third World in the Cold War. His ambassador to the United Nations, Andrew Young, a black rights leader from Atlanta, developed excellent relations with African delegates and helped place Africa's problems in a new perspective. Radical, even anti-American, rhetoric on the part of Africa's leaders could be tolerated without fear that it was necessarily Soviet-inspired. And the survival of independent black regimes was to be encouraged. In 1982 Carter's friend David Rockefeller expressed the attitude in the classic terms of the Open Door: "We [the Chase Manhattan Bank] have found we can deal with just about any kind of government, provided they are orderly and responsible. . . . The more I've seen of countries which are allegedly Marxist in Africa, the more I have a feeling it is more labels and trappings than reality."

Benign and neutral attitudes toward revolution did not always work out, in part because in some parts of the world past policies had created an abiding reservoir of anti-Americanism. In Nicaragua, Carter refused to aid the Somoza dictatorship when it faced an uprising of Sandinista guerrillas. When the Sandinistas triumphed in 1979, the American government expressed the hope that they would establish a democratic regime. Instead, anti-American leftists gained the upper hand in the Nicaraguan government and vowed to export their revolution to other Central American countries. That problem Carter passed on to his successor.

THE HOSTAGE CRISIS

In Iran, the seeds sown in the past produced the bitterest fruit of all. The shah of Iran had been a close friend of the United States ever since a CIA-sponsored coup restored his family to the throne in 1953. During the oil crisis of the mid-1970s, the shah purchased enormous quantities of American arms, which helped the U.S. trade balance and shored up the dollar. The shah's efforts to modernize his country, however, alienated Islamic traditionalists, while the brutal methods of his secret police alienated almost everyone else.

In 1978, President Carter praised the shah as America's firmest friend in the Middle East, but as opposition to the shah mounted, the American government fell silent. The administration hoped that Western-oriented moderates would control the revolution. The shah fled into exile in February 1979, and the Ayatollah Khomeini, leader of the Muslim fundamentalists, came to power. The Ayatollah was still purging his opponents and consolidating his power when in October 1979 Carter made the mistake of admitting the shah to the United States for medical treatment. Enraged Iranian students invaded the American embassy in Teheran and took as hostages over fifty members of the American mission. Instead of repudiating this act of international barbarity, the Khomeini government imposed its own control on the embassy and the hostages as a means of showing its hatred for anything American. It held the hostages for the next fifteen months, the remainder of Carter's term in office.

Only a month after the seizure of the American embassy in Teheran, Soviet troops occupied Afghanistan. Though ostensibly neutral, Afghanistan had had a pro-Communist government for some years. It was unable to control a Muslim-based anti-Communist opposition, however, and the Soviets moved in to shore it up. The Soviets claimed they were invited, but once in Kabul, the capital, they deposed and executed the existing president and installed one of their own. The Soviet move seems to have stemmed not from aggressive instincts, but from fear—fear that Islamic fundamentalism might spread to neighboring Soviet provinces, fear of losing a pro-Soviet regime on their southern frontier. The Carter administration, troubled by the succession of crises, reacted in alarm. Brzezinski linked it to Soviet support for rebels in Somalia on the horn of Africa and talked of an "arc of crisis" along the shores of the Indian Ocean. The administration also became concerned about the potential threat to oil supplies posed by the upheavals in Iran and Afghanistan. In a statement that newspapers soon labeled the "Carter doctrine," the president announced that the United States would guarantee, with force if necessary, the free movement of oil from the Persian Gulf. The threat was directed not only at the Soviets, but at the rulers of Iran.

A sluggish economy at home and insults abroad: The United States in 1980 was reaping the harvest sowed by the mistakes of the past. Carter, though not wholly to blame, was the man at the helm, and public confidence in his leadership, never very high, plummeted to a new low. On April 24, 1980, Carter tried a desperate gamble. He ordered a daring helicopter-born commando raid to rescue the hostages in Teheran. Bad luck and mechanical failures aborted the raid at an airstrip in the Iranian desert, but most Americans approved the try. In the aftermath, Secretary Vance resigned and was replaced by Maine Senator Edmund Muskie. National Security Adviser Brzezinski thereafter had the dominant voice in foreign policy, with a resulting harder line toward the Soviets. In his final budget, Carter, who had earlier opposed appropriations for several new weapons systems, made provision for a substantial increase in defense expenditures. Carter's belligerence toward the Soviets seemed to increase his popularity—itself an indicator of the resurgence of conservatism in the country—and at the Democratic convention that summer he turned aside a challenge from Senator Edward Kennedy and won renomination on the first ballot. It was, as it turned out, his last political win.

SUMMARY

Just as the Kennedy-Johnson policies had built on the programs of Roosevelt and Truman, Richard Nixon built on the Eisenhower philosophy of modern Republicanism. He dismantled what was left of Johnson's antipoverty agencies, and his Supreme Court appointments reflected a conscious desire to steer the Court away from judicial activism. Nixon was not as concerned as Eisenhower had been, however, about military expenditures and budget deficits. Nixon, in fact, claimed that both helped stimulate the economy. His budget deficit for 1971 accordingly was a peacetime record (to that day) of $23 billion.

Nixon and his National Security Adviser Henry Kissinger also broke with Eisenhower on foreign policy. Where Eisenhower and Dulles had sought to order the world, Nixon and Kissinger recognized that American power was limited, a recognition expressed in the Nixon Doctrine of 1969. In line with that pronouncement, Nixon began withdrawing troops from Vietnam, leaving the South Vietnamese army to bear the brunt of the fighting. The American withdrawal emboldened the North Vietnamese, who openly invaded the South. Nixon countered by ordering the bombing of civilian targets in the North, and that eventually forced the North Vietnamese to make concessions in the peace negotiations that had been underway since 1969. In January 1973, a treaty was signed that ended the American role in the fighting. The Communists dropped a demand that they be allowed to participate in the South Vietnamese government, and the United States withdrew the last of its troops without insisting that the North Vietnamese withdraw as well.

The agreement lasted two years. In the spring of 1975, the Communists struck in force and overran South Vietnam and Cambodia in six weeks. The American people, recognizing that they could do nothing to help a people that could not help themselves, accepted it calmly.

A thread of realism ran through the Nixon-Kissinger foreign policy, a recognition that not all Communist countries looked to Moscow, that not all were inimical to American interests. This allowed them to exploit the schism that had developed between the Soviet Union and Communist China, a move that culminated in President Nixon's China visit in February 1972. The new realism also allowed them to explore détente with the Soviet Union, the relaxation of Cold War tensions begun by the Test Ban Treaty and interrupted by the Vietnam war. Negotiations to limit strategic weapons culminated in the SALT I treaty of 1971, and further talks led to a SALT II agreement in 1979. The lessening of Cold War tensions gave Nixon and Kissinger greater flexibility in other areas of foreign policy. In 1973 Kissinger was able to play the role of "honest broker" in a Middle East conflict, and before he left office he opened talks with the government of Panama concerning the return to Panama of the Canal Zone.

These achievements in the field of foreign policy might have earned Nixon history's accolade as a great president, but for Watergate. The scandal that forced Nixon from office resulted from excessive presidential power, the inexperience of Nixon's advisers, and the president's own obsession with secrecy. The nub of the problem was the illegal coverup of a minor burglary committed at the Democratic party headquarters by overzealous employees of Nixon's Committee to Re-elect the President in 1972. The coverup, in which the president was directly involved, lasted through the election of 1972, but then came unraveled in a succession of revelations that ultimately forced Nixon's resignation. He was succeeded by Gerald Ford, whose two years at the helm of the ship of state can best be described as a time of national drift.

The 1970s were not a decade of intellectual ferment or social conscientiousness. Early in the decade, considerable progress was made in protecting and improving the environment, but the legislation resulted from agitation begun in the sixties. State and federal equal opportunity laws benefited women and racial minorities, but the economic progress of both groups was slow, in part because the years after 1973 were ones of slow economic growth and high unemployment.

The prevailing mood of conservatism hampered the efforts of President Jimmy Carter to resurrect American liberalism. Carter was elected in 1976 as an outsider, uncorrupted by power and untainted by scandal. His only prior service had been a single term as governor of Georgia. Being an outsider also proved a hindrance. Congress ignored most of his proposals and emasculated his energy program. As a result, Carter's achievements were mainly in the realm of foreign policy, where he brought the Kissinger initiatives to a successful conclusion by extending diplomatic recognition to China, by signing a treaty returning the Canal Zone to Panama, by arranging a peace between Israel and Egypt, and by completing the SALT II negotiations with the Soviet Union. (That treaty was never ratified, however, due to the 1979 Soviet invasion of Afghanistan.)

Carter's political fall in the election of 1980 was due principally to factors over which he had little or no control—a stagnant economy and the seizure of hostages in the American embassy in Iran.

READING SUGGESTIONS

The most recent survey of America in the 1970s and 1980s is Melvyn Dubofsky and Athan Theoharis, *Imperial Democracy: The United States since 1945* (1983). Christopher Lasch, *The Culture of Narcissism: American Life in the Age of Diminishing Expectations* (1979), is a mildly critical look at the period.

John L. Gaddis, *Strategies of Containment: A Critical Appraisal of Postwar American National Security Policy* (1982), is one of the best of the scholarly reassessments of American foreign policy in the wake of the Vietnam war. The Nixon-Kissinger contribution to this reassessment is surveyed in Lloyd Gardner, *The Great Nixon Turnaround* (1973), and in Tad Szulc, *The Illusion of Peace* (1978).

Preliminary assessments of Watergate include Theodore H. White, *Breach of Faith: The Fall of Richard Nixon* (1975), J. A. Lukas, *Nightmare: The Underside of the Nixon Years* (1976), and Jonathan Schell, *The Time of Illusion* (1976).

Robert T. Hartmann, *Palace Politics: An Inside Account of the Ford Years* (1980), is the memoir of a journalist who was an aide to Gerald Ford. Laurence A. Shoup, *The Carter Presidency and Beyond* (1980), is a New Left critique of Carter. Betty Glad, *Jimmy Carter* (1980), has a wealth of detail, but she brings her story to an end in 1979.

17

TRIUMPH OF CONSERVATISM: 1980–1988

The emerging Republican majority, forecast by Kevin Phillips in 1969, in fact controlled the politics of the 1970s. The Carter presidency was the aberration, not the norm, a brief swing to moderate liberalism made possible by Watergate. Congress, though nominally under the control of Democrats, remained fundamentally conservative, resistant to innovation or reform. Political Action Committees (PACs)—well-financed special interest lobbies—made politics more confusing than ever. They added to the conservative mood because most of their causes—anti-abortion, antipornography and anti-gun control—were supported by conservatives. In the election of 1980, a National Conservative Political Action Committee took aim at a half-dozen liberal Democrats and defeated every one.

⊔ The Reagan Revolution

ELECTION OF 1980

The feeling of malaise that had permeated the 1970s—broken families, wayward children, street violence, drug abuse—produced a fundamentalist revival by the end of the decade. Evangelical Protestants, calling themselves the Moral Majority, demanded anti-abortion and antipornography statutes and prayer in the public schools. In the South and West, there was a new effort to prohibit the teaching of evolution in the schools. In foreign outlook they blamed the Soviet Union for all the world's ills and called for massive defense expenditures. Nixon's "silent majority" was no longer silent.

In Ronald Reagan, the Republicans had a candidate who could bind these conservative threads together. Hero to the Republican right ever since he backed Goldwater in 1964, Reagan had impeccable conservative credentials. He had a visceral hatred of Communists, dating from his 1940s struggle with them for control of the Screen Actors Guild, and he perpetuated the 1950s view of the Soviet Union as evil incarnate. As governor of California (1967–1975) he had appeared to be generally moderate and flexible, which belied his reputation for simplistic solutions. Most important of all, he had a magnetic stage presence, born of long experience in movies and television. He had a sincerity and originality that made the most simple lines meaningful, a ready smile and quick wit that softened the sharpest rhetoric.

On election day Reagan swamped Carter, taking 51 percent of the popular vote to Carter's 41 percent. John Anderson, a liberal independent candidate, managed 7 percent. Turnout was the lowest in thirty years, indicating a certain popular disenchantment with all candidates. Indeed, of all eligible voters, only 28 percent selected Ronald Reagan. But the Republican majority fashioned by Nixon in 1968 was still intact. The Roosevelt coalition—blue collar workers, Catholics, Jews, blacks, and the "solid South"—was shattered. Of the Democratic constituencies, only blacks remained. The Republicans also gained control of the Senate for the first time since the Eisenhower years, and they were able to maintain de facto control of the House by allying with conservative Democrats.

NEOCONSERVATISM

Sharing the Eisenhower-Dulles view of the Soviet menace, while lacking Eisenhower's fiscal caution, Reagan called for the biggest peacetime arms buildup in history: a total of $1.7 trillion in appropriations between 1982 and 1986. The money was to be obtained, so he argued at first, by cutting domestic welfare spending and boost-

---

(*Chapter opening photo*) President Ronald Reagan.

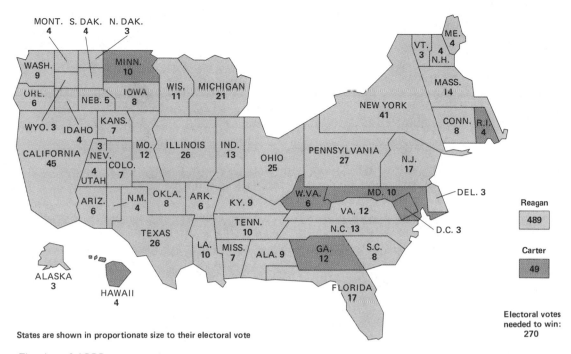

MONT. S. DAK. N. DAK.
4   4   3

WASH.
9

ORE.
6

WYO. 3

CALIFORNIA
45

IDAHO
4

NEV.
3

NEB. 5

COLO.
7

UTAH
4

ARIZ.
6

N.M.
4

KANS.
7

OKLA.
8

TEXAS
26

MINN.
10

IOWA
8

MO.
12

ARK.
6

LA.
10

MISS.
7

WIS,
11

MICHIGAN
21

ILLINOIS
26

IND.
13

KY. 9

TENN.
10

ALA. 9

OHIO
25

GA.
12

W.VA.
6

VA. 12

N.C. 13

S.C.
8

NEW YORK
41

PENNSYLVANIA
27

N.J.
17

MD. 10

D.C. 3

DEL. 3

VT.
3

N.H.
4

ME.
4

MASS.
14

CONN.
8

R.I.
4

ALASKA
3

HAWAII
4

FLORIDA
17

States are shown in proportionate size to their electoral vote

Reagan
489

Carter
49

Electoral votes
needed to win:
270

Election of 1980.

ing the economy to improve government revenues. To stimulate the economy, Reagan proposed cutting income taxes at all income levels. The theory, which Reagan supporters called "supply side" economics, was the reverse of Keynesian "pump priming"—it meant spurring economic recovery by leaving money in the pockets of taxpayers. With more money to spend, consumers were expected to buy goods, which would then stimulate production and employment.

Congress, lacking a liberal leadership and charmed by the Reagan style, went along with the entire program. In 1981 it approved Reagan's military buildup and simultaneously enacted the biggest tax cut in history: $749 billion spread over five years. The budget drastically cut food stamp, legal aid, and other poverty programs, and it virtually eliminated grants for scientific and energy-related research. In effect, the Reagan budget meant a real-

location of resources from the civilian sector to the military, and it benefited the rich at the expense of the poor.

Reagan's most subtle assault on the liberal legacy was in his appointments policy. To head the Department of Energy, created by Congress during the energy crisis of the 1970s, Reagan appointed James Edwards, a dentist and former governor of South Carolina who denied there ever was an energy crisis, favored the unregulated development of nuclear power, and looked forward to dismantling his own department. The most controversial of the Reagan appointments was Secretary of the Interior James Watt, a Wyoming attorney who had previously headed a political lobby that favored exploitation of the public domain. In two years, Watt unraveled much of the conservation legislation of the past twenty years by leasing federal lands to coal and oil companies, allowing offshore oil drilling in environmentally sensitive waters, and narrowing the scope of wilderness preserves. Ultimately his resource giveaways and his outrageous statements (he made racial and religious jokes that might have drawn laughs in the white male atmosphere of a country club lockerroom, but which sounded outrageous when published in the newspapers) forced his resignation in early 1984.

In similar fashion, Anne (Gorsuch) Burford, head of the Environmental Protection Agency, administered water cleanup funds with a political favoritism that ended in a congressional investigation, her resignation, and subsequent criminal indictment. Despite these scandals (and this was only the beginning—by the end of Reagan's presidency more than 100 top presidential appointees had been fired or forced to resign under allegations of wrongdoing), Reagan remained high in public esteem. In frustration, Democrats in Congress began referring to him as the "Teflon President" because dirt never stuck to him. Reagan's success in this role was part luck and part his management style: He worked the presidency as a chairman of the board, giving his appointees broad responsibility and letting them take the blame for failures. It worked for a time, but the dangers in such casual, loose-handed governance would become evident in his second term.

THE DIPLOMACY OF CONFRONTATION

Just as the arms buildup was the centerpiece of Reagan's domestic policy, a crusade against Communist Russia was the focus of his foreign policy. The crusade stemmed from Reagan's ideology rather than from any obvious need. There was little tension in the world when Reagan took office. Iran freed its hostages on Inauguration day. The Soviets, far from conquering Afghanistan and menacing the Middle East, had become bogged down in

a long and costly guerrila war that many called a Soviet Vietnam. The previous summer workers in Poland had won recognition for their non-Communist union Solidarity and extensive rights of free speech. The Polish situation was a standing embarrassment to the Russians, who could not afford to tolerate it any more than they could afford to intervene.

The decision to heat up the Cold War seems, in retrospect, a calculated one. Pointing to the Soviet presence in Afghanistan, Soviet badgering of Poland, and a civil war in El Salvador, Reagan's Secretary of State Alexander Haig blamed all world unrest on Soviet machinations. Reversing Carter's priorities, Haig declared that "international terrorism," which he claimed was aided and abetted by the Soviets, was the world's primary problem, not human rights. Focusing on the civil war in El Salvador, where he claimed the rebels were being supplied by the Sandinista leftists in Nicaragua, Haig invoked the domino theory to justify American intervention. If the government of El Salvador fell, he declared, all Central America was in danger. Mexico, understandably angry, immediately protested that it was quite capable of resisting Communist subversion. The administration nevertheless increased military aid to the ruling Salvadorean junta and sent in over fifty American advisers to train the junta's army. Worried about Soviet-Cuban penetration of Latin America, Haig moved toward closer diplomatic and military relations with two of the continent's most repressive regimes, Argentina and Chile. Their governments, he said, shared a basic value with the United States, "a belief in God."

Within the administration, meanwhile, officials seriously wondered whether a nuclear war was winnable. Their concern was that the nuclear deterrent, to be effective, had to be potentially usable. In a crisis, they wanted the president at least to be able to consider it. Relying heavily on the

UPI/Bettmann.
Demonstration on behalf of the Equal Rights Amendment in front of the Lincoln Memorial, October 12, 1981.

Munich "lesson" and the assumption that the Soviet Union is much like Hitler's Germany, they feared that the danger of appeasement exceeded that of nuclear destruction. A nuclear war could be "won," they concluded, only with an effective civil defense. And there the discussion became murky. One Reagan official responsible for defense policy told journalist Robert Scheerer that the effects of nuclear war were not as devastating as people had been led to believe. Said he: "If there are enough shovels to go around, everybody's going to make it." The shovels were for digging backyard shelters covered with doors and three feet of dirt. "It's the dirt that does it," he explained. Public fears about nuclear war were common throughout Reagan's first year. The president himself claimed it would be possible to limit nuclear war on the European continent to a tactical exchange and offered to situate American medium-range missils in West-

ern Europe. The careless talk and the missile offer breathed new life into European pacifist and ban-the-bomb movements.

The administration's rhetoric chilled Soviet-American relations and threatened détente, but in practical ways the interchange between the two powers continued. In April 1981, Reagan lifted an embargo on grain shipments to the Soviet Union that Carter had imposed after the Soviet invasion of Afghanistan, contending that the embargo had hurt only American farmers, because the Soviet Union had been able to purchase grain elsewhere. Regan did try to impose an embargo on heavy equipment the Soviets planned to use for the construction of a pipeline linking its natural gas wells with consumers in Western Europe. But when Europe objected, Reagan backed down and let the sales continue.

During the 1980 campaign, Reagan denounced Carter's SALT II treaty as too generous to the Soviets, but he kept to the limits it imposed. After some delay he did undertake negotiations on both intermediate-range and strategic weapons, but the discussion yielded nothing. Pressured by Congress, which demanded serious arms negotiations as a condition for the appropriation of funds for a mobile intercontinental missile system (the MX), and anxious to undercut European popular opposition to the deployment of missiles there, the administration in 1983 offered a flurry of new arms limitation proposals.

Before the Soviets could reply in any comprehensive way, a new atrocity deepened the Cold War chill. On September 12, 1983, a Soviet jet fighter shot down a South Korean commercial airliner that had strayed over Soviet territory in the western Pacific, killing all 269 people aboard. Despite worldwide outcry, the Soviets refused to accept the blame and insisted they had shot down an American spy plane. President Reagan denounced the Soviets but continued the arms limitation talks. There was no sign, however, of Soviet concessions. On September 28, 1983, Soviet Premier Yuri Andropov denounced the Reagan administration in language of a sort that had not been heard from a Soviet leader since the days of Nikita Khrushchev. The shrill accusations reminiscent of the 1950s alarmed many Americans, as well as their European allies. The sudden chill also sobered the president, who in January 1984 adopted a more conciliatory tone and accompanied it with hints of new American flexibility in arms control negotiations.

The Middle East proved equally intractable. In the summer of 1982, the Israelis invaded Lebanon in retaliation for Palestine Liberation Organization (PLO) raids. They smashed the PLO bases and forced most of the Palestinian fighters into exile in North Africa. To prevent the Israelis from coming into conflict with the Syrian army, which had occupied eastern Lebanon since 1976, American and UN negotiators arranged a ceasefire. A UN buffer zone, manned by American, British, French, and Italian troops, was created to separate the warring parties. The Reagan administration then negotiated an agreement between the Israelis and the Christian-dominated Lebanese government, which called for an Israeli withdrawal into the southern part of the country. The American government hoped the Syrians would then withdraw as well, but that proved illusory. Not only did the Syrians stay on but they gave arms and encouragement to Muslim militias hostile to the Lebanese government. The result was an effective partition of Lebanon, with the Lebanese government left in control of little but its capital. Worse still, as fighting continued, the Muslims came to see the American Marine contingent in Beirut as supporters of the Christian-dominated government, a perception that President Reagan did nothing to dispel. The Muslims turned their guns and bombs on the Marines, along with the other foreign troops. By year's end, the Marines had suffered more than 300 casualties.

The fact was that, at the end of his first term, President Reagan could not point to a single foreign policy success. His friends predicted that successes would come after the president restored military power and prestige. His critics suggested, instead, that the new weapons available to the president inclined him toward military, rather than diplomatic, solutions to problems, and they cited his tendency to rely on force in both Central America and the Middle East.

RECESSION AND RECOVERY

The president was somewhat more flexible in his domestic undertakings. "Supply side economics" was a failure, and discussion of it was quickly dropped. The economy, already in trouble in Carter's last years, slipped into a major recession in 1981, the

Black America in the Eighties: Progress and Poverty

In some respects, 1983 was a banner year for blacks, Jesse Jackson became the first black presidential candidate in a major political party. Guion Bluford, Jr., became the first black astronaut in space. Vanessa Williams was the first black Miss America. By contrast, the National Urban League's annual survey, "The State of Black America," released in January 1984, revealed how little progress the 28 million blacks in America had actually made. Among its findings:

> In December 1983, when the nation's unemployment rate dropped to 8.2 percent, unemployment among blacks stood at 17.8 percent. Unemployment among black teenagers is nearly 50 percent.
>
> The percentage of black families at or below the government's official poverty line—$9,862 for a family of four—was almost three times that of whites, the worst showing since 1967.
>
> Of all black households, 42 percent were headed by women, three-fifths of whom did not have jobs, and 45 percent of whom were below the poverty line.
>
> Declared Urban League President John E. Jacob: Black American remains "buried in a depression of crushing proportions."

deepest and longest economic downturn since the 1930s. Unemployment in 1982 reached 10 percent, and that included only those who were looking for jobs. Those who had become discouraged and had given up looking were no longer even statistics. The hard times did cut the inflation rate to manageable levels, and toward the end of 1982 the Federal Reserve Board allowed more money to flow into the economy. Interest rates went down, and by the spring of 1983 a recovery was underway.

In the meantime, the government began incurring enormous deficits—ranging above $200 billion a year—as a result of the tax cut and the defense buildup. Despite annual predictions of improvement by the President, the deficits continued year after year. Remarkably, the deficits did not bring back high interest rates or kill the economic boom, largely because of foreign investment. In an uncertain world of war and terrorism, the world's moneymen have come to view the United States as one of the world's most secure invest-

ments. Through the mid-1980s, whenever the Treasury Department went to the money markets to finance a new installment on the deficit, foreign capitalists were there. By the end of his presidency, Reagan will have borrowed more money than all other presidents put together. And the nation will have mortgaged its future to Japanese industrialists and Arab oilmen.

The economic recovery of 1983 led to an extended period of prosperity with steady, if not spectacular, economic growth. Throughout these years inflation was under control, interest rates remained low, and the stock market soared. The Dow-Jones industrial average pushed through the magical 2,000 barrier at the beginning of 1987. Like the Treasury deficits, the stock market boom was fueled in part by foreign investors, who had come to regard American corporations as nearly as secure as the American government. What might happen when foreign capital began to flow the other way was not given much thought in the mid-1980s.

CLIO'S FOCUS: Decision-making in the Reagan White House

Among the conservative idealists attracted by the prospect of a "Reagan Revolution" was David A. Stockman, a 33-year-old congressman from Michigan. Stockman's vision of political economy was as stark and simple as that of Adam Smith 200 years earlier: Eliminate government intervention and lower taxes to promote economic growth, and everyone will prosper. In December 1980, President-elect Reagan made him director of the Office of Management and Budget (OMB), which placed Stockman at the center of Reagan fiscal "revolution." Stockman began his service to the President with great enthusiasm, happily hacking away at government programs, but he soon ran into a stone wall of politics. The President would not tolerate a cut in defense expenditures (the biggest single item in the budget), and in fact increased them substantially. Congress and other Reagan advisers rejected the idea of cutting Social Security benefits (the next largest item in the budget). Because the 1981 tax cut was not balanced by a reduction in expenditures, the budget deficit inherited from Carter doubled in Reagan's first year in office and tripled in the second. In Stockman's view, the "tax and spend" policies of the Democrats had been replaced by an even more irresponsible policy of "borrow and spend." By 1983 he had abandoned hope of a "Reagan Revolution" and was frantically searching for ways to avoid impending bankruptcy. Since neither executive nor Congress was willing to cut expenditures, he concluded that new taxes were the only answer. His effort to convert the President offers a fascinating insight into decision-making in the Reagan White House.

It was January 1983, and Jim Baker [White House chief of staff] and I were in the third-floor residence of the White House, briefing the President.

"You're telling me this trigger tax is actually going to happen, aren't you?" The President sounded crushed.

"Yes," I answered, "I don't see how it can be avoided."

"Oh darn, oh darn. It just can't be. I never thought it would come to this." Slowly he took out his pen and scratched "RR" on the paper I had brought to him. His 1984 budget was thus approved, calling for a tax increase of $50 billion per year, on top of the large tax increase he had approved just a few months earlier. I had never seen him look so utterly dejected.

Ordinarily, Ronald Reagan was an incorrigible optimist. One of his favorite stories was the one about the two boys getting their Christmas presents. The first boy was a pessimist, the second an optimist. The pessimist gets a roomful of toys. He's miserable, because he's sure there's some catch involved. The optimist gets a roomful of horse manure. He's delighted. He digs around in the room for hours on end. With all that horse manure, he figured there just *had* to be a pony in there somewhere!

Well, I had just unloaded several tons of horse manure into the Cabinet Room, and it appeared that Ronald Reagan had finally given up looking for the pony. God knows he had tried. But now even he understood that major tax increases were needed to restore the Treasury's depleted coffers. Over the previous two months I had given him evidence upon evidence that if we didn't impose this trigger tax, the already frightening deficit would soar to $277 billion by 1986. As it stood now, we would accumulate *$1.4 trillion* in red ink over five years. . . . [The new taxes did not reduce the deficit because of further increases in the defense budget and the restoration of social services cut in 1981.]

The 1983 deficit had already come in at $208 billion. The case for a major tax increase was overwhelming, unassailable, inescapable, and self-evident. Not to raise taxes when all other avenues were closed was a willful act of ignorance and grotesque irresponsibility. In the entire twentieth-century fiscal history of the nation there has been nothing to rival it.

Yet nothing was done. Nothing has *yet* been done. Why? Because after the dark days of January 1983, the President renewed his search for the pony. Once the recovery started booming in the spring of 1983, there was not a thing you could tell him to shake his absolute faith that these massive deficits were simply going to vanish. Ronald Reagan is a terminal optimist.

When real GNP expanded at better than 7 percent during the last three quarters of 1983, he began to hear the whinnying. The tax cut was working—the Laffer curve [the theoretical basis for supply-side economics] was happening. The budget deficits were fading. A new era in economic history had started!

In early 1984, Marty Feldstein [chairman of the President's Council of Economic Advisers] and I made one last run at reviving the contingency tax in the next (1985) budget.

This time the President did not say, "Oh darn, oh darn." He came down on us like a ton of bricks with a twenty-minute lecture on economic history and theory.

"There has not been one tax *increase* in history that actually raised revenue," he proclaimed. "And every tax *cut*, from the 1920s to Kennedy's to ours, has produced more.

"We have always warned that the problem is *deficit spending*," he continued. "But 'they' had this theory that it didn't matter because we just owed it to ourselves. So this deficit isn't our fault. It was here before we got here. Now they're all just waiting for us to admit we were wrong so they can go back to tax and spend.

"There is another thing about this that people overlook," the President continued, "the idea that the budget was smaller than when he started. The spending line actually went down.

"It was after that that people forgot what happened. Spending went up four hundred percent but the deficit zoomed up seventeen hundred percent. That point never gets mentioned.

"We never believed in this," he went on. "We always said deficit spending couldn't go on. I still dream of the day when we actually have a surplus, when we can start retiring the national debt. That's what we have to be thinking about; not just cutting the deficit but eliminating it.

"There was a time when government took less than ten percent from the people. But that has gone up and up and up. And that's where all the trouble started. I remember some economists warned about it at the time.

"Some of our people discovered this in California. The state automatically shared part of its revenue with the local governments. And since it wasn't their money, they would spend it on things you never dreamed of. They would hire people for the parks just to stand around and watch other people work.

"So that never has worked. Carter tried it. He came up with the largest tax increase in history for Social Security and it was already bankrupt when we got here."*

"No," the President concluded, "we have to keep faith with the people. Everywhere I go they say, Keep it up! Stick to your guns! Well, isn't that what we came here to do?"

What do you do when your President ignores all the palpable, relevant facts and wanders

---

*Excerpted from David A. Stockman, *The Triumph of Politics: How the Reagan Revolution Failed* (New York: Harper & Row, 1986), pp. 355, 373–75. Reprinted by permission.

in circles. I could not bear to watch this good and decent man go on in this embarrassing way. I buried my head in my plate, and as I looked down, there it was again—the perfect scoop of tuna salad with an olive on top.

This time he was doing all the talking, but his pony made no more sense than my revolution. It was hard to say which was the greater delusion.

The next day I told Jim Baker that I was going to resign. I couldn't defend a planned trillion-dollar deficit; I couldn't defend no taxes; I couldn't defend a policy of fiscal know-nothingism.

"I can't make a fool of myself any longer, Jim," I told him. "This budget is so bad, it's beyond the pale."

Baker came back at me with a voice I hadn't heard since November 12, 1981. It was ice-cold.

"You do that and you'll stab the President right in the back," he said. "The Democrats will have a field day in the 1984 campaign.

"Let me remind you of something, my friend. He stuck by you. Now you stick by him. You've made as many mistakes as the rest of us around here. So stick that unwarranted pride of yours right up your ass, and get back in the trenches with the rest of us."

So I did, because I knew Jim was right. As I shuffled back to my office on that brisk January day in 1984, it seemed ironic that in only four years my Grand Doctrine for remaking the world had turned, finally, into a dutiful loyalty to nonsense. That was the worst lesson of all.

ELECTION OF 1984

Throughout his first term, opinion polls consistently revealed that a majority of Americans perceived Reagan as the friend of the rich and the enemy of the poor. Nevertheless, despite a brief downturn in his ratings during the 1981–82 depression (which he blamed on Carter), his popularity remained high. Indeed, until his ratings in the polls took another downturn in late 1986 in the wake of the Iran scandal, Reagan remained the most consistently popular president of modern times. The root of his popularity, besides his own communication skill, was the public perception that with Reagan at the helm the country was once again "standing tall." Americans had suffered searing humiliations in the 1970s with the Watergate scandal, the collapse of Vietnam, and Iranian hostage crisis. Reagan rebuilt the military and talked of national pride. And though he could not point to any major achievement in any part of the world, he was able to use the nation's power in limited ways that rebuilt the nation's self-confidence—the invasion of the Caribbean island of Granada in 1983, for instance, where American forces overthrew a leftist government, and the bombing of Libya in the spring of 1986 in retaliation for Libya's support of terrorism.

As a result, President Reagan had a broad spectrum of public support when he sought reelection in 1984. Blue-collar workers liked him, even though he had scorned organized labor (when federal air traffic controllers went on strike in 1981, he fired them, breaking the strike and crushing their union). Farmers liked him, even though his farm policies were driving farmers off the land faster than ever before. Businessmen loved his economic policies (though they fretted about the debt); religious evangelicals responded to his support for anti-abortion laws and prayer in the public schools.

Ted Thai/Time, Inc.

Children pledging allegiance in a New York City elementary school. A revival of patriotism was a hallmark of the 1980s.

Only two groups clouded Reagan's political future in 1984: blacks and women, and neither proved decisive. Blacks gave Reagan only 9 percent of their vote in 1980, and Reagan made no effort to attract their support thereafter. Of 450 political appointments made by the president in his first two years, only 30 went to blacks, not one of them of any importance. Oblivious to black concerns, Reagan revoked an Internal Revenue Service ruling that had denied tax exemptions to segregated private colleges, stacked the Civil Rights Commission with white conservatives, and flirted with the idea of weakening the Voting Rights Act until a political firestorm changed his mind. Blacks continued to make some gains on their own as the num-

ber of registered black voters continued to rise. By 1982 there were 220 black mayors in the country, including three of the nation's six largest cities—Chicago, Los Angeles, and Detroit. During the spring primaries of 1984, black voters responded enthusiastically to Jesse Jackson's campaign to win the Democratic nomination. In the fall election, blacks again threw 90 percent of their support to the Democratic candidate, but their numbers were still too small to make a difference.

Women also proved ineffective as a voting bloc in 1984. The major women's organizations had opposed Reagan since 1980, when the Republicans pointedly deleted support for the Equal Rights Amendment from their party platform and Reagan himself opposed it. He did appoint a woman, Sandra Day O'Connor, to the Supreme Court, previously an all-male preserve, and he named a woman, Jeanne Kirkpatrick, ambassador to the United Nations, a post that carries cabinet rank. But positions given to women were otherwise symbolic, rather than central to decision-making.

Opinion polls taken during Reagan's first term showed that women were decidedly less favorable to the Reagan administration than men were. The best explanation seemed to be that women, whom the polls have shown to be more peace-oriented than men, perceived Reagan as a warhawk. By 1984, the women's right organizations were vowing to support "anybody but Reagan." But when the votes were counted, women split evenly between the candidates, thereby cancelling themselves out as an independent political factor.

The Democrats were not an effective opposition party during Reagan's first term, in part because the party had been decapitated in the election of 1980. Conservative political action committees had targeted six of their most prominent congressional leaders, and defeated every one of them. In 1984, a host of Democratic hopefuls entered the spring primaries, but none of

Diana Walker/Time, Inc.

Vice Presidential candidate Geraldine Ferraro flanked by Walter Mondale, addresses a crowd in front of the Mondale home in Elmore, Minnesota.

them caught the public fancy. Minnesota Senator and former Vice-President Walter Mondale emerged from the spring brawl with the party nomination. In tribute to the success of the women's movement and in overt appeal to the women's vote, he chose congresswoman Geraldine Ferraro of New York to be his running mate.

Mondale was a good man and poor candidate. As a public speaker he was the dullest man to run for president since Herbert Hoover. His program, insofar as it could be discerned, involved tax increases in order to finance both social welfare programs and a large defense establishment, all of which was reminiscent of the "guns and butter" policy that had ruined Lyndon Johnson and the nation. Thus, while Reaganism invoked the nostalgia of the nineteenth century when "the eagle screamed," Mondale made nostalgic appeals to the lib-

eralism of Truman, Kennedy, and Johnson. More people bought Reagan's nostalgia than Mondale's. Reagan carried every state but one (Minnesota) and received 59 percent of the popular vote.

Even so, there were some ominous portents for Reagan's future. Talk of a "Reagan revolution," with the long-range implications of the "Roosevelt revolution," became suspect when "exit polls" (interviews with persons as they left the voting booths) showed that 20 percent of those who voted for Reagan had "serious" disagreements with him on domestic issues, while another 20 percent said they voted for the man without concern for issues. Nor was the president able to pull in supporters with his "coattails," as landslide winners had so often in the past. Republicans gained only 14 seats in the House of Representatives in 1984, and they actually

Dennis Brack/Black Star.

The president asks the First Lady to dance during the Second Inaugural Ball, January 1985.

lost 2 seats in the Senate. In the off-year elections of 1986, Democrats regained control of both houses of Congress.

⎵Progress and Poverty

Ronald Reagan was elected president a bit more than a century after Henry George published his famous indictment of the American dream, *Progress and Poverty*. Yet the central social trend of the 1980s was the same as the 1880s—the rich were getting richer and the poor poorer. Much of that was attributable to Reagan's policies— the tax cut of 1981 benefited chiefly the rich; the cuts in domestic spending hit hardest on the poor, especially working women in charge of families.

The administration claimed that newspaper reports of homelessness and malnutrition were oddities dwelt upon by a liberal press; the president countered with a symbolic oddity of his own, the welfare mother who drove a Cadillac. But the statistics gathered by social workers were grim indeed. According to their estimates made in mid-decade, as many as 10,000 people were homeless in the nation's capital, while New York City contained as many as 50,000 who were sleeping in the streets, subway stations, and parks. An estimate by private food charities was that as many as 1.5 million people were going hungry, especially near the end of the month, when government food stamps ran low. The problem of the homeless was made more acute by the policy, begun in the 1970s, of deinstitutionalizing people in mental institutions. The policy had originated in an effort to get marginally competent but nonviolent people out of institutions and into the "mainstream" of society, where what mental facilities they possessed would be challenged and exercised. Advocates envisioned a variety of community-based programs to assist them. Instead the cutbacks in federal spending placed new burdens on the states, and the programs never materialized.

Ignoring the fact that the United States had more poor people in the 1980s than ever before, the Reagan administration emphasized the statistics that showed more people employed than ever before. It is true that in the relatively prosperous years of the mid-1980s, unemployment hovered between 6 and 7 percent and the economy was generating a quarter of a million new jobs a month. But nearly all of the new jobs were in poorly paid services, and three-fourths were part-time. As the nation's economy shifted its focus from steel to hamburgers, men were being let go from jobs paying $20 an hour, while their wives, and perhaps their children, were taking jobs at $6 or $7 an hour.

At the other end of the economic scale, industrial "progress" increasingly took the form of the corporate merger. Businesses had been consolidating into ever-larger units for more than a century. Spurred by Reagan's tax cuts, the rate of corporate mergers in the 1980s was faster than ever before. Reagan's tax policies were intended to encourage investment and growth; instead many businesses used the savings to buy out rivals or insure their sources of supply or demand. At the same time that it was closing outmoded steel plants, U.S. Steel was buying up coal mines and oil fields. Its multiple operations eventually induced it to change its name to the high-tech, internationally neutral logo of USX. In the merger mania, Pepsi swallowed Frito-Lay and made a pass at 7-Up, while Coca-Cola gulped down Dr. Pepper. Spurred by the deregulation of the industry in the 1970s, airlines chased one another with a frenzy that evoked memories of the circus elephant train, each with its tail in the mouth of the one behind.

Besides Reagan's tax policies and general friendliness toward business, the other inducement to corporate merger in the 1980s was the technique of "leveraged buyout," in which a corporate raider (*arbitrager*) could acquire a business with literally billions in loans and little "up front" money of his own. The technique meant that even giant firms could become prey, and they could save themselves from "unfriendly" takeovers either by buying up huge chunks of their own stock (as CBS did in 1985–1986, for instance) or by giving the raider enough stocks or bonds ("greenmail") to persuade him to desist. That many takeovers were achieved unethically, if not illegally, was indicated by the number of "insider" trading (persons with information not available to the public) scandals that swept Wall Street in 1986–1987. The Wall Street corruption was an early signal of a growing crisis of morality that confronted Americans during Reagan's second term in office.

⊔ Losing Momentum, 1984–1988

A strong commitment to ideology and a loose management style that enabled the President to concentrate on public relations were the roots of President Reagan's strength in this first term. By an ironic twist of fortune, these elements of his leadership became sources of weakness in his second term. The President's ideological commitment had attracted to the White House a group of intense men who were convinced that they knew what was best for the country. The President's failure to keep close watch on these aides (or, some think, his concurrence in their plans) led to the tragicomedy of the Iran-Contra affair, which haunted Reagan through his final years in office. Weakened by obvious flaws in his foreign policy decision-making, the President was less able to influence the course of domestic affairs. As in the Eisenhower era 30 years earlier, an otherwise remarkable presidency began to drift aimlessly amidst the winds of scandal.

The two most important domestic programs of Reagan's second term were budgetary reform and tax reform. Both originated in Congress. By 1985 the annual budget deficits, ranging above $200 billion, had become a matter of intense public concern, and the political system seemed unable to cope with the hemorrhage. Democrats and some Republicans in Congress could not bring themselves to make further cuts in social programs; the President would not hear of a slowdown in military expenditures. With neither side willing to cut spending, a tax increase seemed the only answer. Yet the President remained adamantly opposed, and the Democrats, having been badly burned by the issue in the election, were understandably reticent.

Faced with the spectre of national bankruptcy, Congress came forth with a measure that had all the subtlety of a broadaxe. The Gramm-Rudman Act, passed in 1985, was designed to achieve a blanced budget by 1991. To meet this goal it set forth a series of budget ceilings with annually reduced deficits over the 6-year period. If the President and Congresss could not agree on what programs to cut, the act imposed an automatic across-the-board reduction in spending. Harsh as it seemed, the proposal sliced through the barriers of partisanship and parochialism that had blocked previous efforts to cut spending. Conservatives supported it in the hope that it would force further cuts in social programs; liberals favored it because it would necessarily result in lower defense expenditures (defense being the biggest single item in the budget). President Reagan, who had long advocated a constitutional amendment requiring his successors in the White House to maintain balanced budgets, gave it his approval.

The Gramm-Rudman Act never went fully into effect. The Supreme Court gutted the bill by declaring its automatic trigger unconstitutional. Both President and congressional leaders vowed to adhere to its budgetary ceilings; neither did. Some cuts were made, but the federal budget remained all but out of control.

More was accomplished in the field of tax reform. The federal income tax code had not been substantially revised since the withholding system was introduced in the 1940s. Critics of the system pointed to a bewildering variety of loopholes and shelters that were utilized chiefly by business corporations and the wealthy. They suggested a simpler system with fewer loopholes and fewer tax brackets. To succeed in Congress, however, the idea had to have the backing of the President. Reagan gave his support on condition that the result be "revenue neutral"—that is, with neither an increase nor a decrease in the overall tax burden. Passed in August 1986, the act increased taxes on the wealthy by eliminating some deductions, and it eliminated millions of low-income people from the tax rolls altogether. Most other taxpayers were virtually unaffected. If not as mighty an achievement as the President and Congress seemed to think, it was certainly a step forward.

With the President unwilling to make any major assault on such festering problems as acid rain, the global ozone layer, the deterioration in the nation's highway and mass transportation systems, and the decline in America's economic competitiveness—to suggest only a partial agenda—and with the Congress increasingly distracted by the approaching presidential election (which sparked an unusual number of congressional candidacies), it was unlikely that there would be any further legislation of significance in the President's final months in office. Making it more unlikely was a growing scandal, beginning in the fall of 1986, involving the President's foreign policy decision-makers. The exposé caused a lengthy congressional investigation that sapped the president's political strength and undermined his credibility. The story began in Central America.

CENTRAL AMERICAN LABYRINTH

The Reagan administration's initial concern over the battle between rightist and leftist forces in El Salvador lessened after popular elections there in 1984 returned a moderate government that was able to exert its authority over much of the country. That enabled the American government to redirect its attention to Nicaragua, where the Sandinista revolution of 1979 had gone progressively sour. The Sandinistas had come to power promising democratic reforms; instead, they silenced the opposition press and refused to hold elections. As American criticism mounted, they built up their military forces, accepted financial aid and weaponry from the Soviet Union, and offered encouragement to the leftist rebels in El Salvador.

In a press conference in March 1985, President Reagan denounced Nicaragua as a "Communist totalitarian state." He denied that he planned to overthrow the Sandinista government, but he did want to force them to "say 'Uncle.'" Secretary of State George Schultz later explained what that meant. American policy, the secretary said, was to force the Sandinistas to modify their behavior in three areas: by reducing the size of their armed forces (which were by far the largest in the region), cease their support for the insurgents in El Salvador, and introduce democratic reforms within Nicaragua.

The administration's method of achieving these goals was to support a group of Nicaraguan rebels called Contras (so named because, from the point of view of

the Sandinistas, they were contra-revolutionary). The administration had been supplying the Contra movement with money and weapons since 1981. The Contras, many of whom had been officers in the pre-Sandinista right-wing dictatorship, proved unable to win much popular support in Nicaragua, nor were they able to seize and hold any territory. Instead, they camped across the border in neighboring Honduras and conducted sabotage raids into Nicaragua. Distressed by the Contra's tactics, disillusioned by their unwillingness to fight, and fearful of American military involvement in a lost cause, Congress in 1984 prohibited (by the Boland amendment) American intelligence agencies from giving any active support to the Contras. It also reduced American financial aid to "humanitarian" support (food and medical supplies). In May 1985, it cut off aid to the Contras altogether.

The division over Central American policy was a litmus test of political ideology among Americans in the 1980s. Conservatives regarded Nicaragua as a "second Cuba," an agent of the Soviet Union helping to spread world Communism. They argued that American military intervention in Nicaragua would ultimately be necessary unless the Contras forced Nicaragua to modify its behavior. Conservatives also believed that the Contras represented the Nicaraguan people; President Reagan himself described them as "freedom fighters."

Liberals had more doubts about the strength and popularity of the Contras, pointing to their inability to raise any substantial support within Nicaragua. Liberals also favored a diplomatic, rather than a military, solution to the problem of Central America. Liberals supported the efforts of a group of Central and South American countries—the Contradora group, so named from their original meetingplace—to draft a nonaggression pact for the region. The treaty, tentatively approved by

Nicaragua, had been put on ice because of the opposition of the Reagan administration. With respect to Soviet influence in Nicaragua, liberals contended—and some students of Soviet behavior agreed—that the Russians were happy to spend a few rubles to distract Uncle Sam, but they had no strategic interests in Central America.

The President's fervent anticommunism had drawn into his service a number of men who saw their mission as combatting the spread of Communism and Soviet influence throughout the world. Among these was Marine Colonel Oliver North, an official of the National Security Council,* with an office in the White House itself. In the course of 1985 and early 1986, while the congressional ban on funding to the Contras was in effect, Colonel North organized a pipeline of private funds to keep the Contras in weapons. From wealthy Americans and even from foreign countries, he received donations which were channeled to the Contras by way of secret Swiss bank accounts. In one diverting incident, the Sultan of Bahrein,** a tiny, oil-rich principality in the East Indies, gave North $10 million, which North accidentally deposited (by transposing account numbers) in the account of a surprised but happy Swiss businessman. Throughout these months it was common knowledge that the Contras were receiving funds from private sources in the United States and elsewhere. The administration's involvement, in violation of the spirit if not the

---

*The National Security Council, created in 1947 by the same law that created the Central Intelligence Agency, was originally a committee of top officials whose job was to help the President formulate long-range American world strategy. With the evolution of the office of National Security Adviser in the 1960s and 1970s, the Council had become an independent policy-making body within the White House, cooperating with and sometimes competing with the State Department and the CIA.

** That the Sultan was a man with more money than sense is evidenced by his lavish, multi-million dollar palace in a country with no public school system.

letter of the Boland amendment, did not become known until the late fall of 1986. The exposure was a result of the breakdown of another covert operation undertaken by the administration—this time in the Middle East.

THE IRAN-CONTRA AFFAIR

After withdrawing the U.S. Marines from Lebanon in early 1984, the Reagan administration seemed to lose interest in the Middle East. Its display of force had failed; it had no diplomatic initiatives at hand. The catalytic effect of Jimmy Carter's Egypt-Israeli diplomacy had faded, and as America's interest and influence declined, Syria, Jordan, and Israel took turns torpedoing peace proposals. Lebanon, meanwhile, dissolved ever further into anarchy.

A war between Iran and Iraq (begun by Iraq in 1980) further complicated the situation. Arab countries along the Persian Gulf, fearing the spread of Iran's fanatical form of Islamic religion, more or less openly supported Iraq in the bloody struggle. Iran countered by redoubling its efforts to spread religious subversion. In distracted Lebanon, Islamic fanaticism added a new dimension to terrorism. Palestinian terrorism had been directed principally at Israel. In 1984 new terrorist units, professing loyalty to Iran, spread death and destruction around the world. They planted bombs in the major cities of western Europe and Japan, and they began kidnapping westerners residing in Lebanon. By the fall of 1986, terrorists in Lebanon held some 20 hostages, most of them Americans.

Most Americans saw nothing to choose in the bloody war between Iraq and Iran. Iraq had a 20-year history of antiAmericanism; Iran had recently humiliated the United States by holding its embassy staff hostage in Teheran. The administration, however, viewed the conflict in a Cold War

Roland Neven/Gamma-Liaison

Passengers being released by terrorists from a hijacked TWA jetliner in Beirut, Lebanon, June 1985.

context, and it was concerned that the Soviet Union might somehow take advantage of the conflict to increase its own influence in the Persian Gulf. It was already the major supplier of arms to Iraq and Syria. Iran, which bordered the Soviet Union, was an historic American ally. Perhaps, reasoned the administration, it could be made a friend once again. In August 1985, President Reagan approved a limited sale of arms to Iran as a way of strengthening pro-American elements in Iran and improving relations. The sale could not be done publicly, however, because for months the President had been asking leaders of the western world not to traffic with Iran, the fomenter of world terrorism. A scheme was worked out by which Israel sent missiles to Iran on planes supplied by the CIA during the fall of 1985. The United States then resupplied Israel. Iran paid for the arms by depositing money in Swiss bank accounts controlled by the ubiquitous Colo-

nel North and by American arms dealers (retired military officers) who found profit in patriotism.

Since North was already involved in an international intrigue to collect money for the Contras in Nicaragua, the idea of linking the two covert operations must have come naturally. The means was simple enough. In January 1986, President Reagan signed a document authorizing arms sales to Iran from U.S. stockpiles, and a month later the United States made its first direct sale to Iran. North and his compatriots charged Iran an inflated price for the weapons, reimbursed the Pentagon at the list price, and deposited the profit in a Swiss bank account for the benefit of the Contras. (The Contras later complained that they saw very little of the money, and Congress's investigation revealed that most of it stuck to the hands of the arms dealers.)

Whether President Reagan knew about this international shell game was a question that would haunt his presidency. Colonel North did tell his boss, National Security Adviser Robert McFarlane, about the Iran-Contra connection in May 1986. The occasion was a personal—and highly secret—visit that McFarlane and North made to Iran in a plane carrying yet a third shipment of weapons. By this time, the release of hostages in Lebanon had become an additional American objective in the arms sales. McFarlane, in fact, expected a release of all hostages when he landed in Iran; he got none. A month later the United States sent more planeloads of weapons to Iran; in July a single hostage was released. Two more planeloads of weapons were sent in October; again a single hostage was released. By this time it ought to have been evident to all that what had begun as a diplomatic initiative to mend relations had become a rather cynical swap of arms for lives. And there was no end in sight because the terrorists could always kidnap more Americans whenever Iran ran short of currency.

Nor was there any evidence that an avenue of communication had been opened. In early November, the Iranian government made public the arms sales. If there had been any "moderates" in that government, as the President believed, they had been overpowered by the extremists, who saw more to gain in embarrassing the United States.

That it did. The President, who had been pressuring U.S. allies not to sell arms to Iran, was trapped in his own duplicity. Attorney General Edwin Meese was asked to investigate the affair, and discovered the money trail that led from Iran to Nicaragua. President Reagan, steadfastly denying any knowledge of the Iran-Contra connection, fired Colonel North and asked Admiral John Poindexter (who had replaced McFarlane as head of the National Security Council) to resign. On national television, Reagan insisted that his sole purpose in selling arms had been to open communica-

tions with a country important to American interests. Somewhat inconsistently, he blamed the press for exposing the affair and endangering the lives of the hostages in Lebanon.

A congressional investigation in the spring and summer of 1987 brought out the details of the whole sordid mess. As the testimony poured forth, the President's credibility fell (polls showed that a majority of Americans liked him but didn't believe him) and his leadership was weakened. Internationally, by mid-1987, the only bright spot on the horizon was the chance of an arms control agreement with the Soviet Union.

⊔ Arms Control

President Reagan had entered office in 1981 an outspoken critic of the arms limitation agreements negotiated by his predecessors. His program was aimed at arms buildup, rather than limitations. The Soviets, suffering periodic leadership crises with aged, sick, and dying premiers, were in no position to enter serious talks, in any case. Toward the end of his first term, the President softened his rhetoric toward the Soviet Union, and a new round of arms negotiation opened in Geneva in March 1985. That same month, Soviet Premier Konstantin Chernenko died. He was the last of the old guard in the Kremlin, and his 54-year-old successor Mikhail Gorbachev represented a new generation of leadership. A skilled communicator eager to utilize the world's media (in sharp contrast to the dour secretive Russians of the past), Gorbachev presented a novel challenge for the United States.

The change was almost immediately evident when on Easter Sunday 1985, Gorbachev suddenly and dramatically made the arms talks public. He announced a freeze on Soviet deployment of medium range missiles in Europe and proposed a bilateral freeze on intercontinental missiles. He also suggested a summit meeting with President Reagan. "Confrontation," he said, "is not an inborn defect in our relations."

The two nations agreed on a summit conference in Geneva in November 1985. It was President Reagan's first meeting with a Soviet premier. Both went to the meeting with fairly rigid positions, in part because neither side had achieved an internal consensus of what might and might not be yielded. The discussion was candid yet civil, and, as so often in the past, the failure to achieve anything concrete was masked by journalistic talk about the "spirit of Geneva."

Undaunted, Gorbachev kept up the pressure. In January 1986, he called for the elimination of all nuclear weapons by the year 2000. President Reagan was wary

(as well he might in view of the Soviet superiority in conventional forces), but he did not want to appear negative. Throughout the year, the two powers inched toward another summit. Although no specific agreements had been reached (the usual condition for a successful summit), they agreed to meet in Reykjavik, Iceland, in November. Cautioning Americans not to expect too much from the meeting, White House aides described it as a "pre-summit summit."

Landing in Iceland, Gorbachev climaxed his year-long crusade for arms limitation with a breathtaking proposal to immediately cut in half the long-range missiles in the arsenals of the two superpowers and eventually eliminate them altogether. His price was that research on American's Strategic Defense Initiative (a

A grim Reagan takes his departure from Soviet Premier Gorbachev after the failed Reykjavik summit, October 1986.

David Hume Kennerly/Time, Inc.

space-based antimissile defense system that the press had labeled "Star Wars") be confined to the laboratory.* President Reagan was much tempted by the scope of the Russian proposal and the possibilities it might awaken for agreements in other areas; but at the last minute he decided to insist on testing the SDI in space (even though to do so violated the spirit and probably the letter of the anti-ballistic missile treaty negotiated by Nixon in 1972). The meeting broke up in a bitter exchange, and relations cooled temporarily.

Serious negotiations resumed, however, in the spring of 1987 at Geneva. The new focus of attention was the medium range missiles based in Europe. There was much promise of agreement on reducing or eliminating these because they had been installed only within the past decade. In the event of conventional war they could not be used without danger of escalating; in the event of all-out war they were irrelevant. The hope, too, was that the success of a limited agreement might form the basis of mutual trust that could lead to further agreements. Both leaders, moreover, had a stake in successful negotiations. President Reagan reportedly wished to leave office with some sort of legacy of peace. Premier Gorbachev candidly admitted his desire to reduce international tensions so the Soviet Union could focus its energies on improving its own standard of living. Some sort of arms limitation seemed only a question of time—whether it would be achieved during Reagan's "watch" (as he so often referred to his tenure in office) or whether it would be unfinished business passed on to his successor.

---

*The irony is that a majority of American physicists did not think SDI would work, and many felt that even if it could be made to work, it would be a decade before there was any need for tests outside the laboratory. The purpose of immediate testing in space, many suspected, was political: to impress on Congress that progress was rapid enough to justify the enormous cost of the project.

⊔ The National Agenda: Challenge and Opportunity

The slogan "I feel good about myself," born of the "me decade" 1970s and so symbolic of the politics of the 1980s, seemed increasingly hollow as the decade neared its end. Once again the nation's moral fiber was being seriously questioned. The Iran-Contra* hearings drew a picture of a head of state who was actively encouraging his supporters to skirt the law and find ways to thwart the will of Congress. They drew a picture of government policy being carried out by private citizens, who took advantage of the opportunity to line their own pockets. Allegations of corruption also shadowed the administration's domestic policymakers. By the spring of 1987, Attorney General Edwin Meese—the nation's chief law-enforcement officer—was the target of four separate investigations.

Across the Potomac River, the Pentagon was rocked with one spy scandal after another in the mid-1980s. First there was the revelation of a spy ring in the U.S. Navy that had given the Soviets vital information on the operation of American missile submarines. The U.S. Marines, an organization that thrived on honor, had to watch in silent chagrin as one of their own officers, Col. Oliver North, appeared before a committee of Congress in full uniform and took the Fifth Amendment, refusing to answer questions on grounds that he might incriminate himself. In the midst of that, in the winter of 1986–87, came allegations that Marine guards at the U.S. embassy in Moscow had been giving information to Soviet spies. Rarely in the past had

---

*This was the label for the episode generally adopted by the press during the congressional hearings. When the story first broke, many newspapers referred to it as "Irangate," in rather clumsy reference to Nixons Watergate scandal. One newspaper held a contest for a label. This author's favorite entry was "Iranamok."

Drug bust among Wall Street brokers. Suspects being led away from a New York City court.

Bill Foley, *Time Magazine*.

the American military establishment, the principal beneficiary of Reagan's budgetary largesse, had so much cause for embarrassment.

There was mounting evidence outside the government, too, of the breakdown in moral fiber: insider trading in Wall Street, the use of drugs by Wall Street stockbrokers to win customers, and ongoing revelations of the use of narcotics by professional athletes. Indeed, the use of drugs, once confined to "opium dens" and ghetto alleyways, had become a middle-class fancy and threatened to become a national epidemic.

Heroes with feet of clay were a sign of the times, and none was more shocking than the fall of television evangelist Jim Bakker in the spring of 1987. Bakker, head of PTL ("Praise the Lord"), one of the largest of the television ministries with millions in annual donations, resigned after confessing adultery with a church secretary. Investigation revealed that Bakker and his wife collected salaries of over a million dollars a year and maintained lavish households in various parts of the country. The revelations cast a pall over the whole mul-

timillion dollar empire of televised religion and caused a series of "holy wars" among the TV evangelists, who traded allegations of power-broking and skulduggery. Endangered also was the "moral majority" movement, which for more than a decade had sought to impose its conservative social agenda on the nation.

The spread of the deadly AIDS virus raised other moral issues. Only a decade after its first discovery, the disease threatened to become one of the worst world epidemics in history. Because it was invariably fatal and there was no known cure, AIDS presented an enormous challenge to medical science; it also presented society with serious moral decisions because the virus was spread principally by sexual contact. Even nonsexual means of transmission, such as the infected needles of narcotics users, had moral implications. In mid-1987, it was estimated that half of New York City's drug addicts were infected with AIDS. (The disease, of course, could be contracted quite innocently—through blood transfusions, for instance, or by an unborn child from its mother.) Not since syphilis had raced across Europe in the six-teenth century had there been an epidemic so closely related to moral behavior, with a high risk of punishment for wrongdoing. The long-range effect on social mores can only be guessed, but one casualty almost surely will be the sexual license that was a by-product of the liberationist movements of the 1960s.

Perhaps the most serious threat to future well-being was the tendency of the nation to live beyond its means. The federal government spent far more than it received in revenue, and in financing its excesses it soaked up the world's capital. Consumer debt also mounted, and increasingly it represented debt owed to foreign countries. The nations' trade had been unbalanced by the oil crises of the 1970s; instead of righting itself in the stable and prosperous 1980s, it grew steadily worse. Both publicly and privately, by the end of the 1980s, Americans had pawned themselves to the rest of the world.

All of these stormclouds presented challenge enough for the future, but there were also some rays of hope. The free enterprise system, which had been on the defensive around the world for decades, was once more on the march. Its worth had been graphically demonstrated by the glowing success of countries on the Pacific rim—Japan, South Korea, Taiwan, and Singapore. Unabashedly capitalistic, these nations had transformed themselves in a few short years from overpopulated backwaters (with the exception, of course, of Japan, long an industrial power) to the world's fastest-growing economies. In so doing, they became models for the whole "third world." Elsewhere in Asia and Africa, countries that had once embraced "socialism" as a means of allocating capital investment, were dismantling bloated bureaucracies and eagerly seeking international funds. Most stunning of all was China's announcement in the fall of 1985 that the economic theories of Karl Marx were no longer relevant to China's development.

Never before had a country of that size and importance renounced the theory (though not, as yet, the practice) of communism.

Accompanying the revitalization of free enterprise was the spread of political democracy in the Third World (though the two developments should not be equated). The year 1986 provided two spectacular examples as vicious dictatorships were overthrown in the Philippines and in Haiti. The Philippines have since developed a stable democratic government; the future of Haiti (the poorest nation in Latin America) is more problematical. In Latin America, where military rule was once the norm, civilian governments are in control. Elsewhere—as in South Korea—military governments are under attack.

It may be that the most arresting trend of the 1980s was not democracy but decentralization. Bureaucracies everywhere are on the defensive in part because the world has become too complex for centralized management. In the United States it was not simply Reagan's ideology, but a recognition of failure that induced the federal government to turn over many of its social functions to the states and the cities in the 1980s. In Europe, Britain and Scandinavia trimmed the edges of their welfare-state apparatuses. Around the world, business corporations have taken lessons from the Japanese, who encourage employee participation in decision-making and trim management to essentials. Perhaps the most dramatic change of all—though still in its infancy—is taking place in the Soviet Union, where Premier Gorbachev is reducing the role of central planning (a major feature of the Marxist system) and is introducing competitiveness in both the political and the economic systems.

If decentralization is truly the trend of the future, the United States may well be in the vanguard. Americans were pioneers in decentralized government; their culture is built on the worth of the free individual. This may still be "an American century."

SUMMARY

Continuing "stagflation" and the American diplomatic hostages in Iran gave Ronald Reagan a chance to accuse the Carter administration of neglecting both the nation's economy and the nation's defenses. Reagan's election in 1980 reflected a resurgence in the conservative mood that had set in after 1968. He shared Nixon's devotion to national defense and scorn for social programs, and took both to extremes. The combination of high expenditures for defense, a tax cut, and an economic recession produced budget deficits of more than $200 billion a year by Reagan's third year in office. In 1980, Reagan had accused the Democrats of ruining the country with a policy of "tax and spend"; his substitute policy of "borrow and spend" seemed even more ruinous.

Reagan retained the Nixon-Kissinger policies with respect to China and the Middle East, but he reverted to the Eisenhower-Dulles view of the Soviet Union in his first term in office. His verbal attacks on the Soviet Union, coupled with his arms buildup, alarmed the Soviet leadership and brought a new chill to the Cold War. During his second term in office, however, the President softened his rhetoric and sought an arms control agreement with the Soviet Union.

The prevailing mood of conservatism meant that many urgent social needs went unmet—the social infrastructure, such as highways and education, was shortchanged in favor of military expenditures, the number of homeless people increased dramatically, acid rain and the ozone layer were ignored, and only token efforts were made at cleaning up hazardous wastes. Nevertheless, the middle years of the decade were years of prosperity with low inflation, low interest rates, and relatively high employment. Americans, having recovered from the humiliations of the 1970s, felt that their country was once again "standing tall," and they credited the President. He was re-elected in 1984 by one of the largest margins in history.

President Reagan's second term was less successful. The aroma of corruption pervaded the air as one high administration official after another (more than 100 in all) came under investigation or indictment. The Iran-Contra affair, with its revelation of a President openly encouraging his subordinates to skirt the law, cast a pall over the administration and weakened the president's authority in both domestic and foreign affairs. Through it all, the President remained personally popular with the people. Whether history would share their judgment remained to be seen.

READING SUGGESTIONS

There is, as yet, no adequate history of the 1980s or the Reagan Presidency. Almost the only items available are critiques from Reagan's opponents and the memoirs of his disillusioned lieutenants. An example of the first genre is Alan Gartner, Colin Greer and Frank Riessman, eds., *What Reagan Is Doing to Us* (1982); an example of the second is David A. Stockman, *The Triumph of Politics: How the Reagan Revolution Failed* (1986). The story of this chapter has been derived principally from newspapers and newsmagazines; its thesis and conclusions therefore are necessarily tentative.

THE DECLARATION OF INDEPENDENCE

When in the Course of human events, it becomes necessary for one people to dissolve the political bands which have connected them with another, and to assume among the Powers of the earth, the separate and equal station to which the Laws of Nature and of Nature's God entitle them, a decent respect to the opinions of mankind requires that they should declare the causes which impel them to the separation.

We hold these truths to be self-evident, that all men are created equal, that they are endowed by their Creator with certain unalienable Rights, that among these are Life, Liberty and the pursuit of Happiness. That to secure these rights, Governments are instituted among Men, deriving their just powers from the consent of the governed, That whenever any Form of Government becomes destructive of these ends, it is the Right of the people to alter or to abolish it, and to institute new Government, laying its foundation on such principles and organizing its powers in such form, as to them shall seem most likely to effect their Safety and Happiness. Prudence, indeed, will dictate that Governments long established should not be changed for light and transient causes; and accordingly all experience hath shown, that mankind are more disposed to suffer, while evils are sufferable, than to right themselves by abolishing the forms to which they are accustomed. But when a long train of abuses and usurpations, pursuing invariably the same Object evinces a design to reduce them under absolute Despotism, it is their right, it is their duty, to throw off such Government, and to provide new Guards for their future security.—Such has been the patient sufferance of these Colonies; and such is now the necessity which constrains them to alter their former Systems of Government. The history of the present King of Great Britain is a history of repeated injuries and usurpations, all having in direct object the establishment of an absolute Tyranny over these States. To prove this, let Facts be summitted to a candid world.

He has refused his Assent to Laws, the most wholesome and necessary for the public good.

He has forbidden his Governors to pass Laws of immediate and pressing importance, unless suspended in their operation till his Assent should be obtained; and when so suspended, he has utterly neglected to attend to them.

He has refused to pass other Laws for the accommodation of large districts of people, unless those people would relinquish the right of Representation in the Legislature, a right inestimable to them and formidable to tyrants only.

He has called together legislative bodies at places unusual, uncomfortable, and distant from the depository of their public Records, for the sole purpose of fatiguing them into compliance with his measures.

He has dissolved Representative Houses repeatedly, for opposing with manly firmness his invasions on the rights of the people.

He has refused for a long time, after such dissolutions, to cause others to be elected; whereby the Legislative Powers, incapable of Annihilation, have returned to the People at large for their exercise; the State remaining in the mean time exposed to all the dangers of invasion from without, and convulsions within.

He has endeavoured to prevent the population of these States; for that purpose obstructing the Laws of Naturalization of Foreigners; refusing to pass others to encourage their migration hither, and raising the conditions of new Appropriations of Lands.

He has obstructed the Administration of Justice, by refusing his Assent to Laws for establishing Judiciary powers.

He has made Judges dependent on his Will alone, for the tenure of their offices, and the amount and payment of their salaries.

He has erected a multitude of New Offices, and sent hither swarms of Officers to harass our People, and eat out their substance.

He has kept among us in times of peace, Standing Armies without the Consent of our legislature.

He has affected to render the Military independent of and superior to the Civil power.

He has combined with others to subject us to a jurisdiction foreign to our constitution, and unacknowledged by our laws; giving his Assent to their acts of pretended Legislation:

For quartering large bodies of armed troops among us:

For protecting them, by a mock Trial, from punishment for any Murders which they should commit on the Inhabitants of these States:

For cutting off our Trade with all parts of the world:

For imposing taxes on us without our Consent:

For depriving us in many cases, of the benefits of Trial by Jury:

For transporting us beyond Seas to be tried for pretended offences:

For abolishing the free System of English Laws in a neighbouring Province, establishing therein an Arbitrary government, and enlarging its Boundaries so as to render it at once an example and fit instrument for introducing the same absolute rule into these Colonies:

For taking away our Charters, abolishing our most valuable Laws, and altering fundamentally the Forms of our Governments:

For suspending our own Legislature, and declaring themselves invested with Power to legislate for us in all cases whatsoever.

He has abdicated Government here, by declaring us out of his Protection and waging War against us.

He has plundered our seas, ravaged our Coasts, burnt our towns, and destroyed the lives of our people.

He is at this time transporting large Armies of foreign Mercenaries to compleat the works of death, desolation and tyranny, already begun with circumstances of Cruelty & perfidy scarcely paralleled in the most barbarous ages, and totally unworthy the Head of a civilized nation.

He has constrained our fellow Citizens taken Captive on the high Seas to bear Arms against their Country, to become the executioners of their friends and Brethren, or to fall themselves by their Hands.

He has excited domestic insurrections amongst us, and has endeavoured to bring on the inhabitants of our frontiers, the merciless Indian Savages, whose known rule of warfare, is an undistinguished destruction of all ages, sexes and conditions.

In every stage of these Oppressions We have Petitioned for Redress in the most humble terms: Our repeated Petitions have been answered only by repeated injury. A Prince, whose character is thus marked by every act which may define a Tyrant, is unfit to be the ruler of a free People.

Nor have We been wanting in attention to our British brethren. We have warned them from time to time of attempts by their legislature to extend an unwarrantable jurisdiction over us. We have reminded them of the circumstances of our emigration and settlement here. We have appealed to their native justice and magnanimity, and we have conjured them by the ties of our common kindred to disavow these usurpations, which, would inevitably interrupt our connections and correspondence. They too have been deaf to the voice of justice and of consanguinity. We must, therefore, acquiesce in the necessity, which denounces our Separation, and hold them, as we hold the rest of mankind, Enemies in War, in Peace Friends.

We, therefore, the Representatives of the United States of America, in General Congress, Assembled, appealing to the Supreme Judge of the world for the rectitude of our intentions, do, in the Name, and by Authority of the good People of these Colonies, solemnly publish and declare, That these United Colonies are, and of Right ought to be Free and Independent States; that they are Absolved from all Allegiance to the British Crown, and that all political connection between them and the State of Great Britain, is and ought to be totally dissolved; and that as Free and Independent States, they have full Power to levy War, conclude Peace, contract Alliances, establish Commerce, and to do all other Acts and Things which Independent States may of right do. And for the support of this Declaration, with a firm reliance on the protection of divine Providence, we mutually pledge to each other our Lives, our Fortunes and our sacred Honor.

THE CONSTITUTION OF THE UNITED STATES,
And What It Means Today

The Preamble. Chief Justice John Marshall pointed out in 1803 that the Preamble begins "We the people," and not "We the states." Thus the federal government derives its authority directly from the people and not from the states.

We the people of the United States, in Order to form a more perfect Union, establish Justice, insure domestic Tranquility, provide for the common defense, promote the general Welfare, and secure the Blessings of Liberty to ourselves and our Posterity, do ordain and establish this Constitution for the United States of America.

ARTICLE I

Section 1. All legislative powers herein granted shall be vested in a Congress of the United States, which shall consist of a Senate and House of Representatives.

Section 2. The House of Representatives shall be composed of Members chosen every second Year by the People of the several States, and the Electors in each State shall have the Qualifications requisite for Electors of the most numerous Branch of the State Legislature.

No Person shall be a Representative who shall not have attained to the Age of twenty-five Years, and been seven Years a Citizen of the United States, and who shall not, when elected, be an Inhabitant of that State in which he shall be chosen.

Direct taxes. This provision was altered by the Sixteenth Amendment, which allows the federal government to levy an income tax directly on the people.

Apportionment of representation. In 1929 Congress limited the House of Representatives to 435 members, who are allotted among the states on the basis of population. Each ten-year census thus requires a re-arrangement of the House of Representatives. "Three fifths of all other persons" referred to slaves, and it was among the several sectional compromises in the Constitution.

Representatives and direct Taxes shall be apportioned among the several States which may be included within this Union, according to their respective Numbers, which shall be determined by adding to the whole Number of Free Persons, including those bound to Service for a Term of Years, and excluding Indians not taxed, three fifths of all other Persons. The actual Enumeration shall be made within three Years after the first Meeting of the Congress of the United States, and within every subsequent Term of ten Years, in such Manner as they shall by Law direct. The number of Representatives shall not exceed one for every thirty Thousand, but each State shall have at Least one Representative; and until such enumeration shall be made, the State of New Hampshire shall be entitled to chuse three, Massachusetts eight, Rhode Island and Providence Plantations one, Connecticut five, New York six, New Jersey four, Pennsylvania eight, Delaware one, Maryland six, Virginia ten, North Carolina five, South Carolina five, and Georgia three.

When vacancies happen in the Representation from any State, the Executive Authority thereof shall issue Writs of Election to fill such Vacancies.

The House of Representatives shall chuse their Speaker and other Officers; and shall have the sole Power of Impeachment.

Section 3. The Senate of the United States shall be composed of two Senators from each State, chosen by the Legislature thereof, for six Years; and each Senator shall have one Vote.

Immediately after they shall be assembled in Consequence of the first Election, they shall be divided as equally as may be into three Classes. The Seats of the Senators of the first Class shall be vacated at the Expiration of the second Year, of the second Class at the Expiration of the fourth Year, and of the third Class at the Expiration of the sixth Year, so that one-third may be chosen every second Year; and if Vacancies happen by Resignation, or otherwise during the Recess of the Legislature of any State, the Executive thereof may make temporary Appointments until the next Meeting of the Legislature, which shall then fill such Vacancies.

No Person shall be a Senator who shall not have attained to the Age of thirty Years, and been nine Years a Citizen of the United States, and who shall not, when elected, be an Inhabitant of that State in which he shall be chosen.

The Vice President of the United States shall be President of the Senate, but shall have no vote, unless they be equally divided.

The Senate shall choose their Officers, and also a President pro tempore, in the absence of the Vice President, or when he shall exercise the Office of the President of the United States.

The Senate shall have the sole Power to try all Impeachments. When sitting for that purpose, they shall be on Oath or Affirmation. When the President of the United States is tried, the Chief Justice shall preside: And no person shall be convicted without the Concurrence of two thirds of the Members present.

Judgment in Cases of Impeachment shall not extend further than to removal from Office, and disqualification to hold and enjoy any Office of honor, Trust, or Profit under the United States: but the Party convicted shall nevertheless be liable and subject to Indictment, Trial, Judgment, and Punishment, according to Law.

Section 4. The Times, Places and Manner of holding Elections for Senators and Representatives, shall be prescribed in each state by the Legislature thereof; but the Congress may at any time by Law make or alter such Regulations, except as to the Places of Chusing Senators.

The Congress shall assemble at least once in every Year, and such Meeting shall be on the first Monday in December, unless they shall by Law appoint a different Day.

Selection of senators. By the provisions of the Seventeenth Amendment, senators are chosen by the voters rather than by the state legislatures.

The vice president's "casting vote." John Adams cast the first tie-breaking vote in 1789 on a rule that allowed the president to remove important executive officers without the "advice and consent" of the Senate.

Impeachments. The persons subject to impeachment are "civil officers of the United States," which does not include members of Congress. *Impeachment* means an accusation of misconduct, which must first be voted by the House of Representatives. The misconduct must amount to a charge of "treason, bribery, or other high crimes and misdemeanors" (Article II, Section 4). The Senate tries all impeachments, with members of the House serving as the prosecution. A two-thirds majority is required for conviction. It has never been determined whether a person has to be convicted of a crime or simply of "misbehavior." Judges are appointed for life during good behavior (Article III, Section 1), but they can be removed only by impeachment. In all, three persons, all judges, have been convicted and removed under this article.

Qualifications of members. Control over seating was one of the early privileges claimed by the English Parliament, and American legislatures have uniformly claimed the same power. Congress has usually used the power to purge itself of undesirable elements. In 1900 the House refused to seat a representative from Utah because he was guilty of polygamy. In 1919 it refused to seat a Wisconsin congressman because he was a Socialist.

Journal of proceedings. The requirement that each house keep a journal and record roll call votes was intended to ensure that the voters could keep track of the conduct of their representatives and senators.

Immunity. Immunity from arrest while attending sessions and freedom of speech in debate were rights claimed by the English Parliament to protect itself against interference from the crown. In America they have served little purpose other than to protect legislators from libel suits.

Revenue bills. The provision that taxation measures must originate in the House of Representatives was intended to make that house more important. It was part of the large state–small state compromise that based representation in the House by population and in the Senate by states.

The veto. The requirement that the president must sign a bill before it becomes law, and the requirement that each house of Congress must muster a two-thirds vote to override a president's veto, are among the "checks and balances" of the Constitution. The ten-day rule allows a president to give a bill a "pocket veto" simply by withholding his signature until Congress adjourns, if the bill has been sent to him within ten days of the end of the session.

Section 5. Each House shall be the Judge of the Elections, Returns and Qualifications of its own Members, and a Majority of each shall constitute a Quorum to do Business; but a smaller number may adjourn from day to day, and may be authorized to compel the Attendance of absent Members, in such Manner, and under such Penalties, as each House may provide.

Each House may determine the Rules of its Proceedings, punish its Members for disorderly Behaviour, and, with the Concurrence of two thirds, expel a Member.

Each House shall keep a Journal of its Proceedings, and from time to time publish the same, excepting such Parts as may in their Judgment require Secrecy; and the Yeas and Nays of the Members of either House on any question shall, at the Desire of one fifth of those Present, be entered on the Journal.

Neither House, during the Session of Congress, shall, without the Consent of the other, adjourn for more than three days, nor to any other Place than that in which the two Houses shall be sitting.

Section 6. The Senators and Representatives shall receive a Compensation for their Services, to be ascertained by Law, and paid out of the Treasury of the United States. They shall in all Cases, except Treason, Felony, and Breach of the Peace, be privileged from Arrest during their Attendance at the Session of their respective Houses, and in going to and returning from the same; and for any Speech or Debate in either House, they shall not be questioned in any other Place.

No Senator or Representative shall, during the Time for which he was elected, be appointed to any civil Office under the Authority of the United States, which shall have been created, or the Emoluments whereof shall have been increased, during such time; and no Person holding any Office under the United States shall be a Member of either House during his continuance in Office.

Section 7. All Bills for raising Revenue shall originate in the House of Representatives; but the Senate may propose or concur with Amendments as on other Bills.

Every Bill which shall have passed the House of Representatives and the Senate, shall, before it become a Law, be presented to the President of the United States; If he approve he shall sign it, but if not he shall return it, with his Objections, to that House in which it shall have originated, who shall enter the Objections at large on their Journal, and proceed to reconsider it. If after such Reconsideration two thirds of that House shall agree to pass the Bill, it shall be sent, together with the Objections, to the other House, by which it shall likewise be reconsidered, and if approved by two thirds of that House, it shall become a Law. But in all such Cases the Votes of both Houses shall be determined by Yeas and Nays, and the Names of the Persons voting for and against the Bill shall be entered on the Journal of each House respectively. If any Bill shall not be returned by the President within ten Days (Sundays excepted) after it shall have been represented to him, the Same shall be a Law, in like Manner as if he had signed it, unless the Congress by their Adjournment prevent its Return, in which Case it shall not be a Law.

Every Order, Resolution, or Vote to which the Concurrence of the Senate and House of Representatives may be necessary (except on a question of Adjournment) shall be presented to the President of the United States; and before the Same shall take Effect, shall be approved by him, or being disapproved by him, shall be repassed by two thirds of the Senate and House of Representatives, according to the Rules and Limitations prescribed in the Case of a Bill.

Section 8. The Congress shall have Power To lay and collect Taxes, Duties, Imposts and Excises, to pay the Debts and provide for the common Defense and general Welfare of the United States; but all Duties, Imposts and Excises shall be uniform throughout the United States;

To borrow money on the credit of the United States;

To regulate Commerce with foreign Nations, and among the several States, and with the Indian Tribes;

To establish an uniform Rule of Naturalization, and uniform Laws on the subject of Bankruptcies throughout the United States;

To coin Money, regulate the Value thereof, and of foreign Coin, and fix the Standard of Weights and Measures;

To provide for the Punishment of counterfeiting the Securities and current Coin of the United States;

To establish Post Offices and post Roads;

To promote the Progress of Science and useful Arts, by securing for limited Times to Authors and Inventors the exclusive Right to their respective Writings and Discoveries;

To constitute Tribunals inferior to the Supreme Court;

To define and punish Piracies and Felonies committed on the high Seas, and Offenses against the Law of Nations;

To declare War, grant Letters of Marque and Reprisal, and make Rules concerning Captures on Land and Water;

To raise and support Armies, but no Appropriation of Money to that Use shall be for a longer Term than two Years;

To provide and maintain a Navy;

To make Rules for the Government and Regulation of the land and naval forces;

To provide for calling forth the Militia to execute the Laws of the Union, suppress Insurrections and repel Invasions;

To provide for organizing, arming, and disciplining the Militia, and for governing such Part of them as may be employed in the Service of the United States, reserving to the States respectively, the Appointment of the Officers,

The powers of Congress. The phrase "general welfare" in the first paragraph of Section 8 is a limitation on what Congress can do with tax revenue; it does not add to the powers of Congress. The framers of the Constitution intended the powers of Congress to be specific, not general. However, the courts over the years have found within these specifically enumerated powers various "implied powers." For instance, the power to regulate interstate commerce has been interpreted to include social security, Medicare, labor legislation, and civil rights acts. The power to "raise and support armies" includes the power to build interstate highways to facilitate army movements.

and the Authority of training the Militia according to the discipline prescribed by Congress;

To exercise exclusive Legislation in all Cases whatsoever, over such District (not exceeding ten Miles square) as may, by Cession of particular States, and the acceptance of Congress, become the Seat of Government of the United States, and to exercise like Authority over all Places purchased by the Consent of the Legislature of the State in which the Same shall be, for the Erection of Forts, Magazines, Arsenals, dock-Yards, and other needful Buildings;—And

To make all Laws which shall be necessary and proper for carrying into Execution the foregoing Powers, and all other Powers vested by this Constitution in the Government of the United States, or in any Department or Officer thereof.

Section 9. The Migration or Importation of such Persons as any of the States now existing shall think proper to admit, shall not be prohibited by the Congress prior to the Year one thousand eight hundred and eight, but a tax or duty may be imposed on such Importation, not exceeding ten dollars for each Person.

The privilege of the Writ of Habeas Corpus shall not be suspended, unless when in Cases of Rebellion or Invasion the public Safety may require it.

No Bill of Attainder or ex post facto Law shall be passed.

No Capitation, or other direct, Tax shall be laid unless in Proportion to the Census or Enumeration herein before directed to be taken.

No Tax or Duty shall be laid on Articles exported from any State.

No Preference shall be given by any Regulation of Revenue to the Ports of one State over those of another: nor shall Vessels bound to, or from, one State, be obliged to enter, clear, or pay Duties in another.

No Money shall be drawn from the Treasury, but in Consequence of Appropriations made by Law; and a regular Statement and Account of the Receipts and Expenditures of all public Money shall be published from time to time.

No title of Nobility shall be granted by the United States: And no Person holding any Office of Profit or Trust under them, shall, without the Consent of the Congress, accept of any present, Emolument, Office, or Title, of any kind whatever, from any King, Prince, or foreign State.

Section 10. No State shall enter into any Treaty Alliance, or Confederation; grant Letters of Marque and Reprisal; coin Money; emit Bills of Credit; make any Thing but gold and silver Coin a Tender in Payment of Debts; pass any Bill of Attainder, ex post facto Law, or Law impairing the Obligation of Contracts, or grant any Title of Nobility.

No State shall, without the Consent of the Congress, lay any Imposts or Duties on Imports or Exports, except what may be absolutely necessary for exercising its inspec-

---

Necessary and proper. The advocates of "implied powers," beginning with Alexander Hamilton, have always pointed to the final clause of Article I, Section 8, as a catchall intended to give Congress broad legislative authority. John Marshall interpreted the clause thus in 1819: "Let the end be legitimate, let it be within the scope of the Constitution, and all means which are appropriate, which are plainly adapted to that end, which are not prohibited, but consist with the letter and spirit of the Constitution, are constitutional."

Importation of persons. This phrase referred to the importing of slaves from Africa. The requirement that Congress could not prohibit the import until 1808 was one of the sectional compromises in the Constitution. Congress did prohibit the import in 1808, although the government did not seriously enforce the law until the 1840s.

Habeas corpus. This has been called "the most important single safeguard of personal liberty known to Anglo-American law." It means that a person who has been arrested is entitled to have a court inquiry into the cause of his or her detention, and if she or he is not detained for good cause, is entitled to be freed.

Limits on the states. No state shall. . . . This list of restrictions on state powers was intended by the framers to rectify some of the problems that had arisen during and after the revolution. The stricture on bills of credit or making anything but gold or silver legal tender was designed to prevent the states from printing paper money and to prevent them from making tobacco, whiskey, or deerskins a medium of exchange. The stricture on laws "impairing the obligations of contracts" was intended to prevent the states from enacting debtor-relief laws. In 1933, however, the Supreme Court held that a state could, in time of depression, enable debtors to postpone meeting their obligations for a "reasonable" period of time.

The electoral college. This cumbersome method of selecting an executive is unique to the American system of government. The only model of it available at the time the Constitution was drafted was in Maryland, where the upper house was indirectly elected. The original purpose of the electoral college was to ensure qualified leadership (since electors experienced in government were assumed to be better judges of a candidate's qualifications than the voters) and to insulate the executive from popular pressures.

The arrangement that the person with the most electoral votes would be president and the one who came in second would be vice president was altered by the Twelfth Amendment (1804), which established the procedure of nomination by ticket.

The Constitution originally made no provision regarding the reelection of a president. George Washington established a tradition of serving no more than two terms. After Franklin Roosevelt violated the tradition by running for office four times, Congress passed the Twenty-second Amendment, which limits a president to two terms.

tion Laws: and the net Produce of all Duties and Imposts, laid by any State on Imports or Exports, shall be for the Use of the Treasury of the United States; and all such Laws shall be subject to the Revision and Control of the Congress.

No State shall, without the Consent of Congress, lay any duty of Tonnage, keep Troops, or Ships of War in time of Peace, enter into any Agreement or Compact with another State, or with a foreign Power, or engage in War, unless actually invaded, or in such imminent Danger as will not admit of delay.

ARTICLE II

Section 1. The executive Power shall be vested in a President of the United States of America. He shall hold his Office during the Term of four Years, and, together with the Vice President, chosen for the same term, be elected, as follows:

Each State shall appoint, in such Manner as the Legislature thereof may direct, a Number of Electors, equal to the whole Number of Senators and Representatives to which the State may be entitled in the Congress: but no Senator or Representative, or Person holding an Office of Trust or Profit under the United States, shall be appointed an Elector.

The Electors shall meet in their respective States, and vote by Ballot for two Persons, of whom one at least shall not be an Inhabitant of the same State with themselves. And they shall make a list of all the Persons voted for, and of the Number of Votes for each; which List they shall sign and certify, and transmit sealed to the Seat of the Government of the United States, directed to the President of the Senate. The President of the Senate shall, in the Presence of the Senate and House of Representatives, open all the Certificates, and the Votes shall then be counted. The Person having the greatest Number of Votes shall be the President, if such Number be a Majority of the whole Number of Electors appointed; and if there be more than one who have such Majority, and have an equal Number of Votes, then the House of Representatives shall immediately chuse by Ballot one of them for President; and if no Person have a Majority, then from the five highest on the List the said House shall in like Manner chuse the President. But in chusing the President, the Votes shall be taken by States, the Representation from each State having one Vote; a quorum for this Purpose shall consist of a Member or Members from two-thirds of the States, and a Majority of all the States shall be necessary to a Choice. In every Case, after the Choice of the President, the Person having the greatest Number of Votes of the Electors shall be the Vice President. But if there should remain two or more who have equal votes, the Senate shall chuse from them by Ballot the Vice President.

The Congress may determine the Time of chusing

the Electors, and the Day on which they shall give their Votes; which Day shall be the same throughout the United States.

No person except a natural-born citizen, or a Citizen of the United States, at the time of the adoption of this Constitution, shall be eligible to the Office of President; neither shall any Person be eligible to that Office who shall not have attained to the Age of thirty-five Years, and been fourteen Years a Resident within the United States.

In case of the Removal of the President from Office, or of his Death, Resignation, or Inability to discharge the Powers and Duties of the said Office, the same shall devolve on the Vice President, and the Congress may by Law provide for the Case of Removal, Death, Resignation, or Inability, both of the President and Vice President, declaring what Officer shall then act as President, and such Officer shall act accordingly, until the Disability be removed, or a President shall be elected.

The President shall, at stated Times, receive for his Services a Compensation, which shall neither be increased nor diminished during the Period for which he shall have been elected, and he shall not receive within that Period any other Emolument from the United States, or any of them.

Before he enters on the Execution of his Office, he shall take the following Oath or Affirmation:—"I do solemnly swear (or affirm) that I will faithfully execute the Office of President of the United States, and will, to the best of my Ability, preserve, protect, and defend the Constitution of the United States."

Section 2. The President shall be Commander in Chief of the Army and Navy of the United States, and of the Militia of the several States, when called into the actual Service of the United States; he may require the Opinion, in writing, of the principal Officer in each of the executive Departments, upon any subject relating to the Duties of their respective Offices, and he shall have Power to Grant Reprieves and Pardons for Offenses against the United States, except in Cases of Impeachment.

He shall have Power, by and with the Advice and Consent of the Senate, to make Treaties, provided two thirds of the Senators present concur; and he shall nominate, and by and with the Advice and Consent of the Senate, shall appoint Ambassadors, other public Ministers and Consuls, Judges of the supreme Court, and all other Officers of the United States, whose Appointments are not herein otherwise provided for, and which shall be established by Law: but the Congress may by Law vest the Appointment of such inferior Officers, as they think proper, in the President alone, in the Courts of Law, or in the Heads of Departments.

The President shall have Power to fill up all Vacancies that may happen during the Recess of the Senate, by granting Commissions which shall expire at the end of their next Session.

Removal, death, resignation of the president. The first vice president to succeed to the presidency was John Tyler (1841), who established the precedent, since followed, that he was president in fact, rather than merely an "acting president."

Gerald Ford was the only president who was never elected to the office, having been appointed by Richard Nixon as vice president (after Spiro Agnew resigned under criminal indictment) and having succeeded to the presidency on Nixon's resignation.

Congress has established the presidential succession in the event of the death or resignation of both president and vice president as follows: Speaker of the House, president pro-tem of the Senate, and then the members of the cabinet, beginning with the secretary of state.

The powers of the president. The powers given to the executive are fewer than those granted to Congress, but they are less specific. The president is made commander-in-chief of the armed forces, thereby ensuring civilian control of the military. He conducts foreign relations, appoints officials (both with the advice and consent of the Senate), executes the laws, and that's it.

Executive power was much feared at the time the Constitution was drafted, and the framers had no desire to make enemies for their document by endowing the president with visible authority to affect the lives of citizens. Yet in the Constitution's vagueness alone lies enough expandable power to create what has been called the "imperial presidency." The rubbery injunction to "take care that the laws be faithfully executed" alone includes the power to spend money, create bureaus, appoint task forces, mediate labor disputes, set aside forest reserves, ban pesticides, and eavesdrop on suspected subversives.

Section 3. He shall from time to time give to the Congress Information of the State of the Union, and recommend to their Consideration such Measures as he shall judge necessary and expedient; he may, on extraordinary occasions, convene both Houses, or either of them, and in Case of Disagreement between them, with respect to the Time of Adjournment, he may adjourn them to such Time as he shall think proper; he shall receive Ambassadors and other public Ministers; he shall take Care that the Laws be faithfully executed, and shall Commission all the Officers of the United States.

Section 4. The President, Vice President and all civil Officers of the United States, shall be removed from Office on Impeachment for, and Conviction of, Treason, Bribery, or other high Crimes and Misdemeanors.

ARTICLE III

Section 1. The judicial Power of the United States, shall be vested in one supreme Court, and in such inferior Courts as the Congress may from time to time ordain and establish. The Judges, both of the supreme and inferior Courts shall hold their Offices during good Behaviour, and shall, at stated Times, receive for their Services, a Compensation, which shall not be diminished during their Continuance in Office.

Section 2. The judicial Power shall extend to all Cases, in Law and Equity, arising under this Constitution, the Laws of the United States, and Treaties made, or which shall be made, under their Authority;—to all Cases affecting Ambassadors, other public Ministers and Consuls;—to all Cases of admiralty and maritime Jurisdiction;—to Controversies to which the United States shall be a Party;—to Controversies between two or more States;—between a State and Citizens of another State;—between Citizens of the same State claiming Lands under Grants of different States, and between a State, or the Citizens thereof, and foreign States, Citizens or Subjects.

In all Cases affecting Ambassadors, other public Ministers and Consuls, and those in which a State shall be Party, the supreme Court shall have original Jurisdiction. In all the other Cases before mentioned, the supreme Court shall have appellate Jurisdiction, both as to Law and Fact, with such Exceptions, and under such Regulations as the Congress shall make.

The trial of all Crimes, except in Cases of Impeachment, shall be by Jury; and such Trial shall be held in the State where the said Crimes shall have been committed; but when not committed within any State, the Trial shall be at such Place or Places as the Congress may by Law have directed.

Section 3. Treason against the United States, shall consist only in levying War against them, or in adhering to their Enemies, giving them Aid and Comfort. No Person

The judicial power. Courts, judges, and lawyers were as suspect in the United States of the 1780s as kings and ministers. The poor looked upon law courts as agents of the rich, using the power of the state to collect debts and enforce contracts. Article III, which establishes the third branch of government—"the judicial power of the United States"—is therefore deliberately vague. The framers had no desire to stir up a hornet's nest of controversy by outlining a hierarchy of courts staffed by learned judges. Article III specifies only a Supreme Court, and it leaves to Congress the thorny questions concerning the number of "inferior courts" and the extent of their powers.

Congress in 1789 did establish a hierarchy of circuit and district courts—which, expanded in number, remain today—but it cautiously confined their jurisdiction to the "Constitution, laws, and treaties of the United States." Ordinary civil and criminal jurisdiction is left to the state courts. A federal court can take jurisdiction only when a suit involves a federal issue, such as the interpretation of an act of Congress, or when the parties to the suit reside in different states ("diversity of citizenship"). Even then, the Supreme Court declared in 1938 in the case of *Erie Railroad* v. *Tompkins*, federal courts are obliged to apply the law of the forum state. There is no federal common law.

shall be convicted of Treason unless on the Testimony of two Witnesses to the same overt Act, or on Confession in open Court.

The Congress shall have power to declare the Punishment of Treason, but no Attainder of Treason shall work Corruption of Blood, or Forfeiture except during the Life of the Person attainted.

ARTICLE IV

Section 1. Full Faith and Credit shall be given in each State to the public Acts, Records, and judicial Proceedings of every other State. And the Congress may by general Laws prescribe the Manner in which such Acts, Records and Proceedings shall be proved, and the Effect thereof.

Section 2. The Citizens of each State shall be entitled to all Privileges and Immunities of Citizens in the several States.

A Person charged in any State with Treason, Felony, or other Crime, who shall flee from Justice, and be found in another State, shall on demand of the executive Authority of the State from which he fled, be delivered up, to be removed to the State having Jurisdiction of the crime.

No Person held to Service or Labour in one State, under the Laws thereof, escaping into another, shall, in Consequence of any Law or Regulation therein, be discharged from such Service or Labour, but shall be delivered up on Claim of the Party to whom such Service or Labour may be due.

Section 3. New States may be admitted by the Congress into this Union; but no new State shall be formed or erected within the Jurisdiction of any other State; nor any State be formed by the Junction of two or more States, or parts of States, without the Consent of the Legislatures of the States concerned as well as of the Congress.

The Congress shall have Power to dispose of and make all needful Rules and Regulations respecting the Territory or other Property belonging to the United States; and nothing in this Constitution shall be so construed as to Prejudice any Claims of the United States, or of any particular State.

Section 4. The United States shall guarantee to every State in this Union a Republican Form of Government, and shall protect each of them against Invasion; and on Application of the Legislature, or of the Executive (when the Legislature cannot be convened) against domestic Violence.

ARTICLE V

The Congress, whenever two thirds of both Houses shall deem it necessary, shall propose Amendments to this Constitution, or, on the Application of the Legislatures of

Full faith and credit. The intent of this provision is to ensure cooperation and mutual respect among the states. In the twentieth century it has been commonly invoked by people who travel to another state, such as Nevada or Florida, in order to obtain a quick divorce.

New states. The framers of the Constitution contemplated the indefinite expansion of the American union. The organism they created was both a republic and an empire, but it was a unique empire in that the colonies (territories) were expected, upon maturity, to join the Union on a par with the original thirteen states.

Amendments. The framers of the Constitution, with commendable foresight and humility, anticipated that posterity might want to make some changes in their handiwork. But they deliberately made the amendment procedure cumbersome, so that the Constitution would not be subject to popular whim. Amendments must be approved by a two-thirds vote in each house of Congress, and then they have to be ratified by legislatures or conventions in three fourths of the states. The only amendment ratified by specially summoned conventions was the Twenty-first, which repealed prohibition. The first ten amendments (the Bill of Rights) were drafted and approved only four years after the Constitution was written. Since then, only sixteen have been added.

two thirds of the several States, shall call a Convention for proposing Amendments, which, in either Case, shall be valid to all Intents and Purposes, as part of this Constitution, when ratified by the Legislatures of three fourths of the several States, or by Conventions in three fourths thereof, as the one or the other Mode of Ratification may be proposed by the Congress; Provided that no Amendment which may be made prior to the Year One thousand eight hundred and eight shall in any Manner affect the first and fourth Clauses in the Ninth Section of the first Article; and that no State, without its Consent, shall be deprived of its equal Suffrage in the Senate.

ARTICLE VI

All Debts contracted and Engagements entered into, before the Adoption of this Constitution, shall be as valid against the United States under this Constitution, as under the Confederation.

This Constitution, and the Laws of the United States which shall be made in Pursuance thereof: and all Treaties made, or which shall be made, under the Authority of the United States, shall be the supreme Law of the Land; and the Judges in every State shall be bound thereby, any Thing in the Constitution or laws of any State to the Contrary notwithstanding.

The Senators and Representatives before mentioned, and the Members of the several State Legislatures, and all executive and judicial Officers, both of the United States and of the several States, shall be bound by Oath or Affirmation to support this Constitution; but no religious Test shall ever be required as a qualification to any Office or public Trust under the United States.

Ratification. Mindful of the difficulties that had attended efforts to alter the Articles of Confederation in the 1780s, the framers of the Constitution provided that the document would go into effect when only nine of the thirteen states gave their approval. They also bypassed potentially jealous and divided state legislatures by providing that the Constitution was to be approved by specially elected conventions.

ARTICLE VII

The Ratification of the Conventions of nine States shall be sufficient for the Establishment of this Constitution between the States so ratifying the same.

Done in Convention by the Unanimous Consent of the States present the Seventeenth Day of September in the Year of our Lord one thousand seven hundred and Eighty seven and of the Independence of the United States of America the Twelfth. In Witness whereof We have hereunto subscribed our Names.

Articles in Addition to, and Amendment of, the Constitution of the United States of America, Proposed by Congress, and Ratified by the Legislatures of the Several States, Pursuant to the Fifth Article of the Original Constitution.

The Bill of Rights. The first ten amendments were intended as restraints on the power of the federal government. Since 1931, the Supreme Court has progressively applied them to the states under the theory that they are embodied in the "due process" clause of the Fourteenth Amendment.

The First Amendment, which protects the freedom of speech, press, and belief, is clearly the most important. In recognition of this, the Supreme Court places the burden of proof on the government where freedom of speech is in question; that is, the government must demonstrate, when a citizen complains, that its action does *not* inhibit freedom of speech, press, or religion.

The Second and Third amendments are the product of English tradition and American colonial experience. The Fourth through the Eighth amendments are judicial safeguards intended to ensure fair court procedure. The Ninth Amendment is a catchall intended to overcome the misgivings, expressed by James Madison among others, that a listing of human rights would be restrictive—that is, imply that these are the *only* rights people have. The Ninth Amendment has been invoked by the Supreme Court most recently in a decision that overturned a state law restricting the use of contraceptives.

The Tenth Amendment, though drafted and approved with the rest of the Bill of Rights, addresses itself to power, not rights. It is a reminder that the government established by the Constitution is one of specifically delegated powers, and that all other powers reside in the states. This residual power is usually described as the "police power": the power to legislate for the health, safety, welfare, and morals of the people. The Tenth Amendment was long relied on by the advocates of states' rights, but in 1941 the Supreme Court declared the amendment a mere truism that expressed the distribution of power between the federal government and the states without, of itself, restricting the authority of either.

The Eleventh Amendment was the product of a fleeting political controversy involving the efforts of Loyalists to recover property that states had confiscated during the revolution.

The Twelfth Amendment resulted from the tie in the electoral college between Thomas Jefferson and Aaron Burr in 1800. By requiring a "distinct list" of persons running as president and another for those running as vice president, the amendment, to be workable, requires a nominating procedure. It is therefore an indirect recognition of the function of political parties.

AMENDMENT I [1791]

Congress shall make no law respecting an establishment of religion, or prohibiting the free exercise thereof; or abridging the freedom of speech, or of the press; or the right of the people peaceably to assemble, and to petition the Government for a redress of grievances.

AMENDMENT II [1791]

A well regulated Militia, being necessary to the security of a free State, the right of the people to keep and bear Arms, shall not be infringed.

AMENDMENT III [1791]

No Soldier shall, in time of peace, be quartered in any house, without the consent of the Owner, nor in time of war, but in a manner to be prescribed by law.

AMENDMENT IV [1791]

The right of the people to be secure in their persons, houses, papers, and effects, against unreasonable searches and seizures, shall not be violated, and no Warrants shall issue, but upon probable cause, supported by Oath or affirmation, and particularly describing the place to be searched, and the persons or things to be seized.

AMENDMENT V [1791]

No person shall be held to answer for a capital or otherwise infamous crime, unless on a presentment or indictment of a Grand Jury, except in cases arising in the land or naval forces, or in the Militia, when in actual service in time of War or public danger; nor shall any person be subject for the same offence to be twice put in jeopardy of life or limb; nor shall be compelled in any criminal case to be a witness against himself, nor be deprived of life, liberty, or property, without due process of law; nor shall private property be taken for public use, without just compensation.

AMENDMENT VI [1791]

In all criminal prosecutions, the accused shall enjoy the right to a speedy and public trial, by an impartial jury of the State and district wherein the crime shall have been committed, which district shall have been previously ascertained by law, and to be informed of the nature and cause of the accusation, to be confronted with the witnesses against him; to have compulsory process for obtaining witnesses in his favor, and to have the Assistance of Counsel for his defence.

AMENDMENT VII [1791]

In Suits at common law, where the value in controversy shall exceed twenty dollars, the right of trial by jury shall be preserved, and no fact tried by a jury, shall be otherwise re-examined in any Court of the United States, than according to the rules of the common law.

AMENDMENT VIII [1791]

Excessive bail shall not be required, nor excessive fines imposed, nor cruel and unusual punishments inflicted.

AMENDMENT IX [1791]

The enumeration in the Constitution, of certain rights, shall not be construed to deny or disparage others retained by the people.

AMENDMENT X [1791]

The powers not delegated to the United States by the Constitution, nor prohibited by it to the States, are reserved to the States respectively, or to the people.

AMENDMENT XI [1798]

The Judicial power of the United States shall not be construed to extend to any suit in law or equity, commenced or prosecuted against one of the United States by Citizens of another State, or by citizens or Subjects of any Foreign State.

AMENDMENT XII [1804]

The Electors shall meet in their respective States and vote by ballot for President and Vice President, one of whom, at least, shall not be an inhabitant of the same State with themselves; they shall name in their ballots the person voted for as President, and in distinct ballots the person voted for as Vice-President, and they shall make distinct lists of all persons voted for as President, and of all persons voted for as Vice-President, and of the number of votes for each, which lists they shall sign and certify, and transmit sealed to the seat of the government of the United States, directed to the President of the Senate;—The President of the Senate shall, in the presence of the Senate and House of Representatives, open all the certificates and the votes shall then be counted;—The person having the greatest number of votes for President, shall be the President, if such number be a majority of the whole number of Electors appointed; and if no person have such majority, then from the persons having the highest numbers not exceeding three on the list of those voted for as President, the House of Representatives shall choose immediately, by ballot, the President. But in choosing the President, the votes shall be taken by states, the representation from each state having one vote; a quorum for this purpose shall consist of a member or members from two-thirds of the states, and a majority of all the states shall be necessary to a choice. And if the House of Representatives shall not choose a President whenever the right of choice shall devolve upon them, before the fourth day of March next following, then the Vice-President shall act as President, as in the case of the death or other constitutional disability of the President.—The person having the greatest number of votes as Vice-President, shall be the Vice-President, if such number be a majority of the whole number of Electors appointed, and if no person have a majority, then from the two highest numbers on the list, the Senate shall choose the Vice-President; a quorum for the purpose shall consist of two-thirds of the whole number of Senators, and a majority of the whole number shall be necessary to a choice. But no person constitutionally ineligible to the office of the President shall be eligible to that of Vice-President of the United States.

The war amendments. Adopted after the Civil War, the Thirteenth Amendment freed the slaves, the Fourteenth sought to protect their civil rights, and the Fifteenth prevented the states from denying the right to vote on the basis of race.

Due process. The Fourteenth Amendment has, through the years, been the most controversial of the war amendments. The phrase "due process" has been held to include the whole panoply of rights outlined in the first ten amendments. The phrase "equal protection of the laws" has been held to exclude racially segregated facilities and to require periodic reapportionment of state legislatures to ensure that all ballots are of equal weight.

AMENDMENT XIII [1865]

Section 1. Neither slavery nor involuntary servitude, except as a punishment for crime wherof the party shall have been duly convicted, shall exist within the United States, or any place subject to their jurisdiction.

Section 2. Congress shall have the power to enforce this article by appropriate legislation.

AMENDMENT XIV [1868]

Section 1. All persons born or naturalized in the United States, and subject to the jurisdiction thereof, are citizens of the United States and of the State wherein they reside. No state shall make or enforce any law which shall abridge the privileges or immunities of citizens of the United States; nor shall any State deprive any person of life, liberty, or property, without due process of law; nor deny to any person within its jurisdiction the equal protection of the laws.

Section 2. Representatives shall be apportioned among the several States according to their respective numbers, counting the whole number of persons in each State, excluding Indians not taxed. But when the right to vote at any election for the choice of electors for President and Vice President of the United States, Representatives in Congress, the Executive and Judicial officers of a State, or the members of the Legislature thereof, is denied to any of the male inhabitants of such State, being twenty-one years of age, and citizens of the United States, or in any way abridged, except for participation in rebellion, or other crime, the basis of representation therein shall be reduced in the proportion which the number of such male citizens shall bear to the whole number of male citizens twenty-one years of age in such State.

Section 3. No person shall be a Senator or Representative in Congress, or elector of President and Vice President, or hold any office, civil or military, under the United States, or under any State, who, having previously taken an oath, as a member of Congress, or as an officer of the United States, or as a member of any State legislature, or as an executive or judicial officer of any State, to support the Constitution of the United States, shall have engaged in insurrection or rebellion against the same, or given aid or comfort to the enemies thereof. But Congress may by a vote of two-thirds of each House, remove such disability.

Section 4. The validity of the public debt of the United States, authorized by law, including debts incurred for payment of pensions and bounties for services in suppressing insurrection or rebellion, shall not be questioned. But neither the United States nor any State shall assume or pay any debt or obligation incurred in aid of insurrection or rebellion against the United States, or any claim for the loss or emancipation of any slave; but all such debts, obligations, and claims shall be held illegal and void.

Section 5. The Congress shall have the power to enforce, by appropriate legislation, the provisions of this article.

AMENDMENT XV [1870]

Section 1. The right of citizens of the United States to vote shall not be denied or abridged by the United States or by any State on account of race, color, or previous condition of servitude—

Section 2. The Congress shall have the power to enforce this article by appropriate legislation.

AMENDMENT XVI [1913]

The Congress shall have power to lay and collect taxes on incomes, from whatever source derived, without apportionment among the several States, and without regard to any census or enumeration.

Civil rights. Section 5 of the Fourteenth Amendment was clearly intended to give Congress power to pass laws for the protection of civil rights. This Congress attempted to do in 1875 by passing a law forbidding inns, railroads, and theaters from discriminating among persons on the grounds of race. In 1883 the Supreme Court struck down the law on the grounds that the Fourteenth Amendment prohibited only official discrimination, not the private acts of individuals. As a result, modern civil rights legislation, notably the Equal Opportunity Act of 1964, rests on Congress's power to regulate interstate commerce, rather than on the Fourteenth Amendment.

The Fifteenth Amendment. For nearly a century after it was drafted, the Fifteenth Amendment was evaded by various devices that hindered blacks from registering and voting. The Voting Rights Act of 1965 is the most recent attempt to enforce the amendment by providing federal supervision of voter registration in localities with a history of discrimination.

The Progressive amendments. The Sixteenth through Nineteenth amendments were the product of the Progressive movement. The Sixteenth was necessitated by a Supreme Court decision in the 1890s that a federal income tax violated the constitutional requirement that direct taxes (as opposed to excises) had to be apportioned among the states, which in turn would collect from the people. The Seventeenth Amendment was intended to democratize the "millionaires' club," the U.S. Senate, by requiring that its members be elected directly by the people. The Eighteenth Amendment authorized prohibition, and the Nineteenth women's suffrage.

AMENDMENT XVII [1916]

The Senate of the United States shall be composed of two Senators from each State, elected by the people thereof, for six years; and each Senator shall have one vote. The electors in each State shall have the qualifications requisite for electors of the most numerous branch of the State legislatures.

When vacancies happen in the representation of any State in the Senate, the executive authority of such State shall issue writs of election to fill such vacancies: *Provided*, That the legislature of any State may empower the executive thereof to make temporary appointments until the people fill the vacancies by election as the legislature may direct.

This amendment shall not be so construed as to affect the election or term of any Senator chosen before it becomes valid as part of the Constitution.

AMENDMENT XVIII [1919]

Section 1. After one year from the ratification of this article the manufacture, sale, or transportation of intoxicating liquors within, the importation thereof into, or the exportation thereof from the United States and all territory subject to the jurisdiction thereof for beverage purposes is hereby prohibited.

Section 2. The Congress and the several States shall have concurrent power to enforce this article by appropriate legislation.

Section 3. This article shall be inoperative unless it shall have been ratified as an amendment to the Constitution by the legislatures of the several States, as provided in the Constitution, within seven years from the date of the submission hereof to the States by the Congress.

AMENDMENT XIX [1920]

The right of citizens of the United States to vote shall not be denied or abridged by the United States or by any State on account of sex.

Congress shall have power to enforce this article by appropriate legislation.

The lame duck amendment. The Twentieth Amendment did away with an anomaly created by Article I of the Constitution, the requirement that elections would be held in November but inaugurations delayed until March. This resulted in a "lame duck" session of Congress, lasting from December until March in even-numbered years, when members, many of whom had failed to be

AMENDMENT XX [1933]

Section 1. The terms of the President and Vice President shall end at noon on the 20th day of January, and the terms of Senators and Representatives at noon on the 3rd day of January, of the years in which such terms would have ended if this article had not been ratified; and the terms of their successors shall then begin.

reelected and were on their way to private life, were voting on matters of national importance. By moving inauguration day back from March 4 to January 20, the amendment shortens the interval between popular selection and the exercise of presidential and legislative power.

Section 2. The Congress shall assemble at least once in every year, and such meeting shall begin at noon on the 3d day of January, unless they shall by law appoint a different day.

Section 3. If, at the time fixed for the beginning of the term of the President, the President elect shall have died, the Vice President elect shall become President. If a President shall not have been chosen before the time fixed for the beginning of his term, or if the President elect shall have failed to qualify, then the Vice President elect shall act as President until a President shall have qualified; and the Congress may by law provide for the case wherein neither a President elect nor a Vice President elect shall have qualified, declaring who shall then act as President, or the manner in which one who is to act shall be selected, and such person shall act accordingly until a President or Vice President shall have qualified.

Section 4. The Congress may by law provide for the case of the death of any of the persons from whom the House of Representatives may choose a President whenever the right of choice shall have devolved upon them, and for the case of the death of any of the persons from whom the Senate may choose a Vice President whenever the right of choice shall have devolved upon them.

Section 5. Sections 1 and 2 shall take effect on the 15th day of October following the ratification of this article.

Section 6. The article shall be inoperative unless it shall have been ratified as an amendment to the Constitution by the legislatures of three-fourths of the several States within seven years from the date of its submission.

The Twenty-first Amendment. The Twenty-first Amendment repealed the Eighteenth, and thereby repealed prohibition. It is the only amendment that provides for its ratification by specially selected conventions, and it is the only one that has been approved in this way.

AMENDMENT XXI [1933]

Section 1. The eighteenth article of amendment to the Constitution of the United States is hereby repealed.

Section 2. The transportation or importation into any State, Territory, or possession of the United States for delivery or use therein of intoxicating liquors, in violation of the laws thereof, is hereby prohibited.

Section 3. This article shall be inoperative unless it shall have been ratified as an amendment to the Constitution by conventions in the several States, as provided in the Constitution, within seven years from the date of the submission hereof to the States by the Congress.

The Twenty-second Amendment. The Twenty-second Amendment, a belated slap at Roosevelt by a Republican-dominated Congress, limits the president to two terms in office. Ironically, the first president to which it applied was a Republican, Dwight D. Eisenhower.

AMENDMENT XXII [1951]

No person shall be elected to the office of the President more than twice, and no person who has held the office of President, or acted as President, for more than two years of a term to which some other person was elected President shall be elected to the office of the President more than once.

But this Article shall not apply to any person holding the office of President when this Article was proposed by the Congress, and shall not prevent any person who may be holding the office of President, or acting as President, during the term within which this Article becomes operative from holding the office of President or acting as President during the remainder of such term.

AMENDMENT XXIII [1961]

The Twenty-third Amendment. The Twenty-third Amendment allows residents of the District of Columbia to vote in presidential elections.

Section 1. The District constituting the seat of Government of the United States shall appoint in such manner as the Congress may direct:

A number of electors of President and Vice President equal to the whole number of Senators and Representatives in Congress to which the District would be entitled if it were a State, but in no event more than the least populous State; they shall be in addition to those appointed by the States, but they shall be considered, for the purposes of the election of President and Vice President, to be electors appointed by a State; and they shall meet in the District and perform such duties as provided by the twelfth article of amendment.

Section 2. The Congress shall have the power to enforce this article by appropriate legislation.

AMENDMENT XXIV [1964]

The poll tax amendment. The Twenty-fourth Amendment prevents the states from making payment of a poll tax a condition for voting. Common at the time among southern states, the poll tax was a capitation (poll, or head) tax on individuals. A poll tax receipt was often required in order to vote. It was designed to prevent uneducated people, especially blacks, who were unaccustomed to saving receipts, from voting.

Section 1. The right of citizens of the United States to vote in any primary or other election for President or Vice President, for electors for President or Vice President, or for Senator or Representative in Congress, shall not be denied or abridged by the United States or any State by reason of failure to pay any poll tax or other tax.

Section 2. The Congress shall have the power to enforce this article by appropriate legislation.

AMENDMENT XXV [1967]

The Twenty-fifth Amendment. The Twenty-fifth Amendment, inspired by President Eisenhower's heart attack and President Johnson's abdominal surgery, provides for the temporary replacement of a president who is unable to discharge the duties of the office.

Section 1. In case of the removal of the President from office or his death or resignation, the Vice President shall become President.

Section 2. Whenever there is a vacancy in the office of the Vice President, the President shall nominate a Vice President who shall take the office upon confirmation by a majority vote of both houses of Congress.

Section 3. Whenever the President transmits to the President pro tempore of the Senate and the Speaker of the House of Representatives his written declaration that he is unable to discharge the powers and duties of his office, and until he transmits to them a written declaration to the contrary, such powers and duties shall be discharged by the Vice President as Acting President.

Section 4. Whenever the Vice President and a majority of either the principal officers of the executive departments, or of such other body as Congress may by law provide, transmit to the President pro tempore of the Senate and the Speaker of the House of Representatives their written declaration that the President is unable to discharge the powers and duties of his office, the Vice President shall immediately assume the powers and duties of the office as Acting President.

Thereafter, when the President transmits to the President pro tempore of the Senate and the Speaker of the House of Representatives his written declaration that no inability exists, he shall resume the powers and duties of his office unless the Vice President and a majority of either the principal officers of the executive departments, or of such other body as Congress may by law provide, transmit within four days to the President pro tempore of the Senate and the speaker of the House of Representatives their written declaration that the President is unable to discharge the powers and duties of his office. Thereupon Congress shall decide the issue, assembling within 48 hours for that purpose if not in session. If the Congress, within 21 days after receipt of the latter written declaration, or, if Congress is not in session, within 21 days after Congress is required to assemble, determines by two-thirds vote of both houses that the President is unable to discharge the powers and duties of his office, the Vice President shall continue to discharge the same as Acting President; otherwise, the President shall resume the powers and duties of his office.

The Twenty-sixth Amendment. The Twenty-sixth Amendment corrected the anomaly that young men could be drafted and sent to war at the age of eighteen, but not allowed to participate in the nation's democratic processes until they were twenty-one. It extended the vote to eighteen-year-olds.

AMENDMENT XXVI [1971]

Section 1. The rights of citizens of the United States, who are 18 years of age or older, to vote shall not be denied or abridged by the United States or any state on account of age.

Section 2. The Congress shall have the power to enforce this article by appropriate legislation.

PRESIDENTIAL ELECTIONS

YEAR	CANDIDATES	PARTY	POPULAR VOTE	ELECTORAL VOTE
1789	**George Washington**			69
	John Adams			34
	Others			35
1792	**George Washington**			132
	John Adams			77
	George Clinton			50
	Others			5
1796	**John Adams**	Federalist		71
	Thomas Jefferson	Republican		68
	Thomas Pinckney	Federalist		59
	Aaron Burr	Republican		30
	Others			48
1800	**Thomas Jefferson**	Republican		73
	Aaron Burr	Republican		73
	John Adams	Federalist		65
	Charles C. Pinckney	Federalist		64
1804	**Thomas Jefferson**	Republican		162
	Charles C. Pinckney	Federalist		14
1808	**James Madison**	Republican		122
	Charles C. Pinckney	Federalist		47
	George Clinton	Independent-Republican		6
1812	**James Madison**	Republican		128
	DeWitt Clinton	Federalist		89
1816	**James Monroe**	Republican		183
	Rufus King	Federalist		34
1820	**James Monroe**	Democratic-Republican		231
	John Quincy Adams	Independent-Republican		1
1824	**John Quincy Adams**	Republican	108,740	84 (elected by the House of Representatives)
	Andrew Jackson	Republican	153,544	99
	Henry Clay	Republican	47,136	37
	William H. Crawford	Republican	46,618	41
1828	**Andrew Jackson**	Democratic	647,286	178
	John Quincy Adams	National Republican	508,064	83
1832	**Andrew Jackson**	Democratic	688,000	219
	Henry Clay	National Republican	530,000	49
	William Wirt	Anti-Masonic	255,000	7
	John Floyd	National Republican		11
1836	**Martin Van Buren**	Democratic	762,678	170
	William H. Harrison	Whig	549,000	73
	Hugh L. White	Whig	146,000	26
	Daniel Webster	Whig	41,000	14
1840	**William H. Harrison**	Whig	1,275,017	234
	Martin Van Buren	Democratic	1,128,702	60

1844	**James K. Polk**	Democratic	1,337,243	170
	Henry Clay	Whig	1,299,068	105
	James G. Birney	Liberty	62,300	
1848	**Zachary Taylor**	Whig	1,360,101	163
	Lewis Cass	Democratic	1,220,544	127
	Martin Van Buren	Free-Soil	291,263	
1852	**Franklin Pierce**	Democratic	1,601,274	254
	Winfield Scott	Whig	1,386,580	42
1856	**James Buchanan**	Democratic	1,838,169	174
	John C. Frémont	Republican	1,335,264	114
	Millard Fillmore	American	874,534	8
1860	**Abraham Lincoln**	Republican	1,866,452	180
	Stephen A. Douglas	Democratic	1,375,157	12
	John C. Breckinridge	Democratic	847,953	72
	John Bell	Constitutional Union	592,631	39
1864	**Abraham Lincoln**	Republican	2,213,665	212
	George B. McClellan	Democratic	1,805,237	21
1868	**Ulysses S. Grant**	Republican	3,012,833	214
	Horatio Seymour	Democratic	2,703,249	80
1872	**Ulysses S. Grant**	Republican	3,596,745	286
	Horace Greeley	Democratic	2,843,446	66
1876	**Rutherford B. Hayes**	Republican	4,036,572	185
	Samuel J. Tilden	Democratic	4,284,020	184
1880	**James A. Garfield**	Republican	4,449,053	214
	Winfield S. Hancock	Democratic	4,442,032	155
	James B. Weaver	Greenback-Labor	308,578	
1884	**Grover Cleveland**	Democratic	4,874,986	219
	James G. Blaine	Republican	4,851,981	182
	Benjamin F. Butler	Greenback-Labor	175,370	
1888	**Benjamin Harrison**	Republican	5,444,337	233
	Grover Cleveland	Democratic	5,540,050	168
1892	**Grover Cleveland**	Democratic	5,554,414	277
	Benjamin Harrison	Republican	5,190,802	145
	James B. Weaver	People's	1,027,329	22
1896	**William McKinley**	Republican	7,104,779	271
	William J. Bryan	Democratic; Populist	6,502,925	176
1900	**William McKinley**	Republican	7,219,530	292
	William J. Bryan	Democratic; Populist	6,356,734	155
1904	**Theodore Roosevelt**	Republican	7,628,834	336
	Alton B. Parker	Democratic	5,084,401	140
	Eugene V. Debs	Socialist	402,460	
1908	**William H. Taft**	Republican	7,679,006	321
	William J. Bryan	Democratic	6,409,106	162
	Eugene V. Debs	Socialist	420,820	
1912	**Woodrow Wilson**	Democratic	6,293,454	435
	Theodore Roosevelt	Progressive	4,119,538	88
	William H. Taft	Republican	3,484,980	8
	Eugene V. Debs	Socialist	897,011	

1916	**Woodrow Wilson**	Democratic	9,129,606	277
	Charles E. Hughes	Republican	8,538,221	254
1920	**Warren G. Harding**	Republican	16,152,200	404
	James M. Cox	Democratic	9,147,353	127
	Eugene V. Debs	Socialist	919,799	
1924	**Calvin Coolidge**	Republican	15,725,016	382
	John W. Davis	Democratic	8,385,586	136
	Robert M. LaFollette	Progressive	4,822,856	13
1928	**Herbert C. Hoover**	Republican	21,392,190	444
	Alfred E. Smith	Democratic	15,016,443	87
1932	**Franklin D. Roosevelt**	Democratic	22,809,638	472
	Herbert C. Hoover	Republican	15,758,901	59
	Norman Thomas	Socialist	881,951	
1936	**Franklin D. Roosevelt**	Democratic	27,751,612	523
	Alfred M. Landon	Republican	16,618,913	8
	William Lemke	Union	891,858	
1940	**Franklin D. Roosevelt**	Democratic	27,243,466	449
	Wendell L. Willkie	Republican	22,304,755	82
1944	**Franklin D. Roosevelt**	Democratic	25,602,505	432
	Thomas E. Dewey	Republican	22,006,278	99
1948	**Harry S. Truman**	Democratic	24,105,812	303
	Thomas E. Dewey	Republican	21,970,065	189
	J. Strom Thurmond	States' Rights	1,169,063	39
	Henry A. Wallace	Progressive	1,157,172	
1952	**Dwight D. Eisenhower**	Republican	33,936,234	442
	Adlai E. Stevenson	Democratic	27,314,992	89
1956	**Dwight D. Eisenhower**	Republican	35,590,472	457
	Adlai E. Stevenson	Democratic	26,022,752	73
1960	**John F. Kennedy**	Democratic	34,227,096	303
	Richard M. Nixon	Republican	34,108,546	219
1964	**Lyndon B. Johnson**	Democratic	43,126,233	486
	Barry M. Goldwater	Republican	27,174,989	53
1968	**Richard M. Nixon**	Republican	31,783,783	301
	Hubert H. Humphrey	Democratic	31,271,839	191
	George C. Wallace	Amer. Independent	9,899,557	46
1972	**Richard M. Nixon**	Republican	47,168,963	520
	George S. McGovern	Democratic	29,169,615	17
	John Hospers	Republican (noncandidate)		1
1976	**Jimmy Carter**	Democratic	40,827,292	297
	Gerald R. Ford	Republican	39,146,157	240
	Ronald Reagan	Republican (noncandidate)		1
1980	**Ronald Reagan**	Republican	43,899,248	489
	Jimmy Carter	Democratic	35,481,435	49
	John Anderson	Independent	5,719,437	
1984	**Ronald Reagan**	Republican	53,428,357	525
	Walter Mondale	Democratic	36,930,923	13

INDEX

Wagner Act, 264, 353
Wake Island, 136
Wallace, George, 382, 406, 418
Wallace, Henry A., 353–54
Wall Street, 178, 244–45
Wanamaker, John, 118n
Ward, Lester Frank, 62
War Department, 352
War Industries Board (1917), 205, 222
War Labor Board (1942), 295
War on Poverty, 384–85
War Powers Act (1973), 410
War Production Board (1942), 294
Warren, Earl, 365–66, 406–7
Washington (state), 190–91
Washington, Booker T., 156–57, 165
Washington, D.C., and city beautiful
    movement, 160
Washington Treaty, 281–82
Watergate scandal, 410–12
Watson, Thomas, 118, 157
Watt, James (secretary of the interior),
    429
Watts, riot in, 391
Wealth, distribution of:
    in 1929, 344
    in 1945, 344
Weathermen (1960s), 401n
Weaver, James B., 103, 105
Welles, Orson, 287–88
Weyler, Gen. Valeriano, 131
Wheeler, "Fighting Joe," 134
Wherry, Kenneth, 327
Whiskey Ring, 41–42
White, Walter, 273
White, William Allen, 149, 225
White citizen councils, 363
Whiteman, Paul, 228–29
"White Man's Burden," 128
Wilderness, preservation of:
    in Progressive period, 113–15, 169–70
    in 1970s, 421
    in 1980s, 430
Wiley, Alexander, 335
Willard, Frances, 153

Williams, Vanessa, 433
Willkie, Wendell, 290
Wilson, Charles E., 332
Wilson, Woodrow:
    early life, 174
    election of 1912, 174–76
    president:
        domestic policies, 176–80, 184
        Latin American policy, 169–71
        and World War I, 199–204
        and Versailles Treaty, 209–18
Wisconsin:
    and Progressive movement, 163–64
    University of, 113, 151, 154, 401
Women:
    and Progressive movement, 153–55,
        180–88
    in World War I, 186–87
    in 1920s, 231–32
    and New Deal, 272–73
    in World War II, 347–51
    in 1950s, 357–58
    in 1960s, 398–400
    in 1970s, 417–19
    in 1980s, 437
    in the temperance movement, 153, 180–
        81
    work of, 69–70, 155, 358, 400, 416
    (See also Women's rights movement;
        Women's suffrage)
Women's Christian Temperance Union,
    153, 180
Women's club movement, 153–54
Women's rights movement:
    in Progressive movement, 180–88
    in 1960s, 398–99
    in 1970s, 417–18
    in 1980s, 437
Women's suffrage, 183, 185–88
Women's Suffrage Association, 186
Women's vote:
    in 1920s, 187–88
    in 1980s, 437
Wood, Gen. Leonard, 134
Woodhull, Victoria, 30

Work, concept of, 69–71
Workers, hours and conditions of,
    67–71, 180, 189, 223 (See also
    Labor)
Workers' compensation laws, 163, 175,
    180
Workingmen's Party, 71
Works Progress Administration (WPA),
    263–64, 275
World Bank, 313, 337
World War I:
    U.S. entry into, 194–204
    mobilization for, 204–7
    military events of, 207–9
World War II:
    events leading to, 283–94
    home front, 294–95
    military operations:
        Europe, 295–301
        Far East, 301–5
    diplomacy of, 309–15
Wounded Knee:
    massacre, 80–81
    seizure of, 400

Yale University, 229
Yalta conference, 311–13
Yankees (New York), 228
Yates v. *United States*, 366
Yellow-dog contracts, 252
"Yellow press," 131
Yellowstone National Park, 79
York, Sgt. Alvin C., 212–14
Yosemite National Park, 114
Young, Andrew, 423
Young Plan, 281
Youth:
    in 1950s, 359–61
    in 1960s, 401–2
    in 1970s, 416

Zapata, Emilio, 198
Zimmermann note, 199, 209
Zoot suits, 345–46